D1616878

JOY IN WORK, GERMAN WORK

JOY IN WORK, GERMAN WORK

THE NATIONAL DEBATE,

1800–1945

JOAN CAMPBELL

PRINCETON UNIVERSITY PRESS

PRINCETON, NEW JERSEY

This book has been composed in Linotron Goudy type

Clothbound editions of Princeton University Press books are printed
on acid-free paper, and binding materials are chosen for strength
and durability. Paperbacks, although satisfactory for personal
collections, are not usually suitable for library rebinding

Printed in the United States of America
by Princeton University Press,
Princeton, New Jersey

*Library of Congress
Cataloging-in-Publication Data*
Campbell, Joan, 1929–
Joy in work, German work : the national debate,
1800–1945 / Joan Campbell.
p. cm.
Bibliography: p.
Includes index.
ISBN 0-691-05569-6
1. Work ethic—Germany—History. 2. Work—Psychological
aspects. 3. Industrial sociology—Germany—History. I. Title.
HD8450.C33 1989
306'.36'0943—dc19 88-37120

CONTENTS

PREFACE

THE IDEA for this book originated in the early 1970s, when I was working on a history of the German Werkbund. Founded in 1907, the Werkbund brought together artists, craftsmen, progressive industrialists and others who hoped to revitalize German culture through an alliance between art and industry. Werkbund reformers wanted not only to improve the quality and design of German goods, but also to solve the "social question" by restoring dignity and joy to labor. In the revolutionary aftermath of the First World War, joy in work became a major preoccupation of the Werkbund which devoted its annual meeting of 1922 to the topic. This led me to examine how widely held this notion was, and what it entailed. The question was timely, for social critics in North America in the 1970s were also arguing about joy in work and its converse, alienated labor, with German authorities figuring prominently in the debate. German theorists—Karl Marx, Max Weber, Herbert Marcuse, and Jürgen Habermas—had taken the problem of alienated labor particularly to heart. Were alienation and joyful work in some sense "German" ideas?

In this book I attempt to uncover the roots of the Werkbund ideal of *Arbeitsfreude*, "joy in work," and to establish the role it played outside the Werkbund among Germans who sought to address the problem of work in modern society. At some other point it may be possible to compare German thinking about the nature and future of work with that in other countries faced with the consequences of industrialization.

My search took me back to the end of the eighteenth century and forward to the present. It enabled me to read some of the great works of German intellectual history, but also led me to a mass of lesser writings and to a rapidly expanding secondary literature. Grants from the Social Science and Humanities Research Council of Canada, the Historische Kommission zu Berlin, and Wilfrid Laurier University allowed me to visit Germany, as well as to make use of the collections of German sources in the New York Public Library and the Library of Congress in Washington. Essential to my work has been the interlibrary loan service of the following Canadian universities: Queen's, Toronto, Western Ontario, and Wilfrid Laurier. I would like to thank their staffs as well as those of the special libraries and archives listed in the Bibliography.

I should also like to thank all those who provided information and needed encouragement, whether in person or by letter, particularly Dr. Adolf Birke (German Historical Institute, London), Dr. Wolfram Fischer (Free University, Berlin), Dorothée Friedrich (Traunstein), and Dr. Hans Mommsen (Ruhr-Universität Bochum). Among Canadian scholars, I owe a special debt to the late John Sherwood of Queen's University who was present at the genesis of this project, and to E. J. Hundert of the University of British Columbia whose detailed critique of my first grant application helped to give it direction. At a later stage, my manuscript benefitted greatly from critical readings by Frank Trommler (University of Pennsylvania) and Alfred Kelly (Hamilton College). Finally, thanks go to my husband, Dugal Campbell, for his invaluable criticism and unfailing moral support through the years.

ABBREVIATIONS

ADGB	Allgemeine Deutsche Gewerkschaftsbund (German Trade Union Federation, free trade unions)
AEG	Allegemeine Elektrizitätsgesellschaft (German General Electric Company)
AfA	Anstalt für Arbeitskunde (Institute for Work Study)
AS	*Archiv für Sozialgeschichte*
ASS	*Archiv für Sozialwissenschaft und Sozialpolitik*
AWI	Arbeitswissenschaftliches Institut (Science of Work Institute, DAF)
BA	Bundesarchiv, Koblenz
Ber.Ev.	Diakonische Werk der Evangelischen Kirche, Berlin, Central-Bibliothek der Inneren Mission
BDC	Berlin Document Center
BH	*Biographisches Handbuch der deutschsprachigen Emigration* (see IBD/CE)
BNW	Bund für Nationalwirtschaft und Werksgemeinschaft (Association for a Planned Economy and Works Community)
DAF	Deutsche Arbeitsfront (German Labor Front)
DATSCH	Deutsche Ausschuss für Technisches Schulwesen (German Bureau for Technical Education)
DDP	Deutsche Demokratische Partei (German Democratic Party)
DF	Dorothée Friedrich
DHV	Deutschnationaler Handlungsgehilfenverband (German National Union of Commercial Employees)
Dinta	Deutsches Institut für Technische Arbeitsschulung (German Institute for Technical Industrial Training); from 1933 to 1945 Deutsches Institut für Nationalsozialistische Technische Arbeitsforschung und-schulung (German Institute for National Socialist Technical Labor Research and Training)
DNVP	Deutschnationale Volkspartei (German National People's Party)
ESK	Evangelisch-Soziale Kongress
FAD	Freiwillige Arbeitsdienst (Voluntary Labor Service)
FRG	Federal Republic of Germany
FuA	Freude und Arbeit (Joy and Work)
GDR	German Democratic Republic
GSR	Gesellschaft für soziale Reform (Social Reform Association)
GWS	Gesellschaft für deutsche Wirtschafts-und Sozialpolitik (Society for German Economic and Social Policy)
HA	*Handwörterbuch der Arbeitswissenschaft*

ABBREVIATIONS

HJ	Hitler Jugend (Hitler Youth)
IBD/CE	*International Biographical Dictionary of Central European Emigrés 1933–1945*
IfZ	Institut für Zeitgeschichte (Institute of Contemporary History, Munich)
ILO	International Labor Office
IWK	*Internationale Wissenschaftliche Korrespondenz zur Geschichte der deutschen Arbeiterbewegung, Berlin.*
JCH	*Journal of Contemporary History*
JMH	*Journal of Modern History*
JNS	*Jahrbücher für Nationalökonomie und Statistik*
KdF	Kraft durch Freude (Strength through Joy)
KPD	Kommunistische Partei Deutschlands (German Communist Party)
KSB	Kirchlich-Soziale Bund (Church Social Association)
LC	Library of Congress
NDB	*Neue Deutsche Biographie*
NN	New York Public Library
NSBO	Nationalsozialistische Betriebszellenorganisation (National Socialist Factory Cell Organization)
NSDAP	Nationalsozialistische Deutsche Arbeiter Partei (National Socialist German Workers' Party)
RDI	Reichsverband der Deutschen Industrie (Federal Association of German Industry)
RKW	Reichskuratorium für Wirtschaftlichkeit (Federal Council for Economic Efficiency)
RGG	*Die Religion in Geschichte und Gegenwart*
RWR	Reichswirtschaftsrat (Federal Economic Council)
SA	Sturmabteilung (Storm troopers)
SdA	Schönheit der Arbeit (Beauty of Work)
SOPADE	*Deutschland-Berichte der Sozialdemokratischen Partei Deutschlands*
SP	*Soziale Praxis*
SPD	Sozialistische Partei Deutschlands (German Social Democratic Party)
SS	Schutzstaffel (NSDAP elite paramilitary force)
TH	Technische Hochschule (College of Technology)
VB	Volksverein Bibliothek, Mönchengladbach
VdA	Vereinigung deutscher Arbeitgeberverbände (Association of German Employer Organizations)
VdI	Verein deutscher Ingenieure (Society of German Engineers)
VfS	Verein für Sozialpolitik (Social Policy Association)
VfZ	*Vierteljahrshefte für Zeitgeschichte*

ABBREVIATIONS

VVVD	Vereinigte vaterländische Verbände Deutschlands (Associated German Patriotic Organizations)
ZAG	Zentralarbeitsgemeinschaft (Central Working Alliance)
ZCGD	*Zentralblatt der Christlichen Gewerkschaften Deutschlands*

NOTE: I have tried to supply the dates of birth and death of the more important individuals discussed. A question mark indicates that I was unable to find the date of death.

JOY IN WORK, GERMAN WORK

INTRODUCTION

THROUGHOUT much of history Germans have been regarded, by themselves and by others, as superior workers. If one wished to establish if Germans do work harder than others and, if so, how this is related to their ideas about work, it would be necessary to embark upon a comparative investigation covering several centuries and involving many disciplines. One would also have to take account of the regional and religious differences that persisted after Germany became a nation state in 1870, and to look at the attitudes toward work of all classes of the population, including the largely inarticulate mass of manual laborers whose thoughts and feelings can be discerned only obscurely. This book has a more modest aim: to set forth what educated Germans thought about work and to examine how these ideas changed under the impact of industrialization. Our survey, which ends with the collapse of Hitler's Germany, will give special attention to the debates about modern work that flourished between the two world wars, and, although it will cover the whole spectrum of opinion, will focus on those thinkers who went beyond criticism to seek out solutions in a constructive spirit. Germany undoubtedly contributed to the pessimistic European antimodernist tradition centered on the notion of alienated labor,[1] but it also produced a surprising number of individuals determined to come to terms with modernity and convinced that it was possible to restore a positive relationship between human beings and their work.

In the debate about the nature and ethical value of work that formed the backdrop to the efforts of German reformers one can isolate two key themes. The first, and central, notion is that of *Arbeitsfreude*, or "joy in work." While Germans hold no monopoly of this concept, nowhere else has it been given greater emotional content, nor has any other country made a more determined effort to explore its applicability to modern industrial society. Intertwined with Arbeitsfreude is a second theme, that of *Deutsche Arbeit*, German work. During the nineteenth century, as German nationalism acquired shape and intensity, the national self-image came to involve the conviction that Germans possessed a special, and indeed superior, approach to work, one cen-

---

[1] For a comparative view, see David Meakin, *Man and Work* (London: Methuen, 1976). British anti-modernism is analyzed in Martin J. Wiener, *English Culture and the Decline of the Industrial Spirit 1850–1980* (Cambridge: Cambridge University Press, 1981).

tered on the idea that work is its own best reward, and is alone capable of giving meaning to human existence. When this glorified concept of work was first expressed at the end of the eighteenth century, many writers expressed doubts about the ability of ordinary people to experience joy in work; the discrepancy between ideal and reality, however, aroused widespread concern only from the 1850s on, when extensive industrialization began, and particularly after the creation of the Second Reich in 1870, when the rapid growth of German cities made manifest the religious, ethical, and social implications of modern work. As the First World War approached, a number of patriotic Germans felt impelled to seek ways to restore joy in work as a way of solving the "social question" that threatened domestic stability and the potential power of the new nation.

It was not social unrest but defeat in war that led to the collapse of the imperial regime. Saddled with an unpopular peace and faced with a revolutionary situation aggravated by a deepening economic crisis, its successor, the impoverished and embattled Weimar Republic, struggled to restore the nation's economy and to achieve legitimacy in the eyes of its own citizens and of foreign nations. On the economic front, the best way forward seemed to be to reinforce the modernizing process which had been significantly furthered during the war. Weimar governments therefore supported "rationalization" that drew on American ideas of scientific management and had a major impact on most branches of commerce and industry. Not surprisingly, this reinvigorated the national debate about work. In the course of the 1920s, the "new" disciplines of sociology and psychology, only now acquiring academic respectability, enriched the science of work—*Arbeitswissenschaft*—that had begun systematically to address problems of work organization and motivation before the war. Industrialists, engineers, educators, churchmen, artists, trade unionists, and politicians joined in the effort to increase the productivity of German labor while improving the quality of working life.

Although the reform of work and of attitudes to work were given a higher priority than ever before in the Weimar years, no agreement emerged on how to create—or restore—joy in work. The fact that the need to do so was widely recognized as essential for the health of the nation enabled the National Socialists to capitalize on this issue in order to win support from all sectors of the community. What is more, once in power they made Joy in Work a national objective, thereby completing the identification between Arbeitsfreude and Deutsche Arbeit.

By tracing the development of German ideas about work from the beginning of the nineteenth century, this book contributes to modern German intellectual history. By analyzing the role of Arbeitsfreude and Deutsche Arbeit in early National Socialist ideology, and describing the efforts made after 1933 to embed these concepts into the institutional structure of the Third Reich, it also sheds light on the nature of National Socialism and its place in German history.

Although the ideology of work that I have sought to delineate at first found its most eloquent spokesmen among socialists who wished to overturn the existing order, it was quickly appropriated by defenders of that order who molded it to their own purposes and tended to emphasize its uniquely "German" character. However, it is important to remember that questions about the meaning of work and its ideal relation to life have arisen in all societies where the traditional order has been called into question by the changes associated with modern industry. Germans who sought answers to these questions frequently drew on the thinking of their contemporaries elsewhere, and many of the conclusions they reached influenced thinking in other lands. Indeed, "German" ideas continue to inspire efforts to reconcile modern people with their work in both industrialized and developing countries around the world. For these reasons, an historical account of how Germans tried to tackle this problem not only deepens our understanding of that country but illuminates a problem of vital interest to us all.

FROM the methodological point of view, this book can be described as a social history of ideas. In order to understand the development of German thinking about the problem of modern work, it is essential to take into account the reciprocal relationship between ideas and social realities, and to give due weight to elements of both continuity and change. My subject is not the idea of joy in work itself. Rather, I shall be dealing with such questions as the reasons for its emergence in Germany, why it was adopted as a reform slogan by certain people, how they used it, who opposed them, and why the proposed solutions were or were not realized at various times. This makes it necessary to discuss not only the major German theorists of work who enjoy an international reputation, but also the lesser individuals who joined in the national debate because they claimed to have answers to the problem of modern work. Indeed, most of what was written in Germany about alienated labor and joy in work was produced by essentially derivative authors content to use the ideas of others, so long as these met their own needs or those of the interests they served.

The historian must wonder at times whether it is worthwhile to take such pronouncements seriously. Faced with particularly incoherent, ambiguous, or self-serving arguments, one is tempted to leave their author in deserved obscurity. The ideas of humanity's great thinkers, however, frequently exert their greatest influence in forms imposed on them by less gifted epigones. Nor does superior intellectual endowment, even when combined with genuine commitment, guarantee effective practical thinking. Those involved in the everyday world, although less articulate, are often better able to develop an understanding of issues and contribute to the solution of current problems than their more eloquent academic contemporaries. For this reason, it is essential to cover the whole range of debate.

Similar considerations made it necessary to expand the chronological scope of this inquiry. If one wishes to understand what happened in Germany in the years between the two world wars, it is not possible to begin in 1918 or even with the fascinating years around the turn of the century, years that saw the birth of so many of the ideas and ideals that shaped events in the following decades. For background, one must go to the beginning of the nineteenth century, when the problem of work was first formulated in something approaching modern terms. Ideally one would also wish to take the story forward beyond 1945, in order to assess to what extent the idea of "German" work, including its Nazi manifestation, has influenced subsequent thinking about the problem of alienation in the successor states that have come to represent the German nation since the demise of the Third Reich. That there are significant continuities cannot be doubted, and much could be learned from a comparison of postwar developments in the Federal Republic with those in the Democratic Republic. For practical reasons, however, it has seemed advisable to confine this account to the period from Hegel to Hitler.

I

THE PROBLEM OF WORK

FOR THE MAJORITY of people throughout recorded history, work has been inseparable from existence. Most of those who reflected upon work regarded it as a burden, a necessary evil to be avoided or at least kept to a minimum by employing slaves, women, beasts, or machines to carry out the labor needed to supply their wants. Furthermore, the rewards for hard, manual work have everywhere tended to be low, providing a firm basis in everyday life for the negative valuation of work. This "common sense" view was elegantly formulated by the classical poets and philosophers. The Greeks regarded manual labor as incompatible with full citizenship because leisure was deemed the prerequisite for the cultivation of the human spirit. While classical authors on occasion sang the praises of agricultural labor, they did not honor work for its own sake, much less place it at the core of human existence. For them, it had merit only to the extent that it created the economic basis for civilized living.[1]

The Judeo-Christian tradition substantially modified the classical position by giving manual labor a limited but hallowed place in God's plan. Adam, even in Eden, was enjoined to cultivate his garden in imitation of his creator. When he was cast out, work accompanied him, attended by sorrow and suffering as punishment for his disobedience. Christianity stressed that hard labor was the lot of human beings because of Adam's sin, but it also maintained that work was a potential source of merit, if it was done with love for God and one's fellow human being. St. Paul not only maintained that all must work; extending the concept of work beyond manual labor, he decreed that the maxim "he who will not work, neither shall he eat" applied to rich and poor, cler-

[1] Werner Conze, "Arbeit," in *Geschichtliche Grundbegriffe. Historisches Lexikon zur Politisch-Sozialen Sprache in Deutschland*, ed. Otto Brunner *et al.* (Stuttgart: Klett Cotta, 1972), 1:155–58; Sebastian de Grazia, *Of Time, Work, and Leisure* (Garden City, N.Y.: Doubleday, 1962); Adriano Tilgher, *Work: What It Has Meant to Men Through the Ages* (London: G. G. Harrap, [1930], reprinted New York: Arno Press, 1977).

ics and laymen. In Christian theory from the time of St. Paul on all work was honorable if done in a spirit of Christian service. To this St. Augustine and the other Church fathers added the notion of work as a continuation of God's act of creation and so a positive good even after the Fall.[2]

The Christian emphasis on work found notable expression in medieval monasticism, but it was the Protestant Reformation, centered in Germany and Switzerland, which gave it resonance in the wider community. Luther, Zwingli, and Calvin all proclaimed work's value as a safeguard against idleness and sin and deemed pursuit of a calling as a major expression of faith, a form of worship in no way inferior to contemplation and prayer.[3] In its most extreme Puritan version, Protestantism produced an ethic of work characterized by asceticism and the notion of vocation (in German, *Beruf*), an ethic that could easily reconcile itself with, if it did not give rise to, capitalism.[4]

From the time of the Reformation, Catholics as well as Protestants regarded hard work as both important and meritorious,[5] but it was only in the eighteenth century that the Augustinian notion of work as a positive good resurfaced as a significant element of the Christian tradition. The agent of this transformation was Pietism, a movement within German Protestantism which propagated the idea of work as a spiritual and a psychological necessity. The Pietists put work on a level with prayer as a means to the soul's salvation, or even promoted it as a surrogate for prayer; they maintained that work performed in conscious fulfillment of God's injunction to help one's neighbor could be expected to give rise to a sense of blessedness, a feeling of joy.[6] But although Pietists stressed the significance of work for the individual psyche, they never valued it *because* of its contribution to human hap-

---

[2] Konrad Wiedemann, *Arbeit und Bürgertum. Die Entwicklung des Arbeitsbegriffs in der Literatur Deutschlands an der Wende zur Neuzeit* (Heidelberg: Carl Winter, 1979), 83–88.

[3] Conze, "Arbeit," 163–67. Conze, "Beruf," 490–507.

[4] Few today would accept the argument of Max Weber's classic "Die protestantische Ethik und der Geist des Kapitalismus," first published in *ASS* (1905) and translated into English as *The Protestant Ethic and the Spirit of Capitalism* (New York: Scribners, 1930). In any case, ascetic Calvinism, central to Weber's analysis, never became important in Germany. See Wiedemann, *Arbeit und Bürgertum*, 289–94.

[5] Keith Thomas, "Work and Leisure in Pre-Industrial Society," *Past and Present* 29 (1964): 58–59.

[6] Klara Vontobel, *Das Arbeitsethos des deutschen Protestantismus von der nachreformatorischen Zeit bis zur Aufklärung* (Bern: A. Francke, 1946), 42–45; Carl Hinrichs, *Preussentum und Pietismus. Der Pietismus in Brandenburg Preussen als religiös-soziale Reformbewegung* (Göttingen: Vandenhoeck & Ruprecht, 1971), 313–15 and 342–51; Anthony J. La Vopa, "Vocations, Careers, and Talent. Lutheran Pietism and Sponsored Mobility in Eighteenth-Century Germany," *Comparative Studies in Society and History* 28 (1986): 255–86.

piness. Salvation in the world to come rather than happiness in this life remained the Christian's goal; at its best, therefore, work constituted a means of salvation, not an end in itself.

Adherents of the traditional Christian view of work might be inspired to look for less onerous ways to produce goods, but the idea of humanizing work and raising the quality of working life is largely predicated on the post-Christian assumption that individual happiness in this world is of prime importance. Christian concern did lead to denunciations of the evils attributable to greed and exploitation and to injunctions that one should work towards ends pleasing to God. Sometimes it also inspired a search for more equitable ways to distribute the proceeds of labor. But only after Christianity itself began to be called into question was work perceived as a "problem" requiring urgent solution. Serious efforts to give individuals satisfaction in and through work were inspired by the ideals of the Enlightenment, which played a critical role in the evolution of Western thinking about work. The "age of reason" defined work in an essentially positive way, as the instrument of human mastery over nature, the basis of culture, the creator of community and the source of social progress. At the same time, by proclaiming individual happiness in this life to be a legitimate goal of human endeavor, it made possible a conception of joy *through* work, or even joy *in* work that went far beyond anything in the Christian tradition.

Because advancing secularization introduced new ways of conceiving the relationship between human beings and the natural world, it can be called on to explain why Arbeitsfreude emerged as a major theme near the start of the German debate about work. Yet concern with the topic would probably not have reached the level it did in the nineteenth century had the character of work not undergone a transformation. How secularization and industrialization were linked has never been satisfactorily resolved; nor has it been established which of these processes was primarily responsible for altering the way western Europeans thought about work. In the German case, however, it seems certain that the new attitude to work emerged well before the industrial revolution had significantly changed the mode of production. The men of letters, poets, and philosophers whose speculations were to influence thinking about work in and outside Germany as industrial capitalism came to dominate economic life were the products of an essentially "pre-industrial" society. Their contributions were those shaped by Enlightenment and early Romantic re-evaluations of the human situation rather than by personal experience or observation of a radically altered world of work.

J. G. Herder, a leading spokesman of the German Enlightenment, reflected the new mood:

> Work, you wise ones of the people, further your own joy and that of the masses! Where dwells true tranquillity? Where the blessing of a loving God? Only in work![7]

Herder still thought of work in Christian terms, as a means to keep from idleness and sin and distract oneself from the miseries of this world, but he added the secular idea of diligent effort in the service of humanity as a source of individual happiness. Similarly, the jurist Justus Möser wrote of work as "the source of all true joy," and the poet Johann Andreas Cramer insisted that "work is not slavery, but the joy of humanity."[8]

The most eloquent and frequently quoted statement of the new outlook was Friedrich Schiller's "The Bell" which praised the human capacity to respond with the heart to what the hand creates and proclaimed that "Work is the Bürger's honor, blessedness his labor's wage."[9] Goethe, too, contributed to the exaltation of work when he declared that nothing is more benighted than a man without work and praised the labor of the craftsman as the source of all art. Indeed, Goethe's Faust has come to symbolize the Western drive to create and to seek joy, freedom, and immortality in productive labor.[10] At a more prosaic level, an instructional manual of 1798 urged young Germans not to think of work as something oppressive. Instead, it promised that the development of good work habits would teach them how to derive great pleasure from labor, to the point where they would no longer wish to live without it.[11]

The German idealist philosophers did most to shape the new ethos of work. Admittedly, the founder of German idealism, Immanuel Kant (1724–1804), had little to say on the subject, and his moral philosophy reinforced the Christian concept of work as duty (*Pflicht*) instead of encouraging contemporaries to regard it as a source of human happiness.[12] Nor did his disciple Fichte (1762–1814) accept the equation of productive labor with happiness. Instead, he valued work as a source of material progress, which would make possible the leisure to make in-

---

[7] Eberhard Schmieder, "Arbeitsethos: eine Einführung in seine Geschichte," *Schmollers Jahrbuch* 79 (1959): 432.

[8] Conze, "Arbeit," 172.

[9] Friedrich Schiller, "Das Lied von der Glocke," *Sämtliche Werke* (3d ed.; Munich: Carl Hanser, 1962), 1:430, 439.

[10] Schmieder, "Arbeitsethos," 435.   [11] Conze, "Arbeit," 172.

[12] Conze, "Arbeit," 184.

dividuals truly free. Nonetheless, Fichte did help to shape the secular modern work ethic, for he insisted that free, purposeful activity, especially intellectual work, both shaped man as an individual and produced the moral order:

> You are not in this world for contemplation nor for introspective examination of your spiritual state—no, you are here to act, and your activity . . . alone determines your worth.[13]

In sum, Fichte rejected both the inwardness of the Romantics and the preference for a life of contemplation over one of action that had led many Christians to a quietist position. Influenced by classical humanism, he argued for a balanced existence in which work would be done by choice, although in moderation, so as to benefit society and to lay the economic basis for the free spiritual and intellectual growth of the individual.[14]

It was Hegel (1770–1831), representing the apogée of Germany's idealist tradition, who incorporated into his system the theoretically most extreme positive valuation of work. But even while giving Arbeit the highest possible status, Hegel, like Herder and Fichte, generally used the term to denote a type of activity far removed from the realm of ordinary labor or from economic life. In his abstract philosophizing work is variously described as the defining characteristic of humanity, the means used by Spirit to master matter, and a progressive force related to the will of God.[15] Seen in this light, all work becomes honorable, even that of slaves who, as Hegel maintained, through work become the masters of their non-laboring masters.[16] Work, and only work, is the source of the highest good, freedom. From this it was just a short step to the glorification of the worker as the "father of mankind." Thus one of Hegel's disciples could argue that human beings create themselves as *human* through work, and that all work has value insofar as it allows people to develop themselves physically and mentally, to subject nature to human purposes, and to ennoble humanity.[17]

[13] Schmieder, "Arbeitsethos," 499.

[14] Conze, "Arbeit," 185. On Fichte's ideas about work, see also Zwi Batscha, "Die Arbeit in der Sozialphilosophie Johann Gottlieb Fichtes," AS 12 (1972): 1–54.

[15] Karl Löwith, *From Hegel to Nietzsche* (Garden City, N.Y.: Doubleday, 1967), 262; Conze, "Arbeit," 186; Hans Freyer, *Die Bewertung der Wirtschaft im philosophischen Denken des 19. Jahrhunderts* (Leipzig, 1921, reprinted Hildesheim: Georg Olms, 1966), 57–58; Schmieder, "Arbeitsethos," 499.

[16] For expositions of Hegel's views on the master-slave relationship as propounded in his *Phenomenology of the Spirit* (1807), see Alexander Kojeve, *Introduction to the Reading of Hegel* (New York: Basic Books, 1969), 20–24, and Eugen Fink, *Grundphänomene des menschlichen Daseins* (Freiburg: Karl Alber, 1979), 276–80.

[17] A. Ruge, cited by Schmieder, "Arbeitsethos," 441–42.

By assigning work a central role in the development of both the individual and society, German idealist philosophers at once reflected and provided theoretical justification for the Enlightenment's faith in the progress of humanity towards the goal of freedom. Work remained a means to an end, but the fulfillment of humanity's potential within the historical process rather than salvation in the life to come was now the goal. Yet German idealism, while giving work an exalted status beyond anything proposed earlier, also drew attention to its problematic nature. Compared with the free, creative, intellectually stimulating, socially useful, personally fulfilling "work" praised by the philosophers and the humanist poets, most labor in the real world was bound to appear unsatisfactory: impersonal, mechanical, deadening, and destructive of higher values.

Unlike Fichte, who preferred not to dwell on the gulf between ideal and reality, Hegel, at least in his early writing, showed himself to be keenly aware of the discrepancy between the "is" and the "ought" of work. His Jena lectures of 1805/6 contained an analysis of the problem of work that stressed the devastating effects of industrial labor on the individual and on society. Basing his indictment of modern work largely on Adam Smith's famous account of specialized labor in a pin factory in *The Wealth of Nations* (1776), Hegel foretold the development of a factory proletariat. Increasing mechanization and division of labor would create a class of workers deprived of their skills, whose work would consequently be devalued and ill-rewarded, and who would depend for their livelihood on the caprice of impersonal market forces.[18]

Having formulated the problem of modern work as part of a critique of industrialism, Hegel withdrew once more into the realm of abstraction. His *Phenomenology of the Spirit* of the following year still deplored alienation and reification, but these were now described as inescapable features of human progress rather than as related to specific—and therefore potentially remediable—contemporary developments. Indeed, at no time did Hegel make an effort to move from analysis to prescription when dealing with the problem of work. Evading the issue, he argued that productive labor, the source of human alienation, would itself, in dialectical fashion, become the means to overcome alien-

[18] Georg Wilhelm Friedrich Hegel, *Jenaer Realphilosophie* (Hamburg: Felix Meiner, 1967), 232; Schlomo Avineri, "Labor, Alienation, and Social Classes," in J. J. O'Malley *et al.*, eds., *The Legacy of Hegel* (The Hague: Martinus Nijhoff, 1973), 201–207; Alasdair Clayre, *Work and Play. Ideas and Experience of Work and Leisure* (London: Weidenfeld and Nicolson, 1974), 36.

ation.[19] When combined with the abstract nature of his argumentation, this approach rendered Hegel's treatment of the problem of work virtually useless to the social critic or would-be reformer.

Hegel turned to the topic of work for a third and last time in his *Philosophy of Right* (1821). By then he had abandoned the effort to clarify contemporary trends by juxtaposing the ideal with reality. Instead, he sought to do away with the entire problem by reconciling his theoretical conception of unalienated spiritual or intellectual labor with the circumstances of economic life. Thus he argued that human beings not only create themselves and their culture through work, but that productive labor could be regarded as "culturally educative" because it accustomed people to be busy and to take the will of others into account. In other words, the habit of work freed the civilized human being from the laziness and subjective individualism of the barbarian. What is more, Hegel, who had condemned the process of mechanization in his Jena lectures, now claimed that the machine, by forcing workers to a higher level of abstraction, contributed to their spiritual and ethical elevation. Having thus "solved" the problem of work at the speculative level, Hegel henceforth gave little thought to the hardships endured by his laboring contemporaries, although he did grant the state a limited role in the alleviation of economic distress through the regulation of foreign trade and the institution of poor relief.[20]

Romanticism was the third strand of thought that in combination with classical humanism and philosophical idealism helped to create the intellectual context within which Germans addressed the problems of society in the early nineteenth century. Usually conservative in their outlook, German romantics compared the modern world unfavorably with the organic, Christian community of the Middle Ages. By painting an idealized picture of medieval artist-craftsmen and their guilds, romantic writers added a persistent element to the critique of modern work and contributed to the positive ideal of Arbeitsfreude. Nevertheless, it would be a mistake to equate belief in the possibility of joyful work with romantic conservatism. Hegel's acknowledgement that work had deteriorated from an earlier state of rich complexity did not make him a romantic, nor did it induce him to join the reactionaries in advocating a return to earlier modes of production. Likewise Schiller (1759–1805), following in Rousseau's footsteps, joined the romantics

[19] Georg Wilhelm Friedrich Hegel, *Phänomenologie des Geistes*. Theorie Werkausgabe, vol. 3 (Frankfurt: Suhrkamp, 1973).

[20] Georg Wilhelm Friedrich Hegel, *Grundlinien der Philosophie des Rechts* (1821), in *Werke* (Frankfurt: Suhrkamp, 1970) 7:351–53; Löwith, *From Hegel to Nietzsche*, 266–67; Avineri, "Labor," 207.

in complaining that the advance of culture had "made a breach between state and church, laws and customs, and separated enjoyment from work, means from ends, effort from its reward."[21] But instead of demanding the restoration of the old order, he argued that humanity must move forward to a time when all would be able to engage in free, joyful, activity. Thus, although the ideal of Arbeitsfreude was generally accompanied by nostalgia, it could also inspire longing for a new and better society. Romanticism and socialism proved to be just as compatible as romanticism and conservatism.

It is also significant that not all who thought of themselves as romantics adopted the idea of joy in work. The more conservative among them emphasized the importance of Christian community, and were therefore firmly opposed to an ethic based on individual gratification. Typically, Adam Müller (1779–1829), a leading voice of German conservatism, did not base his preference for a stable agricultural and artisan economy on the belief that these modes of production were particularly conducive to joyful work. Concerned that ethical values be placed above material ones, Müller looked forward to the day when human beings and their work would once more be firmly rooted in a society that valued honor, duty, and Christian love above riches.[22] At most, the dogma of joyful labor gave conservative romantics one more weapon with which to combat the industrial capitalism that was associated in their minds with an atheistic, materialistic, and rational-utilitarian ethos destructive of the Christian organic world view.

By the time of Hegel's death in 1831 work had become an important literary and philosophical theme. Germans had begun to debate many topics that were to loom large in subsequent discussions: the significance of work for the individual and the community, the cultural implications of mechanization and rationalization, the educational potential of work and the need to educate people for work, and the relationship of work and leisure. What is more, some of the difficulties had already become apparent. These included the seeming impossibility of agreeing on definitions of "work" and "worker," and the tendency of intellectuals to apply a standard derived from their experience of "mental work" or creative activity to manual labor.

But if the early nineteenth-century German debate about work foreshadowed things to come, it also exhibited some distinctive features. The topic was treated at an extraordinary level of abstraction, as a

[21] Friedrich Schiller, *Über die äesthetische Erziehung des Menschen in einer Reihe von Briefen* (Stuttgart, 1967), 22.
[22] Conze, "Arbeit," 194–95.

problem facing "humanity" as a whole rather than particular classes or nations. And although a start had been made in noting the psychological, economic, and social aspects of the question, work was still discussed in the first instance as an ethical problem. Disturbed by the negative features of modern developments, writers tended to call for ethical renewal rather than pressing for the reorganization of society or the reform of work itself.

There was also a reluctance to develop the theoretical implications of their ideas. Thus, although many German romantics and idealists assigned an enormous significance to work, they stopped short of proclaiming it a supreme value. In part this can be explained by the strength of the classical humanist tradition, with its emphasis on the need for moderation in all things and its belief in the culture-bearing value of free activity. When combined with the romantic distaste for utility and mechanism, this prevented thinkers like Schiller and Fichte from turning their exaltation of creative activity into a glorification of work *per se*. But even more instrumental in discouraging the emergence of a full-fledged gospel of work at this time was the continuing influence of Christianity. For the Christian, valuing work for the joy it brings to the producer carries with it a danger that individuals will give their own wellbeing precedence over the needs of the Christian community and prefer the quest for happiness in this world to the search for salvation in the next. But even if one does not stress the potential of work as a source of happiness, insisting on its central importance to human existence increases the risk that people will devote time and energy to their work to the detriment of Christian worship. No wonder, then, that most Germans who contributed to the development of a new ethic of work in the early nineteenth century recoiled from the consequences of their ideas. In the event, it needed the influx of foreign ideas, combined with a marked intensification of social tensions, to reveal fully just how subversive of inherited Christian values was the new way of thinking about work.

II

WORK AND REVOLUTION

BETWEEN Hegel's death in 1831 and the upheavals of 1848–50, important changes took place in the way people discussed the problem of work. The perception that German society was in crisis lent a new urgency to the debate, which for the first time addressed itself to specifically German circumstances. Although observers could not agree on either causes or cures, they noted the rapid growth of a *Stand* or social estate that fell outside the traditional order and posed a potential threat to its stability: the poverty-stricken mass of would-be laborers composed largely of landless farm workers and newly dependent craftsmen. In an economy with limited employment opportunities, even those who got jobs were frequently forced to accept below-subsistence wages, to put up with abysmal working conditions, and to rely on the earnings of their wives and children to make ends meet. Faced with this burgeoning class of the uprooted, to which the term "proletariat" was increasingly applied,[1] the literate public reacted with alarm. The result was a flood of newspapers and pamphlets analyzing the origins of the problem and proposing solutions.

By creating additional employment opportunities, the factories that were beginning to appear in parts of Germany were actually less a cause of social distress than a palliative of economic misery. Nevertheless, reform-minded individuals in Germany were apprehensive about the advance of the factory system because they saw what had happened elsewhere. Attributing the social tensions so evident in England and the political instability of contemporary France to the industrial revolution which had proceeded much further in those countries, they felt challenged to discover a uniquely German path to modernity that would make it possible to reap the benefits of progress without paying its penalties.

[1] Werner Conze, "Vom 'Pöbel' zum 'Proletariat': Sozialgeschichtliche Voraussetzungen für den Sozialismus in Deutschland," in Hans-Ulrich Wehler, ed., *Moderne deutsche Sozialgeschichte* (Cologne: Kiepenheuer & Witsch, 1968), 117.

Germany's would-be revolutionaries also looked abroad. The growth of self-conscious working-class movements in England and France, and the accompanying wave of socialist and communist theorizing, helped to convert radicals like Wilhelm Weitling, Moses Hess, Friedrich Engels, and Karl Marx to socialism. In close contact with disaffected workers and intellectuals in other lands, these men incorporated significant foreign elements into their prescriptions for the thoroughgoing reorganization of German society.

It was the radicals who introduced to Germany the writings of Charles Fourier and Thomas Carlyle, two of the most original contributors to the modern ideology of work. Fourier (1772–1837), a leading French utopian, propagated the idea of *travail attrayant*, "pleasing work," as a way of motivating the inhabitants of his new communities or phalansteries. Although he believed that "natural man" liked to be active, Fourier posited no innate desire to work.[2] To render work attractive, society had to be thoroughly restructured so as to enable individuals both to engage in tasks suited to their temperament and talents and to indulge their natural love of variation. In Fourier's new society, the tedium of unavoidably repetitive tasks was to be allayed by changing jobs, while the division of labor, far from engendering a sense of alienation, was expected to create a cooperative system of production that would allow all members of the community to develop their individuality. Working at a variety of tasks suited to his nature, "socialist man" would be spurred on by group rather than individual competition and by the desire to complete projects from which all would benefit. Unprecedented wealth would be created through effective and enjoyable labor.

Fourier's vision of a society based on joyful work appealed to the early German socialists, including Wilhelm Weitling (1808–1871), who came into contact with Fourier's ideas and those of his disciple, Considerant, when he lived in Paris from 1837 to 1841.[3] Influenced by French theory, this self-educated tailor elaborated plans for a society organized around a system of production that would allow most workers "to follow several occupations, thus eliminating monotony by rotating

[2] Nicholas V. Riasanovsky, *The Teaching of Charles Fourier* (Berkeley: University of California Press, 1969), 225.

[3] Biographical details are from Carl Frederick Wittke, *The Utopian Communist. A Biography of Wilhelm Weitling, Nineteenth-Century Reformer* (Baton Rouge, La.: Louisiana State University Press, 1950). Weitling's role in linking German with French communism was noted by a contemporary, Lorenz von Stein. See his "Blicke auf den Sozialismus und Communismus in Deutschland und ihre Zukunft (1844)," in *Lorenz von Stein*, ed. E. Pankoke (Darmstadt: Wissenschaftliche Buchgesellschaft, 1974), 50–51.

the tasks assigned every two hours."[4] But although Weitling agreed that productivity could be improved by getting people to work joyfully, he was convinced that individuals needed to be *taught* to work for the good of their fellows and to find joy in so doing. He therefore suggested a comprehensive system of schools to inculcate appropriate attitudes to work while offering training in a variety of skills. The educational process was to culminate in three years of compulsory service in an industrial army organized on military lines, during which all able-bodied members of the community between the ages of fifteen and eighteen would learn the skills and discipline needed for farm and factory. As adult citizens, they would then be fitted into the complex occupational structure of Weitling's utopia.

Weitling followed Fourier in designing a society in which the subdivision of labor would be so great and the hours of work so limited that people would be able to escape boredom by engaging in a variety of activities. But his more rigid scheme ruled out the unlimited transfers from job to job envisioned by Fourier. Moreover, Weitling departed from Fourier's ideal of work carried on joyfully for its own sake or in a spirit of gentle group competition. To provide the necessary material inducements he devised a system of work credits which individuals could earn through labor, and which could be used to purchase goods produced by others. The aim was to encourage people to continue working in their free time, that is, after the completion of hours required by their primary occupation.

Weitling's writings were widely distributed during his lifetime, and his reputation exceeded that of any other German socialist in the years before 1848. His emigration to the United States after the failure of the German revolutions opened the way for Marx's theoretically more sophisticated "scientific" socialism which in any case proved better suited to the atmosphere for "realism" that prevailed after 1850 than Weitling's quasi-religious utopianism. Yet it is important to recall that in its formative stages "Marxism," the creation of Karl Marx (1818–1883) and Friedrich Engels (1820–1895), was shaped by many of the same utopian influences that had contributed to Weitling's doctrines.

These included the ideas of Fourier, which came to Marx and Engels through Moses Hess (1812–1875). A convinced communist while Marx and Engels still held to the democratic republicanism of their youth, Hess had set himself the task of combining German idealist philosophy with French socialism, Hegel and Feuerbach with Fourier. In his *21 Bogen aus der Schweiz* of 1843 he praised French communism for

---

[4] Wittke, *Utopian Communist*, 59.

insisting that the new society would abolish the conflict between enjoyment (*Genuss*) and work, thus giving practical realization to the philosophical ethic which proclaimed free activity as the only true joy and highest goal of humanity.[5] Two years later Hess defined socialism as the society in which production and consumption, work and pleasure, are no longer distinct. Work was bound to be alienated in a system based on private property; only communism would enable human beings to move from the realm of necessity to that of freedom by providing work that would at last be both self-determined and social. After the advent of the new social order and the total abolition of wage labor, people would work in a truly human fashion, motivated to realize their full potential by an inner drive rather than by external rewards.[6]

Hess denounced the communist proposal for tackling the problem of work by giving everyone an equal measure of work and pleasure. In his view, such a scheme could never create an organic bond between labor and enjoyment. Attempts to implement the ideas of men like Weitling and the French utopian communist Cabet upon whom Weitling had drawn would inevitably lead to the reinstitution of the master-slave relationship in altered form. Similarly, Hess felt that the French socialists, including Fourier, were in error because they failed to denounce wage labor and thus to free themselves from dependence on the market and the pernicious system of interest and money. While acknowledging that German radicals lagged behind the French in the practical realm, he believed that the latter had failed to move beyond a prettified version of bourgeois commercialism because they lacked the benefits of German philosophy. Convinced of the superiority of the German ideology of work, he preached the need for a thorough-going implementation of its highest ideals.[7]

Like Hess, the young Marx evolved an ideal of work that combined elements of German humanism and philosophical idealism with French socialism. Before moving to Paris, where he lived from late 1843 to 1845, Marx was already a critic of contemporary society, given to denouncing its dehumanizing aspects and advocating political remedies. By 1844 personal contact with French socialists and radical workers and the study of French and British political economy had converted him to the view that the alienation of labor was the chief root of dehumanization. From this it was but a short step to designating the proletariat, the product of alienated labor, as the historical agent of the revolution

[5] Moses Hess, *Philosophische und Sozialistische Schriften 1837–1850. Eine Auswahl*, ed. Auguste Cornu and Wolfgang Mönke (Berlin: Akademie-Verlag, 1961), 204.

[6] Hess, *Schriften*, 322–23.   [7] Hess, *Schriften*, 323–25.

that would shortly overthrow bourgeois capitalism. Marx's analysis of alienated labor, central to his critique of capitalism, inspired him to become the theorist of proletarian revolution. From the mid-1840s on he gave priority to economics in his "programme of gaining mastery over the various causal factors involved," with the aim of "practically superseding alienation in all spheres of life."[8]

The complexity of the young Marx's thinking about work and alienation, and the fact that many of his most revealing remarks on the topic contained in his *Economic and Philosophical Manuscripts* of 1844 were not published until the 1930s, meant that his views on work had little influence on his contemporaries. Nevertheless, it is worth looking at some of his early pronouncements on the subject. Of particular interest are his attempts to come to terms with Fourier. Fourier's notion of pleasurable labor appealed strongly to Marx. It fitted in with his belief, derived from German idealism, that human beings are essentially producers who, through their work, transform nature and in the process form themselves. Like the Young Hegelians, Marx maintained that people could fulfill themselves through work—and only through work. People were thought not only to possess the capacity to engage in free, creative activity, but also to have a real need to do so. Thwarting this drive would inevitably produce a sense of alienation. An important element in Marx's indictment of wage labor in modern industrial capitalism was his conviction that it entailed the "disappearance of all creativity and joy from work, and thus was psychologically damaging."[9] How much of this Marx derived from his study of Hegel and Hess and how much from what he read and heard while in Paris is a matter of dispute. In either case, the influence of Fourier is evident in his insistence that "a properly organized, humane and rational society would ensure that labor was varied and enjoyable, and that this should be one of the chief goals of socialism."[10]

Marx argued that work in capitalist society fails to approach the ideal for several reasons: the exploitation of labor by capital, the workers' lack of control over both the process and the product of their efforts, but, above all, the excessive division of labor. Thus in *The German*

[8] Istvan Mészáros, *Marx's Theory of Alienation* (London: Merlin Press, 1970), 232–33. The most complete historical discussion of the young Marx's ideas on work is in Edward David Gregory, "The Influence of French and English Socialism on the early Thought of Friedrich Engels and Karl Marx, 1835–1847" (unpublished Ph.D. diss., Queen's University, Kingston, Ontario, 1978).

[9] Karl Marx, "The Economic and Philosophical Manuscripts of 1844," in Robert C. Tucker, *The Marx-Engels Reader* (2d ed.; New York: Norton, 1978), 70–81; Gregory, "French and English Socialism," 454–56.

[10] Gregory, "French and English Socialism," 565.

Ideology (1845/46), written together with Engels at whose urging he had recently undertaken a systematic study of Fourier's works,[11] Marx expressed the hope that under communism it would prove possible to render work less monotonous and stultifying by cutting down the number of hours at any one task and allowing individuals to engage in a variety of occupations. This would permit people to experience their labor as a social activity satisfying natural human needs and to cultivate all facets of their personality.[12]

Although he never again spoke with such longing of a society in which he could "do one thing today and another tomorrow, to hunt in the morning, fish in the afternoon, rear cattle in the evening, criticize after dinner, just as I have a mind, without ever becoming hunter, fisherman, shepherd or critic,"[13] the possibility of unalienated labor continued to find a place in Marx's thinking long after he had outgrown his romantic youth. As late as 1875 he spoke of a final stage of communism "after the enslaving subordination of the individual to the division of labor" had been overcome, along with "the antithesis between mental and physical labor," making work "not only a means of life but life's prime want."[14]

Marx rejected the traditional Christian view of work as essentially a burden or sacrifice which had been upheld by the classical economists, and which had been reasserted in secular form by Hegel who regarded alienation as an inescapable feature of the human condition rather than the by-product of a particular socio-economic system. Instead, he joined Fourier in advocating a new ethic that would liberate, not repress, human impulses and passions, and have room for the concept of joyful labor. However, Marx was too puritanical—and, perhaps, too "German"—to follow Fourier all the way. As he wrote in his notebooks of the late 1850s, "Labour cannot become play, as Fourier would like."[15]

For his part, Marx preferred to close the gap between labor and leisure not by turning work into play but by transforming leisure into something closer to creative work. In its ideal form human activity, whether directed to the production of the necessities of life or to the creation of ideas and objects of beauty, remained a serious matter, one that in Marx's view required both discipline and effort. The satisfaction

[11] Gregory, "French and English Socialism," 532.

[12] Gregory, "French and English Socialism," 469.

[13] Marx, "The German Ideology," in Tucker, *Marx-Engels Reader*, 160.

[14] Tucker, *Marx-Engels Reader*, 531. This passage appeared in Marx's critique of the German Social Democratic Party's Gotha program, republished by Engels in 1891.

[15] Tucker, *Marx-Engels Reader*, 290, excerpt from *The Grundrisse*.

to be derived from work at its best was not mere pleasure but an earnest kind of joy closely linked with the fulfillment of a project or purpose. Not Playboy but Prometheus was Marx's model: a heroic individual engaged in a variety of challenging, self-directed activities of social value which, taken together, allowed the full utilization of all mental and physical powers and the development of a total personality.[16] One must conclude that Marx's view of work was influenced as much by Schiller and the German romantics as by Fourier. Moreover, it remained essentially an intellectual's vision, derived from speculation about human nature rather than close observation of the world of work and with little apparent applicability to the realities of industrial labor.

To determine the contribution of Marxism to the German ideology of work one must examine the ideas of Engels, who influenced "Marxism" from the beginning and became the doctrine's chief propagandist and interpreter in Germany after Marx's death in 1883. Engels drew on the same romantic-idealist tradition that had inspired Hess and Marx, but his idea of work was also influenced by industrial Manchester where he completed his business training in the early 1840s and established contacts with British Chartists, socialists, and social critics. Although Engels admired Fourier's critique of commercial capitalism, he was convinced that the British utopian Robert Owen had a better grasp of the social problems produced by industrialization. His view of what work might be like under communism therefore combined a "Fourierist vision of a cooperative association in which work was voluntary and joyous with Owen's conviction that an industrial commune would be able to take full advantage of new technology to reduce working hours and raise living standards."[17]

In England, Engels also came under the influence of Thomas Carlyle (1795–1881) whose *Past and Present*, published in 1843, he reviewed for the *Deutsch-Französische Jahrbücher*. Steeped in the literature of German romanticism and idealist philosophy, Carlyle judged the ills of society from a standpoint closer to that of the young Engels than to the "orthodoxies of Ricardian political economy and Malthusian social thought."[18] Engels found it easy to admire the brilliance of Carlyle's attack on Mammon and on the utilitarianism of a fragmented society which reduced the individual to a soulless atom. However, he differed from the British writer on almost all points of substance. Whereas En-

[16] John McMurtry, *The Structure of Marx's World View* (Princeton: Princeton University Press, 1978), 31–35.

[17] Gregory, "French and English Socialism," 330.

[18] Gregory, "French and English Socialism," 305; Steven Marcus, *Engels, Manchester and the Working Class* (New York: Vintage Books, 1975), 212–13.

gels thought nothing more terrible than labor performed for money alone, or involving the execution of monotonous, specialized tasks under exploitative conditions, Carlyle proclaimed the value of *all* work and explicitly rejected the idea that people should strive for happiness, or that work should give pleasure:

> All work, even cotton-spinning, is noble; work is alone noble. . . . And in like manner too, all dignity is painful; a life of ease is not for any man, nor for any god . . . the one unhappiness of a man that he cannot get his destiny as a man fulfilled.[19]

Given the strenuous nature of Carlyle's gospel of work, it is no wonder that the critique of working conditions took second place in his writings to an indictment of idleness on the one hand and of Mammonism on the other. Carlyle's devastating picture of contemporary society entailed no program that could lead to improvements in the quality of working life, and his work ideal proved best adapted to the purposes of those who defended the status quo. Engels could follow Carlyle when he asserted that work is a blessing and idleness the source of despair, but as a socialist he could not accept the gospel of work in its entirety without abandoning his radical convictions.

Engels's first-hand acquaintance with the terrible plight of the workers in the mills of Manchester, described for German readers in his *The Condition of the Working Class in England* of 1845, persuaded him that wage labor under capitalism was irredeemably evil. Only in the future communist society would compulsory, meaningless, and stunting labor gradually make way, through the application of modern technology, to work that was freely undertaken and capable of developing all one's mental and physical powers. Carlyle's criticism of capitalism ended with praise for the heroic captains of industry; Engels's denunciation of dehumanizing labor in capitalist society culminated in a call for the destruction of that society. Instrumental in drawing the attention of German socialists to both Fourier and Carlyle, the young Engels found the "libertarian" socialism of the French utopian more congenial than Carlyle's romantic Toryism.[20]

The failure of the revolutions of 1848 and the subsequent acceleration of social and economic change profoundly effected both Marx and Engels. Like most of their intellectual contemporaries, they now repudiated utopianism and turned to "science" as the instrument of prog-

[19] Thomas Carlyle, *Past and Present* (1843, reprinted London: J. M. Dent & Sons, 1912), 147, 150.
[20] David Gregory, "What Marx and Engels Knew of French Socialism," *Historical Reflections* 10 no. 1 (Spring 1983): 156–57, 159.

ress. Their revolutionary goals remained unchanged, as did their belief that labor would one day be transformed from a tool of subjugation to a "means of emancipation, by offering each individual the opportunity to develop all his faculties, physical and mental, in all directions and exercise them to the full," making work a "pleasure instead of a burden."[21] Nevertheless, there were significant alterations in their treatment of the problem of work.

While still attacking the division of labor and excessive specialization, Marx and Engels increasingly saw modern industry and technology not as a source of these evils but as their potential cure. In the *Communist Manifesto* of 1848 they had blamed modern industry—equated with mechanization, the division of labor, and factory regimentation—for turning the proletarian into an appendage of the machine and thereby reducing work "to the most simple, most monotonous, and most easily acquired knack."[22] By contrast, the first volume of Marx's *Das Kapital* which appeared in 1867 prophesied that modern industry would in time

> replace the detail-worker of today, crippled by lifelong repetition of one and the same trivial operation, and thus reduced to a mere fragment of a man, by the fully developed individual fit for a variety of labors, ready to face any change of production, and to whom the different social functions he performs are but so many modes of giving free scope to his own natural powers.[23]

Similarly, Engels, in his *Anti-Dühring* of 1878, cited Marx to the effect that technological progress would put a premium on "variation of labour, fluency of function, [and] universal mobility of the labourer."[24] The implication was that a prime task of the socialist revolution would be to liberate the beneficent tendencies within modern technology from the fossilizing specialization imposed by an anachronistic capitalist system. Drawing on Marx's later writings, Engels stressed that automation would progressively reduce the physical burden of labor, that modern industry, once freed from its capitalist shackles, would offer full scope to scientific creativity and technical ingenuity and thus bridge the gap between mental and physical labor, and that work would become a humanizing force even as the productive capacity of industry increased for the benefit of society. In other words, the romantic humanism of the pre-1848 writings had yielded to a "technical

---

[21] Friedrich Engels, "Anti-Dühring" (1878), in Tucker, 720.
[22] Tucker, *Marx-Engels Reader*, 479.   [23] Tucker, *Marx-Engels Reader*, 413–14.
[24] Tucker, *Marx-Engels Reader*, 721.

humanism" that took as its model the work of the scientist and engineer rather than that of poet, artist, or craftsman, and held out the promise that further changes in the mode and relations of production would in time vanquish alienation.[25]

When the German Social Democrats turned to Marx in the last decades of the nineteenth century, they virtually ignored that strain in Marxism which sought to transform work itself into a free creative activity, "life's prime want." Forced to fight for tolerable conditions of employment and basic civil rights, their Marxism had little room for the notion of joy in work. The Social Democratic Party (SPD) did value work highly as the source of all wealth and culture. Subscribing to a secularized version of St. Paul's dictum that "He who will not work, neither shall he eat," it showed little sympathy for the ideas of Marx's French son-in-law, Paul Lafargue, who equated leisure with culture and work with slavery.[26] At most, Social Democrats expressed a longing for a world in which advanced technology would minimize the need for burdensome work and enlarge the "realm of freedom" in which truly human activity could flourish.

Their tendency to disregard the "joy in work" aspect of Marxism was partly due to the influence of Engels, who tended to play down this feature of his friend's doctrine. Engels believed that some of the distasteful feature of work in the modern factory, most notably the need for discipline and hierarchy, would persist even after the destruction of the bourgeois capitalist order because they were innate features of industrial production. Moreover, instead of dwelling on socialism's potential to provide satisfying work, he stressed that higher productivity would make it possible greatly to reduce labor time.[27] Marx had been ambivalent about whether the goal of communism should be to humanize labor or to abolish it;[28] Engels's prompting helped to ensure that not joy *in* work but more free time for enjoyment *after* work became the prime objective of German Marxists.

This interpretation of Marxism was reinforced by Engels's protégé and friend Karl Kautsky (1845–1938), the SPD's chief theoretician who categorically declared in 1892 that

[25] Conze, "Arbeit," 203, and Helmut Klages, *Technischer Humanismus. Philosophie und Soziologie der Arbeit bei Karl Marx* (Stuttgart: Ferdinand Enke, 1964).

[26] Michael J. Neufeld, " 'He Who Will Not Work, Neither Shall He Eat': German Social Democratic Attitudes to Labour 1880–1914" (unpublished M.A. diss., University of British Columbia, 1976); Wolfgang Nahrstedt, *Die Entstehung der Freizeit* (Göttingen: Vandenhoeck & Ruprecht, 1972), 263–64.

[27] "Anti-Dühring," in Tucker, *Marx-Engels Reader*, 721.

[28] John Maguire, *Marx's Paris Writings: An Analysis* (Dublin: Gill & Macmillan, 1972), 79–82.

not freedom of work, but liberation from work as rendered possible to a large extent by mechanization in a socialist society, will give humanity freedom of life, the freedom of artistic and scientific activity, the freedom of most noble enjoyment.[29]

By doing so, Kautsky gave support to the German labor movement's inclination to focus on higher pay and shorter hours, rather than promote the reform of work. It may be an oversimplification to maintain that German Social Democrats equated freedom with free time and denied the humanizing potential of work, but by the end of the century their view does seem to have been that work, even under communism, would remain an effortful activity requiring discipline and willing submission to authority, a duty rather than a source of pleasure.

Even those who hoped that workers would labor joyously in the future socialist society regarded Arbeitsfreude as something to be taught and learned rather than as a spontaneous expression of human nature that would at last find release in the post-revolutionary world. Socialist educators who were unaware of or simply ignored Marx's belief in the innate longing for meaningful work stressed the necessity of training the young to recognize in work the "duty and honour of human beings."[30] Meanwhile, those German Marxists who held to the goal of individual self-fulfillment tended to view human beings in the first instance as consumers rather than producers as Marx had done, and so projected a socialism that would make it possible for people to enjoy the abundant fruits of rationalized production and a full measure of society's cultural goods in their non-working hours.

Whatever their reasons may have been, by failing to espouse the ideal of unalienated labor the Social Democrats contributed to the decline in revolutionary fervor within the German labor movement. Had they called for a radical transformation of the workplace in order to maximize opportunities for joyful work, they might well have turned the widespread desire for Arbeitsfreude into a potent element of their rhetorical assault on the capitalist system. Instead, the SPD's unromantic, "materialist," view of work reinforced already powerful evolutionary and reformist tendencies on the German left.

Convinced that capitalism would become more productive and more "social" with the passage of time, the Social Democrats increasingly focused their reforming efforts on the democratization of state power. The SPD evidently hoped that a more democratic government would

[29] Cited by Conze, "Arbeit," 204.
[30] Neufeld, "He Who Will Not Work," 103; Käte Duncker, "Die Schulreform der Sozialdemokratie," *Die Neue Zeit* 29/2 (1910–11): 697–704.

allot to the workers a fair share of the new wealth created by their labor, and therefore concentrated on building up its organizational strength, extending its political base, and raising the consciousness and educational level of the workers, while backing the struggle of the affiliated trade unions for shorter hours and better pay. All in all, the German socialists by the turn of the century put democracy before socialism, preferred reform to revolution—and longed for liberation from, rather than through, work. It was left to the bourgeois enemies of socialism to take up the early socialist critique of industrial society in terms of alienation, and to develop the notion of joyful work as an inspiration for social change.

III

THE BOURGEOIS ETHIC
OF WORK

THE IDEAL of joyful labor that Marx had specified as a prime objective of revolutionary socialism was adopted by spokesmen for the middle classes who sought to end alienation in order to *avert* social upheaval. Their aim was not to bring the international proletariat to power but rather to dissolve it and to reintegrate manual workers into the larger national community. There was no consensus among "bourgeois" thinkers[1] on how this was to be achieved or on the nature of the resulting social order, but whether they looked back to the pre-industrial past or forward to a technological utopia, they agreed that it was essential to solve the problem of work if social stability was to be restored.

The anti-Marxist ideology of work based on Arbeitsfreude that was to emerge with particular force in the 1920s and 1930s originated with several contemporaries of Marx and Engels whose views overlapped to a remarkable degree with those of their socialist compatriots. The shared heritage of romanticism, idealism, and Hegelianism meant that mid-nineteenth-century opponents of proletarian revolution cast their critique of modern industrial work in terms hardly distinguishable from those employed by its proponents, and came to similar conclusions about work and alienation.

An example is Lorenz von Stein (1815–1890), best known for his *Der Sozialismus und Communismus des heutigen Frankreichs* (1842), which introduced the German public to advanced French social thought. Von Stein defined work as that which allows the individual person to master the natural world and, in so doing, to become truly

[1] By this I mean non-working-class, antisocialist thinkers who proudly proclaimed what they felt were middle-class values. I do not use "bourgeois" to denote class status. It should be recalled that most socialist intellectuals, including Marx and Engels, were of middle-class origin.

autonomous.[2] It was the drive to engage in creative work—the capacity to invent, compose, form, design, experiment—that differentiated human beings from animals. Drawing on Hegel, von Stein further claimed that such "free" activity carried forward the work of the Spirit in its progress towards self-realization by producing durable goods to be enjoyed and, at the same time, satisfying an inborn human need to act upon the environment.[3] Contrasting the labor demanded by industrial society with this ideal, von Stein found it wanting. In mechanized production, workers were ruled by, rather than mastering, their tools. Condemned by the lowly nature of their work to earn just enough to reproduce themselves, they were also deprived of the means to satisfy their legitimate desires and to develop their personalities.[4]

To free human beings from mechanical, soul-destroying, and ill-paid work was as much von Stein's goal as it was that of the young Marx. He, too, argued the need to overcome the gap between mental and physical labor, and regarded the highest form of work as a blend of the two. Ideally, the human mind would achieve mastery over the natural world and "raise material work to the level of spirit, while transforming external satisfactions into inward fulfillment."[5] Also like Marx, von Stein sensed the disruptive potential of the growing proletariat. But whereas Marx urged the workers to solve the problem of work by destroying private property and the capitalist market economy, von Stein sought to analyze their legitimate aspirations and devise ways to satisfy them within the existing social order.

In particular, he advocated the expansion of public education and government support for technological innovation. By improving the workers' mental and physical capacities, education would fit individuals for work capable of generating greater material and spiritual rewards. Meanwhile, the advance of technology would enable machines to do much of the burdensome "natural" work of the world, and thereby liberate people to engage in the "free" activities for which their better training would qualify them. Thus the problem of work would be solved without the necessity of revising property relations or redistributing the profits of labor.[6]

[2] Lorenz von Stein, *Blicke auf den Sozialismus und Communismus in Deutschland und ihre Zukunft*; Der Begriff der Arbeit und die Principien des Arbeitslohnes in ihrem Verhältnisse zum Sozialismus und Communismus, in *Blicke auf den Sozialismus und Communismus in Deutschland*, ed. Eckart Pankoke (Darmstadt: Wissenschaftliche Buchgesellschaft, 1974), 99.

[3] Stein, "Begriff der Arbeit," 107.   [4] Stein, "Begriff der Arbeit," 112.

[5] von Stein, "Begriff der Arbeit," 106. A similar abstract analysis, culminating in a glorification of work in its ideal form, is contained in von Stein' popular *Lehrbuch der Nationalökonomie* (3d ed., Vienna, 1887), 46–64.

[6] Stein, "Begriff der Arbeit," 119.

Not all anti-socialist economists and social theorists of the pre-1848 period were as optimistic as von Stein. The liberal political theorist Robert von Mohl (1799–1875), who was to play a prominent role during the 1848 revolution, depicted the negative consequences of modern production in terms fully as stark as those employed by Engels. Almost a decade before Engels's book on what was happening in England, von Mohl concluded that massive industrialization was bound to lead to the moral and physical degradation of the workers and demanded the abandonment of laissez-faire principles. Advocating a comprehensive program of reforms to mitigate the most glaring evils of proletarian existence, including state regulation of wages and hours and government promotion of profit-sharing arrangements, he also favored universal education to raise the cultural level of the masses and provide the ethical training no longer supplied by the majority of families. Nevertheless, he remained convinced that none of these proposed changes, nor all of them taken together, would solve the problem of work. So long as the modern system of production prevailed, society would be burdened with a "mass of ignorant, poor individuals, exhausted daily by joyless work."[7]

A more hopeful view of workers' prospects for a life of joyful labor was propagated by the economist Johann Heinrich von Thünen (1785–1850). Like Marx, he foresaw a time when human beings would spend their life "not in idleness but in moderate activity, exercising both mind and body and strengthening health and enjoyment (*Frohsinn*)."[8] However, in Malthusian fashion, von Thünen put most of the blame for their misery on the workers themselves and concluded that their condition would only improve if proletarians began to think like the bourgeoisie. In particular, the workers must come to value learning sufficiently to postpone marriage, and thereafter produce only as many children as they could afford to educate. What was required, in essence, was a complete reformation of the *Volk* character.

Von Thünen acknowledged that this was unlikely to come about in the absence of a higher standard of living and a system of compulsory state education. He was as determined as any socialist, however, to

[7] Robert von Mohl, "Über die Nachteile, welche sowohl den Arbeitern selbst als dem Wohlstande und der Sicherheit der gesamten bürgerlichen Gesellschaft von dem fabrikmässigen Betrieb der Industrie zugehen und über die Notwendigkeit gründlicher Vorbeugungsmittel" (1835), in Carl Jantke and Dietrich Hilger, eds., *Die Eigentumslosen. Der deutsche Pauperismus und die Emanzipationskrise in Darstellungen und Deutungen der zeitgenössischen Literatur* (Freiburg: Karl Alber, 1965), 294–318.

[8] Johann Heinrich von Thünen, "Die konstitutionellen Staaten und das Los der Arbeiter" (1826), from *Der isolierte Staat in Beziehung auf Landwirtschaft und Nationalökonomie*, 2d ed. (1842–50), in Jantke and Hilger, *Eigentumslosen*, 282.

break the vicious cycle of poverty and ignorance and accepted the legitimacy of the workers' aspirations to a better life, including their right to better paid, more secure employment and to meaningful work. Where he differed from Marx was in his conviction that the destruction of private property would not solve the problem of alienation. Rather, the route to the utopia of joyful work lay along the "humble, thorny, path of scientific research."[9] Von Thünen therefore embarked on empirical studies intended to lay the foundation for a social science that would combine economics with ethics. He also argued, and tried to prove scientifically, that employers who raised wages above the subsistence level, far from increasing unemployment, would improve the workers' standard of living, enable them to adopt a bourgeois standard of morality, and thereby guarantee industrial peace and social harmony.

More sanguine still was the economist Bruno Hildebrand (1812–1878). Hildebrand, who fled from Germany to Switzerland at the time of the 1848 revolution, returned to Jena in 1861 as professor, founded the prestigious *Jahrbuch für Nationalökonomie und Statistik*, and won a reputation as one of the fathers of the historical school of political economy. Although aware of the negative social effects of industrial progress, he denied Engels's charge that recent changes in the method of production *caused* the misery of the lower classes. Instead he maintained that these developments had merely brought the underlying problem of poverty to public attention.

Hildebrand also rejected Engels's argument that industrial work was morally degrading, for he was impressed by the way the majority of English workers accepted the need for further mechanization, were active in the establishment of producer cooperatives, and supported trade unions that cooperated with employers to promote honest work.[10] Hildebrand reported that the English trade unions fined workers who insulted their employers and in general adhered to a high ethic of diligent labor. From this he concluded, correctly, that England would avoid the revolutionary upheavals threatening its less developed neighbors.

Determined to cast the future in a positive light, Hildebrand depicted the impact of factory labor on the working class in terms remarkably similar to those Marx employed in *Das Kapital* to describe the humanistic potential of modern work in socialist society. According to Hildebrand, industrial labor accustomed people to "regular activity,

[9] Thünen, "Konstitutionelle Staaten," 283–85.

[10] Bruno Hildebrand, "Die Nationalökonomie der Gegenwart und Zukunft" (1848), in *Die Nationalökonomie der Gegenwart und Zukunft und andere gesammelte Schriften*, ed. Prof. Dr. Hans Gehrig (Jena: G. Fischer, 1922), 1:187–90.

persistence and conscientious utilization of their time," while nurturing their "drive and strength of will." By forcing individuals to move from one occupation to another, industrialization also encouraged mental versatility and self-confidence and broadened the workers' outlook, while the machine developed the workers' humanity by stimulating a sense of solidarity. Lifting the working classes "out of indolence and ignorance," modernization endowed them with the "consciousness of their strength, with perseverance in work and with the spirit of enter-prise," encouraged them to strive for a more dignified and worthy place in history, and thus turned them into active collaborators in the his-torical process.[11] In Hegelian fashion, he concluded that labor in mod-ern industry would prepare the workers to become fully integrated members of bourgeois or "civil" society, while the advance of mecha-nization would make it possible for them to share in the material re-wards of increased prosperity.

In sum, Hildebrand believed that the new spirit of confidence awak-ening among the workers, together with greater awareness of the plight of the impoverished masses on the part of the educated classes, would suffice to overcome what he judged to be the miseries of a period of transition, the necessary birth-pangs of a better future.[12] Enlightened as to their true interests, the newly-awakened working classes would enter into rationally calculated cooperation with their employers, adopt the bourgeois work ethic, and transform the labor movement from a potentially destructive to a culture-bearing force.

By mid-century, a considerable number of respected and respectable German scholars had recognized the problem of work as a major com-ponent of the "social question" and had sketched out non-revolution-ary ways of resolving it. Yet it was only in 1861, with the publication of Wilhelm Heinrich Riehl's *Die deutsche Arbeit*, that the subject was given extended treatment from a bourgeois perspective.[13] Riehl (1823–1897) more than any other nineteenth-century German removed the question of alienation from the socialist domain and made the ideal of Arbeitsfreude part of the anti-socialist arsenal. Although his contribu-tion to the philosophy and sociology of work in no way ranks with that of Hegel or Marx,[14] Riehl was to influence all who favored a character-

[11] Hildebrand, "Nationalökonomie," 184–85.
[12] Hildebrand, "Nationalökonomie," 185.
[13] Wilhelm Heinrich Riehl, *Die Deutsche Arbeit* (Stuttgart: J. G. Cotta, 1861). A third, revised edition appeared in 1883 and was repeatedly reissued. Unless otherwise indicated, page references are to the undated fourth edition, an unaltered reprint of the third.
[14] But see Christian von Ferber, *Arbeitsfreude. Wirklichkeit und Ideologie. Ein Beitrag zur Soziologie der Arbeit in der industriellen Gesellschaft* (Stuttgart: Friedrich Enke, 1959), 71, where the author takes Karl Löwith to task for asserting in his *From Hegel to Nietzsche* that no one

istically German approach to the social question. This, combined with the originality of his approach to the problem of work, justifies extensive treatment of his ideas.

Riehl never mentioned Marx, while Marx disdainfully dismissed Riehl's contribution to the study of society as inconsequential.[15] Nevertheless, much can be learned from a comparison between Riehl's views on the problem of work and those of his great socialist contemporary. For although these two educated middle-class Germans evolved opposing social ideologies, they had much in common as individuals and held similar views on important aspects of the problem of work.

Like Marx, Riehl was a Rhinelander by birth, and studied at a number of German universities where he came into contact with Hegelian philosophy and with the writings of the leading social theorists of post-Napoleonic Europe. The revolutions of 1848 exerted a decisive influence on the political and social outlook and subsequent career of both men. However, in other important respects their backgrounds differed. Marx came from a wealthy Jewish professional family; Riehl's forebears were Protestant, middle-class, and poor.[16] Had it not been for the determination of his widowed mother and his own energy and ability, his father's suicide in 1839 would have ended Riehl's hopes for a university education. Like many ambitious young men of limited means, Riehl sought to better his status by training for the Lutheran ministry. However, his interests gradually shifted away from theology to philosophy and then to cultural history. Soon after graduation, he abandoned his original plan of becoming a village parson and decided, instead, to devote his life to the study of the German Volk and its customs.

Both Marx and Riehl found academic careers closed to them. Marx was prevented from obtaining a university post by his radical religious and political views; a lack of money forced Riehl to set aside his dream of becoming a professor. Like Marx, he found a substitute in journalism. As founding editor of the *Nassauische Allgemeine Chronik* of his home province, Riehl kept himself and his readers informed of political and social events by journeying through the countryside on foot to at-

---

after Hegel and Marx made a major contribution to the ideology of work. In Ferber's view, both Riehl and Max Weber deserve to be placed in this illustrious company.

[15] Siegfried A. Peter, *Arbeit und Beruf bei Wilhelm Heinrich Riehl. Ein psychologisch-soziologischer Beitrag zur Entwicklung des Berufsgedankens im 19. Jahrhundert* (Inaugural diss., Erlangen, 1964), 262.

[16] The fullest account of Riehl's life is Viktor Ritter von Geramb, *Wilhelm Heinrich Riehl: Leben und Wirken 1823–1897* (Salzburg: Otto Müller Verlag, 1954). See also H. Simonsfeld, "Wilhelm Heinrich Riehl," *Allgemeine Deutsche Bibliographie* (Leipzig, 1907), 53:362–83. Biographies of Marx are legion. A good treatment of his early years can be found in David McLellan, *Karl Marx, His Life and Thought* (London: Macmillan, 1973).

tend popular assemblies and observe the courts at work. By the time revolution broke out in March 1848, he knew a great deal, at first hand, about the contemporary situation. But unlike Marx who was transformed by events into a revolutionary activist, Riehl was cured of any desire to get personally involved in politics. Social disorder and the failure of the Liberals to bring about the unification of the country under a constitutional regime convinced him, along with many of his contemporaries, that underlying social problems had to be resolved before any further restructuring of political life could begin.[17]

During the reaction that followed, Riehl finally turned his back on the youthful radicalism that he had inherited from his artist father—a Free Mason and enthusiast for the French Revolution. Instead, he adopted the conservative outlook of his Pietist maternal grandfather whose years of service as an estate manager had given a rural-aristocratic tinge to his essentially bourgeois character. Marx, in permanent exile, dedicated himself henceforth to the cause of international socialism; Riehl put down roots and concentrated on revealing the intellectual and popular sources of his beloved German heritage.

His conservatism was reinforced by his transfer from the Prussian Rhineland to Bavaria, still relatively untouched by modernization. In 1851, his publisher and friend, Freiherr Georg von Cotta, invited Riehl to Augsburg where he spent several productive years working for Germany's leading newspaper, the *Allgemeine Zeitung*, and publishing his first serious books: *Die bürgerliche Gesellschaft*, *Land und Leute*, and *Musikalische Charakterköpfe*. In 1854 he was called to Munich by Maximilian II, who put him in charge of the royal information services. In 1857 he began on a multi-volume descriptive survey of Bavarian life, and by 1859 he was professor of cultural history and statistics at the University, thus fulfilling his youthful ambitions. In 1885 he became director of the Bavarian National Museum and conservator of monuments and antiquities for the kingdom.

As a member of Maximilian's intimate circle, Riehl attended the court and produced memoranda on topics of public concern. But his activities were not confined to Bavaria. An effective and popular public speaker, between 1871 and 1885 he calculated that he had delivered 487 lectures on 112 themes in 106 German cities to more than 180,000 listeners.[18]

---

[17] Geramb, *Riehl*, 131, 185–91. For an interesting discussion of Riehl's response to the revolution, see Andrew Lees, *Revolution and Reflection: Intellectual Change in Germany during the 1850's* (The Hague: Martinus Nijhoff, 1974), 102, 147–53.

[18] Simonsfeld, "Riehl," 370. Meanwhile, a series of popular historical novella won Riehl a national reputation as a man of letters.

Deutsche Arbeit, the last of Riehl's major works to deal with social issues, may be regarded as the logical conclusion of his *Natural History of the Volk as the Foundation for German Social Policy,* in which he had sought to counter liberalism and socialism, ideologies deemed pernicious to the sound and organic development of German society.[19] Instead of appealing to abstract reason and focusing on material issues, Riehl set out to elucidate the nation's popular traditions in all their diversity as the basis for a social policy capable of serving as an antidote to radicalism and disorder.

In *Deutsche Arbeit,* too, his aim was not to write objective history or anthropology but to draw attention to the strength of inherited social forms and attitudes. Arguing that a nation's character is best revealed in its attitudes to work, and that Germany was *the* nation of work, Riehl set out to explore his subject from a folk-historical perspective. Granting only limited utility to economics and statistics, he insisted that the best way to grasp the spirit of German work was by examining folk customs, songs, and proverbs.[20] With these as sources, he set out to delineate the national ethos of work that seemed to be emerging from the traditions of the diverse regions, estates, and professions which together comprised the Germany of his day.[21]

The main characteristic of this "German" work ethic was its high idealism, involving the belief that work should be done for its own sake and for the good of the Volk, rather than for profit. Riehl shared the anti-capitalist ethos prevalent among his academic contemporaries,[22] and had nothing but disdain for the money-grubbing business elements—"Jews" or "Yankees." Instead of striving for the external rewards of labor like these worshipers of Mammon, the true German derived satisfaction from the sense of duty accomplished and work well done. Here he was in essential agreement with Marx, except that the latter would probably have substituted "socialist" for "German" in the previous sentence.[23]

Like Marx, over time Riehl became somewhat less idealistic in his

[19] Wilhelm Heinrich Riehl, *Die Naturgeschichte des Volkes als Grundlage einer deutschen Sozialpolitik* (Stuttgart, 1854–69), 4 vols. On the genesis of these works, see Günther Ipsen, "Die Soziale Volkskunde W. H. Riehls," in Ipsen, ed., *W. H. Riehl: Die Naturgeschichte des deutschen Volkes* (Stuttgart: Alfred Kröner, 1935). This volume contains excerpts from the *Naturgeschichte* as well as essays and articles on related themes.

[20] Riehl, *Deutsche Arbeit,* 1–9.   [21] Riehl, *Deutsche Arbeit,* 46–94.

[22] For comparable views on work of Riehl's bourgeois liberal contemporaries, notably the historian Droysen, see Wolfgang Hock, *Liberales Denken im Zeitalter der Paulskirche. Droysen und die Frankfurter Mitte* (Münster: Aschendorff, 1957), 108–111.

[23] For Marx's equation of the capitalist work ethic with the Jewish spirit, see especially his essay of 1843, "On the Jewish Question," in Tucker, *Marx-Engels Reader,* 26–52.

views on work. His youthful review of a book on the ethos of the Reformation made no mention of "German" work, and cited a number of foreign authors with approval, including Carlyle and Rousseau on the virtue of work and the iniquity of idleness, and Fourier on the right of everyone to find work which will give him joy.[24] In a passage very similar in tone and content to Marx's description of unalienated labor in the classless society of the future, Riehl here spoke of a time when mental and physical labor would be shared, enabling everyone to obtain both bread and culture (*Brot und Bildung*), and when crime would disappear along with the need for government repression, because all would have suitable and purposeful work. Even at this stage, however, Riehl argued that private property constituted the only way to preserve individual identity. He also rejected the popular socialist slogan of the "organization of labor," on the grounds that reform could not be engineered. Not a socialist restructuring of economic life but an ethical rebirth was needed to restore social harmony through the provision of joyful work for all.

The openness to foreign ideas and the utopian belief in the capacity of workers in all walks of life to experience joy in work were notably absent from Riehl's post-revolutionary writings. When he returned to the theme of work in the 1850s, he no longer dealt with it in universal terms. But he continued to believe in the importance of ethical as opposed to economic or political reform, and in the overriding need to reconcile people with their work.

In his widely read *Die Bürgerliche Gesellschaft*, conceived between 1848 and 1851, Riehl analyzed German society in terms of four estates or *Stände*, of which two—the peasantry and the aristocracy—represented the forces of resistance, while the other two—the *Bürger* class (itself divided into conservative and progressive elements) and the Fourth Estate—represented the forces of movement. In order to maintain the traditional order, he argued that it was necessary to reverse the trend to proletarianization that was creating a fourth estate out of rootless renegades from the three legitimate orders. Praising the German peasant as the best exemplar of German work, he assigned the peasantry, the landed aristocracy, and the middle-class artisanate key roles in the preservation of inherited values.

Nonetheless, Riehl cannot be fairly categorized as an outright reac-

[24] Review of *Die philosophische Weltanschauung der Reformationszeit in ihren Beziehungen zur Gegenwart* by M. Carriere, 13 March 1847, cited in Geramb, *Riehl*, 140–42. Riehl also approved of Fichte for insisting that the state has the duty to ensure that all people can live from their work and have sufficient leisure to develop all aspects of their humanity.

tionary,[25] for he acknowledged the inevitability and irreversibility of social change, refused to condemn all progressive elements outright, and conceded the need for substantial reforms. By the time *Deutsche Arbeit* appeared, Riehl had become reconciled to the relative decline of his "forces of resistance" and was prepared to draw the consequences: the Bürger, representative of the "forces of movement," now replaced the peasant as the hero of his tale, and was cast as the chief exponent of German values, the creator of the highest ideal of work. Riehl acknowledged that the peasants could only show what Germans had been.[26] Studying peasant life might enable his compatriots to evaluate the gains and losses incurred in the evolution of the modern economy, but it could not provide guideposts for future conduct.[27]

The work ethic outlined in *Deutsche Arbeit* was anything but a glorification of the medieval world view. Steeped as he was in the Pietist tradition, Riehl believed that the Reformation had performed a signal service when it destroyed the Catholic Weltanschauung that had measured the value and dignity of work in accordance with the social status of the worker. Since then, intellectuals who reflected on the relationship between status and profession (Stand and Beruf) had developed new criteria, so that in the modern world labor was judged by its nature and results alone. Terming this a "liberating" idea, Riehl argued that it corresponded to the increased complexity of society; but he attributed it neither to the impersonal working of economic forces nor to Volk instinct. Rather, it had taken the conscious effort of generations of Protestant teachers and preachers to free German work by destroying the guild system, and win general acceptance for the belief that all work is honorable.[28]

Riehl was also "progressive" in his insistence that the German work ethic had achieved its ideal form not in the countryside but in the towns. It was the Bürger, not the peasant, who was Germany's most productive and representative worker, and it was the city that provided

---

[25] See, e.g., Ernest K. Bramsted, *Aristocracy and the Middle Classes in Germany* (rev. ed.; Chicago: The University of Chicago Press, 1964), 326; T. S. Hamerow, *The Social Foundations of German Unification 1858–1871: Ideas and Institutions* (Princeton: Princeton University Press, 1969), 183, 208–209; George L. Mosse, *The Crisis of German Ideology: Intellectual Origins of the Third Reich* (London: Weidenfeld and Nicolson, 1970), 19–24; Eckart Pankoke, *Soziale Bewegung—Soziale Frage—Soziale Politik. Grundfragen der deutschen 'Socialwissenschaft'* *im 19. Jahrhundert* (Stuttgart: Ernst Klett, 1970), 61–66; Lees, *Revolution and Reflection*, 146–47. The more progressive elements in Riehl are brought out by Karl Buchheim, *Deutsche Kultur zwischen 1830 und 1870* (Frankfurt: Akademische Verlagsgesellschaft Athenaion, 1966), 9, 217, 220–21.
[26] Riehl, *Deutsche Arbeit*, 113.   [27] Riehl, *Deutsche Arbeit*, 69.
[28] Riehl, *Deutsche Arbeit*, 16–20.

the greatest stimulation and variety of opportunity. By opening education to all, the urban centers created a competitive climate that enforced superior work discipline and a faster tempo of labor.[29] Above all, it was intellectual work (*Geistesarbeit*), characteristically the product of urban life, that best exemplified the national character. Spreading from the towns to the countryside, the new *ethic* of work had produced a new *practice* of work "from the studies of philosophers and scientists to the peasants' huts."[30] In sum, the work ethic Riehl prized was the product of the Protestant urban middle classes, and could only be expected gradually to permeate the lower strata of the social hierarchy.

By attributing the national work ethic to the bourgeoisie Riehl could explain why the folk songs he studied failed to reveal an elevated ideal of work. Largely the creation of peasants or even of herders, their tendency to praise poverty and to depict paradise as the realm of undiluted leisure rendered them irrelevant to the modernizing economy of his day.[31] On the other hand, Riehl was not prepared to dismiss the material he had so lovingly collected. Instead, he drew attention to the fact that many popular sayings and customs either presaged or reflected the bourgeois values of diligence and hard work. Moreover, the popular tradition differentiated among *Erfolg* ("achievement" or "success"), *Gewinn* ("gain" or "reward"), and *Profit* in a distinctively German way fully consonant with the new bourgeois ethic. While praising and encouraging energetic labor, the folk wisdom warned against work done for the sake of external rewards alone, expressed distaste for greed, and condemned concentration on work to the exclusion of worship.[32]

In a chapter on "Work and the Bible," Riehl discussed the important role played by the Scriptures in shaping German ethical concepts. Distinguishing between Old (Mosaic) and New (Christian) attitudes to work, he maintained that the Old Testament described work as God's punishment for the sin of Adam, an inescapable feature of life after Man's exclusion from paradise, but that the story of the Creation showed God himself as a worker who enjoined Man to labor six days and rest on the seventh in imitation of his Maker.[33] The Old Testament also contributed to the modern work ethic by praising hard work, castigating idleness, and stressing the utility and rewards of labor for both individual and community. Nevertheless, Riehl judged the New Testament to be far superior. For Christ, while praising hard work, had also warned against the worship of Mammon. Taking seriously the Gos-

[29] Riehl, *Deutsche Arbeit*, 256–59.   [30] Riehl, *Deutsche Arbeit*, 252.

[31] Riehl, *Deutsche Arbeit*, 109.   [32] Riehl, *Deutsche Arbeit*, 115–17, 176–94.

[33] Riehl, *Deutsche Arbeit*, 147.

pels' anti-capitalist strictures, Riehl dwelt on those passages that valued work for its ethical content rather than its outcome.[34] It was this aspect of the Bible that he believed had been particularly potent among the Germans, who had learned from the Scriptures that work is blessed quite apart from its effects, and that huckstering, profiteering, and the love of lucre (Schacher, Profitmacherei, Geldfresserei) are evil.[35]

Riehl's "Christian" ideal of work, directly opposed to the spirit of capitalism, was by extension also antithetical to the theory and practice of the Jews, whom he accused of exhibiting the capitalist love of lucre in its most extreme form. On the other hand, Riehl praised Jews as workers, argued that they had been forced into usury by their exclusion from industry and agriculture, and maintained that conversion, assimilation, and the adoption of German work habits and ideas about work would in time dissipate the "semitic" and medieval characteristics which he disliked.[36] Thus Riehl's antisemitism, unlike that which began to take hold in the 1880s, was based on religious and nationalistic rather than racist grounds.[37]

As far as Riehl was concerned, socialism was as alien to the Christian work-ethic as capitalism. Distancing himself from the atheist critics of the status quo, he condemned those "prophets of the proletariat" who declared work to be holy and "would have us not work and pray, but work instead of worshipping."[38] While he acknowledged that artists or intellectuals, in their finest moments, might experience work as prayer, in general the two were separate. "We work for ourselves and others, but we pray only for ourselves." Moreover, Riehl stressed the psychological importance to the individual of limiting the demands of work: the more mechanical the occupation, the more the worker requires periods of quiet and self-communion. Finally, Riehl feared that those who preached the holiness of labor were treating applied ethics as a surrogate for religious faith. This, he insisted, might attract the half-educated, but was alien both to the truly cultured individual and to the general populace, which rightly condemned excessive glorification of labor as an impoverishment of ethical and religious life.[39] Riehl thus rejected the "gospel of labor," which is usually designated as *the* bourgeois ethic of work although it was just as often espoused by socialists.[40]

[34] Riehl, *Deutsche Arbeit*, 159–60.   [35] Riehl, *Deutsche Arbeit*, 161.

[36] Riehl, *Deutsche Arbeit*, 53–54.

[37] On the varieties of German antisemitism, see Uriel Tal, *Christians and Jews in Germany. Religion, Politics, and Ideology in the Second Reich, 1870–1914* (Ithaca, N.Y.: Cornell University Press, 1975).

[38] Riehl, *Deutsche Arbeit*, 28.   [39] Riehl, *Deutsche Arbeit*, 29.

[40] On the nineteenth-century bourgeois work ethic in Germany, Bramsted, *Aristocracy*, 109–119, and Martin Halter, *Sklaven der Arbeit-Ritter vom Geiste. Arbeit und Arbeiter im*

Riehl also objected strongly to the egalitarian element in socialism. While he accepted the modern view that all work is honorable, he denied that all was equally worthy of honor. Instead, there existed a natural hierarchy of work based on the degree to which each type of labor incorporated an element of mental effort (*Geist*). At the top of this hierarchy stood the creative artist and the scholar, for he believed that intellectual work (*Geistesarbeit*) was at once most individual and most "national." Convinced that literature and the applied arts were among the "products" that could tell most about a nation's character, he urged Germans to develop their own forms of artistic expression instead of borrowing continuously from others. His idea of German work was thus closely allied with cultural nationalism. On the other hand, Riehl recognized that *Geist* was also important in the world of modern industry: because of the large element of intellect in their work, Riehl placed entrepreneurs, managers, and inventors just below pure intellectuals in the hierarchy of labor.[41]

It was the manual worker—glorified by Riehl's socialist contemporaries—whom he found most difficult to place in the hierarchy of honorable work. Peasants and artisans, the entrepreneurial and professional middle classes, even the aristocrats, had made and would continue to make a valuable contribution not only to national production but also to the German ethic of work.[42] The factory worker, by contrast, seemed to stand right outside the social order. Uprooted from popular folkways, the worker in modern industry no longer obeyed the "natural" division of labor between man, woman, and child. Instead, the factory system imposed an artificial division of labor that inevitably produced a sense of alienation. While undoubtedly enriching the nation, industrialization created a class of people for whom work was impersonal and therefore a perpetual source of individual dissatisfaction and social disaffection.[43] How different was harmonious, freely chosen intellectual work, which, if not pursued to excess, ennobled both mind and body by strengthening the will and with it the entire nervous sys-

deutschen Sozialroman zwischen 1840 und 1880 (Frankfurt: Peter Lang, 1983), especially 123–24, 431 n.71. According to Halter, from the utopian socialists on, the labor movement increasingly adopted the religion of work, whereas the bourgeoisie tended to abandon it after 1870. As it became the new leisure class, the latter either went on the defensive or adopted aristocratic modes of thought. Meanwhile, the German Social Democrats came to pride themselves on their superior work ethic.

[41] Riehl, *Deutsche Arbeit*, 23, 75. Riehl commented that the gap between the industrial manager and the ordinary factory worker was much greater than that which had obtained between the master craftsman and the medieval journeyman.

[42] Riehl, *Deutsche Arbeit*, 192–93, 209–221.   [43] Riehl, *Deutsche Arbeit*, 92–93.

tem. For the *Geistesarbeiter* work continued to constitute life's chief pleasure, and even the agony of creative effort was a source of joy, although he might on occasion envy manual workers for the limited nature of the demands made on them.[44] Indeed, it was the joy they derived from their work that made intellectuals the supreme apostles of the German work ethic.

When *Deutsche Arbeit* first appeared, Riehl still believed it might prove possible to preserve a harmonious balance between the different types of work and to minimize those with undesirable characteristics by slowing the rate of industrialization and limiting its extent. He also assumed that proletarianization could be stemmed by encouraging sound family life, fostering a spirit of solidarity through cooperative housing, and enabling workers to put down roots in a place of employment structured along patriarchal lines. Above all, better education, including moral and religious training, would serve to counter socialist propaganda that drew attention to the inequality of rewards under capitalism and advocated class struggle in the name of social justice. For Riehl was convinced that people could be taught to view poverty positively, as a spur to labor and a source of Christian humility. The Fourierist ideal of joy in work, still upheld as relevant to people at the apex of the hierarchy of work, Riehl condemned as bestial when applied to the lower orders.[45] Rather than fighting for better wages or aspiring to Arbeitsfreude, the workers should practice the old virtues of self-restraint and moderation and create a place for themselves as an honorable estate within the corporate order of society.[46]

By 1883, when Riehl published a revised version of *Deutsche Arbeit*, his views had somewhat altered. Although he was now more reconciled to the spread of modern industrialism, which was especially rapid after the unification of Germany in 1870–1871, he was less sanguine about the possibility of converting the factory workers to his bourgeois ethic of work. In a new passage, he acknowledged that whatever might be done to raise wages or to shield the new proletarians against illness and old age, their work by its very nature was bound to remain a source of discontent.[47] His only consolation was the knowledge that, although the industrial proletariat had greatly increased, so had the number of intellectual workers. The proliferation of professions and occupations in which individuals could develop their potential had created a larger class of people capable of deriving personal satisfaction from work. As

[44] Riehl, *Deutsche Arbeit*, 232–36.   [45] Riehl, *Deutsche Arbeit*, 104.

[46] Riehl, *Deutsche Arbeit*, 219–21. See also, Geramb, *Riehl*, 326, and Pankoke, *Soziale Bewegung*, 64.

[47] Riehl, *Deutsche Arbeit*, 93.

the new leaders of society, these people had a special duty to eschew materialism and uphold a high national work ideal. Riehl still hoped that their example might spread to the bulk of German workers, because even the lowliest workers still knew instinctively that their work, inspired as it was by the altruistic desire to serve their families and neighbors, was at least in part an ethical deed. Building on this foundation, Riehl thought that the workers could be taught that they could contribute something of value to the nation and help to determine its character.[48] If alienated labor was a fundamental fact of modern life, in Germany, at least, it should prove possible to inculcate a compensatory spirit of community based on the concept of service to the Volk.

By treating Arbeitsfreude as a component of a distinctive national work ethic, Riehl's *Deutsche Arbeit* made a significant contribution to the debate about work, although its full impact was delayed until after the First World War.[49] It can also be seen as a serious attempt to approach its subject in a novel manner. In some ways, Riehl's treatment of work is as "scientific" as that of Marx. Thus Riehl based his discussion of the role of the Protestant Reformation and the French Revolution in creating the modern work ethic on what he knew of the intellectual history of the preceding centuries and demonstrated comprehension of the fundamental political, social, and economic developments that separated his own world from that of the Middle Ages. His use of folk customs, songs, and literature, and his analysis of Biblical elements in the folk tradition provided Riehl with an empirical basis for generalizations about German work, and established him as the founding father of the new discipline of *Volkskunde* ("cultural ethnography").[50]

Never content to ground his judgments regarding popular attitudes on documentary sources alone, Riehl throughout his life spent holidays on walking tours designed to familiarize him with the land and its people. This enabled him to combine first-hand knowledge with more traditional literary and semi-literary sources. Marx undoubtedly developed

[48] Riehl, *Deutsche Arbeit*, 94.

[49] The book was frequently dismissed before 1914 as the creation of a literary artist rather than a serious historian or social scientist. See, e.g., Paul Heyse, *Jugenderinnerungen und Bekenntnisse*, 5th ed. (Stuttgart, 1912), 222, cited in Geramb, *Riehl*, 530–31.

[50] For a discussion of Riehl's contribution to empirical social science in Germany, see Anthony Oberschall, *Empirical Social Research in Germany 1848–1914* (Paris: Mouton, 1965), 65–68, and Pankoke, *Sociale Bewegung*, 114–16. The former stresses the empirical and the latter the conceptual features of Riehl's methodology. See also Holm Gottschalch, "Historische Stationen auf dem Leidensweg der Arbeitsfreude im Spiegel psychologischer Theorien und empirischer Erhebungen. Materialsammlung und Typologie zum Arbeiterbewusstsein," *Soziale Welt* 30 (1979): 439–45.

a more theoretically coherent picture of industrial society based on a penetrating grasp of underlying forces, but Riehl, captivated by the particular, may well have come to a more realistic understanding of the needs, aspirations, and ideals of ordinary German workers.

There were limits to Riehl's method. His wanderings produced superficial impressions of life in the regions he visited. Moreover, he preferred to spend his time in rural areas and therefore was much better acquainted with the traditional Germany of the countryside than with the world of industry and commerce. Especially after his move to Bavaria, he had little occasion to observe the modern entrepreneur or factory worker. On the other hand, Riehl was not as ignorant of current economic and social developments as is often claimed. His memorandum for Maximilian II entitled "Three Recommendations for Dealing with the Proletarian Problem" led to his appointment to a royal commission which studied the condition of the proletariat throughout Germany in the 1850s, and which reported on social welfare provisions in the different jurisdictions. This assignment undoubtedly deepened Riehl's understanding of the social question and provided valuable background material for his *Deutsche Arbeit*.[51]

Riehl's emphasis on the traditional aspects of German society was thus a matter of choice rather than the result of ignorance. Although aware of the magnitude of social change and conscious that modern society rested on new principles, he nevertheless thought it dangerous to focus exclusively on the revolutionary features of the age. In theory, the world had been fundamentally altered since the French Revolution, but in reality Riehl maintained that nineteenth-century society was like a new building in whose structure many older elements had been incorporated, elements that social scientists could not afford to ignore and social reformers overlooked at their peril.[52]

Contemptuous of those liberals and socialists who believed it possible to reconstruct society on purely rational lines without taking into account inherited institutions and attitudes, Riehl also opposed the tendency of the modern state to impose uniformity from above. It is perhaps paradoxical that the author of a major study of "German" work, an ardent patriot who urged his fellows to labor for the greater glory of the national community, should have been highly ambivalent about the new Germany created by William I and Bismarck. Before unification had become a reality, Riehl had maintained that the German idea of work was superior to that of other nations precisely because nature and history had prevented the evolution of a unitary racial state.

[51] Geramb, *Riehl*, 276–79.   [52] Riehl, *Deutsche Arbeit*, 23.

Instead, every German city had a unique character and acted as a school of work for the surrounding region; each branch of the Germanic people had its own characteristic approach to work, and each social grouping could make its particular contribution to the national ethos. While he admitted that a centralized nation-state would be able to organize work on more rational lines and thus achieve greater prosperity, he nevertheless rejected unification as an overriding goal. The Germany he favored was a cultural entity that preserved and cherished historical diversity, rather than a political power demanding conformity to a single set of rationally determined values. In his view, Germany could best prove its superiority not by becoming richer and more powerful than other nations, but by evolving the most elevated ideal of work and propagating it successfully among all elements of the population.[53]

Because he valued diversity as a source of both personal liberty and German greatness, Riehl continued to battle against bureaucratic and political intervention once the Second Reich had been established.[54] In particular, while acknowledging that the state could not stay entirely aloof, Riehl argued that social policy should be directed in the first instance to preserving traditional institutions in all their rich complexity. Riehl's dislike of bureaucracy and centralization eventually led him to warn that the "creeping socialism" of state welfare in Bismarck's Germany was potentially a greater danger than the subversive propaganda of the socialists themselves.[55]

One cannot deny that Marx, the father of "scientific socialism" and Riehl, the founder of Volkskunde, were at one level diametrically opposed to one another. Whereas Marx advocated revolution to realize his vision of an egalitarian, classless society, Riehl clung to an essentially hierarchical model of the social order and favored organic growth. Marx cast the proletariat as the chief agent of change and bearer of a new ethic of work valid for all nations; Riehl assigned the leading role to the bourgeoisie and denied the relevance of foreign experience to the evolution of the German work ethic. Finally, while Marx continued to hope that alienation could be overcome with the establishment of true communism, Riehl subscribed to the more modest goal of increasing the scope for joyful work within the framework of an evolving economy—thus showing himself to be less of a visionary than the man who insisted that his socialism transcended utopianism.

[53] Riehl, *Deutsche Arbeit*, 268–69.   [54] Buchheim, *Deutsche Kultur*, 8–9.

[55] Wilhelm Heinrich Riehl, "Zur inneren Geschichte des Sozialismus," in *Raumers Historisches Taschenbuch*, Folge 5, Jahrgang 10 (Leipzig, 1880): 309–315.

Nevertheless, there are striking similarities in the way these two men formulated the problem of work. Exposed in their youth to classical humanism, philosophical idealism, and literary romanticism, both extolled the virtues of freely chosen intellectual work and considered it life's chief pleasure. Having derived their notions of joy in work from their own experience as intellectuals, both used this ideal to judge and find wanting the mechanical, mindless, impersonal labor imposed by the increasing division of labor on the working masses. Both recognized that there was no turning back from the path to modernity. Both differentiated between the true working class, to which honor was due, and that stratum of society which Marx termed the *Lumpenproletariat* and Riehl described as the irredeemably depraved elements of the Volk.

Although initially attracted to Fourier's idea of attractive labor, both ultimately rejected the equation of work and play and agreed that work became a potential source of satisfaction to the degree that it involved strenuous effort. On the other hand, although both Marx and Riehl were impressed by Carlyle's gospel of labor, neither believed that life should be given over entirely to work. According to Marx, under communism all people would be given not only satisfying work, but also sufficient free time to develop their human potential to the full. For his part, Riehl stressed the need to allow time for contemplation and Christian worship, as well as for participation in the life of the community. Furthermore, both denounced those who made the ideal of joyful work an excuse for insufficient pay or exploitative hours of work. As Riehl put it, even the intellectual who loved to work deserved to be paid, and in a truly just society the highest monetary rewards would go to those whose work was intrinsically least satisfying.[56]

One could develop the comparison further, but perhaps enough has been said to demonstrate that Marx and Riehl, although temperamentally, ideologically, and politically poles apart, shared a significant set of beliefs about work, including an ideal of joyful labor and a work ethic that kept them at their self-appointed tasks to the end of their days. There is little evidence that this ethic owed anything to the changing modes of production as the Marxist analysis would posit. Rather, one could argue as Riehl would have done that participation in a distinctively German bourgeois intellectual tradition was the best explanations for common features of the two men's thinking about work.

Because this tradition antedated the coming of industrial capitalism, it is not surprising that towards the end of their lives both Marx and Riehl found their ideals of work either misused or pushed aside as irrel-

[56] Riehl, "Zur inneren Geschichte," 187–90.

evant by a society which respected only efficiency and power. Marx's followers tended to repudiate the fundamental idealism of the original communist program in the name of science. Riehl's natural allies, the bourgeois reformers, increasingly shied away from examining the deeper religious, moral, psychological, and cultural implications of the problem of work. Riehl's books, including *Deutsche Arbeit*, were available and were occasionally cited, but, in a pragmatic and positivist age, their message tended to be overlooked.

Only in the twentieth century, particularly in the period between the two world wars, was there a significant "Riehl revival" involving a return to the twin ideals of joy in work and "German" work, and it should not be too surprising in the light of what we have said about the relationship between nineteenth-century socialist and bourgeois ideology in Germany that this coincided with a renewed interest among socialist intellectuals in the ethical and ideal dimensions of their own creed.

IV

THE SOCIAL QUESTION
AND THE REFORM OF WORK IN
IMPERIAL GERMANY

SPURRED by political unification, the forces of change that had gathered impetus since the 1850s reached most areas of Germany and, directly or indirectly, affected all strata of the population. The development of large enterprises applying modern technology to the production of goods for an expanding domestic and international market was matched by the growth of a disciplined labor movement closely allied with Europe's mightiest socialist party. As the economic balance shifted from the rural-agrarian to the urban-industrial sector, for the first time big business and organized labor played a major role within what was becoming the most advanced and powerful economy on the continent.

These changes affected not only how Germans worked, but also how they thought about work. Instead of producing religious and ethical disquisitions about the meaning of work for human beings in general, the growing number of reformers tended to confine their concern to manual wage laborers employed in large-scale mechanized factories producing for the capitalist market—this despite the fact that such workers still represented only a minority of gainfully employed Germans. Accepting the socialist agenda, progressive intellectuals now dealt with the predicament of the urban proletariat as an economic and political problem, a conflict between "capital" and "labor" centering on wages, hours, working conditions, and the right of workers to organize. Ignoring the objections of older theorists of work like Riehl, they narrowed the "social question" down to the "labor question" or *Arbeiterfrage*.[1] So

[1] Riehl continued to insist that all classes were affected by the problem of work, and that it was wrong to equate the social question with the worker question. See Riehl, "Zur inneren Geschichte," 273, and Heinz Roscher, *Der Volksforscher W. H. Riehl und seine soziale Politik*

defined, it produced a search for technical or legal solutions, rather inspiring deeper analyses of the implications of recent changes in the nature of work for the individual and society. Conservatives continued to complain about the effects of modernization on society as a whole, but it was not until the decade immediately preceding the First World War that reformers once more discussed work as a problem for both the laboring masses and the nation's elite.

If the intervening period deserves a place in our story, it is because it produced several reform associations which both reflected and helped to shape the national work ethic. This chapter will deal with five of these societies, focusing on the motives that inspired their formation, the methods they favored, and the assumptions about work that underlay their reform efforts. It will also assess the contributions of several individuals who, operating within this institutional context, significantly influenced German thinking about work and its reform in the period between the founding of the Second Reich and the outbreak of the First World War.

The first social reform association seriously to address the problem of work was the Verein für Sozialpolitik (VfS), founded in 1872. Appropriately labelled *Kathedersozialisten* ("Socialists of the Chair") by their critics, its most active members were academics, overwhelmingly economists, who believed that the state had the right and duty to intervene in economic life in order to harmonize interests and regulate conflicts, and who favored the implementation of a comprehensive and progressive social policy. As Gustav Schmoller (1838–1917), president of the VfS from 1890 until his death, explained to its founding congress, the aim of the new society was to find ways to integrate the workers into the body of the nation through "moderate but firmly carried-out factory legislation" combined with a variety of other measures that would mitigate the worst evils of contemporary capitalism and ensure increasing popular participation in the "higher possessions of culture, in education, and in well-being."[2] In addition to academics, the VfS included civil servants, representatives of industry, prominent politicians from several parties, religious leaders, and publicists. Its congresses and publications strove for a "scientific" consensus in favor of specific government measures designed to dampen the conflict between capital and labor and between the traditional and modernizing elements in German society.

(Inaugural diss., Hamburg University; Buna-Leipzig: Universitätsverlag Robert Noske, 1927), 25–26.

[2] Cited in Koppel S. Pinson, *Modern Germany* (2d ed.; New York: Macmillan, 1966), 243–44.

A number of assumptions about work differentiated the VfS from both the Marxist proponents of social revolution and those advocates of laissez-faire who, with Riehl, condemned state-sponsored social reform as "socialism" in disguise.[3] Against the Marxists, the VfS maintained that the division of labor was a permanent and necessary feature of any advanced economy, and that every modern society was bound to be a class society because of the differential valuation of the various occupations. Even those of its members who were influenced by Marx's economic writings were convinced that a degree of hierarchy and authority would always be essential to maintain social order and that it was utopian to aim for equality, absolute freedom, and the end of alienation. VfS spokesmen also disputed Marx's prediction that class disparities would increase and transform the proletariat into a revolutionary force dedicated to the overthrow of bourgeois capitalism. Instead, they argued that an enlightened social policy could successfully undercut the revolutionary impulse and eventually reintegrate the proletariat into the nation without sacrificing the benefits of industrial capitalism.

Despite the VfS's explicit repudiation of socialism, proponents of laissez-faire had good grounds for regarding it with deep suspicion. The VfS favored government intervention on behalf of the weaker elements in society and argued for the creation of a state-run system of universal education. Although the VfS intended the public schools to propagate largely traditional attitudes to family, church, and state under the aegis of the educated elite who were thought to have an obligation to control and mold those beneath them in the social hierarchy,[4] its anti-socialist critics were not appeased. For example, the historian Heinrich von Treitschke (1834–1896) argued that the higher culture was not only the product of the leisured few but also their exclusive preserve. He also insisted that the laboring masses were condemned to a life of intensive labor for minimal rewards under any regime and that no social reform would ever "bring greater blessings to the working classes than

[3] The following is largely based on the VfS *Schriften*, selected volumes of its journal, the *Archiv für Sozialwissenschaft und Sozialpolitik* (ASS), Else Conrad, *Der Verein für Sozialpolitik und seine Wirksamkeit auf dem Gebiet der gewerblichen Arbeiterfrage* (Jena: G. Fischer, 1906), and Franz Boese, *Geschichte des Vereins für Sozialpolitik 1872–1932*. Schriften des Vereins für Sozialpolitik, 188 (Berlin: Duncker & Humblot, 1939). See also Abraham Ascher, "Professors as Propagandists: The Politics of the Kathedersozialisten," *Journal of Central European Affairs* 23 (1963): 282–302.

[4] Gustav Schmoller, "Das Wesen der Arbeitsteilung und der sozialen Klassenbildung," *Schmollers Jahrbuch*, 14 (1890): 103. On the elitism of the German professoriat, see Fritz K. Ringer, *The Decline of the German Mandarins* (Cambridge, Mass.: Harvard University Press, 1969) and Walter Struve, *Elites against Democracy* (Princeton: Princeton University Press, 1973).

the old and simple admonition: pray and work."[5] Treitschke, who regarded himself as a liberal, in this respect was at one with the most reactionary opponents of the VfS who supported the anti-socialist legislation in effect from 1878 until Bismarck's fall from power in 1890 because they were convinced that social revolution could only be averted by forceful repression of the labor movement.

Although the VfS accepted the premise that all rule is inevitably based on might as well as right and therefore did not directly oppose the anti-socialist laws, it maintained that judicious concessions to the workers could do as much or more than outright repression to establish the state's legitimacy in their eyes. Its members therefore backed Bismarck's elaborate social insurance program which was initiated in the hope of pacifying the working class, and helped to ensure its successful implementation by proffering constructive suggestions and providing the statistical basis for many of the government's measures. In addition, the VfS developed theoretical arguments to counter the doctrinaire liberals and reactionary extremists who opposed social legislation on principle.

Members of the VfS tended to agree on the importance of overcoming social divisions to strengthen the new nation, on the obligation of governments to harmonize social conflicts, on the responsibility of bourgeois intellectuals to formulate necessary reforms, and on the ability of "science" to lay the basis for a progressive social policy. Yet these strong bonds, reinforced as time went on by a number of professional and personal ties, still did not suffice to achieve a VfS consensus on questions of program, methodology, or tactics. Divisions appeared between conservatives and liberals, pessimists and optimists, paternalists and advocates of working-class initiative, supporters of a value-free approach to social questions and those who favored an avowedly ethical stance. Unable to speak with one voice on practical reforms, the VfS increasingly confined itself to academic debates about questions of principle and method and so failed to exert as much influence as its founders had hoped or as the prestige and ability of its members would lead one to expect. Its 1881 decision to cease voting on resolutions at its annual meetings publicly confirmed the inability of VfS members to reconcile their differences on controversial issues.[6]

Although the economic upswing of the early 1870s was interrupted by a period of fluctuating fortunes, in the 1890s economic growth became impressive and sustained. This intensified the problems created

---

[5] Pinson, *Modern Germany*, 245; Conze, "Arbeit," 207–208.
[6] Boese, *Geschichte des VfS*, 45.

by technological and organizational change, but it also produced circumstances favorable to the cause of reform. Moreover, the abrogation of the anti-socialist laws that marked the end of the Bismarck era enabled an ever stronger, more self-confident working class to claim as a right reforms which bourgeois intellectuals in the preceding decades had urged governments to grant as a favor. Yet the Reich in this period notably failed to accept responsibility for solving the worker question. Under pressure from conservative interests, Emperor William II did little to extend the social legislation of the Bismarck era, concentrating instead on military and foreign political questions. As a result, a number of bourgeois reformers came to acknowledge what the Social Democrats had long maintained, namely that political reform was an essential precondition for a progressive and effective social program.

At the VfS's Mannheim Congress of 1905, Friedrich Naumann (1860–1919), a young Protestant pastor turned politician, "explicitly challenged the dogma that the state, now in the hands of reactionary landlords and bourgeois, could be regarded as a champion of social policy."[7] Only a democratization of political life, achieved in cooperation with the organized working class, could prepare the ground for further reforms. Naumann was supported by the economist Lujo Brentano (1844–1931), who argued that governments must legislate the framework for the resolution of industrial conflicts, with the workers providing the major impetus for improvements in their conditions of labor. Against the VfS's old guard, Brentano advocated a system of industrial relations on the British model, including compulsory unionization, collective bargaining, and arbitration, so that the workers might more nearly match the power of their employers in the giant enterprises that were coming to dominate the economy.[8]

A few years later Alfred Weber (1868–1958), one of Brentano's pupils, went even further. Speaking for a growing number of the association's younger members, Weber argued that the bureaucratic state constituted as great a threat as unrestrained capitalism to individual freedom and cultural progress. Bureaucracy had to be fought, even if this meant cutting back on the state's paternalistic role in social policy. The only way to secure reforms without sacrificing essential freedoms was to circumvent the government by expanding trade unionism and collective bargaining.[9]

The new generation within the VfS also addressed an aspect of the

---

[7] Ringer, *Decline of the German Mandarins*, 161.   [8] Boese, *Geschichte des VfS*, 106–109.
[9] Ringer, *Decline of the German Mandarins*, 160.

problem of work that had heretofore been largely neglected, namely the effect of industrial labor on the workers' psyche. In its early years, the VfS had concentrated on remedying such obvious deficiencies as job insecurity, excessive hours of work, insalubrious and dangerous working and living conditions, and inadequate educational opportunities. By the early 1900s, however, it had become evident that neither the reform legislation nor the rising level of real wages of the preceding decades had gone to the roots of worker disaffection. Instead, the industrial workers had turned in greater numbers to the SPD with its program of class war and proletarian revolution. Given the failure of the proletariat to come to terms with the "system" even when it had begun to satisfy their material interests, a number of VfS spokesmen concluded that it was necessary to think once more about the deeper causes of social conflict. This led them to posit alienation as a major element in proletarian discontent, and to reintroduce the ideal of joyful labor and of salvation through work into VfS discussions.

First to do so was the Austrian-born political economist, Heinrich Herkner (1863–1932). In his early writings on the worker question, Herkner, too, had paid little attention to the problem of alienation. His *Die Arbeiterfrage*, first published in 1894, outlined a social policy that stressed economics and favored higher wages and shorter hours. However, even at this stage Herkner emphasized the need to take seriously workers' quest for job security and for a work setting that respected their personal freedom.[10] Soon he came to recognize that noneconomic factors were a major cause of worker disaffection and to insist on the "high importance of Arbeitsfreude for the occupational and personal well-being of the worker."[11]

The result was his pathbreaking *The Importance of Joy in Work for the Theory and Practice of Political Economy* of 1905.[12] This short book started with a theoretical treatment of the problem of work and went on to analyze the psychological effects of modern work processes and industrial organization on the individual employee. It concluded with a number of reform proposals designed to improve the ratio between the satisfactions and dissatisfactions of work. Modestly, Herkner ad-

[10] Heinrich Herkner, *Die Arbeiterfrage* (Berlin: Guttentag, 1894), 185–96.

[11] Charlotte Leubuscher, "Heinrich Herkner als Sozialpolitiker," *Schmollers Jahrbuch*, 57 (1933): 23–24. Like many of his contemporaries, Herkner was greatly influenced by Ruskin's cultural criticism and social reform ideals. See Heinrich Herkner, "John Ruskin als Sozialreformer," *Neue Deutsche Rundschau* (1901) 1:225–37; Herkner, "Der Lebenslauf eines 'Kathedersozialisten'" in *Die Volkswirtschaftslehre der Gegenwart in Selbstdarstellungen*, ed. Felix Meiner (Leipzig, 1924), 1:24–25.

[12] Heinrich Herkner, *Die Bedeutung der Arbeitsfreude in Theorie und Praxis der Volkswirtschaft* (Dresden: Zahn & Jaensch, 1905).

mitted that his conclusions were based on rather primitive theorizing and insufficient facts, and that the romantics were wrong to believe that work had ever been, or could ever be, a source of undiluted joy for the mass of workers. Nevertheless, he emphasized the importance of investigating the psychological costs of labor, as a preliminary to initiating reforms that would minimize these costs to the individual and so guarantee social stability and cultural progress.

Like most intellectuals, Herkner viewed industrial work with aversion and spoke from the heart when he described its damaging effects on the mental and physical wellbeing of the laboring classes. Unlike many academic critics of industrialism, however, his stance was based on experience. The scenes of urban distress that he had witnessed as the son of a Bohemian factory owner produced in Herkner a decided preference for rural life and a lifelong interest in agrarian questions, demonstrated by his advocacy of land reform and other measures to halt the flight to the cities. His studies at the universities of Vienna, Leipzig, Berlin, Freiburg, and Strasbourg strengthened his belief in the negative effects of urbanization and industrial concentration, notably the loss of independent employment, increasingly mechanical and specialized work, and harsher workshop discipline.[13]

Herkner regretfully agreed with his fellow economist, Werner Sombart (1863–1941), that the trend toward modernization was irreversible. But he rejected Sombart's pessimistic conclusion that it was therefore impossible to restore joy in work.[14] Instead, he insisted that many workers still loved their jobs and that current developments were increasing the scope for joyful labor. Moreover, he noted that although work on the farm was "objectively" healthier and more satisfying than factory labor, many wage earners, above all women, actually preferred urban employment. Despite his concern about the accelerated division of labor, he also maintained that occupational specialization, by developing skills, might in fact increase Arbeitsfreude. Even his worry about the unfortunate effects of monotonous, repetitive tasks on the unskilled majority was qualified by his conviction that some races, notably the Anglo-Saxon, had an innate affinity for such work and could adapt to boring jobs without psychological damage.[15]

Herkner's approach to the problem of work was remarkably similar to that of Riehl, to whom he paid tribute in the opening pages of his book on Arbeitsfreude. Although he gave greater weight to economic

[13] Herkner, "Lebenslauf," 86–90.
[14] See especially Werner Sombart, Das Proletariat. Bilder und Studien. Die Gesellschaft, ed. Martin Buber (Frankfurt: Rütten & Loening, 1906), 1.
[15] Herkner, Arbeitsfreude, 14–17.

factors, Herkner, too, stressed the ethical and psychological components of the problem. Like Riehl, he insisted that modern society still offered many opportunities for work that demanded skill, gave scope to individuality, and allowed people to maintain a significant degree of involvement in the productive process.[16] Finally, he agreed with Riehl that the bourgeois reformer had a responsibility neither to capital nor to labor but, in the first instance, to the nation as a whole. This stance allowed him to condemn union leaders who sought to raise revolutionary consciousness by rooting out the remnants of occupational pride and stripping away the consolations of religion; it also led him to acknowledge the positive role of the labor movement in pressing for needed reforms, providing the workers with new pride in their status, and giving numerous individuals an opportunity for personal development.[17] In sum, Herkner believed rising productivity could be combined with social progress, high profits with high wages, greater joy in work with the benefits of an advanced, technologically sophisticated, industrial capitalism.[18]

Herkner, nevertheless, went beyond Riehl in two significant ways. Rather than confining himself to a combination of description with ethical exhortation, he listed a number of specific measures designed to improve the lot of the workers and to minimize the subjective feelings of displeasure arising from modern work. These included such traditional remedies as limitation of working hours, monetary incentives to compensate for the monotony of industrial labor, and extension of health and safety regulations. More "modern" were his proposals for vocational guidance to place workers in appropriate jobs, greater mobility of labor and better training to maximize the element of occupational choice and raise the general level of skills, improvements in the work environment including the use of color and music to enhance the physical surroundings, and reorganization of the work process to lessen monotony and increase opportunities for social interaction. As far as the non-working portion of the laborers' lives was concerned, he proposed that inferior recreational pursuits—such as excessive drinking, which so often accompanied joyless work—be replaced by organized leisure activities capable of absorbing surplus intellectual and spiritual energies. He also suggested that industries be established in rural settings so that employees might devote their spare time to healthful and joyful agricultural tasks.[19] But because his main objective was to enable

[16] Herkner, *Arbeitsfreude*, 19.   [17] Herkner, *Arbeitsfreude*, 23–24.
[18] Herkner, *Arbeitsfreude*, 186–91.   [19] Herkner, *Arbeitsfreude*, 30–31.

more people to experience joy in *work*, he laid greater stress on systematically encouraging industries engaged in the production of quality goods, thereby increasing the number of jobs capable of fully utilizing German skills and creativity.[20]

The second way in which Herkner departed from Riehl was in advocating the systematic study of the physiology and psychology of work. Whereas Riehl had hoped to use ethical training and elite example to change popular attitudes to work revealed in folk customs, songs, and sayings, Herkner sought to increase the emotional bond between people and their work through reforms based on research into the effect of work on body, mind, and spirit.[21] His reintroduction of the *Arbeitsfreude* theme into public discussion of the labor question therefore encouraged the emergence of a science of work that would give due weight to the psychological aspects of the subject.

Around the turn of the century, concern that the VfS had become too academic to constitute an effective agent of reform led to the founding of several rival associations determined to tackle the social question. While sharing the VfS's basic objectives, each added a distinctive note to the social policy debate based on its own diagnosis of the problem of work. Members of the VfS played major roles in all of them, and the VfS itself continued to make a significant contribution, but it no longer held the preeminent position within the bourgeois reform movement that it had enjoyed during the first quarter century of its existence.

Of the new societies, the most active was the *Gesellschaft für Soziale Reform* (GSR). Founded in 1901, it soon became the focal point of the social policy reform movement.[22] Although close to the VfS in its basic purpose, the GSR differed from the older association with respect to organization, membership, and stated objectives. That it was started by a prominent civil servant rather than by a professor symbolizes the disparity between them. Freiherr von Berlepsch (1843–1926), recently forced to abandon his post as Prussian Minister of Trade under pressure from a strong alliance of interests opposed to his vigorous reform efforts

[20] Herkner, *Arbeitsfreude*, 33.

[21] Herkner, *Arbeitsfreude*, conclusion, 35–40. Herkner acknowledged his debt to Ernst Engel of Dresden, who had already drawn attention in the 1860s to the importance of psychological factors in establishing the "price of labor." Ernst Engel, *Der Preis der Arbeit. Zwei Vorlesungen* (Berlin: Lüderitz, 1866). Engel's seminars had impressed Brentano who in turn influenced Herkner. See Erich Angermann, *Robert von Mohl 1799–1875. Leben und Werk eines altliberalen Staatsgelehrten* (Neuwied: Hermann Luchterhand, 1962), 323.

[22] See, most recently, Ursula Ratz, *Sozial Reform und Arbeiterschaft. Die 'Gesellschaft für Soziale Reform' und die sozialdemokratische Arbeiterbewegung von der Jahrhundertwende bis zum Ausbruch des Ersten Weltkrieges* (Berlin: Colloquium, 1980).

on behalf of the workers, hoped that the GSR and its affiliated journal, *Soziale Praxis (SP)*, would generate public support for a more radical social policy specifically tailored to meet the needs of the industrial proletariat.[23] Whereas the VfS devoted considerable attention to the problems of peasants, craftsmen, and small shopkeepers, all of whom were currently appealing to the public for sympathy and to the government for help, von Berlepsch argued that the urban working class which constituted nearly half the country's population was markedly worse off than other sectors of society and so deserved the full attention of reformers. He therefore insisted that the GSR concentrate on the worker question, narrowly defined, rather than dissipating its energies as he felt the VfS was inclined to do.[24] Moreover, his conviction that improvements in the material and intellectual condition of the workers would eradicate class hatred only if reformers emphasized social justice rather than public and private charity and replaced paternalism with worker participation, led him to insist that the GSR support rather than undercut worker initiatives for the emancipation of the proletariat.[25]

The GSR's particular orientation was reflected in its membership policy. In addition to encouraging participation by prominent political and religious leaders, progressive academics, and enlightened industrialists, it actively sought mass support. By 1906, it had succeeded in involving trade union leaders who between them represented over half a million workers.[26] As the Christian unions discouraged the socialist Free Unions from applying for formal GSR membership, these were drawn primarily from the non-socialist union movement. However, individual Free Union leaders played an active role in the association's affairs, and a number of leading Social Democrats were also prepared to voice the standpoint of socialist labor within the GSR.[27] Eager to cooperate with elements still regarded as subversive by most educated Germans in and outside the government, the GSR evidently hoped it

[23] Ernst Schraepler, ed., *Quellen zur Geschichte der sozialen Frage in Deutschland* (Göttingen: Musterschmidt-Verlag, 1956), 2:4–5.

[24] Dr. Freiherrn von Berlepsch, "Warum betreiben wir die soziale Reform?" (1903), *Schriften der GSR*, 11 (Jena: G. Fischer, 1906), 4.

[25] Speech at the twelfth meeting of the Evangelisch-Soziale Kongress (ESK), 1901, quoted in Gerhard A. Ritter, *Staat, Arbeiterschaft und Arbeiterbewegung in Deutschland* (Berlin: J.H.W. Dietz, 1980), 57.

[26] Dieter Fricke, "Bürgerliche Sozialreformer und die Zersplitterung der antisozialistischen Arbeiterorganisationen vor 1914," *Zeitschrift für Geschichtswissenschaft* 23 (1975): 1181. By 1910 the worker organizations within the GSR represented 1,600,000 people. See Ratz, *Sozial Reform*, 250.

[27] Ratz, *Sozial Reform*, 237, 248–59.

would be possible to induce the SPD to become a genuine workers' party: one that would abjure class hate, call off its war to the death against the existing order, and instead use gradualist tactics to win for the workers the place in the sun to which, as German subjects, they were entitled.[28] In so doing, the GSR built on the nineteenth-century reform tradition represented by such people as von Mohl and Riehl, who had been convinced that an effective social policy would make it possible to integrate the workers into the national community.

Although condemned by doctrinaire socialists as a pseudo-liberal undermining tactic,[29] the GSR's policies clearly struck a responsive chord among both reformist trade unionists and SPD "revisionists" who exerted increasing influence over the German labor movement in the years before the war. While it is impossible to estimate to what extent the GSR's stand influenced German labor's move to the right, the very vehemence of left-wing opposition suggests that the association strengthened that portion of the organized working class prepared to envision a peaceful transformation of the existing order in cooperation with reform-minded individuals from other sectors of society.

In its efforts to counteract the influence of powerful industrial and agrarian interest groups, the GSR established local branches in many parts of the country. It also helped form the *Büro für Sozialpolitik* in Berlin as a clearing-house for reform ideas and sought to enhance its prestige by serving as the German section of the International Association for Factory Reform Legislation, precursor of the International Labor Organization (ILO).[30] Nonetheless, the GSR failed to win the significant popular following it needed in order to impose new directions on German social policy or secure fundamental changes in the pattern of industrial relations. In the last peace-time years of the Second Reich some legislative reforms were implemented, but these were generally cautious extensions of earlier measures rather than fundamental improvements.[31] Likewise, attempts to replace the dominant authoritarian paternalism with a more democratic model of industrial control centered on worker committees (*Arbeiterausschüsse*) ran into stiff opposition not only from the employers but also from union leaders who regarded the committees as devices to diminish the ability of unions to negotiate on an industry-wide basis, and thus make the workers more

[28] Von Berlepsch, "Warum betreiben wir die soziale Reform?" 27.

[29] Fricke, "Bürgerliche Sozialreformer," 1779–81.

[30] Friedrich Karrenberg, "Geschichte der sozialen Ideen im deutschen Protestantismus," in Helga Grebing, ed., *Geschichte der sozialen Ideen in Deutschland* (Munich: Günter Olzog, 1969), 607.

[31] Ritter, *Staat, Arbeiterschaft und Arbeiterbewegung*, 58–64.

subservient to management. At best, the reform agitation of the GSR prevented the further erosion of government and trade union restraints on employer prerogatives.

Because the GSR deliberately eschewed theoretical debate in order to concentrate on practical reform, its publications made no significant contribution to the German ideology of work. Nevertheless, it is of interest to examine the beliefs about work of its guiding spirits. The chief determinant of these beliefs was German Protestantism. Appalled by the continuing erosion of the church's hold on the working class, many Protestants had become convinced that the process of secularization could only be reversed if the churches addressed themselves to social issues. Their organizational focus was the Evangelisch-Soziale Kongress (ESK) of which von Berlepsch was a leading member. Founded in 1890, the ESK provided a forum in which clerics and laymen of diverse persuasions and from all walks of life could present their views on how best to counter the attraction that atheist socialism held for the workers. Within it there gradually emerged a nucleus of people prepared to combat the social conservatism of the church, to accept the process of modernization, and to question traditional attitudes with regard to the rights and duties of the workers and the responsibility of Christian employers for their welfare.[32] While compassion and charity were the prime motivation, these reformers realized that a social policy based solely on the Christian virtues could not meet the contemporary challenge. As a result, the ESK eventually supported trade union activity and other self-help efforts of the proletariat, including cooperatives.

The ESK also took a great interest in various profit-sharing and worker-participation schemes initiated by Protestant industrialists. At its tenth annual congress of 1899 in Kiel, the industrialist Heinrich Freese gave an address on the "constitutional system" he had successfully introduced into his own factories. Thereupon the ESK passed a resolution welcoming this first attempt to restructure a major firm along constitutional lines and expressing the hope that government-run enterprises would set an example by setting up worker consultative committees similar to those with which Freese was experimenting.[33] To its proponents, the introduction of an element of democracy into industry seemed ideally designed to ensure the employers a stable, loyal work force and to give employees a sense of belonging and at least a limited degree of control over their fate. Combined with higher wages, shorter

[32] On the ESK, Gottfried Kretschmar, *Der Evangelisch-Soziale Kongress. Der deutsche Protestantismus und die soziale Frage* (Stuttgart: Evangelisches Verlagswerk, 1972).

[33] Kretschmar, *ESK*, 112; Heinrich Freese, *Die konstitutionelle Fabrik* (Jena: G. Fischer, 1909).

hours, and improved working conditions, it was hoped such reforms would encourage the workers to take advantage of educational and cultural opportunities, turn them into fully participating members of bourgeois society, and so make them receptive, once more, to the Christian message.

This optimistic vision of a proletariat delivered from crass materialism and class hatred undoubtedly inspired the reform efforts of von Berlepsch and his friends, but the majority of German Protestants thought it impossible substantially to improve the lot of industrial workers, and so took no part in the movement to do so. Some, like Treitschke, favored industrial modernization based on unrestrained capitalism and preached a gospel of duty and selfless service in order to ensure the peaceful submission of the lower orders. Others followed the lead of Adolf Wagner (1835–1917), co-founder of the VfS and the ESK, who argued that no amount of tinkering could overcome the "plutocracy, greed for profit, speculation, envy, discontent and revolution" associated with industrial capitalism.[34] Wagner's solution to the problem of work was state action to reverse the process of industrialization and strengthen the peasantry and the Mittelstand of craftsmen and small shopkeepers, which was regarded as the backbone of a healthy and moral Christian nation. The tendency of both Treitschke and Wagner to neglect the specific problems of modern industrial labor while urging Christian love and obedience on the workers gravely hampered the active minority of Protestant reformers centered on the ESK.[35]

Although individual Protestants played a leading role in the social reform movement of the Second Reich, the contribution of German Catholicism should not be overlooked. Catholics helped to develop new ideas about work in industrial society, encouraged the spread of worker associations and Christian trade unionism, and pressed for legislation to improve and regulate working conditions. The chief agency of Catholic reform in Germany before 1914 was the Volksverein für das katholische Deutschland (National Organization for Catholic Germany).[36] This Catholic counterpart of the ESK, was also established in 1890, but it differed significantly from the Protestant group in both concept and purpose. Regarding itself from the start as a mass organi-

[34] Kenneth D. Barkin, "Conflict and Concord in Wilhelmian Social Thought," *Central European History* 5 (1972), 64.

[35] See E. I. Kouri, *Der Deutsche Protestantismus und die soziale Frage 1870–1919. Zur Sozialpolitik im Bildungsbürgertum* (Berlin: Walter de Gruyter, 1984).

[36] See Horstwalter Heitzer, *Der Volksverein für das katholische Deutschland im Kaiserreich 1890–1918* (Mainz: Matthias-Grünewald, 1979), and *Der Volksverein für das katholische Deutschland 1890–1933*, ed. Georg Schoelen (Mönchengladbach: Stadtbibliothek, 1974).

zation, it proceeded to establish a nation-wide network of people's bureaus and worker secretariats. Headquarters in Mönchengladbach organized short social work courses and somewhat longer ones on economics, while a massive publishing program included both specialized literature and popular publications, the chief of which, *Der Volksverein*, had a circulation of 800,000 by 1914.[37]

The Volksverein also put less reliance than the ESK on state social policy. Although it was not averse to pursuing its goals by political means, self-help and education figured more prominently than legislation in its attack on the worker question. The Volksverein's chief objective was to convert both employers and workers to a sense of Christian responsibility and solidarity in the spirit of Leo XIII's encyclical *Rerum Novarum* of 1891. To this end, it declared itself ready to cooperate with non-Catholics, actively encouraged the organization of trade unions open to members of all Christian denominations, and gave full support to the Protestant-led GSR.

Just as the ESK represented only a limited segment of Protestant opinion, however, so the Volksverein, despite its mass following, spoke only for a portion of German Catholics. It ran into stiff opposition from the church hierarchy. Insisting on absolute clerical control of the social movement, conservative church leaders preferred purely Catholic worker associations to the non-denominational Christian unions favored by the Volksverein. They also disapproved of the latter's willingness to back their members' demands by striking against recalcitrant employers.

Despite opposition from church authorities, Catholic reformers found it somewhat easier to win mass support for their efforts to solve the worker question than did their Protestant contemporaries. This was partly because German Catholics tended to be treated as outsiders even after their Centre party entered into political alliance with the governing elites of the Second Reich in the mid-1890s. Discrimination freed them to challenge the prerogatives of the powerful in the name of the common people in a way not open to members of the Protestant establishment. What is more, the majority of leading German industrialists were Protestant, while the artisans and "workers" in some of the main centers of German industrial growth, notably the Ruhr and Rhine dis-

Franz Josef Stegmann, "Geschichte der sozialen Ideen im Deutschen Katholizismus," in Grebing, *Geschichte der sozialen Ideen*, 418–19; Hubert Mockenhaupt, ed., *Katholische Sozialpolitik im 20. Jahrhundert. Ausgewählte Aufsätze und Reden von Heinrich Brauns* (Mainz: Matthias-Grünewald, 1976), 14–17, 38–43. Membership of the Volksverein rose from 109,000 in 1891 to 805,000 in 1914.

tricts, were predominantly Catholic. Finally, the Catholic church had a longer, more vital tradition of social concern than did Protestantism.

This tradition, dating back to the period before 1848, emphasized the duty of the clergy to minister to the physical and mental needs of those entrusted to their care, as well as seeking to save their souls. Its major figure was Bishop Ketteler of Mainz (1811–1877). In the 1850s Ketteler had maintained that producer cooperatives along the lines proposed by the founder of German Social Democracy, Ferdinand Lassalle, were the answer to the problem of work. However, by 1866 he had recognized that voluntary self-help associations could not meet the needs of the growing factory proletariat and therefore looked increasingly to the state to regulate the conditions of labor.[38] Although he was flexible in his approach to the worker question and was prepared to adapt his social prescriptions to the realities of a society in transition, Ketteler rejected the easy enjoyment and luxurious living he believed to be the goals of liberal policy. Upholding a traditional and somewhat puritanical work ethic, he insisted that only effortful human labor, combined with the exercise of practical Christian virtues, could raise the level of public welfare.

Ketteler asserted that Man had been fashioned by God for work rather than for idleness; nonetheless, he refused to sanction the full-blown nineteenth-century gospel of work. The latter enabled reactionaries to argue that earthly happiness and wellbeing distracted Man from his true objective, the preparation of his eternal soul for the life to come, whereas abstinence and renunciation, the struggle against lust and repression of all selfish tendencies, cleansed and ennobled him and allowed him to experience the deep satisfaction derived from assuaging the hunger and fatigue produced by long hours of honest toil, as well as the joy that is the reward for duty done.[39] Instead, Ketteler wanted women excluded from factory employment, opposed the extension of working hours as inhumane, and deemed the Sabbath essential for health and family life as well as for the fulfillment of religious obligations.[40] Thereby, he laid the basis for a Catholic reform program that sought to restrict hours of labor and improve working conditions

[38] Stegmann, "Geschichte der sozialen Ideen," 383.

[39] Günther Wachtler, *Humanisierung der Arbeit und Industriesoziologie: eine soziologische Analyse historischer Vorstellungen humaner Arbeitsgestaltung* (Stuttgart: W. Kohlhammer, 1979), 51–52.

[40] Karl Heinz Grenner, *Wirtschaftsliberalismus und katholisches Denken* (Cologne: J. P. Bachem, 1967), 218–20; Goetz Briefs, ed., *Das Bild des Arbeiters in der katholischen Sozialbewegung* (Cologne: Balduin Pick, 1960), 9–22.

through the efforts of Christian employers, where necessary supplemented by legislative controls.

After Ketteler's death, the process of adaptation gathered momentum. Social Catholicism continued to uphold the ideal of a decentralized Christian commonwealth organized on corporative lines, based on the family and firmly rooted in the soil, and it never ceased to encourage private charity, worker self-help associations, and voluntary cooperation between employers and employees. But its leaders, having accepted capitalist industrial society and the centralized state as facts of modern life, recognized the necessity of discovering new ways to integrate the industrial workers into the national community. This combination of social conservatism with adaptive realism characterized the approach of Franz Hitze (1851–1921), the Volksverein's leading figure in its early years. Hitze, too, believed that work was essentially God's punishment for Adam's disobedience; his Christian repudiation of the Arbeitsfreude ideal was reinforced by his experiences as general secretary of the Volksverein's precursor, *Arbeiterwohl* ("workers' welfare"), an association of socially minded entrepreneurs that brought him into close touch with the worker question and shattered any illusions he might have had about the possibility of turning industrial labor into a source of joy.

On the other hand, Hitze's work ethic lacked the puritanical features so evident in Ketteler's pronouncements. Thus, in a lecture of 1877 on "The Right to Work," Hitze wrote sympathetically of contemporary labor's aspirations to job satisfaction:

> The old Roman wanted enjoyment without work, the modern worker wants joy in and with his work and is ethically advanced enough to give primacy to work.[41]

Denying that labor was a commodity like any other, Hitze called for the right to work, for adequate material rewards, and for restricted hours so as to allow time for education and worship. He also insisted that

> work must not be allowed to bestialize the worker or reduce him to a mechanism. As intended by the creator, work should be a means for man to educate and develop himself, not a means to oppress and dehumanize; a punishment for sin—bitter medicine—but medicine for all that.[42]

Although the germs of the later concern with the quality of working life were already present in the thinking of its leaders, neither the

[41] Franz Hitze, *Kapital und Arbeit* (Paderborn: J. W. Schröder, 1880), 148.
[42] Hitze, *Kapital und Arbeit*, 152.

Volksverein nor the GSR, in which prominent Catholics like Hitze and the Christian trade union leader Johannes Giesberts (1865–1938) played an active part, addressed themselves seriously at this time to the humanization of work. Acting on the assumption that work was a necessary evil, they concentrated on alleviating its damaging side-effects rather than tackling the problem of alienation at its point of origin in the workplace.

In this respect the Catholic and Protestant positions were scarcely distinguishable. Social reformers in both camps agreed that most people work in order to live rather than for the satisfaction to be derived from their activity. Yet they also valued work as a determinant of individuality and community. Involving service to God and his fellow men, a worker's vocation was deemed a legitimate, if indirect, source of personal satisfaction.[43] This notion of vocation dominated the thinking of both Catholics and Protestants as they attempted to reconcile the Christian concept of work with the demands of modern industry; it also spurred the search for ways to preserve occupational and professional distinctions in the face of developments that threatened to transform the majority of workers into a mass of unskilled, anonymous, and interchangeable units.

Impressed by the ability of industrial capitalism to raise living standards and productivity, by the end of the century most Christian reformers confined their efforts to making the capitalist system more equitable and humane, rather than attempting to restructure the economic and social order. This "conservative" tendency was reinforced by the conviction that Marxist socialism represented a greater threat than capitalism. Although they tended to agree that the socialist critique of liberal capitalism had considerable merit, both Catholic and Protestant reformers maintained that property based on work and entrepreneurial skills was productive, socially valuable, and therefore worthy of preservation. Thus, although Hitze lashed out as Ketteler had done against a stock market capitalism without a basis in productive enterprise and against a liberalism that gave employers absolute power over their workers, he firmly defended the rights of inherited property against socialist attack. In his view, a healthy social policy would be based on the belief that both work and property were holy and would seek to create a just balance between them.[44]

Quite a number of Christian reformers recognized that the quasi-

[43] Conze, "Beruf," 490–507. For a contemporary exposition of the Lutheran position see Hauptprediger Dr. Christian Geyer, *Religion und Arbeit*. Vortrag in der Vortragsreihe 'Die Religion im Leben der Gegenwart', Nürnberg 1912/13 (Ulm: Heinrich Kerler, 1914).

[44] Hitze, *Kapital und Arbeit*, 158.

feudal paternalistic model of industrial relations, based on authority and submission, was an anachronism. Some suggested that the enterprise should be reorganized as a *Werksgemeinschaft* or works community. The latter, representing the shared interests of employers and workers, was portrayed as an intermediate body between the family and the nation. Alternative suggestions for giving the workers a greater sense of belonging were profit-sharing, worker committees, and welfare programs. However, no agreement with respect to industrial organization and management was achieved. For example, some argued that it was wrong to make the works community the exclusive focus of employee loyalties. Torn between the entrepreneurial and the anticapitalist standpoints, they recognized the advantages of establishing a sense of community in the workplace, but felt that unions and trade associations were needed as checks on the power of capitalist firms over the lives of their employees. Others warned that company welfare policies were dangerous if they chained workers to the enterprise through pensions and tied housing.

One thing on which Protestant and Catholic reformers could agree was the need to supplement those institutional reforms designed to reduce conflicts between individuals and classes with education. The importance of education as a major instrument of social regeneration was universally recognized. Pulpit and school were assigned the task of converting the proletariat to Christian values of discipline and hard work while inculcating a sense of social responsibility in the minds of the privileged. Germans of all classes were to be imbued with a uniform, essentially "bourgeois," ethic of work, to counter both the "intellectual coarseness and deficient moral discipline of the lower orders stemming from absence of cultivation [*Unkultur*]" and the "physical debility and moral corruption of the upper classes due to their excessive refinement [*Überkultur*]."[45]

In the early twentieth century, the call for universal elementary education to inculcate traditional values was frequently combined with demands for a new type of schooling in which work would itself become the key educative element. The latter educational model owed much to the pioneering efforts of Georg Kerschensteiner (1854–1932), for many years director of education in Munich. Developing the idea of the *Arbeitsschule* or "work" school, Kerschensteiner introduced the principle of learning by doing into the schools under his control. In his view, the educational system had a duty to train the young for the working world by teaching "trade efficiency and love of work" and certain

[45] Schmoller, "Wesen der Arbeitsteilung," 102–4. Heitzer, *Volksverein*, 80–101.

"elementary virtues": diligence and industry, carefulness and attention to detail, cleanliness, honesty, and a determination to succeed.[46] Although a Catholic himself, Kerschensteiner greatly admired Carlyle and frequently cited that Protestant Englishman's views on work as blessing and salvation.[47] Propounding ideas equally congenial to Protestants and Catholics, he lived to see his Bavarian reforms of elementary and vocational education widely imitated in other parts of Germany.

Although Kerschensteiner insisted that education should make it possible for people to enjoy their jobs, he knew that modern industry provided few tasks capable of yielding the intrinsic satisfactions of skilled manual or intellectual work.[48] He therefore concluded that schools could only meet the needs of the factory proletariat if in addition to developing manual dexterity they also taught the patriotic and social virtues of citizenship through group activity. Only thus could individuals forced into occupations bereft of scope for Arbeitsfreude learn to moderate their natural egotism sufficiently to derive pleasure from helping their families, colleagues, and the nation as a whole.

Kerschensteiner's conviction that work must be regarded as a duty to the state was inspired by, and confirmed, the traditional Christian principle of vocation. Similarly, his belief in the educational value of manual training and group work reinforced the Christian view that even the lowliest occupation, if carried out in the proper spirit, constituted a service to the community and so possessed moral worth. A certain ambivalence crept into his work ethic as the notion of work as duty came into conflict with belief in its intrinsic value as a source of personal enrichment.[49] But on the whole Kerschensteiner combined reform enthusiasm with a reasonably realistic view of what improved moral and vocational training could do about the problem of worker alienation. An innovator in education, but a traditionalist where ethical values were concerned, he was representative of mainstream progressive Christianity.[50]

Whereas Catholic reformers operated within the framework of a highly organized national church with international affiliations and a strong tradition of social concern, their Protestant counterparts could

[46] Diane Simons, *Georg Kerschensteiner. His Thought and Its Relevance Today* (London: Methuen, 1966), 34–35, 49.

[47] E.g., Georg Kerschensteiner, *Grundfragen der Schulorganization* (Leipzig: B. G. Teubner, 1907), 42–43, 73.

[48] Kerschensteiner, *Grundfragen der Schulorganization*, 65.

[49] Particularly in his postwar writings, Kerschensteiner put a quasi-utopian emphasis on inner vocation and individual self-fulfillment. Simons, *Kerschensteiner*, 131–32.

[50] Ringer, *Decline of the German Mandarins*, 269–74.

not look to any central organization for support and guidance. Forced to develop their social policy positions in accordance with their individual consciences and to pit their personal convictions against the predominantly conservative ethos of their regionally diverse clerical establishments, Protestants found it extremely difficult to achieve consensus on the social question.[51] But if this was a source of weakness on the practical level, it also meant that Protestants were freer than Catholics to develop an innovative approach to the problem of work.

Among those who took advantage of this situation was Naumann. Naumann regarded the unfortunate aspects of modern industrialism as temporary features of a transitional stage in the historical process. From a perspective shaped by the tradition of German idealism, he and his friends not only accepted the machine as an economic necessity but extolled its virtues as an agent of social and cultural progress. Thus a close associate of Naumann, the liberal cleric Gottfried Traub (1869–1956), tried to persuade the ESK in 1904 that automation could be counted on eventually to diminish the monotony currently characteristic of factory production while enabling the mass of workers to develop their potential as individuals.[52]

The Protestant advocates of reform were also less hesitant than the Catholics to associate themselves politically with the organized labor movement, although few actually joined the SPD. One who did take this step was Paul Göhre (1864–1928), Naumann's deputy in the National-Soziale Verein and the first General Secretary of the ESK. Göhre joined the SPD in 1900 and represented that party in the Reichstag in 1903 and then again from 1910. Although Naumann decided not to follow suit, he continued to believe in the possibility of creating a genuine alliance, based on shared national and social values, between the progressive middle class and German Social Democracy.[53] Again, it was Traub who best expressed the assumptions on which Naumann's policy of collaboration rested. Traub emphasized the idealistic potential of the socialist working class which the majority of Catholic and Protestants regarded as a hotbed of materialism and atheism. Rather than interpreting labor's concentration on higher wages and shorter

[51] On the different strands within the Protestant reform camp, Kouri, *Deutscher Protestantismus*, 99–146.

[52] Gottfried Traub, "Organisation der Arbeit in ihrer Wirkung auf die Persönlichkeit," in ESK, *Breslau 1904. Verhandlungen* (Göttingen: Vandenhoeck & Ruprecht, 1904), 57–82.

[53] Kretschmar, *ESK*, 32–34, claims it was Göhre who dissuaded Naumann from joining the SPD, on the grounds that he could do more for the workers from within the bourgeois democratic camp. On Göhre, see also E. Pikart, in *NDB* 6:513–14 and Georg Bollenbeck, *Zur Theorie und Geschichte der frühen Arbeiterlebenserinnerungen* (Kronberg: Skriptor, 1976), 244–48.

hours as evidence of greed, Traub claimed that it bore witness to the thirst of the German working class for culture; for it was undeniable that true culture or Bildung required a reasonable standard of living and a degree of leisure time. Similarly, he argued that the labor movement's support for modernization demonstrated a certain willingness to engage in more intellectually demanding kinds of work. Finally, he maintained that the labor organizations, by awakening a spirit of class solidarity, lifted individuals above private egoism and directed them towards higher goals. Indeed, if the workers were still to some extent selfish and materialistic, this was because the employers, with a few honorable exceptions, subscribed to the principle of profit maximization and exploited the workers for their own ends. Traub believed firmly that German workers were prepared to collaborate in raising industrial productivity and that enlightened entrepreneurs would encourage their participation in decision making. Treated with respect, organized labor would eventually make a positive contribution to the "de-materialization" (*Entmaterialisierung*) of the work process.[54]

While Traub echoed the traditional Christian belief in the value of work done for its own sake and for its contribution to the community, he thought it both unrealistic and immoral to carry this to extremes, for example, in expecting nurses to work for inadequate pay.[55] He also maintained that it was not the division of labor which gave rise to disgust with modern work, but the injustice of a society that allowed some to grow rich without working. The remedy for alienation was to pay people enough for their work so that they need not constantly worry about money. Like Göhre and Naumann he saw no obstacle to practical collaboration between bourgeois progressives and socialist workers. Based on a common ethic of work, joint efforts would eventually solve the religious, ethical, and cultural problems of the modern world.[56]

If Protestantism was somewhat more open to innovation than Catholicism, the Protestant establishment proved at least as rigid as the Catholic church. Protestant radicals soon found themselves in conflict with those who thought that the challenge of modernity could best be met by insisting on theological as well as social conformity. As a result, a number of Naumann's friends were eventually forced to withdraw

[54] Gottfried Traub, "Arbeit und Arbeiterorganisation," in *Festgaben für F. J. Neumann* (Tübingen: Verlag der H. Laupp'schen Buchhandlung, 1905), 139–42.

[55] Gottfried Traub, "Arbeit und Arbeiterorganisation," 129–30.

[56] Gottfried Traub, "Arbeit und Arbeiterorganisation," 132; Kretschmar, ESK, 36. Traub never joined the SPD. A Progressive deputy in the Prussian Landtag before 1914, he moved sharply to the Right during the war, and joined the German National People's Party (DNVP) in 1919. See Gottfried Traub, *Erinnerungen* (Munich: R. Oldenburg, 1949).

from the Church or were formally ejected.[57] For those who remained within the Protestant fold there were two possible courses of action. Either one could try to develop a new theology consistent with the requirements of modern thought,[58] or one could argue that theological and social issues were in principle distinct.

The chief advocate of the second, "secular," approach was Naumann. Initiated into the reform camp as a young Protestant pastor working among the urban poor, Naumann, a protégé of the Court pastor Adolf Stöcker, founder of the Christian-Social movement, turned to political action when he realized that religion alone provided no adequate answer to the worker question. He and his friends continued to hope that labor could be reconverted to active Christianity, but their social reform program avoided any explicit appeal to religious sentiment. In 1895 Naumann formed his own National-Social party, and when this failed, he joined the Progressives whom he represented in the Reichstag from 1906.[59] Meanwhile, his growing awareness of the need to comprehend social developments led him to study the economists, including Marx, and to participate in the activities of the VfS as well as of the ESK.

Naumann decided to abandon a purely ethical and religious approach to the social question, but he was far from confident that political action and economic reform could deal with it in all its dimensions. A keen amateur artist and prolific writer of art criticism, Naumann was acutely conscious of the "cultural" determinants and implications of the contemporary crisis. Influenced by Ruskin and Morris, he became aware of the intimate link between art and life and, consequently, of the close connection between cultural-artistic revival on the one hand

[57] Göhre resigned from the Church in 1906 in protest against its social conservatism and in due course abandoned Christianity entirely, although not his concern with religion. A year later Max Maurenbrecher left the Church and joined Göhre in the SPD. In 1912 Traub was disciplined and deprived of his right to preach because of his support for the liberal theologian Jatho. Kretschmar ESK, 34–36. Maurenbrecher broke with the SPD on patriotic grounds during the war and was reinstated in the Church in 1917; Traub, too, returned to Lutheran orthodoxy and was reinstated in 1918.

[58] E.g., a Pastor Liebster who tried to persuade both the Church and the ESK that German workers could be won back to Christianity if the church adopted his "dialectical" theology. See Manfred Schick, *Kulturprotestantismus und soziale Frage. Versuch zur Begründung der Sozialethik, vornehmlich in der Zeit von der Gründung des Evangelisch-sozialen Kongresses bis zum Ausbruch des ersten Weltkrieges (1870–1914)* (Tübingen: J.C.B. Mohr, 1970), 136; Friedrich Naumann, "Die Industrialisierung des Christentums" (1910), in Friedrich Naumann. *Werke*, ed. Walter Uhsadel (Cologne: Westdeutscher Verlag, 1964), 1:819–24.

[59] On Naumann, see the biography by Theodor Heuss, *Friedrich Naumann. Der Mann, das Werk, die Zeit* (2d rev. ed.; Stuttgart: Rainer Wunderlich Verlag Hermann Leins, 1949) and the editor's introductions to the six volumes of Naumann's *Werke*.

and social reform on the other.[60] It was these ideas that led Naumann to play a major role in founding the German Werkbund, a society of artists and progressive industrialists dedicated to raising the standard of German work in the applied arts. Established in 1907, the Werkbund sought both to produce a harmonious national style in tune with the spirit of the modern age and to restore dignity and joy to work. Naumann was instrumental in formulating the society's initial manifesto and made it an adjunct to his social reform program. Through the Werkbund he was able both to influence sectors of German society not otherwise accessible to his ideas and also to win disciples among members of the educated public who felt ill at ease with his party-political approach to social issues.[61]

There were two distinct strands in Naumann's thinking on the "worker question" and the problem of work. On the one hand, he advocated the democratization of industrial relations in order to give the workers a sense of belonging that would "immunize" them against Marxist class-conflict propaganda; on the other, he propagated the ideal of quality work as a means of restoring joy and dignity to labor. The idea of industrial democracy was emphasized in the pages of his weekly, *Die Hilfe*, constituted the burden of his message when addressing the VfS and the ESK, and informed his political program. The quality idea accounted for his involvement with the Werkbund. Both had a single root: his belief that alienation had its source in the workplace and that it had to be tackled there, if the working class was ever to become a full partner in the creation of a strong and united nation.

Naumann, as one of the earliest and most consistent German propagandists for worker participation in industry, rejected both the military model of industrial management with its emphasis on command and obedience and the patriarchal approach favored by many leading industrialists. Instead, he insisted that reformers must increase workers' rights and liberties and combat the "industrial feudalism" of the large firms which often provided better-than-average working conditions but tended to limit their employees' freedom.[62] A strong supporter of the "constitutional factory" idea sponsored by progressive industrialists like Abbe and Freese, he hoped that the works councils would in time be

[60] Joan Campbell, "Social Idealism and Cultural Reform in the German Arts and Crafts 1900–1914," *The Turn of the Century. German Literature and Art 1890–1915* (Bonn: Bouvier, 1981), 319–22.

[61] On the founding of the Werkbund and its evolution to 1914, Joan Campbell, *The German Werkbund: The Politics of Reform in the Applied Arts* (Princeton: Princeton University Press, 1978), Chapters 1 and 2.

[62] Naumann, "Neudeutsche Wirtschaftspolitik" (1906), *Werke* 3:428–29.

transformed from purely advisory bodies into organs of democratic control over management and foresaw a time when industry would be fully
democratized and ownership transferred to the organized community of
workers.[63]

Although he wanted to extend the power of the councils, Naumann
thought it important that this should be done in such a way as to safeguard the position of the trade unions. He therefore recommended that
the latter be involved as advisers to the councils in large concerns,
while continuing to speak directly for the employees in smaller enterprises. Similarly, although he regarded company patriotism (*Betriebs-
patriotismus*) as an important by-product of the democratization of
work, his desire to promote a sense of community within industry
through the spread of "industrial parliamentarism" was always tem-
pered by the fear that the employers might use the increased authority
derived from reform to exploit their workers or to impose conditions
detrimental to their health and wellbeing. As a liberal, Naumann was
determined to protect the autonomy of individual workers as well as to
encourage their integration into the community of producers.[64]

Respect for the individual also inspired the second aspect of Naumann's reform program: the maximization of Arbeitsfreude. Like Ruskin and Morris, Naumann was convinced that work could be truly joyful only if it was creative, demanded skill, and satisfied the instinct for
beauty. Where he differed from the English reformers was in his belief
that joy in work was a realizable objective not just for artists and artisans, but also for modern industrial workers employing machines to
produce for a mass market, provided only that industry adopted the
ideal of quality. To this end, he sought to persuade German manufacturers, especially in the art industries, to concentrate on the production
of well-designed objects satisfying to make as well as to use. Although
this might mean abjuring quick profits, he argued that it would pay off
in the long run by helping to overcome labor alienation, a major obstacle to higher productivity and to genuine social and cultural progress.

It was Naumann's updated version of the English Arts and Crafts
ideal of joyful labor that lay beneath the German Werkbund's efforts to
forge an alliance between art and industry. His slogan of "quality work"
appealed both to those interested in raising the level of design for aesthetic reasons and to the many others, in and outside the Werkbund,
who adopted the cause of reform above all for social or patriotic motives. By arguing that quality production would both improve the na-

[63] Naumann, "Neudeutsche Wirtschaftspolitik," 418–23.
[64] Naumann, "Neudeutsche Wirtschaftspolitik," 425–26.

tion's artistic culture and help to overcome the alienation of the workers, Naumann provided the Werkbund with a program capable of holding together its highly disparate membership and so enabled it to play a prominent role in the movement for cultural and social reform.

Building on the ideas of Riehl and Herkner, Naumann stressed the importance of Arbeitsfreude for the health of society and sought to direct social policy towards the creation of additional opportunities for joyful labor. Yet he was realist enough to recognize that the quality ideal, key to both true art and joy in work, was an appropriate standard only within the art industries, and that, even there, economic factors set limits to its achievement. He knew that the mass-market manufacturers of consumer goods and *objets d'art* would find it difficult to devote themselves exclusively to the production of goods of outstanding merit. At best, they could be expected to strive for the gradual improvement of the quality of materials, workmanship and design. In heavy industry, and wherever utility rather than beauty was the prime consideration, Naumann argued that good pay and improved industrial relations were especially vital to compensate for the fact that the majority of workers could not hope to derive joy from the work itself.

Naumann and his Werkbund friends never thought to make joyful labor a substitute for adequate material rewards. Giving due weight to the motivational power of money, they tried to convince the employers that putting quality ahead of profits would eventually pay off, and the operatives that high-quality skilled work would enable them to earn enough so that they could enjoy the fruits of their labor and participate in the national culture. Such arguments supported the contention that quality production would help to overcome alienation, buttress the social order, and raise the level of artistic culture. But Naumann insisted that these ends would be achieved only if the quality ideal was combined with reforms in the organization of work that involved workers in decision-making and gave them a fair share in the profits of production.[65]

Aware that the production of useful and beautiful goods was only a partial answer to alienation, Werkbund members also tackled other facets of the social question that had a direct bearing on the physical and mental wellbeing of the working classes, and an important, if indirect, relationship to joy in work. Thus some addressed the task of beautifying the workplace, while others designed healthful, attractive housing for

[65] In addition to Naumann's "Neudeutsche Wirtschaftspolitik," see his "Deutsche Gewerbekunst" (1908), *Werke* 6:275–77; "Kunst und Volkswirtschaft" (1912), *Werke* 6:290–316; and "Werkbund und Handel," *Werke* 6:316–31.

the industrial workforce. Such Werkbund efforts notwithstanding, however, it is fair to conclude that concern with the quality of working life played only a subsidiary role in the thinking of German social reformers in the period before 1914. The notion of Arbeitsfreude cropped up frequently in discussions of the worker question, but little was done to define the concept or to explore its relevance in the context of modern industrial society. The few who did analyze this topic with some degree of rigor quickly discovered that they were entering a realm where even the basic facts had yet to be established. No wonder that many were tempted to conclude that joy in work was unattainable under modern capitalism and so not worth worrying about. This was the position adopted by most German socialists, and by those of their bourgeois opponents in whom the devastating effects of modernization had induced a mood of cultural despair.[66] The alternative was to argue, with Herkner, that serious examination of the facts would make it possible to replace prevalent quasi-religious or self-serving generalizations about Arbeitsfreude with "scientifically" grounded conclusions about the actual and potential relationship between industrial Man and his work, and thereby lay the basis for effective steps to counter alienation.

[66] See Fritz Stern, *The Politics of Cultural Despair. A Study in the Rise of the Germanic Ideology* (New York: Doubleday, 1965).

V

THE SCIENCE OF WORK BEFORE
THE FIRST WORLD WAR

THE EARLY twentieth century saw the emergence of a new science of work (*Arbeitswissenschaft*) which attempted to shed light on work in all its facets by integrating the findings of a wide spectrum of disciplines.[1] In this endeavor, Germany lagged behind other industrial nations. By 1914 the scientific study of the relationship between human beings and their work in the age of the machine was more advanced in Belgium, France, and the United States than in Germany, particularly from the methodological point of view.[2] Yet by placing greater stress than did their colleagues elsewhere on the problem of alienation, Germans did make an important contribution. In Germany, the desire to identify the reasons for the loss or absence of Arbeitsfreude played a major role in guiding the research even of those who regarded themselves as objective scholars, free of romantic illusions about the prospects for joy in work in the modern context.

Whereas parallel movements elsewhere tended to concentrate on productivity and profits, German Arbeitswissenschaft dedicated itself to the discovery of fundamental principles. Disdainful of those whose main concern was with the practical application of research, German professors long sought to maintain the elevated status of their institutions by relegating applied work to the colleges of technology (*Technische Hochschulen*, TH). So eager were most of them to preserve their academic purity and scholarly integrity that they proclaimed their neutrality in the struggle between capital and labor.

What is more, German scholars who engaged in the new science of work were increasingly inclined to stay aloof from the social reform movement. Subscribing to the notion of "value-free" learning, they

[1] Fritz Giese, "Arbeitswissenschaft," HA 1:418–23.
[2] Anthony Oberschall, *Empirical Social Research in Germany 1848–1914* (Paris: Mouton, 1965), 133.

73

used it to add an aura of academic respectability to their endeavors and to justify their abstention from political involvement.[3] Yet this stance had serious drawbacks. For one thing, it limited the support that Arbeitswissenschaft obtained from industry. For another, by restricting academic access to the workplace, it accentuated the gulf that separated intellectuals from office and factory and reinforced their tendency to think about the problem of work in abstract terms. In turn, this increased skepticism about the new science expressed by those in industry and government.

Had it not been for the growing conviction among social reformers that "science" held the key to the problem of modern work, there would have been little or no organized support for Arbeitswissenschaft in Germany before 1914. Thanks to the encouragement of associations like the VfS, a number of German academics did proceed to investigate the psychotechnical and psychosocial components of work, thereby laying the groundwork for impressive achievements in these areas after the war. This chapter will examine the extent to which concern about the loss of Arbeitsfreude, as well as attitudes to work inherited from earlier times, influenced the efforts of progressive researchers to deal "objectively" with the problem of work.

One of the most original progenitors of the twentieth-century science of work was Karl Bücher (1847–1930), a professor of economic history at Leipzig and an active member of the VfS. In his *Arbeit und Rhythmus*,[4] Bücher, in a manner reminiscent of Riehl, combined archaeological, anthropological and historical evidence to shed light on the nature of work and its evolution since primitive times. But whereas Riehl had stressed national differences, Bücher surveyed past and present attitudes and practices of peoples around the world and sought to establish generalizations that would be valid for humanity as a whole. Bücher concluded that work, art, and play had been united for primitive people, that all three had been linked by a natural rhythm that rendered them intrinsically pleasurable. Humanity had quickly learned that music could enhance the rhythmic character of manual labor, and that rhythm, by making work more nearly automatic, eased fatigue, increased the effectiveness of labor, and rendered work more enjoyable for the individual.

---

[3] For a brief summary of the controversy about the role of values in the social sciences, see Harald Winkel, *Die deutsche Nationalökonomie im 19. Jahrhundert* (Darmstadt: Wissenschaftliche Buchgesellschaft, 1977), 151–58. On Max Weber's role, see also Ringer, 161–62.

[4] Karl Bücher, *Arbeit und Rhythmus* (Leipzig: B. G. Teubner, 1896). Unless otherwise indicated, page references are to the sixth edition of 1924, which included extra examples but was substantially the same as previous editions.

Bücher's observations led him to challenge the general view of German intellectuals that repetitive manual labor was bound to evoke feelings of monotony and a sense of alienation. Instead, he insisted that physical work was essentially pleasurable—at least so long as workers were able to assimilate it to their own natural rhythms and exercise some control over its tempo and duration.[5] His anthropological evidence also led him to contradict the interpretations of other scholars about the nature of primitive people, for example those of the Austrian positivist, Gustav Ratzenhofer (1842–1904), who maintained that "natural man," far from taking pleasure in his work, instinctively shied away from labor, and engaged in it only when compelled to do so.[6] Whereas Ratzenhofer concluded that Arbeitsfreude was a product of advanced culture, Bücher maintained that joy in work, characteristic of early society, had diminished in the course of evolution.

Adopting a position characteristic of German idealism, and language close to that of the young Marx, Bücher traced the degeneration of an initial paradise of joyful work into the noisy, soulless, mechanical world of the modern factory. Thanks to an extreme division of labor, joy in work, once the birthright of every human being, now appeared reserved for the fortunate few: artists, poets, and scholars.[7] The problem was compounded by the evolution of technology which had given rise to both mechanized industry and a market economy based on the ownership of the means of production by a minority. The machine enslaved the worker by destroying the natural rhythm of work and imposing its own non-human pace; the capitalist system subjected the worker to the will of others.[8]

In the guise of an anthropological and historical treatise on the relationships among labor, music, and art, *Arbeit und Rhythmus* constituted an indictment of modern industrial society. Yet Bücher neither joined those who called for a return to pre-industrial modes of production nor supported the Marxist crusade against the capitalist system. Opting for a middle ground, he consoled himself for the decline of Arbeitsfreude by pointing to the improved standard of living that modern technology and economic organization had made possible. Nor did he abandon the hope that joy in work might be restored. For Bücher believed that his "discoveries" might be used to reform the sphere of industrial labor so as to reverse the progress of alienation. Although he portrayed a world where art itself "went in search of bread" and work

[5] Bücher, *Arbeit und Rhythmus*, 443.

[6] Gustav Ratzenhofer, *Die Soziologische Erkenntnis. Positive Philosophie des sozialen Lebens* (Leipzig: F. A. Brockhaus, 1898), 141–42.

[7] Bücher, *Arbeit und Rhythmus*, 15–16.   [8] Bücher, *Arbeit und Rhythmus*, 456–57.

was "no longer cheerful play nor joyful pleasure but serious duty and often painful renunciation," he dreamed of a time when technology and art would be reconciled in a "higher rhythmic unity" capable of "giving the spirit back that joyous cheer, and the body that harmonious development, which characterizes the best of the primitive peoples."[9]

Insisting that his sole purpose was to lay bare the hidden forces behind humanity's economic and social evolution, Bücher made no attempt to implement the semi-utopian conclusion of *Arbeit und Rhythmus* by outlining specific measures to counteract alienation. Yet his book both reflected and gave legitimacy to that strain of progressive idealism which inspired contemporary reformers like Herkner or the members of the Werkbund to search for ways to restore joy and dignity to labor. At the same time, the "scientific" character of his treatise, including its innovative use of anthropological evidence, stimulated the academic study of the nature and meaning of modern work. Above all, *Arbeit und Rhythmus* was important because it directed attention to manual work as a major potential source of Arbeitsfreude. The majority of German idealists assumed a positive correlation between the intellectual content of a task and joy in its execution. Bücher showed that physical work could also be pleasurable, and encouraged his fellow scientists to investigate the psychophysiology of manual labor.

The person who did most to inaugurate experimental research in this area was a colleague of Bücher's at the University of Leipzig, Wilhelm Wundt (1832–1920). A man of wide learning and interests who ranged beyond the confines of any single discipline in his attempt to make sense of the world, Wundt, who admired Carlyle and Kant, firmly believed that the nation's educated elite had a mission to lead the way to a new order based on German idealism.[10] His Institute of Experimental Psychology, established in 1892, sponsored laboratory studies that closely mirrored Bücher's concerns. For example, attempts were made to test the link between the organic and psychic effects of rhythm, and between physical fatigue and boredom.[11] Bücher himself acknowledged the relevance of Wundt's work, while the latter paid tribute to Bücher's contribution.[12]

Significantly, Wundt had sought to address the problem of work long

[9] Bücher, *Arbeit und Rhythmus*, 463.
[10] For Wundt's intellectual development and career see his autobiography, *Erlebtes und Erkanntes* (Stuttgart: Kröner, 1920).
[11] Ernst Meumann, *Untersuchungen zur Psychologie und Aesthetik des Rhythmus* (Leipzig: Wilhelm Engelmann, 1894), first published as vol. 10 of Wundt's *Philosophische Studien*.
[12] Bücher, *Arbeit und Rhythmus* (1902), 376; Wilhelm Wundt, *Grundzüge der Physiologischen Psychologie* (Leipzig: Wilhelm Engelmann, 1903), 3:40–41.

before he turned from philosophy to experimental psychology. In his *Ethics* of 1886 he had attributed the origins of Arbeitsfreude to the development of the aesthetic sensibility and had expatiated on the moral value of the crafts, portraying them as the last bulwark of professional honor and pride in a world increasingly at odds with traditional norms.[13] Some years later, he examined the relationship between work and religion from an ethnographical perspective.[14] Wundt's chief contribution to the subject, however, stemmed from his influence on those who passed through his psychological laboratory.

Of these, the most distinguished was the psychiatrist Emil Kraepelin (1865–1926). A professor at Heidelberg from 1891 to 1903, Kraepelin moved to Munich where he founded his own psychiatric research institute in 1917. At Heidelberg he inaugurated a series of experimental studies of mental activity and fatigue which enabled him to derive "work curves" that took into account such psychological aspects of work performance as stimulation, habituation, and motivation.[15] Yet, like Wundt, Kraepelin is important primarily because his example stimulated others to push the psychology of work in new directions.

The person who made explicit the connection between Arbeitswissenschaft and joy in work was Kraepelin's pupil Hugo Münsterberg (1863–1916). After completing his doctorate in psychology under Wundt in 1885, Münsterberg spent two years with Kraepelin in Heidelberg. Equipped with these excellent credentials, he went to Harvard in 1892 as visiting professor and, after failing to obtain a full professorship at a European university, accepted a chair there five years later. At Harvard, he pioneered in the application of psychology to industry and helped to create the new discipline of "psychotechnics."

Although Münsterberg remained at Harvard until his death and so is frequently thought of as an American psychologist, he maintained close links with the German world of learning. His writings on the psychology of industrial labor cannot be understood without reference to his German background, and it is no coincidence that his first book on industrial psychology, *Psychology and Industrial Efficiency*, was based on a series of lectures given at the University of Berlin in 1910–11.[16]

[13] Wilhelm Wundt, *Ethik. Eine Untersuchung der Thatsachen und Gesetze des sittlichen Lebens* (Stuttgart: Ferdinand Enke, 1886), 134, 515–16.

[14] Wilhelm Wundt, *Völkerpsychologie*, 2 vols. (Leipzig: Wilhelm Engelmann, 1909).

[15] See Emil Kraepelin, *Über Geistige Arbeit* (2d ed.; Jena: Gustav Fischer, 1897), a popular lecture originally given in 1893. Kraepelin's research helped lay the basis for Wundt's own discussion of work. See especially his section on "Geistige Arbeit und Arbeitskurven" in Wundt, *Grundzüge*, 3:615–24.

[16] Hugo Münsterberg, *Psychologie und Wirtschaftsleben* (Leipzig: Johann Ambrosius Barth, 1912); translated as *Psychology and Industrial Efficiency* (Boston: Houghton Mifflin, 1913).

On the other hand, this text also reflected the influence of its author's adopted country. Münsterberg owed much to the America vocational guidance movement and the "scientific management" ideas of the industrial engineer Frederick Taylor. Similarly "American" was his insistence that science must put itself at the service of business. In the German edition, he made a point of condemning intellectual prejudice against economic activity and in a passage omitted from the American translation urged his German readers to put their science to practical use.[17] Defining the new type of "industrial psychologist" in a pragmatic way, he maintained that his job was to select people whose mental qualities best fitted them for particular occupations, to determine under what psychological conditions they would be most productive, and to discover how to motivate them to give their utmost to the enterprise.[18]

Münsterberg never rejected the heritage of his country of origin, nor did he abandon his belief in the superiority of German science. Indeed, he particularly relished his role as an intermediary between two cultures.[19] For example, while approving Taylor's aim of rationalizing industrial work, Münsterberg accused scientific management of naiveté and "helpless psychological dilettantism" in comparison with his own approach, which was based on the latest German experimental findings.[20] In the American edition of his text, he stressed the importance of the scientist's autonomy: applied psychology must "speak the language of exact science, independent of economic opinions and debatable partisan interest."[21] Even more "German" was his concluding passage where he dropped the pose of pragmatic, value-free expert concerned purely with means rather than ends to expatiate on "the cultural gain which will come to the total economic life of the nation, as soon as everyone can be brought to the place where his best energies may be unfolded and his greatest personal satisfaction secured."[22] Far from contenting himself with finding solutions for technical problems in the name of efficiency and higher profits, Münsterberg's industrial

See Matthew Hale, Jr., *Human Science and Social Order. Hugo Münsterberg and the Origins of Applied Psychology* (Philadelphia: Temple University Press, 1980), especially Chapter 10: "Industrial Efficiency," 148–63.

[17] Münsterberg, *Psychologie und Wirtschaftsleben*, 181.

[18] Münsterberg, *Psychology and Industrial Efficiency*, 23.

[19] According to R. W. Rieber, "Wundt and the Americans," in *Wilhelm Wundt and the Making of a Scientific Psychology*, ed. Rieber et al. (New York: Plenum, 1980), 138–39 n.2, Wundt was "one of the major forces that facilitated the Americanization of psychology during this period."

[20] Münsterberg, *Psychology and Industrial Efficiency*, 55–56; Hale, *Human Science and Social Order*, 150–52; Loren Baritz, *The Servants of Power. A History of the Use of Social Science in American Industry* (Middletown, Conn.: Wesleyan University Press, 1960), 35–36.

[21] Münsterberg, *Psychology and Industrial Efficiency*, 19.

[22] Münsterberg, *Psychology and Industrial Efficiency*, 309.

psychologist would strive to adjust work and psyche so that "mental dissatisfaction in the work, mental depression and discouragement, may be replaced in our social community by overflowing joy and perfect inner harmony."[23] The American Münsterberg might be content to accept material wellbeing as a legitimate objective, but the German placed himself in the service of a higher ideal: that of securing the good of the individual and the national community through the restoration of joy in work.[24]

There is no way to ascertain whether the "real" Münsterberg was the one who sold American business on the importance of psychology by emphasizing the improved profits to be derived from the employment of happy workers or the one who argued that the maximization of joy in work was important for the sake of the worker and the good of society. Undoubtedly there are sections in *Psychology and Industrial Efficiency* which treat the enhancement of joy in work in purely instrumental fashion. Nevertheless, one must reject the contention of some of Münsterberg's critics that the passage about joy in work at the end of the book should be dismissed as a mere "panacean flourish."[25] To do so is to make the unwarranted assumption that the Münsterberg of *Psychology and Industrial Efficiency* no longer had anything in common with the man who in 1908 had published a neo-Fichtean philosophical treatise on ethics which described work in typically idealist fashion as a major and unfailing source of joy.[26] It also fails to give sufficient weight to the fact that Münsterberg repeatedly demonstrated his concern for the psychic wellbeing of the individual worker, for example when he recommended that the machine be adapted to accommodate the natural bodily and psychological rhythms of the operative, along the lines suggested by Bücher's *Arbeit und Rhythmus*, in order to enhance the employee's work experience.[27] All in all, there is no reason to question the fundamental idealism of Münsterberg's enterprise, with its typically German emphasis on joy in work as an independent value.[28]

[23] Münsterberg, *Psychology and Industrial Efficiency*, 309.

[24] See also his *Grundzüge der Psychotechnik* (2d ed.; Leipzig: Barth, 1920), 359–60. Originally published in 1914, this was the first general textbook of applied psychology.

[25] Baritz, *Servants of Power*, 37; Frieda Wunderlich, *Hugo Münsterbergs Bedeutung für die Nationalökonomie* (Jena: Gustav Fischer, 1920), 78, citing a review by Willy Hellpach.

[26] Hugo Münsterberg, *Philosophie der Werte. Grundzüge einer Weltanschauung* (Leipzig: Barth, 1908), 231; English translation: *The Eternal Values* (Boston: Houghton Mifflin, 1909), 200. See Richard Hamann and Jost Hermand, *Stilkunst um 1900, Epochen deutscher Kultur von 1870 bis zur Gegenwart*, vol. 4 (Munich: Nymphenburger Verlagshandlung, 1975), 83–84.

[27] Münsterberg, *Psychology and Industrial Efficiency*, 162–64; *Psychologie und Wirtschaftsleben*, 94–96; Hale, *Human Science and Social Order*, 157–58.

[28] Harvard's Charles Eliot made very similar statements about joy in work. See James B. Gilbert, *Work without Salvation. America's Intellectuals and Industrial Alienation, 1880–1910*

While some of the contradictions in Münsterberg's analysis of the problem of work stemmed from the conflict between German and American values, the intrinsic difficulty of what he was attempting must also be taken into account: German theorists of work, those uncorrupted by the utilitarian world of American capitalism, also failed to produce internally consistent statements on the potential for Arbeitsfreude in industrial society. If Hegel and Marx, Riehl and Bücher were all unable to define the problem of modern work clearly or propose satisfactory solutions, it is no wonder that Münsterberg, a man whose gifts were in any case essentially practical rather than theoretical, did no better.

Münsterberg's statements on work deserve closer examination, for they mirrored assumptions general among his German academic contemporaries, and, along with his 'findings,' played a considerable role in the postwar German debate about rationalization and scientific management. Perhaps the most striking characteristic of his industrial psychology was its optimism. Münsterberg assumed that for every individual there existed some "best work" and for every task a "best man," so that the expert, having assessed the worker's physical and psychological capacities and analyzed the requirements of the available jobs, could bring the two together. The workshops of the nation provided a niche for those who adapted well to repetitive tasks and for those who required alternation in their activities and even the most seemingly boring jobs were attractive to certain persons.

Once steps were taken to match the right person with the right job, monotony ceased to be a problem.[29] But Münsterberg also believed that proper vocational training, emphasizing the development of motor skills while inculcating improved work attitudes, could beneficially affect both industrial efficiency and joy in work.[30] The industrial psychologist as tester assumed that capacities were innate; as educator he posited the physical and psychic malleability of human beings.

Münsterberg's antideterminist outlook was most forcefully revealed in his essay on socialism, where he argued that the first priority must be to change workers' habits of thought. The problem of work would be solved if the workers came to realize that their labors, hard as they were, served the "ideal purpose of civilized mankind, the development

---

(Baltimore: Johns Hopkins, 1977), 124–31, and "Charles W. Eliot and the Quest for Joyful Labor," in Daniel T. Rodgers, *The Work Ethic in Industrial America 1850–1920* (Chicago: University of Chicago Press, 1978), 233–42. As his stance was not typical of contemporary American opinion, it would be interesting to know if he was influenced by Münsterberg.

[29] See the chapter on monotony in *Psychology and Industrial Efficiency*.
[30] Münsterberg, *Grundzüge*, 374–75.

of economic civilization. . . . Give to the workingman the right kind of ideas, the right attitude towards his work, and all the hardship becomes blessedness and the suffering glory."[31] Neither poverty nor the nature of modern work was to blame for the loss of joy in work. The labor leaders were culpable, because they had "persuaded the workman to look on the movements which he is to perform in the factory" and to ignore "the higher interest and aim of the civilization which he is helping to serve."[32] Denying that rationalized work transformed people into mere machines, Münsterberg asserted that it was only necessary to "change the theory about uniformity, and you remove monotony from the industrial world. Monotony is only the uniformity which is hated."[33]

Münsterberg knew that harmony would be difficult to realize in practice, and that it might not always be possible to match every worker with an appropriate task,[34] or achieve an "ideal distribution of wage earners among the various commercial and industrial positions."[35] He was also aware of contemporary German studies showing that workers who liked their jobs least were often the most productive, thus calling in question the correlation between Arbeitsfreude and productivity.[36] Indeed, in the short run, he had to admit that the new "scientific" methods of work while increasing productivity, might actually decrease joy in work, and would assuredly put many out of work.[37] Nevertheless, "from the point of view of the whole community," psychotechnics would in the long run serve the general good, even if for the present it might be necessary to sacrifice the full development of some workers' personalities and social adjustment in the name of "civilization."[38] As he put it in his essay on socialism, industrial workers might envy scholars in their laboratories, but

> there is under no factory roof a workman so forlorn that the work of his hands is not aiding the fulfillment of an equally great and equally ideal purpose of civilized mankind, the development of economic civilization.[39]

To deal with the possibility that his science might hinder the achievement of Arbeitsfreude, Münsterberg drew on supplementary

---

[31] Hugo Münsterberg, *Psychology and Social Sanity* (Garden City, N.Y.: Doubleday, 1914), 71–110.

[32] Münsterberg, *Psychology and Social Sanity*, 103.

[33] Münsterberg, *Psychology and Social Sanity*, 106.   [34] Münsterberg, *Grundzüge*, 373.

[35] Münsterberg, *Psychology and Industrial Efficiency*, 126.

[36] Münsterberg, *Psychology and Industrial Efficiency*, 127.

[37] Münsterberg, *Psychology and Industrial Efficiency*, 143–44.; *Grundzüge*, 400.

[38] Münsterberg, *Psychology and Industrial Efficiency*, 144.

[39] Münsterberg, *Psychology and Social Sanity*, 103.

arguments from his ideological arsenal to buttress his faith in the fundamental harmony of the social order. All would yet be well if the entire industrial community became "inspired by the belief in the ideal value of work as work and as a necessary contribution to the progress of mankind."[40] But in any case, he insisted, people were wrong to regard a rising standard of living as a genuine source of happiness. Instead, all must be taught to find their highest satisfaction in the joy of duty done.[41] On occasion, Münsterberg acknowledged the role of material motivators in improving worker morale and admitted that the best incentive to higher productivity remained the prospect of higher income.[42] But momentary concessions to the utilitarian ethic could not obscure his fundamental idealism. By redefining the quest for joy in work in terms of an ethic of duty and service, Münsterberg was able to reconcile demands for sacrifice on the part of the workers with belief in the essential compatibility of individual and society, and in the possibility of reconciling ethical with economic ends.

It is probable that Münsterberg's tone of determined optimism helped him to market his own students, the trained psychologists he claimed industry needed to create a happy, efficient labor force. However, his desire to believe that happy workers were better workers and his confidence in the fundamental harmony of economic interests led him to slight evidence contrary to his argument. To the end of his life, he reiterated his conviction that joy in work, industrial efficiency, and cultural progress were compatible, and that the industrial psychologist, applying the latest scientific techniques and insights, was the person best equipped to guide society in the right direction.[43]

As a scientist, Münsterberg took from others what suited his purposes rather than developing a method of his own. To solve the problems of industrial society, he used the experience of industrial managers and the observations of skilled psychologists operating in the workplace. In addition, he stressed the relevance of experimental laboratory investigations and even planned a social survey to obtain information on worker attitudes regarding job satisfaction and motivation.[44] Generally speaking, his aim was to blend theory and practice:

[40] Münsterberg, *Psychology and Social Sanity*, 108; Hale, *Human Science and Social Order*, 160–62.

[41] Münsterberg, *Philosophie der Werte*, 232.   [42] Münsterberg, *Grundzüge*, 402.

[43] Münsterberg, *Grundzüge*, 359.

[44] Münsterberg, *Psychology and Industrial Efficiency*, 124; Hale, *Human Science and Social Order*, 159–60. The latter describes a questionnaire Münsterberg intended to distribute to 15,000 factory and mill workers, but which was never used because Harvard thought its good name might be tarnished thereby.

The mere trying and trying again in practical life can never reach the maximum effects which may be secured by systematic, scientifically conducted efforts. On the other side, the studies of the theoretical scholars can never yield the highest values for civilization if the problems which offer themselves in practical life are ignored. . . . As long as industrial managers have no contact with the experiments of the laboratory and the experimentalists are shy of any contact with the industrial reality, humanity will pass through social suffering. The hope of mankind will be realized by the mutual fertilization of knowing and doing.[45]

Thus Münsterberg proposed an industrial psychology that blended German theoretical science with American pragmatic experimentalism, the whole dedicated to the service of an essentially German cultural ideal and based on faith in the ability of science to transform that ideal into reality.

Another of Kraepelin's pupils, Willy Hellpach (1877–1955), presents a striking temperamental contrast to Münsterberg. Hellpach, too, first studied with Wundt at Leipzig in the 1890s before moving on to Heidelberg where he served as assistant to Kraepelin and studied medicine. In 1904 he settled in Karlsruhe as a practicing psychiatrist and two years later completed an advanced degree in psychology at the local college of technology. In 1911 he joined the staff of the Karlsruhe TH, and in 1920 was appointed professor of applied psychology and director of its new Institute for Social Psychology—the first of its kind in Germany.[46]

Hellpach had addressed himself to the problem of work as early as 1902, some years before Münsterberg, and returned to the subject at intervals throughout his life. Throughout, he rejected not only Münsterberg's optimism about the possibility of reconciling modern people with their work, but also Bücher's belief that human beings in their natural state had experienced joy in work. Like Ratzenhofer, he was convinced that primitive man hated work, and that only the need for self-preservation, operating over thousands of years, had succeeded in habituating people to sustained labor and had enabled them to derive a certain satisfaction from it. At the same time, following Bücher whom he greatly admired, he condemned modern industrial society for its negative effects on work. Although he admitted that the process of occupational specialization had made it possible for those with inborn talents to find increased satisfaction in the urban professions, he maintained that, for the vast majority, the advancing division of labor and fragmentation of tasks meant a diminution of Arbeitsfreude to the

---

[45] Münsterberg, *Psychology and Industrial Efficiency*, 215.　　[46] *NDB* 8:487–88.

point where labor was once more as painful as it had been for primitive people.[47]

Arbeitsfreude was the theme of Hellpach's inaugural lecture at Karlsruhe in 1906.[48] Addressing himself to the relationship between technical progress and mental health, he drew on his experience as a physician to paint a gloomy picture of the psychic state of the German proletariat. In particular, he noted that industrial workers regularly demonstrated their abhorrence of the work they were compelled to do by prolonging their absence from their jobs after bouts of illness, despite the fact that sick-pay lagged well behind wages. The explanation seemed plain: mechanization was rendering factory labor ever more "bleak, monotonous and joyless" by fragmenting the productive process, robbing work of all elements of creative spontaneity, and making it impossible for the worker to develop any feeling for the whole. Hellpach agreed with Bücher that the machine's tendency to subject the worker to its own rhythm was in part responsible for the loss of joy in work. Enslaved by the machine and unable to see the meaning of their efforts, it was no wonder that many workers rebelled and were content to work less, even if this meant a drop in earnings.[49] Herkner and others might attribute this type of behavior to the persistence of pre-industrial attitudes, but to Hellpach it represented a natural and rational response to the deterioration of modern work.[50]

Although Hellpach denied that the decline of joy in work was specific to any particular class, he stressed that the class to suffer most was the urban proletariat. The swelling ranks of low-level white-collar workers were engaged in tasks just as monotonous and deadening as those imposed on industrial labor, but he noted that these workers had on the whole managed to keep some control over the tempo of work and, more important, enjoyed a degree of job security and pension rights that helped compensate for the loss of joy in work.[51] The increase in neurotic illness among the bourgeoisie could best be explained by

[47] Willy Hellpach, *Die Grenzwissenschaften der Psychologie* (Leipzig: Verlag der Dürr'schen Buchhandlung, 1902), 480–85.

[48] The occasion is described in his autobiographical *Wirken in Wirren. Lebenserinnerungen* (Hamburg: C. Wegner, 1948), 1:499.

[49] Willy Hellpach, *Technischer Fortschritt und seelische Gesundheit* (Halle: C. Marhold, 1907), 21–22.

[50] Herkner, *Arbeiterfrage*, 187–88; Max Weber, *The Protestant Ethic and the Spirit of Capitalism* (New York: Scribners, 1930), 60–61, maintained that resistance to the intensification of work was a characteristic of "traditionalism." See also Reinhard Bendix, *Max Weber: An Intellectual Portrait* (New York: Doubleday, 1962), 51–52; and Peter Stearns, "The Effort at Continuity in Working-Class Culture," *JMH* 52 (December 1980): 633.

[51] Hellpach, *Technischer Fortschritt*, 22.

the greater pace of modern life and the increased pressures associated with the urban environment rather than by changes in the nature of work; in any case, the damage was more superficial than that which afflicted the industrial proletariat.[52]

Hellpach also argued that the capitalist system itself was partly responsible for limiting Arbeitsfreude because it linked the most unpleasant work with the greatest degree of stress and insecurity. Whereas Münsterberg upheld the economic order because he believed it capable of initiating the progressive reforms needed to fulfill its ideal goals, the young Hellpach introduced a strong anticapitalist component into his critique of industrial society. This first led him to place his hopes in the revisionist wing of the SPD, and then brought him into the orbit of Friedrich Naumann during the latter's National Social phase. But by 1903, when the revisionists were defeated at the Dresden Congress of the SPD, Hellpach's hope for the emergence of some kind of "German" or ethical socialism as an alternative to Marxist orthodoxy had faded; at the same time, he felt that Naumann had "betrayed" the cause by going over to the liberal camp.[53]

Even as he lost faith in the possibility of transforming society by political means, Hellpach took heart from the fact that economists like Herkner were beginning to concern themselves with the problem of modern work and to call for scientific study of the psychological and psychopathological features of industrial labor. Convinced of the social and personal costs of technological progress, he wanted to believe that systematic examination of the relationship between technical change and the loss of joy in work could help to provide a scientific basis for needed reforms.[54] His own research on the connection between accident proneness and Arbeitsfreude was designed in this spirit.[55] Hellpach thought it utopian to hope that joy in work might be restored through a restructuring of the labor process. Indeed, he was convinced that the process of modernization could not be halted and that as it gained momentum, Arbeitsfreude would become ever less accessible to the average wage earner.[56] He therefore assigned to the science of work the more modest task of depicting the adverse effects of rationalization, so that countervailing measures might be devised to minimize the dam-

[52] Hellpach, *Technischer Fortschritt*, 16–17.

[53] Hellpach, *Wirken in Wirren*, 1:249, 396–403.

[54] Hellpach, *Technischer Fortschritt*, 23.

[55] Willy Hellpach, "Unfallneurosen und Arbeitsfreude," *Neurologisches Zentralblatt* (Leipzig), 25 (1906): 605–609. Cf. Wladimir Eliasberg, "Richtungen und Entwicklungstendenzen in der Arbeitswissenschaft," ASS 56 (1926): 701–702.

[56] Hellpach, *Technischer Fortschritt*, 28.

age and to compensate, where possible, for the inevitable loss of joy in work.[57]

As an example of such compensations, he noted that improved transport facilities would enable people to live further from their places of employment and thus enjoy more salubrious surroundings without expending more time and energy travelling to and from their work. He also hoped that automation of housework would ease their daily labors and that the provision of more and better consumer goods at lower prices would make up for the negative impact of rationalization on their jobs. Despite his stress on the drawbacks of modern industrial developments for the individual, Hellpach thus agreed with Naumann that the working class had a direct interest in technological progress, on balance stood to benefit from the machine age, and would help to determine its culture.

Hellpach's evidence about the damaging effects of modern work on the health of German workers and his generalizations from clinical practice about the psychic state of the German working class, added a new dimension to the scientific study of the industrial proletariat. By bringing abnormal and social psychology to bear on the problem of work, he supplemented the efforts of economists like Sombart, Bücher, and Herkner, and provided a corrective to the narrowly psychotechnical approach of Münsterberg. By insisting that manual and mental work were very different, Hellpach also cast doubt on the relevance of Kraepelin-style laboratory investigations of mental function for the understanding of factory labor and emphasized the need for an experimental psychology more closely tied to the specific problems of modern industry.[58] On the other hand, the fact that Hellpach based his own conclusions largely on observation of the mentally ill limited the extent to which his approach could shed light on the state of mind of "normal" workers; in addition, his fundamental pessimism prevented him from effectively promoting specific reforms of work or of social policy. Thus, while Hellpach did contribute to the development of Arbeitswissenschaft, the methods he favored were unable to do justice to the complexities of worker alienation or to serve as a basis for a reform program capable of "curing" the condition he helped to diagnose.

A third academic whose efforts to advance the scientific study of

[57] Willy Hellpach, review of Münsterberg, *Psychologie und Wirtschaftsleben*, 2d ed., 1913, in *Zeitschrift für angewandte Psychologie und Charakterkunde* 10 (1914): 573. Hellpach criticized Münsterberg for encouraging employers to introduce Taylorist methods, the source of much of the problem.

[58] Willy Hellpach, "Die Arbeitsteilung im geistigen Leben: eine Untersuchung ihrer hauptsächlichen Formen, Gesetze und Triebkräfte," ASS 35 (1912): 678–79.

modern work were greatly stimulated by the researches of Kraepelin was the Heidelberg professor Max Weber (1864–1920). Weber had commented on the psychology of work as early as 1892, in an essay on the peasant problem east of the Elbe: his famous *The Protestant Ethic and the Spirit of Capitalism* (1904/5) contained several suggestive passages on labor motivation and attitudes to work.[59] But it was only in 1908 that Weber developed ideas with direct impact on the new Arbeitswissenschaft.[60] After summarizing what had so far been learned about the psychophysics of industrial labor, and acknowledging his debt to the physiological and psychological researches of Kraepelin and his school, he outlined a scheme for sociological-empirical investigations that would pay more attention to such psychological factors affecting performance as boredom and its converse, joy in work.[61]

Weber had already argued in *The Protestant Ethic* that education and Weltanschauung were important determinants of attitudes to work and, in turn, influenced individual output. Now, as evidence, he noted the superior productivity of two groups of workers: women with Pietist backgrounds and men enrolled in socialist trade unions.[62] The mechanisms that underlay this phenomenon, he concluded, could not be explored scientifically in the laboratory but required the study of large numbers of workers in their places of work.[63] Laboratory experiments, although useful for hypothesis-building, could not shed much light on the extent to which "impulses of will" affected output and fatigue. What he recommended was a series of long-term, factory-based, team investigations to provide both statistical and survey evidence on a number of industries. Their aim would be to establish the special characteristics of intellectual, economic, and psychological motivators, as well as to determine how, and how much, each factor influenced productivity.[64]

Weber's "Zur Psychophysik der industriellen Arbeit" was in fact the second of two papers meant to prepare the ground for just such an effort. The first, on methodology, was originally presented in manuscript to the VfS in 1908; it was to serve as background for a projected survey

[59] Arthur Mitzman, *The Iron Cage: An Historical Interpretation of Max Weber* (New York: Knopf, 1970), 99–102, 171–77.

[60] Max Weber, "Zur Psychophysik der industriellen Arbeit," ASS 27 (1908): 730–70; 28 (1909): 219–77, 719–61; 29 (1909): 513–42. References below are to the version in Max Weber, *Gesammelte Aufsätze zur Soziologie und Sozialpolitik* (Tübingen: Mohr, 1924).

[61] Max Weber, "Zur Psychophysik," 92; Oberschall, *Empirical Social Research*, 111–34; Wachtler, *Humanisierung der Arbeit*, 42–60.

[62] Max Weber, "Zur Psychophysik," 160–61.

[63] Max Weber, "Zur Psychophysik," 239–40.

[64] Max Weber, "Zur Psychophysik," 93, 111–13, 241, 255.

of industrial labor which Max Weber's brother Alfred had initiated at a meeting of the VfS in September 1907.[65] Following up Herkner's plea for a re-examination of the nation's economic life from the perspective of Arbeitsfreude, Alfred Weber had called for a study of the factors influencing productivity in large-scale enterprises. This was approved by the VfS congress, and detailed planning began in late 1908 under the direction of Bücher. When the latter withdrew for personal reasons, the study was carried to completion under the aegis of a committee comprising Alfred Weber, Schmoller, and Herkner.[66] Inevitably, the experimental design reflected the concerns of all these men, but it was shaped most of all by Max Weber who welcomed the VfS initiative as an opportunity to explore the effects of worker attitudes on performance and, conversely, the impact of factory labor on the worker's psyche.[67]

In view of the close involvement with the project of Herkner and Max Weber, both of whom specifically mentioned Arbeitsfreude as one of the factors to be examined, it is somewhat surprising that the VfS survey (completed between 1909 and 1911) made little effort to study worker attitudes towards work in mechanized and rationalized industry.[68] Of the twenty-seven items in the questionnaire, only two tried to elicit responses regarding aspirations and feelings: No. 10 on reasons for taking up the present occupation, and No. 27 on life goals.[69] The remainder sought objective personal information to supplement "hard" data derived from factory records in order to produce a psychophysical analysis of earning and output figures, to provide material for a survey of the occupational history and life-fate of proletarians (Alfred Weber's prime interest), and to test hypotheses put forward by Max Weber on the influence of hereditary factors.[70] Admittedly, the investigators were encouraged to go beyond the questionnaire to examine motivation and related issues, but

> the whole area of the social organization of the factory floor, of the preference of the different groups of workers for different types of occupations,

[65] Max Weber, "Methodologische Einleitung für die Erhebungen des Vereins für Sozialpolitik über Auslese und Anpassung (Berufswahlen und Berufsschicksal) der Arbeiterschaft der geschlossenen Grossindustrie (1908)," *Gesammelte Aufsätze zur Soziologie und Sozialpolitik*, 1–60.

[66] Oberschall, *Empirical Social Research*, 111–16; Marie Bernays, *Auslese und Anpassung der Arbeiterschaft der geschlossenen Grossindustrie* (Leipzig: Duncker & Humblodt, 1910), Foreword and Author's Introduction. The questionnaire that was used by the researchers is reproduced by Bernays, xii–xiv.

[67] Max Weber, "Methodologische Einleitung," 1.

[68] Oberschall, *Empirical Social Research*, 122–23.

[69] Oberschall, *Empirical Social Research*, 125–26.

[70] Max Weber, "Methodologische Einleitung," Pt. 2; "Zur Psychophysik," 242–55.

of their attitude towards advancement and their satisfaction with the pay and the work, of their relationship with fellow workers . . . was not the focus of the analysis and received only secondary attention in the design of the study.[71]

The failure of most of the dozen or so investigators to administer the questionnaire to more than a fraction of the workers in any factory also diminished the survey's value. The one exception was Max Weber's protégé Marie Bernays, who managed to overcome the initial hostility of the employees in a textile factory by posing as a fellow worker. Her four months on the shop floor not only gave her insight into the life of the firm through direct experience and observation; they also enabled her to win the trust of the workers and thus to obtain a higher percentage of responses to the questionnaire.[72]

In her report, Bernays dealt twice with worker attitudes. In a section on the shop community, she analyzed the relationship between the textile worker and his or her work. These jobs were characterized by an extreme division of labor and a piece-rate wage structure. Bernays observed that many workers actually preferred this method of payment because they felt that it allowed them to work at their own pace and so freed them to some extent from external control. Moreover, time seemed to pass more quickly when one's thoughts were concentrated on maximizing earnings rather than dwelling on the aridity of the task in hand.[73] Indeed, apart from a few skilled operatives, the textile workers whom Bernays studied seem to have regarded their jobs purely as a means of making money:

Every movement embodied for them a minute fraction of their wage; their joy in work, where it appeared at all, was in essence joy in pay.[74]

Viewing everything in quantitative terms, these workers lacked appreciation for quality and were without any inner relationship to their work. In Bernays's judgment, theirs was a colorless existence within a monotonous and noise-filled environment, devoid of variation or hope for improvement.

Bernays's second treatment of the question of Arbeitsfreude occurred in a later section on the psychophysics of textile work. Exploring the effect of attitudes on output through a series of cross tabulations, she used responses to the life-goals item in the questionnaire to measure the workers' subjective adaptation to their current employment against

[71] Oberschall, *Empirical Social Research*, 127.

[72] Oberschall, *Empirical Social Research*, 127–29.

[73] Bernays, *Auslese und Anpassung*, 188.

[74] Bernays, *Auslese und Anpassung*, 189. Bernays contrasted Arbeitsfreude with *Lohnfreude* ("joy in pay").

their productivity (indicated by the level and stability of each individual's earnings). She first divided the respondents into three groups on the basis of their replies to questions regarding their youthful and present feelings about different occupations: those who were satisfied with factory work and aspired to nothing else, those who expressed their dissatisfaction and dreamed of escape to non-factory jobs, and those who were intent on bettering themselves by moving up within the firm. What she found was that apart from a group of largely unskilled women who claimed to like their work and were good at it, there was an inverse relationship between job satisfaction and work performance, rather than the expected positive correlation.[75]

As far as her textile workers were concerned, Bernays concluded that the ethical and intellectual qualities which enabled the male wage earner to undertake complex tasks and so raise his wages were the same ones which psychologically disqualified him from deriving genuine satisfaction from factory work. Indeed, the more complicated the task, the greater the discrepancy between inner and outward adaptation: individuals who claimed to be tired, tense, and dissatisfied with their work generally out-performed their more contented co-workers. This paradoxical finding gave rise to the hypothesis that high-grade workers were sufficiently intelligent to recognize the essential meaninglessness of the job they were required to do and to be irritated and bored by tasks which failed to make full use of their potential. Conversely, "contented" workers lacked either the intellectual or the ethical capacity to rebel against joyless work.[76]

Although she recognized that her results and explanations required further testing, the care with which Bernays analyzed her data would indicate that she believed in her method. Yet given the difficulty of ascertaining inner feelings even with today's more sophisticated questionnaires, it is unlikely that the responses to Bernays's questions accurately reflected what the workers thought about their work. Moreover, whatever the question about life-goals was measuring, it was not Arbeitsfreude in the full sense, but merely the extent to which the individual had successfully adapted to a type of labor which Bernays, along with most of her respondents, regarded as intrinsically incapable of producing joy in work. If contemporaries like Münsterberg were sufficiently impressed by Bernays's evidence to develop doubts about the positive correlation between Arbeitsfreude and productivity, this is a tribute to the aura of scientific respectability surrounding her study

[75] Bernays, *Auslese und Anpassung*, 344–48.
[76] Bernays, *Auslese und Anpassung*, 348–49.

rather than testimony to the validity of her results. It is also necessary to emphasize once more that in Bernays's study, as in the VfS survey in general, the question of Arbeitsfreude was secondary to more narrowly conceived economic and psychophysical concerns, including the derivation and analysis of productivity curves along the lines of Kraepelin.

In the final report on the project which Herkner presented to the VfS congress at Nuremberg in 1911, the difficulties met in realizing the objectives of the surveys were fully acknowledged. But although Herkner admitted that the results were far from conclusive, he nevertheless proceeded to generalize about worker psychology. With respect to Arbeitsfreude, he claimed that the studies demonstrated that joy in work had *not* declined to the extent generally supposed. Virtually ignoring Bernays's contrary findings, he noted that many workers claimed to like their jobs and the machines they served. Moreover, few complained about monotony and those who did find repetitive tasks displeasing tended to counteract boredom by striving to earn more, or by utilizing the opportunities for social interaction still present in many places of work. Workers demonstrated their job satisfaction by preferring to stay with their own work group and accustomed task, rather than accepting more interesting and responsible jobs within the firm. [77]

In the debate that followed Herkner's presentation, it became apparent that not everyone shared his optimistic assessment of the evidence. Thus the General Secretary of the Gewerkverein der deutschen Maschinenbau- und Metallarbeiter (Union for German Machine-Tool and Metal Workers) insisted that the majority of workers in big industry had been assigned to specialized tasks that ruled out joy in work. If they put up with such jobs without demur, it was because their occupations had dulled them to the point that they no longer had an interest in advancement or any inclination to improve their skills. [78] Similarly Alfred Weber believed the surveys had demonstrated that only a minority of skilled workers could still hope to improve their work situation and that no member of the industrial proletariat could consider a job a source of true Arbeitsfreude because the work was not self-determined. [79]

Edgar Jaffé, editor of the *Archiv für Sozialwissenschaft und Sozialpolitik* (ASS), went beyond a critique of Herkner to mount a fundamental attack on the very notion of joy in work. Rather than being specific to

---

[77] Heinrich Herkner, *Probleme der Arbeiterpsychologie mit besonderer Rücksichtnahme auf Methoden und Ergebnisse der Vereinserhebungen*, Verhandlungen des Vereins für Sozialpolitik in Nürnberg 1911. Pt. 2 (Leipzig: Duncker & Humblot, 1912), 133.

[78] Herkner, *Probleme der Arbeiterpsychologie*, 164–65.

[79] Herkner, *Probleme der Arbeiterpsychologie*, 156.

the modern proletarian condition, as Alfred Weber suggested, according to Jaffé the inability to experience Arbeitsfreude had been the fate of all but a few artists, artist-craftsmen, and professionals since Adam and Eve. Although he was prepared to acknowledge that modern capitalism had compounded the problem, in Jaffé's judgment all labor was a struggle against nature undertaken quite simply in order to survive. He conceded that it had perhaps been necessary for a poor country like Germany to cloak the fulfillment of occupational duty with an appeal to higher ethical principles in order to raise national production. But even if one could understand why the ideal of joy in work was so strongly held in Germany, Jaffé concluded that it was impossible to realize, and that reformers should therefore concentrate not on humanizing work but on rendering it more efficient. By making it possible to shorten the working day, this would free people to satisfy their cultural needs outside working hours.[80]

Although the fourteen published monographs resulting from the VfS survey contained a wealth of empirical data on the composition of the labor force in several industries and touched on a number of topics that bore directly on the social and psychological adaptation of German workers to new production methods, they failed to establish scientifically valid conclusions with respect to the subjective relationship between human beings and their work. They were therefore unable to resolve differences among the association's members regarding the potential for preserving or extending Arbeitsfreude in the context of modern industry. The observations the monographs made on the problem of work can tell us more about the preconceptions and hopes of the VfS researchers than about the attitudes of German industrial wage earners in the pre-1914 period.

The eagerness of contemporaries to discover what the workers really thought and felt extended beyond VfS circles. Although the VfS study was the most extensive and academically respectable attempt to illuminate the subject, it was not the only source for those who sought to understand what work meant to the industrial proletariat. Paralleling the VfS's efforts was a large-scale attitude survey undertaken by Adolf Levenstein, a non-academic of working-class background who hoped, through a questionnaire, to elicit information about working class hopes and sentiments. Levenstein, who published his findings in 1912,[81] was fully aware of his lack of academic credentials, and indeed had approached Max Weber for help at an early stage of his research.

[80] Herkner, *Probleme der Arbeiterpsychologie*, 188.

[81] Adolf Levenstein, *Die Arbeiterfrage, mit besonderer Berücksichtigung der sozialpsychologischen Seite des modernen Grossbetriebes und der psychophysischen Einwirkungen auf die Arbeiter* (Munich: E. Reinhardt, 1912).

92

But although the latter recognized the potential value of the material Levenstein had gathered among workers in the textile, mining, and metalworking industries, he was skeptical about Levenstein's ability to make proper scientific use of it.[82] In the end Levenstein incorporated some of Weber's suggestions, but failed to do the detailed calculations urged upon him and refused to make the questionnaires themselves available to other scholars so that his results could be verified.[83]

It was easy to criticize Levenstein's questionnaire, his sample, and the way he presented his data, and the VfS researchers did so, not without patronizing comments on Levenstein's good intentions. Yet the VfS studies were themselves open to criticism on many of the same counts.[84] Indeed, Levenstein's effort was superior in certain respects, for like Bernays he had managed to establish a rapport with a large number of workers and had achieved a relatively high (63 percent) response to his questionnaire: of the 8,000 copies distributed, 5,040 were returned, although only 1,811 contained a significant amount of information.[85] Levenstein's questionnaire also contained a greater number of items bearing on worker perceptions of monotony and fatigue, their feelings about their machines, and the presence or absence of Arbeitsfreude than did the VfS protocol. Finally, even those unimpressed by the statistical aspects of his *Die Arbeiterfrage* ("The Worker Question") acknowledged the value of the selected questionnaire responses which Levenstein included in his publication together with excerpts from the many letters he had received from members of his sample.[86] All in all, one must conclude that Levenstein's *Die Arbeiterfrage*, despite the author's lack of methodological sophistication, made a contribution to the social psychology of work at least equal to that of the VfS surveys, while presenting more material relevant to the problem of alienation.

Among the many writers who drew on Levenstein to substantiate

[82] Max Weber, "Zur Methodik sozialpsychologischer Enqueten und ihrer Bearbeitung," ASS 29 (1909): 949–58.

[83] Oberschall, *Empirical Social Research*, 95–106.

[84] See, e.g., Ernst Bernhard, "Auslese und Anpassung der Arbeiterschaft. Kritische Betrachtungen zu den Untersuchungen des Vereins für Sozialpolitik," *Schmollers Jahrbuch* 35 (1911): 1399–1432.

[85] Heinrich Herkner, "Soziale Frage," *JNS* 99 (1912): 698–702. Levenstein himself placed the 64.1 percent of respondents who failed to give detailed answers into a category labeled the "mass stratum" (*Massenschicht*) and virtually ignored them in the subsequent analysis. Levenstein, *Arbeiterfrage*, 13.

[86] Herkner, *Probleme der Arbeiterpsychologie*, 700; Levenstein, *Arbeiterfrage*, 6. Some of these letters had been previously published by Levenstein as *Aus der Tiefe. Beiträge zur Seelen-Analyse moderner Arbeiter* (Berlin: Morgen-Verlag, 1909). See the reviews by Max Weber in ASS 29 (1909): 949–58, and by Herkner in *Schmollers Jahrbuch* 33 (1909): 1332–35, and *Preussische Jahrbücher* 140 (1910): 393–412: "Seelenleben und Lebenslauf in der Arbeiterklasse."

their arguments about Arbeitsfreude were Alfred Weber, Münsterberg, and Hellpach. When Alfred Weber wrote about working-class life and attitudes, he based his judgments more on Levenstein than on the VfS studies he himself had initiated. Münsterberg quoted Levenstein repeatedly on such matters as fatigue, joy in work, and thoughts during work and leisure, and he closely followed Levenstein's example when designing a questionnaire of his own in 1913.[87] But the most positive appreciation of Levenstein came from Hellpach who regarded *Die Arbeiterfrage* as a valuable documentary source on the thoughts, feelings, and wishes of German workers and a significant event in the development of social psychology.[88]

On the other hand, when it came to interpreting the message of Levenstein's survey, academic opinion was just as divided as in the case of the VfS studies. Herkner and Münsterberg, who wished to believe that many industrial workers continued to enjoy a positive relationship with their work, claimed to find support for their optimism in Levenstein. But Hellpach was able to seize on passages in which the respondents emphasized the monotony and fatigue associated with their jobs to substantiate his pessimistic prognosis for modern industrial labor and to prove that the negative reaction to mechanized work was not a product of the intellectuals' fancy but a painful reality for the workers. Although he admitted that as many workers in Levenstein's sample were indifferent to their work as were seriously disturbed by its lack of meaningful content, Hellpach stressed those portions of the evidence that confirmed his own belief that the absence of Arbeitsfreude was a major source of worker disaffection.[89]

Although Levenstein himself tried to give his results a scientific veneer, he never claimed to be an unbiased student of the subject. Rather, his avowed aim was to expose the pathological features of working-class life and thereby arouse sympathy for the plight of the individuals whose attitudes he portrayed. His sense of commitment was demonstrated even more openly in the two publications that preceded *Die Arbeiterfrage*, an anthology of worker philosophy and poetry, and *Aus der Tiefe* ("From the Depths"), a collection of excerpted letters of workers contacted in the course of his "scientific" survey. In *Arbeiter-Philosophen und-Dichter* and *Aus der Tiefe* Levenstein had provided a self-

[87] Hale, *Human Science and Social Order*, 159–60.
[88] Hellpach, in *ASS* 36 (1913): 929–39. Hellpach's review followed a highly critical one by Bernays who, the editors felt, had not taken the socio-psychological implications of Levenstein's work sufficiently into account. Ibid., 929. Levenstein cited Hellpach admiringly in *Die Arbeiterfrage*, 53 and 406.
[89] Hellpach, in *ASS* 36 (1909): 932.

selected group of more or less literate workers with an opportunity to express their feelings about life and work.

A comparable anthology of worker writings appeared in 1910 under the title *Das moderne Proletariat.*[90] Prepared by Rudolf Broda (1880–1932) and Julius Deutsch (1884–1968), two Austrian Social Democrats active in the international workers' movement, it included excerpts from essays by German, Austrian, and Swiss workers who had been encouraged to write on topics of their own choosing. The primary aim of the editors, like that of Levenstein, was not to encourage the development of worker literature, but to shed light on the social psychology of the working class in order to stimulate reform. In the long introduction that makes up the bulk of the book, they insisted that the absence of Arbeitsfreude was a major factor shaping the proletarian psyche: forced to engage in joyless labor, the workers became embittered, indifferent to ethical and aesthetic values, and intellectually impoverished. Unlike Levenstein, however, Broda and Deutsch drew heavily on socialist authors like Engels and Otto Bauer, and on Werner Sombart's recently published study of the proletariat, to create a theoretical-historical framework for their material. Thus they attributed the degeneration of the workers to the fact that modern industry transformed "unripe human beings into mere machines for the production of surplus value."[91] But whereas Sombart saw nothing but gloom ahead, these Social Democrats predicted a bright future:

> The monotony of labor presses the wage earner to the ground, but the solidarity of class conflict overcomes oppression and once more lifts him to the heights.[92]

A class-conscious proletariat would arise from the wilderness of drunkenness, sexual aberration, and loss of family feeling. Joyless labor undoubtedly constituted a serious problem, but they were convinced that belief in, and the struggle for, socialism, and this alone, could provide the saving force capable of transforming dehumanized, debased, and rootless individuals into ethical beings who would strive for ever more education to expand their own personalities, while proudly producing good work and developing a unique proletarian culture.[93]

[90] Rudolf Broda and Julius Deutsch, *Das moderne Proletariat. Eine sozialpsychologische Studie* (Berlin: Reimer, 1910).

[91] Broda and Deutsch, *Modernes Proletariat,* 22.

[92] Broda and Deutsch, *Modernes Proletariat,* 129.

[93] Frank Trommler, *Sozialistische Literatur in Deutschland: ein historischer Überblick* (Stuttgart: Alfred Kröner, 1976), 348. For information on Deutsch, see *BH* 1; on Broda, see Julius Deutsch, *Ein weiter Weg. Lebenserinnerungen* (Zürich: Amalthea-Verlag, 1960), 37, 67, and entries in *Wer ist's?* for 1922 and 1928. The Austrian socialist context is explained in Ernst

Das moderne Proletariat, which appeared in both French and German, was intended as a significant contribution to science on a Marxist foundation. Nevertheless, one can argue that Levenstein's less pretentious efforts shed greater light on the psyche of the ordinary worker. Although the people to whom Levenstein gave voice for the most part also belonged to the organized labor movement, he refrained from using his authority as editor to press his contributors into a uniform "proletarian" mold. Indeed, he made a point of stressing their residual humanity and individuality rather than presenting them simply as representatives of their class.[94] In any event, non-socialist intellectuals concerned with the problem of work considered Levenstein's writers as more authentic "voices from below" than the writers assembled by Broda and Deutsch.

They also drew heavily on the worker autobiographies that were beginning to appear at the time, pioneered by the evangelical theologian and ESK activist Paul Göhre. Already wellknown for a popular account published in 1891 of his own experiences as a factory worker,[95] Göhre had proceeded to edit a series of worker autobiographies under the Diederichs imprint.[96] His example was soon followed by Naumann and others who hoped in this way to document the social and psychological realities of working-class life. Together with the autobiographies of Social Democratic notables like August Bebel and Adelheid Popp, these accounts of heretofore unknown individuals from the lower strata of society seemed to provide a wealth of material on which "scientists" and social reformers alike could draw.[97]

To what extent workers' memoirs could be relied upon to tell the truth about proletarian attitudes was hotly debated at the time and has continued to be a subject of controversy.[98] Because these personal ac-

---

Glaser, *Im Umfeld des Austromarxismus: Ein Beitrag zur Geistesgeschichte des österreichischen Sozialismus* (Vienna: Europa, 1981).

[94] Levenstein, *Die Arbeiterfrage*, 13; Oberschall, *Empirical Social Research*, 95.

[95] Paul Göhre, *Drei Monate Fabrikarbeiter und Handwerksbursche* (1891), abridged and ed. Joachim Brenning and Christian Gremmels (Gütersloh: Gerd Mohn, 1978).

[96] On Ernst Diederichs's role, see Gary P. Stark, *Entrepreneurs of Ideology. Neoconservative Publishers in Germany 1890–1933* (Chapel Hill: University of North Carolina Press, 1981), 99–100.

[97] For a short list of German worker memoirs, see Martin H. Ludwig, *Arbeiterliteratur in Deutschland* (Stuttgart: J. B. Metzler, 1976), 28. Selected texts, with useful biographical data, are reproduced in Wolfgang Emmerich, ed., *Proletarische Lebensläufe*, 2 vols. (Reinbek bei Hamburg: Rowalt, 1974). Vol. 1 deals with the period before 1914.

[98] Bollenbeck, *Zur Theorie und Geschichte der frühen Arbeiterlebenserinnerungen*, passim; Wolfram Fischer, "Arbeitermemoiren als Quellen für Geschichte und Volkskunde der industriellen Gesellschaft," in Wolfram Fischer, *Wirtschaft und Gesellschaft im Zeitalter der Industrialisierung. Aufsätze-Studien-Vorträge* (Göttingen: Vandenhoeck & Ruprecht, 1972), 214–23; Alfred Kelly, ed., *The German Worker. Working-Class Autobiographies from the Age of Indus-*

counts revealed important differences between individuals, one must question whether it was legitimate for contemporary scholars to base generalizations about worker attitudes on them. In any event, the autobiographies had relatively little to say about the kind of mechanized, rationalized factory labor whose effect on the workers' psyche was of particular concern to the new science. Alfred Weber noted in 1912 that no autobiography by a skilled industrial worker had appeared.[99] Most were written by people whose origin, temperament, ambition, literary background, and circumstances placed them at some distance from the world of modern industry. They generally portrayed unskilled, frequently casual, manual labor of a traditional or quasi-traditional kind, and expressed attitudes to work that reflected values acquired during their authors' pre-industrial, often rural childhood and youth, rather than bearing witness to a "proletarian" outlook shaped by the modern factory.[100] Above all, they were produced by unusually articulate men and women, many of them influenced by socialist or anarchist ideals, so that one could not automatically assume that what they had to say about attitudes to work was shared by the average laborer.[101]

Despite reservations about their reliability or their representative character, middle-class scholars welcomed workers' memoirs as a potentially valuable source of information on the proletarian psyche.[102] Even such a hard-headed academic as Max Weber, although critical of the carelessness with which these documents were frequently interpreted, was prepared to acknowledge their worth.[103] Yet with regard to the specific question of worker alienation this autobiographical material proved to be just as ambiguous, and as subject to conflicting interpretations, as were the VfS and Levenstein surveys. Thus the strongly antisocialist Herkner saw no evidence of the uniform "proletarian" mentality described by a Marx or a Sombart. Because workers' attitudes toward their jobs seemed to be shaped as much by their background, sex, religion, psychological makeup, political affiliation, and life experience as by the industrial environment or the nature of the work itself, the cause of restoring Arbeitsfreude in modern industrial society was far from hopeless.[104]

trialization (Berkeley: University of California Press, 1987), 1–49. For a recent attempt to use this material as an historical source see Otfried Scholz, *Arbeiterselbstbild und Arbeiterfremdbild zur Zeit der industriellen Revolution* (Berlin: Colloquium, 1980).

[99] Alfred Weber, "Das Berufsschicksal der Industriearbeiter," ASS 35 (1912): 378.
[100] Trommler, *Sozialistische Literatur*, 353–54.
[101] Herkner, "Seelenleben und Lebenslauf in der Arbeiterklasse," 400–401.
[102] Bollenbeck, *Zur Theorie und Geschichte*, 233–42.
[103] Weber, "Zur Methodik" (1909), 952–53.
[104] Herkner, "Seelenleben und Lebenslauf in der Arbeiterklasse," 400; Herkner, "Soziale

Looked at from the socialist perspective, however, the same material supported the view of Broda and Deutsch that alienated labor was a universal feature of capitalist industrialism whose stultifying effects on the individual could only be mitigated by participation in the socialist movement. An intermediate position was that of Alfred Weber, who hoped to reconcile socialists with non-socialists. Alfred Weber agreed with the socialists that all the evidence pointed to the essential unity of proletarian existence, but maintained that work could be humanized within modern capitalism and that individual workers could meanwhile save their sanity and stave off alienation by frequent job changes.[105]

While German academics seized on worker literature, in particular the worker autobiographies, as a valuable adjunct to their scholarly assault on the problem of work, they tended to neglect another possibly more useful source, namely the views of those actually involved in organizing the productive process: entrepreneurs, managers, and engineers. This choice reflected the disdain for money-making shared by those most active in creating the new science of work, as well as their ambivalence about modern technology. Only a few were prepared to look at the problem of work from the managerial perspective.

Of these, one of the most able was Philipp Stein (1870–?), a political economist closely associated with the *Soziales Museum*, which had been founded in the 1890s by the Frankfurt philanthropic industrialist Wilhelm Merton to further the reconciliation between employers and workers, and which was administered by the sociologist and social reform advocate Leopold von Wiese (1876–1969).[106] Stein, who liked to regard himself as a mediator between factory and academe, thought it important to persuade future technicians and managers to become conversant with the findings of modern Arbeitswissenschaft: he believed that Arbeitswissenschaft could supply insights into the mentality of workers which would secure their voluntary compliance with the discipline essential to the modern factory. At the same time, he tried to convince Germany's armchair academics that "educated observation" of worker behavior could provide a vitally important supplement and corrective to the subjective reports of worker attitudes contained in

Frage," a review of Levenstein's *Die Arbeiterfrage*, JNS 99 (1912): 698–99. The idea that modern work inevitably led to homogenization of the workers and, in turn, to the creation of a uniform proletariat with a unique work ethic had been prevalent in the VfS since the publication of Sombart's *Das Proletariat*; the VfS survey was itself in part designed to test the validity of Sombart's claim. See L. Sinzheimer in Herkner, *Probleme der Arbeiterpsychologie*, 182.

[105] Weber, "Berufsschicksal der Industriearbeiter," 379–80.

[106] Hans Achinger, *Wilhelm Merton in seiner Zeit* (Frankfurt: Waldemar Kramer, 1965); on von Wiese, Ringer, *Decline of the German Mandarins*, 229 and passim.

social surveys, worker memoirs, and similar sources on which academics were inclined to rely.[107]

Stein frankly regarded *Arbeiterkunde*—the systematic study of labor—as a tool of management rather than as a basis for social policy. He also differed from the majority of German academics in his willingness to stress the positive features of modern industrialism. While he acknowledged that the jobs of the bulk of factory workers tended to be uniform and monotonous and required only a minimum of training, he denied that they necessarily produced a sense of alienation. For one thing, even the simplest task required some skill. Indeed, Stein claimed that although modern work made fewer physical demands, it called for superior determination, energy, reliability, and attentiveness.[108] What is more, like the Werkbund proponents of modern work, Stein argued that well-designed high-quality precision products turned out by machine could be just as attractive and functional as goods created by expensive traditional handicraft methods, and so equally capable of giving satisfaction to their makers.

Like Herkner, Stein took issue with those who, under Marxist influence, stressed the unity of the proletariat. In his view, the tendency to occupational specialization was breaking up the masses into an ever greater number of sub-groups, while the development of large-scale enterprises, combined with the growth of industrial cities, fostered diversity and so made it possible for each individual to find a niche in the economic structure.[109] Stein also denied that the modern factory had depersonalized the relationship between capital and labor. On the contrary, he noted that the traditional patriarchal model of industrial relations persisted in some firms, and that many types intermediate between it and the most modern, impersonal employer-employee pattern continued to flourish. The picture Stein drew was of a workforce characterized by a high degree of individual, occupational, and regional variation, of workers for whom work and life remained closely linked, and of a workplace in which the human element continued to play a major role. The task of Arbeiterkunde was to describe and analyze the realm of productive labor in all its colorful diversity, thereby helping management to raise productivity, counter centralizing pressures, and neutralize the political and trade union elements that endangered industrial peace by preaching the inevitability of conflict between employer and worker.[110]

---

[107] Philipp Stein, "Arbeiterkunde und Fabrikorganisation," in Leopold von Wiese und Kaiserwaldau, *Wirtschaft und Recht der Gegenwart* (Tübingen: Mohr, 1912), 2:179–80.

[108] Philipp Stein, "Arbeiterkunde und Fabrikorganisation," 178.

[109] Philipp Stein, "Arbeiterkunde und Fabrikorganisation," 177.

[110] Philipp Stein, "Arbeiterkunde und Fabrikorganisation," 184.

In his antisocialism, his eagerness to put science in the service of industry, and above all his emphasis on the importance of the expert in the development of a "scientific" management, Stein was perhaps closest to Münsterberg. But whereas the latter stressed the crucial role of psychology, Stein, under the influence of von Wiese, looked to sociology as the key to a new, applied science of work. Yet his model was not free of contradictions. Following in the tradition of Riehl, he hoped that the industrial worker could eventually be integrated once more into the body of the Volk. This led him to interpret Arbeiterkunde as a branch of Volkskunde and to stress the continuities between traditional and modern kinds of work. On the other hand, Stein acknowledged that the laboring classes differed significantly from the bourgeoisie with respect to work, family, and social and public roles, and that this gap was permanent. He even suggested that it be reinforced by giving the workers a different, more practical education. Although he praised modern industry for providing individual workers with the opportunity to rise, Stein clearly did not wish them to rise above their station. His final picture was of a society in which a cohesive bourgeois stratum stood above, and distinct from, a highly differentiated lower class whose traditional, occupational, and regional variations were to be valued, preserved, and exploited in the interests of management. Against the "proletariat" of Marxist theory, Stein sketched the contours of what came to be called the *Arbeitertum*: the collectivity of genuine German workers, rooted firmly in the Volk community and prepared to labor loyally within the framework of the modern industrial enterprise whose interests they identified with their own.

Stein disdained Max Weber's plea for a value-free social science and ignored his warnings against the premature utilization of the findings of the new science of work. Instead, he presented Arbeiterkunde as a body of transmittable knowledge with immediate applications and, despite genuine concern with the wellbeing of the workers, focused on Arbeitsfreude principally because its absence prevented the efficient and harmonious utilization of labor in large-scale industry. On the other hand, Stein shared Weber's preference for hard facts over subjective reports or "empathy" as a way of coming to grips with the problem of work, as well as his desire to establish empirically the relationship between attitudes to work and industrial output. His motives may have differed from those characteristic of the majority of reform-minded academics, but his scholarly approach, as well as his connection with von Wiese, the Merton circle in Frankfurt, and the GSR, placed him solidly within the ambit of the pre-1914 reform movement.

This was not true of some other academics who took up a pro-entrepreneurial position at this time, notably Richard Ehrenberg (1857–1921). A professor of economics at the University of Rostock, Ehrenberg became notorious for his sustained attack on the socialists and their bourgeois accomplices, the *Kathedersozialisten* ("Socialists of the Chair"), whom he accused of maintaining a virtual monopoly of university professorships and of using the VfS and the GSR to propagate anticapitalist judgments based solely on moral indignation. Calling for an "objective" economics and a social science from which ethical considerations were to be rigidly excluded, he turned Max Weber's arguments for a value-free social science against the latter's friends and associates in the social reform movement.[111]

Ehrenberg purported to ground his own economics in a combination of statistical analysis and observation. Taking as his model the nineteenth-century pioneer of industrial sociology, Johann Heinrich von Thünen, Ehrenberg established in 1905 his own journal, the *Thünen-Archiv*,[112] wrote detailed histories of the Siemens and Krupp enterprises, and laid elaborate plans for an Institute of Empirical Economic Research. The latter came to fruition in 1910, thanks to financial support from industrial supporters who welcomed his attack from within on the reform-oriented academic establishment.[113]

Nonetheless, Ehrenberg saw himself not as a paid propagandist of big business, but rather as a scientist whose views were based solely on the "facts." Thus, he argued that Brentano and Schmoller were simply in error when they asserted that the modern employer-employee relationship was a purely contractual one based on money, and that whatever failed to fit the confrontational model could be attributed to survivals from an earlier, patriarchal phase of capitalism. According to Ehrenberg, one could document the emergence in modern industry of a genuine community of interest between entrepreneurs and workers, a community of work or *Arbeitsgemeinschaft* that found natural expression in a stable, contented, and highly efficient workforce. In effect, Ehrenberg denied that alienated labor was a necessary by-product of modern capitalism, and that the workers could therefore improve their condition only by engaging in a struggle with their employers. On the contrary, he used historical evidence to demonstrate that the workers served their own best interests when they abandoned the strike weapon and collective bargaining, and that higher productivity, based on in-

[111] Rudiger vom Bruch, *Wissenschaft, Politik und öffentliche Meinung. Gelehrtenpolitik im Wilhelminischen Deutschland (1890–1914)* (Husum: Matthiesen, 1980), 160–61.

[112] From 1909 on, this journal appeared as *Archiv für exakte Wirtschaftsforschung*.

[113] Klaus Saul, *Staat, Industrie, Arbeiterbewegung im Kaiserreich* (Düsseldorf: Bertelsmann, 1974), 363–65; Bruch, *Wissenschaft*, 297–301.

dustrial peace, was the best guarantee of permanent improvements in the standard of living.[114]

Ehrenberg's defense of the Arbeitsgemeinschaft model of industrial relations was designed to give academic respectability to the industry-sponsored *Werkverein* ("company-union") movement that made considerable headway in the years immediately before the war.[115] Moreover, some of his students took a leading part in organizing such unions in accordance with their teacher's theories.[116] The business community therefore had every reason to be delighted with this professor who claimed to have established scientifically that only the meddling of socialists and trade unions, spurred on by the academic advocates of social reform, prevented the development of a genuine work community capable of serving the best interests of all engaged in the productive process, and of the nation as a whole.

As an opponent of the trade unions and advocate of a social policy that aimed to increase the national product through greater efficiency rather than to redistribute that product in the name of social justice, Ehrenberg naturally found himself treated with suspicion by the more ardent reformers among his contemporaries. But he also failed to win his colleagues' approval of his methodological innovations. Even those who sympathized with his attack on the *Kathedersozialisten* remained dubious about his anti-theoretical bias. Ready to admit that Ehrenberg's innovative business histories were not without value, his critics pointed out that he was better at reconstructing the past than at shedding light on current problems and practices. Moreover, they argued that what had worked for large firms like Krupp and Siemens, headed by outstanding individuals, was not necessarily appropriate to the multitude of medium and small enterprises that dominated German economic life. Above all, Ehrenberg's focus on the individual firm and, within it, on the key figure of the successful entrepreneur, in their view could not replace careful analysis of economic developments on the national level.[117]

[114] Richard Ehrenberg, "Das Arbeitsverhältnis als Arbeitsgemeinschaft," *Archiv für exakte Wirtschaftsforschung* 2 (1909): 176–209.

[115] See Hermann P. Schäfer, "Die 'Gelben Gewerkschaften' am Beispiel des Unterstützungsvereins der Siemens-Werke, Berlin," *Vierteljahrschrift für Sozial- und Wirtschaftsgeschichte* 59 (1972): 41–76; Wolfgang Friedrich and Joachim Rückert, "Betriebliche Arbeiterausschüsse in Deutschland, mit einem Vergleich zu Grossbritannien und Frankreich," in Norbert Horn and Jürgen Kocka, eds., *Recht und Entwicklung des Grossunternehmen im 19. und frühen 20. Jahrhundert* (Göttingen: Vandenhoeck & Ruprecht, 1979), 489–508.

[116] Saul, *Staat, Industrie*, 363–64; K. J. Mattheier, "Werkvereine und wirtschaftsfriedlich-nationale (gelbe) Arbeiterbewegung im Ruhrgebiet," in Jürgen Reulecke, ed., *Arbeiterbewegung an Rhein und Ruhr* (Wuppertal: Peter Hammer, 1974), 179–87.

[117] Bruch, *Wissenschaft*, 295.

As his academic reputation faltered, Ehrenberg became ever more dependent on financial help from outside sources and increasingly strident in his defense of agrarian and industrial interests, making it even easier for his scholarly opponents to challenge his academic integrity. Ironically, the diminution of his scholarly standing decreased his value to the business community. Unlike Philipp Stein who managed to balance industrial and academic roles, Ehrenberg in the end was unable to win the trust and respect of either camp.[118]

Another economist who attacked the ethically-motivated social reformers for giving the emerging Arbeitswissenschaft an anticapitalist bias was the Cologne economist Adolf Weber (1876–?), who was appointed to a professorship at Breslau in 1913 and subsequently enjoyed a successful career at Frankfurt and Munich. Like Ehrenberg, Adolf Weber defended the entrepreneurs against their high-minded critics and blamed the socialist unions and their bourgeois defenders, rather than capitalist exploitation, for the growth of industrial conflict. But Adolf Weber was much less sanguine than Ehrenberg, who had believed that the workers, if left to themselves, could be integrated into the work community with relative ease, and that industry-sponsored Werkvereine would soon displace the trade unions. This was primarily because, unlike Ehrenberg, he regarded the loss of joy in work as a major factor behind the emergence and continued strength of the socialist workers' movement.

In his much quoted *The Fight between Capital and Labor*,[119] Adolf Weber stressed that changing attitudes to work played an important part in fomenting social discontent. Tracing the emergence in the nineteenth century of a cult of labor that posited work as the key to social status and propagated the idea of salvation through work, he went on to note the paradox that the same period had replaced the idealistic valuation of labor with a materialistic one: "Now one lives off one's work . . . but that one also lives, can live, must live *in* work is generally overlooked."[120] While this was true even of the educated classes, Adolf Weber argued that the modern proletariat, in particular, had become thoroughly materialistic. Rejecting all ideologies as weapons of the ruling class, it had turned its back on religion and patriotism and scorned the idealistic view of labor that was needed if Arbeitsfreude was to become a reality.

To prove his point about the degeneration of the concept of work,

[118] Bruch, *Wissenschaft*, 296–99, 438–39. See also Dieter Lindenlaub, "Firmengeschichte und Sozialpolitik," in *Wissenschaft, Wirtschaft und Technik*, ed. Karl-Heinz Manegold (Munich: Bruckmann, 1969), 272–85.

[119] Adolf Weber, *Der Kampf zwischen Kapital und Arbeit* (Tübingen: J.C.B. Mohr, 1910).

[120] Adolf Weber, *Der Kampf*, 59.

Adolf Weber contrasted statements by the early French socialist Saint-Simon and the leading theoretician of contemporary German Marxism, Karl Kautsky. Whereas Saint-Simon had spoken of work as something of intrinsic value, capable—like love—of evoking enthusiasm, Kautsky bleakly asserted that

> The wage earner sells his labor power in order to live. The main thing for him is his wages. The work itself is for him a secondary concern. Were it possible to receive the pay without work, he would have no objection whatsoever.[121]

When combined with the loss of traditional religious and ethical values, Adolf Weber maintained that the Marxists, by juxtaposing a cult of labor with rejection of the ideal of joyful work, tended to produce a latent sense of dissatisfaction among workers for which no obvious remedy existed.[122]

Because Adolf Weber believed that alienation had roots deep in the modern psyche and that the problem of work represented a major element in the current social crisis, he was unable to share Ehrenberg's simplistic conviction that the creation of an objective, empirical, economic and social science could help to restore social harmony. "Science" might assist in defining the contours of the social question, but was incapable of providing solutions. At best, Arbeitswissenschaft could mitigate the miseries of alienated labor by encouraging industry-sponsored reforms, but to reverse the downward trend would require an ethical and religious revival that touched the workers themselves and led them to reject both Marxist class-conflict teachings and proletarian materialism. Only the willingness to accept and adapt to the realities of capitalist production, combined with a drastic change in attitudes to work, could allow the notion of a community of work to gain ground, and thus make it possible to reconcile the conflicting individual and group interests characteristic of modern life.[123]

Stein, Ehrenberg, and Adolf Weber represented a minority position in the years before the war, but the well-publicized views of these men, and of others who shared their general outlook, were not without influence, and their scholarly critique of the social reform camp demonstrated clearly that there was as yet no consensus on the basic features of the new Arbeitswissenschaft. A start had been made in redefining the problem of work and experimenting with new methods for getting at the "facts" relevant to its resolution, and there was general agreement on the potential of an interdisciplinary approach involving the

---

[121] Adolf Weber, Der Kampf, 60, quoting Kautsky in Vorwärts no. 257, 1905.
[122] Adolf Weber, Der Kampf, 66.   [123] Adolf Weber, Der Kampf, 78.

relatively new sciences of psychology and sociology alongside such established disciplines as philosophy, economics, anthropology, and physiology. Indeed, psychology and sociology both gained status at this time partly because they gave prominence to the problem of alienated labor and seemed capable of contributing significantly to Arbeitswissenschaft: psychology by investigating worker motivation and the effects of mechanization and monotonous labor on the worker, sociology and social psychology by studying the influence of changing modes of production on social relations inside and outside the workplace.

Perhaps the greatest achievement of the period, however, was that people developed a healthy awareness of the difficulties—both conceptual and methodological—that faced the new science of work. The relationship between human beings and their work proved to be more complex than had been expected, attitudes harder to measure and study, the implications of research findings more difficult to interpret, and their possible uses in modifying individual and group behavior or redefining social policy more controversial. The effects of mechanization and the division of labor on the human psyche were still in dispute, as was the importance of joy in work for worker motivation and productivity. Indeed, most investigators who devoted themselves to discovering ways of restoring Arbeitsfreude themselves harbored doubts about the possibility of joyful work for the laboring masses, while a few, notably, Sombart and Jaffé, openly conceded that joyful work for all was a chimera in a world increasingly based on scientific rationality. In other words, even while they strove to increase the body of knowledge bearing on the problem of work, many suspected that "science" was more likely to intensify the crisis of contemporary society than to cure its ills.

It also became increasingly difficult to remain confident that further knowledge would eventually lead to practical reforms. Max Weber's warning in 1911 that only a multitude of detailed, long-term studies could be expected to resolve the issues raised by the investigations of recent years must have had a discouraging effect on potential researchers. To persevere in the face of this prospect required either total dedication to the pursuit of knowledge for its own sake or a belief that science alone could improve society. Max Weber seems to have combined these traits, but most contributors to the science of work in its first phase were not motivated by scientific curiosity so much as by strong religious, ethical, cultural, or patriotic concern. Once Arbeitswissenschaft proved slow to fulfill its early promise, such individuals tended to abandon it in favor of alternative methods for combating alienation and restoring social harmony.

In the last years before 1914 growing opposition to social reform in government circles and intensified conflict between capital and labor as employers organized to resist further encroachment on the prerogatives of management also helped to weaken the social reform impulse that had initially sustained the science of work. Arbeitswissenschaft did not die, nor was the quest for Arbeitsfreude abandoned, but those few who persisted in it increasingly looked not to science but to religion, moral philosophy, education, and art to restore meaning and joy to work.

VI

THE QUEST FOR UTOPIA

THE FIRST WORLD WAR induced massive changes in the conditions of German work. The need to make efficient use of the nation's resources, including human labor, accelerated the shift from rural to urban occupations, the trend toward mechanization and standardization, and the application of science to industrial production. Indeed, it was during the war that rationalization and scientific management won significant government backing and captured the attention of the general public for the first time. So did efforts to counteract the damaging physical and psychic effects of modern industrial work on a weary, undernourished, labor force, through psychotechnical innovation and to adapt the organization of production to the capacities of new categories of workers, notably unskilled women and wounded war veterans.

After the war, advocates of a scientific approach to the problem of work found it easier to persuade both employers and organized labor that rationalization was not only inevitable but potentially the cure for many of the nation's economic, social, and political ills. Yet there were others in whom the horrifying experience of modern warfare intensified opposition to the emerging industrial society. To them, it seemed evident that the war itself was the result of the same "materialism" that in the nineteenth century had inspired the limitless worship of science and the development of a ruthless capitalism. Building on foundations already laid down by the prewar intellectual avant-garde, these social critics pitted idealism against materialism, art against science, emotion and will against reason, ethics against knowledge, the crafts against the machine.

The result was a revival of romantic longings for utopia. This was true in other countries as well, but nowhere were the circumstances more conducive to the propagation of radical schemes and dreams than in postwar Germany. Following the virtual collapse of the old political and social order, the defeated nation experienced a period of revolutionary turmoil and economic chaos, culminating in an inflation of staggering proportions. This time of troubles produced a climate of opinion that fluctuated between hope and desperation, and that proved ideally suited to nurturing proposals for a total transformation of society based on a revaluation of values.

It was against this background that a number of Germans, whose views covered the spectrum from extreme left to extreme right, set forth the ideal of a society to be inhabited by a "new man" (neuer Mensch) for whom work would once more become "the essence of life and its supreme honor."[1] Committing themselves to the radical goal of ending the alienation of labor, these Germans explored a variety of paths to the utopia of joyful work.

It is not easy to do justice to the character and richness of utopian thought about work in the aftermath of the First World War. Given a mass of literary utopias, utopian experiments seeking to change the world by example, reform proposals dedicated to utopian goals, optimistic visions of a perfect future society, and despairing critiques of the present through application of a utopian yardstick, how is one to decide what the concept of utopianism does and does not include?[2] In addition, the multiplicity of motivations that inspired postwar utopians, the enormous variety of political, social, and intellectual standpoints represented, and the wide range of 'solutions' to the problem of work that emerged in this period, render arbitrary any grouping or selection. Nonetheless, these utopias of joyful work are of interest because of what they reveal about the contemporary intellectual mood, and because they left a residue of aspirations and ideals that continued to influence the German debate about work throughout the Weimar period.

Most of them were produced by people who regarded themselves as socialists, yet were highly critical of Marxist orthodoxy for failing to tackle the problem of modern work energetically enough. The prime example was the intellectual anarchist Gustav Landauer (1870–1919), who had already emerged before 1914 as a major critic of contemporary society and social theory, with fully developed views about the nature and future of work. Landauer's participation in the Bavarian socialist revolution of 1919 and his martyrdom in the "white terror" that ended this extraordinary episode stimulated interest in his prewar writings.[3]

[1] David Meakin, "Decadence and the Devaluation of Work: The Revolt of Sorel, Péguy and the German Expressionists," *European Studies Review* 1 (1971): 56.

[2] For an extended discussion of this problem, see Frank E. Manuel and Fritzie P. Manuel, *Utopian Thought in the Western World* (Oxford: Basil Blackwell, 1979).

[3] These were republished posthumously. See Gustav Landauer, *Der werdende Mensch. Aufsätze über Leben und Schrifttum*, ed. Martin Buber (Potsdam: Gustav Kiepenheuer, 1921). Buber was himself a prominent utopian socialist.

Landauer argued that under capitalism everyone, whether dependent on profits or wages, engaged in completely "useless, unproductive,
superfluous work" and became enmeshed in an exploitative relationship incapable of providing the individual with a truly human existence.[4] It was the task of socialism to create a genuine community
within which people would once more experience joyous, creative labor and thus find both security and freedom. Landauer supported the
trade unions' struggle for a shorter working day and sympathized with
their preference for hourly wages over piece rates, but he insisted that
it would be possible to get to the root of the current crisis only if one
recognized that the real human need was not "recreation, rest and joy
in the evening," but work that would serve as "a playful unwinding of
all our energies."[5] No cure could therefore be expected from organized
labor which, if anything, reinforced the contrary tendency of the age
to transform "sport, the unproductive, playful activity of muscles and
nerves, into a sort of work or profession."[6]

Landauer also rejected the Marxist belief that socialism would grow
inexorably out of fully developed capitalism in crisis, through the
agency of an aroused proletariat. In his view, the struggles of the proletariat to overthrow bourgeois capitalism merely served to stabilize this
decadent system and perpetuate its values. The victory of socialism depended on the refusal by individuals of all classes to put up with the
condition of joyless work. People would have to band together in voluntary communities, go back to the land, and learn once more how to
work. Work alone was capable of leading them "out of the petrified
world of greed and hardship," a kind of work that reunited "agriculture,
industry and crafts, mental and physical work, teaching and apprenticeship."[7] As the Russian anarchist Peter Kropotkin had put it:

> Whoever wants to do something for socialism, must set to work out of a
> premonition of an intuited, yet unknown joy and happiness. We still have
> everything to learn: the joy of work, of common interest, of mutual for-
> bearance.[8]

[4] Gustav Landauer, *For Socialism* (1911), ed. Russell Berman and Tim Luke, trans. David
J. Parent (St. Louis, Mo.: Telos Press, 1978), 98–99.

[5] Landauer, *For Socialism*, 95.

[6] Landauer, *For Socialism*, 95. Although creative activity had also been the ultimate goal
of communism for Marx, Landauer made much of the fact that the program of the SPD and
its affiliated unions did not reflect concern with the problem of joyless labor during these
years. See Eugene Lunn, *Prophet of Community. The Romantic Socialism of Gustav Landauer*
(Berkeley: University of California Press, 1973), 212.

[7] Landauer, *For Socialism*, 136–37.   [8] Landauer, *For Socialism*, 138, citing Kropotkin.

In an essay of 1913 that summed up his personal ideal of work,[9] Landauer adopted the Fourierist equation of joyful work with play as the final goal of communism, but acknowledged that this was utopian in the present time of transition. For the present, he encouraged his contemporaries to seek happiness through effort and struggle, reminding them that in medieval times the very harshness of labor had rendered it a means to bliss and salvation.

The themes Landauer introduced before the war were raised with greater frequency after 1918. In both socialist and non-socialist writings on the problem of work, the central demand now was for non-alienating alternatives to mechanized wage labor. This demand was linked to the quest for community as a prerequisite to individual and cultural renewal, an emphasis on quality rather than quantity in production, and a search for ways to bridge the gaps between mental and physical labor, town and country, producer and consumer. When combined with a new willingness to engage in social experimentation, this kind of thinking prepared the ground for a revival of communitarianism along the lines sketched out in the nineteenth century by such utopian forerunners as Fourier and Proudhon.

Of the numerous attempts to establish voluntary communes capable of implementing Landauer's vision, the most notable was the community conceived by the Bremen artist Heinrich Vogeler (1872–1942). The son of a rich iron merchant, Vogeler was trained in painting and architecture and initially devoted himself totally to art; like so many of his contemporaries, however, he was awakened to the importance of politics by his war experience. Discharged after an apparent psychological breakdown, he returned home in November 1918 a convert to pacifism and communism and was immediately elected to the local revolutionary workers and soldiers council. By 1919, he had joined the left communist opposition. At the same time, he proceeded to transform his estate, the Gut Barkenhoff in Worpswede near Bremen, into a workers' commune and school. What had been a center for progressive artists since 1894 now became a refuge for persecuted revolutionaries.[10]

As an *Arbeitsschule* (work school), Vogeler's commune was dedicated to educating the "new man" in order to prepare the way for further attempts at political or social revolution, but it also claimed to constitute a cell of the new, classless, society in the making. Vogeler's

---

[9] Landauer, "Arbeitsselig," in *Werdender Mensch*, 84–88.

[10] Hans Manfred Bock, *Syndikalismus und Linkskommunismus von 1918–1923* (Maisenheim am Glan: Anton Hain, 1969), 443; Walter Fähnders und Martin Rector, *Linksradikalismus und Literatur*, vol. 1 (Reinbeck: Rowolt, 1974), 150–57; Hans Hackmack, *Leben und Wirken Heinrich Vogelers seit dem Ersten Weltkrieg*, ed. Karl-Robert Schütze (Berlin, 1980).

experiment had its practical side: his commune was based on agriculture not because of the romantic anti-urbanism that led many contemporaries to return to the land but because food was desperately needed
in the face of current shortages. Nevertheless, the primary impetus behind his experiment was a typically utopian longing for ethical renewal.
Working and learning together in a spirit of brotherhood, the members
of his community were to submit themselves to no authority other than
the laws of life and love, and were to experience the joy and fulfillment
of free labor.[11]

Vogeler's Arbeitsschule Barkenhoff provided the model for the utopian community described in 1921 by the Viennese expressionist Paul
Robien. In a pamphlet appropriately titled *Arbeitsfreude*, which appeared in a series entitled "New Building for a Free World" brought out
by an avant-garde publisher (whose list included works by Bakunin and
periodicals addressed to the "Free Generation" and the "Working
Woman"), the tract's expressionist cover depicted naked construction
workers building a house, to symbolize the simple life of cooperative
manual labor. Like Vogeler, Robien celebrated the artist as savior of
society on the grounds that artistic production alone could serve as a
model of free, creative work. He attributed the misery of the age to the
fact that Mammonism and greed had instigated the production of unneeded goods, thereby condemning human beings to ceaseless drudgery. In war, work was murder; in times of peace, it only served to support a mass of parasites. In either case, unnecessary labor was sinful.
The cure for the ills of society was therefore to create an artists' commune in which the inhabitants, by performing all essential agricultural
and crafts tasks themselves, would cease to work for the benefit of the
"drones, rulers, money devils, mass murderers, world betrayers, bureau-
crats with their hatred of manual labor."[12]

Set in a birdwatcher's paradise (in the hope that it would achieve a
secure financial base by attracting people of means interested in scientific study as well as artists), Robien's commune, like Vogeler's Arbeitsschule, was meant to become the nucleus of a new, rational society
after the imminent collapse of the old urban world in which work
yielded no satisfaction. Dispersed into scattered small communities and
directed by sensible, unselfish, and nature-loving leaders, human
beings would learn to live an austere but natural and sun-filled exis-

[11] Heinrich Vogeler, *Die Arbeitsschule als Aufbauzelle der klassenlosen menschlichen Gesellschaft* (Hamburg: Konrad Hanf, 1921), 1–19.
[12] Paul Robien (alias Rathke or Ruttke), *Arbeitsfreude* (Vienna: Rudolf Cerny, 1921), 1.

tence in total harmony with their environment, and to experience peace and joy in work.[13]

Although the communitarianism advocated by anarchist socialists like Landauer, Vogeler, and Robien reflected attitudes that were widespread among artists and intellectuals after the war, not all who shared the anarchist vision accepted communalism as an efficacious way to transform the social and moral order. Indeed, not even Landauer and Vogeler put all their eggs in the communitarian basket: both eventually resorted to political activism.[14] One who took the political route from the start was Rudolf Rocker (1873–1958), the leading theoretician of German anarchism after Landauer, and the chief spokesman of the syndicalist international which he helped to organize in 1922.[15] Like Landauer, Rocker drew on Fourier to buttress his contention that the primary task was to end the alienation of labor and criticized the Marxists for failing to address themselves to this issue in the face of the dehumanization associated with modern rationalized production. Convinced that the crisis of work, and hence of society, was psychological rather than economic in origin, he believed with Kropotkin that a practical and constructive socialism would reverse the centralization of industry, and restore the link between mental and manual labor by educating human beings for both intellectual and physical work. Like the artist-utopians, he insisted that humanity must be taught to regard work not just as a necessity but as an outpouring of creative activity, and to judge the value of an individual's work not by the hours devoted to labor but by "the sum of joy and inner satisfaction his work could yield."[16] But while he shared the utopian goals of the men discussed so far, Rocker rejected the communalist belief that a small elite of intellectuals and artists could show the way to the new society by their example. Instead, he attempted to organize and educate the masses and to mobilize the utopian enthusiasm of youth to build a new and better world.[17]

Anti-Marxist socialists like Landauer or Rocker were decidedly more prone than their Marxist contemporaries to project a society centered

---

[13] Robien, *Arbeitsfreude*, 15–16.

[14] In Vogeler's case, this took the form of union agitation and participation in party politics, first as a syndicalist and, from 1924 on, as a member of the German Communist party. Bock, *Syndikalismus und Linkskommunismus*, 443.

[15] Bock, *Syndikalismus und Linkskommunismus*, 439.

[16] Rudolf Rocker, *Die Rationalisierung der Wirtschaft und die Arbeiterklasse* (Berlin: Verlag 'Der Syndikalist', F. Kater, 1927), 46–47.

[17] Rocker asserted the right of the young to chase after utopias. See his "Ich liebe die Jugend," *Der Syndikalist* 2 (1920): 28, quoted in Ulrich Linse, *Anarchistische und anarchosyndikalistische Jugendbewegung 1918–1933* (Frankfurt: Dipa, 1975), 162.

on joy in work. However, the latter were not entirely immune to this tendency. Even before the war, August Bebel, the outstanding leader of German Social Democracy, had made a point of stressing that the socialist society of the future would incorporate the ideal of joy in work, and others had joined him in propagating this "utopian" vision. As one SPD commentator put it:

> Everyone is drawn into the work force. . . . Work is not a burden but a joy. It will be performed joyfully by a race which has been educated for work and which through its work influences its own fate.[18]

However, it was only when the overthrow of the Kaiser had raised hopes for a revolutionary breakthrough that voices within the socialist labor movement began to demand immediate measures to realize the utopia of joyful work.

The new mood, symbolized by the re-publication in 1921 of Bebel's 1907 study of Fourier,[19] was particularly strong among those working class activists who had come under the influence of the pre-war German Youth Movement. Of these, one of the most eloquent was the worker poet Karl Bröger (1886–1944), who created a stir in 1919 with an essay on "The New Meaning of Work" in the quarterly journal of the *Bund für schöpferische Arbeit* ("Society for Creative Work").[20] The son of a building laborer, Bröger was a prominent member of the *Jungsozialisten*, an organization of young workers affiliated with the Social Democratic party.[21] What he wanted was a revolutionary transformation of society leading to a quasi-corporatist order expressed politically in an economic parliament, but he argued that this revolution could only come about if it was preceded by a human transformation. He therefore called on the young to have courage for utopia (*Mut zur Utopie*) and, in particular, to reject materialistic ideas about work—the notion that labor was a commodity to be bought and sold, that personal gain was the primary motivator of human endeavor, and that technical progress was the answer to everything. Such attitudes could only lead

[18] Robert Danneberg, *Was will die Sozialdemokratie?* (Vienna, 1912), 11–13, as quoted in Kenneth R. Calkins, "The Uses of Utopianism," *Central European History* 15 (June 1982): 137.

[19] August Bebel, *Charles Fourier. Sein Leben und seine Theorien* (4th ed., 1921, reprinted Berlin: J.H.W. Dietz Nachf., 1973). Bebel's study had originally been published to celebrate the hundredth anniversary of Fourier's first book.

[20] Karl Bröger, "Vom neuen Sinn der Arbeit," *Nyland* (1919) 3:228–36. See Trommler, *Sozialistische Literatur*, 388–97.

[21] Gudrun Heinsen Becker, *Karl Bröger und die Arbeiterdichtung unserer Zeit* (Nürnberg: Stadtbibliothek, 1977); Franz Osterroth, *Biographisches Lexicon des Sozialismus* (Hannover: Dietz, 1960); Franz Osterroth, "Der Hofgeismarkreis der Jungsozialisten," *AS* 4 (1964): 525–69. Bröger edited the *Jungsozialistische Blätter* between 1921 and 1924.

to chaos. Instead, he urged his contemporaries to regard work as the strength which produces joy (*Kraft zur Freude*), a combination of spirit and act, idea and physical effort, brain and brawn, and he insisted that they must learn to give equal honor to all who labor.[22] Only such a revolutionary ethic of work would make it possible to restore peace and joy to daily labor, and, by once more giving work its rightful value and dignity, produce a genuine *Kultur* in place of a spurious *Zivilisation*.

In this one short essay, Bröger assembled most of the elements common to the postwar utopias of joyful work: the appeal to youth, the call for a new idealism, the notion of Arbeitsfreude as the chief source of social harmony and cultural salvation, the identification of work with creative activity, the reconciliation of intellectual with manual labor. He even put a religious gloss on the whole by maintaining that work was "striving to regain a human face, in which the Godhead would be reflected."[23] But it was not clear how this vision was to be implemented. In an effort to do so, Bröger established contact with the *Bund entschiedener Schulreformer* ("Association of Determined School Reformers"), a group of socialist educators who called for a radical restructuring of the German school. For its part, the Bund welcomed the support of this youthful and popular working-class prophet of joyful labor. Bröger was invited to address its 1921 convention in Frankfurt on the theme of the vocational crisis facing youth,[24] and in 1923 the Bund published his pamphlet on *Imagination and Education*, an impassioned plea for a new school that would stimulate creativity and spontaneity and produce people capable of both work and play in the spirit of Schiller's *Aesthetic Letters*. Such individuals, Bröger reasoned, would be incapable of accommodating to a world that regarded children purely as potential members of the workforce, and so would become the revolutionary agents of a new humanist culture and society.[25]

The idea of a school based on creative activity instead of drill, one designed to produce rebels in place of conformists, was not Bröger's invention, nor, indeed, was it a product of the postwar crisis. Otto Rühle, a leading advocate of "proletarian" education, had propounded similar views as early as 1904.[26] The years before 1914 had also seen

[22] Bröger, "Vom neuen Sinn der Arbeit," 235: "Arbeit ist die Ehre, die allen zukommt in gleichem Masse. Arbeit ist Geist und Tat, Idee und Handgriff, Hirn und Faust."

[23] Bröger, "Vom neuen Sinn der Arbeit," 236.

[24] Karl Bröger, "Die Berufsnot der Jugend," in Olga Essig, *Beruf und Menschentum* (2d ed., rev. and enl.; Berlin: C. H. Schwetschke & Sohn, 1924), 22–26.

[25] Karl Bröger, *Phantasie und Erziehung. Ein Versuch zur Besinnung auf Grundlagen der Pädagogik* (Leipzig: Ernst Oldenburg, 1923).

[26] Otto Rühle, *Arbeit und Erziehung. Eine pädagogische Studie* (Munich: B. Birk & Co., 1904).

the development of radical movements for school reform in the bourgeois camp, of which the most striking were associated with the name of Gustav Wyneken, a man closely linked with progressive elements in the Youth Movement and with revolutionary Expressionism.[27] Finally, it should be recalled that although Germany lagged behind the United States, France, England, Switzerland, and Scandinavia in reforming its system of vocational training, the idea of education based on the child's activity rather than on passive learning, incorporated in the concept of the Arbeitsschule and vigorously propagated by Kerschensteiner, had already won a degree of acceptance before 1914.[28] Nevertheless, it was only after the war that such ideas became an important component of socialist educational theory, and it was only then that socialist educators achieved a significant, if still limited, role within the Social Democratic movement.[29]

Paul Oestreich and Olga Essig of the *Bund entschiedener Schulreformer* were among the most vocal "Marxist" proponents of the Arbeitsschule as an instrument of social regeneration. Essig not only attributed to Karl Marx the utopian ideal of the end of alienation but followed him in insisting that the overthrow of capitalism was essential to realize this vision. Nevertheless, she rejected political revolution as a means, instead calling for the immediate implementation of educational reforms to produce the new socialist man who would be free, creative, joyfully productive, and capable of cooperating with their fellows.[30]

The most important socialist theoretician to deal with the problem of education during these years was the Austrian Marxist Max Adler.

[27] George L. Mosse, *The Crisis of German Ideology* (London: Weidenfeld and Nicolson, 1970), 184–88.

[28] Rühle, *Arbeit und Erziehung*, 79–80; Kurt Löwenstein, "Sozialistische Schul- und Erziehungsfragen" (1919), in Kurt Löwenstein, *Sozialismus und Erziehung. Eine Auswahl aus den Schriften 1919–1933*, ed. Ferdinand Brandecker and Hildegard Feidel-Mertz (Berlin: J.H.W. Dietz, 1976), 80–81; Heinrich Schulz, *Die Schulreform der Sozialdemokratie* (Dresden: von Kaden & Co., 1911), 8–13. For an analysis of pre-1914 Social Democratic educational theory and policy, see Ulrich Bendele, *Sozialdemokratische Schulpolitik und Pädagogik im Wilhelminischen Deutschland* (Frankfurt: Campus, 1979).

[29] Wolfgang W. Wittwer, *Die Sozialdemokratische Schulpolitik in der Weimarer Republik* (Berlin: Colloquium, 1980).

[30] Essig, *Beruf und Menschentum*, 9. Cf. Anna Siemsen, "Erziehung zum Gemeinschaftsgeist" (excerpt) in *Arbeiterkulturbewegung in der Weimarer Republic*, ed. Wilfried van der Will and Rob Burns (Frankfurt: Ullstein, 1982), 32–39. A socialist activist who listed "joy in work, order, life, beauty, community" as basic human needs increasingly thwarted by capitalist industry, Siemsen complained that the nation's schools repressed the young through excessive emphasis on specialized skills training. Pending the seizure of political power that would open the way to both the socialization of the means of production and the radical reform of education, she advocated the creation of schools in which the children would engage in independent, self-directed labor while learning to cooperate for the common good.

Adler combined elements of Kantian idealism, the utopian tradition, the heritage of the bourgeois reformers from Rousseau through Fichte (portrayed as the first German socialist!) to Wyneken, and insights supplied by Marxism. The latter led him to deny that changed attitudes alone could change society; nor did he concede Wyneken's claim that schools could be politically neutral. But he also opposed the idea that education under capitalism necessarily reflected bourgeois values. Instead, he insisted that education could be transformed into a class tool for the emancipation of the proletariat. What was needed were schools that would equip the workers with the skills and qualities of character needed for survival in today's world, while creating a new type of individual inwardly at odds with existing society and so prepared to struggle for utopia.[31]

Kurt Löwenstein (1885–1939), the individual who did most to realize these socialist educational ideals in the Weimar years, sought to turn the nation's schools into small coeducational, secular, and self-governing communities in which young people would be educated, through work, to meet the requirements of a democratic republic, while learning to aspire to a future in which they would be free to satisfy their natural urge for activity and fully to develop their intellectual and physical capacities in the production of socially useful goods.[32] Posing as a hard-headed Marxist, Löwenstein claimed that the school reforms he advocated were a "realistic" alternative to sectarian communitarianism. He also acknowledged that his goals could only be attained over the long term, and even admitted that the need for work education would persist after the socialist revolution, because inherited patterns of thought and behavior would continue to inhibit the full flowering of unalienated labor. But his deliberate repudiation of utopianism could not obscure the fact that his entire program was inspired by the utopian ideal of a socialist community of joyful work.

Although socialists of various persuasions took the lead in proposing utopian solutions for the problem of work in the early postwar period, a number of people on the political Right also believed that the revolutionary crisis could be exploited to reverse the debasement of work and restore genuine community. Among those who were led to espouse an antisocialist utopianism by concern with the problem of alienation were two members of the German Werkbund, Karl Ernst Osthaus (1874–1921) and Karl Scheffler (1869–1951). At the Werkbund's first postwar convention in October 1919, Osthaus, a noted patron of the

---

[31] Max Adler, *Neue Menschen* (Berlin: E. Laub'sche Verlagsbuchlandlung, 1924). See also Glaser, *Im Umfeld des Austromarxismus*, pp. 317–22.

[32] Löwenstein, "Sozialistische Schul- und Erziehungsfragen," 31–40.

arts and friend of the expressionist avant-garde, argued that industrial capitalism and socialism were both imbued with a materialistic spirit devoid of aesthetic sensibility and joy, and that both tended to undermine German culture because they defined work purely in terms of effort and reward. Osthaus called for an ethical revolution that would restore work to its true meaning as *Schaffen*, creative activity, something one engages in without counting the hours, something capable of carrying the individual towards light and beauty.[33] But apart from urging the Werkbund to renew its commitment to artistic quality and give full support to its young radicals, Osthaus gave no hint as to how the desired ethical revolution could be effected.[34]

By contrast, Karl Scheffler the noted art critic and editor of *Kunst und Künstler* ("Art and Artists"), offered a detailed reform program to the Werkbund. Scheffler was not content with vague appeals for a return to idealism, nor did he believe that the artistic avant-garde could lead the way to salvation. An anti-modernist in both cultural and social matters, he argued instead that the nation's only hope lay in a revival of the crafts (*Handwerk*). Unlike the Marxists who cast the proletariat as chief agents and beneficiaries of the revolutionary crisis, Scheffler was convinced that the virtual collapse of German industry had created a unique opportunity for the resurgence of the artisanate and, more generally, of the middle classes (Mittelstand) on whom the lasting wellbeing of society must rest. Carried forward by these sectors of the nation, the "revolution" would destroy the overpowering influence of the metropolis, extend to all occupations the quality ideal associated with the crafts, and make possible a "re-aristocratization" of society. Once industry's predominance over the crafts and agriculture had been destroyed, the machine would lose its baneful influence on thought and feeling; this, in turn, would allow idealism to revive and would save Germany from the industrial slavery projected for it by England and America.[35]

The crafts romanticism with which Scheffler's schemes were imbued, although a product of the prewar period, reached its full flowering in the years of crisis following Germany's defeat. Under its influence, the Werkbund virtually repudiated its prewar program of forging an alliance between art and industry and instead sought ways to revive Germany's artistic culture and restore joy in work through cooperation with the

[33] Karl Ernst Osthaus, "Deutscher Werkbund," *Das Hohe Ufer*, vol. 10 (October 1919): 239–40.
[34] Campbell, *German Werkbund*, 133–40.
[35] Karl Scheffler, *Die Zukunft der Deutschen Kunst* (Berlin: Bruno Cassirer, 1919), 36; Campbell, *German Werkbund*, 127–32.

CHAPTER VI

artisans.[36] The strength of the handicraft mystique was revealed in 1922 when the Werkbund made joy in work the theme of its annual meeting. Although the keynote speaker tackled the question of alienated labor from the standpoint of industrial work, most of those who addressed the conference were convinced that only promotion of skilled quality work and the traditional crafts would make possible the restoration of Arbeitsfreude.[37] Idealization of the crafts also inspired the first phase of the Bauhaus, the experimental school of applied arts established in Weimar by Walter Gropius in 1919. Although the Bauhaus a few years later came to be identified with architectural modernism and played a major role in the development of industrial design, its initial manifesto reflected the contemporary resurgence of "medievalizing" romanticism: depicting the school as a community of artistic workers engaged in building the cathedral of the future, it proclaimed the "unity of art and craft."[38]

Outside the artistic community, the craft ideal won support not only from spokesmen of the handicraft organizations, but also from the churches. Typically, a pamphlet published in 1920 by the Catholic youth association, the *Grossdeutsche Jugend*, argued for a rejection of modern industry and the mass consumption associated with it. Concerned with the spread of Mammonism and the growing rift between life and work, it urged the nation's youth to draw inspiration from the spirit of the medieval crafts which the author identified with Catholicism.[39] More specifically, it recommended a return to nature combined with a search for new forms of economic organization such as work communities to enable labor to recover its ethical dimension.[40] Only by reaching back to the true Catholic faith, as embodied in the medieval guilds, could Germans hope to move forward to a new and better world of meaningful work. Condemning the gospel of work which it identified with Protestantism, it argued that undue emphasis on work was inimical to both religion and genuine culture. As it put it, the "Neopolitan's 'dolce far niente' " was to be preferred to the Englishman's "time is money." In this Catholic utopia, work and life were to be reconciled without enthroning the former as life's highest good.[41]

[36] Scheffler, *Zukunft der Deutschen Kunst*, Chapter 6, describes the Werkbund's pro-handicraft phase.
[37] Scheffler, *Zukunft der Deutschen Kunst*, 161–62.
[38] On this phase of the Bauhaus, see Marcel Franciscono, *Walter Gropius and the Creation of the Bauhaus in Weimar* (Urbana, Ill.: University of Illinois Press, 1971).
[39] Josef Scherer, *Die Arbeit, von ihrem Geist und Wesen* (Paderborn: Jungermann, 1920), 36–37.
[40] Scherer, *Arbeit*, 24, 43–44.   [41] Scherer, *Arbeit*, 45.

A diametrically opposed viewpoint was espoused by Heinrich Lhotsky (1859–1930), a wellknown Protestant theologian and antisemite whose works of fiction and essays on contemporary issues reached a wide audience.[42] Much as he wanted to believe that Germany could return to an economy dominated by farmers and craftsmen, Lhotsky recognized that this was impossible and so was not prepared to condemn modern industrial capitalism outright. Instead, he drew a distinction, characteristic of antisemitic writings, between productive indigenous industrialism and evil foreign finance. Arguing that the bourgeois retained what the proletarian had lost, namely belief in the German idea of work, he cast the *entire* German bourgeoisie—entrepreneurs, civil servants, the Mittelstand—in the role of the nation's saviour. In a patriotic tract of 1919 entitled *Work, Only Work!*, Lhotsky inveighed against socialists, democrats, and anarchists, whom he portrayed as allies of those alien princes of Mammon who were out to destroy Germany by undermining its will to work.[43] If the nation was to recover its former grandeur, he insisted that the masses must once more be taught that work is at the heart of a meaningful existence, because it alone enables people to experience, and therefore comprehend, the world, their fellows, truth, God.[44] With utopian conviction, he rested his hopes on the very group most utopians were inclined to blame for the deterioration of work: the industrial capitalists. Under the patriarchal guidance of their employers, the nation's industrial workers must be persuaded to adopt the German ethic of hard and joyful work, thus bringing about the recovery of German industrial production for the benefit of all.[45]

That this kind of thinking was not confined to the extreme right is demonstrated by Paul Rohrbach's essay on Germany's future published in 1921.[46] Rohrbach (1869–1956), a democratic publicist active in the DDP, shared Lhotsky's intense nationalism, but combined it with a somewhat less reactionary set of social views. As befitted a disciple of

[42] *Wer ist's?* (1928), 944; *NDB* 14:440–41. The latter gives his date of birth as 1850. On Lhotsky (whom, however, he incorrectly cites as Chotsky), see also Peter Hinrichs, *Um die Seele des Arbeiters. Arbeitspsychologie, Industrie- und Betriebssoziologie in Deutschland* (Cologne: Pahl-Rugenstein, 1981), 149–51.

[43] Heinrich Lhotsky, *Arbeiten, nichts als arbeiten* (Stuttgart: J. Engelhorns Nachf., 1919).

[44] Lhotsky, *Arbeiten*, 107.

[45] Lhotsky would have been gratified to know that a year after his death the company newspaper of Siemens, one of the country's largest electrical firms, published an excerpt from his writings on the German work ethic for the edification of its employees. "Die Arbeit als sittliche Tat," *Das Werk* (1931): 481.

[46] Paul Rohrbach, "Deutschlands Zukunft," in *Deutschlands Zukunft im Urteil führender Männer*, ed. Klemens Löffler (Halle: H. Dickman, 1921), 123–36.

Friedrich Naumann (who had died in 1920 shortly after helping to found the DDP), Rohrbach called for a just social order based on national and Christian principles that would concentrate on restoring Germany to greatness by reversing the *Entseelung* ("despiritualization") of German work. Rather than focus on improvements to the workers' standard of living or seek to embellish social welfare programs, Rohrbach insisted that social reformers must place the spiritual needs of the workers above the material. What was required, above all, was a revolution in attitudes (*Revolution der Gesinnung*) to ensure that workers would be treated in a Christian manner, as an end and never as a means, and thus be delivered from soulless labor and provided with a positive relationship to their work. At the same time, the redistribution of land would enable industrial workers not only to acquire homes of their own but also some soil to work in their spare time. This would not only restore the contact with nature so necessary for physical and mental health, but also drive out the commercial spirit (*Krämergeist*) and overcome the limitless receptivity to unhealthy sensations characteristic of a rootless urban existence.[47] Reintegrated into the nation, the proletariat would abandon its dreams of social revolution and cooperate in rebuilding the economy.

Like Lhotsky, Rohrbach favored the end of alienation through the restoration of joy in work as a means to revive German power and prosperity, but he did not think it sufficient to rebuild the nation's military and economic strength. To become great once more, according to Rohrbach, Germany had to fulfill its ideal mission to the world. It could do this by showing other nations the way to a harmonious society in which there would no longer be employers and employees, but only workers in a common cause, enjoying equality of opportunity and rewarded in accordance with their contribution to society.[48] In effect, Rohrbach preached a "national" socialism in which the creation of a Volk community (*Volksgemeinschaft*) through the transformation of work would enable Germany to regain its rightful place in the community of nations and thus undo the verdict of Versailles.

Rohrbach failed to make clear just how his "revolution of attitudes" was to be effected and who its agents were to be, but there is evidence that he believed that the answer might lie, in part, in the ranks of the *Werkstudenten*. These were middle-class youths who had been forced by the loss of their families' savings to work their way through university, generally at menial jobs. A new phenomenon in Germany, the work

[47] Rohrbach, "Deutschlands Zukunft," 136.
[48] Rohrbach, "Deutschlands Zukunft," 135.

student was the product more of economic necessity than choice during a period when escalating inflation was wiping out the savings that heretofore had enabled the sons of the middle classes to attend university.[49] Nevertheless, there were many, inside and outside the universities, who were prepared to take a positive view of this development. Thus, in an English language publication of 1924 edited by Rohrbach and financed by a Charles Lange of Cincinnati, Professor von Blume of Tübingen University described the work student as the "new man"

> who combines in one person the mental and manual worker. . . . The combination of mental and manual work brings forth a connection between mental and manual workers. For many years students and laborers have been enemies. Now they are beginning to know and esteem each other better. Great progress has been made towards social reconciliation.[50]

Here major aspects of the utopian vision of the Left, including the longing for a rapprochement between intellectuals and workers and the desire to close the gap between mental and manual labor, reappeared under patriotic and anti-socialist auspices. It soon became apparent, however, that a considerable element of wishful thinking was involved: middle-class students, working side by side with uneducated laborers on the factory floor, found it difficult to maintain their belief in the possibility or even desirability of class reconciliation. Proximity frequently led students to feel disgust at the "materialism" of their proletarian workmates, who gave little sign of valuing work for its own sake and lacked appreciation for the higher things in life. Surrounded by people who thought the ideal job was one that produced a maximum of pay for minimum effort, even those work students originally motivated to some extent by social idealism developed a more realistic view of wage labor. The hope that Germany's academic youth would help to bridge the gulf between classes and overcome a mutual distrust bred of

---

[49] Michael H. Kater, "The Work Student: A Socio-Economic Phenomenon of early Weimar Germany," *Journal of Contemporary History* 10 (1975) 1:71–94.

[50] Von Blume, in *The German Work-Student*, ed. Paul Rohrbach (Dresden: Wirtschaftshilfe der Deutschen Studentenschaft, 1924), 14. See also Wilhelm Tafel, *Arbeitszwang und Arbeitslust* (Gotha: F. A. Perthes, 1919). Speaking to the local society of engineers, Tafel, a professor at the Breslau TH, argued that it was essential to dismantle the bureaucratic restrictions imposed during the war, improve the workers' attitudes, and restore the habit of work. Although he advocated a variety of practical measures, his main plea was for a new spirit of cooperation based on mutual respect and understanding between mental and manual labor, employers and workers, a spirit allegedly demonstrated by the Werkstudenten. By their example he hoped the latter would persuade the workers to abandon their apparent willingness to settle for a life *without* work and instead seek joy *in* work.

ignorance[51] proved a typically short-lived product of the utopian phase that coincided with the birthpangs of the Weimar Republic.[52]

The most imaginative, radical, and best publicized proposals for creating a cohesive national community in which manual workers and intellectuals would cooperate for the common good were put forward at this time by Walther Rathenau (1867–1922). Like Rohrbach a member of the new DDP, Rathenau was a trained engineer, successful author, and wellknown public figure who in 1915 had succeeded his father as head of the German General Electric Company (AEG). Despite his position as one of Germany's leading industrialists, Rathenau identified the fact that a large portion of the workforce was condemned to a lifetime of mindless, repetitive manual labor as the fundamental evil of modern society.[53] Like the Marxists, he recognized that social and economic life would have to be totally restructured if the problem of work was to be solved and rejected as romantic nonsense all the talk of overcoming alienation by returning to pre-industrial forms.

Although he was convinced that the society of the future must rest on a progressive economic foundation that made full use of innovative technology and rational organization to maximize production, Rathenau also turned his back on the "technological utopianism" of those who argued that the triumph of the machine would spell the liberation of human beings from soulless labor. Automation might indeed obviate the need for a great deal of unpleasant work and change the balance between mechanical and supervisory occupations in favor of the latter.[54] But at best this would be a long process, and only a partial one, for a certain amount of sheer hard work would always be required, and no amount of external tinkering could free this kind of work from its debilitating effects on body and spirit.[55] Nor did Rathenau believe that it was possible to compensate people for the miseries of modern work by enriching their leisure. In his judgment, people whose working lives were spent in purely mechanical tasks suffered a fatigue of the spirit that rendered them incapable of using their free time for peaceful relax-

[51] Hans Maier, "The Work-Student System, a Way to Social Labour," in Rohrbach, German Work-Student, 71–75.

[52] By soliciting funds for student assistance, the Rohrbach book itself acknowledged that it was desirable to free students as much as possible from the necessity of earning a living!

[53] Walther Rathenau, "Arbeit," in Walther Rathenau, Der Neue Staat (Berlin: S. Fischer, 1919), 49–74; "Die Neue Gesellschaft" (Sept. 1919), in Walther Rathenau, Gesammelte Schriften, vol. 5 (Berlin: S. Fischer, 1925), 339–456, especially 424–38 on work and the reform of work; Walther Rathenau, Autonome Wirtschaft (Jena: Eugen Diederichs, 1919).

[54] Rathenau, Autonome Wirtschaft, 7; Harry, Graf Kessler, Walther Rathenau: sein Leben und sein Werk (Berlin: Hermann Klemm, 1928), 197.

[55] Rathenau, "Neue Gesellschaft," 425.

ation and culturally valuable recreation. For this reason, among others, he rejected the socialist solution of higher wages and shorter hours: this would merely replace joyless work with *Bummelei* ("loafing") and do nothing to address the economic and cultural problems of the nation or to effect the desired reconciliation between people and their work, and between mechanical and intellectual labor.[56]

Yet Rathenau himself was not immune to the utopian temptation. Refusing to accept that the problem of work was insoluble, he advocated the creation of a just society in which hereditary wealth and unearned income would be taxed away, private ownership would yield to democratic management of productive enterprises reorganized into autonomous units supervised by guilds and, ultimately, by the state, and all would be granted an equal opportunity to develop their talents.[57] Beyond this, he proferred as a panacea *Arbeitsausgleich*, the equalization of work, to counteract the unavoidable division of labor between manual and mental labor. In his utopia the individual would be able to partake of both kinds of work. Rotating between jobs, manual workers with the requisite natural ability would spend part of the day in suitable intellectual activities and would have the option at any stage of life to acquire the knowledge and training needed to make this alternate occupation (*Gegenberuf*) their primary one.[58] At the same time, all but the handful of intellectual workers engaged in vital tasks would be obligated to devote some hours of each day to manual labor. After a protracted time of transition, during which young people of both sexes would undergo a year at compulsory labor that would prepare them for a society based on the new concept of work, Rathenau envisaged the emergence of an ideal society in which all who so desired would be able to learn and to put their knowledge to productive use, and in which everyone capable of developing inborn talents would in fact wish to do so.[59]

Rohrbach had hoped to reconcile the classes with one another; Rathenau desired their dissolution.[60] His goal was a classless society based on the principle of careers open to talent, and an organization of work that would compel the occupational ranks to mingle. In this way, he hoped to reconcile human beings and work, and to create an organic

---

[56] Rathenau, "Neue Gesellschaft," 427.   [57] Rathenau, *Autonome Wirtschaft*, passim.

[58] Rathenau, "Neue Gesellschaft," 436.

[59] Rathenau, "Neue Gesellschaft," 369 on the long path to utopia; 438 on the utopian goal.

[60] Rathenau, "Neue Gesellschaft," 424, speaks of *Klassenaufhebung* instead of *Klassenversöhnung*.

community of the spirit in which *Schaffen*, creativity activity, would cease to be material and formal, and instead acquire meaning and intrinsic value.[61] Where Rathenau agreed with Rohrbach was in his insistence that the primary objective in resolving the problem of work must be to ensure the welfare of society as a whole, rather than to further the happiness and wellbeing of the individual citizen. The economic and social transformation he envisaged was not designed to provide joyful or even profitable and secure jobs, so much as ones involving a balanced blend of activities that would develop people's capacities, and thus enable them fully to participate in, and contribute to the national culture. As a result, Rathenau gave an even more utopian twist to Rohrbach's notion of the national mission: as *the* land of the spirit and of education (*Geist und Geistesbildung*), Germany was not only to show other nations how to solve the social question, but also to initiate them into the life of the mind. Only by dedicating itself to the "German idea" (*deutsche Gedanke*) of a unified higher culture embracing the entire Volk could the new republic develop the internal cohesion needed to bind the various interest groups together, and regain the respect and friendship of foreign countries, which had been forfeited by Germany's disastrous policies of the previous hundred years.[62]

Rathenau was well aware that words could not of themselves spark off the social transformation required to realize his radical notions of work.[63] But because he failed to mobilize the backing of either big business or organized labor during the revolutionary years, he was forced to content himself with preaching and prophecy. One can also criticize Rathenau for resting his proposal regarding job equalization on the unsubstantiated assumption that a manual worker who spent part of the day on administrative tasks would experience a sense of liberation. This result was unlikely to occur in view of the fact, noted by many of his contemporaries, that "intellectual" and white collar work was increasingly devoid of "Geist," and therefore just as likely as "mechanical" work to be soul-destroying. Alternation between equally unsatisfactory occupations could hardly be expected to produce the beneficial effects that Rathenau posited. For this and other reasons, although there continued to be considerable interest in Rathenau's suggestions for job rotation and equalization, even after the utopian mood that inspired them had waned, his ideas were generally rejected as ill-conceived and

---

[61] Rathenau, "Neue Gesellschaft," 440.
[62] Rathenau, "Neue Gesellschaft," 455–56; *Autonome Wirtschaft*, 28.
[63] Rathenau, "Neue Gesellschaft," 29.

impracticable. Nor did Rathenau himself follow up his proposals for the reform of work. Having failed to win an appointment to the Socialization Commission where he might have been able to pursue his socio-economic reform ideas, he eventually came to serve the new democratic Germany in a political capacity, first as Minister for Reconstruction and then as Foreign Minister. Assassinated in 1922 while in office, he did not live to face the challenge that was soon to confront his fellow utopians: that of finding a way to adapt their dreams to the reality of the post-revolutionary Germany that emerged from the years of political and financial crisis with its fundamental social and economic structures virtually intact.[64]

As we have seen, the theme of reconciliation between manual and mental work cropped up repeatedly in the utopian projects of both right and left. It was generally assumed that the industrial worker suffered most from labor alienation, and that the intellectual and artist were privileged to enjoy work and could act as sympathetic reformers and guides to those less fortunate. However, a number of writers rejected the fashionable view that only manual labour was "real" work and sought remedies for what they diagnosed as a significant aspect of the current crisis, namely the deterioration of intellectual work and the attendant loss of status of the intellectual worker.

One person who viewed the problem of work in this way was Erich Ruckhaber (1876–?). A Monist in the materialist sense propagated by Ernst Haeckel,[65] Ruckhaber, in a pamphlet on "The Correct Valuation of Physical and Mental Work" that went into eight printings in 1920,[66] claimed that his own work constituted a breakthrough in the understanding of mental activity, or *Geistesarbeit*. In his view, the difference between mental and physical work was one of quantity rather than quality, because the former, involving eye movements in memory, was itself always physical. Convinced that all work involves an element of compulsion and is associated with unpleasant, even painful, sensations, Ruckhaber also claimed that the tendency of the majority to shun mental activity demonstrated that such work was actually more burdensome than physical labor.[67]

---

[64] On the tenacity of the old regime and its reconstruction after the First World War, Charles S. Maier, *Recasting Bourgeois Europe: Stabilization in France, Germany and Italy in the Decade after World War I* (Princeton: Princeton University Press, 1975).

[65] On Monism, Daniel Gasman, *The Scientific Origins of National Socialism. Social Darwinism in Ernst Haeckel and the German Monist League* (London: Macdonald), 1971.

[66] Erich Ruckhaber, *Die richtige Bewertung der Körper- und Geistes-Arbeit* (3d ed.; Berlin: Verlag der 'Neuen Weltanschauung,' 1920). Ruckhaber was the author of several books on "Biomechanics."

[67] Ruckhaber, *Richtige Bewertung*, 12. Ruckhaber maintained that the most onerous occu-

Although Ruckhaber made suggestions for ameliorating the lot of ordinary workers, he was therefore more concerned about what the revolution could and should do for the intellectuals. The aim must be to abolish the "academic proletariat," create a rational society that would apportion work efficiently according to merit and give brain workers the support they required in terms of extra free time, books, and travel. Arguing that the final goal was an increase in individual happiness, particularly for the thinking person, Ruckhaber hoped to achieve this by transforming Arbeit into *Tätigkeit*, free activity. In his view, it was the duty of the state to encourage joyful labor, instead of allowing society to transform people into beasts of burden for some alleged common good.[68] Consequently, in his post-revolutionary utopia, capitalism would be modified by abolition of the stock exchange, nationalization of the banks and key industries, and tax reform: rationalization would create a society of plenty in which it would be possible to end exploitation, shorten the working day, and assign tasks according to individual inclination and ability.

The attitudes revealed in Ruckhaber's pamphlet were not atypical. Even among those intellectuals sympathetic to the working class, there was concern lest the increasingly desperate plight of Germany's brain-workers and artists be overlooked by the socialist revolutionaries and their special problems forgotten. It seemed essential to remind people that the post-revolutionary society must also meet the needs of the nation's intellectuals. This is what Martin Luserke, a popular novelist and educator, tried to do in an essay on work motivation published in 1919 as part of a series *Praktischer Sozialismus* ("Practical Socialism") edited by the philosopher Karl Korsch.[69] Like Ruckhaber, Luserke thought it wrong to make a distinction between mental and physical labor. This led him to call for a "socialist" ethic of work to replace the bourgeois-idealist one based on this distinction, which only helped to perpetuate the hierarchy of classes. Under socialism, people of all walks of life would be taught to work for one another and to accept discipline in order to achieve common goals.

Where Luserke chiefly differed from Ruckhaber is in his belief that intellectual "work" is hardly work at all, but rather intrinsically pleasurable activity and therefore in some sense its own reward.[70] As a re-

---

pations were those of the machine-minder or cashier, in other words jobs entailing mechanical work that required the operative's full attention.

[68] Ruckhaber, *Richtige Bewertung*, 15.

[69] Martin Luserke, *Warum arbeitet der Mensch? Eine sozialistische Ideologie der Arbeit* (Hannover: Freies Deutschland, 1919). The previous volume in the series was by Bernard Shaw.

[70] Luserke, *Warum arbeitet der Mensch?*, 26. The contemporary debate on whether what

sult, he was not particularly concerned with improving the remuneration of intellectuals or cutting back on their hours of work. But he did think that workers of the mind needed special conditions if they were to serve society effectively. To make their different treatment acceptable to the majority of workers whose days were spent in hard, routine, labor, it was necessary to adopt the principle of meritocracy: in Luserke's utopia, examinations would be used to select the few needed for intellectual tasks, and these individuals would then be given non-monetary privileges and rewards, including the opportunity to experience joy in work.[71]

The intellectuals' concern lest the ordinary workers, who had been transformed by the new democracy into their masters, should fail to recognize the legitimacy of their special status was soon reinforced by the realization that the revolution had failed to institutionalize the ideal of cooperation between brain and hand, generally deemed a prerequisite for the restoration of community and the flourishing of Arbeitsfreude. Given the continuation of political and social strife, it was not long before many who had initially welcomed the revolution concluded that the obstacles to drastic reform of the existing order were insurmountable. Socialist intellectuals and artists who had thought themselves destined to lead society to a brighter future in alliance with the working masses found it difficult to maintain faith in the spontaneous idealism of the proletariat, or to ignore the fact that most craftsmen, whom the radical artists had assumed to be kindred spirits, failed to share their work ethic.

The process of disillusionment can be clearly traced in the revolutionary weekly, *Die Brücke*, which began publication in Chemnitz in 1919. In the introductory issue, the publisher, Alfred Fellisch, gave voice to his utopian vision: "brawny workmen, arm in arm with knights of the intellect" marching into the Reich of the future

> in which the socialist spirit has created a human community filled with joy and justice, an economic order based on equality and a temple for work that gives joy. And all who dwell therein are content. . . . As the sinewy working hand lays itself lovingly on the brow of the thinker and the intellectual producer feels himself at one with the man of the workbench and factory, and both are filled with the great, all-embracing and invincible socialist concept, we will construct the spiritual bridge into this beautiful land.

---

the intellectual does is work or not, was summarized by Karl Elster, "Was ist 'Arbeit'?" *JNS* (1919): 609–627.

[71] Luserke, *Warum arbeitet der Mensch?* 28.

Singing the praises of the proletariat, Fellisch saw Germany's collapse as an opportunity to bridge the gap between intelligentsia and workers by creating a "Werkbund" or productive alliance between intellectual converts to socialism like himself and Germany's working class elite.[72]

But the utopianism that had originally inspired the journal quickly dissolved when its editors found themselves faced with the realities of a world inhabited by workers largely unresponsive to the ideal of diligent, selfless, and joyful labor. Writing in the same periodical less than a year later, the playwright Gustav Slekow sorrowfully noted a deplorable deterioration in worker attitudes. The continuing lack of discipline and social turmoil led him to conclude that it would take time, coupled with better education, to complete

> the ethical conversion of the German worker from exploited wage slave to responsible individual, capable of recognizing in productive work the salvation and joy of all earthly beings, the source of all contentment and the creative force of all human culture.[73]

Ironically, it was Germany's *failure* to take a leap into the socialist future of joyful work that gave rise to the most elaborate postwar literary utopia centered on Arbeitsfreude. In his *Der Güterberg* ("The Commodity Mountain"), subtitled "Letters from a Land of Work and Joyful Labor,"[74] Julius Lerche (1867–?), an engineer and Prussian civil servant, told of a communal experiment on a small island off the coast of Greenland which he called Ludwigsland. Here a band of craftsmen, with only their tools and under the leadership of a beloved "Master," set out to create a new society in which everyone would contribute, through joyful work, to the community's wealth represented by the *Güterberg*. Whereas most utopias describe the advance of the imagined society towards its proclaimed goals, Lerche depicted the progressive deterioration of his ideal community into something closely resembling the real world. In the course of his story, Ludwigsland society becomes ever more complex and non-egalitarian. Envy and discord are reborn, along with the other social evils which its inhabitants had sought to escape, such as mechanization, night work, and crime. Yet all is not lost. After the Master's death, the colony, now under the humble lead-

---

[72] Alfred Fellisch, "Über den Abgrund!" *Die Brücke* 1 (1919–1920), 1–4. The periodical was subtitled "Wochenschrift zur Förderung sozialer Erkenntnis" and was a weekly for the promotion of social understanding.

[73] Gustav Slekow, "Arbeitsfreude und Klassenbewusstsein," *Die Brücke* 1 (1919–1920): 337–40.

[74] Julius Lerche, *Der Güterberg. Briefe aus dem Lande der Arbeit und der Arbeitsfreude* (Stuttgart: K. Thienemanns, 1921). An expanded second edition was published by J. Springer in Stuttgart and Berlin in 1922.

ership of the narrator, continues to possess one great advantage over
the Motherland: the inhabitants do not labor under compulsion or regard work purely as a means to earn their daily bread, but experience
joy in creation and have the satisfaction of knowing that together they
are building a better future for themselves and their children. Lerche's
purpose was clearly to encourage Germans to follow the example of the
citizens of Ludwigsland, whose ethic of work and community spirit enabled them to build a viable society from the ground up. His readers
were led to believe that by adopting the ethic of joyful work, Germany
might once more become "a great, united Volk," win back its former
place in the world through the "customary diligence and thoroughness
and the quality of work" of its people, and thus most effectively wipe
out the evils visited on it by "stupidity, hatred, and hypocrisy."[75]

Lerche seems never to have participated in the socialist euphoria
that after the war briefly induced many German intellectuals to adopt
the cause of the proletariat as their own. For him as for many other
patriotic Germans joy in work was neither a means to create utopia nor
the longed-for outcome of a revolutionary social transformation, but
rather a necessary instrument in the struggle for national recovery. Nor
did he concern himself unduly with the contemporary debate on how
to reconcile manual and mental labor. Instead, he simply chose to focus
on people like himself, for whom work was a matter of applying intelligence to the constructive solution of challenging tasks.[76]

While Lerche's stress on the importance of leadership and the need
to subordinate individual welfare to the requirements of the Volk
placed him firmly in the conservative nationalist camp, he can also be
seen as representative of the practical people of action who increasingly
replaced artists and literati in the forefront of discussions about the reform of work.[77] The tendency of the latter to withdraw rather than to
engage in the compromises required of participants in the public arena
coincided with and contributed to the waning of utopianism. The
change in intellectual fashion had begun even before the currency reform of 1923 made it possible to restore a semblance of stability to economic and political life. In the mid-1920s, as Expressionism in litera-

[75] Lerche, Güterberg, 127–28.

[76] See Julius Lerche, Arbeiter unter Tarnkappen. Ein Buch von Werkleuten und ihrem Schaffen
(Stuttgart: K. Thienemanns, 1919; 2d ed.; Berlin: J. Springer, 1920), a collection of short
stories about men at work that included inventors, engineers, architects, and machine de-
signers.

[77] See the review of Der Güterberg in the journal of the VdI, Technik und Wirtschaft 14
(1921): 772.

ture and the arts gave way to *Neue Sachlichkeit* ("New Objectivity"),[78] the domain of social thought underwent a parallel transformation. The problem of work continued to command attention, but attempts to tackle it and the related social question now were generally characterized by a "new sobriety" that denounced extreme hopes as outdated romanticism and promoted objectivity, empiricism, and pragmatism as better routes to progress.[79] The goals of joy in work and social harmony were not abandoned, but sober second thought convinced most people, even in the socialist camp, that neither society nor human nature could be radically transformed overnight. Only in the early 1930s, when the onset of the Great Depression once more called into question the stability of the existing order, was there to be a significant revival of utopianism.

[78] For an excellent brief account of these two movements, see Wolfgang Sauer, "Weimar Culture: Experiments in Modernism," *Social Research* 39 (Summer 1972): 254–84.

[79] John Willett, *Art and Politics in the Weimar Period: The New Sobriety 1917–1933* (New York: Pantheon, 1978).

VII

THE RATIONALIZATION OF
PRODUCTION AND THE
HUMANIZATION OF WORK

THE STABILIZATION of the mark in 1923 raised hopes that the post-war crisis was finally over and that the country could look forward to a period of sustained growth and prosperity. Taking stock of significant recent alterations in the social, political, and legal context of German work—notably the pact of November 1918 between the trade unions and employer organizations (*Zentralarbeitsgemeinschaft*, ZAG) and the works council legislation of 1920 (*Betriebsrätegesetz*)—many individuals concluded that it made sense to abjure revolutionary utopianism and instead respond constructively to current problems in a spirit of cool realism. Their decision to work within the framework of the status quo also included a greater willingness to make use of, and build on, the body of knowledge produced by the prewar science of work.

The task that faced reformers in the era of Neue Sachlichkeit was no easy one. The major complicating factor was a rapid acceleration in the rate of technological and economic change, as additional sectors of German industry sought to "rationalize" their administrative, production, and marketing procedures. Although many of its methods and practices were borrowed from abroad, especially from the United States, the *concept* of rationalization—and the term itself—both seem to have originated in Germany.[1] *Rationalisierung* was first widely used as an economic term to designate the weeding out of inefficient firms or their absorption by more efficient rivals. Particularly during the inflation period, this kind of rationalization strengthened the prewar trend to concentration in German industry. In its extreme form, it led to the

[1] Robert A. Brady, *The Rationalization Movement in German Industry* (Berkeley: University of California Press, 1933), 6–7; Lyndall Urwick, *The Meaning of Rationalization* (London: Nisbet, 1929), 13–15.

creation of producer cartels more inclined to limit output so as to maintain prices than to maximize profits by increasing production and expanding markets. But by the mid-1920s "rationalization" had also come
to designate technological innovation and organizational change, as
more and more businesses attempted to improve labor productivity
through the introduction of standardized mass production.[2]

Rationalization, in this second sense, won support for the first time
from a broad coalition of interests, including "labor and capital, industrialists and agriculturists, producers and consumers, private traders and
the state."[3] From the early 1920s on, the media alerted the general
public to the issues, while specialists in and outside the universities
worked to perfect the new methods and adapt them to German needs.
Numerous private and government-subsidized agencies also furthered
the rationalization movement, with the *Reichskuratorium für Wirtschaft-
lichkeit* (Federal Council for Economic Efficiency, RKW), founded in
1921, in the forefront by the middle of the decade.[4]

Contributing to the vogue of rationalization in Germany after the
war was a relatively greater openness to foreign influences. The concept
of *Deutsche Arbeit* continued to influence the way developments in
other countries were perceived, and it was occasionally used to assess
which of them would prove acceptable to German workers, but for a
few years, in the mid-1920s, the inclination to stress the uniqueness of
German work was pushed into the background. The turn to "internationalism" in the debate about work can be explained in part by the
widespread revulsion against the horrors of the Great War. However, a
new willingness to look at what other countries were doing was also
demonstrated by many German nationalists who felt the need to analyze, explain, and match the impressive industrial achievements of the
victors. Reinforcing this tendency was the Dawes Plan of 1924 which
multiplied contacts between Germany and the United States and produced an infusion of U.S. capital. America, perceived by both admirers
and critics as the leading industrial power, was generally thought to
represent the future. As a consequence, what people believed was happening there had a major impact on the way Germans thought about
work throughout the 1920s.[5]

[2] On the question of definition, in addition to Brady and Urwick, cited above, see also
"Rationalisierung" in *HA* 2:3619–31.

[3] Brady, *Rationalization Movement*, 3.

[4] Bruno Birnbaum, *Organisation der Rationalisierung Amerika-Deutschland* (Berlin: R. Hobbing, 1927), 76–87; Urwick, *Meaning of Rationalization*, 15, 129–30; Hans Wolfgang Büttner,
Das Rationalisierungs-Kuratorium der deutschen Wirtschaft (Düsseldorf: Droste, 1973), 11–23.

[5] Peter Berg, *Deutschland und Amerika* (Lübeck: Matthiesen, 1963), 96–97; Jost Hermand

Interest in the American experience both produced and was stimulated by a plethora of eye-witness reports on industrial life in the
United States, such as that published in 1925 by Paul Riebensahm, an
engineering professor at the Berlin TH.[6] In addition, books by Taylor,
Ford, and other trans-Atlantic prophets of rationalization were either
reprinted or published in translation. Frederick Taylor's *The Principles
of Scientific Management,*[7] first published in 1918, had sold over 30,000
copies in Germany by 1922; a German version of Henry Ford's autobiography, *Mein Leben und Werk* was republished over thirty times between 1923 and 1939.[8] Rationalization became virtually synonymous
with the ideas of scientific management associated with Taylor and the
assembly-line system of production pioneered by Ford. This led to the
emergence of *Taylorismus* and *Fordismus* as cults among those who believed it essential to abandon traditional methods in favor of more scientific, rational ones, if Germany's industries were to produce and sell
enough to carry the burden of reparations, raise material and cultural
standards, and restore Germany to the position in the world due to its
numbers and natural talents.[9]

Throughout the decade those who cheered on the rationalization
movement found themselves under attack from others who denounced
it because of its negative effects on conditions of work and on the human capacity to experience Arbeitsfreude. As the more thoughtful proponents of rationalization were themselves aware of its potential dangers for the individual and society, it is not surprising that the search
for creative solutions to the problem of modern work became a major
concern of German reformers at this time. Somehow, a way had to be
found to combine necessary rationalization with changes aimed at "humanizing" industrial life.

Like rationalization (and, indeed, Arbeitsfreude), humanization

---

and Frank Trommler, *Die Kultur der Weimarer Republik* (Munich: Nymphenburger Verlagshandlung, 1978), 49–64.

[6] Paul Riebensahm, *Der Zug nach U.S.A. Gedanken einer Amerikareise 1924* (Berlin: Julius
Springer, 1925).

[7] F. W. Taylor, *Die Grundsätze wissenschaftlicher Betriebsführung* (Munich, 1918). Taylor's
Shop Management had already been widely available in German before the war, with a third
edition appearing in 1914.

[8] Henry Ford, *Mein Leben und Werk* (Leipzig: P. List, [1923]). Even more popular was Ford's
antisemitic tract, *Der Internationale Jude;* published in two volumes in 1922 (Leipzig: Ham-
mer-Verlag), it had run through twenty-nine editions by 1933 and a further four by 1937.
Although much quoted, his *Philosophie der Arbeit* (Dresden: P. Aretz, 1929), a paean to the
value of rationalization and the inevitability of progress, was less of a publishing triumph,
possibly because its appearance coincided with the onset of the Depression!

[9] Birnbaum, *Organisation der Rationalisierung*, 88–89; Charles S. Maier, "Between Taylorism and Technocracy," *JCH* 5 (1970): 54.

(*Humanisierung*) meant different things to different people. Many found it impossible to exult in, or even accept without protest, the increasing dominance of science and technology, the growing mechanization and the specialization of labor, the impersonality of the modern factory (often itself but a small constituent of a vast corporate structure), and the widening gap between work life and the rest of existence. In the face of these tendencies, these people responded to rationalization with a desire to humanize work. It seemed essential to discover ways to put people once more at the center of things and to allow their humanity—including both its rational and its irrational elements—to flourish.

Beyond this, however, the leading exponents of humanization in Germany failed to agree among themselves. Motives differed widely, as did estimates regarding the prospects for success. What is more, the exact relationship among rationalization, humanization, and Arbeitsfreude remained unclear. Did humanization represent the perfection of rationalization or entail its reversal? Could it be equated with the promotion of joy in work, or should it be pursued in order to compensate the workers for the inescapable loss of Arbeitsfreude? Unable to reach a theoretical consensus, German reformers failed to develop a coherent program for the humanization of work in the 1920s. All that emerged from the Weimar debate was an array of partly overlapping, partly conflicting proposals. What is more, few of these schemes were implemented, and none managed to influence a significant proportion of German enterprises. Yet these German projects are worth reviewing, for they not only anticipated the American "Human Relations" movement associated with the name of Elton Mayo,[10] but also laid the basis for several reforms initiated by the National Socialists in the 1930s and prepared the ground for more elaborate efforts to humanize the workplace and improve the quality of working life after the Second World War.[11]

For analytical purposes, it is helpful to deal separately with two closely interrelated aspects of the attempt to humanize rationalized industry in Weimar Germany. This chapter will examine the ideas of those who hoped to reconcile modern people with their work by restructuring the productive process. The following chapter will focus on efforts to achieve the same end by reorganizing industrial relations. In

[10] See Elton Mayo, *The Human Problems of an Industrial Civilization* (New York: Macmillan, 1933), describing the path-breaking experiments carried out between 1927 and 1932 at the Hawthorne works of the Western Electric Company.

[11] Friedrich Dorsch, *Geschichte und Probleme der angewandten Psychologie* (Bern: H. Huber, 1963), 94–98.

both, a sub-theme is the close connection between the Neue Sach-lichkeit of the mid-1920s and the utopianism it purported to replace.

This link is certainly evident in the thinking of those reformers who believed that a more intensive and consistent application of science to industry, far from aggravating the problem of work, would constitute its cure. Engineers, many of whom assumed that it was the mission of their profession to lead the way to a better world, were especially prone to this kind of "technological utopianism." An excellent exemplar was Georg Schlesinger (1874–1949), from 1904 on professor of mechanical engineering at the Berlin TH. Founder in 1907 of the specialist journal *Werkstattechnik* ("Workshop Technology"), and author of several books on industrial management, Schlesinger had derived the fundamental principles of Taylorism—that the accurate and objective measurement of work performance, leading to the establishment of a just and accept-able wage rate, constituted the key to both improved productivity and industrial peace—from his own experience in the early 1900s and had become a leading expositor and proponent of Taylorism in Germany before the First World War.

Yet Schlesinger refused simply to equate scientific management with Taylorism. Instead, he maintained that the road to progress lay in com-bining the rather mechanistic ideas of Taylor and his followers with the latest findings of German sociology and psychology.[12] As early as 1920, in a treatise on psychotechnics and management, he argued that sci-entific management could achieve its potential only if it de-emphasized technical solutions and instead focused on the careful selection, train-ing, and placement of individuals.[13] Sharing the optimism of Münster-berg, on whose work he drew, and influenced by the utopian euphoria of his contemporaries, Schlesinger maintained that Taylorist time-and-motion studies, when combined with improved methods of psycholog-ical testing, selection, and guidance, would eventually enable manage-ment to place everyone in the right job. This, in turn, would not only make it possible to reconcile the interests of employers, wage earners, and consumers by optimizing production, but would also permit the individual worker once more to experience joy in work.

Schlesinger recognized that the first step was to improve psycho-technical methods. To overcome the current imperfections of psycho-

---

[12] Hans Ebert and Karin Hausen, "Georg Schlesinger und die Rationalisierungsbewegung in Deutschland," in Reinhard Rürup, ed., *Wissenschaft und Gesellschaft. Beiträge zur Geschichte der Technischen Universität Berlin, 1879–1979* (Berlin: Springer, 1979), 1:326–27.

[13] Georg Schlesinger, *Psychotechnik und Betriebswissenschaft* (Leipzig: S. Hirzel, 1920), 20–21. An early version appeared under the same title in October 1919, as the opening piece in *Praktische Psychologie*, a journal edited by Schlesinger's colleague, Walther Moede.

technical tests and to ensure their objectivity, he advocated their removal to neutral testing stations. Far from the influence of school, employer, or paymaster, such centers would not only make selection and guidance more effective, but would also encourage greater collaboration between employers and workers. Similarly, the cooperation of all involved was required if time and motion studies were to serve a constructive purpose.[14] Without abandoning the Taylorist belief that workers, in the last analysis, had to subordinate themselves to management and follow the instructions of the engineer-cum-psychotechnician, he recommended that the experts make a practice of consulting with those affected by their decisions, rather than demanding unquestioning compliance with solutions imposed from above. In other words, Schlesinger accepted the democratic revolution and acknowledged the basic principles of worker participation and equality of rights in industry.[15]

Schlesinger also insisted that joy in work depended on linking good work organization and proper job placement with hygienic and attractive working conditions, reasonable supervision that respected the individual's human dignity, and, not least, proper wages and monetary incentives.[16] Before the war he had argued that Germans, unlike Americans, did not work only for material gain, and so could be expected to make do with lower wages in order to preserve the competitiveness of German industry,[17] but he now admitted the importance of

[14] Schlesinger, *Psychotechnik und Betriebswissenschaft*, 33–36.

[15] In this respect he differed significantly from Wichard von Moellendorff (1881–1937), another prominent engineer and "technological utopian" whose views on the potential of scientific management to solve the problem of work were very similar to Schlesinger's. After the revolution of 1918, as undersecretary in the Reich Ministry of Economics, Moellendorff collaborated with the socialist Rudolf Wissell to implement a program of "practical socialization" with the aim of creating a new order based on corporatist principles and superior to both capitalism and Marxist socialism, but when their proposals were rejected in the summer of 1919, he concluded that his dream of a "conservative" or "German" socialism would not be realized in the near future. While Schlesinger remained in the thick of the struggle, Moellendorff henceforth turned his back on the Weimar republic, which he and his fellow "conservative revolutionaries" regarded as unworthy of the German nation. See Wichard von Moellendorff, *Konservativer Sozialismus* (Hamburg: Hanseatische Verlags-Anstalt, 1932); Klaus Braun, *Konservatismus und Gemeinwirtschaft. Eine Studie über Wichard von Moellendorff* (Duisburg: Walter Braun, 1978); Lothar Burchardt, "Technischer Fortschritt und sozialer Wandel. Das Beispiel der Taylorismus-Rezeption," in *Deutsche Technikgeschichte*, ed. Wilhelm Treue (Göttingen: Vandenhoeck & Ruprecht, 1977), 77; and Jeffrey Herf's chapter, "Engineers as Ideologues," in his *Reactionary Modernism. Technology, Culture and Politics in Weimar and the Third Reich* (Cambridge: Cambridge University Press, 1984), 152–88. Moellendorff, not discussed by Herf, was a typical "reactionary modernist."

[16] Schlesinger, *Psychotechnik und Betriebswirtschaft*, 27.

[17] Georg Schlesinger, "Betriebsführung und Betriebswissenschaft," *Technik und Wirtschaft* 6 (1913): 545 and 568, cited in Hinrichs, *Um die Seele*, 67–68.

adequate pay as a motivator and therefore supported trade union demands for higher wages and shorter hours.[18]

Although he consistently maintained that rationalization and the humanization of work were essentially compatible, Schlesinger's nearly utopian faith in the progressive character of the rationalization process was balanced by the practical engineer's awareness of its darker side. On the one hand, he insisted that the increasing specialization and mechanization involved in the rationalization process, far from leading to spiritual impoverishment (*geistige Verödung*) of the workers, would create enhanced opportunities for satisfying work, while scientific management would make it possible to maintain a degree of Arbeitsfreude in rationalized industry.[19] On the other hand, he acknowledged that many large mechanized factories were creating jobs that were irredeemably boring, fatiguing, and impersonal, and that only certain workers, generally those drawn from rural areas, could withstand the monotony and stress they entailed.[20] In addition, he admitted that scientific management as currently practiced was not yet capable of engineering joy in work and social harmony, that the science of psychotechnics was still in its infancy, and that greater efforts, involving both academics and practitioners, would be needed to discover satisfactory ways to entrench Arbeitsfreude in rationalized industry.[21]

The rationalization movement in Germany counted engineers among its chief proponents, but this did not mean that the majority of engineers shared Schlesinger's enthusiasm for scientific management. Typical of the skeptics was the industrial engineer Gustav Frenz, who published a critique of Taylorism in 1920. Frenz insisted that German workers would never accept the Taylorist incentive and premium system, nor adapt willingly to a psychotechnical selection process that disregarded the individual's wishes or was designed to weed out the "unfit." Moreover he argued that, because only happy workers were truly productive, the aim of good management must be to find satisfying work for the *majority* of workers, not just for a pre-selected elite. Overspecialization and "de-skilling," the inevitable accompaniments of Taylorism, were bound to result in a diminution of Arbeitsfreude for which neither higher pay nor intensified supervision could compensate.[22]

As remedies, Frenz advocated decentralization of industry and the search for alternatives to the Taylorist organization of work. But his

---

[18] Ebert and Hausen, "Schlesinger," 330.   [19] Ebert and Hausen, "Schlesinger," 330.
[20] Schlesinger, *Psychotechnik und Betriebswissenschaft*, 96–98.
[21] Schlesinger, *Psychotechnik und Betriebswissenschaft*, 156.
[22] Gustav Frenz, *Kritik des Taylor-Systems* (Berlin: Julius Springer, 1920), 38–45.

main concern was to warn against an overly intellectual approach to the problems of industry. Expressing views undoubtedly widespread among people whose traditional methods of work were threatened by the advance of rationalization, including practicing engineers, skilled workers, and supervisory personnel, he denied the claim of academically trained engineers like Schlesinger that *more* scientific knowledge was needed to solve the problem of work. In Frenz's view, higher education was of little value to the practitioner. He therefore suggested that the growing gap between planning and execution could best be overcome not by upgrading engineering studies or engaging in research but by forming industrial engineers, promoted from the shop floor, into a corps of "Pioneers of Labor."[23]

Opposition to Taylorism among German engineers also had other sources. By the mid-1920s, those who remained true to the technocratic ideal were more inclined to tout the American automobile magnate Henry Ford rather than the industrial engineer Taylor as the best guide to a future of improved productive efficiency, social harmony, and humanized work.[24] One of the first to change allegiance was Paul Rieppel, an academic engineer who in 1925 published an account of the Ford works. In his book, Rieppel praised that industrialist's organizational achievements and attributed Ford's alleged success in overcoming the conflict between labor and management to the fact that he treated the workers as human beings, got them interested in their own work, allowed them to share in the success of the company, and persuaded them that he and they were working together for the good of the country. Through high wages, opportunities for advancement, and stress on the greatness of the common goal, Ford raised their standard of living and was said also to have given the workers satisfaction and joy in work.[25]

Fordismus was not confined to engineers. This was demonstrated publicly at an academic conference on the theme of Ford and the Germans sponsored by the Soziales Museum in Frankfurt in 1926, which brought together speakers from a variety of disciplines.[26] Indeed, the person who did most to proclaim Ford as the new prophet of rationalization was an Austrian-born economist, Friedrich von Gottl-Ottlilien-

[23] Frenz, *Kritik des Taylor-Systems*, 112–13.

[24] Maier, "Between Taylorism and Technocracy," 54–55; Walter G. Waffenschmidt, "Ford und Ford Literatur," *ASS* 53 (1925): 232–39.

[25] Paul Rieppel, *Ford-Betriebe und Ford-Methoden* (Munich, 1925), 23–33, cited in Berg, *Deutschland und Amerika*, 101–102.

[26] Frankfurt, Soziales Museum, *Ford und Wir. Fünf Beiträge zur deutschen Umstellung. Vorträge auf der 'Sechsten Tagung für Werkspolitik' in Frankfurt a. M. am 4. und 5. Juni 1926* (Berlin: Industrieverlag Spaeth und Linde, 1926).

feld (1868–1958). Gottl, professor of theoretical economics at the University of Berlin from 1926, had been one of the first people before the war to employ the term "rationalization" in Germany.[27] In the 1920s, his pamphlet *Fordismus?*[28] did much to shape the German debate on scientific management. In it, Gottl accused Taylor's German followers of having debased the latter's original message by pushing technical considerations to the point where they became opposed to good sense. The resulting *Taylorei* (which he contrasted with Taylorism proper) had turned the factory into a soulless mechanism, in which the personality of the worker was exterminated.[29] A paradise for the unskilled, it was the source of tragedy for the skilled worker; nor did it help the consumer because it failed to lower prices.

According to Gottl, Lenin's attempt to impose Taylorism on backward Russia was bound to fail: although it did provide work suitable for Russian coolies, it required a higher degree of previous industrial development than was present in the Soviet Union. On the other hand, Gottl agreed with Frenz that German workers were too sophisticated to adapt to Taylorism, and so concluded that Taylor's approach was also unsuited to the much more advanced German situation. He concluded that Taylorei could in no way solve the problems of economic and technological rationalization, much less overcome conflict in the sphere of industrial relations.[30]

By contrast, Gottl believed that Fordismus constituted a true amalgam of economic and technical reason.[31] Echoing Rieppel, he maintained that Ford, far from squelching the intellect and initiative of his workers, demanded these qualities and so encouraged the development of his employees' personalities. Moreover, the workers in his factories were well-paid, had enjoyed an eight-hour day since 1914, and could take pleasure in being part of an exciting organization that offered interesting work and the satisfaction of serving society. Finally, the Ford concern passed on the lower costs due to self-financing to its workers in the form of higher wages and to consumers in the form of lower prices, thereby increasing the size of the market for its product and benefiting all concerned.[32]

Gottl also went into raptures about the innovations in production

[27] Giese, "Rationalisierung," in HA 2:3620.

[28] Friedrich von Gottl-Ottlilienfeld, *Fordismus. Von Frederick W. Taylor zu Henry Ford* (2d rev. ed.; Jena: Gustav Fischer, 1925). The book was first published in 1924. A third edition in 1926, subtitled "Über Industrie und technische Vernunft," was expanded by over one hundred pages to include a number of related writings. References below are to the second edition.

[29] Gottl, *Fordismus*, 5–6.   [30] Gottl, *Fordismus*, 7–9.   [31] Gottl, *Fordismus*, 10.

[32] Gottl, *Fordismus*, 14–23.

methods introduced by Ford. The assembly line with its conveyor belt was said to enable even unskilled workers to see themselves as part of a significant whole. Admittedly, many of the tasks such workers had to do were simple, but even in these cases skills could be improved by attention to detail, as Münsterberg had shown. What was mercifully absent was the element of drill insisted on by Taylor. Moreover, the possibility of advancement was ever present, although Gottl acknowledged that the majority of Ford workers showed little inclination to take advantage of their opportunities.[33]

Although Gottl praised many aspects of the Fordist organization of production, it was Ford's superior management style and ideology that seemed to him the greatest improvement over Taylorei. The Ford of Fordismus was a tireless worker who knew that work represented effort and was therefore capable of inspiring a spirit of work which to a great extent transformed the hardship of labor into "joy in achievement and in the common task," thus retaining "work as the content of life in place of mere sacrifice for that life."[34] Because firm and effective leadership enabled all Ford workers to see themselves as collaborators in a vast and worthwhile endeavor, they could freely accept the authority of management. Above all, by replacing the profit motive with an ethic of service,[35] Ford had created a new model of industrial relations based on the leader-follower principle.[36] Imposed from above by managers implementing a dictatorship of technical reason, Fordismus released a "joyfully activist spirit," the source of true community.[37] The result amounted to a "white socialism" ideally designed to counter Bolshevism.

Equalling Gottl in enthusiasm for Fordismus was Goetz Briefs (1889–1974), an influential economist-cum-sociologist who in 1928 established Germany's first Institute for Industrial Sociology at the Berlin TH.[38] Because German workers refused to be treated purely as factors of production, and because they were denied the opportunities for upward mobility required to make Taylorism work, Briefs like Gottl, judged Taylorism to be ill-adapted to Germany. What is more, he denied that Taylorist methods were equally suited to every kind of firm.[39] By contrast, he had only praise for Ford, the first capitalist who, in

[33] Gottl, *Fordismus*, 12–13.   [34] Gottl, *Fordismus*, 27.   [35] Gottl, *Fordismus*, 28–29.
[36] "Führer-Gefolgschaft." Gottl, *Fordismus*, 33.   [37] Gottl, *Fordismus*, 35.
[38] See Manfred Wilke, "Goetz Briefs und das Institut für Betriebssoziologie an der Technischen Hochschule Berlin," in Rürup, *Wissenschaft und Gesellschaft*, 1:335–51.
[39] Goetz Briefs, "Rationalisierung der Arbeit" in Industrie- und Handelskammer zu Berlin, *Die Bedeutung der Rationalisierung für das deutsche Wirtschaftsleben* (Berlin: Georg Stilke, 1928), 40.

pursuit of profit, had managed to realize the social potential of capitalism with respect to both worker and consumer.[40]

What Briefs chiefly admired about the American auto magnate was not his management philosophy and ethic of service, but the fact that Ford had abandoned Taylor's exaggerated rationalism and contributed to the humanization of work by successfully integrating the worker into the "higher rhythm" of the conveyor belt. True, assembly-line workers had to subordinate themselves to the tempo of the conveyor belt, but Briefs maintained that there nevertheless was room in a Ford plant for reflection and for participation. He also claimed that by abolishing the powerful estimating department that Taylor had relied on to coordinate all subordinate functions, Ford had brought workers once more into direct contact with their work.

Germany's academic engineers, economists, and industrial sociologists, represented by Schlesinger, Gottl, and Briefs, contributed a great deal to the rationalization movement of the 1920s and to the expansion of Arbeitswissenschaft. The growth of Arbeitswissenschaft owed much to their belief that it was essential to learn more about the complex relationship between human beings and their work if the productive efficiency of the German economy were to increase without doing permanent damage to the individual and society. It was accompanied by increasing overlap between Arbeitswissenschaft and Arbeitskunde.[41] This phenomenon can be clearly demonstrated in the case of German psychology, which at this time came to play a key role in the science of work.

Whereas most academic psychologists before the war had prided themselves on their status as "pure" scientists, after 1918 their successors—particularly the heirs to the tradition of psychophysics associated with Wundt, Meumann, and Kraepelin—willingly used their research, teaching, and publications to address the everyday concerns of industry and had few compunctions about accepting financial support from business.[42] Psychotechnicians continued to take the lead in applying psychological knowledge to the problems of industry, but experimental psychologists and psychophysiologists as well, impelled by concern with the manifold practical problems facing the nation, were prepared to make a practical contribution. For their part, the psychotechnicians, even when employed directly by industrial enterprises and keen to

[40] Briefs, "Rationalisierung der Arbeit," 41.

[41] See "Arbeitswissenschaft" in HA, 1:418–23, and Johannes Riedel, ed., Arbeitskunde. Grundlagen, Bedingungen and Ziele der wirtschaftlichen Arbeit (Leipzig: B. G. Teubner, 1925).

[42] Paul Devinat, Scientific Management in Europe. ILO Studies and Reports, Series B, no. 17 (Geneva, 1927), 33.

prove their economic worth, continued to stress their academic credentials and generally presented themselves as independent experts dedicated to the general welfare rather than as agents of management. The result was a rapprochement between pure and applied psychology, based on the belief that rationalization was a national imperative, potentially of benefit to all classes, and that psychology could help to overcome, or at least minimize, any conflict between the requirements of higher productivity and the human needs of the individual worker. The ethos of the psychologists was thus very like that of the academic engineers with whom they often worked in tandem along the lines advocated by Schlesinger.

Weimar psychologists who contributed to the science of work in the interwar period were obsessed with the question of whether it was possible to reconcile human beings with their work in rationalized industry, and, if so, how this might best be done. Prominent among them was Walther Moede (1888–1958), Schlesinger's colleague at the Berlin TH. Founder of Germany's first Institute for Industrial Psychotechnics, editor of numerous journals, including *Praktische Psychologie* and *Industrielle Psychotechnik*, psychological adviser to the German railways, and active teacher and researcher, Moede was well placed to influence the way Germans thought about work. He set about tackling the problem of alienation and used his influence to propagate the view that psychology could and should play a major part in the humanization of work and the restoration of Arbeitsfreude.[43]

Together with his colleagues and pupils, who included both psychologists and industrial engineers, Moede used experimental and statistical techniques to develop better vocational tests and selection procedures. But he also encouraged efforts to create a healthy, attractive work environment, to improve industrial training, and to restructure work so as to minimize its psychological costs. On the assumption that there was no inherent conflict between the requirements of productive efficiency and the psychological wellbeing of the individual—or at least that these could be brought into an acceptable balance—he assigned psychotechnics the mission of arranging work to best advantage from the standpoint of safety, economic efficiency, and the worker's welfare.[44]

Even more enthusiastic about the contribution psychology could

[43] Like Münsterberg, Moede believed that industrial psychology was important "for the welfare, joy and satisfaction of each individual and the community." Walther Moede, *Arbeitstechnik. Die Arbeitskraft: Schutz, Erhaltung, Steigerung* (Stuttgart: Ferdinand Enke, 1935), 262, citing the 1930 edition of his text.
[44] Moede, *Arbeitstechnik*, 1–7.

make to the rationalization of work, and rationalization to the welfare of humanity, was Professor Hans Rupp (1880–?) of the University of Berlin. Rupp believed that psychological theory, in particular the analysis of motivation in terms of drives, had implications for all types of work. In the case of the intrinsically unsatisfying jobs of the unskilled industrial labor force, particularly conveyor-assembly line work (*Fliessarbeit*), he favored further rationalization and automation on the grounds that far from setting intolerable limits to individual freedom, these actually rendered work less stressful and therefore freer.[45] Modern workers of this type could be motivated to do their best by the exercise of objective but firm control, a purposeful and sensible subdivision of tasks, the introduction of pauses to break up worktime, and the provision of carefully devised and timed non-monetary positive reinforcements to foster a sense of achievement that would, in turn, serve as an incentive to improved performance.[46]

In Rupp's view, people employed in higher professional, organizational work and in creative occupations were also in need of positive reinforcement. Unlike factory workers, such individuals were thought to perform better if they were largely freed from external controls and allowed to participate in the work design. But Rupp insisted that whatever their station, all workers had a right to be placed in accordance with their abilities and level of aspirations, to experience success, to be shown their place in the larger scheme of things, and to be treated with respect. Above all, it was essential to ensure that all work was fairly remunerated; despite his belief that German and European workers had a stronger creative drive than Americans (who were spurred on more by personal ambition and preferred high earnings above security), Rupp was convinced that monetary incentives provided the prime stimulus for good performance, also in Germany.[47]

Although Rupp stressed that increased productivity rested on a correct balance between incentives and compulsion and between monetary and non-monetary incentives, he, too, insisted that the end goal of rationalization was not economic efficiency but human welfare. The goal of psychotechnics must be to restructure work not so much to save energy as to satisfy the individual's essential need (*Lebensbedürfnis*) to keep busy, grow, move towards higher goals, and become personally involved with the task in hand. With a final rhetorical flourish, he set

[45] Hans Rupp, "Die Aufgaben der psychotechnischen Arbeitsrationalisierung," *Psychotechnische Zeitschrift* 3 (1928): 178.

[46] Rupp, "Aufgaben," 173–75. Rupp opposed premium wage schemes on the grounds that these led to premature exhaustion through exaggerated intensification of work.

[47] Rupp, "Aufgaben," 180–81.

psychotechnics the task of rationalizing not only work, but also leisure, and, in the long run, all the manifold activities of Life.[48]

Fritz Giese (1890–1935), director of a psychotechnical laboratory at the TH in Stuttgart and a specialist in vocational testing, similarly assigned industrial psychology and psychotechnics major roles in solving the modern dilemma. He was active as a consultant, wrote textbooks, and contributed to the leading psychotechnical journals, but he also worked to extend the range of Arbeitswissenschaft as a whole,[49] for he was convinced that the problem of work was best tackled in an interdisciplinary fashion, by drawing on everything from medicine to psychology, sociology, and philosophy.[50] Indeed, Giese maintained that despite the substantial contribution of German scientists to the psychology of work, particularly in his own eminently practical area of vocational testing, the land of Hegel, Marx, and Engels had most to offer the world in the speculative realm.[51]

At the other extreme from the metaphysically oriented Giese, and more in tune with the spirit of Neue Sachlichkeit, was the psychophysical experimentalist Edgar Atzler (1887–1938), head of the Kaiser-Wilhelm-Institut für Arbeitsphysiologie ("physiology of work"). Founded in 1913 out of concern for the welfare of the workers, Atzler's institute after the war sponsored numerous laboratory studies dealing with the biological and medical aspects of work, especially the effects of fatigue and monotony on productivity.[52] In view of the practical implications of this research, and prompted by the desire to see the institute's findings used to solve real problems, Atzler in 1929 transferred his activities from Berlin to Dortmund, a city in the heartland of German heavy industry.[53]

[48] Hans Rupp, "Die Aufgaben der psychotechnischen Arbeits Rationalisierung," *Psychotechnische Zeitschrift* 4 (1929): 17–19.
[49] Giese edited a two-volume *Handwörterbuch der Arbeitswissenschaft* (1927–30) and the series, *Handbuch der Arbeitswissenschaft*.
[50] Fritz Giese, *Philosophie der Arbeit*, vol. 10 of *Handbuch der Arbeitswissenschaft* (Halle: Carl Marhold, 1932), 73. Among other broad issues of the day, Giese addressed himself to "educational ideals in the machine age." See his *Bildungsideale im Maschinenzeitalter*, vol. 7 of the *Handbuch der Arbeitswissenschaft* (Halle: Carl Marhold, 1931).
[51] Giese, *Philosophie der Arbeit*, 77–78.   [52] Hinrichs, *Um die Seele*, 84–85.
[53] Hinrichs, *Um die Seele*, 84 n.172. Like most German students of work, Atzler claimed to be neutral in the conflict between capital and labor, and therefore denied that he had sold out to big business. In point of fact, the institute's move, although assisted by funds proffered by industry, was met with suspicion by some employers as well as union leaders, the former fearing that they would be subjected to socio-ethical lectures, the latter worried lest his scientific findings be used to intensify the exploitation of labor. See Richard Woldt, *Arbeitswandlungen in der Industriewelt*. Betriebssoziologische Studien 1 (Münster: Wirtschafts- und Sozialwissenschaftlicher Verlag, 1933), 115.

Acting on the assumption that the essential interests of business were fully compatible with, and indeed best served by, the humanization of work, Atzler and his associates rejected the Taylorist principle of *maximum* output generally subscribed to by the psychotechnicians and instead urged employers to adopt an *optimal* work design that would maintain and enhance the wellbeing of their labor force over the long term. As Professor Durig of Vienna explained in a compendium edited by Atzler, reforms introduced on the basis of psychophysical experimental research addressing the problem of fatigue were meant to improve the physical and mental health of the workers and increase their Arbeitsfreude, as well as enhance productivity and profits.[54] Specifically, Durig recommended the adaptation of machines to people, redesign of the workplace to take into account the workers' natural rhythm and to avoid one-sided wear and tear, the institution of breaks and alternation of tasks, the abolition of all unnecessary drudgery and, above all, an end to the intensification and speeding up of work.[55]

Without denying that psychotechnicians and psychophysiologists could contribute to the humanization of rationalized production, other psychologists felt that this goal could only be achieved if a real effort was also made to reform industrial training. One of the pioneers in this regard was Johannes Riedel (1889–1971), a graduate engineer who had also studied law, economics, philosophy, and psychology at the universities of Leipzig and Dresden, and who had familiarized himself with the problems of industry before the war by working as an engineering consultant.[56] The experience of revolution turned Riedel, like many other educated German patriots, into a determined antisocialist. Convinced that socialism both encouraged and fed on the distressing negativism about work currently characteristic of German labor, he decided to analyze worker motivation in the hope of discovering a way to restore the German will to work.[57]

In his *Der Wille zur Arbeit* Riedel sought to flesh out the theory first propounded in 1905 by Herkner who had emphasized the close link between motivation and economic success in his *Bedeutung der Arbeitsfreude*. His aim was to achieve a rational organization of labor in mechanized industry that would be compatible if not with Arbeitsfreude,

[54] Dr. Arnold Durig, "Die Ermüdung im praktischen Betrieb," in Edgar Atzler, ed., *Körper und Arbeit. Handbuch der Arbeitsphysiologie* (Leipzig: Georg Thieme, 1927), 524–25.

[55] Durig, "Ermüdung im praktischen Betrieb," 516–17.

[56] See Martin Kipp, *Arbeitspädagogik in Deutschland: Johannes Riedel* (Hannover: Hermann Schroedel, 1978), 25.

[57] See also Ferdinand Graf von Degenfeld-Schonburg, *Die Motive des volkswirtschaftlichen Handelns und der deutsche Marxismus* (Tübingen: J.C.B. Mohr, 1920). A conservative economist, Degenfeld was led to the study of motivation by the same concerns as was Riedel.

then at least with *Arbeitsfreudigkeit*, a positive attitude to work.[58] In his view, placing the right person in the right job was just the first step toward a rational reordering of work.[59] Thereafter, proper supervision, the creation of a good work environment, and above all on-the-job training to improve skills and inculcate a positive attitude to work were essential to maintain and enhance motivation. Indeed, Riedel became convinced that education was one of the most constructive ways to reconcile productive efficiency with the needs of the individual worker. He therefore advocated the institution of extensive company-sponsored educational programs, including regular lectures during working hours. Supplemented by slides, films, and demonstrations, these were designed to inform the workers about technological developments, the products of the competition, and other relevant topics. In addition, instructors would help individual workers to improve their performance, for example by showing them instances of good and bad work and by teaching them how to monitor their work. Steps would also be taken both to persuade supervisors and managers that it was their responsibility to discover and overcome dissatisfactions before these had a chance to affect performance and also to equip them with the human-relations skills that would enable them to lead the workers to produce willingly and well.[60]

Riedel's views on the problem of work reached a wider public through the major compendium on Arbeitskunde which he edited for publication in 1925, but it was only towards the end of the decade, when he had become associated with Weimar Germany's most important center for the reform of industrial training, the *Deutsches Institut für Technische Arbeitsschulung* (Dinta), that his pedagogic ideas became truly influential.[61] Moreover, although Riedel and his Dinta colleagues stressed the importance of the "human factor" in industry and employed the rhetoric of Arbeitsfreude, they were more interested in raising productivity and averting social discord than in minimizing the psychological trauma experienced by the individual worker engaged in rationalized production. The opposite can be said of Adolf Friedrich (1892–1963), a practicing engineer who, like Riedel, looked to psychology for answers to the problems of modern industry and shared the latter's belief that proper industrial training was of critical importance if modern humanity was to be reconciled with work.[62]

[58] Johannes Riedel, *Der Wille zur Arbeit* (Dresden: Zahn & Jaensch, 1921).
[59] Riedel, *Wille zur Arbeit*, 19–32.   [60] Riedel, *Wille zur Arbeit*, 43–51.
[61] Gerhardt P. Bunk, *Erziehung und Industriearbeit. Modelle betrieblichen Lernens und Arbeitens Erwachsener* (Weinheim: Beltz, 1972), 217–19.
[62] On Friedrich, see Bunk, *Erziehung und Industriearbeit*, 79–185. Additional information

After obtaining an engineering diploma from the Braunschweig TH, Friedrich became an employee at Krupp, where he eventually headed a 250-person division for applied psychotechnics. During the war, his laboratory sought new ways to raise the quality of the labor force by releasing the latent strengths of the company's employees.[63] Resuming his studies, Friedrich worked under Moede in Berlin and acquired the academic credentials in psychology that qualified him to leave Krupp for an instructorship at the TH in Hannover in 1922. By 1924 he was professor of psychology and head of the Institute for Social Psychology at Karlsruhe. A doer rather than a researcher by inclination, Friedrich also acted as consultant for a number of major firms, including Siemens and Hanomag.[64]

Like many other German psychotechnicians, Friedrich rejected the "American" emphasis on purely material values and immediate profits in favor of an ethical approach and put long-term productivity in the course of the worker's lifetime above short-term profit. He therefore recommended that instead of using pre-testing to weed out the unfit, existing employees be tested as a preliminary to personal counselling that would help them to make full use of their abilities. Similarly, his aim was to train *Tatmenschen*, practical and flexible activists, rather than using drill to produce highly specialized and biddable operatives as Taylor had recommended. In sum, what he advocated was a "healthy" Taylorism that would combine the quest for technical efficiency with respect for the human factor.[65] Imbued with the utopian spirit of the time, Friedrich insisted that joy in work was an essential component of a truly human existence as well as a prerequisite for efficient work: he convinced himself that he would be able to persuade employers, engineers, and the public at large to make it a reality for every industrial worker through skills enhancement (*Berufsertüchti-*

---

was obtained from his daughter, Dorothée Friedrich, whom I visited in Landshut February 7 and 8, 1981. In addition to answering my questions in an extended interview, Fräulein Friedrich gave me access to the small Adolf Friedrich archive in her possession.

[63] "Die Beseelung des Arbeitsprozesses. Ein Besuch des psychotechnischen Instituts der Firma Krupp. Messung der Arbeitseignung. Heranbildung von Qualitätsarbeitern," *Essener Anzeiger*, 17 August 1922, 3.; Peter Hinrichs and Lothar Peter, *Industrielle Friede. Arbeitswissenschaft, Rationalisierung und Arbeiterbewegung in der Weimarer Republik* (Cologne: Pahl-Rugenstein, 1976), 51.

[64] Devinat, *Scientific Management*, 81 n.1. Friedrich's lucrative but time-consuming extra-academic activities were deplored by Willy Hellpach, his predecessor at the Institute of Social Psychology. Hellpach, impressed by Friedrich's work at Krupp, had been instrumental in securing his appointment, but soon regretted his choice, because Friedrich showed no taste for academic teaching or experimental research and eventually allowed the institute to collapse. Willy Hellpach, *Wirken in Wirren*, 2:167–68.

[65] Bunk, *Erziehung und Industriearbeit*, 85.

gung) combined with thoughtful structuring of work (*Arbeitsgestaltung*). Together, these would make it possible for people once more to master their means of production, as in the days of the crafts.

On the assumption that every individual possessed an innate drive to Arbeitsfreude or *Schaffensfreude* ("joy in creating"), Friedrich argued that the restoration of joy in work could be achieved quite simply by abolishing anything that hindered the full development of the worker's natural capacities. For this reason, even workers destined for tasks requiring minimal skills were to be given careful prior training, as well as ample opportunities to practice what they had learned, to improve on their past performance, and, wherever possible, to monitor their own progress—all under the guidance of organizational engineers who would act as role models and spokesmen for those in their charge.[66] Good management by people trained to motivate and lead could eventually be expected to produce a stress-free, harmonious work environment, and a truly rational organization of production.[67]

Friedrich's views up to this point were firmly rooted in his own experience at Krupp, where, during the war, he had developed techniques for expeditiously training workers newly arrived from the country, as well as wounded veterans and the handicapped. For the rest, his thinking echoed ideas current among his socially conscious contemporaries. But by 1925, when the rationalization movement hit its stride and Sachlichkeit was in vogue, Friedrich moved in the opposite direction. Converted to Christian Science, he took as his motto "*Gott-Mensch-Arbeit*" ("God-Man-Work"), and henceforth approached the problem of joyless work in a quasi-mystical manner derived from belief in the power of mind over matter.[68] Perhaps under the influence of his wife who went into analysis in the early 1920s,[69] he also began to employ psychoanalytical concepts when discussing human motivation, for example talking of a frequently "unconscious" striving towards the Good or God, referring to education as therapy, and urging management to help workers overcome their inner resistance to assigned tasks.[70]

Notwithstanding the religious and metaphysical language in which he presented his argument, Friedrich managed to persuade a number of

[66] Adolf Friedrich, "Menschenwirtschaft," *Wirtschaftliche Nachrichten aus dem Ruhrbezirk*, 5 April 1923, 72–73.
[67] Adolf Friedrich, "Menschenwirtschaft," a talk to the VDI in Hannover, *Zeitschrift des VDI* 68 (April 1924): 1–9. Offprint, DF.
[68] Adolf Friedrich, "Gott—Mensch—Arbeit," *Der Arbeitgeber*, 15, no. 20 (1925): 490–94, elaborated in *Gott, Mensch und Arbeit* (Freiburg: Magnum Opus, 1926). Friedrich's theology at this time appears to have combined Christian Science with Zen Buddhism.
[69] DF, interview.
[70] Adolf Friedrich, "Befreiende Arbeit," *Reichsarbeitsblatt*, 25 April 1925, 266–68.

industrialists engaged in the process of rationalization to experiment with his ideas. His chief instrument was the *Anstalt für Arbeitskunde* (AfA) which he established in 1927 with the initial support of fourteen Saarland industrial concerns.[71] Within three years most of these had introduced training facilities and counselling services for their employees along the lines advocated by Friedrich. It also pressed on member firms the results of its own psychotechnical laboratory and undertook research to improve work methods. Finally, it encouraged the training of supervisory personnel to provide the skilled leadership on which Friedrich's entire scheme depended.

While its most immediate impact was on the industry of the Saar, the activities of the AfA were widely and favorably reported in the German and international press. Thus the *Frankfurter Zeitung* in 1929, noting Friedrich's success in getting employers to take up his plans, praised him for making the technical and personal needs of the individual the starting point for concrete efforts to overcome the problems of industrial work.[72] In the same year, the International Rationalization Institute in Geneva described the work of the AfA in its trilingual monthly, commented on its skillful psychological educational activities, and noted that the workers seemed to appreciate the chance to improve their skills, raise earnings, and experience job satisfaction (*Arbeitsbefriedigung*). According to this report, the Saar experiments were paying for themselves, in the process demonstrating the secret of harmonious American industrial relations hitherto regarded by skeptical Europeans as utopian.[73]

Friedrich did not confine his efforts to the AfA. In 1929 he gave a three-day course on the problems of rationalization and humanization to the vocational school association of Saxony, in which he stressed the importance of a human-centered educational and industrial policy that would regard increased productive efficiency merely as a by-product of its chief objective, the full flowering of the individual.[74] Later that year, he lectured the membership of the Association of German Employer Organizations (VdA) on the responsibility of management

[71] Another firm joined in 1929. See Bunk, *Erziehung und Industriearbeit*, 167–68, n.140, for details on the membership and aims of the AfA.

[72] "Der Arbeiter und seine Arbeit. Neue Versuche zur Überwindung der Problematik der Industriearbeit," *Frankfurter Zeitung*, 15 January 1925.

[73] H. von Haan, "Menschenwirtschaftlich orientierte Rationalisierungstätigkeit im Saargebiet," *Mitteilungen des internationalen Rationalisierungs Institutes* (Geneva). 3 (January 1929): 11–14.

[74] M. Rossberg, "Psychologie der Arbeit und Berufsschule. Zum Kursus Prof. Dr. Ing. A. Friedrich, Karlsruhe vom 25. bis 27. März in Leipzig," *Die Deutsche Berufsschule* 38 (1929): 327–39.

for establishing a link between people and their work *through* work, by allowing individuals as much as possible to exercise personal control over their jobs and thus develop their full potential.[75] Then in 1931 he published two short books on scientific management in which he once more gave the restoration of joy in work a central place.[76] Finally, in 1932, he gave this theme its most eloquent expression in *Die Arbeits-freude des Lebens,* based on a talk to officials of the United Steel Company's Mining Division in Hamborn. Summing up his position on the interrelationships among Arbeitsfreude, rationalization, and the current national crisis, this pamphlet reaffirmed Friedrich's belief that good teaching, leadership, and supervision could solve the problem of work and thereby the social question.[77]

Friedrich developed a number of practical ways to motivate workers and restore their capacity for joyful work, and he also had a degree of success in convincing industry to give primacy to the needs and desires of the individual in its training and management programs. Nevertheless, many of his fellow psychologists were not convinced that Friedrich's method was suited to achieve his ends: they tended increasingly to believe that the problem of work derived from flaws in the relationship between people or groups of people rather than between people and their work, and that alienation could therefore never be overcome by dealing only with individual workers.

An important role in the transition to this new approach was played by the social psychologist Willy Hellpach, whose contribution to the prewar science of work we have already described. Long concerned with the effect of modernization on mental health, Hellpach, as first director of the Institute of Applied Psychology established at Karlsruhe in 1921, remained true to the spirit that had motivated his involvement in the social question before the war. However, the rapid advance of the rationalization movement after 1918, which he interpreted as the Americanization of industrial work under the influence of Taylor and Ford, led him to redirect his research efforts.

In a far-sighted article of 1921 in the engineering journal *Technik und Wirtschaft,* Hellpach denied that he was an obscurantist advocating a return to an irrecoverable past, but warned that cold rationality (*Sachlichkeit*) was an inadequate approach to current problems: the rationalization movement could only achieve its own objective of increased productive efficiency if it took the human factor fully into account and took note of the impact on individual performance of such qualities as practice, motivation, interest, and enthusiasm.[78] At the same time, however, Hellpach maintained that the social component of the problem of work was critical, and so raised questions about the methodology of experimental psychotechnics as currently practiced by scholar's like Moede. In his view, the socio-psychological aspects of industrial work could only be grasped by those willing to subordinate experimentation and the compilation of statistics to a new "scholarly" method based on "experience, understanding and explanation."[79]

Gruppenproduktion, "group production," the first publication of Hellpach's institute, was itself an example of the approach he favored. A brief description of a practical experiment carried out in 1919 at the Daimler-Benz automotive factory in Stuttgart by a company engineer, Richard Lang, was followed by an interpretative essay in which Hellpach expanded on the significance and implications of Lang's findings. Lang, attempting to combine the advantages of pure mass production with those of the small workshop, had separated an independent group from the remainder of the factory floor and given it the task of producing a set of components from raw materials to finished object. Among the potential disadvantages of the new organization of work was the need for more space, a certain duplication of machines and tools, and, possibly, the need for more supervisors. Among the advantages he listed were decreased transport costs, increased effectiveness of supervision, and better quality control. As a by-product, the workers were expected to demonstrate an increased sense of responsibility and greater *Arbeitslust* ("zest for work"), because they could now more readily see the contribution each individual was making to the final product. The workers would still be condemned to do uniform and monot-

[78] Willy Hellpach, "Die geistigen Kräfte der Wirtschaft," *Technik und Wirtschaft* 14, no. 1, reprinted in *Willy Hugo Hellpach, Universitas Litterarum*, ed. Gerhard Hess and Wilhelm Witte (Stuttgart: F. Enke, 1948), 184–85.

[79] "Das wesentlich Sozialpsychische ist überwiegend nur mit der 'geisteswissenschaftlichen' Methodik des Erlebens, Verstehens und Deutens zu packen." Willy Hellpach, "Geleitwort," in Richard Lang and Willy Hellpach, *Gruppenfabrikation*. Sozialpsychologische Forschungen des Instituts für Sozialpsychologie an der Technischen Hochschule Karlsruhe, 1 (Berlin: Julius Springer, 1922), vi. *Gruppenproduktion* is discussed sympathetically in Günther Wachtler, *Humanisierung der Arbeit und Industriesoziologie* (Stuttgart: Kohlhammer, 1979), 73–80, and from a critical Marxist viewpoint in Hinrichs, *Erziehung und Industriearbeit*, 170–79.

onous work, but it was hoped that a greater sense of group participation would compensate for the fact that their jobs lacked intrinsic interest.[80]

Hellpach began his commentary with an analysis of what he termed the "factory problem." Arguing that the evil effects of the factory system had been discussed seriously only by backward-looking economic romantics and a few bourgeois social reformers,[81] he maintained that no one before Lang had attempted to restructure the factory while retaining, or even enhancing, the advantages conferred by mechanization and the division of labor. According to Hellpach, Lang's experiment called into question the generally held assumption that modern industry had to take the form of large factories in which anonymous masses were assembled in a single work-space, with disastrous results both for the individual and society. Even from the point of view of the rationalized concern (as Ford, alone, had to some extent recognized), it was of the utmost importance to overcome the atomization of factory production and to turn the work space once more into a genuine living space, a *Lebensraum*.[82]

Despite his belief that group production as outlined by Lang could help to solve the factory problem, Hellpach was gloomy about the chances of its adoption by German industry, which tended to run its affairs on the basis of short-term calculations of profitability. At best, reforms designed to humanize work could be implemented surreptitiously under the guise of measures to enhance productive efficiency.[83] Nor did Hellpach share Lang's optimism regarding the psychological benefits of his scheme. Although he, personally, found the apparently effortless flow of the productive process enthralling as his eyes followed the work at the conveyor belt, he acknowledged that the apathy and lack of emotion on the faces of Lang's workers gave no evidence that these operatives shared these feelings; nor did they demonstrate any more attachment to their work or their workplace than did their compatriots in the standard Taylorized factory.[84] Reluctantly, he concluded that the prevailing attitudes of the workers, bred by their previous experiences and reinforced by the trade unions, for the time being, made it impossible to achieve the recovery of Arbeitsfreude by this route, and that the transformation of worker attitudes through a reformed system of education must precede any successful assault on the factory problem.

[80] Lang and Hellpach, *Gruppenfabrikation*, 3–4.
[81] Lang and Hellpach, *Gruppenfabrikation*, 7.
[82] Lang and Hellpach, *Gruppenfabrikation*, 8–27.
[83] Lang and Hellpach, *Gruppenfabrikation*, 53.
[84] Lang and Hellpach, *Gruppenfabrikation*, 57.

By the time Hellpach returned to this theme in an address to the German Werkbund's 1924 annual convention, he had followed the logic of his analysis and abandoned academe to pursue his educational reform ideas as Minister of Culture and Education for Baden.[85] He then turned to politics: after a term as Minister-President of Baden and an unsuccessful attempt to win the Federal presidency in 1925, he served in the Reichstag from 1928 to 1930. Although he accepted a professorship at Heidelberg in 1926 and continued to write prolifically, his academic interests shifted away from industrial psychology. Nevertheless, the notion of group work as a method of humanizing rationalized production continued to be associated with his name throughout the 1920s, when it was actively debated as a possible solution to the problem of work despite a lack of response on the part of German industry.

The second publication of Hellpach's institute, Eugen Rosenstock's *Werkstattaussiedlung*, was usually mentioned in the same breath with *Gruppenproduktion* in Weimar discussions of the problem of work.[86] Both books proposed to solve the problem of modern work by reorganizing the modern factory so as to integrate the individual into a smaller productive group. Moreover, both consisted of a commentary by an academically trained outsider on an experiment initiated by an individual personally involved in the productive process. In the case of Werkstattaussiedlung, the experimenter was a skilled turner, Eugen May, who like Taylor had worked his way up from the workbench to a supervisory position, and then, after years of increasingly unsatisfactory employment in a large factory setting, had decided to go out on his own. May described how he and two associates established an independent workshop near his home, in which they produced goods under contract for the firm of Kessler, using machines supplied by the parent company. According to May, he and his friends not only out-produced traditional workers by a large margin, but also, for the first time, were able to experience Arbeitsfreude and enjoy a decent family life.[87]

Whereas Hellpach subjected Lang's experiment to a critical appraisal, Rosenstock (1888–1973) used May's experience as the basis for a detailed scheme of industrial decentralization, whose aim was to enable individual laborers once more to bring their life and work into harmonious accord. A jurist by training, Rosenstock had originally spe-

[85] Hugo Borst und Willy Hellpach, *Das Problem der Industriearbeit. Zwei Vorträge gehalten auf der Sommertagung 1924 des Deutschen Werkbundes* (Berlin: Julius Springer, 1924), 39–70.

[86] Eugen Friedrich Moritz Rosenstock-Huessy, with Eugen May and Martin Grünberg, *Werkstattaussiedlung* (Berlin: Julius Springer, 1922).

[87] Eugen May, "Mein Lebenslauf," *Werkstattaussiedlung*, 16–71. See Hinrichs, *Erziehung und Industriearbeit*, 179–87, and Wachtler, *Humanisierung der Arbeit*, 80–83.

cialized in legal history, but the influence of the youth movement and his wartime experiences deflected him from this path. Persuaded by the revolutionary situation at war's end of the paramount need to find a non-Marxist solution to the problems of industrial society, he turned down chances for an academic, political, or clerical career, and instead accepted a position as co-editor (with Paul Riebensahm) of the newly established Daimler-Benz works newspaper in Stuttgart.[88] However, his non-academic career was brief. By 1921, he had already resigned from Daimler to become the first director of the newly established Academy of Labor in Frankfurt. This was followed in 1922 by a short period as a sociology student and instructor at the Darmstadt Technical University, and by his appointment in 1923 to the chair of legal history and sociology at Breslau University, a post he retained until his dismissal by the National Socialists in 1933.

During his time as a Daimler employee Rosenstock, who appears to have shared Hellpach's belief that personal involvement was a superior and more "scientific" source of insight than the traditional methods of Arbeitswissenschaft, came into direct contact with industrialists, engineers, technicians, and skilled workers, among them May and Richard Lang, whose group work experiment was originally described in the first issue of the Daimler company paper. On the basis of this brief experience in the world of industry, he concluded that the deterioration of work in the industrial age, which he regarded as the main cause of social unrest and cultural decline, did not stem from mechanization, or even from the division of labor, but rather from the fact that "man works to live, but where he works, he does not truly live."[89] Only his wage, linking the two worlds, enabled the modern worker to step out of the factory where he was a slave, into the realm of freedom. But, Rosenstock maintained, the freedom to spend money, to consume, could never form the basis of a satisfactory existence, especially for Germans. To realize true freedom and full humanity, it was necessary to restore meaning to work and to give work once more a central place in the life pattern of individuals.

Although he was in essential agreement with Hellpach on this point, Rosenstock could not share the latter's hope of transforming the Taylorized factory into a Lebensraum because he firmly believed that the modern factory, no matter how drastically restructured, could only pro-

---

[88] Eugen Rosenstock-Huessy, *Ja und Nein. Autobiographische Fragmente* (Heidelberg: Lambert Schneider, 1968), 77–78. Rosenstock, from a Jewish family, was a convert to Protestantism who devoted much of his later life to philosophical and theological matters. For biographical information, see *IBD/CE*, 2.

[89] Rosenstock, *Werkstattaussiedlung*, 5.

vide the majority of its employees with inferior work. Filled with nostalgia for the pre-industrial world of joyful work, Rosenstock proposed a thoroughly utopian solution: destruction of the current factory system and its replacement by a network of small quasi-independent workshops like that of May. Situated in close proximity to the workers' homes, these satellite shops would enable their employees to organize their own work and, ideally, to pass on their jobs to their sons as in former times.

A typical representative of Weimar's utopian phase, Rosenstock believed that it was necessary only to establish the truth of ideas by example in order to secure their adoption. Once his model shops had established the *Werkstatt* principle, he assumed that people would reject their previous false attitudes to work and dedicate themselves to implementing his ideals. Yet, like Hellpach, he made a point of insisting that he was not a reactionary utopian intent on turning the clock back to the pre-industrial age. Rather, his proposal would make it possible to restore the link between work and life without sacrificing the advantages of modern machine production. He also was realist enough to recognize that his scheme could only meet the needs of an elite of skilled, mature, male workers.

Rosenstock continued to defend his concepts for some time after utopianism had gone out of vogue. In a second book on the subject published in 1926[90] he once more conceded the purely exemplary character of his proposed workshops,[91] but, in an apparent concession to the contemporary enthusiasm for Sachlichkeit, he abandoned the purely normative mode employed in *Werkstattaussiedlung* and attempted to produce "evidence" to prove that current developments were going his way. He also represented his proposals as simply one variant of a broader humanization movement which he claimed was gaining support especially among social psychologists and Catholic academics.[92] Rosenstock admitted that both management and labor in Germany continued to be indifferent or even hostile to his ideas, but pointed with satisfaction to efforts to tackle the problem of labor alienation and Arbeitsfreude in other European countries. He also insisted that even the Americans, including Ford himself, were having second thoughts about the virtues of scale and were turning to the idea of smaller production units.[93]

[90] Eugen Rosenstock, *Lebensarbeit in der Industrie und Aufgaben einer europäischen Arbeitsfront* (Berlin: Julius Springer, 1926).

[91] Rosenstock, *Lebensarbeit in der Industrie*, 53–54.

[92] Rosenstock, *Lebensarbeit in der Industrie*, 43.

[93] Rosenstock, *Lebensarbeit in der Industrie*, 47.

In a further effort to dissociate his scheme from the reactionary agrarian romanticism characteristic of the utopian period, Rosenstock changed the designation of his workshops from *Siedlung* to *commandite*. Taken from the French, *commandite* was chosen to emphasize the affinity of his concept to experiments initiated among printers and subsequently extended to other trades through the pioneering efforts of Henri Dubreuil, who enjoyed the support of the ILO's Albert Thomas.[94] According to Rosenstock, the emergence of the *commandite*, an independent group employing the latest technology, proved that at least some European workers now saw their interests as distinct from the mass and were willing to cooperate with their employers in pursuit of these interests.[95]

Rosenstock argued that it was the commandite rather than Fordismus that represented the wave of the future. Showing the way to a new constitution of work that would span the generations by creating inheritable jobs, it promised to combine stability with opportunity for advancement, and to avoid the wasteful exploitation of physical and human resources characteristic of the American economy.[96] By following this route, he believed that Europe would be able to create a "new front," a "third way" between Americanism and Marxist communism, both of which continued to uphold the "outdated" principles of bourgeois scientific management.[97]

Despite his best efforts, Rosenstock was unable to convince his contemporaries that his approach was realistic. Forced to conclude that the ills of modern society could not be solved by reforming the organization of industrial work, he soon began with equal vigor to propagate the notion that the only possible sphere of human redemption was that part of a person's life spent away from work.[98] While still concerned to save at least some individuals from the barren fate industrial society had in store for them, after 1926 his main objective was to "free the soul from the straitjacket [*Panzer*] of work," using the power of education and religious faith to enrich leisure time and so bind up the wounds of the "soldiers of labor." Rosenstock still thought that the sense of community that would result from shared leisure activities might indirectly prepare the ground for an eventual reform of the productive process,[99]

[94] Rosenstock, *Lebensarbeit in der Industrie*, 43.

[95] Rosenstock, *Lebensarbeit in der Industrie*, 27–28.

[96] Rosenstock, *Lebensarbeit in der Industrie*, 41.

[97] Rosenstock, *Lebensarbeit in der Industrie*, 33–37.

[98] See, for example, Eugen Rosenstock, "Leben und Arbeit," *Zeitwende*, 4 (April 1928): 341–53, an expanded version of a talk given to the Kirchlich-Soziale Kongress in Düsseldorf, 5 October 1927.

[99] Rosenstock, "Leben und Arbeit," 353.

but he made no further effort to reform work as such, and left to others the task of elaborating the idea fundamental to both *Gruppenproduktion* and *Werkstattaussiedlung*: the critical importance of taking the social dimension into account in any attempt to solve the problem of modern work by humanizing rationalized production.

VIII

THE HUMANIZATION
OF INDUSTRIAL RELATIONS

ALTHOUGH Hellpach and Rosenstock failed to persuade contemporaries that alterations in the productive process were needed to overcome alienation and bridge the gap between work and life, their emphasis on the social dimensions of the problem of work had a decided impact on the movement for the humanization of work. The relation between the individual and work continued to be a major concern, but as the decade wore on the focus of reform efforts shifted to the areas of industrial relations and management practices. Those who agreed on the need to restore the "human factor" to a central place in rationalized production now thought primarily in terms of furthering a sense of community within the workplace, both among the workers and between labor and management.

Among academic disciplines, the main contributors to this endeavor were social psychology and sociology, but economics, labor law, and political science also played important roles. So did several new university departments and institutes of management studies founded in the 1920s to study the implications of the burgeoning science of work for the individual enterprise and to transmit the latest findings to people in a position to apply them. Finally, reform proposals came from people directly involved in the productive process who recognized the need for improving cooperation in the workplace, including spokesmen for both labor and employer associations, engineers, managers, and social workers.

The main question was whether the required reforms could be engineered by altering the organization of industrial relations or whether ways of thinking would have to change *before* institutions could be effectively modified to bring about the desired end of greater social harmony. When one examines reform efforts inspired by the former view, they seem to fall into three main groups. The first, which drew support largely from the organized labor movement and its sympathizers, involved attempts to humanize rationalized production by giving the workers a greater role in the decision-making process. The second assigned the responsibility for initiating changes to the employers, thereby preserving the essential prerogatives of management. The third argued that because only the state represented the interests of the nation as a whole, it had a duty to re-shape the legislation under which labor and management could resolve their conflicts.

There was, of course, a degree of overlap between these categories, as well as great diversity of opinion within each group. Moreover, the ensuing debate, although lively and productive of useful insights, was once again marred by the failure to define clearly what was meant by "rationalization" and "humanization," and produced no agreement on the key questions: Was humanization compatible with greater efficiency? And could it lead to the recovery of Arbeitsfreude?

By the early 1920s Germany had effectively turned its back on socialism. Capitalism not only survived the revolution that created the democratic Weimar Republic, but emerged triumphant from the inflationary crisis; in the era of relative stability that followed, German business was even able to retract some of the concessions made earlier to a militant working class. Although radicals of various stripes continued to advocate drastic changes in the status quo, under these circumstances a growing number of socialists thought it more realistic to join their non-socialist contemporaries in seeking to reform work within the framework of the capitalist economy.

Their willingness to settle for immediate reforms was strengthened by the fact that German workers had undeniably made important gains since 1918. These included the establishment of a parliamentary republic and at least theoretical acceptance by the employers of collective bargaining and the eight-hour day. In addition, the Works Council legislation of 1920 established the principle of elected worker representation in industry, and set out rules for its institutionalization.[1] Admittedly, the new councils, or Betriebsräte, represented a compromise from the point of view of the radical workers, but the employers likewise had to make concessions. The former had to abandon the idea of worker control that had been incorporated in the revolutionary Arbeiterräte, and content themselves with the hope that it would prove possible gradually to increase worker participation in decision-making, and so move towards genuine industrial democracy and a socialist new order.

[1] Claude William Guillebaud, The Works Council. A German Experiment in Industrial Democracy (Cambridge: Cambridge University Press, 1928), Appendix 1. The fullest recent treatment is Die Betriebsräte in der Weimarer Republik. Von der Selbstverwaltung zur Mitbestimmung. Dokumente und Analysen, ed. R. Crusius, G. Schiefelbein and M. Wilke. 2 vols. (Berlin: Olle & Wolter, 1978).

The latter had to accept the end of patriarchalism, and modernize their methods so as to achieve a *modus vivendi* with the councils.

Fears lest the works councils serve as bridgeheads for the extension of trade union power and the erosion of managerial authority led anti-socialist observers to play down their revolutionary origins and instead to stress their historical roots in the prewar works committees. Moreover, it proved possible in practice to limit the scope of the Betriebs-räte. Prevented from interfering with major corporate decisions, they were even used, on occasion, to counter trade union influence at the plant level.[2] But if the council legislation failed fundamentally to alter the balance of power between management and labor in favor of the latter, the Betriebsräte did keep the concept of industrial democracy alive. Reinforcing the fact that Germany now had a democratic state, the new laws held out the promise that the interests of the employees would henceforth be taken into account when companies attempted to increase productivity through technical and organizational rationalization in the name of "scientific management." At least initially, many friends of labor had reason to believe that the councils would enable workers to exercise a degree of control over matters not covered by collective bargaining and so help to reconcile rationalization with humanization.[3]

Whether the councils could also help to recover joy in work was another question. One who answered it in the affirmative was the social psychologist Kurt Lewin (1890–1947). In an essay of 1920 on the "socialization of the Taylor system," he acknowledged that it would not be possible to turn every unpleasant job into something truly desirable even under socialism, but argued that works councils, in cooperation with management and state-supported psychological advisers, could do much to enrich and humanize work, achieve a correct balance between the demands of productive efficiency and the right to satisfying occupations, and help to restore Arbeitsfreude.[4] Less confident about the value of the works councils in this context was the economist and social

[2] S. Aufhäuser, "Betriebsrat-Werksgemeinschaft," *Die Arbeit* 1 (1924): 272–75. See also Ludwig Preller, *Sozialpolitik in der Weimarer Republik* (Stuttgart: F. Mittelbach, 1949; reprint Düsseldorf: Droste, 1978), 137–39, 249–51.

[3] See the talk by Richard Woldt, then adviser to the Prussian Ministry of Education and instructor in Management Science at the University of Münster, on *Betriebsräteschulung* ("the education of works council members"), in *Bericht über eine Sachverständigenkonferenz*, GSR Schriften 10, no. 74 (Jena: Gustav Fischer, 1921), 1–24, and discussion, 24–56; also, *Betriebsrat und Arbeitswissenschaft. Eine arbeitswissenschaftliche Besprechung an der Berliner Betriebsräteschule*, ed. Hans Krauss (Berlin-Fichtenau: Gesellschaft und Erziehung, 1922).

[4] Kurt Lewin, *Die Sozialisierung des Taylorsystems*, vol. 4, *Praktischer Sozialismus*, ed. Karl Korsch (Berlin, 1920), 16–22.

policy specialist Robert Wilbrandt (1875–?), a member of the Socialization Commission whose concern with the problem of work dated back to his involvement with the prewar VfS. Wilbrandt started the decade as an active proponent of industrial democracy and other reforms designed to reconcile rationalization and Arbeitsfreude. However, he soon lost faith in the possibility of solving the problem of alienated labor in this manner, and, instead, defended worker participation as a way of giving employees a feeling of control lacking in their jobs, a compensation for the *loss* of joy in work.[5]

Richard Woldt (1878–1952), one of the few trade union supporters who consistently expressed deep concern about the subjective implications of rationalization and the problem of inter-personal relations in the workplace, shared Wilbrandt's outlook. Woldt, a trained engineer who had worked for the German Metalworkers Union and taken an active part in VfS debates before the war, became influential after 1918 as adviser to several ministers and as an instructor on the sociology of work and management at the University of Münster, the Berlin TH, and the Academy of Labor at Frankfurt. Although Woldt defended the councils as instruments of democracy capable of transforming the worker from subject to citizen, he, too, regarded it as unrealistic to expect them to abolish the alienation of labor and restore Arbeitsfreude.[6] Recommending moderation with regard to means as well as ends, Woldt advised both trade unions and councils to abandon the confrontational approach. Instead he advocated more subtle and informed ways to ensure that the new production techniques were not used to exploit the workforce, but rather resulted in both better pay and a more human pace and conditions of work.[7]

The works councils were only one of several ways in which proponents of industrial democracy sought to implement their ideals. In the early 1920s, there was considerable interest in British guild socialism, an attempt to transfer the ideal of joyful work associated with the medieval guilds to the world of modern rationalized production "by de-

[5] Robert Wilbrandt, "Die Kulturkrise der Arbeit," *Die Arbeit* 2 (1925): 321–27; *Die moderne Industriearbeiterschaft. Eine Einführung in die Grundfragen der Sozialreform* (Stuttgart: Ernst Heinrich Moritz, 1926), 59–71, 171–203; and "Das Betriebsräte system als Grundlage zur Schaffung einer Interessensolidarität zwischen Unternehmer und Arbeiter im Betriebe," in *Wege zum Wirtschaftsfrieden*, GWS Schriften 3 (1928), 26–41.

[6] Woldt, "Betriebsräteschulung," 12–13.

[7] Richard Woldt, *Der Werkmeister im Wirtschaftskampfe* (Munich: Werkmeister-Buchhandlung, 1920), 9, 14–15; and "Betriebslehre und Arbeitswissenschaft. Die Betriebslehre in Forschung und Unterricht," *Gewerkschafts-Archiv* 1 (1924): 270–76. On Woldt, see Gunnar Stollberg, *Die Rationalisierungsdebatte 1908–1933. Freie Gewerkschaften zwischen Mitwirkung und Gegenwehr* (Frankfurt: Campus, 1981), 77–78, 82–83, 99–100, and 151 n.80.

mocratizing the conditions under which [work] was performed."[8] This was stimulated by the publication in translation of the English psychologist Frank Watts's *An Introduction to the Psychological Problems of Industry* (1921), in which guild socialism was examined as one of several devices for ensuring cooperation in industry through worker participation.[9] By 1922, when Theodor Plaut devoted his inaugural lecture at the University of Hamburg to the subject, he was able to claim that the idea of guild socialism was making greater headway in Germany than in Britain, although admittedly in substantially modified form.[10] However, despite its attractiveness to people longing for a restoration of Arbeitsfreude,[11] guild socialism had no enduring impact on German industrial relations, and soon faded out of the debate about work.[12]

Somewhat more sustained was interest in the "constitutional factory" and profit-sharing as ways of involving workers in the fate of the firms that employed them. For one thing, these reforms had been pioneered before the war by German industrialists like Ernst Abbe (1840–1905) and Heinrich Freese (1853–1944), and so were assumed to be more suited to German circumstances than such imports as guild socialism, syndicalism, or Fordismus.[13] Also working in their favor was the fact that these proposals were the products of non-socialists.[14] By generalizing what Freese, Abbe, and other progressive employers had pioneered before the war, the Betriebsräte legislation appeared to have

[8] Anthony W. Wright, "Guild Socialism Revisited," *JCH* 9/1 (1974): 179–80.

[9] Frank Watts, *Die psychologischen Probleme der Industrie* (Berlin: Julius Springer, 1922).

[10] Theodor Plaut, *Wesen und Bedeutung des Gildensozialismus* (Jena: Gustav Fischer, 1922).

[11] See, e.g., the pedagogue Adolf Reichwein's essay, "Die Gilde. Ein Weg zur Einheit von Bildung und Arbeit" (1924), in *Ausgewählte Pädagogische Schriften*, ed. Herbert E. Ruppert and Horst E. Wittig (Paderborn: Ferdinand Schöningh, 1978), 9–15.

[12] See the entries "Gildensozialismus" by Johannes Gerhardt of the University of Munich, and "Demokratie des Betriebes" by Arthur Dissinger, *HA* 1:2265–66 and 1288–91, respectively.

[13] E.g., Karl Diehl, *Über Sozialismus, Kommunismus und Anarchismus* (4th ed.; Jena: Gustav Fischer, 1922), 426–27, who argued that each nation would have to produce its own socialism; and Karl Christian Thalheim, *Sozialkritik und Sozialreform bei Abbe, Rathenau und Ford* (Berlin: R. Hobbing, 1929).

[14] Thus Günther Axhausen, in a study of the ideological sources of the council movement, concluded that Germany would do better to take as a model Freese's constitutional factory rather than to imitate the French Fourierist Godin's communalism. Identifying industrial democracy with the constitutional factory, he recommended that the council legislation be supplemented with compulsory profit-sharing in order to nudge the employers in Freese's direction. Günther Axhausen, *Utopie und Realismus im Betriebsrätegedanken. Eine Studie nach Freese und Godin* (Berlin: Emil Ebering, 1920). See also Friedrich Edler von Braun, "Wege zu Deutschlands Wiederaufbau," in Löffler, ed., *Deutschlands Zukunft*, 38–39. Here the author, a member of the Reichstag and president of the Federal Economic Council (RWR), advocated profit-sharing because he feared that without this additional link between the workers and the enterprise, the councils might exacerbate rather than contain class conflict.

laid the groundwork for effective cooperation between labor and management.[15] But, in any event, German enterprises showed little inclination to adopt the ideal of the constitutional factory, the labor movement directed its attention elsewhere, and successive governments failed to strengthen industrial democracy through further legislative action. Even Abbe's own firm, Zeiss of Jena, thought it necessary after 1918 to back away from some of his basic principles, with the result that its works council came to be dominated by a majority favoring the class-war standpoint.[16]

Organized labor as a whole showed little enthusiasm for the idea of industrial democracy. The socialist parties and their affiliated trade unions did not believe that it addressed the major problems facing the working class under capitalism. They also tended to reject two assumptions on which its bourgeois supporters based their advocacy: that the democratization of industry would help to create a true spirit of community between labor and management within the workplace, and that the resulting practical cooperation would serve the best interests of the workers. Catholic social thinkers and the Christian unions were also ambivalent about industrial democracy and certainly never made it the exclusive focus of their reform program, but they were somewhat more inclined to regard with favor the idea of cooperation between management and labor in the works community, and to explore its potential for humanizing rationalized production.

The only workers' associations to give unqualified support to the works community or Werksgemeinschaft concept were those affiliated with the anti-democratic *Wirtschaftsfriedliche* ("economic-peace-oriented") movement. Comprised of company or "yellow" unions—the *Werkvereine*—together with a number of church-affiliated *Arbeitervereine* and associations of agricultural workers, this movement was held together by nationalism and anti-Marxism. Its chief distinguishing features were opposition to use of the strike weapon and advocacy of pay according to performance, the so-called *Leistungslohn*. Of considerable importance before 1914, the movement lost membership during the war and disintegrated with the collapse of the Second Reich. Attempts to revive it after 1918 were hampered by the ZAG agreement of that year by which the central organizations of employers withdrew support from the company unions and recognized the trade unions as ex-

[15] Wilbrandt, *Moderne Industriearbeiterschaft*, 67.
[16] Hilde Weiss, *Abbe und Ford. Pläne für die Errichtung sozialer Betriebe* (Inaugural diss., University of Frankfurt; Berlin: Progres, 1927). Weiss had worked for Zeiss while studying at Jena under Korsch.

clusive bargaining partners, a principle incorporated into the Weimar Constitution.[17]

The Betriebsräte legislation of 1920, which sought to institutionalize the community of interest between employers and workers at the level of the individual enterprise, at first glance appeared more favorable to the Werksgemeinschaft movement, but in practice the works councils proved only moderately effective as agents of social harmony: while the owners stubbornly upheld their exclusive rights to manage the enterprise, most councils were dominated by socialist trade unionists who refused on principle to equate the workers' interests with those of their employers.[18]

Despite these and other obstacles, the Werkvereine reemerged in the early 1920s. Under Fritz Geisler (1890–?) and Wilhelm Schmidt (1878–1945), associations such as the Vereinigte vaterländische Verbände Deutschlands (VVVD),[19] the Nationalverband Deutscher Berufsverbände, the Reichsbund vaterländischer Arbeiter- und Werkvereine, and the Reichsausschuss werksgemeinschaftlicher Verbände claimed to represent a genuine, independent, and significant working-class constituency, and attempted to create a national presence through the weekly *Deutsche Gemeinschaft*, published in Berlin between 1924 and 1933 with the motto "For Free Labor! For a Free Economy!" However, these societies, plagued as they were by internal divisions and problems of leadership, were never able to mobilize more than a small fraction of German workers behind the principle of industrial peace through Werksgemeinschaft. Consequently, they found it necessary to rely for support on employer and agrarian sources, and on the parties of the political right.[20]

---

[17] Nathan Reich, *Labor Relations in Republican Germany. An Experiment in Industrial Democracy, 1918–1933* (New York: Oxford University Press, 1938), 38–39. Chapter 2 analyzes the Weimar constitution's economic provisions.

[18] Reich, *Labor Relations*, 202–203.

[19] See James M. Diehl, "Von der 'Vaterlandspartei' zur 'Nationalen Revolution': Die 'Vereinigten vaterländischen Verbände Deutschlands (VVVD)' 1922–1932," *VfZ* 33 (1985): 617–39.

[20] Preller, 194–96, 340–41; Reich, *Labor Relations*, 78–82. The link between the DNVP and the "Wirtschaftsfriedliche" is analyzed by Amrei Stupperich, *Volksgemeinschaft oder Arbeitersolidarität. Studien zur Arbeitnehmerpolitik in der Deutsch-nationalen Volkspartei, 1918–1933* (Göttingen, 1982); Stupperich gives useful short biographies of Geisler and Schmidt, 260 and 265 respectively. See also Fritz Geisler, in *Die Vaterländische-Soziale Arbeitnehmerbewegung* (Berlin: Reichsgeschäftsstelle des Nationalverbandes Deutscher Berufsverbände, 1925) and Wilhelm Schmidt, *Die Deutsche Arbeiterbewegung der Vorkriegs- und der Revolutionsjahre in besonderer Berücksichtigung des Werksgemeinschafts-Gedankens* (Berlin: Reichsbund vaterländischer Arbeitervereine, [1925]). For a positive appraisal of the movement's prospects, see Karl Vorwerck, *Die wirtschaftsfriedliche Arbeitnehmerbewegung Deutschlands in ihrem Werden und in ihrem Kampf um Anerkennung. Eine kritische Untersuchung* (Jena: Gustav Fischer, 1926).

In the end, the chief proponents of Werksgemeinschaft or Betriebs-gemeinschaft as a way of solving the problem of modern work by re-structuring industrial relations within the firm along non-confronta-tional lines were employers and managers concerned to maximize company profits, as well as the new class of management specialists who hoped through the creation of a community of work to salvage the hu-manist ideal of Arbeitsfreude in an era of rationalized production. Among the former were a number of industrialists, predominantly from the Ruhr, who were convinced that if sufficient workers could be con-verted to the Werksgemeinschaft ideology, the new Betriebsräte could be manipulated in the interests of management. This belief led a num-ber of Ruhr enterprises to pay selected workers—frequently works council members—to attend the Deutsche Volkshochschule in Berlin-Treptow, which had been founded in January 1921 under the auspices of the conservative Deutsche Vereinigung[21] and which was staffed by teachers paid by the Werkvereine.[22]

The most vigorous proponent of the idea that the works councils could be rendered harmless or even turned to good use by management was Josef Winschuh (1897–1970), an academically trained progressive businessman and publicist. In his *Practical Company Politics* of 1923 Winschuh surveyed measures German employers might adopt to counter the drive towards industrial democracy without directly con-fronting the works councils or the unions. Although educational pro-grams to persuade potential worker leaders of the benefits to be derived from cooperation, along the lines of the Deutsche Volkshochschule, had a role to play, Winschuh argued that it was also necessary to im-prove working conditions and raise the tone of labor-management re-lations, in order to deprive radicalism of all sustenance.[23] Properly han-dled, he was convinced that the works councils could be persuaded to relinquish the ideal of participatory democracy and to accept the need for authority, discipline, and hierarchy within the firm; the employers, for their part, would have to abandon the prewar patriarchal model of industrial relations. It was Winschuh's hope that the reforms he sug-gested would buttress the communality of interests between workers and management at the plant level and enable them to enter into a

[21] See, on its origins, Dr. Erich Sperling, *Die wirtschaftsfriedliche nationale Arbeiterbewegung im Lichte der Kritik* (Berlin: Deutsche Vereinigung, 1918).

[22] Mattheier, in Reulecke, *Arbeiterbewegung*, 199–204. For a critical description of the Deutsche Volkshochschule see Fritz Fricke, *Sie suchen die Seele* (11th enl. ed.; Berlin: Ver-lagsgesellschaft des ADGB, 1927), 35–39.

[23] Josef Winschuh, *Praktische Werkspolitik. Darstellung einer planmässigen Arbeitspolitik im modernen Fabrikbetriebe* (Berlin: Industrieverlag Spaeth & Linde, 1923).

constructive relationship based on the principle of "constitutional monarchy."[24] The lack of interest shown by most councils in the improvement of methods of work notwithstanding, he continued to argue that progressive entrepreneurs could use the Betriebsräte to ensure worker cooperation in the quest for higher productivity, and to believe that modern industrial management practices, by renouncing both outdated romantic notions of Werksgemeinschaft and impractical ideas of industrial democracy, would succeed in turning the enterprise into a conflict-free social space in which cooperation and Arbeitsfreude would thrive.[25]

Winschuh described the motives for undertaking Werkspolitik as a blend of the selfish and the social; as an employer however, he saw nothing wrong in giving primacy to economic considerations: companies that fostered positive attitudes on the part of the workers, improved benefits, hygiene, housing, and company-sponsored social and recreational activities would be rewarded by greater loyalty and willingness to work hard on the part of its labor force. At relatively little cost, such measures would create an atmosphere in which it was possible to work, lead, and produce with a minimum of friction, and so increase profits.[26] Winschuh did not claim originality for the specific measures he advocated. Firms like Krupp in Germany or Ford in the United States had recognized the need to reduce absenteeism, stabilize the workforce, prevent accidents, enhance skills, and develop company welfare policies well before the First World War. What was new was his insistence that patriarchalism was out of fashion, and that employers interested in reaping the benefits of rationalization would have to adapt their outlook and methods to a world in which parliamentary democracy, works councils, and a strong trade union movement were facts of life.

Although Winschuh's writings were designed to appeal to the business community,[27] they may well have had more impact in academic circles newly receptive to the idea of company-based social policies as an appropriate response to the problem of worker alienation. Before the war, Richard Ehrenberg had been virtually isolated when he advocated the restoration of the works community as a means to resolve social tensions and restore Arbeitsfreude. Now this idea was taken up by a

[24] Josef Winschuh, "Die Psychologischen Grundlagen der Werksarbeitsgemeinschaft," Die sozialen Probleme des Betriebes, ed. Heinz Potthoff (Berlin: Industrieverlag Spaeth & Linde, 1925), 268–69.
[25] Josef Winschuh, "Zehn Jahre Betriebsrätegesetz," SP 39 (1930): 232–35; and "Gedanken zum Problem einer neuen Werkspolitik," in Probleme der sozialen Betriebspolitik, ed. Goetz Briefs (Berlin: Julius Springer, 1930), 144–53.
[26] Winschuh, Praktische Werkspolitik, 9–10.   [27] Hinrichs, Um die Seele, 169.

number of academics who, by extending the scope of Arbeitswissenschaft to include social psychology, industrial sociology, and management science, hoped to contribute to the reform of industrial relations and thereby solve the problem of modern work. A degree of disillusionment about the ability of the state to sponsor social policies that would significantly improve the relationship between people and their work also contributed to their willingness to regard private enterprise as a possible agent of reform.

Both motives were at work in the thinking of Goetz Briefs, the Ford enthusiast whose Institute of Industrial Sociology at the Berlin TH became the most important center for this endeavor. As a Catholic, Briefs was heir to a strong tradition of social concern that gave a religious-humanitarian coloring to his proposals for restructuring social relations within the workplace and prevented his pronounced anti-Marxism from turning either into a one-sided defense of liberal capitalism or into an attack on trade unionism as such.[28] Indeed, Briefs regarded the labor movement and the radicalism of the revolution as understandable reactions to the worker alienation produced over four generations by the development of rationalized production under capitalist auspices. Persuaded that the proletarian threat was not the product of any particular system of property relations but had its chief locus in the workplace, Briefs sought ways to counteract the trend to impersonal rationality (*Versachlichung*) of social interaction in enterprise (*Betrieb*), and advocated company social policies designed to help alleviate the harshness of working class existence.[29]

Briefs felt that neither the labor movement nor the social reformers had given the social problems of the firm sufficient attention in the past, apart from a few individuals such as Robert Owen, Gustav Schmoller, and Richard Ehrenberg and, since the war, Rosenstock, Hellpach, and Winschuh. However, public opinion was coming around, and industry, too, was beginning to recognize that it might not

[28] Goetz Briefs, "Die geistige und soziale Achsendrehung im Unternehmertum und in der Arbeiterschaft," *ZCGD* 25/13 (1925): 178–79, and 25/14:187–90. Earlier, he had even advocated an amalgamation of Christianity and socialism. See his "Der soziale Volksstaat und der Sozialismus," in *Soziale Arbeit im neuen Deutschland. Festschrift zum 70. Geburtstag Franz Hitze* (Mönchen Gladbach: Volksverein Verlag, 1921), 61–84. See also Hinrichs, *Um die Seele*, 264–70, who, however, fails to take due note of the Catholic element in Briefs's thought, or to credit him with sincere humanitarian impulses.

[29] Goetz Briefs, "Betriebsoziologie" in *Handwörterbuch der Soziologie*, ed. Alfred Vierkandt (Stuttgart, 1931), 32; "Betriebssoziologie" in *Jahrbuch für Sozialpolitik* (1931), 115. Briefs played some part in initiating the works council legislation of 1920, although there is disagreement about the exact nature of his role. See Wilke, "Briefs," 337. For his views on proletarian attitudes, see Goetz Briefs, "Das gewerbliche Proletariat" in *Grundriss der Sozialökonomik* 9 (Tübingen, 1926), 1:143–240, and *The Proletariat: A Challenge to Western Civilization* (New York: McGraw-Hill, 1937).

be truly "rational" to ignore the workers' need for a sense of belonging and for some degree of Arbeitsfreude. Through his institute, Briefs sought both to draw on and expand what practical industrial engineers knew about social relations within the enterprise, and to develop an industrial sociology that would answer some of the outstanding questions. By examining how modern work could be made more tolerable and the workplace livable, if it was in fact possible for people to retain their humanity over the long term within the large enterprise, how the nature of social interaction within the Betrieb was influenced by and had an impact on the larger society, and similar topics, he hoped to develop prescriptions for effective company social policies to supplement state efforts.[30] In addition to publishing the work of its researchers,[31] Briefs's Institute attempted to influence opinion by bringing together representatives of labor and management to thrash out the problems of company social policy.[32]

On a different level, the questions raised by Briefs and his associates were addressed in these years by the Institute for Applied Sociology. Also located in Berlin, this organization had been founded in 1924 by Karl Dunkmann (1868–1932), a former minister, student of philosophy, and professor of theology at Greifswald. Dunkmann turned to sociology after the war when he became convinced that religion by itself could not solve the nation's pressing social and economic problems. By 1921 he had abandoned his professorship to become an instructor in sociology at the Berlin TH. His limited academic standing in this field, combined with the fact that his institute was largely funded by industry, led his opponents to dismiss him as a propagandist for big business. However, while Dunkmann's work was subsidized by the VDA, the chief employers' association dealing with labor-management relations, this was also true of numerous entirely reputable academic institutions and individuals, whose scholarly integrity no one could call in question.[33] In point of fact, several highly regarded sociologists, including

[30] Briefs, "Betriebsoziologie," *Jahrbuch für Sozialpolitik*, 119–20.

[31] See Ludwig Heinrich Adolf Geck, *Die sozialen Arbeitsverhältnisse im Wandel der Zeit. Eine geschichtliche Einführung in die Betriebssoziolgie* (Berlin: Julius Springer, 1931); Walter Jost, *Das Sozialleben des industriellen Betriebes* (Berlin: Julius Springer, 1932); Rudolf Schwenger, *Die betriebliche Sozialpolitik einzelner Industriezweige*, ed. Goetz Briefs, VfS Schriften 186, 2 vols. (Munich: Duncker & Humblot, 1932 and 1934).

[32] The proceedings of one such gathering, held in February 1930, are recorded in *Probleme der sozialen Betriebspolitik*, ed. Goetz Briefs (Berlin: Julius Springer, 1930). Co-sponsored by the Berlin TH's extension office, this conference was widely reported in the press. See, e.g., Walter Jost, "Die soziale Betriebspolitik industrieller Unternehmungen," in *Ruhr und Rhein* 11/15 (1930): 482–86.

[33] For details on financial assistance to German Arbeitswissenschaft distributed by industry through the *Stifterverband der Notgemeinschaft der Deutschen Wissenschaft*, see VdA, *Geschäfts-*

Ferdinand Tönnies at Kiel, and Alfred Vierkandt and Leopold von Wiese of the Research Institute for Social Studies at Cologne, indicated publicly that they took Dunkmann seriously, or at least respected his sincerity, even when they disagreed with some of the positions he adopted.[34]

Dunkmann as early as 1921 had called for a new social policy based on sociology and Christianity. Adopting Tönnies's *Gemeinschaft Gesellschaft* ("Community-Society") terminology, he spoke of the need to replace the chaos of materialistic *Gesellschaft* with a genuine *Volksgemeinschaft* that would satisfy the longing for community produced by the advance of modernity.[35] Initially he maintained that the recovery of community could be centered on the family, but he quickly realized that the family had lost its productive role, and that reform efforts would therefore have to focus on the world of work. As rationalized industry represented the future, it was necessary to counter its evils and to transform the Betrieb into a true community where the workers could feel at home and cooperate harmoniously with management to maximize production.[36]

Dunkmann thus became an advocate of Werksgemeinschaft, defined as the institutional expression of the implicit solidarity of interests that lay at the heart of every profitable enterprise. To achieve reconciliation at the level of the firm, industrial relations would have to be depoliticized and management reforms instituted to restore joy in work and foster a sense of common purpose. Success in achieving a spirit of Werksgemeinschaft would, in turn, make it possible to reverse the disintegration of modern society and rebuild the national community.[37]

---

bericht 1927/1929, 24 (Berlin, 1930): 395–400. The Briefs-Riebensahm Institute, Adolf Friedrich at Karlsruhe, Poppelreuter at Bonn, Rupp in Berlin, and Lechtape at Münster were among those deemed worthy of support.

[34] Von Wiese, describing the founding of the Institute in the news section of the *Kölner Vierteljahrshefte für Soziologie* 4, 3/4 (1925): 330–31, named Vierkandt and Tönnies as co-workers. Both contributed essays after Dunkmann's death to a memorial issue of the *Archiv für angewandte Soziologie* 5, 3/4 (1933), edited by Dunkmann's associate Dr. Heinz Sauermann. An obituary by Sauermann, in the same volume, no. 2 (1932/3): 77–84, provides useful biographical detail on Dunkmann.

[35] Karl Dunkmann, "Gemeinschaft und Gesellschaft," in *Soziale Arbeit im neuen Deutschland*, 20–37. On Tönnies, see Arthur Mitzman, *Sociology and Estrangement* (New York: Knopf, 1973), Pt. 2. Tönnies's *Gemeinschaft und Gesellschaft*, first published in 1887, was reprinted six times before his death in 1936. Mitzman, *Sociology and Estrangement*, 39.

[36] Karl Dunkmann, *Die Lehre vom Beruf* (Berlin: Trowitzsch & Sohn, 1922); *Volksgemeinschaft, Sozialpolitik und Geisteskultur* (Duisburg: Echo-Verlag, 1922); *Soziologie der Arbeit*, Handbuch der Arbeitswissenschaft 8/9 (Halle: Carl Marhold, 1933).

[37] Karl Dunkmann, "Werksgemeinschaft als Organisationsproblem. Eine soziologische Untersuchung," in Karl Vorwerck und D. K. Dunkmann, *Die Werksgemeinschaft in historischer und soziologischer Beleuchtung* (Berlin: J. Springer, 1928), 63–130.

Whereas Briefs could hope to influence developments through his students, Dunkmann and his associates had to go directly to the public with their message. This was attempted through educational newsletters, the *Unterrichtsbriefe*, supplanted in 1928 by the bi-monthly *Archiv für angewandte Soziologie*. Dunkmann claimed these were read by workers, engineers, entrepreneurs, economists and other academics, and politicians, with all groups given an opportunity to voice their opinions.[38] He also spoke frequently at church and business meetings, and took part in symposia such as the one sponsored in 1925 by the influential Association of Iron and Steel Producers on "Human Labor in the Productive Process," to which he spoke on "Mass Psychology and Worker Productivity."[39] Finally he contributed frequently to the bi-weekly newsletter of the Gesellschaft für Deutsche Wirtschafts- und Sozialpolitik (GWS), founded in 1926 by his friend Dr. Karl Vorwerck. A conservative counterpart to the GSR, the GWS had close links with industry, gave primacy to the economy over the state in social policy matters, and dedicated itself to the dual ideas of Werksgemeinschaft and *Qualitätsarbeit* ("quality production").[40]

Both Briefs and Dunkmann to some extent operated on the academic periphery. However, the Werksgemeinschaft ideal also found supporters within the universities. These included Gerhard Albrecht (1889–1971), from 1927 professor of political science at Jena, and Friedrich Lent (1882–1960), a law professor at the University of Erlangen, as well as younger scholars like Heinrich Lechtape (1896–1936), an instructor in sociology at the University of Münster, Karl Christian Thalheim (1900–?), who taught at the Commercial University (*Handelshochschule*) in Leipzig from 1928, and Theodor Lüddecke (1900–?), a political economist at the University of Halle. All believed that the social tensions produced by modern rationalized production could best be addressed from within the firm, and that management-sponsored company social policies could play an important part in fostering the spirit of cooperation needed to humanize work and ensure industrial peace.[41] Whether they described their subject as *Soziale Betriebspolitik*,

[38] GWS *Mitteilungen* 1 (March 1927), report of the "Wissenschaftliche Ausschuss der GWS."

[39] Karl Dunkmann, "Massenpsychologie und Arbeitserfolg," in Verein deutscher Eisenhüttenleute, *Die menschliche Arbeitskraft im Produktionsvorgang. Drei Vorträge, gehalten auf der Gemeinschaftsitzung der Fachausschüsse des Vereins deutscher Eisenhüttenleute in Bonn am 24. Mai. 1925* (Düsseldorf: Verlag Stahleisen, 1925), 3–9. The other two speakers were the psychologist Walther Poppelreuter of Bonn University and Karl Arnhold, head of the Dinta.

[40] The GWS was renamed the Gesellschaft Neue Wirtschaft in 1931.

[41] See, e.g., Gerhard Albrecht, *Vom Klassenkampf zum sozialen Frieden* (Jena: Gustav Fischer, 1932; Friedrich Lent, *Werksgemeinschaft als Kulturproblem*. Auftrag gehalten auf dem

betriebliche Sozialpolitik or, with Thalheim, *autonome Sozialpolitik*, they were at one in assigning it a major, if not exclusive, role in tackling the problems of modern industrial society.

They were also in agreement that it was desirable to minimize the role of state social policy, although their reasons for this varied. Whereas some argued from principle that it was essential to reduce the role of the state in economic matters, others urged industry to solve its own problems on the grounds that the existing state was incompetent to address the issues they thought crucial, or that its interventions would be detrimental to the efficient and profitable development of rationalized industry. Still others were influenced by the conservative trend that was leading even some erstwhile supporters of state social policy, like Herkner, to oppose government programs designed to assist the laboring classes. Herkner, who had done much to place Arbeits-freude on the social policy agenda before the war, after 1918 not only rejected socialization in all its forms, but also argued that Germany could no longer afford to undertake social reforms to promote joy in work at the expense of productivity. While his objective remained the cultural advancement of the Volk, he now maintained that this could only be attained by maximizing productive efficiency and restoring the seriously endangered capitalist system to full health. Accusing the VfS of being too pro-labor and of inhibiting his scholarly independence, he resigned from that body in November 1922.[42]

The drift of Herkner and others away from the cause of social policy reform may have been attributable in part to the mistaken belief that labor, as the main beneficiary of the revolution, no longer needed outside help. Moreover, in the words of Robert Wilbrandt, "When one thrives, one has sympathy for others; if one suffers, one pities oneself."[43] Conscious of their personal difficulties and those of their mid-

---

2. Reichsbundestage des Reichsbund vaterländischer Arbeiter- und Werkvereine, Vorsitz Wilh. Schmidt (2d ed.; Berlin: Deutschland Verlag, 1926); Heinrich Lechtape, *Die menschliche Arbeit als Objekt der wissenschaftlichen Sozialpolitik* (Jena: Gustav Fischer, 1929); Thalheim, *Sozialkritik und Sozialreform bei Abbe, Rathenau und Ford,* and "Grundfragen der betrieblichen Sozialpolitik," in *Archiv für angewandte Soziologie,* 4/1 (1931): 121–32; Jerome Davis and Theodor Lüddecke, *Industrieller Friede, Ein Symposium* (Leipzig: P. List, 1928), and Lüddecke, *Meisterung der Maschinenwelt* (Leipzig: P. List, [1931]).

[42] Heinrich Herkner, "Lebenslauf eines Kathedersozialisten," 36–38. Immediately after the war Herkner had headed both the VfS and the GSR, as well as serving on the social policy committee of the provisional RWR.

[43] Wilbrandt, *Moderne Industriearbeiterschaft,* 27. See also "Die Not der geistigen Arbeiter" ("The Distress of the Intellectual Workers"), in *Verhandlungen der Generalversammlung in Eisenach 20. und 21. September 1922,* VfS Schriften 163 (Munich: Duncker & Humblot, 1923), 165–259. Wilbrandt cited Professor Adolph Günther's declaration at this conference that the worker question was no longer current as evidence of the contemporary reaction.

dle-class contemporaries in a time of political unrest and rampant inflation, German academics were no longer inclined to equate the social
question with the worker question or to view the problem of work primarily as one affecting the laboring masses. Wilbrandt acknowledged
that some, like Herkner or Phillip Stein, sincerely believed that economic policy was now the only social policy, because only a strengthened and more productive economy could solve the nation's problems
and thus improve the condition of the workers. But he deplored the
tendency of contemporaries to spend more time complaining about the
alleged unwillingness of the workers to work, than seeking ways to explain and reverse the loss of proletarian joy in work: the industrial
worker "has need today of a Carlyle, and instead finds impoverished
academics who, since the time of revolution and inflation, have become jealous of him."[44]

The bourgeois social reform movement that emerged from the postwar crisis did not in fact abandon the workers. But few reformers still
believed that the state had an important role to play as far as the problem of alienation was concerned. Successive Weimar governments legislated extensively on such matters as wages and hours, pensions and
unemployment insurance; a system of labor courts was established in
1926; and the state intervened in the collective bargaining process
through an elaborate and controversial procedure of voluntary media-
tion and binding arbitration.[45] But nothing significant was done by the
Republic to expand the powers of the works councils or otherwise to
transform industrial relations within the enterprise from absolutism to
constitutionalism, as had been intended by the 1919 draft legislation
detailing the respective duties of employers and workers in the collective labor contract.[46]

The author of this draft was Dr. Heinz Potthoff (1875–1945), a leading expert on labor law who, although no democrat himself, realized
that it would be necessary to apply to the economy and the law the
same principles that underlay the new constitution: the primacy of the
working person, and the democratic principle of individual autonomy.[47] Potthoff never ceased to argue that legislation could help to

[44] Wilbrandt, *Moderne Industriearbeiterschaft*, 201. On the debate about the "crisis of social
policy" and the correct relationship between social reform and the economy, see also Preller,
Sozialpolitik, 204–218.

[45] Preller, *Sozialpolitik*, 341–90 on the period 1926–1928; Reich, *Labor Relations*, Chapter
4 on collective bargaining and Chapter 7 on the labor courts. Also, Otto Kahn-Freund,
Labour Law and Politics in the Weimar Republic, ed. Roy Lewis (Oxford: Blackwell, 1981).

[46] Preller, *Sozialpolitik*, 257.

[47] Heinz Potthoff, "Die sozialen Probleme des Betriebes," in *Die sozialen Probleme des Betriebes*, ed. Heinz Potthoff, 16.

bring about the spirit of cooperation among entrepreneurs, salaried workers, and labor needed in order to raise the productivity of industry to its highest pitch; but he quickly became convinced that no further progress would be made until there was a change of attitudes, particularly among the nation's employers, and that true Werksgemeinschaft could not be legislated.[48] Similarly, Heinrich Brauns (1868–1939), the Catholic reformer who headed the Reich Ministry of Labor from 1920 to 1928, believed that governments could do little to humanize the world of work, because humanization required first and foremost the development of mutual understanding between capital and labor and the creation of a sense of solidarity between employers and workers.[49]

Also disappointing were the results of institutionalized cooperation between the various groups in the economy through the mechanism of the Reichswirtschaftsrat. Efforts to turn the RWR into a genuine economic parliament came to nothing, and even as an advisory body it accomplished little.[50] The RWR did contribute to the work of a governmental commission of enquiry set up in 1926 to investigate the German economy, and a subcommittee of this studied the hotly-disputed issue of the relationship between productivity on the one hand and working hours and methods of establishing wages on the other.[51] But research was halted in 1930 when funding was cut off, and, by the time the committee's report appeared, the depression had altered the picture to such an extent that no practical conclusions could be drawn.[52] A similar fate awaited the semi-official RKW's major study of the human implications of the rationalization process. The report on this investigation was meant to be the first of a series on a topic whose importance was clearly recognized, but it, too, was robbed of its full effect by the fact that it appeared in 1931, at the height of the crisis.[53]

The only area where many people continued to look to the central government for leadership and positive action was the sphere of education. The federal authorities found it impossible to respond effec-

[48] Potthoff, *Soziale Probleme*, 336–40.

[49] Karl Josef Rivinius, *Die soziale Bewegung im Deutschland des neunzehnten Jahrhunderts* (Munich: Heinz Moos, 1978), 131. During his period of office, Brauns had little opportunity to foster these attitudes, and his resignation coincided with a renewal of large-scale industrial conflict.

[50] Preller, *Sozialpolitik*, 251–52, 324–25, 481–82.   [51] Preller, *Sozialpolitik*, 348–49.

[52] *Die innere Verflechtung der deutschen Wirtschaft*. Bericht des Enquete-Ausschusses des Deutschen Reichstags (Berlin, 1930).

[53] RKW, *Der Mensch und die Rationalisierung*, 1, RKW *Veröffentlichungen* 71 (Berlin, 1931). In any case, the RKW study had always been seen as a tool for influencing public opinion rather than as a direct stimulus to legislative reform.

tively, however, in large part because responsibility for schooling was traditionally reserved to the states and municipalities. In any case, with respect to vocational training, where reform was most likely to have a direct and positive impact on the world of work, there was a growing tendency in the 1920s to prefer industrial or trade union initiatives to government action.

The gradual loss of faith in state social policy as a way of restoring joy in work can be traced in the writings of Bruno Rauecker (1887–?), one of Weimar Germany's leading social policy specialists. A trained economist close to the Naumann circle and the German Werkbund before the war, Rauecker, during the 1920s, repeatedly bemoaned the loss of meaning in work due to rationalization and energetically canvassed ways to counter this *Entleerung* ("emptying").[54] A frequent contributor to a variety of social reform and trade union periodicals and author of several books on social policy, Rauecker examined and abandoned in turn the entire gamut of measures proposed by his contemporaries for reconciling human beings with their work.

Rauecker believed at first that the state had an important role to play. Welcoming the new labor law, above all the works council legislation, he argued that greater worker participation would be particularly important in those industries producing quality consumer goods: rescued from their fate as a mechanized unit of production, skilled workers would cease to threaten social peace.[55] Rauecker also urged the government to foster quality production for export, on the grounds that workers in this type of industry required and could expect to achieve better than average wages and conditions of work, and that this example would exert an upward pull on wages and working conditions for labor in other areas of the economy.[56]

Once the rationalization movement was in full swing, Rauecker abandoned the somewhat utopian idea of quality production as a key to social reform. Instead, he advocated legislation to support the eight-hour day and urged state intervention to protect workers from excessive intensification of work and capitalist exploitation. In other words, he now advocated policies directed less at restoring joy in work than at limiting work and preserving the physical and mental strength of the workers so that they might share in general culture.[57] He also wanted

[54] Stollberg, *Rationalisierungsdebatte*, 97.
[55] Bruno Rauecker, "Qualitätsarbeit und Sozialpolitik," in *Deutscher Werkbund Mitteilungen* (1919), no. 2: 58–63.
[56] Bruno Rauecker, "Sozialpolitik durch Produktionspolitik IV," SP 33 (1924): 766–67.
[57] Bruno Rauecker, *Rationalisierung und Sozialpolitik* (Berlin: Sieben Stäbe, 1926), 67–88; "Rationalisierung und Religion," SP 37 (1928): 175.

the works council legislation strengthened and the works councils more closely linked with the trade unions. In particular, he argued that steps must be taken to ensure that the trade unions retained the right to select council members, on the grounds that only the unions were able to educate people properly for these important posts.[58]

Finally, Rauecker called for a reformed and expanded educational system to counterbalance the adverse tendencies associated with rationalization, although he was critical of Hellpach's singleminded promotion of educational reform as the way to tackle the problem of alienation and believed that continued efforts should be made to humanize work itself.[59] Impressed by the Arbeitsschule ideas propagated by Kerschensteiner and others, Rauecker welcomed Article 148 of the Weimar constitution which made vocational training compulsory in the schools.[60] Beyond this, he urged the establishment of facilities specifically designed to develop work skills, overcome the shortage of skilled workers caused in part by a temporary decrease in wage differentials immediately after the war, and produce people able to enjoy their work in a way and to an extent denied to ordinary laborers enmeshed in the toils of the Taylorized factory or subject to control by the Ford-style conveyor belt.[61] In addition, enhanced opportunities for adult education, notably in the new *Volkshochschulen* or People's Universities, could be expected to produce better workers and citizens and help to compensate for the joyless labor that was the lot of an ever larger segment of the population.[62] Thus Rauecker envisaged quite a number of ways in which the state could contribute to solving the problem of work.

Nevertheless, he recognized from the start that there were strict limits to what could be achieved through government social policy, and so was prepared to look in other directions. Immediately after the war he had had high hopes for non-profit producer cooperatives as agents of

[58] Bruno Rauecker, *Rationalisierung als Kulturfaktor* (Berlin: Reimar Hobbing, [1929]), 38.

[59] Bruno Rauecker, "Die seelischen Wirkungen der Mechanisierung und Rationalisierung der Industriearbeit. Bemerkungen zu dem gleichnamigen Vortrag des Staatspräsidenten Prof. Dr. Hellpach auf dem evangelisch-sozialen Kongress," *SP* 34 (1925): 627–28.

[60] Bruno Rauecker, *Versittlichung des Arbeitslebens. Wege zur Wiedererweckung der Berufsfreude und der Arbeitslust* (Munich: Duncker & Humblot, 1920), 9.

[61] Rauecker, "Sozialpolitik durch Produktionspolitik," 766; "Stärkung der Arbeitsfreude im Wirtschaftsleben der Gegenwart," *Soziale Revue* 22 (1922): 211; "Monotonie Problem und Sozialpolitik," *Die Arbeit* 4 (1927): 8–9, dismissing Gottl-Ottlilienfeld's assertion that Ford's assembly-line production enabled workers to feel themselves part of a significant whole and so saved them from the depersonalization characteristic of Taylorism.

[62] Bruno Rauecker, *Die Berufsfreude im modernen Wirtschaftsleben* (Berlin: Zentralverlag Staat und Wirtschaft, 1922), 49–53; Rauecker, "Stärkung der Arbeitsfreude," 215; Rauecker, "Die seelischen Wirkungen," 609–612, 625–28; *Rationalisierung als Kulturfaktor*, 159–61.

joy in work and had shared in the widespread belief that cooperation between intellectuals and workers in all branches of industry could help to overcome alienation.[63] Once the utopian mood had passed, he gave greater attention to "scientific" ways of solving the problem of work. Thus, in 1924 he argued that psychotechnical methods, if monitored by government, could do much to humanize Taylorist scientific management, and that industrial psychology could and should devote its efforts in the first instance to nurturing Arbeitsfreude rather than to maximizing productive efficiency and profits.[64]

By 1926, Rauecker virtually abandoned the notion that it made sense to pursue the ideal of joy in work, having concluded that workers, under the influence of Neue Sachlichkeit, no longer wanted to develop close personal links with their jobs, and were prepared to adapt to the world created by rationalization.[65] For similar reasons, he rejected the idea of Werksgemeinschaft as an outdated and potentially pernicious romanticism. Nevertheless, he looked for solutions ever more to private industry rather than to the state, insisting that companies, through internal educational programs and Werkspolitik, should do what they could to give the workers a greater understanding of and sense of involvement with the enterprise that employed them, thereby decreasing labor alienation while at the same time stabilizing the workforce.[66]

Finally, Rauecker was typical in his growing awareness that if the aim was to humanize rationalized production, it was necessary not only to adapt work to human beings, but also to change people to fit the new world of work. Gradually, it dawned on people that needed reforms were not likely to occur unless there was a prior alteration of attitudes to work on the part of both employers and workers. The situation was well summed up as early as 1924 by Professor Otto von Zwiedineck-Südenhorst (1871–1957) of the University of Munich. A major contributor to the social policy debate in the early years of the Weimar

[63] Rauecker, *Versittlichung des Arbeitslebens* (1920), 24–26, quoting manifestos issued by the *Reichsverband gemeinnütziger Arbeitsgenossenschaften* and the *Deutsche Arbeitsbund* in which both organizations dedicated themselves to the restoration of the love of work (*Arbeitslust*).

[64] Bruno Rauecker, "Die sozialpolitische Bedeutung der Wirtschaftspsychologie," *SP* 33 (1924): 88–89, 109–111.

[65] Bruno Rauecker, "Zur Psychologie der mechanisierten Industriearbeit," *SP* 37 (1928), 1177–78. Rauecker had developed the same argument in the early 1920s, e.g., in his *Die Berufsfreude im modernen Wirtschaftsleben* of 1922, 1929, but at that time he still sought by various means to restore Berufsfreude or even Arbeitsfreude.

[66] Rauecker, *Rationalisierung als Kulturfaktor*, 27–30; "Zur Psychologie der mechanisierten Industriearbeit," 1178; *Rationalisierung und Sozialpolitik*, 70–71.

Republic,[67] Zwiedineck believed that for the sake of the nation, "joy in work must be made into a keystone of the social structure" and that "everything possible must be done to ensure that work is seen not only as an economic factor but rather . . . as the soul of the economy."[68] To achieve this, he favored the idea of converting from serial to group production along the lines suggested by Hellpach, but, like Hellpach, he recognized that this and other desirable reforms necessitated new ways of thinking. The employers "must come to see their highest vocation in restructuring work to make it capable of giving joy to their workers,"[69] while the workers, for their part, must learn that it was in their own interests to operate within the system. An effective social policy could be developed only if Germans learned to think as one and accepted responsibility for probing to its depths the social question which their country was fated to experience more acutely than other nations.[70]

Just how this was to be accomplished Zwiedineck did not explain. But quite a number of his socially conscious contemporaries thought it a useful first step to ascertain what Germans currently thought about work. The following chapters will analyze the efforts of reformers to establish what the German attitude to modern work was, what it should be, and what might be done to inculcate the appropriate ideas into the hearts and minds of German workers.

[67] See Preller, *Sozialpolitik*, 212–13.

[68] Otto von Zwiedineck-Südenhorst, "Zum Schicksal der Sozialpolitik in Deutschland," (*Schmollers Jahrbuch*, 1924), reprinted in *Mensch und Gesellschaft* (Berlin: Duncker & Humblot, 1961), ed. Otto Neuloh, 160.

[69] Zwiedineck-Südenhorst, "Zum Schicksal," 160.

[70] Zwiedineck-Südenhorst, "Zum Schicksal," 161.

IX

ATTITUDES TOWARDS
MODERN WORK

GERMAN REFORMERS who set themselves the task of humanizing modern work either by changing the process of production or by reorganizing industrial relations, recognized that conflicts of interest and institutional inertia constituted major obstacles to the attainment of their goal. But many of them became convinced that the chief barrier to further progress was the persistence of attitudes inimical to industrial peace and social harmony. Before determining how such attitudes might best be modified, it seemed logical to discover what German workers actually thought about work and society.

The result was a large number of studies that built on what had been done before the war and used ingenious methods to probe opinion. Disappointingly, no clear picture emerged. Examining a selection of these attempts enables one to see why even the most "scientific" study failed to produce conclusive results. It also allows one to establish what educated Germans *thought* could be demonstrated about the attitudes of their fellow citizens to work. The latter is particularly important, for it was perceptions rather than "facts" that shaped contemporary attempts to delineate a work ethic more in tune with the realities of modern life, and to bring the 'is' and the 'ought' into accord with one another.

Undoubtedly the most influential of many attempts to deal empirically with the question of attitudes to work in the era of Neue Sachlichkeit was an investigation by the Belgian socialist Hendrik de Man (1885–1953), reported as "The Struggle for Joy in Work."[1] The son of a bourgeois family who had early been attracted to Marxism, de Man first came to Germany in 1905 as a reporter for a Belgian socialist newspaper to cover the Jena Congress of the SPD. When he was offered a job with the *Leipziger Volkszeitung*, he decided to stay in Germany. By

[1] Hendrik de Man, *Der Kampf um die Arbeitsfreude* (Jena: Eugen Diederichs, 1927). References in the text are to this edition. An English translation, entitled *Joy in Work*, was published in 1929 by Allen & Unwin in London.

1907 he was first secretary of the Socialist Youth International, which he had helped to found, and had become actively involved with both the Belgian and German socialist parties. Meanwhile, he had enrolled at the university in Leipzig, where he came into contact with Wilhelm Wundt, Karl Bücher, and the art historian Karl Lamprecht.[2] After concluding his studies, he spent nearly a year in England, then returned home to help build the Belgian workers' education movement.

It was his experiences during the First World War, in which he fought against Germany, that led de Man to abandon Marxist orthodoxy and develop his own brand of socialism. De Man had been sent as a representative of the Belgian government first to Kerensky's Russia and, in the last six months of the war, to the United States. There, as part of a team investigating the possible application of American industrial methods in postwar reconstruction, he became a convert to political democracy and decided to make the United States his home. After a short period as instructor in social psychology at the University of Washington, however, his left-wing activities cost him his job. By 1922, having fallen out of favor with the Belgian socialists as well, de Man chose to settle in Germany where he taught for four years at the Frankfurt Academy of Labor before assuming the newly created chair of social psychology at the University of Frankfurt in 1929.

Even before his *Joy in Work* appeared, de Man had brought out two important books directly related to the problem of modern work. In the first, he drew on what he had learned in the United States to explore the social consequences of scientific management.[3] This initial attempt to tackle the problem of "how man can find happiness, not only through work, but in work,"[4] was followed up in his controversial *The Psychology of Socialism* of 1926.[5] Here, de Man sought to describe the state of mind of the industrial proletariat without resort to the Marxist notion of class consciousness. Instead, he employed concepts derived from psychology and psychoanalysis, or, as one reviewer put it, used Wundt and Freud as a corrective to Marx.[6]

[2] Peter Dodge, *Beyond Marxism: The Faith and Works of Hendrik de Man* (The Hague: Martinus Nijhoff, 1966), 22–24. The biographical information on de Man is drawn from Dodge except where otherwise indicated. De Man wrote a doctoral thesis, along thoroughly Marxist lines, on the Ghent textile industry in the Middle Ages

[3] Hendrik de Man, *Au Pays du Taylorisme* (Brussels: Le Peuple, 1919).

[4] Dodge, *Beyond Marxism*, 117. The quotation is from de Man's *Zur Psychologie des Sozialismus* (Jena: Eugen Diederichs, 1926), 45.

[5] Hendrik de Man, *Zur Psychologie des Sozialismus* (2d ed.: Jena: Eugen Diederichs, 1927; reprinted Bonn: Hohwacht, 1976). An English translation, *The Psychology of Socialism*, was published in 1928 by Allen & Unwin and in 1929 in New York by Henry Holt.

[6] Theodor Heuss, "Zur Psychologie des Sozialismus," *Berliner Börsen-Courier*, 23 May 1926. Heuss welcomed de Man's emphasis on the problem of work, but found his descriptive passages more valuable than his theorizing. A more critical review by Dr. Franz Müller in the

Joy in Work was thus the product of de Man's experience in the socialist and trade union movements, his first-hand observation of modern industrialism, and his considerable theoretical reflection on worker motivation. Yet what most impressed contemporaries was the fact that its conclusions were ostensibly based on a scientific survey designed to test in Germany hypotheses de Man had arrived at on the basis of his Belgian, English, and North American experience. The book included seventy-eight edited protocols summarizing questionnaires completed by students from his social psychology classes at the Frankfurt Academy of Labor in 1924–25 and 1925–26.[7] The students answered questions about career, education, changes of work, job description with specific reference to qualifications, scope for initiative, variety, methods of payment, hygiene, average wages, vacation provisions, work hierarchy, and social and other aspects of their work environment that had a direct bearing on their state of mind. The questionnaire also sought to probe feelings: about the machines and tools, colleagues, superiors, the job in general, and preferred leisure activities. Optional questions dealt with any perceived connection between joy in work and participation in the works councils or unions on the one hand, and general social attitudes on the other. Finally, respondents were encouraged to indicate how they thought Arbeitsfreude might best be increased, whether by changing the work process, the organization of the firm, or the social order as a whole.[8] Interviews were used to supplement the written protocols, each of which, de Man stressed, represented a *person*.[9]

De Man knew that his students were unrepresentative of German workers. Drawn from the younger generation (most were between the ages of twenty and thirty), his sample was above average with respect to intelligence and included a disproportionate number of individuals who had been sent to the Academy by their trade union, were active in the organized labor movement, and had considerable job experience. Moreover, although the sample covered a wide range of blue and white collar occupations and included both skilled and unskilled workers, some branches of industry, notably metalworking and the printing trades, were over-represented.[10] De Man acknowledged that the questionnaires would have to be assessed in a qualitative rather than a quantitative manner, but also insisted on the value of his evidence: if his

Catholic *Soziale Revue* 27 (1927): 479–80, correctly pointed out that de Man was no Freudian, but rather adhered to a form of "drive psychology."

[7] For the book, de Man shortened the protocols and paraphrased the material, only occasionally including direct quotations. De Man, *Kampf um die Arbeitsfreude*, 7.

[8] De Man, *Kampf um die Arbeitsfreude*, 4–5.

[9] De Man, *Kampf um die Arbeitsfreude*, 9. [10] De Man, *Kampf um die Arbeitsfreude*, 5–6.

respondents did not reflect the present sentiments of the bulk of workers, in his judgment they constituted a vocal elite whose views indicated the direction in which the masses were moving.[11]

Although he made no claim for the statistical validity of his findings, de Man like Levenstein before him tried to make his generalizations look more scientific by calculating percentages. Thus he noted that whereas positive attitudes to work were expressed by only 11 percent of the unskilled, 44 percent of the semi-skilled, and 67 percent of the skilled workers in his sample, every member of the group reported experiencing joy in work at some point.[12] From this he optimistically concluded that every worker possessed an autogenous psychic drive to Arbeitsfreude, that this drive was the natural possession of all normal individuals, and that the circumstances which either encouraged or thwarted its practical fulfillment were under human control.[13] He then proceeded to tabulate the motives which in varying degrees led the individual to seek joy in work, as well as the factors that inhibited its flourishing.[14]

De Man broke down Arbeitsfreude into seven fundamental components, five incidental motives, and the sense of social obligation. The factors inhibiting Arbeitsfreude he divided more simply into just three groups: those deriving from the work situation, including technological constraints, those involving social conditions in the workplace, and still others connected with extraneous social factors. By expanding on each of these categories, de Man was able to develop a complex picture of the German worker's psyche.

Although his findings were presented in a reasonably clear and "scientific" manner, their implications were not as straightforward as de Man must have wished. It was not at all obvious that socialism, even in the revised version that he advocated, would be able to address the problem of work more successfully than a humanized capitalism incorporating some features of industrial democracy. In fact, the book provided a great deal of 'evidence' that German workers were on good terms with their machines and were prepared to welcome opportunities to utilize and master the latest technology, as long as they were treated with respect by their superiors. In de Man's own words, "Not the machine, but rather the supervisor is the worker's chief enemy. Among the causes of worker disaffection social conditions outweigh the tech-

---

[11] De Man, *Kampf um die Arbeitsfreude*, 7.   [12] De Man, *Kampf um die Arbeitsfreude*, 147.
[13] De Man, *Kampf um die Arbeitsfreude*, 149.
[14] De Man, *Kampf um die Arbeitsfreude*, 150.

nical, and among the social factors an autocratic works hierarchy stands in first place."[15]

De Man also concluded that German workers were more willing than their peers in other countries passively to accept poor wages and working conditions, and that they were surprisingly uninfluenced by Marxist class consciousness, continuing to derive pleasure from their actual work even while verbally condemning capitalism as 75 percent of his sample did.[16] No wonder, then, that *Joy in Work* was welcomed enthusiastically by those who hoped to preserve the essential features of the status quo based on the principle of private property.

Even more cheering to conservatively-inclined contemporaries was de Man's assertion that the workers still demonstrated remnants of a strong belief in the duty to work for the good of society.[17] Admittedly only a minority, composed of individuals who retained a religious sense of community or believed in a socialist future, was sufficiently moved by ethical considerations to be able to transform a socially conditioned distaste for work into a higher pleasure in work out of a sense of social duty.[18] But de Man acknowledged that because most people wanted to look good in the eyes of their co-workers and immediate superiors, they tried to avoid appearing sloppy or lazy in their presence. Traditional habits of respect for those in authority reinforced a tendency to uphold the unspoken contract between employer and employee and to accept the superior social status of the ruling classes. They helped to sanction ethical values that made it difficult for any anticapitalist ideology to destroy the feeling of obligation to work and work well.[19]

Convinced that a strong normative belief in the obligation to work for the general good was capable of overcoming rational counter-arguments as well as individual instincts inhibiting the desire to work,[20] de Man maintained that the propagation of a new ethic of work centered on duty could help to solve the problem of Arbeitsfreude. In particular, he argued that nationalism—the only sentiment still potent enough to influence the masses at a time when religion had virtually ceased positively to affect feelings about work—could be used to strengthen their sense of duty.[21]

Such arguments seemed ideally suited to encourage those who

[15] De Man, *Kampf um die Arbeitsfreude*, 275.
[16] De Man, *Kampf um die Arbeitsfreude*, 250–51, 286.
[17] De Man, *Kampf um die Arbeitsfreude*, 177.
[18] De Man, *Kampf um die Arbeitsfreude*, 189.
[19] De Man, *Kampf um die Arbeitsfreude*, 178–80.
[20] De Man, *Kampf um die Arbeitsfreude*, 177, 184.
[21] De Man, *Kampf um die Arbeitsfreude*, 181–88.

wished to believe that the workers might be weaned away from Marxism, integrated into the works community, and motivated to do their best without the need to embark on a serious program of reform. Yet when de Man stressed the importance of environmental factors in shaping attitudes and behavior or emphasized the persistence of proletarian consciousness, he gave comfort to his fellow socialists. This facet of the book was reinforced by his insistence that industrial work would continue to be regarded as socially inferior by others and by the workers themselves so long as it was done by people at the bottom of the social hierarchy from the point of view of intelligence and education. Individuals doomed to this fate were bound to develop a proletarian inferiority complex and remain wedded to it in the absence of genuine institutional change. Overall, de Man concluded that the problem of work must be tackled in the first instance by reforming the conditions that inhibited Arbeitsfreude, particularly in the sphere of industrial relations, rather than by influencing attitudes directly. The new work ethic for which he called, the spirit of social obligation that alone could overcome the final obstacles to joy in work, would emerge only if a genuine community was first established in the enterprise:

> No works spirit without Works Community, no Works Community without a community of will and interest, no community of will without co-determination, no community of interest without power sharing.[22]

These were the sentiments that de Man chose to emphasize a few years later in an entry on "worker psychology" in Giese's *Handwörterbuch der Arbeitswissenschaft*.[23] To counteract the optimism regarding the potential for Arbeitsfreude in rationalized industry which *Joy in Work* had encouraged, de Man devoted much of this article to explaining just how psychological and situational factors differentiated the "proletarian" attitude to work from that of the rest of the population. Arguing that factory workers were chiefly motivated by economic need and fear of unemployment, de Man here gave center stage to the physical and psychological consequences of poverty and to the unconscious *ressentiment* or social inferiority complex that underlay proletarian class consciousness. Now he explained worker disaffection more in terms of the

---

[22] De Man, *Kampf um die Arbeitsfreude*, 188. De Man was here restating a position he had already developed in 1921. Addressing a group of Belgian trade unionists, he had insisted that ordinary workers would come to experience the joy in work that already motivated the creative technician only when the democratic re-organization of industry would allow them to participate once more in planning the productive process. Hendrik de Man, "Workers' Control," in *A Documentary Study of Hendrik de Man, Socialist Critic of Marxism*, ed. Peter Dodge (Princeton: Princeton University Press, 1979), 127.

[23] HA, 1 (1930): 199–217.

thwarted need to "count" in and through work rather than attributing it to the frustrated drive to experience joy in work. After describing how ordinary workers sought to compensate for their inability to salvage their self-esteem on the job by free-time work in house and garden, or by exercising their native talents in trade union activity, he maintained that real change would have to come from the workers themselves, and that the only hope lay in further developing the new ethical pride of caste spawned by socialism and the labor movement. Reform attempts that underestimated or ignored the sense of solidarity and class consciousness of the workers would be rejected by them and so come to nothing.[24]

Worried that his contemporaries were drawing the wrong conclusions from *Joy in Work*, de Man also recognized the study's methodological limitations and therefore sought better ways to gain insight into the worker's psyche. This led him to conduct a model investigation of a single enterprise, using interviews with a large number of workers over a considerable period of time, but the results of this study were never published, allegedly because the company involved insisted on secrecy.[25] He also experimented with radio interviews, which seemed to present a unique method for eliciting revealing material of a social psychological nature. Subjects were pre-selected and questioned in their place of work so as to enable the interviewer to formulate relevant questions and also to provide a basis for assessing the validity of the answers they gave on air. They were kept in ignorance of the questions they would be asked so as to maintain spontaneity.[26]

If the resulting interviews made good radio, it is doubtful that they added much to what was known about worker attitudes. The fact that de Man's interviewees, although representing a variety of types of work, were selected on the advice of the trade unions largely for their ability to verbalize feelings, laid his radio survey open to the same criticism that had been leveled against his earlier efforts, namely that the views expressed were atypical. Moreover, it is unlikely that they reflected the deeper attitudes and personal experience even of the individuals with whom he talked. What went on the air were the opinions adopted by a set of exceptionally intelligent and articulate people influenced by contact with the socialist labor movement.[27] As far as de Man himself

---

[24] HA, 1 (1930): 215.

[25] Hendrik de Man, "Mensch und Maschine," in *Die Akademie der Arbeit in der Universität Frankfurt a. M. 1921–1931*, ed. Ernst Michel (Frankfurt: Union-Druckerei, 1931), 149.

[26] De Man, "Mensch und Maschine," 149–53.

[27] De Man, "Mensch und Maschine," 150.

was concerned, the evidence from the radio experiment reinforced convictions already formed on the basis of his earlier researches.

Although antisocialists found much in his writings to encourage them in their fight for the soul of the worker, de Man's perspective on the problem of work and the question of worker attitudes throughout this period remained that of a socialist dedicated to the humanization of work through extension of worker power in the workplace and in society. This was recognized at the time by the socialist and trade union press which gave his books respectful treatment, despite the fact that his revisionism rendered him suspect in the eyes of doctrinaire Marxists. Thus a popular Social Democratic catalogue of suggested reading for workers described his *Zur Psychologie des Sozialismus* as "insightful" if wrong in a number of ways;[28] while several socialists cited *Joy in Work* in support of their beliefs. One was the socialist educator Richard Seidel who praised de Man for successfully dispelling the clouds with which the voluminous literature about *Entseelung*, with its anachronistic romanticization of the crafts, had surrounded the subject of modern work.[29] By contrast, Julius Fries of Hamburg thought de Man had demonstrated the growing discrepancy between the workers' longing for joyful work and their actual situation, a discrepancy that would increasingly turn them against capitalism and strengthen their desire for a new socialist order.[30]

De Man's emphasis on the need to restore (or liberate) joy in work, combined with his attempt to illuminate worker attitudes with the help of psychological theories and empirical data, placed him in the direct succession of Riehl, Herkner, and Levenstein,[31] and made him the most important contributor to this aspect of the science of work to emerge in the 1920s. But he was not the first Weimar investigator to use the questionnaire to probe worker attitudes in a "scientific" manner. A year before the publication of *Joy in Work* Hermann Bues, a vocational counselor in Harburg on the Elbe, reported on an extensive study of youth and work that covered vocational students from thirty-five trades as well as four categories of unskilled workers drawn from Harburg and three neighboring towns.[32] In total, 3,523 young people between the ages of fourteen and eighteen were asked a series of open-

[28] *Das Buch des Arbeiters. Ein Wegweiser für alle Schaffenden* (Dresden, 1926/27).

[29] Richard Seidel, "Psychologie im Dienste der Arbeitswissenschaft," *Die Arbeit* 4 (1927): 805–18.

[30] Julius Fries, "Gibt es noch Arbeitsfreude? Die Erbschaft des bürokratisch-militärischen Obrigkeitsstaates," *Gewerkschafts-Archiv* 13 (1930): 193–99.

[31] See Gottschalch, "Historische Stationen," 459–67.

[32] Hermann Bues, *Die Stellung der Jugendlichen zum Beruf und zur Arbeit* (Bernau bei Berlin: Grüner, 1926).

ended questions about the light and dark sides of their chosen occupation. Although some refused to complete the survey or did so only reluctantly, most complied.[33] Scoring was done by counting, tabulating, and then calculating the percentage of positive and negative statements in each protocol, without any effort to weight or evaluate them.

Bues, too, gave a central place to the concept of Arbeitsfreude, which he attempted to break down into more manageable components. He first tabulated the "positive" responses to the work itself under such headings as joy in work for its own sake and pleasure in independence and responsibility, joy in the finished product, and joy in the opportunity to impose aesthetic standards. This was followed by a section dealing with the pleasures to be derived from the work environment and another on vocational prospects. The same three major categories were used to group the negative statements.

The unsophisticated nature of Bues's analysis, coupled with the fact that some subgroups of his sample were too small to give statistically meaningful results, limited the value of the survey.[34] Nevertheless, the material did enable Bues to make suggestive comparisons between occupational groupings and between skilled and unskilled work. Thus he claimed to have demonstrated that among the unskilled, factory workers were considerably less likely to derive joy from work than such people as messenger boys or servants,[35] and that a somewhat greater number of industrial trainees (6.9 percent) than crafts apprentices (3.3 percent) expressed genuine enthusiasm for their specific occupations.[36]

Although Bues was clearly disappointed that only 0.17 percent of those preparing for the skilled trades named social motives among the reasons for their job satisfaction, and only 0.5 percent indicated any degree of vocational pride, he drew comfort from the fact that a few individuals with a sense of calling could be found in even the lowliest occupations. What is more, he was convinced that pride in work would gradually develop as young workers came under the influence of the trade unions and of such excellent institutions as the Borsig company paper, which devoted itself to nurturing both vocational pride and a sense of Werkgemeinschaft.[37]

He was also optimistic in his interpretation of the evidence relating

[33] Bues, *Stellung der Jugendlichen*, 18.

[34] Reviewing Bues's study in *Jugend und Beruf* 1 (1926): 263–64, Richard Liebenberg recommended it to vocational counselors and others, but argued that more could be learned from small group discussions such as those he had held with young trade unionists the previous winter, and that spiritual matters could in any case not be quantified. Cf. the enthusiastic review in *Technik und Kultur* (1926): 186–87.

[35] Bues, *Stellung der Jugendlichen*, 31.   [36] Bues, *Stellung der Jugendlichen*, 43.

[37] Bues, *Stellung der Jugendlichen*, 64–67.

to his sub-sample of school leavers employed in unskilled factory jobs. Bues noted that individuals did not choose this type of work, but were forced to engage in such unsatisfying occupations by external circumstances, above all by their families' inability to finance further training: over two-thirds of the 129 Altona factory workers questioned and over three-quarters of the 179 in Harburg said that they had wanted to train for a trade at the conclusion of their schooling, and a high percentage of these still wished to do so after three years in the workforce.[38] This led Bues to recommend the introduction of a state-assisted system of compulsory one-year apprenticeships. Combined with improved job counselling, such a system would enable the 80 percent of young people held back only by lack of funds to enter into occupations capable of giving joy in work. In this way, it would be possible to make full use of the nation's human resources, and so enable Germany to compete successfully in the world market for quality goods.[39]

Given Bues's professional interests, it is hardly surprising that he supported the extension of subsidized compulsory vocational training and guidance. It is also likely that he would have favored this scheme even if he had never undertaken his survey, for he could point to similar steps taken by the Belgians, Swiss, and French.[40] Like de Man and others who studied the question of joy in work empirically, Bues interpreted his evidence so as to make it conform with judgments arrived at by other means and used it to strengthen the case for reforms appropriate to his social role and in line with his particular set of ideals. Yet there is no reason to doubt that Bues embarked on his research with a genuine desire to shed new light on the workers' psyche. In any event, his work was taken seriously by contemporary scholars.[41]

Among the most methodologically innovative researchers to examine proletarian youth from the perspective of joy in work were Günther Dehn (1882–1970) and Ernst Lau (1893–?). A controversial Protestant pastor and one of the founders of the group of religious socialists, Dehn was primarily interested in the workers' spiritual life. In 1921–1922, together with the psychologist Lau, he required sixty-four classes of pupils in Berlin's further education schools to produce essays on their attitudes towards work. Asked to write either on "Work-Joy-Unemploy-

[38] Bues, *Stellung der Jugendlichen*, 269–72, 278–82.
[39] Bues, *Stellung der Jugendlichen*, 299–304.   [40] Bues, *Stellung der Jugendlichen*, 302–303.
[41] E.g., Paul Felix Lazarsfeld, *Jugend und Beruf. Kritik und Material* (Jena: Gustav Fischer, 1931), and Hilde Rosenberg, *Die Berufsvorbereitung des Industriearbeiters und ihre Bedeutung im Kampf um die Arbeitsfreude* (Cologne: M. DuMont-Schauberg, 1930). Rosenberg drew heavily on Bues although she was critical of his methodology and strongly disagreed with his conclusions and recommendations.

ment" or "Work-Joy-Anger," all but two classes (where the teacher's political views were said to have influenced the outcome) were thought to have responded with sincerity.[42] Dehn and Lau also questioned the boys and girls in person regarding the reasons for their choice of occupation, their hopes for the future, and their religious views, about which Dehn reported separately in 1923.[43] These conversations were judged to be particularly fruitful: the students, who apparently thought they were talking to union officials or people interested in assessing their intellectual abilities, were pleased that someone was taking them seriously and so spoke freely.

Breaking the sample down by occupational category, Lau noted for each the chief motivation for work and associated virtues. Although he recognized that everyone worked for money, he found it interesting that each group seemed to have its own approach to earning and a distinctive vocational outlook.[44] But Lau failed to make clear just what, if anything, followed from this set of findings. He also was justifiably defensive about the methodological shortcomings of the study, but this did not prevent him from generalizing about the strength of his young subjects' unconscious will to work (*Arbeitswillen*), which he claimed was closely correlated with their feelings about Arbeitsfreude. His chief conclusion, namely that there was a striking contrast between the skilled and the unskilled, was subsequently confirmed by Bues and others.[45] On the other hand, Lau found that few in the latter group complained about their work being too hard, nor did they suffer from monotony or find their jobs demeaning.[46] Indeed, it was just this total adaptation to undemanding and intrinsically unsatisfying work and the low level of aspiration it demonstrated that Lau deplored.

Lau maintained that attitudes to work were environmentally determined, with the first job often playing a critical role;[47] but he acknowl-

[42] Ernst Lau, "Die Berliner Jugend und ihr Beruf," in *Beiträge zur Psychologie der Jugend. Moral-und-sozial-psychologische Untersuchungen auf experimenteller Grundlage* (4th ed.; Langensalza: Julius Beltz, 1930), 46.

[43] Originally published as Günther Dehn, *Die religiöse Gedankenwelt der Proletarierjugend*, this went into several editions and was eventually reprinted as Part 2 of Dehn's *Proletarische Jugend* (Berlin: Furche, 1929).

[44] According to Lau, the unskilled worked to earn money for themselves and their families and were characterized by a willingness to take on every kind of job, while clerks were proud to work and earn independently and had the virtue of conscientiousness.

[45] Those training for a specific occupation or Beruf revealed positive attitudes to work; the unskilled, irrespective of their sex, regarded their work as Arbeit in the classical sense of burden, and therefore were indifferent to their jobs. Lau, "Berliner Jugend," 83.

[46] Lau, "Berliner Jugend," 49–52.

[47] This was confirmed experimentally in a psychotechnical study of 650 Württemberg vo-

edged that an outside observer could easily mistake such an acquired disposition of the will (*Willensleben*) for an inborn drive, and therefore urged readers to continue to "will to change the will," rather than allowing gloomy thoughts about the evil nature of humanity to deter them from this attempt.[48] Unlike Bues, however, whose findings he cited in confirmation of his own, Lau did not explain how joy in work might be inculcated in the face of the overwhelmingly materialistic attitudes revealed by his study and the strength of environmental forces.

By contrast, his co-researcher emerged undaunted from this early experiment. Subsequent contacts with young proletarians and a second series of school visits in 1929 led Dehn to the optimistic conclusion not only that many trades still impressed their distinctive traits on workers, but also that the work ethic was far from dead and that a considerable store of "healthy Volk power" persisted among skilled proletarians.[49] Specifically, he argued that the youth movement, which preached the need for a new man and a new ethic, was helping to restore faith in human creativity. If people came to believe in their ability to construct a world in which all could be happy, a new ethical socialism might emerge that would lead the way to a better society.[50]

Using Lau's methods to study the problem of monotony, Dieck, an industrial training instructor in the Harburg/Elbe district where Bues had undertaken his survey two years earlier,[51] experimentally confirmed Lau's findings that money was the chief motivator and that as they grew older, people came to accept or even to like or, occasionally, prefer monotonous jobs. However, Dieck questioned whether the young were inwardly as satisfied as the evidence seemed to indicate. Building on Lau's suggestion about the impact of the first job, he argued instead that the abrupt transition from school to factory constituted a trauma that inhibited the individual's natural psychic development and accounted for the subsequent apathetic acceptance of stagnation. The answer, in his view, was to keep young people of impressionable years away from monotonous work in the interests of their mental health by extending schooling to the age of eighteen. If this were done, even the unskilled, presumably after a period of instruction by people like himself, would

---

cational pupils. See Erich Wagner, *Berufsumwelt und geistige Leistung bei Jugendlichen* (Halle: C. Marhold, 1930).

[48] Lau, "Berliner Jugend," 84.   [49] Dehn, *Proletarische Jugend*, Preface, and 66–67.

[50] Dehn, *Proletarische Jugend*, 56–58.

[51] F. Dieck, "Beiträge zum Verständnis der Industriejugend," *Jugend und Beruf* 2 (1927): 229–30, 271–73, 309–310, 348–49. Dieck gave his pupils the key words: work-joy-money, and asked them to write essays linking "work" with either "joy" or "money."

enter the workforce as fully developed, educated individuals capable of understanding the importance of rationalization to the economy and the national community, and so able to engage in their boring jobs with minimal psychic damage.[52]

A somewhat different approach to the challenge of determining worker attitudes was that of the Catholic educator Heinrich Kautz (1892–?), who was convinced that the deteriorating condition of industrial humanity was the key problem of the day, and that the question of how best to educate people for work in industry was the prime concern not just of German but of European pedagogy. Published in 1926, two years before Kautz graduated in sociology, economic history, and philosophy from the University of Cologne, his *In the Shadow of the Smoke Stack* used unsystematically assembled material on the workers' physical and psychological condition to assess the industrial milieu of the Rhineland as it affected individuals, families, and groups (types).[53]

Although Kautz used questionnaires, interviews, and personal observation to prepare his book, he admitted that his attempt to delineate the state of mind of industrial man was not fully scientific. Just the same, he claimed that his *Seelenkunde*, the study of souls, broke new ground in industrial psychology and was a methodological improvement on pre-1914 studies. Kautz tried to take into account the circumstances under which questions were answered and therefore avoided handing out questionnaires on weekends or holidays when people had time to think too much and consult with friends and neighbors. He also thought it best to select a small sample and to administer tests without warning so as to avoid intervention by outside groups such as trade unions.[54] Finally, he believed it legitimate and necessary to supplement survey results with insights derived from a whole range of other approaches, including the study of industrial fables and the social novel.[55]

Kautz vividly described the evil consequences of modernization and analyzed in gloomy detail the enormous environmental stresses that shaped the mentality of the industrial worker. On the basis of his re-

[52] Dieck, "Beiträge," 348–49.

[53] Heinrich Kautz, *Im Schatten der Schlote. Versuche zur Seelenkunde der Industriejugend* (Einsiedeln: Benziger, 1926), 10. Biographical information can be gleaned from the back cover of Heinrich Kautz's postwar *Das Zerschlagene Menschenbild. Prinzipien und Ideen zur Wirklichkeit und Ideologie des Nationalsozialismus* (Sankt Augustin, Verlag Wort und Werk, 1977), and from his *Lebenslauf* in BDC, personnel records of the Reichsschulungsamt.

[54] Heinrich Kautz, *Industrie formt Menschen. Versuch einer Normierung der Industriepädagogik* (Einsiedeln: Benziger, 1929), 256–59.

[55] Kautz's *Lebenslauf* in BDC lists among his publications *Industriemärchen* (1927), an analysis of industrial fables, and *Das Ende der sozialen Frage* (1932) in which Kautz discussed social novels. I was unable to examine either of these books.

search he concluded that workers were in danger of succumbing to materialism, socialism, excessive politicization, and secularism and needed to be inoculated against these dangers if revolution was to be averted. Calling for a *völkisch* approach not only to education but also to pastoral work, he urged that *all* young people in industrial areas, not just the proletarians, be taught the importance of working for the family, the community, and the nation.[56] In the essential task of changing people's attitudes, educators had an important part to play. It was the industrial pedagogue's responsibility to bring the workers back to a true sense of community and traditional values, or at least to reconcile them to the realities of depersonalized work by inculcating a spirit of heroic selflessness.[57] At the same time, Kautz's dislike of the Weimar Republic, which he regarded as a class state under socialist influence,[58] led him to deny that the public school system could serve as the appropriate instrument of this "fight against deformation and for reformation."[59] Instead, he assigned the Catholic church and its schools a central role in the fight for the soul of the "worker" in the broader sense that included all active members of industrial society. He also cooperated from the start with the Dinta's industry-sponsored efforts to have a direct influence on the attitudes of those involved in modern rationalized production.[60]

In addition to educators and psychologists, Protestant and Catholic reform groups and a number of trade unions sponsored attitude surveys in the 1920s. Although none used very sophisticated methods, they played a major role in shaping attempts to formulate and solve the problem of work.

The major Protestant effort along these lines was a survey of 1926 in which the ESK gathered information about the living and work conditions of the young, using evidence from people who had professional dealings with their subjects, such as ministers, youth group leaders, teachers, welfare workers, and trade union officials.[61] The only generalization about attitudes to work that emerged from this study was that

[56] Kautz, *Im Schatten der Schlote*, 245–62. Kautz recognized that not everything could be reduced to morality and Weltanschauung, and that education was no panacea for the miserable conditions he described. He advocated an active state social policy and scientifically based company welfare programs, and insisted that capitalist exploitation must be overcome, possibly through some form of Christian Solidarism. Kautz, *Industrie formt Menschen*, 12, 78–87, 232–33.

[57] Kautz, *Industrie formt Menschen*, 231–32.   [58] Kautz, *Im Schatten der Schlote*, 294–95.
[59] Kautz, *Industrie formt Menschen*, 27.
[60] According to his *Lebenslauf*, 19 February 1942, 4, in BDC, Kautz lectured in the Dinta's engineering school from 1925 to 1938. On the Dinta, see Chapter 11, below.
[61] See Wilhelm Hülssner, "Die Lebens- und Arbeitsverhältnisse der erwerbstätigen Jugend," *Evangelisch-Sozial* (1927, nos. 1–4; 1928, no. 2; 1929, nos. 1 and 4).

it was wrong to generalize: while some young people were reported as liking their work and experiencing Arbeitsfreude, others appeared to be completely alienated.

Not surprisingly, this conclusion echoed the views of Waldemar Zimmermann (1876–1963), professor of economics at Hamburg, whose numerous books and articles dealing with the effects of rationalization on the workers' psyche emphasized the importance of individual differences.[62] Fully conversant with the earlier work of Levenstein, Herkner, Lau, and others, Zimmermann evidently hoped that the ESK survey, in whose design he had played a major role, would add to the body of knowledge about worker attitudes, but it is hard to see what he expected it to contribute. Its chief purpose may have been to draw attention to the problems of the young workers, and so act as a stimulus to reform; in this it seems to have succeeded.[63]

Methodologically, the ESK study closely paralleled one undertaken in the same year by the Catholic Arbeitervereine (worker associations). But unlike the Protestant survey which focused specifically on young factory workers, the latter was designed to elicit information about the thinking of workers of all ages and several occupations, including craftsmen and agricultural laborers. Reporting on its findings, Josef Joos (1878–1965), himself a skilled carpenter and one of the chief organizers of the Catholic worker association movement, came to conclusions about the plight of "industrial man" very similar to those of Kautz.[64] He also noted that the growing concentration of industry and mass unemployment were adversely affecting the spiritual life of Catholic workers.[65] People no longer took pride in their work or displayed a

---

[62] See especially Waldemar Zimmermann, "Das Problem der rationalisierten Industriearbeit in sozial psychologischer Betrachtung," Schmollers Jahrbuch 49 (1925): 107–118; "Erwerbsarbeit und berufliche Erziehung im Lichte sozialer Politik," in Die Aufgaben de neuen Berufsschulwesens und die Berufsschulgemeinde im Lichte der Jugendkunde und sozialer Politik, ed. Peter Petersen and Waldemar Zimmermann (Weimar: Hermann Bölaus Nachfolger, 1925), 1–65; and "Arbeiter und Arbeiterfragen," in Handwörterbuch der Staatswissenschaft (4th ed., 1928), 387–90.

[63] Hülssner, "Lebens- und Arbeitsverhältnisse," 161–66.

[64] Josef Joos, "Ergebnisse der Umfrage über die gegenwärtige seelische Lage der katholischen Arbeiter in Deutschland," Diözanleitung der katholischen Arbeitervereine der Erzdiözese Köln, Mitteilungen an die Arbeiterpraesides, 4, no. 3 (1926), 34–43, and Joos's review of Kautz's Im Schatten der Schlote, "Von proletarischen Menschen," Deutsche Republik 1 (1926/27) 9:1–4. Like Kautz, Joos found that people living in industrial areas were depressingly materialistic, tended to lack respect for authority, adopted extreme political and social attitudes, and lost their sense of ethical values. On Joos, see the entry in NDB, and Oswald Wachtling, Joseph Joos. Journalist-Arbeiterführer-Zentrumspolitiker. Politische Biographie 1878–1933 (Mainz: Matthias-Grünewald, 1974), especially 137–47 describing his activities as a worker leader.

[65] Joos, "Ergebnisse," 36.

high occupational ethic. Although a contributory factor was the insecurity bred by war, defeat, and inflation, which made the situation particularly bad in Germany, Joos maintained that the main culprit was a general depersonalization and dehumanization of work, felt most strongly by wage laborers, as well as the loss of contact between intellectuals and workers.[66]

The survey results did not tell Joos anything he did not know. Already before the war he had written about the deleterious effects of industrial wage labor on the German work ethic and had warned that the church would have to engage in a fight for the soul of the worker: in addition to offering religious instruction as a means to grace, it had a duty to wean the workers from low-grade leisure pursuits such as pubs, cinemas, and music halls, and to teach them how to lead good, family-oriented, "human" lives within the framework of the modern economic and productive system.[67] And in 1922 Joos had stressed the need for restoring the link between work and life and had urged the church to persuade both workers and intellectuals to change their attitudes in preparation for a concerted effort to restore pride and joy in work.[68] Thus the 1926 Arbeiterverein survey merely supplied its sponsors with "empirical" evidence to buttress their previously held beliefs.

Somewhat more revealing was a questionnaire administered by the Christian Metal Workers Union. This survey, which addressed itself to the specific problem of monotonous labor and approached the workers directly, provided the data for a thesis by Liselotte Imhof of the University of Cologne. Imhof also drew heavily on the Levenstein and de Man findings.[69] According to her summary in the union's journal,[70] a small number of respondents said that they preferred monotonous work because it allowed them to think of other things, and a somewhat larger group worked out of a sense of duty, but the majority felt oppressed by routine tasks. On the other hand, many who claimed to find mechanized work monotonous were unclear about what they meant by this, or were critical of features of their work and life situation that had nothing to do with the nature of the job in itself. In fact, Imhof insisted, not a single worker covered by this study opposed technical progress as such or wished to halt the process of technical rationalization.

[66] Joos, "Ergebnisse," 36–41.

[67] Joos, *Industrie und Arbeiterseele*. Flugschriften des Sekretariats sozialer Studentenarbeit 7 [1914].

[68] Joos, *Der Berufsgedanke und die industrielle Lohnarbeit* (Mönchen-Gladbach: Volksvereins-Verlag, 1922).

[69] Liselotte Imhof, *Technischer Fortschritt und Arbeiterschaft* (Duisburg: Echo, 1930).

[70] Liselotte Imhof, "Arbeiterschaft und technischer Fortschritt," *Der Deutsche Metallarbeiter* (1929): 290–92, 309–310.

In her conclusion Imhof joined the ranks of those who argued that "social education," the inculcation of correct attitudes to work, could help to solve the problem of work. Unlike Joos and Kautz, however, she refused to give the recovery of joy in work or the "fight for the soul of the worker" top priority. Instead, adopting the trade union standpoint, she maintained that the *first* task must be to do away with the social and economic evils—including insufficient wages, exploitation, and onerous supervision—that led many workers to voice concern about technical progress. She also called for the reform of industrial relations through restoration of a genuine community of work between organized workers and organized employers, in order to further rationalization through voluntary cooperation.

Whereas the wide-ranging surveys sponsored by the churches and the trade unions threw only indirect light on Joy in Work, Arbeitsfreude was central to the investigation carried out by Karl Miedbrodt (1895–?). A turner employed in a large Berlin works which he regarded as typical of modern industry, Miedbrodt began in the late 1920s to examine his own attitudes to work.[71] Introspection revealed that he regarded work as a duty, but also believed himself to have a right to a bit of associated joy. Curious whether his views were shared by others, he studied the results of earlier opinion research. These left him dissatisfied, however, and he therefore determined to discover for himself what his fellow workers felt about their work. Because he wished to question both trade union members and non-union workers, as well as people of different political persuasions, he rejected the idea of turning to an outside organization for support. Fortunately, he got the subsidy he needed to print his five thousand questionnaires and publish his results from a clergyman who took an interest in his project and, Miedbrodt claimed, gave him full freedom in his inquiries.

Despite the fact that he was a worker speaking to workers, Miedbrodt received back only one hundred questionnaires instead of the three thousand he had hoped to get. Simply assuming these to be representative, he selected fifty to include in his published account. No numerical or statistical analysis was attempted. Instead, the individuals were grouped in accordance with their response to the last question, on their Weltanschauung. Answers to the other fifteen questions were briefly

[71] Karl Miedbrodt, *So denkt der Arbeiter. Eine Sammlung von Fragebogen und Arbeiterbriefen* (Berlin-Tegel: im Selbstverlag, n.d.). The copy in the library of the Free University in Berlin gives the date as "um 1920," but internal evidence, including references to de Man's *Kampf um die Arbeitsfreude*, places it around 1929. A preliminary report on Miedbrodt's results appeared under the title "Geist der Belegschaft," in *Archiv für angewandte Soziologie* 1, no. 2/3 (1928–29): 28–34, 40–45.

summarized. At the end of the book, Miedbrodt reproduced letters which several respondents had attached to their protocols.

Much to Miedbrodt's delight, Question 11, which asked whether the individual had any longing for joy in work, evoked a positive response. Clearly, others besides himself believed that work was not just a question of earning wages and that Arbeitsfreude mattered. Quite a few individuals claimed to enjoy their jobs, and several said that payment by results made work more interesting, but the majority admitted to suffering in one way or another from the lack of consonance between their life and work. Like many middle-class reformers, Miedbrodt concluded that alienation represented the greatest source of working-class malaise.[72] Interpreting his findings as a warning to those who continually put new obstacles in the path of reconciliation between people and their work, he argued that it was more important to transform work and industrial relations than to reshape attitudes.[73]

If Miedbrodt's efforts were regarded with suspicion by his working-class contemporaries, this was probably less because of the amateurish nature of his investigation than because he was associated in their minds with Dunkmann's Institute for Applied Sociology, well known for its anti-trade-union stance. The Institute, which had published one of Miedbrodt's essays on attitudes to the machine, conducted its own survey of worker opinion designed to give the "unorganized minority" a chance to speak out.[74] To what extent the Institute actually supported Miedbrodt, and exactly how his study and Dunkmann's were related, remains unclear.[75] In any event, the Berlin laborer's exceedingly gloomy conclusions about the prospects for joy in work under the present dispensation, identical with the sentiments of the Young Socialists around Bröger with whom Miedbrodt had been connected to 1922,[76]

[72] Miedbrodt, So denkt der Arbeiter, 6: "Die grösste Not unserer Arbeiterschaft ist eine Bewusstseins Not."

[73] Miedbrodt, So denkt der Arbeiter, 59–60 and passim.

[74] Miedbrodt, "Mensch und Maschine," in Unterrichts-Briefe des Instituts für angewandte Soziologie, Series A, no. 10 (1926/27): 18–22; Karl Dunkmann, "Erklärung zur 'Sozialen Praxis' no. 16," in ibid, no. 7: 2–3. Dunkmann was defending himself against an article in the GSR's Soziale Praxis, which had not only condemned his attitude survey, said to be completely unscientific, but had also attacked the Institute as such and urged Dunkmann to return to theology!

[75] According to Miedbrodt, "Geist der Belegschaft," his survey was to be published in full as vol. 2 in the Institute's publication series.

[76] BDC, Miedbrodt file, transcript (copy) of police interrogation report dated 4 May 1937. Miedbrodt here claimed to be a long-time anti-Bolshevik and antisemite. After 1933, he became a propagandist first for the Stahlhelm and then for the National Socialists. See also the twenty-page autobiographical piece dated January 1937, in the same file, and a police report of 21 October 1936 which described Miedbrodt as a member of the SA reserve.

could have done little to cheer those, like Dunkmann or Vorwerck, who hoped to win the battle for the workers' souls without undermining the capitalist status quo.

Dunkmann's attempts to throw light on worker attitudes ran parallel to similar efforts undertaken by sociologists associated with the Frankfurt Institute for Social Research, which represented the opposite end of the political spectrum. Established in 1923 by a group of self-proclaimed neo-Marxists, the Frankfurt Institute undertook in 1929 to explore the social and psychological condition of the working class in Germany through an ambitious survey modelled on Levenstein's investigations. The investigation, as planned by the Freudian Erich Fromm (1900–1980) and carried out with the assistance of Hilde Weiss, was intended to improve on Levenstein in both scale and method. A relatively sophisticated attempt at empirical attitude research on a large scale,[77] it purported to reveal the "psychic structure" that underlay the conscious attitudes expressed by respondents to a lengthy questionnaire.[78]

Although the Frankfurt study had the potential to shed light on important correlations between social and political beliefs on the one hand and psychological makeup on the other, it did not appear in time to influence the Weimar debate about work. The analysis of the protocols was delayed for a variety of reasons, and the project was pushed to one side when the Institute was forced to emigrate to the United States after 1933. But even if the research had proceeded as planned, it would have contributed little to our topic. For only one short section of this study of the German worker dealt with work-related attitudes![79] And, as might have been expected of a survey originating from the Left and supported by the trade unions, it made no attempt to elicit the subjects' views on Arbeitsfreude as such.[80]

Also too late to have an impact on Weimar thinking about the problem of work was Rexford Hersey's study of German railway workers, the last attempt in pre-Hitler Germany to examine worker attitudes using

[77] Of the 3,300 questionnaires distributed to workers in both manual and white-collar jobs, an impressive 1,100 were eventually returned.

[78] See Wolfgang Bonss's introduction to Erich Fromm, *The Working Class in Weimar Germany: A Psychological & Sociological Study* (Cambridge: Harvard University Press, 1984, translated for Berg Publishers Ltd. from the German edition published Stuttgart: Deutsche Verlagsanstalt, 1980), 1–33.

[79] Fromm, *The Working Class*, 101–158. The remainder dealt with political, social and cultural aspects of the respondents' lives.

[80] The questionnaire is reproduced in Fromm, *The Working Class*, Appendix 2. Closest to our topic were Question 135, which asked about attitudes towards rationalization, and Questions 154 through 156, which dealt with job preferences.

survey methods.[81] An American industrial psychologist who had already done research for the Pennsylvania railroad, Hersey was invited to carry out a thorough investigation of the German railways in 1932. Concern about the *Entgeistigung* ("de-spiritualization") of work due to rationalization, mechanization, and the division of labor led Hersey to examine the pre-conditions of Arbeitsfreude as a step towards removing the obstacles to its realization.[82] Employing questionnaires to confirm findings derived from shop-floor and laboratory studies, he concluded that although positive feelings about work did little to raise productivity, negative ones produced a decided drop in output.

So far we have virtually omitted any discussion of women's work. This is because most Germans who wrote about the problem of modern work and agonized over the loss of Arbeitsfreude confined their concern to male workers. This remained true during the Weimar years, despite the fact that more women than ever were entering paid employment and that many of them were engaged in precisely those jobs regarded by social critics as most monotonous and soul-destroying. The trend to increased female participation in the workforce, firmly established before 1914, was greatly accelerated by the war; attempts after 1918 to return women to the home were largely unsuccessful. There were simply too many single women and widows dependent on wages for their own support, while the aging of the population due to a decline in the birth rate, already evident before 1914, increased the demand for women workers. Reinforcing this trend was the rationalization of factory and office, which created a mass of low-paid jobs demanding limited skills, precisely the kind of work for which women were thought ideally suited. Together, these factors led women, many of them married, to join the industrial workforce in unprecedented numbers and to make even more startling advances in the nation's shops and offices.[83]

---

[81] An article by Hersey on factors influencing attitudes to work did appear in the last volume of *Die Arbeit*, but this was based on his studies of American workers. See Rexford Hersey, "Betriebliche und ausserbetriebliche Bedingungen der inneren Einstellung des Arbeiters zur Arbeit," *Die Arbeit* 10 (1933): 32–39. Because his German findings were not published until 1935, it was left to the National Socialists to examine the reform implications of this research. See Rexford Hersey, *Seele und Gefühl des Arbeiters. Psychologie der Menschenführung.* Mit einem Geleitwort von Reichsorganisationsleiter Dr. Robert Ley. (Leipzig: Koncordia-Verlag, 1935). In *Zest for Work: Industry Rediscovers the Individual* (New York: Harper, 1955), which drew on his German research along with investigations carried out between 1927 and 1954 in the United States, Hersey noted that *Seele und Gefühl des Arbeiters* remained the required text for training foremen on German Railways to 1943! Appendix C, 250–57 reports on the "Reaction of German Workers to the Great Depression and Adolf Hitler, 1932–1933."

[82] Hersey, *Seele und Gefühl*, 3.

[83] Preller, *Sozialpolitik*, 120–25, statistically demonstrates the growing role of women in the German workforce between 1907 and 1933.

Meanwhile, middle-class educated women were pressing into the professions and claiming a right to vocational fulfillment.[84]

These changes in the composition of the German labor force made it a matter of some urgency to discover how women responded to their work situation and approached their jobs. Employers, reformers, and advocates of women's rights all had an interest in determining whether women differed significantly from men in their relationship to their work and in exploring the implications of any distinctive features for the training of women and their treatment in the workplace. A few people also began to wonder whether it might not be necessary to encourage new attitudes towards women's work, not least among women themselves.

All this led to some discussion of how women ought to feel about paid employment outside the home. In turn, the debate about the ideology of women's work spurred efforts to learn more about the actual and potential capacity of girls and women to achieve full participation in the world of modern work. Nevertheless, it is striking that the majority of writers and academics pontificated on the subject of women and work without worrying too much about the actual situation. Only a very few, for the most part women, recognized the value of fact-gathering as a preliminary to decision-taking and therefore engaged in empirical research to determine women's attitudes to work. Before 1914, Marie Bernays had made an important contribution to the subject within the framework of the VfS studies, and a few others had given thought to the problem of women's work, but much had changed since then, and new evidence was needed. During the 1920s this was recognized by people engaged in psychological testing and vocational guidance, as well as by teachers, social workers, physicians, and trade union organizers, all of whom did collect a certain amount of relevant information. Yet surprisingly little systematic empirical research was done to establish women's attitudes to work, and the quality of these studies tended to be even lower than that of similar investigations focusing on male workers or on young people.

Although several of the surveys we have examined did deal with both men and women, these shed little light on the question of sex differences or the special problem of women's work. Thus Lau noted that when questioned about the pleasures associated with their jobs, girls in the vocational schools were more likely than boys to express

[84] See Jill McIntyre, "Women and the Professions in Germany, 1930–1940," in *German Democracy and the Triumph of Hitler*, ed. Anthony Nicholls and Erich Matthias (London: George Allen and Unwin, 1971), 175–213.

positive attitudes even to routine work. He also thought girls went to work a bit more cheerfully. However, he insisted that many boys, too, preferred routine and had low job aspirations, while members of both sexes tended to enjoy their work, especially its social aspects.[85] After reviewing contrary evidence, he came to the conclusion that as far as the unskilled were concerned, there was no significant difference between boys and girls:

> Despite the great difference in the ethical-religious and family spheres, there is a minimal difference in the attitude to work. In matters of vocational engagement, we are dealing with a zone of adaptable and moldable volitional activity relatively independent of gender.[86]

De Man likewise detected no real difference between men and women as far as attitudes to work and capacity for job satisfaction were concerned. Although hardly in a position to generalize on the basis of the few female typists and sales clerks in his sample, he did suggest that women seemed to be more conscientious and motivated than their male colleagues because they frequently had a somewhat erotic relationship with their male supervisors, but he acknowledged that many male workers also demonstrated their unconscious pleasure in subordination by shying away from responsibility.[87]

It is only when women began to look at the subject of sex differences with respect to work that more interesting aspects of the question came to light. One of the few systematically to examine the subject was Charlotte Bühler (1893–1974), an educational and clinical psychologist who has been termed the founder of adolescent psychology.[88] Bühler's clinical investigations of adolescents, begun in the early 1920s,[89] convinced her that the vocational attitudes of men and women are not the same. She assumed that everyone, male and female, had the desire to create, and possessed both male and female characteristics, but the way men and women chose to fulfill their creative drive, as well as the opportunities for doing so, were manifestly different. The widely-deplored lack of career-mindedness demonstrated by many young girls she attributed *not* to woman's nature as such, but to the fact that girls matured later than boys. Because they remained open longer to new interests and experiences, they were slower to make a career choice.[90]

---

[85] Lau, "Berliner Jugend," 49–53.   [86] Lau, "Berliner Jugend," 83.

[87] De Man, *Kampf um die Arbeitsfreude*, 170.   [88] See *IBD/CE*, s.v. Charlotte Buhler.

[89] See Charlotte Bühler, *Das Seelenleben der Jugendlichen. Versuch einer Analyse und Theorie der psychischen Pubertät* (Jena: G. Fischer, 1922).

[90] Charlotte Bühler, "Zum Berufsproblem der Frau," in Lazarsfeld, *Jugend und Beruf*, 198–200.

Similarly, Bühler tried to explain away the "fact" that girls seemed more interested in human problems than boys who tended towards technical, material speculation, by arguing that the "typically female callings" required greater maturity and experience of life.[91] A fervent advocate of women's professionalization, Bühler claimed that the evidence was not yet in on the question of whether marriages gain or lose through the careers of wives, but thought that if education inculcated appropriate underlying attitudes, it would be possible to reconcile work and marriage.[92]

Bühler's clinical approach to the problem of women's work rested on certain theoretical assumptions about human development that were hard to test. Moreover, her conclusions had little obvious relevance to the majority of women destined for jobs rather than careers. An attempt to remedy this by examining the attitudes to work of a broader cross-section of the female population was made a few years later by another psychologist, Else Schillfarth. Schillfarth, whose interest was in the education of women, used essays on such topics as "my vocation" or "my mother" or "how do I envisage a happy life" to elicit evidence from a sample of pupils in girls' schools that included some who were headed for the factory.[93]

The first German study directed specifically at young female factory workers was undertaken by Hildegard Jüngst and adopted a somewhat different method. Although acknowledging her debt to de Man as well as to Schillfarth, Jüngst rejected surveys that demanded oral or written responses as inappropriate to her subject. Instead, in imitation of Paul Göhre who before the war had disguised himself as a factory worker in order to observe proletarian life at first hand, she worked for two months in a candy factory situated in a small city. To supplement what she could learn by personal contact during the short time at her disposal, she did use a questionnaire, but this was to be completed not by the girls themselves but by factory social workers. She also relied on oral and written communications from women involved in social work, occupational training, and so forth to help her evaluate her evidence. All in all, she believed her method allowed the girls to express their feelings more naturally and spontaneously than was possible in studies employing more traditional procedures.[94]

[91] Bühler, "Zum Berufsproblem der Frau," 202.
[92] Bühler, "Zum Berufsproblem der Frau," 205.
[93] Else Schillfarth, Die psychologischen Grundlagen der heutigen Mädchenbildung (Leipzig, 1926), described in Hildegard Jüngst, Die jugendliche Fabrikarbeiterin (Paderborn: Ferdinand Schöningh, 1929), 14–16.
[94] Jüngst, Jugendliche Fabrikarbeiterin, 31–34. Jüngst believed that her own working-class

Jüngst's main conclusion was that men and women did differ in certain important respects. Women were less interested in objective facts and circumstances and more in personal relations, and because they saw their chief vocation to be that of wife and mother, they thought of their jobs as purely temporary. Moreover, she confirmed the observations of Münsterberg and others that women could carry out incredibly boring work with great devotion to the task in hand, and that some individuals liked or even preferred monotonous tasks. On the other hand, Jüngst asserted that the tension between the psyche and the demands of the factory was even greater in the case of women than of men. [95] She found few instances of the genuine liking for the "worker profession" that Schillfarth had reported. Some might take pleasure in the work itself, but, in the last analysis, the main motivating factor that drove girls into the factory and kept them there was money; the only joy in work that they demonstrated was a joy in earning, be it to help their families, to gratify their own desires, or to win a degree of freedom. [96] Whatever its shortcomings, [97] as far as working women were concerned Jüngst's *Die jugendliche Arbeiterin* stands out as one of the very few serious attempts during this period to get at the facts regarding the attitudes to work of ordinary women workers.

Also worth mentioning are two studies carried out under the auspices of the predominantly female Textile Workers Union. The first, involving young workers of both sexes, was an essay competition on the subject of "A Day in the Factory." Divided equally between males and females, the forty-five responses were difficult to interpret. The girls apparently showed more imagination in their essays, were more inclined to say they enjoyed their work, and took great pleasure in the feeling of independence wage earning gave them, but they seemed even

background enabled her to make sense of what she saw, as well as giving her access to the homes of several of the girls.

[95] Jüngst, *Jugendliche Fabrikarbeiterin*, 55–58.

[96] Jüngst, *Jugendliche Fabrikarbeiterin*, 62–69. Citing Lau in support of her negative conclusions, Jüngst described how the girls, displaying varying degrees of fortitude, courage, humor, and determination to enjoy what they could, came to accept that their occupations would always be just work rather than vocation, and sought diversion and stimulation in their free time to compensate for the essential monotony of their jobs. Jüngst, *Jugendliche Fabrikarbeiterin*, 76–78. The remainder of Jüngst's book dealt with family and education, including education for motherhood, and suggested a number of reforms.

[97] The left-wing sociologist Theodor Geiger (1891–1952), one of the pioneers of empirical social research, described Jüngst's work as a model of how *not* to do an attitude study, and thought that only a romantic sentimentalist would find depressing her conclusion that girls work chiefly for money. Theodor Geiger, "Zur Kritik der arbeiter-psychologischen Forschung" (1931), in Theodor Geiger, *Arbeiten zur Soziologie*, ed. Paul Trappe. Soziologische Texte, vol. 7 (Neuwied: Hermann Luchterhand, 1962), 164–65.

more alienated than their male co-workers. According to one commentator, this was because their drive to motherhood stood in stark contrast with the impersonal-objective atmosphere on the factory floor.[98] The second, also an essay contest, was sponsored by the union's Women's Secretariat. Undertaken in the fall of 1928, this prize competition involved only women and elicited 150 essays on the theme "My Working Day, My Weekend." The main finding, not surprisingly, was that working-class women, and in particular the large proportion who were married and had families to care for, were not especially distressed by the monotony of their jobs, but were much too badly paid and overburdened to report any degree of positive joy in work.[99]

The only major survey of female industrial workers in German-speaking Europe during this period was organized by the Women's Branch of the Viennese Worker Council headed by Käthe Leichter (1895–1942), a left-wing activist in the Austrian Social Democratic Party.[100] Reporting at the height of the depression on the testimony of 1,320 women who completed a questionnaire distributed in July 1931 to 4,000 individuals in a variety of occupations, Leichter analyzed the problems facing women as workers, homemakers, and mothers.[101]

In a chapter on attitudes to work, Leichter dealt explicitly with vocational choice, motivation, and job satisfaction.[102] Assuming that quantification was possible despite the great variation among occupations and individuals revealed by her data, she reported that only about 20 percent of the women had exercised real occupational choice: the remainder had been thrown into their jobs by necessity or chance. What is more, 85 percent would have preferred not to work outside the home, while as many as 95.3 percent of the married respondents said they would stop working if their husbands earned enough to support

[98] I was unable to examine this study. The above account is based on Ernst Niekisch, "Jugend und Arbeit," *Jugend und Beruf* 1 (1926): 361–73.

[99] Deutsche Textilarbeiter-Verband, *Mein Arbeitstag—mein Wochenende. 150 Berichte von Textilarbeiterinnen* (Berlin: Verlag Textilpraxis, 1931). Documents from this collection are reproduced in *European Women. A Documentary History, 1789–1945*, ed. Eleanor S. Riemer and John C. Fout (New York: Schocken Books, 1980), 55–56, and 161–62.

[100] Glaser, *Im Umfeld des Austromarxismus*, 222–24, 355–57.

[101] Käthe Leichter, *So leben wir . . . 1320 Industriearbeiterinnen berichten über ihr Leben* (Vienna: Verlag "Arbeit und Wirtschaft," 1932), 1–5. Leichter claimed there had been only two previous attempts to establish facts about working women in a systematic fashion: an Austrian survey of 1896 and the recently published *Mein Arbeitstag-mein Wochenende*. She attributed the relatively high response rate and the amount of detail received to the fact that a number of trade union officials had approached the women personally, helped them to complete the questionnaires, and encouraged oral comment.

[102] Leichter, *So leben wir*, 52–71.

the family.[103] On the other hand, one-third of the unmarried women worked because they wanted to, and the majority of seamstresses said that they preferred working to staying at home. She also noted that the younger women expected more from work than had their mothers and were more prone to change jobs on a whim. Leichter concluded that the results of the survey might have been different had more intrinsically interesting female jobs been available.

Commenting on de Man's claim that all workers enjoy their work if not prevented from doing so, Leichter pointed out that women were subject to many more factors inhibiting Arbeitsfreude than men. Because of the double burden of work and home, women workers frequently were too exhausted to concentrate on their jobs. Moreover, they were generally treated as subordinate, subjected to critical, niggling supervision, and given work that was particularly dependent, badly paid, monotonous, repetitive, mechanized, dirty, and unhealthy. Since women had little choice of occupation and minimal security or opportunity for advancement, it was hardly surprising that over two-thirds insisted that *nothing* about their jobs gave them joy. An additional 10 percent or so thought their wages the only positive aspect of their work. Of the remaining 20 percent who had good things to say about their jobs, some were involved in tasks that provided opportunities for variation and creativity, while others took pleasure in their own skill or the status attached to their work; only a very few, however, liked their tools, in this differing from men who frequently expressed positive feelings about their machines.

One of Leichter's most interesting findings was that those occupations of which many complained were also the ones most capable of giving joy. A prime example was the printing trade, where poor working conditions prevailed, but where women often said they enjoyed their work because they were given an opportunity to exercise taste and skill. Conversely, it was the mature skilled workers who expressed themselves as most dissatisfied with their jobs, presumably because their work encouraged them to develop aspirations for Arbeitsfreude that were seldom met. The chief positive correlation was between choice of occupation and Arbeitsfreude. That is, a woman who had chosen her career was more likely to find it satisfying. Leichter's overall conclusion was that the general misery of modern women's work was due not to paid employment as such, but to the capitalist organization of work, combined with extra-work burdens. Her vision was of a future

[103] Cf. Miedbrodt, *So denkt der Arbeiter*, who noted that the few married women in his sample were unanimous as to this issue.

socialist order in which women worked because they wished to, not because they had to.

The inability of Weimar attitude studies, including those dealing with specific groups such as young people or women, to yield clear-cut results was due not only to their lack of methodological sophistication, but also to the preconceptions about work and society of the people who designed them, and who tended to use their "research" to support generalizations arrived at by other means. Yet these pioneers of empirical attitude research made a contribution to the debate about work which compares favorably with that of their contemporaries who felt free to dispense with empirical data on the assumption that an intuitive or theoretical approach to the topic could produce results as good or better. At the least, the survey researchers deserve credit for making a sincere attempt to tackle a difficult subject scientifically.

An outstanding exponent of the non-empirical "method" was the sociologist Heinz Marr (1876–1940). Marr published two books on the psychology of German workers in the early 1920s and continued to pronounce on the subject periodically thereafter, without ever making any systematic study of the subject. Because he had been compelled by circumstances to spend over four years in the 1890s working in a factory,[104] he did have some qualifications for judging proletarian sentiments, but one must question if this early exposure to working class life fitted Marr to interpret the workers' response to the accelerated rationalization of the postwar period. In any event, he soon returned to his proper station in life. Completing a first degree at the University of Leipzig in 1902, he eventually became professor of sociology and social policy at the University of Frankfurt and director of the Frankfurt Soziales Museum. While his university appointment gave Marr academic status, his position with the Soziales Museum enabled him to have an active influence on the debate about work by organizing conferences on such topics as Fordismus (1926) and industrial training (1930).

When Marr first outlined the psychology of the proletariat in 1920 to audiences seeking to understand the mental world of the modern industrial worker,[105] he acknowledged the influence of such theorists of mass society as Le Bon, Michels, Simmel, and Tönnies. Explicitly rejecting Levenstein's method of gathering testimony from individuals on the grounds that every mass movement is more than the sum of its

[104] Heinz Marr, in Frankfurt, Soziales Museum, *Industrielle Arbeitsschulung als Problem* (Berlin: Industrie Verlag Spaeth & Linde, 1931), 63–66.
[105] Heinz Marr, *Proletarisches Verlangen. Ein Beitrag zur Psychologie der Massen* (Jena: Eugen Diederichs, 1921). This was based on four talks given in 1920 to groups of Protestant ministers and others concerned with the worker question.

parts[106] he chose to present instead a theoretical analysis of the changing relationship between the German working class and Marxism. Marr argued that the latter was essentially materialistic and individualistic, the product not of modern capitalism but of the rationalism that had taken hold since medieval times. He acknowledged that Marxism had served a critical purpose, but insisted it was gravely flawed as an ideal because among other things it demonstrated an insufficient understanding of intellectual work and left no room for joy and fervor.[107] Marr also maintained that Marxism had originally appealed to German workers not because but in spite of its claims to scientific validity. To them, it had appeared to be a substitute religion capable of satisfying their deepest longings. But the Marxist faith was now outdated, for the war had made it impossible to maintain the optimism of the pre-1914 era that had sustained it.[108]

According to Marr, the prewar proletarian youth movement had injected a new idealism into socialism that ruled out support for communism.[109] Since then, the revolutionary council movement, rejecting both Leninism and western-style parliamentarism, had signalled the emergence of a new German mass-ideal based on the notion of an organic, democratic Volk community. Deeply ingrained in the Volk, this accounted for the remarkable affinity of sentiment revealed by the slogans of the extremes of Right and Left.[110] Although the long-dominant "Prussian-Marxist collectivism" still held some appeal for the masses enraged by the evils of Mammonism and capitalist excesses, he claimed that the German people possessed an "unconscious longing" for such an organic democracy.[111] For Marr was convinced that the era of the masses was coming to an end. Drawing on sources as diverse as Marx (who had initially wanted to conquer the state only in order to abolish it) and Tolstoy, the masses were beginning to recognize the wretchedness of their condition and to seek remedies through such devices as decentralization, or the concept of the works community.[112]

Marr never repudiated the main ideas expressed in *Proletarisches Verlangen*, nor did he abandon his abstract, non-empirical approach to the problem of work. Even after the turn away from utopianism he hankered for the good old days, but he now recognized that it was necessary to come to terms with the realities of modern industrialism and so de-

[106] Marr, *Proletarisches Verlangen*, 11.   [107] Marr, *Proletarisches Verlangen*, 24.
[108] Marr, *Proletarisches Verlangen*, 18, 33.   [109] Marr, *Proletarisches Verlangen*, 58.
[110] Marr, *Proletarisches Verlangen*, 61.   [111] Marr, *Proletarisches Verlangen*, 63–64.
[112] Marr, *Proletarisches Verlangen*, 66–67. Marr prophesied the creation of a polity based on the "new (but in reality age-old) supra-individual German notion of calling," a genuine community able to contain the reality of conflicting interests. Marr, *Proletarisches Verlangen*, 65.

CHAPTER IX

nounced the religious-aesthetic valuation of work of contemporary romantics and life-reformers as an anachronism. In his view, whoever protested against the curse of work in the machine age was endangering modern industry without contributing to the solution of the Man-Machine problem.[113] Fortunately, he argued, the vast majority of Germans did not aspire to joy in work, but labored at their jobs out of a "Prussian," indeed "Kantian," sense of duty to the whole.[114] Because of this, he remained confident that they could be brought to understand that employers and workers were both in fact "socialists," children of the same Volk, united by a common, Prussian, view of the meaning and purpose of work.[115]

Compared with Marr's abstractions, what Alfred Striemer (1879–?) had to say about worker attitudes seems realistic, although the latter also dispensed with systematic fact gathering and analysis in his 1923 publication on the German industrial worker.[116] A graduate of the University of Halle in law and political science and a trained engineer, Striemer had some opportunity to develop a practical understanding of his subject as editor first of the free trade union's *Betriebsrätezeitung*, and then of the *Borsig-Zeitung*, the company newspaper of one of Berlin's largest industrial firms.[117] Experience convinced him that the mass of wage earners regarded work purely as a necessary evil, and that they were right to do so given the nature of their jobs. For this reason, he thought them fully justified in pressing for the eight-hour day and in demanding wages commensurate with the value of their work and level of skill. At the same time, however, he insisted that Arbeitsfreude continued to be a matter of the utmost concern to the German industrial laborers: what drove them to organize and agitate was not an egotistic desire for higher living standards so much as a natural reaction against

[113] Heinz Marr, *Von der Arbeitsgesinnung unserer industriellen Massen. Ein Beitrag zur Frage: Mensch und Maschine* (Frankfurt a. M.: Englert und Schlosser, 1924), 14–15. This was Marr's inaugural lecture at the University of Frankfurt.

[114] Marr, *Von der Arbeitsgesinnung*, 15–17.

[115] Marr, *Von der Arbeitsgesinnung*, 17. See also Heinz Marr, "Die Moral des 'Fordismus,' " in Frankfurt, Soziales Museum, *Ford und wir*, 65–82. Marr here contradicted Gottl-Ottlilienfeld and others who wished to adopt not just Ford's technical innovations but also his service ethic as a basis for their "white socialism." Marr thought Ford's secular, individualistic, and Anglo-Saxon Puritan ethos totally inappropriate for Germany because German workers possessed a civil-service ethos involving subordination to the whole. Without bringing forward any evidence, Marr asserted that "our people cannot and do not wish to become blessed in the Anglo-Saxon individualistic manner."

[116] Alfred Striemer, *Der Industriearbeiter* (Breslau: Ferdinand Hirt, 1923). The book formed part of the popular *Jedermanns Bücherei* ("Everyman's Library").

[117] *Kürschners Gelehrten-Kalender*, 1925; Clemens Nörpel, "Der Mensch im Arbeiter," *Gewerkschafts-Archiv* 2 (1925): 139.

deadening detail work. Advocating reforms that would enable capitalism truly to serve the public interest,[118] he insisted that efforts must be made to overcome labor alienation. Only in this way could the workers be weaned away from Marxism and transformed from beasts of burden into human beings capable of experiencing joy in work.

People dissatisfied with survey research but wanting more direct evidence about workers' attitudes than could be gleaned from middle-class observers like Marr or Striemer frequently turned to worker literature. In the 1920s, as before the war, worker memoirs and poetry and prose produced by workers continued to be mined as a source of insight into the mentality of the proletariat. We have already seen how Rosenstock used the worker May's statement in his much-discussed *Werkstattaussiedlung*. Also widely distributed were the autobiographical writings of August Winnig (1878–1956), a one-time mason, trade-union leader, and Social Democratic activist, who by 1920 had deserted the socialist cause to join the German Nationalist party.[119] Among worker poets, Karl Bröger, Max Barthel, Hermann Lersch, and Paul Ernst continued to be popular. Yet, in the era of Neue Sachlichkeit, there was somewhat less inclination than before the war to regard poetry as a good source of evidence about the feelings of the typical worker. Moreover, doctrinaire Marxists tended to be suspicious of the worker poets on principle. For although their writings seemed well-designed to strengthen the proletarian self-image and raise working-class consciousness,[120] the lyrical glorification of work and the worker in many of these poems and the tendency of most worker poets to concentrate on the private experience of work instead of illuminating the social conditions of the working class meant that their utterances were of little use to promoters of the revolutionary socialist cause.[121]

---

[118] Although he had coauthored a book on the need for economic planning with Rudolf Wissell a few years earlier, Striemer was no socialist. See Rudolf Wissell and Alfred Striemer, *Ohne Planwirtschaft kein Aufbau* (1921).

[119] Donald Ray Richards, *The German Bestseller in the Twentieth Century* (Bern, 1968), 244–45; Fischer, "Die Soziale Problematik der Industrialisierung," 222.

[120] Prime examples were the anthem of the Austrian Social Democrats and the worker poetry of Alfons Petzold, reproduced in Glaser, *Im Umfeld des Austromarxismus*, 140–41, 382–85.

[121] Christoph Rülcker, *Ideologie der Arbeiterdichtung 1914–1933* (Stuttgart: J. B. Metzler, 1970), 87. According to Rülcker, 80–104, the worker-poets falsified the meaning of proletarian life because of their integrationist ideology. The Communists did encourage proletarian authors to contribute as correspondents to the left-wing press and to Communist works newspapers specifically designed to counter the company papers which proliferated during the 1920s. The DDR scholar Alfred Klein argues that only the Communist writings, entirely free of positive references to the value of work prevalent in Social Democratic literature, represented the true thoughts of the revolutionary proletariat. However, such "worker" literature

Somewhat more credible as a source of evidence about worker attitudes in the postwar period were the writings of the Werkstudenten.
Among those who believed that this experience qualified them to speak
with authority about the attitudes of ordinary workers was Dr. Hans
Hümmeler. The son of a miner who became a Catholic youth worker,
Hümmeler extrapolated from his personal experience to argue that
while industrial work is hard rather than joyful in itself, it can yield
Arbeitsfreude if done in the right spirit. This led him to publish a series
of articles and pamphlets, some of them under the pseudonym "Hans
Sauerland," in which he expounded on the psychology of factory youth
in the Ruhr and prescribed ways to change attitudes so as to restore joy
in work.[122]

Although the work-student experience was undoubtedly a valuable
source of insight, there were problems with this approach. No matter
how wellmeaning, work-students were bound to experience work in a
different way than did the average wage earner. As Marr had already
discovered in the 1890s,[123] intellectuals who engage in manual labor
are likely to suffer greater psychic strain than is experienced by born
proletarians. On the other hand, intellectuals can always comfort
themselves with the knowledge that they can terminate their suffering,
if they so choose. As the sociologist Theodor Geiger pointed out at the
time, what caused workers the most anguish was not the nature of their
jobs or even the deprivations of their life, but the fact that there was
no escape from the total situation that seemed to be their fate. No
outsider could fully empathize with this experience, nor could it be
replicated experimentally. An individual forced to share the proletarian's fate would most probably fail the test and end up not as a genuine
working proletarian but as a member of the Lumpenproletariat.[124]

Geiger notwithstanding, the testimony of work students undoubt-

---

could easily be discounted by anti-Marxists as pure propaganda, and therefore did not figure
prominently in the contemporary debate about the problem of work. See Alfred Klein, "Zur
Entwicklung der sozialistischen Literatur in Deutschland 1918–1933," in Literatur der
Arbeiterklasse (Berlin-Ost: Aufbau Verlag, 1974), 17–117; Elizabeth Simons, "Der Bund pro-
letarisch-revolutionärer Schriftsteller Deutschlands und sein Verhältnis zur Kommunistischen Partei Deutschlands," in Literatur der Arbeiterklasse, 118–90, and Klein's contributions to Deutsche Akademie der Künste, Berlin, Literatur im Klassenkampf. Beiträge zur
sozialistischen Literatur der Weimarer Republik (Dortmund: Weltkreis-Verlag, 1973), 12–31,
73–94.

[122] See Hans Sauerland, Die Seele des Industriearbeiters (Hildesheim: Franz Borkmeyer,
n.d.), and "Die Lebenswelt der werktätigen Industriejugend in psychologischer Betrachtung," Jugend-Führung 15 (1928): 172–82, 203–216. Under his own name, Hümmeler published Jugend an der Maschine (Freiburg i. B.: Herder, 1932).

[123] Marr, in Frankfurt, Soziales Museum, Industrielle Arbeitsschulung als Problem, 65.

[124] See Geiger, "Zur Kritik der Arbeiter-psychologischen Forschung," 165–67.

edly influenced their contemporaries, albeit in contradictory ways. Thus some social reformers took comfort from the statements of those returnees from the world of the proletariat who confirmed that ways could be found to reconcile modern workers with their apparently soulless work without the need to resort to social revolution. Yet the same work-study experience transformed others into Communists[125] or enthusiastic technocrats who advocated a revolution from the Right that would culminate in an Italian-style corporate state.[126] In other words, the Werkstudenten signally failed to agree with one another about worker attitudes and prospects and so produced widely divergent prescriptions for dealing with the problem of work.

Towards the end of the Weimar period another way of establishing what the urbanized industrial proletariat thought about work was canvassed. This involved applying to the modern worker techniques of Volkskunde hitherto reserved for the study of rural and small-town Germany. Following in Riehl's footsteps, such writers as Will-Erich Peuckert, Max Rumpf, and Wilhelm Brepohl emphasized the extent to which current attitudes and customs had roots in the variegated traditions of the past; they also stressed, however, that worker culture was in many ways unique, tended to uniformity, and so had to be studied on its own terms.[127] Thus Peuckert used regional studies of nineteenth-century Silesian textile operatives to generalize about the psychological state of the "new breed" of urban factory workers.[128] The idea of shedding light on worker attitudes by studying worker behavior was a good one, and there is no doubt that Volkskunde had the potential to serve as a valuable corrective to generalizations about "the worker" that failed to take regional variations and traditional habits and values into account.

[125] E.g., Graf Alexander Stenbock-Fermor, whose *Deutschland von unten. Reise durch die proletarische Provinz* (Stuttgart, 1931; reprint Lucerne: C. J. Bucher, 1980) painted a totally devastating picture of the plight of the working masses of depression Germany.

[126] E.g., Heinrich Hauser. See Helmut Lethen, *Neue Sachlichkeit 1924–1932. Studien zur Literatur des 'Weissen Sozialismus'* (Stuttgart: J. B. Merzlersche Verlagsbuchhandlung, 1970), 71–72.

[127] For a theoretical analysis of the new approach, see Max Rumpf, *Volkssoziologie im Rahmen einer sozialen Lebenslehre* (Nürnberg: Verlag der Hochschulbuchhandlung Krische & Co., 1931).

[128] Peuckert claimed that, in certain regions, the nineteenth-century factory proletariat had already overcome its earlier reluctance to work (*Arbeitsscheu*) and begun to display the diligence and alertness (*Fleiss und Regsamkeit*) characteristic of the modern urban worker. Will-Erich Peuckert, *Aufgang der proletarischen Kultur*, vol. 1 of *Volkskunde des Proletariats* (Frankfurt a. M.: Neuer Frankfurter Verlag, 1931), 142–44. His source for this positive appraisal of the proletarian work ethic was the report of a Protestant minister, printed in Alexander Schneer, *Über die Zustände der arbeitenden Klassen in Breslau mit Benutzung der amtlichen Quellen* (1845)!

Yet because it was only in its infancy, it failed to contribute significantly to the Weimar debate about work.[129]

The only systematic attempt during the Weimar years to find out about worker attitudes by observing behavior on the job grew out of a massive enquiry into German economic and social conditions initiated in 1926 by the Reichstag and carried out by the RWR.[130] This study was the work of the project's labor productivity subcommittee, chaired by the sociologist Ludwig Heyde (1888–1961) of the University of Kiel. The committee included academics, trade unionists, representatives of Handwerk, and factory owners, as well as members of both Reichstag and RWR. Its scientific secretariat was headed by Otto Lipmann (1880–1933), director of the Institute of Applied Psychology in Berlin, who was convinced that objective, non-partisan research could achieve results acceptable to both employers and workers and eventually lead to the development of a truly rational organization of work.[131] Using numerous experts as field workers, the enquiry amassed an impressive quantity of empirical evidence on wages, hours, and productivity. From this material, the project's initiators hoped to derive statistically valid generalizations with regard to the impact of rationalization on performance. The final report, however, published in 1930, failed to resolve the questions about wages and hours that had inspired the project and produced little in the way of agreed conclusions about the relationship between the disposition to work and productivity.[132]

In his textbooks on the science of work, Lipmann himself had posited that worker attitudes were an important factor in productivity.[133] On the other hand, he believed that genuine Arbeitsfreude could be

[129] According to Gottfried Korff, "Volkskultur und Arbeiterkultur: Überlegungen am Beispiel der sozialistischen Maifesttradition," *Geschichte und Gesellschaft* 5 (1979): 83–87, Göhre had called for an *Arbeitervolkskunde* as early as 1909, but, with these few exceptions, his lead was not followed up until the 1970s. See also Wolfgang Emmerich, *Zur Kritik der Volkstumsideologie* (Frankfurt a. M.: Suhrkamp, 1971), 104. The problems associated with the study of worker culture in its everyday aspects are briefly discussed in Alf Lüdtke, "Erfahrung von Industriearbeitern. Thesen zu einer vernachlässigten Dimension der Arbeitergeschichte," in Werner Conze and Ulrich Engelhardt, eds., *Arbeiter im Industrialisierungsprozess: Herkunft, Lage und Verhalten* (Stuttgart: Klett-Cotta, 1979), 494–512.

[130] Preller, *Sozialpolitik*, 252, 348.

[131] Otto Lipmann, "Zur Methodik der Arbeitswissenschaft," *Die Arbeit* 2 (1925): 476–78. On Lipmann, NDB 14:645–46, and Dorsch, *Geschichte und Probleme*, 69–70.

[132] [Otto Lipmann], *Zusammenfassender Bericht über die Ergebnisse der Arbeiten des Arbeitsleistungsausschusses*, Verhandlungen und Berichte des Unterausschusses für Arbeitsleistung (IV. Unterausschuss) 9 (Berlin: E. S. Mittler & Sohn, 1930); Otto Lipmann, "The Relation Between Industrial Production and the Worker's Disposition to Performance," *International Labor Review* 23 (June 1931): 835–52.

[133] Otto Lipmann, *Grundriss der Arbeitswissenschaft* (Jena: Gustav Fischer, 1926), 26–31, 42–45; *Lehrbuch der Arbeitswissenschaft* (Jena: Gustav Fischer, 1932), 376–92.

elicited only by self-determined activity, and therefore maintained that it was nonsense to speak of it in the context of Taylorized work.[134] Moreover, because Taylorism and Fordism were depriving ever larger numbers of workers of all control over the pace and outcome of their efforts, he knew that increasing the will to work would not automatically result in improved productivity.[135]

Lipmann warned against drawing too many conclusions from the RWR study. Conditions had changed so much during the four years that had elapsed since it began that comparisons were difficult to make, and individual factors had proved almost impossible to isolate. Although he felt justified in stating that worker attitudes had *some* influence on their willingness to perform and, conversely, that there was a psychological component in workers' reaction to changes in the wage and earnings structure,[136] this was a far cry from claiming that an intimate relationship existed between attitudes and performance. Nor did there seem to be a positive correlation between morale (*Stimmung*) and willingness to work, as the Arbeitsfreude theorists tended to claim. Rather, the figures showed that the disposition to work could be influenced by appropriate wage incentives, that monetary rewards were effective even in cases where workers were decidedly dissatisfied with their jobs, and that the fear of unemployment was the best stimulant to hard work.[137]

In the end, the chief finding of this ambitious behavioral study, the most important empirical investigation of German work since the prewar VfS efforts, was that given the complexity of the real world, no general conclusions could be reached about the attitudinal factors affecting worker productivity without further research! Far from establishing a "scientific" and therefore mutually acceptable basis for the organization of rationalized production and the conduct of industrial relations, the RWR enquiry succeeded only in casting doubts on the major assumption that underlay contemporary reform efforts, namely that the reconciliation between human beings and their work would benefit not only the individual worker but also the employer and society as a whole.

[134] Lipmann, *Lehrbuch*, 387–91, citing the research of Bühler, Bues, and others, showed that most workers, even the young, were reconciled to rationalized work, but insisted that this did not entail joy in work, and denied that there existed a "willingness to work" (*Arbeitswillen*) directed to work as such.

[135] Lipmann, "Zusammenfassender Bericht," Introduction and 227–28.

[136] Lipmann, "Zusammenfassender Bericht," 67–68, 199–200.

[137] Poor morale was shown to make a measurable difference in the area of health. Unhappy workers were clearly more accident-prone. Lipmann, "Zusammenfassender Bericht," 220.

In any event, before the implications of the enquiry's report could be explored, the depression and the electoral successes of Hitler's National Socialists diverted attention elsewhere. Together, these developments once more altered the context within which the debate about Arbeitsfreude and German work would henceforth be carried on.

X

THE WORK ETHIC RECONSIDERED

THE SAME technological, economic, and social changes that stimulated research into worker attitudes in the 1920s also led to a reconsideration of the national work ethic. We have seen that those who wished to establish what German workers thought about work had their own ideas about what men and women *ought* to think, but there were also a number of individuals who, seeing themselves as moral "experts," focused their efforts on the latter question. This chapter will examine the ideas about work generated by those professional philosophers, theologians, and educators who thought they could best contribute to solving the alienation by developing an ethic of work suited to contemporary requirements.

If one sets aside those whose response to the pressures of modernity was resignation or a quietist withdrawal into the inner life, and the even smaller group that proposed a modern ethic of life based on leisure to supersede the traditional ethic of work, one can distinguish two main tendencies, centered respectively on Arbeitsfreude and Arbeitspflicht ("the duty of work"). People either stressed the importance of restoring meaning and joy to work or argued that only an ethic of duty and service could meet the needs of the day. But even so, there was no clearcut separation between these positions—individuals espoused both in turn or even tried to effect a reconciliation between the two. Nor was consensus reached on the question of where the primary responsibility for promoting the modern work ethic lay.

The theories of work propounded in the 1920s were not particularly original. Not only did they reflect traditional attitudes to a surprising extent; they also drew heavily on intellectual strains inherited from earlier times. In addition to the great nineteenth-century moralists, these predecessors included several turn-of-century critics of modern society who had demanded a systematic reconsideration of work.

One of the most influential was the academic philosopher and Nobel Prize winner, Rudolf Eucken (1846–1926), whose reflections on life and work reached beyond his students at the University of Jena to a wider public. Determined to combat the positivism, materialism, and loss of spirituality of the age, Eucken, before the war, had propounded an idealist philosophy that combined respect for the achievements of science with belief in the existence of eternal values. Eucken analyzed the dilemma created for work by the process of modernization: work, defined as "the activity which grasps an object and shapes it to man's ends," had become the "central fact" of modern life; therefore, if life was to have meaning in the contemporary world, this could only derive from work.[1] Yet modern work was indifferent to workers' welfare, valuing the worker only as a means, a tool.[2] Involving as it did the creation of specialized jobs that utilized a fraction of the individual's total energy, modern work produced dissatisfaction and led to the "distraction and unsettlement" reflected in the social movements of the day. Under these circumstances, the soul might "easily come to regard work as a foe,"[3] with evil consequences for all spheres of life:

> Everywhere there is the same danger lest, through too exclusive a devotion to work, we gain the world and lose our soul, lest the victories of labor should mean a lowered standard of vitality, a weakened sense of responsibility, and, therefore, of necessity, an impoverished spiritual life.[4]

Eucken proffered no solution to this dilemma. Making a fetish of work would "degrade us to mere beasts of burden."[5] Nor was it possible to "derive a meaning for life from the medley of old and new—the chaos of conflicting tendencies—which is all that present-day mediocrity can offer us."[6] Only a moral transformation, a renewed regard for the transcendental, could restore meaning and value to life, and it was this that Eucken and others who espoused *Lebensphilosophie* ("philosophy of life") sought to bring about.

What Eucken attempted to accomplish through a personal crusade, his contemporary Paul Natorp (1854–1924) hoped to achieve by revitalizing the educational system.[7] The grandson of an educational reformer who, with Humboldt, had helped to transform the Prussian

[1] Rudolf Eucken, *The Meaning and Value of Life* (London: Adam and Charles Black, 1913), 19. The German original had appeared in 1908.

[2] Eucken, *The Meaning and Value of Life*, 21.

[3] Eucken, *The Meaning and Value of Life*, 22.

[4] Eucken, *The Meaning and Value of Life*. See also Ringer, *Decline of the German Mandarins*, 254–55.

[5] Eucken, *The Meaning and Value of Life*, 23.

[6] Eucken, *The Meaning and Value of Life*, 25.

[7] Thomas E. Willey, *Back to Kant. The Revival of Kantianism in German Social and Historical Thought, 1860–1914* (Detroit: Wayne State University Press, 1978), 117–24; Ringer, *Decline of the German Mandarins*, 277–78.

school system a century earlier, Natorp, professor of philosophy at Marburg, was one of those who hoped to close the gap between manual workers and intellectuals and to overcome class conflict associated with this through a "socialist" education common to Germans of all classes and regions.

Natorp lived just long enough to make a direct contribution to the Weimar debate about work. During the war, he had "plunged into the vagaries of a mystical Germanism" and virtually abandoned Kantian moral individualism in favor of a quasi-Hegelian metaphysics that emphasized the organic community.[8] From this followed naturally his utopian proposal of 1920 for the reintegration of mental with manual labor through the creation of small, socially mixed, and preferably semirural communities, in which work "would recover some meaning, and intellectual activity, even language itself, would draw vital nourishment from its roots in the concrete realities of productive work and communal life."[9] Perpetuated by the youth movement, with which he had identified from its beginnings, Natorp's mystical-religious "socialism" continued to influence educational theorists and other intellectuals after his death.

Another prewar thinker frequently quoted in Weimar Germany was Georg Simmel (1858–1918). Although Simmel never founded a "school" and remained on the fringes of the academic world,[10] his public lectures and writings established his reputation as one of Germany's major philosophers. Like Eucken and Natorp Simmel was heir to the German idealist tradition and perceived the crisis of work largely in terms of the troubled relationship between mental and physical activity. His analysis of alienation owed much to Marx, but he rejected Marxist solutions, for, like Hegel, he was convinced that the needs of the individual and the forms imposed by objective development were bound to conflict, no matter what the social system.[11]

[8] Willey, Back to Kant, 122–23. However, Natorp remained critical of the Germans' tendencies to racism and exaggerated idealism. Paul Natorp, Die Seele des Deutschen, vol. 1/2 of Deutscher Weltruf. Geschichtliche Richtlinien (Jena: Eugen Diederichs, 1918), 131.

[9] Ringer, Decline of the German Mandarins, 277–78, summarizing Natorp's Genossenschaftliche Erziehung als Grundlage zum Neubau des Volkstums und des Menschentums (Berlin, 1920).

[10] Lewis A. Coser, "Introduction," 1–26, and "The Stranger in the Academy," 29–37, in Georg Simmel, ed. Lewis A. Coser (Englewood Cliffs, N.J.: Prentice-Hall, 1965). Coser attributes Simmel's failure to attain academic acceptance to the latent antisemitism in academe, combined with his own failure to concentrate on a single topic for any length of time. The University of Berlin, where he taught for many years, refused to give him a permanent professorship. Simmel did finally become a full professor at Strasbourg in 1914.

[11] Raymond Aron, "Culture and Life," in Coser, Simmel, 138–41. Simmel was also convinced that the Marxist labor theory of value, with its materialistic-positivist foundation, constituted a major threat to intellectual life and culture.

On the other hand, Simmel was immunized by the influence of British liberal progressive ideas against the cultural pessimism that this belief seemed to entail.[12] His "solution" was to develop an alternative value system that included a single psychic scale indicating the relative value of various intellectual and manual occupations. This rested on the assumption that all work is burdensome because one must expend some degree of mental or spiritual effort to overcome one's inner resistance to it, and that it is this psychic component that gives work moral value.[13] Whereas the socialists sought to reduce work to the necessary and useful, to the detriment of culture, Simmel urged that efforts be made to elaborate a culture in which Geist ("intellect, spirit") would master all the conditions of production, while the will to justice would determine the rewards of labor in accordance with his new value system.[14]

Perhaps the most innovative German philosopher to address himself seriously to the problem of work in the early twentieth century was Max Scheler (1874–1928). Son of a Jewish mother and a Lutheran father, Scheler converted to Catholicism in his youth and is generally regarded as a Catholic philosopher. After some years of teaching at Jena he was appointed to a professorship at the University of Munich in 1906, but in 1910, as a result of a scandal, he was forbidden to teach. Scheler resumed his academic career after the war as professor of philosophy and sociology at the predominantly Catholic University of Cologne, where he helped Leopold von Wiese found the Research Institute for the Social Sciences. This appointment, however, from which both sides had hoped to profit, proved a disappointment both to Scheler and to the Catholic Church. Further scandals involving his tempestuous personal life led Church authorities in 1922 to forbid Catholic students to attend his lectures. Embarking on a third marriage, Scheler now broke with the Church and began to develop a non-Catholic philosophical position. Finally, in 1928, the year of his death, he left Cologne for Frankfurt where he hoped to find greater freedom to develop his new secular and pluralist social theories.[15]

Today Scheler is chiefly thought of as an originator, with Edmund Husserl (1859–1938), of phenomenology and existentialism, but before

[12] Coser, "Introduction," 18.

[13] Georg Simmel, "Zur Philosophie der Arbeit," *Neue Deutsche Rundschau* 10 (1899): 449–63.

[14] Simmel, "Zur Philosophie der Arbeit," 463.

[15] See John Raphael Staude, *Max Scheler. An Intellectual Portrait* (New York: Free Press, 1967), and John H. Nota, *Max Scheler. The Man and His Work* (Chicago, Ill.: Franciscan Herald Press, 1983).

THE WORK ETHIC RECONSIDERED

and immediately after the First World War, his most important role was as the leading popularizer of a religiously-tinged version of *Lebensphilosophie*. Scheler's ethical views on work, formulated at the beginning of his academic career, represent an attempt to blend ideas derived from Nietzsche and Marx with others taken from the idealist and Catholic traditions. His essay of 1899 on "Work and Ethics" criticized both Marxist materialism and German idealism for insisting dogmatically on the absolute validity of their own position.[16] Scheler's critique of Marxism echoed that of Simmel and other anti-positivists.[17] On the other hand, he accused the idealists of lacking a firm basis in contemporary reality and so chose to stress the essential link between economics and philosophy, and to insist that Arbeit was in the first instance an economic category.[18] Yet in the remainder of his essay, he, too, left "reality" far behind. Rejecting the humanist's glorification of work based on an identification between personality and nature, he called for a work ethic based on faith: only a transcendental power setting laws for humanity and prescribing duties could give work its ethical justification.

When he took up the question of work once more in 1920, Scheler maintained that a new work ethic was desperately needed to enable Germany to cope with the harsh realities of the day. Unlike many of his conservative contemporaries, however, he denied that the required ethos could be based on the old Prussian conviction that human beings were made for work, not work for human beings. Arguing that the "too much" of prewar days and the "too little" of the present could be traced back to the same inner moral-psychological flaw, he called for conversion to a Christian, that is, a Catholic, conception of work.[19] Because work was essentially burden and curse, a punishment for the Fall, the consistent Catholic could never subscribe to the Fourierist view of work as pleasure. But because his faith valued contemplation above action, he was also bound to reject the Protestant ethic with its emphasis on work as the primary means of salvation. This, he argued, led directly to such social evils as capitalism and economic imperialism.

[16] Max Scheler, "Arbeit und Ethik," reprinted in Max Scheler, *Schriften zur Soziologie und Weltanschauungslehre* (Leipzig, 1924) and reproduced in Max Scheler, *Liebe und Erkenntnis* (Bern: Francke, 1955), 91–128.

[17] Scheler had studied with Dilthey and Simmel in Berlin and with Eucken in Jena.

[18] Scheler here reversed the procedure of the nineteenth-century German economist Lorenz von Stein, whose popular textbook prefaced a discussion of the economic category "work" with a philosophical discourse on the "Idea of Work!" See Lorenz Jakob von Stein, *Lehrbuch der Nationalökonomie* (3d rev. ed.; Vienna, 1887), 46–56.

[19] Max Scheler, "Wert und Würde der christlichen Arbeit," in *Jahrbuch der deutschen Katholiken* (Augsburg: Haas und Grabber, 1920/21), 75–89. This essay is printed as "Arbeit und Weltanschauung" in Max Scheler, *Gesammelte Werke*, vol. 6 (2d ed.; Bern: A. Francke, 1963), 273–89.

Nonetheless determined to salvage the work ethic, Scheler insisted that there was room in a Christian view of work for the concept of Arbeitsfreude. Joy in work was said to derive not from work itself but from the attitude of the worker. Done in the right spirit, work could make individuals more selfless, just, and humble, and enable them to participate in God's task of Creation by producing things of quality. Work one must, but one was free to choose whether to labor as an unwilling slave or, by adopting a spiritual-religious ethic, to work as a free human being.[20]

The general philosophical outlook Scheler had developed before the war, by emphasizing the power and freedom of the human will, gave comfort to all who hoped to bring about the restoration of a non-materialistic ethic of work. Also in tune with the times were his postwar sociological writings which promoted "Solidarism," a form of Christian socialism, as an alternative to both capitalism and socialism.[21] Finally, Scheler's rejection of relativism, psychologism, and the notion of a value-free sociology in favor of an absolute Christian ethic based on contact with reality made his approach attractive to Catholics and Protestants alike.[22]

However, the harsher "Prussian" work ethic against which Scheler inveighed continued to dominate the universities. For the most part academic philosophers and theologians preferred to equate the German work ethic with Protestantism in its Lutheran version, as reinforced by the idealism of Kant and Fichte. Based on the notion of calling or vocation and strongly emphasizing duty (*Pflicht*) to the community, this ethic seemed ideally suited to persuade Germans in an era of rapid rationalization to work long and hard for little reward and, if necessary, to sacrifice their personal preferences to the attempt to restore the nation to prosperity and greatness. The authority of the nineteenth-century idealist philosopher Wilhelm Dilthey (1833–1911), whose collected works were published in the 1920s, was frequently invoked to

[20] Scheler, *Wert und Würde*, 82.   [21] Nota, *Scheler*, 113–14, 118–20.

[22] Thus Theodor Brauer (1880–1942), Scheler's colleague at the University of Cologne who played a major role in shaping the ideology of the Christian trade union movement, maintained that Scheler, along with Husserl, had provided the philosophical underpinnings of Catholic economics, sociology, and ethics. Theodor Brauer, *Produktionsfactor Arbeit* (Jena: Gustav Fischer, 1925), 194–201. Also influenced by Scheler's particular version of the Catholic position on work was his friend, the industrial sociologist Goetz Briefs. On the Protestant side, see Dedo Müller, "Das Problem der Arbeitsfreude in der modernen Wirtschaft," *Evangelisch-Sozial* 33 (1928): 101–17. Müller, a minister in Leipzig, praised Scheler, alongside Protestant thinkers like Simmel, Dilthey, and Troeltsch, for awakening the German soul to the need for Arbeitsfreude, and for creating a religiously-inspired reform impetus to overcome the fatalism inspired by the current crisis of work.

buttress this position. Dilthey had made explicit the connection between German work and Protestantism, arguing that the latter was itself a product of the "Germanic" personalities of Luther and Zwingli. These two had insisted that individuals had an indestructible right to come to terms with the unseen relationship of things through their own efforts. It was this belief that had driven Luther and Zwingli to break with the Church hierarchy that represented a "demonic mechanism preventing the free access of the soul to God."[23] Dilthey also claimed that it was Luther, his Germanic activism repelled by the other-worldliness of Catholic monks and priests, who had first proclaimed that everyday occupations were the sphere in which the God-given power of faith could find its fullest scope.[24]

Whereas Dilthey's version of the Protestant work ethic emphasized Luther, Max Weber's influential essays on the Protestant ethic and the spirit of capitalism assigned a key role to Calvin. Weber's friend and colleague, the theologian Ernst Troeltsch (1865–1923), elaborated these ideas in his comprehensive survey of Christian social teaching which greatly influenced Weimar theorists of work.[25] Troeltsch claimed that "Ascetic Protestantism," by emphasizing the duty to work for the service of God, led to the "inner severance of feeling and enjoyment from all the objects of labour,"[26] and produced both "energetic and courageous entrepreneurs and men who were willing to endure exploitation if only they could get work."[27] He showed in detail how the Calvinist ethic differed from that of Catholicism, Lutheranism, and even from that of Puritanism with which it was frequently confused. But Troeltsch went on to deny the practical relevance of both medieval Catholicism and Ascetic Protestantism. Convinced that these forces had exhausted themselves, he acknowledged that new thinking was required if Christian principles were to meet the needs of the modern age.[28] On the other hand, he doubted the church's ability to change worker attitudes, because German labor increasingly turned its back on organized religion, while the Protestant work ethic, with its emphasis on duty and service, had lost its appeal even to those who remained within the church.[29]

[23] Wilhelm Dilthey, "Leibniz und sein Zeitalter," Gesammelte Schriften (Leipzig: B. G. Teubner, 1927–1929), vol. 3, Studien zur Geschichte des deutschen Geistes, 8–9.

[24] Dilthey, Gesammelte Schriften, vol. 2, Weltanschauung und Analyse des Menschen seit Renaissance und Reformation (3d ed., 1923), 215.

[25] Ernst Troeltsch, The Social Teaching of the Christian Churches (London: George Allen & Unwin, 1931), 2:808–15.

[26] Troeltsch, Social Teaching, 808–809.

[27] Troeltsch, Social Teaching, 813.   [28] Troeltsch, Social Teaching, 1101.

[29] Troeltsch, discussion comment at a conference on the work ethic and vocational train-

Even more gloomy than Troeltsch about the possibility of rescuing the Protestant work ethic in the modern period was the sociologist Werner Sombart. In a keynote address of 1927 to the twentieth Congress of the Kirchlich-Soziale Bund (KSB) in Düsseldorf, attended by over 1,100 Protestant clerics and lay people, Sombart related rationalization to "rationalism," which he held responsible for the intellectualization and disenchantment (*Entzauberung*) of the modern world.[30] For the vast majority of industrial workers, rationalization diminished the possibility of finding satisfaction in work and completely ruled out the experience of true vocation. Sombart admitted that a privileged minority of skilled workers, and the over 50 percent of Germans in agriculture or in small and medium businesses had so far largely escaped the proletarian fate. Agriculture in particular could not be Taylorized and so was secure, in his view, from the process of rationalization. Without spelling out the remedial measures to be taken, he also conceded that something could be done to soften the impact of rationalization on the workers. But, taken as a whole, his speech was couched in an emotive terminology that belied his claim to objectivity and exuded pessimism.

The Congress nonetheless refused to be discouraged in its efforts to convert the workers back to the idea of "vocation," and proceeded to set up a working group for social ethics.[31] This was perhaps because the speaker who followed Sombart was the much more optimistic Max Schlenker, executive director of the "Langnamverein" representing the iron and steel industrialists of the Ruhr.[32] Schlenker acknowledged that modernization created difficulties for the workers, but insisted that these were blown out of all proportion by German intellectuals whom he accused of a tendency to turn tasks into problems.[33] It was Schlenker

---

ing sponsored by the GSR, in *Berufsethos und praktische Berufserziehung*. Schriften der GSR, vol. 10 (Jena: Gustav Fischer, 1921), 85–87. While he favored shorter hours, worker education, and industrial democracy, Troeltsch did not believe that such reforms would restore either the spirit of community or joy in work.

[30] On the congress, Jagow, "Düsseldorf," in *Kirchlich-Soziale Blätter* (January 1928): 7, and *Leben und Arbeit. Eine Aussprache*, Kirchlich-Soziales Heft 68 (Leipzig, 1928). Sombart's address was also published separately as Werner Sombart, *Die Rationalisierung in der Wirtschaft* (Leipzig, 1928). The KSB grew out of the organization founded by Stöcker in 1897 when he left the ESK. It represented the conservative and theologically orthodox elements within German Protestantism, and had close links with the Inner Mission. However, it never broke off contact completely with the ESK. From 1909 it was headed by Reinhold Seeberg. See *RGG*, 3d ed., 3:1622–23.

[31] Jagow, "Düsseldorf," 11.

[32] See Henry Ashby Turner, *German Big Business and the Rise of Hitler* (New York: Oxford University Press, 1985), 42.

[33] An expanded version of Schlenker's talk was published as Max Schlenker, "Leben und Arbeit," in *Mitteilungen des Vereins zur Wahrung der gemeinsamen wirtschaftlichen Interessen in Rheinland und Westfalen*, no. 4 (1927): 21–38.

rather than Sombart who captured the mood of the Congress: although the majority of Protestants assembled at Düsseldorf shared Sombart's negative assessment of modernity, they were nevertheless determined to meet its challenges. Subscribing to the Lutheran rather than Calvinist version of the Protestant ethic, they remained convinced that hard work in a calling could yield psychological satisfaction as well as bringing one closer to God, and so refused to despair of restoring the nation's enthusiasm for work or of bringing life and work once more into some kind of harmony. Encouraged by the proponents of *Lebensphilosophie* to believe that the human soul had not yet been entirely destroyed by the process of rationalization, they argued the need to preserve and enhance the individual's capacity to find, if not joy in work, then at least the satisfaction to be derived from service to the community and the knowledge of duty done. What was in dispute was not so much the goal, but rather how it might best be attained, and, in particular, what role the church should play in solving the problem of work.

On this point, Protestant theologians differed widely. At one extreme, Wilhelm Herbst (1891–?) of Greifswald concluded that the church had no role to play in reforming industrial relations or in restoring Arbeitsfreude.[34] At the other, Carl Stange (1870–1959), professor of theology and philosophy at Göttingen and editor of the *Zeitschrift für systematische Theologie*, maintained that the church, by convincing human beings that they still had an inner life, could bring about the ethical reformation that alone could solve the problem of work.[35] Similarly, Professor Arthur Titius (1864–1936) of the University of Berlin, addressing the ESK in 1929, argued that Sachlichkeit was enjoined by God and that religion had a duty to cooperate with science and industry to solve the problem of alienation. Convinced that both employers and workers could be converted to a modern ethic of work that incorporated the Protestant idea of vocation, Titius urged Germans to combine realism with brotherliness in Christ, so as to cre-

[34] Wilhelm Herbst, "Das Problem der industriellen Arbeit und die christliche Ethik," *Reinhold-Seeberg-Festschrift*, vol. 2, *Zur Praxis des Christentums* (Leipzig: A. Deichertsche Verlagsbuchhandlung D. Werner Scholl, 1929), 331–33. On the basis of an exceedingly abstract analysis of Christian ethics in relation to industrial work, Herbst insisted that good Christians must reconcile themselves to modern technology, and that the machine could even strengthen human virtue by teaching respect for, and obedience to, outside forces, thus preparing the way for obedience and subordination to God. But there was little that the Church itself could do to solve the problem of work. Rather, Herbst turned the argument around: because joyless work weakened faith, it would have to be abolished; only with the end of alienation would the workers return to the bosom of the church.

[35] According to Carl Stange, "Die Ethik der Arbeit," *Zeitschrift für systematische Theologie* 4 (1926/27): 712, "Whoever does his work in a spirit of responsibility will derive joy from it and can, through work, become intimately linked with the life of the community."

ate the "new humane and religious sense of calling" sorely needed by mankind.[36]

In general, the Protestant thinkers who addressed social issues remained hopeful throughout the 1920s about the possibility of reconciling human beings with their work. Most expected the Church to turn its back on outdated romanticism and, in a spirit of Sachlichkeit, to teach a religiously-based work ethic centered on a modernized version of the idea of calling. With the ESK once more in the lead, there was also some attempt to mobilize religion in support of efforts to tackle the social question through the humanization of work.[37] Nevertheless, Protestants were particularly prone to a fatalism derived from existential despair of the kind revealed in Karl Jaspers's *The Spiritual State of the Contemporary Age* of 1931. Convinced that the idea of *Beruf* ("vocation"), and with it the opportunities for Arbeitsfreude, in the face of a technologically oriented mass society were dying out even for people in the professions, Jaspers concluded that there was no hope for a solution to the modern predicament.[38]

German Catholics were consistently more sanguine than German Protestants about their church's capacity to make a positive contribution to the restoration of joy in work.[39] Thus in 1921, at the very same GSR Congress that heard Troeltsch express doubts about the continuing relevance of the Christian work ethic, the Catholic August Pieper (1866–1942) insisted that the German sense of vocation could be revitalized despite rationalization and mechanization. According to Pieper, until recently head of the Volksverein's central office, even the

---

[36] Prof. D. Arthur Titius, in ESK, *Verhandlungen* (Frankfurt, 1929), 32–44.

[37] See, e.g., Jacob Schoell, "Der Evangelische Berufsgedanke und das Arbeitsleben der Gegenwart," in *Die soziale Botschaft der evangelischen Kirche* (Berlin: Evangelischer Pressverband für Deutschland, 1924), 34–52. Prelate Schoell of Stuttgart called for external reforms to supplement a new idea of calling based on acceptance of the reality of modern work. He acknowledged that the struggle to restore faith was important, but also urged the church to formulate ethical guidelines applicable to the business world as well as the sphere of private morality. Based on the principle that the welfare of the whole takes precedence over that of the individual—*Volkswohl geht vor Einzelwohl*—this new ethic was needed to improve the tone of public and working life in the contemporary world.

[38] Karl Jaspers, "Das Problem der Arbeitsfreude," in *Die geistige Situation der Zeit* (5th ed., 1932; reprinted Berlin: Walter de Gruyter, 1979), 57–60. Jaspers (1883–1969), professor of philosophy at the University of Heidelberg, had come to philosophy by way of medicine and psychology. He used the example of hard-working modern physicians who derived no joy from their profession to demonstrate that the problem of work was no longer confined to the industrial worker or the person employed in a rationalized office.

[39] Troeltsch himself suggested that it was their ability to latch onto the tradition of the Middle Ages that made it somewhat easier for Catholics than for individualist Protestants to believe in community as the source and center of the vocational ethic. Troeltsch, "Comment," in *Berufsethos und praktische Berufserziehung*, 87.

modern industrial worker employed in routine production could be taught to experience, if not Arbeitsfreude, then at least Berufsfreude, defined as the satisfaction derived from having fulfilled one's duty to the Volk community.[40] Unashamedly backward-looking, he took the vocational ethic of the independent craftsman or skilled worker as a model and yearned for the restoration of small-scale quality production and sound family life. Throughout the Weimar years he hammered home the message that it was possible through appropriate education to resurrect the idea of calling as a source of community by building on the remnants of the traditional work ethic carried over from pre-industrial times.[41] But he stressed that the industrial workers would also have to be taught to protest against the dehumanizing conditions of labor to which they were being subjected, rather than settling for shorter hours and higher wages which could never compensate for the loss of meaningful work.[42]

Pieper's sense of mission clearly inspired the work of Anton Heinen (1869–1934), a Catholic educational specialist closely associated with the Volksverein. Co-founder of the Hohenrodter Bund which was dedicated to educational reform, and of the Deutsche Schule für Volksforschung und Erwachsenenbildung (German School for Study of the Volk and Adult Education), of which Eugen Rosenstock was academic director, Heinen strove to develop forms of popular education that would instill in all walks of life the ethical notion of Volksgemeinschaft.[43] Assuming that vocation was central to a meaningful life, he concluded that individuals had to be enabled to be fully "human" first of all in the workplace. Only from that "Archimedean standpoint" would it be possible for people to find their way back to an appreciation of the wider context of their work, and become capable of taking a

[40] August Pieper, "Die Berufserziehung des Arbeiters," in Berufsethos und praktische Berufserziehung, 63–77. The primary community that counted for Pieper was the Volksgemeinschaft, the nation, but like most Catholics and many conservative Protestants, he also laid great stress on the family, the workplace, and the trade association as spheres within which modern people could develop a sense of working for and with others, and so satisfy their longing for status and experience joy.

[41] E.g., August Pieper, Berufsgedanke und Berufsstand im Wirtschaftsleben (Mönchen-Gladbach: Volksverein, 1925); "Berufsfreude, Beruf und Berufsstand," ZCGD 25 (17 April 1925): 113–19; "Arbeitsethos der persönlichen Ehre und soziales Berufsethos als Träger einer neuen Berufssittlichkeit," SP 38 (1929): 473–76; Berufsethos. Gesammelte Aufsätze (Mönchen-Gladbach: Volksverein, 1929.

[42] Pieper warned the workers to resist the tendency to excessive materialism as consumers, and instead urged them to develop a healthy, modest lifestyle in imitation of the educated classes and the Mittelstand. Berufsethos. Gesammelte Aufsätze, 86–87.

[43] See Karl Bozek, Anton Heinen und die Deutsche Volkshochschulbewegung (Stuttgart: Ernst Klett, 1963).

degree of responsibility for it.[44] Citing Riehl to the effect that the curse of work concealed within itself a secret blessing because it had the capacity to develop human ethical potential, Heinen maintained that education inside and outside the workplace could help turn the workers into fully developed individuals prepared both to cooperate freely and knowledgeably for the good of the economy and also to demonstrate a true spirit of work community in full awareness of their duties as well as of their rights.[45]

Although most Catholics subscribed to essentially conservative views on vocation and community, by 1929 even Pieper had come to realize that it might not be possible to stem the trend to modernity, and that the workers must be taught to master "the laws of rationality," lest they become subservient to them.[46] Others went further, arguing that genuine Arbeitsfreude could be experienced within modern industry. Indeed, a survey of the latest developments in psychotechnics in the Catholic international monthly *Soziale Revue* concluded that Arbeitsfreude was actually on the increase, because the rationalization movement demanded reforms that in earlier times had been inspired only by ethical considerations. Starting out with references to Bishop Keppler's *Freudenbuch* ("Book of Joys") of 1909, the author ended with quotations from Fritz Giese on the economic importance of restoring joy in work.[47]

The man who went furthest in adapting Catholicism to the world of modern work was the Centre party politician Friedrich Dessauer (1881–1963). Dessauer, who was director of the University of Frankfurt's Institute for Medical Physics, and, from 1923 to 1935 published the *Rhein-Mainische Volkszeitung*, organ of the Catholic-left Republicans,[48] proclaimed the existence a "Fourth Reich" of technology on a par with the domains of law, beauty, and will. Agents of this realm, which was said to possess an ethical value of its own, were the inventors who realized nature's potential and the entrepreneurs and engineers who put it in the service of humanity.[49] Dessauer also praised Ford's

---

[44] Anton Heinen, "Das Problem der Arbeiterbildung," *Deutsche Arbeit* 13 (1928): 341.

[45] Heinen, "Das Problem der Arbeiterbildung," 505–511; Bozek, *Heinen*, 100–102.

[46] August Pieper, "Die Stellung der Gewerkschaften zum Berufsethos," *Führer-Korrespondenz* 42 (1929) 3:136–41.

[47] Oskar Meister, "Neuere Untersuchungen über die Arbeitsfreude," *Soziale Revue* 28 (1928): 547–49.

[48] See *IBD/CE* 1.

[49] Friedrich Dessauer, *Philosophie der Technik. Das Problem der Realisierung* (Bonn: Friedrich Cohen, 1927). See also Heinrich Popitz, "Das Problem der Technik und die Fragestellung der Untersuchung," in *Technik und Industriearbeit* (2d ed.; Tübingen: J.C.B. Mohr, 1964), 4–5; Herf, *Reactionary Modernism*, 170–72; Lethen, *Neue Sachlichkert*, 59.

new ideal of technical service because it led away from the excessive individualism promoted by laissez-faire liberalism. Dessauer, himself an entrepreneur on a small scale, was in no position to condemn the profit motive entirely. Indeed, he defended the desire for profit as a stimulant to inventiveness. But best results, also from the financial standpoint, would be obtained if inventiveness were then given full reign.[50] Unfettered technology encouraged the spirit of national community and worked for peace by increasing human interdependence. Far from producing alienation, it transformed all who served it into potentially humanized servants of a higher good. This was true even of the most humble industrial workers who could take part, if only indirectly, by identifying with the spirit of their machines. Finally, technological progress opened up new spheres of human culture and made possible enormous advances in such areas as music and architecture.[51]

There can be no doubt about the influence of Dessauer's extreme pro-modernism on Catholic opinion. For example, the entry on "work" in the *Lexikon für Theologie und Kirche* published by the Bishop of Regensburg maintained that the most effective way to counter the damaging effects of rationalization on industrial labor was to give such work a deeper meaning along the lines proposed by people like Dessauer.[52] On the other hand, the *Lexikon* felt it necessary to reiterate the traditional Catholic warning against the gospel of work associated with Protestantism, stressed the ethical value of non-economic human activities, and insisted that the chief end of humanity lay in the afterlife.

The modernists' challenge was also taken up by Chaplain Dr. Franz Landmesser (1890–?) of Aachen. Landmesser, prominent in the Association of Catholic Academics,[53] inveighed against the Protestant work ethic, particularly in its Calvinist ascetic version. Arguing that Calvinism had produced the modern materialistic concept of work incorporated in both Liberalism and Marxism, he blamed this idea of work for the inexorable advance of the mechanized capitalist economy with all its evils. On the same grounds, he opposed the *Fortschritts-katholizismus* ("progressive Catholicism") of people like Dessauer. To treat work as an end in itself in the "modern" manner was counterproductive as well as grounded on error, Landmesser insisted. Only a religious revival

---

[50] Friedrich Dessauer, "Der unternehmende Mensch," *SP* 38 (1929): 470–73.

[51] On the close relationship between technology and art, Dessauer, *Philosophie der Technik,* 141–42, and Dessauer's address to the 1929 Breslau annual meeting of the German Werkbund, "Technik-Kultur-Kunst," *Die Form* 4 (1929): 479–86.

[52] F. X. Gruber, "Arbeit," *Lexikon für Theologie und Kirche* (2d ed.; Freiburg i. B.: Herdern, 1931), 1:599–602.

[53] See Alois Baumgartner, *Sehnsucht nach Gemeinschaft. Ideen und Strömungen im Sozialkatholizismus der Weimarer Republik* (Paderborn: Ferdinand Schöningh, 1977), 133–44.

could lead to true economic and cultural progress. Landmesser did express some sympathy for current efforts to restore the connection between work and life through changes in the workplace, and was prepared to recommend Rosenstock's Werkstattaussiedlung to his readers despite the fact that its proponent was a Protestant. He concluded, however, that such reforms could produce positive results only on the basis of a prior reformation of attitudes to work on the part of both employers and employees.[54]

Landmesser was not alone in seeking to combat Liberalism and Marxism by developing a characteristically "Catholic" version of the work ethic. This was also the purpose of Johannes Haessle's 1923 study of work in the thought of Thomas Aquinas and Leo XIII. Haessle showed that Pope Leo had rejected as utopian the Arbeitsfreude ideal in its Marxist version. Against Marx and Bebel, who had believed that work, once organized in freedom and equality, would generate great productive energies, or Kautsky, who predicted that work under socialism would cease to be a burden and instead become a pleasure which human beings would seek even without pay, the Pope had insisted that no return to paradise was possible in this sinful world.[55] But if "Christ in no way removed the cross and suffering from work," the Savior did transform it into a "means of strengthening virtue and a source of merit."[56] Pope Leo urged the workers to work hard and earn what they needed, but warned them to limit their demands to those appropriate to their station, and on no account to treat money-making as an end in itself. Only such self-limitation would enable work to produce the human virtues which in turn would make possible the building of a genuine community within which the individual would find inner satisfaction.[57]

Haessle himself went further. Concerned about the diminution of the German will to work since the war, he was loath to abandon the Arbeitsfreude ideal and so argued that work could become at least a relative joy. Strengthened by God and a religiously-based work ethic, individuals could be reconciled with their work and helped to develop a sense of duty to fellow laborers and community, as well as a greater

---

[54] Franz Xavier Landmesser, "Das Problem der Arbeit in den Weltanschauungen des Liberalismus, Socialismus und Christentums," *Soziale Revue* 23 (1923): 145–55; "Sozialistische Bewegung," *Soziale Revue* 24 (1924): 49–56; "Christus und das moderne Arbeitsleben," in *Kirche und Gesellschaft*, vol. 2, *Volkserziehung und Industrie. Die Vorträge und Ausprache der Gelsenkirchener Industriepädagogischen Tagung 1929 des Katholischen Akademikerverbandes* (Augsburg: Haas und Grabherr, 1930), 40–60.

[55] Johannes Haessle, *Das Arbeitsethos der Kirche nach Thomas von Aquin und Leo XIII* (Freiburg i. B.: Herder, 1923), 45.

[56] Haessle, *Arbeitsethos der Kirche*, 47.   [57] Haessle, *Arbeitsethos der Kirche*, 86–91.

sense of self-worth as responsible human beings.[58] And even granting that the social question was at heart a metaphysical-ethical matter and so not amenable to solution through external reforms, he insisted that cooperation between church, state, and workers could help to resolve current tensions and produce a higher form of capitalism based on the ideal of quality work.[59] Haessle thus contributed to the formation of a modernized Catholic work ethic compatible with the dominant Protestant culture and appropriate to the world of rationalized industrial capitalism. At the popular level, this rapprochement with Protestantism was reflected in a widely distributed Catholic tract entitled *Holy Work*, which insisted that idleness is the beginning of all transgression and preached the gospel of work in its full Carlylean version as both salvation and penance.[60]

Paradoxically, while German Catholics increasingly subscribed to something hardly distinguishable from the "Protestant" work ethic, Protestants tended to jettison the gospel of work in favor of a position similar to that of moderate Catholicism. Partly responsible for this was the revival of Protestant orthodoxy which emphasized the primacy of the individual's inner life in the quest for salvation and insisted on the holiness of the Sabbath. Theologians like Emil Brunner, Karl Holl, and Karl Barth reinforced the view that work, while important and valuable, should not be allowed to become the center of human life.[61]

[58] Haessle, *Arbeitsethos der Kirche*, 243–44.

[59] Haessle, *Arbeitsethos der Kirche*, 109, 242, 252. Haessle's explication of Pope Leo's stand on the problem of modern work and the social question reinforced the effect of a prewar study of St. Augustine by the Catholic theologian Heinrich Weinand. Weinand had argued that Max Weber and Troeltsch were wrong in attributing current positive attitudes to work solely to the Protestant Reformation, for St. Augustine in his day had persuaded the Church to stand up for work and had inspired the "exhausted arms of a tired world" to new efforts, producing the mighty economic development of the Middle Ages on which the modern world itself was built. Heinrich Weinand, *Antike und moderne Gedanken über die Arbeit, dargestellt am Problem der Arbeit beim h. Augustinus* (Mönchen-Gladbach: Volksverein, 1911), 59. For a further instance of this line of argument, see Helmut Holzapfel, *Die sittliche Wertung der körperlichen Arbeit im christlichen Altertum* (Würzburg: Verlag für katholisches Schriftum, 1941). Written under the Nazis, Holzapfel's prize-winning entry in a competition sponsored by Würzburg's theological faculty showed that the Church Fathers had transcended both the classical and Jewish work ethic with their high valuation of work, and that Christianity as such, rather than medieval monasticism or the Protestant reformation, had transformed work into both a potential source of salvation and a blessing.

[60] Joseph Lucas, *Heilige Arbeit. Ein Büchlein für alle, die ihre Arbeit wertvoll und schön gestalten wollen* (Limburg: Pallotiner-Verlag, 1930). A new printing of 10,000 in 1949, by the Lahn Verlag of Limburg, indicates that 30,000 copies had been previously distributed.

[61] See e.g., Karl Holl, "Die Geschichte des Worts 'Beruf'," in *Gesammelte Aufsätze zur Kirchengeschichte* (Tübingen: J.C.B. Mohr, 1928, reprinted Darmstadt: Wissenschaftliche Buchgesellschaft, 1965), 3:189–219; Karl Barth, "Die Arbeit als Problem der theologischen Ethik," *Theologische Blätter* 9 (1931): 250–56. See also Paul Marshall, "Vocation, Work, and

Also contributing to this shift of emphasis was a perception that recent changes in the workplace made it essential to rethink the relationship between work and leisure. Given the monotony and stress associated with modern work, it seemed self-evident that more time was
needed for religious and cultural pursuits. This belief strengthened the
hand of those who regarded as legitimate the claim for shorter working
hours put forward by both the socialist and Christian trade unions. The
eight-hour day, it was now argued, would not only enhance workers'
productivity and will to work, but also would help to compensate them
for the loss of Arbeitsfreude by providing a "creative pause" in which
individuals could recover their freedom, develop their human capacities, fulfill family, trade union, and political obligations, and worship
their God.[62]

Conversely, the movement to humanize work gained impetus from a
growing realization that only those who derived some degree of fulfillment from their jobs were capable of making good use of their leisure.[63]
For the increased appreciation for the importance of leisure did not
involve downgrading work in most cases, but rather stimulated a search
for some new kind of balance and a better link between work and life.
Typically, Joachim Sindermann of the Riehlbund, writing in support
of Rosenstock's scheme for Werkstattaussiedlung in a pamphlet devoted to family reform, argued that the recovery of the family was intimately linked with the transformation of work, and that it was therefore of primary importance to restore Arbeitsfreude by providing people
with free, responsible work and job stability. Only by freeing the human being in the worker would it become possible to liberate the time,
space, and force needed to restore the family to health.[64]

The intimate connection between the realms of work and leisure was
emphasized from the perspective of the church by pastor Dedo Müller.
Müller deplored the fact that his contemporaries responded to the
breach between religion and work in the modern world either by making work an end in itself, expecting it to give meaning to life, or by
turning their backs on it completely. Although like Jaspers he acknowledged that the stress of modern working life was felt not just by the

---

Jobs," in *Labour of Love. Essays on Work*, ed. Paul Marshall *et al.* (Toronto: Wedge Publishing
Foundation, 1980), 1–19. Commenting on Barth, Marshall appositely concludes that "Here
we have Augustine and Aquinas, or even Seneca and Aristotle, in new garb." Marshall,
"Vocation, Work, and Jobs," 14.

[62] See Fritz Klatt, *Die schöpferische Pause* (Jena: Eugen Diederichs, 1925).

[63] See, e.g., Otto Donath, *Vom Ethos rationalisierter Arbeit* (inaugural diss., Halle-Witten-
berg, 1927), 111–12.

[64] Joachim Sindermann, *Die Familie und die Arbeit*. Riehlbundheft 6 (Schweidnitz: A. Kaiser, 1926).

factory worker but also by professors, physicians, ministers, and others, he nevertheless warned against succumbing to fatalism. Rather than dwelling on the deterioration of work and leisure, Christians should undertake the reform of both: they should support the efforts of Rosenstock, Dessauer, and others to salvage the souls of the skilled workers by restructuring work and also encourage people engaged in repetitive tasks to do their jobs as mechanically as possible and to seek nourishment for the soul in expanded periods of leisure. Adopting a position more often found among Catholics,[65] Müller concluded that it was necessary both to give meaning to work and to restore content and purpose to leisure. The contemporary Christian's slogan should be *Bete und Arbeite* ("pray and work"), rather than *Arbeiten und Nicht Verzweifeln* ("work and don't despair"), as prescribed by the gospel of work.[66]

To appreciate the radicalism of Müller's defense of leisure from the Protestant perspective, one must remind oneself of the traditional position upheld just a few years earlier by such a relatively progressive thinker as the theologian and pastor Ludwig Weber (1846–1922). Concerned with the social question since the 1880s, and an active member of the ESK,[67] Ludwig Weber still preached in the early 1920s the holiness of work and backed this up with historical arguments that firmly attributed the ethical valuation of work to Protestantism.[68] He did call for preservation of the Sabbath as a day of rest, but qualified even this concession to non-work life by warning against the misuse of the resulting leisure.[69] Keeping work at the center, Ludwig Weber reminded employees of their duty to render obedience, work diligently, and respect the rights of property, while urging employers to acknowledge the obligations of ownership and accept the right of the state to intervene in the workplace for the general welfare.[70]

Just how far even those Protestants who insisted that work must remain the focus of human life had moved away from Ludwig Weber's position by the end of the decade is illustrated by the most exalted paean to work to come out of Weimar Germany, János Czirják's *The Meaning of Work*.[71] In this dissertation, Czirják, a Hungarian Calvinist

[65] See, e.g., Eugen Zimmermann, "Arbeitsethos," *Soziale Revue* (1930): 66–70. While insisting with considerable eloquence that religion and work were inseparable, and that with the right attitude, work could still be a blessing, Zimmermann stressed the duty to work but also the importance of setting limits.

[66] Müller, "Das Problem der Arbeitsfreude in der modernen Wirtschaft," 101–117.

[67] See *RGG*, 2d ed., 5:1775.

[68] Ludwig Weber, *Christentum und Arbeit* (Mönchen-Gladbach: n.p., [circa 1921]).

[69] Ludwig Weber, *Christentum und Arbeit*, 27.

[70] Ludwig Weber, *Christentum und Arbeit*, 19–20, 24.

[71] János Czirják, *Der Sinn der Arbeit, im Anschluss an die neue Literatur* (Bonn: J. Duckwitz, 1934).

who had studied in Switzerland with Emil Brunner and Karl Barth, insisted that only the one who finds joy in work finds it anywhere, and cited Carlyle and Henry Ford on the need to affirm modernity and to work hard.[72] Yet he went on to maintain that higher productivity had ethical value only to the extent that it freed additional time for culture.[73] It made no sense to work for the sake of working, because the final meaning of work, as indeed of life itself, rested in God.[74] Warning that it was wrong for human beings to allow themselves to be tyrannized by their jobs, he maintained that individuals must be allowed to choose their work, or even to choose *not* to work.[75]

To reject the cult of work was one thing. To argue that leisure was what really counted was quite another. Imbued with the notion that meaningful work was at the core of a truly human life, hardly any middle-class Germans took this further step. Ironically, one of the few prepared to argue that a "modern" ethic could be based on a divorce between work and life and that it would be possible to restore meaning to human existence through a reform of leisure was Eugen Rosenstock. In 1927, having abandoned hope of bringing workplace and living space into conjunction once more by reorganizing the former, Rosenstock tried to persuade the church that it had a duty to assist in the creation of new communities *outside* the workplace, to serve as a refuge from the world of alienated labor and a locus of spiritual renewal.[76] Using the sociologist Ferdinand Tönnies's distinction between society and community, he asserted that

> Life and church today belong together as allies in opposition to social-rationalized work, thanks to the unique circumstance that the contemporary soul can be returned to life only through the intermediary of a spiritual community.[77]

Rosenstock tried to persuade his fellow Protestants that the notion of calling or vocation was no longer relevant in the modern world, and that the church would never succeed in making contact with modern humanity so long as it persisted in preaching this outdated ideal.[78] Indeed, efforts to reintroduce soul into the world of work were not only bound to fail, but would result in an undesirable idolization of work

[72] Czirják, *Sinn der Arbeit*, 17, 34.   [73] Czirják, *Sinn der Arbeit*, 42.
[74] Czirják, *Sinn der Arbeit*, 57.   [75] Czirják, *Sinn der Arbeit*, 47–49.
[76] Eugen Rosenstock, " 'Leben und Arbeit.' Rede auf dem kirchlich-sozialen Kongress in Düsseldorf 1927," in *Politische Reden. Vierklang aus Volk, Gesellschaft, Staat und Kirche* (Berlin: Lambert Schneider, 1929), 42–55. Citations are from this version. The speech was also published under the same title in *Zeitwende* (Munich), 4 (1928): 341–53.
[77] Rosenstock, "Leben und Arbeit," 53.
[78] Eugen Rosenstock, "Kirche und Beruf," *Soziale Praxis* 38 (1929): 468–70.

(*Werkgötzendienst*) that would exact a tribute in the form of a wild, unhealthy work-fever. Rosenstock did not deny that the individual could derive a certain sense of exaltation even from intrinsically unsatisfying work if it served the welfare of the group, and so had no objection to the word Beruf if used in the sense of service, but he suggested that it might be better to replace it with *Auftrag* ("commission") to indicate awareness of the fact that the world had changed.

Since the problem of modern work could not be solved from within the workplace, Rosenstock concluded that the Protestant *work* ethic should be jettisoned in favor of an ethic centered on *leisure*. Transferring his reform enthusiasm to the latter, he now sought to restore meaning to life by transforming adult education.[79] Through carefully-devised educational experiences in leisure hours, ones modelled on the youth movement, he hoped to appeal to the sense of community and shared fate of the nation's young people in order to create new communities within which workers would be able to achieve their full development as independent adults.[80]

Rosenstock's efforts were effectively seconded by Fritz Klatt (1888– 1945), his collaborator in the movement for adult and leisure education reform. A pedagogic radical prominent in the Weimar youth movement, Klatt established his own boarding school in 1921 and from 1931 on was a professor at the Teachers' Training Academy in Hamburg. Between 1930 and 1933, he also edited the *Neue Blätter für den Sozialismus*, the mouthpiece of the religious socialists.[81] His educational philosophy was geared to developing individuality and creativity rather than producing good workers,[82] for he too was convinced that modern work could no longer give life meaning, and that education would have to provide alternative focuses for human existence. Nevertheless, Klatt thought it important to prepare Germany's young people for their working lives. Insisting that the child should be helped to overcome an inborn dislike of work by moving from play to creative effort under the guidance of a supportive teacher,[83] he called in the late 1920s for improved general education to supply the individual with contemporary

[79] On Rosenstock's role in worker education see most recently Norbert Reichling, *Akademische Arbeiterbildung in der Weimarer Republik* (Münster: LIT, 1983), 64–72, 161–64.

[80] Eugen Rosenstock, "Erwachsenenbildung und Betriebspolitik," in *Sozialrechtliches Jahrbuch*, ed. Theodor Brauer (Mannheim: J. Bensheimer, 1930), 1:135–50.

[81] See *NDB*, s.v. "Klatt, Fritz," by Winfried Böhm.

[82] See Fritz Klatt, *Beruf und Bildung* (Potsdam: Protte, 1929), excerpted in Fritz Klatt, *Beruf und Bildung. Ausgewählte pädagogische Schriften*, ed. Hermann Lorenzen (Paderborn: Ferdinand Schöningh, 1966), 46–74. References are to the 1966 edition.

[83] Klatt, *Schöpferische Pause*, 46–49. Between 1925 and 1936 this book was reprinted twenty-five times.

values, including realistic acceptance of modern technology and a determination to become its master. Klatt also stressed the importance in
the modern curriculum of physical training, communication skills, and
basic science to prepare graduates for a world dominated by the machine. For those already in the workforce he favored improved leisure
education. To this end he cooperated with Rosenstock and others in
establishing holiday camps where problems of both work and leisure
could be discussed.[84]

The socialist educational reformer Adolf Reichwein (1898–1944)[85]
shared Rosenstock's and Klatt's general outlook. Although he believed
that socialism would eventually make it possible to restore human mastery of the machine, he recognized that for the present freedom and
autonomy were possible only during the holidays. But this meant treating vacations not just as periods of recreation but as times of human
transformation, in which individuals would shake loose the "ghost of
work" that tended to pursue them into their scanty leisure hours and
experience a true "time of freedom" (*Freizeit*) in which their spirits
could shed all encumbrances and constrictions carried over from the
battlefield (*Kampfraum*) of work.[86]

Rosenstock, Klatt, and Reichwein started from different positions,
but by the late 1920s all had largely transferred their hope for the recovery of moral and spiritual values from the sphere of work to that of
leisure. In their efforts to expand opportunities for education outside
the workplace and to improve the quality of leisure education, they
could count on church circles for some support.[87] But even their care-

[84] See *Freizeitgestaltung. Grundsätze und Erfahrungen zur Erziehung des berufsgebundenen
Menschen*, ed. Fritz Klatt (Stuttgart: Silberburg, 1929). Along with essays by Rosenstock on
the leisure of academics, Hans Freyer on academic and popular education, Carl Mennicke on
the organization of leisure, and Adolf Reichwein on the leisure of young workers, this book
included the transcript of a discussion of Rosenstock's *Werkstattaussiedlung* by a group of young
booksellers at a summer holiday camp in 1925, 148–56, which made it clear that the campers
failed to share the optimism Rosenstock then still felt about the possibility of meaningful
work in the machine age.

[85] Reichwein's career paralleled that of Klatt in many respects. The main difference was
that Reichwein actually joined the SPD in 1930 whereas Klatt remained determinedly aloof
from politics. See Adolf Reichwein, *Ausgewählte Pädagogische Schriften*, ed. Herbert E. Ruppert and Horst E. Wittig (Paderborn: Ferdinand Schöningh, 1978), and the brief handwritten
Lebenslauf, dated 9 June 1941, in the BDC. In the Nazi era Reichwein eventually became
part of the Kreisau circle and engaged in resistance activities which led to his death in October 1944.

[86] Adolf Reichwein, "Jungarbeiter-Freizeit," in *Freizeitgestaltung*, 27–35.

[87] Thus, the *Kirchlich-Soziale Kongress*, in response to an appeal by Rosenstock, in 1927
passed a resolution in favor of legally established holidays for young workers. See "Urlaub der
Jugend," *Kirchlich-Soziale Blätter* 32 (1928): 41–43.

fully circumscribed attempt to modify the German ethic of work put them at odds with the majority of their fellows.

The only Germans prepared to subscribe to the leisure ethic without reservation were the few who became involved with the Technocracy movement. By urging the substitution of machines for people wherever possible in the productive process, Technocracy, an American import, deliberately minimized the ethical value of work.[88] Among its supporters were disciples of the Nobel Prize winner Wilhelm Ostwald (1853–1932), president of the Monist League, who already before the war had been an outspoken advocate of scientific management on the grounds that it would increase productive efficiency and help to free the workers for truly human activities.[89] Thus Edgar Herbst, president of the Research Foundation for Scientific Management in Vienna, was firmly convinced that the workers had more to gain from scientific management as consumers than they had to lose as producers and so urged that the old ideology of work be abandoned and the masses allowed to find compensation in leisure for the absence of joy in work.[90]

If Technocacy never achieved the importance in Germany that it attained in the United States, this was largely because it ran counter to the prevailing German work ethic. Indeed, the German proponents of scientific management favored it precisely because they thought in this way to restore the work ethic and the nation's will to work. For example, Gustav A. Winter, vice-president of the society "Die Brücke" founded by Ostwald in 1911, was motivated by patriotism rather than by a desire to free German workers from the burden of labor when he sought to convert Germans to Taylorism after the war.[91] For their part, the supporters of Fordismus were more attracted by Ford's service ethic and the alleged sense of a community to be derived from work on the assembly line than by his promise to raise wages and lower prices. In other words, they chose to emphasize those parts of Ford's message and methods that related to people as producers rather than as consumers.

[88] See Erich Kraemer, *Was ist Technokratie* (Berlin: K. Wolff, 1933), 13. Kraemer was critical of the movement he described and analyzed.

[89] Wilhelm Ostwald, "Wissenschaftliche Betriebsleitung," *Monistische Sonntagspredigten* (Leipzig) 86 (9.8.1913): 146–59.

[90] Edgar Herbst, *Taylorismus als Hilfe in unserer Wirtschaftsnot* (2d. rev. ed; Leipzig: Anzengruber, 1920). Herbst praised both Taylor and Ford for basing their systems on Ostwald's principle of the preservation of energy.

[91] Gustav A. Winter, *Das Taylorsystem und wie man es einführt in Deutschland* (Leipzig: Carl Findeisen, 1919), and *Der Taylorismus* (Leipzig: S. Hirzel, 1920). Winter's enthusiasm for scientific management did not survive the introduction of Fordismus: in his view, Ford was a "false messiah" who aimed to intensify work in order to enhance profits at the expense of the workers' physical and mental health. Gustav A. Winter, *Der Falsche Messias Henry Ford* (Leipzig: Verlag 'Freie Meinung', 1924).

CHAPTER X

The situation was different within the Social Democratic sub-culture. Because German Social Democracy had traditionally asserted that work in capitalist society was a necessary evil to be limited as much as possible and rewarded as well as possible, it was easier for its adherents to think in terms of a leisure ethic. In 1924 Hugo Sinzheimer (1875–1945), the SPD's leading specialist in labor law, quoted Marx to the effect that shorter working time was the best way to freedom and human development.[92] This dictum was taken to heart by the trade unions. Thus Fritz Tarnow, head of the Wood Workers' Union, addressing the ESK in 1929 on the work ethic of the employee, insisted that neither a new religious ethos nor the nationalization of industry could solve the problem of work created by the inevitable progress of rationalization. He conceded that the application of psychological and physiological findings could improve working conditions and that proper counselling, when backed by systematic aptitude testing, could help people find their place in the occupational structure; in the last analysis, however, he maintained that only full employment, higher wages, and shorter hours could counteract and compensate for the negative effects of technical change. Rejecting the Lutheran work ethic as inapplicable to capitalist society, Tarnow concluded that the final goal of the reformer must now be to maximize Joy in Life (*Lebensfreude*) rather than Joy in Work.[93]

Although trade unionists accepted the joylessness of work as an unavoidable facet of rationalization and gave the demand for more leisure time a prominent place in their program, they received little theoretical support from socialist intellectuals. The only important German-speaking Marxist to dispute the primacy of work in the interwar period was the Austrian Ernst Fischer (1899–1972). Greatly influenced by

[92] Hugo Sinzheimer, "Die geistige Fortbildung der Berufstätigen im gegenwärtigen Augenblick," in Essig, *Beruf und Menschentum*, 77–80. Sinzheimer was a professor at the University of Frankfurt and taught at the Frankfurt Academy of Labor.

[93] Fritz Tarnow, "Das Berufsethos des Arbeitnehmers," *Die Arbeit* 6 (1929): 374–84. The talk, under the title "Die Berufsethik des Arbeitnehmers," also appeared in ESK, *Verhandlungen*, Frankfurt, May 1929, 102–155, along with a rebuttal by August Springer, an anti-Marxist who refused to accept Tarnow's argument that the meaning of life should be transferred to leisure time and instead called for efforts to inculcate ideals of duty and service, and downgrade happiness as the goal of life! See also Kranold (Jena), "Zur Problematik des Achtstundentages," *Gewerkschafts-Archiv* 1 (1924): 210–13. Kranold argued that the eight-hour day was the sole alternative to revolution because only increased leisure could compensate the bulk of the working class for the ill effects of capitalist rationalization on their jobs and enable them to participate in cultural life. More generally on the trade union position, Alois Hoff, "Strategien der Gewerkschaften zur Kompensation der Rationalisierungsauswirkungen auf die Arbeitskraft," *Gewerkschaften und Rationalisierung* (Dissertation, Diplom.-Volkswirt, Berlin, 1975), 111–18.

Freud, who in contrast to Marx regarded "natural man" as an indolent being, Fischer condemned the gospel of work as a bourgeois construct which workers under capitalism would do best to eschew.[94] Most Marxists in the Weimar years were reluctant to write off *Arbeitsfreude* in the here and now as a lost cause, and therefore favored efforts to humanize work within capitalism through the application of Arbeitswissenschaft, which they regarded as a class-neutral means of coping with the evils attendant on mechanization and rationalization, pending the advent of the socialist new world and the true end of alienation.

Meanwhile, Socialist educators, by stressing the continued importance of good work and of inculcating pride in work along with a sense of occupational worth, helped to preserve the vocational ethic of German labor, and furthered the process of adaptation to capitalist society. The tendency to accommodation with the existing system was also strengthened by the courses mounted to educate works council members. Such efforts tended to produce men and women eager to participate in all aspects of the evolving democratic industrial society, rather than social revolutionaries.

Enmeshed in such practical activities, German Social Democrats contributed little to the Weimar debate about work in the period of stabilization. The Communists also stood aside from this debate. Although more inclined than Social Democrats to decry the baneful effects of capitalist rationalization on the working class, their firm belief that Marxism entailed hard-headed support for technological progress led them to shy away from ethical issues.[95] Yet it would be wrong to overlook the handful of Weimar intellectuals who preferred to stress the ethical and humanist component in Marx's thought rather than dwell on the scientific and "progressive" aspects of his doctrine. Ambivalent about "science" despite the vogue of the Neue Sachlichkeit, these Marxists found attractive such alternative sources of "truth" as Lebensphilosophie and phenomenology.[96]

The initial impetus to this revisionism came from Karl Korsch's *Marxism and Philosophy* and Georg Lukács's *History and Class Consciousness*. First published in 1923, both of these books dealt with alienation and reification, that is, with the Hegelian element in Marx's think-

[94] Glaser, *Im Umfeld des Austromarxismus*, 147, quoting from Fischer's *Arbeitsgesinnung und Sozialismus* of 1931.

[95] See, for example, Jacob Walcher, *Ford oder Marx* (Berlin: Neuer Deutscher Verlag, 1925), summarized in Stollberg, *Rationalisierungsdebatte*, 105–108.

[96] See Erich Heller, *The Disinherited Mind. Essays in Modern German Literature and Thought* (3d ed.; New York: Barnes & Noble, 1971), 108–109.

ing.[97] The appearance in 1932 of the first full German edition of Marx's "Economic and Philosophical Manuscripts" of 1844 also encouraged Marxists to focus attention on the problem of work. But even before publication of these works by the "young Marx," a few socialists attempted to legitimize their concern with labor alienation by drawing on what they knew of Marxist philosophy. Thus de Man, speaking at the Heppenheim Congress of young socialists in 1928, used *The Communist Manifesto* and other available texts to demonstrate that Marx had started out as an ethical socialist and had remained a "romantic '48er" at heart, despite his subsequent, unsuccessful efforts to diguise this.[98] Similarly, the author of an article on "the problem of work in contemporary German philosophy" published in the journal of the Federation of Free Trade Unions explicitly based his argument on a study of Marx's early writings. It was his claim that Scheler and Heidegger, in developing a "universal anthropology of man in action" that included the workaday world, were engaged in the very endeavor that had occupied Marx in his early philosophical period, before he got sidetracked into economics.[99]

Efforts to effect a rapprochement between German philosophy and Marxism based on their common preoccupation with the problem of work were paralleled by attempts to reconcile Marxism with the findings of psychoanalysis. Apart from Erich Fromm and Ernst Fischer, whose attempts to combine Freud and Marx have already been noted, socialists concerned with the problem of work tended to find the psychologist Alfred Adler (1870–1937) more congenial. This preference was undoubtedly strengthened by the fact that Adler, unlike Freud with whom he had broken by 1911, devoted a great deal of attention to social issues, and his "Individual Psychology" had as one of its main objectives the search for ways to bring "human beings into harmony with their social environment."[100]

[97] Karl Korsch, *Marxism and Philosophy* (reprinted, London: 1970); Georg Lukács, *History and Class Consciousness. Studies in Marxist Dialectics* (reprinted, Cambridge, Mass.: MIT Press, 1971). Korsch was on the left of the KPD from which he was expelled in 1926. Lukács wrote his book in Viennese exile after the failure of the Hungarian Soviet Republic of 1919 in which he had played a leading role. Their arguments are conveniently summarized in David McLellan, *Marxism after Marx* (2d. ed.; London: Macmillan, 1979), Chapters 10 and 11.

[98] *Sozialismus aus dem Glauben.* Verhandlungen der sozialistischen Tagung in Heppenheim a. B., Pfingstwoche 1928 (Zürich: Rotapfel Verlag, 1929), 35–37

[99] J. P. Mayer, "Das Problem der Arbeit in der deutschen Philosophie der Gegenwart," *Die Arbeit* 8 (1931): 128–35.

[100] Geoffrey Cocks, *Psychotherapy in the Third Reich. The Göring Institute* (New York: Oxford University Press, 1985), 37.

Although Adler himself maintained a certain distance from Marxism, this was not true of all his disciples. Thus many Marxist educators accepted Erwin Wexberg's claim that Adler had shown the way to a socialist education that would train the individual in habits of freedom, equality, and brotherhood.[101] Among them were Otto and Alice Rühle who in 1925 created a working group of Marxist individual psychologists in Dresden,[102] and Hermann Mönch who argued that it was the task of the socialist labor movement not only to reform the economic basis of society but also to transform the human soul. Eager to combine Marx with Adler, Mönch maintained that a social pedagogy based on progressive sociology and psychology could help to restore community spirit and forge harmonious bonds between the individual and society.[103]

Wexberg himself dealt specifically with the problem of work in his *Arbeit und Gemeinschaft* of 1932, the second volume of a trilogy covering all aspects of life. Although endorsing Freud's view that human beings do not possess a natural work drive, he went on to show that, with their domestication, they had come to desire meaningful work and to realize that joy in work was worth striving for. Wexberg was confident that individuals, inspired by the community spirit currently on the increase, could overcome their natural laziness through a sense of duty and self-discipline and that it was important for them to do so for the sake of their mental health. The sense of human solidarity might not be so strong as to enable people to derive Arbeitsfreude from otherwise joyless work, but even congenital work evaders might be persuaded to take up the burden of such labor if they could believe that thereby they were helping to bring about a better future.[104]

If there was little to distinguish the "ethical Marxism" propagated in the 1920s by people like Lukács, the Rühles, Mönch, or Wexberg from the ethical socialism of those like de Man who believed it necessary to go beyond Marx, the boundary between de Man's position and that of the frequently anti-Marxist "religious socialists" who regarded ethical reform as the primary or even exclusive means of achieving the desired new order was even less clear.[105] We have already discussed the ideas

---

[101] Erwin Wexberg, "Alfred Adlers Individualpsychologie und die sozialistische Erziehung," quoted by Glaser, *Im Umfeld des Austromarxismus*, 328–29.

[102] Glaser, *Im Umfeld des Austromarxismus*, 276.

[103] Hermann Mönch, "Gemeinwirtschaft-Seelengemeinschaft. Ein Beitrag zur Klärung, Ermutigung und Lösung," *Gewerkschafts-Archiv* 7 (1927): 191–96.

[104] Erwin Wexberg, *Arbeit und Gemeinschaft* (Leipzig: Hirzel, 1932), 8, 31–33, 96. Chapters 2 and 3 deal with Arbeitsfreude and the psychopathology of work respectively.

[105] On the religious socialists see W. R. Ward, *Theology, Sociology and Politics. The German*

about work of one member of this group, Fritz Klatt. Another religious socialist to call for a new ethic of work was Emil Fuchs (1874–1971), a Protestant minister who in the 1920s urged the youth movement to explore new opportunities for community in the modern world. Convinced that a new society in which all would serve the community while preserving their individual dignity and freedom would only be born if the workers' movement adopted a new ethic of responsibility, Fuchs called on the proletariat to fight for joy in work within the context of mechanized, rationalized industry. [106]

The new attitude toward work was also actively promoted by Carl Mennicke (1887–1959), a sociologist who edited the *Blätter für den religiösen Sozialismus* and taught philosophy and education at the University of Frankfurt from 1930 to his dismissal by the National Socialists in 1933. [107] Mennicke accepted the Marxist critique of capitalist society and used the Marxist historical scheme to dismiss attempts by antisocialists like Hellpach, Rosenstock, and Marr to restore Arbeitsfreude as romantic anachronisms. [108] Nevertheless, Mennicke became one of Weimar Germany's foremost proponents of humanization, arguing that socialism could win the confidence of the masses only if it tackled concrete present-day problems in a constructive spirit. [109]

He also insisted that it was necessary to go beyond Marxist orthodoxy on the theoretical level, to replace the economic materialism Marxism shared with capitalism by a moral perspective that stressed religion, a sense of community, and an ethic of duty. [110] To be effective, socialism would have to combine the ethical and cultural concerns of bourgeois intellectuals with the principles of the traditional proletarian workers' movement. This led logically to Mennicke's personal involvement

---

Social Conscience 1890–1933 (Bern: Peter Lang, 1979), Chapter 6; and Renate Breipohl, *Religiöser Sozialismus und bürgerliches Geschichtsbewusstsein zur Zeit der Weimarer Republik* (Zürich: Theologischer Verlag, 1971). Coming to the fore after 1918, religious socialism never disappeared entirely from the Weimar stage and experienced a revival in the last years of the Republic, particularly among Protestant intellectuals.

[106] Emil Fuchs, "Sozialismus und persönliche Lebensgestaltung," in *Sozialismus aus dem Glauben*, 186–203.

[107] See the entry on Mennicke in *IBD/CE*, 2.

[108] Carl Mennicke, "Der Romantische Abweg," *Die Arbeit* 2 (1925), 467–76.

[109] Carl Mennicke, *Das Problem der sittlichen Idee in der marxistischen Diskussion der Gegenwart* (Potsdam: Alfred Protte, 1927). While he endorsed labor's demands for better wages and shorter hours, Mennicke also demonstrated a lingering faith in the ability of Arbeitswissenschaft significantly to improve working conditions. See Carl Mennicke, *Der Sozialismus als Bewegung und Aufgabe* (Berlin: Quäker-Verlag/Heinrich Becker, 1926), 69; "Das Arbeitsschicksal des Proletariats," *Kulturwille* 3 (1926): 174–75; and "Das Problem der Arbeit in der angelsächsischen Welt," *Die Arbeit* 1 (1924): 276–83, an enthusiastic review of Frank Watts's book on industrial psychology, recently translated into German.

[110] Carl Mennicke, "Religiöser Sozialismus," *Soziale Praxis* 35 (1926): 462–63.

with the adult education movement. As lecturer at the *Deutsche Hochschule für Politik* in Berlin and director of the Economic School associated with its Social Policy Seminar, he tried to serve the cause of ethical socialism by educating people to desire—and to be capable of—work that challenged their potential.[111]

Joy in work was also a central concern of Eduard Heimann (1889–1967), professor of economics at the University of Hamburg and from 1930 on, co-editor with Fritz Klatt and the theologian Paul Tillich of the *Neue Blätter für den Sozialismus*. Insisting that Marx's real goal had been to restore the dignity of labor rather than abolish private property or even extend leisure time,[112] Heimann advocated socialization of property because only then would it be possible to emancipate humanity from the despotism of things and to replace capitalist alienation with the self-realization of the individual.[113] Like Mennicke, Heimann hoped to extend social policy and improve working conditions pending the creation of a socialist new order; he believed that socialists, by pressing for such reforms, would help to bring the capitalist era to its close.[114] On the other hand, he did not share Mennicke's belief that a decrease in the hours of work could significantly improve the quality of life: a drastic reduction of the working day was not only unrealistic from the economic standpoint but also undesirable, because even the most fulfilling leisure pursuits could never compensate a person for the loss of meaningful work. Arguing that no matter how effective the national program for leisure education, the majority of people would always experience culture in a passive way rather than as an opportunity for creativity, he insisted that the first priority must be to provide people with opportunities for purposeful activity during working hours.[115]

[111] Carl Mennicke, "Die Wirtschaftschule des Sozialpolitischen Seminars," *Berichte der Deutschen Hochschule für Politik, Mitteilungen*, 5 (1927): 9–14, in *Zeitschrift für Politik* 17 (1927/28).
[112] Eduard Heimann, "Die Begründung des Sozialismus," *Sozialismus aus dem Glauben*, 73. On Heimann, see the editor's introduction to Eduard Heimann, *Sozialismus im Wandel der modernen Gesellschaft. Erinnerungsband*, ed. Heinz-Dietrich Ortlieb (Berlin: J.H.W. Dietz, 1975) and the entry in *IBD/CE*, 2.
[113] Eduard Heimann, *Sozialistische Wirtschafts- und Arbeitsordnung* (Potsdam: Alfred Protte, 1932), 51. See also Dr. Paul Piechowski, "Proletarische Areitsfreude," *SP* 38 (1929): 479. While acknowledging the importance of joy in work, Piechowski warned that it was an illusion to believe that anything short of social revolution would transform proletarian distaste for work into Arbeitsfreude.
[114] Heimann, "Begründung," 74–78; Eduard Heimann, *Soziale Theorie des Kapitalismus* (Tübingen, 1929), 167, as cited in Rudolf Schwenger, *Die Betriebliche Sozialpolitik im Ruhrkohlenbergbau*, Schriften des VfS 186/1 (1932), 7; Eduard Heimann, "Soziale Betriebsarbeit II," *Neue Blätter für den Sozialismus* 1 (1930): 220–26.
[115] Heimann, *Sozialistische Wirtschafts- und Arbeitsordnung*, 55–56.

What Klatt, Fuchs, Mennicke, and Heimann had in common was their desire to solve the problem of work by changing the attitudes of trade unionists and of those intellectuals associated with the labor movement. A somewhat different approach was adopted by their fellow religious socialist, Georg Wünsch (1887–1964), professor of theology at Marburg and editor of the *Zeitschrift für Religion und Sozialismus*. Wünsch was less interested in persuading wage earners to change their view of work than in converting their employers and the church to a new economic ethic. Wünsch, too, believed that people need meaningful work for their mental and physical health, in order to develop their character and to establish their social status. Without such work, the human being would "degenerate, suffer from boredom and find his life and his pleasures shallow and an intolerable burden."[116] Yet he acknowledged that alienation was a fact of life in the modern world and insisted on the necessity of accepting rationalization and mechanization rather than hankering for a return to an irrecoverable past.

In the face of this dilemma, he spoke out for the humanization of work.[117] But he also promoted a return to the Lutheran idea of vocation. The foundation of the entire Christian social ethic, this idea enjoined obedience on the worker, but also demanded love and service from those in authority.[118] Convinced that it was the spirit of capitalism rather than the nature of modern work that was to blame for such characteristics of the modern economy as the excessive division of labor and the production of useless luxury goods, Wünsch insisted that it was the task of the church to promote a Christian business ethic that would conquer the profit-seeking ethos from which all evil flowed and thereby liberate the force needed to bring about the reforms that would make it possible for the masses once more to experience their lowly tasks as meaningful work or calling.[119] By arguing that the pursuit of practical reforms would have to be accompanied by a religiously-founded ethical renewal, with each reinforcing the other, Wünsch developed a "religious socialism" barely distinguishable from the outlook espoused by the more socially minded conservatives among his Christian contemporaries.[120]

---

[116] Georg Wünsch, *Evangelische Wirtschaftsethik* (Tübingen: J.C.B. Mohr, 1927), 539–40. However Wünsch acknowledged that increased wages and shorter hours might be required to compensate individuals for the alienating character of much modern work. Wünsch, *Evangelische Wirtschaftsethik*, 551, 592–93, 610.

[117] Wünsch, *Evangelische Wirtschaftsethik*, 558–59.

[118] Wünsch, *Evangelische Wirtschaftsethik*, 566–68.

[119] Wünsch, *Evangelische Wirtschaftsethik*, 574–80.

[120] See, e.g., *Kirche und Industrie. Vorträge bei der ersten Tagung von Pfarrern aus Industrie-*

All in all, the efforts of Weimar moralists to develop a work ethic appropriate to the age of rationalized production proved remarkably unfruitful. Their heavy reliance on diagnoses of the problem of work dating back to the nineteenth century and the persistence of attitudes and beliefs deeply rooted in the Christian tradition made it difficult even for those most aware of the need for change to develop genuinely new ideas. Just how difficult it was to come to terms with modernity can be seen in their response to what was perhaps the most important change requiring a reconsideration of the German work ethic, namely the rapid expansion of women's work.

Only a few individuals, mostly professional women, seriously addressed the question of what the vocational ethos of the modern working woman should be. Even radical proponents of a new approach to the problem of modern work tended to confine their discussion of the ethical crisis of work to men. Some undoubtedly assumed that what they had to say about "man" would be interpreted as applicable to both sexes. But most, whether consciously or unconsciously, failed to take up the challenge to extend the German work ethic to include the contemporary woman: they shared the traditional view that women could only find their vocation, and therefore true happiness, as wives and mothers. It was recognized that women were often compelled by necessity to work outside the home, or chose to do so in the years before marriage, but as they were not expected to aspire to joy in work, no ethical problem was thought to be involved. This meant that even during the depression when the question of women's work became a significant public issue, it tended to be dealt with on a practical or political rather than on a theoretical level.

As far as working men were concerned, the theoretical debate about the work ethic in Weimar Germany also left something to be desired. Nowhere was the confusing pluralism of Weimar cultural life more evident than with respect to the ideology of work. Despite the widespread longing for a unified national perspective, what Germans had to say about the meaning and future of work and leisure was heavily influenced by class, occupation, political orientation, and religious affiliation, as well as by regional and psychological factors. As a result, there were almost as many positions on the key issues as there were thinkers

---

gemeinden in Mitteldeutschland, ed. Wolfgang Stämmler (Sangerhausen: August Schneider, 1927), especially Pfarrer Geibel (Wittenberg), "Das Ethos des deutschen Unternehmers," 55–71.

willing to pronounce upon them. But it became fully apparent just how unsatisfactory the situation was only when some Germans abandoned the theoretical realm and actually tried to change the "German work ethic" to accord with current ideas about what modern work could and should be.

XI

THE FIGHT FOR THE SOUL
OF THE WORKER

AFTER THE COLLAPSE of the Second Reich, German employers had to come to terms with the unwelcome fact that labor relations would have to be carried on within a democratic political framework that at least on the surface gave the working masses a privileged position. Even after the threat of socialist revolution had evaporated labor unrest continued. The situation was further complicated by the Treaty of Versailles and the reparations burden imposed by the victors, which most businessmen saw as unwarranted constraints on Germany's legitimate efforts to compete in world markets. To meet these challenges the more progressive businessmen and industrialists rested their hopes on further mechanization, rationalization, and cartelization, combined with positive measures to secure the willing cooperation of German workers.

From the employers' perspective, the chief obstacle to success in the latter venture was organized labor. The labor movement seemed determined to press for ever higher wages, shorter hours, and more extensive and expensive social programs, using strikes and political action to secure compliance. By preaching worker solidarity and engaging in a Marxist rhetoric of class conflict, the free trade unions in particular seemed determined to undermine morale and aggravate grievances, instead of helping to resolve them.

In this chapter we will describe some of the steps taken by industry to counteract what was perceived to be a socialist offensive designed to win the German worker over to the anticapitalist and revolutionary cause. Because the prime agent of this counter-offensive was the Dinta, we shall analyze the motives and aims of its founders, describe its efforts to reconquer the workers' soul and restore the ethic of work, and discuss the controversy to which the Dinta gave rise. Our emphasis will not be on the Dinta as such, but on what it reveals about the German work ethic and attitudes to work.

The Dinta was founded in 1925 by a group of Ruhr industrialists headed by Albert Vögler (1877–1945), General Director of the German Luxembourg Mining AG, and Chairman of the Rhineland-Westphalian Coal Syndicate.[1] Ostensibly an attempt by the Ruhr mining industry to take the initiative in worker training so as to overcome a shortage of skilled labor, the Dinta from its origins had a more ambitious aim: to raise productivity by winning over the hearts and minds of the workers. Both organization and program expanded rapidly under the direction of Karl Arnhold (1884–1970), an ambitious engineer in Vögler's employ who headed the Dinta throughout the Weimar years and eventually led it into the Third Reich.[2]

When one examines the sources from which the Dinta's originators drew their inspiration, what stands out most vividly is the diversity and, indeed, the contradictory nature of the ideas that led to its creation. Best known of the ideologues who prepared the ground for the Dinta was the "philosopher" Oswald Spengler (1880–1936), a schoolteacher and freelance writer who had gained a large popular following with the publication, in 1918, of his pessimistic cultural history of western civilization, *The Decline of the West*. Spengler followed this up in 1920 with a political tract entitled *Prussianism and Socialism*, in which he used material from *Decline of the West* to demonstrate that the spirit of Old Prussia and the "socialist" attitude were in fact one and the same, if one interpreted socialism in its true, idealistic, sense.[3] Spengler's was a "national" socialism, one that rested on the spirit of a solidarity and a common destiny that bridged class divisions. Such a socialism, he claimed, had inspired the great men of Prussia from Frederick William to Bismarck and Hindenburg, as well as true working-class leaders like August Bebel, in whose day the German socialist party had been distinguished from those of other countries by "the clattering footsteps of workers' battalions, a calm sense of determination, good discipline, and the courage to die for a transcendent principle."[4]

---

[1] Robert Wistrich, *Who's Who in Nazi Germany* (London: Weidenfeld & Nicolson, 1982), 327–28; Gert von Klass, *Albert Vögler. Einer der Grossen des Ruhrreviers* (Tübingen: Rainer Wunderlich, 1957), 288–95.

[2] For a brief account of Arnhold's career, see Bunk, *Erziehung und Industriearbeit*, 269–70, n. 3, and GEFA [Gesellschaft für Arbeitspädagogik], *Ein Leben für die Deutsche Wirtschaft. Karl Arnhold zu seinem 80. Geburtstag* (Witten, 1964).

[3] Oswald Spengler, *Preussentum und Sozialismus* (Munich, 1920), translated as "Prussianism and Socialism" by Donald O. White, in Oswald Spengler, *Selected Essays* (Chicago: Henry Regnery, 1967), 1–131. References in the text are to the English version. See the discussion in Herman Lebovics, *Social Conservatism and the Middle Classes in Germany, 1914–1933* (Princeton: Princeton University Press, 1969), 160–63.

[4] Spengler, *Prussianism and Socialism*, 10.

As far as attitudes to work were concerned, Spengler argued that the despised English sought money and profits, whereas Prussians regarded work as a vocation, a Divine Commandment, to be carried on for its own sake. While the English capitalist ethic said "Get rich, and then you won't have to work any more,"[5] Prussian socialists strove to "overcome man's inborn lethargy" by proclaiming that people should do their duty by doing their work. No wonder, then, that the true German worker instinctively rejected Marx, an "exclusively English thinker" who had "inoculated his proletariat with a contempt for work."[6] Convinced that Marxism had had its day, Spengler insisted that under proper leadership German workers would once again do their duty in the old Prussian-Lutheran spirit.

Like many of his contemporaries, Spengler was obsessed with the problem of leadership in a modern state. To restore German unity and power the nation needed new leaders who, like the "workers" beneath them in the social hierarchy,[7] would draw on the Prussian civil service and military traditions and on the heritage of the Teutonic orders. Consequently he proposed that industrial management be put in the hands of a knightly order of engineers,[8] an order comprised of men of enterprise and ability imbued with a sense of mission at once political and religious, an elite that would accept status and power rather than wealth as a reward for its labors.

Spengler was able to deliver this message in person to Vögler and Arnhold, when at the end of 1924 these men made a pilgrimage to Munich to discuss their industrial training concepts with the Prussian sage.[9] Subsequently Vögler used Spengler's reputation to get the Dinta off the ground by inviting him to speak at the 1926 opening of the Dinta headquarters in Düsseldorf,[10] and Arnhold, who frequently cited Spengler, claimed that the latter's concept lay behind much of the Dinta's practice.[11]

Another prominent intellectual whose concern with the problem of work led to involvement with the Dinta was the religious philosopher Professor Ernst Horneffer (1871–1954) of the University of Giessen.

---

[5] Spengler, *Prussianism and Socialism*, 53–54.

[6] Spengler, *Prussianism and Socialism*, 95, 99.

[7] Spengler, *Prussianism and Socialism*, 102.

[8] Bunk, *Erziehung und Industriearbeit*, 196, citing Spengler's *Neubau des Deutschen Reiches* (1924).

[9] Bunk, *Erziehung und Industriearbeit*, 193.   [10] Bunk, *Erziehung und Industriearbeit*, 196.

[11] Bunk, *Erziehung und Industriearbeit*, 194. Struve, *Elites Against Democracy*, 242, dismisses as mere rumor the assertion that Spengler played a "direct role in the founding and development of DINTA," but acknowledges that the Dinta fitted in with Spengler's ideas and recommendations.

Horneffer, a leading exponent of Nietzschean thought, had given the funeral oration at Nietzsche's grave in 1900 and was editor of the Nietzsche papers. In 1909, he and his brother August founded the weekly *Die Tat*. He was also active as a religious speaker and educator. Having defined the social question in ethical and cultural terms, Horneffer sought to solve it by creating a new leadership elite that would hasten the spiritual transformation of the nation.[12]

Horneffer's approach to the problem of work was significantly affected by his conversion around 1910 to Free Masonry.[13] The Masons, who linked onto the work traditions of the medieval building guilds, grounded their vocational ethic in a full-fledged "religious" cult of work.[14] The Horneffer brothers adopted the Masonic view of labor as the source of truth, morality, and faith, and transmitted it to the postwar world in combination with elements derived from German idealism and Nietzschean elitism.

August made the Masonic connection explicit in a pamphlet of 1919 entitled *Heilige Arbeit*, "Holy Work." Attributing the loss of the German will to work to the exhaustion, undernourishment, and loss of discipline resulting from the war as well as the demoralization of defeat, he nonetheless insisted that the problem had deeper roots in cultural decline, materialist individualism, class envy and hatred, and the loss of Arbeitsfreude—all of which produced a hectic search for pleasure in consumption.[15] While it was necessary to tackle material problems and provide adequate leisure for recreation, the real solution for Germany lay in education for work on a religious-ethical basis. Necessary for the restoration of the nation's strength was the kind of work which the Masons designated the "royal art": activity conducive to physical and mental health that would perfect the individual personality, serve the brotherhood of man, and complete God's plan.

August's ideal was the simple, natural life where those who could would enjoy their jobs, while the rest would treat work as a national duty and a means to self-discovery and discipline.[16] The task ahead was

---

[12] Hamann and Hermand, *Stilkunst um 1900*, 44–45. One of his disciples at this time was the young Ernst Niekisch who joined a group for "free religious" instruction led by Horneffer and wrote some pieces for the Horneffer brothers' monthly *Unsichtbare Tempel* without knowing that this was a Masonic periodical. See Ernst Niekisch, *Erinnerungen eines Deutschen Revolutionärs* (Cologne: Verlag Wissenschaft und Politik, 1974), 1:24.

[13] IfZ, MA-141/6. Aktenotiz: Betrifft Freimaurermitgliedschaft von Prof. Ernst Horneffer. 25 March 1942, from Kreisleitung Welterau to Gauleitung Hessen-Nassau.

[14] Arthur Salz, "Zur Geschichte der Berufsidee," ASS 37 (1913): 421 n.21.

[15] August Horneffer, *Heilige Arbeit*, Am Bau: Freimaurerische Flugschriften, 2 (Munich: Ernst Reinhardt, 1919), 3–5.

[16] Horneffer, *Heilige Arbeit*, 5–15.

to instill in the ordinary person the philosophy of duty so well expounded by Kant and Fichte. Arguing that it was easier to start by reforming leisure than by reshaping the working world directly, he advocated free-time adult education in Volk High Schools to teach people to view their jobs in a broader context. This was to be supplemented by non-denominational gatherings and festivities in Volk Houses, community centers dedicated to the renewal of Arbeitsfreude and brotherhood and organized by the state in cooperation with a national association, an expanded Masonic lodge.[17]

Although less active than August in the postwar Masonic movement, Ernst Horneffer essentially shared his brother's ideal of work. As he explained in an essay of 1922, the decisive event in human history had taken place when human beings ceased to regard themselves just as children of God but became his collaborator in building the temple of beauty. Citing Luther, Goethe's Faust, and Nietzsche's Zarathustra, he designated Germans as the *Genie-Volk der Arbeit*, the genius race of work, whose salvation lay in adopting as its own the Masonic religion of human creativity.[18]

Had he confined himself to such statements, Ernst Horneffer would simply have been one more voice in the postwar chorus that called for an ethical revival to culminate in a utopia of joyful work. It was the nature of the specific proposals that he outlined for solving the current crisis that set him apart. Unlike his brother he was convinced that reform had to start in the workplace and maintained that the main agents of change must be the employers and engineers rather than the churches, the state, or independent organizations devoted to moral education. Determined to salvage capitalism as the locus of creative work and source of progress, he chose to take his message to German industry.

Horneffer called upon the employers to initiate a fight for the soul of their workers. Arguing that a new approach to management was required if the socialist movement was to be successfully undermined, he urged business leaders to learn the common secret of Europe's two most successful political institutions, the English aristocracy and the Papacy—the ability to yield and adapt to new circumstances. Specifically, he recommended that employers "divide the masses" by tying exemplary workers to their company through promises of job security and opportunities for personal development. Undeterred by critics who charged him with utopianism and denied the applicability of philoso-

[17] Horneffer, *Heilige Arbeit*, 16–20.
[18] Ernst Horneffer, "Die Religion der Arbeit," *Deutsche Pfeiler* 2 (1922/23): 5–13.

CHAPTER XI

phy to the problems of the business world,[19] he also promoted the creation of a modern managerial ideology to counter Marxist proletarianism. Only through cooperation between theorists (like himself!) and practitioners, between social science and economics, would it be possible to reconcile people with their work, render work once more humanity's religion, restore the German Volk to its traditional supremacy as a people of work, and, wiping out the distinction between manual and mental labor, enable all to do their part with enthusiasm and joy.[20]

In the leading business journal, *Der Arbeitgeber*, Horneffer also outlined a new social policy to replace that of the prewar Reich which had clearly failed to overcome worker alienation. Because the state was too remote from the workplace, he argued that social policy henceforth must be based on the company (*Betrieb*) or the plant (*Werk*). Blaming Marxism for having directed social policy into universalist, abstract, and statist channels, he maintained that Nietzsche's individualistic Lebensphilosophie provided a vastly superior guide.[21] Moreover, Nietzsche's ideas were said to represent the best cure for the "fundamental sickness of the entire epoch," namely the generalized rejection of leadership (*Führertum*) that lay behind many attacks on capitalism. If the nation wanted genuine leaders capable of raising economic productivity it would have to approve the material conditions they required, including "the free, totally independent and individual power to mobilize massive economic values."[22]

When the nation's entrepreneurs proved insufficiently responsive to his message, Horneffer turned to the engineers. By 1926 he was telling the Dinta engineers that it was their duty to reeducate the nation.[23]

[19] E.g., Dr. Bovenschen, "Prof. Horneffers Ideen in ihrer praktischen Durchführbarkeit," *Der Arbeitgeber* 12 (1922): 381–84, and Robert Liefmann, "Der soziale Gegensatz und seine Überwindung," *Der Arbeitgeber* 13 (1923): 118–19. Liefmann, professor of economics at Freiburg, denied that Nietzsche provided the answer to Marx, dismissed Horneffer's economic arguments as simplistic, and accused him of empty sloganeering.

[20] Ernst Horneffer, *Der soziale Gegensatz und seine Überwindung*. Vortrag Oct. 1922. Schriften der VdA, 3 (Berlin: Verlag 'Offene Worte,' n.d.), 21–23. This was a condensed version of his *Die Grosse Wunde. Psychologische Betrachtungen zum Verhältnis von Kapital und Arbeit* (Munich: R. Oldenbourg, 1922). Horneffer repeated the religious argument in "Wirtschaft und Religion," *Der Arbeitgeber* (1924): 293–94, and "Die Religion der Arbeit," Ibid., 308–310.

[21] Ernst Horneffer, "Das soziale Problem," *Der Arbeitgeber* 13 (1923): 2–6, and "Die Vormacht des Staates," ibid., 258–59.

[22] Ernst Horneffer, "Das soziale Problem im Lichte von Philosophie und Einzelforschung," *Der Arbeitgeber* 13 (1923): 132–35.

[23] Ernst Horneffer, *Der Ingenieur als Erzieher*. Vortrag gehalten im Institut für Technische Arbeitsschulung in Gelsenkirchen (Essen: G. D. Baedeker, 1926). The talk was reproduced in *Das Werk* 6 (April–December 1926): 243–46, 292–98, 341–45. *Das Werk* was the monthly of the Vereinigte Stahlwerke AG, newly founded by the Dinta enthusiast Vögler, himself a trained chemist and engineer.

Appealing to the elitist pretensions of his auditors, whom he described as members of a young profession that had yet to claim its rightful place,[24] he declared that the performance principle (*Leistungsprinzip*) should replace democracy with its "false egalitarianism." In former times, the state, church, and army had shaped men and educated them for work; now it was time for industry itself to undertake this task, because the state was in inferior hands, the nation's shrunken officer corps too small to handle the job, and the churches unsuited to deal effectively with the specific problems of modern work.[25] Only engineers, scientifically trained and in close touch with wide sections of the general population, could serve as the new *Volkserzieher*, educators of the people.[26]

Horneffer also counted on engineers to adapt the medieval guild principle and its associated cult of work to modern industry. What he envisioned was the creation of new guilds, complete with slogans, ceremonies, and common rites, to reveal work's inner nature. Based on the Masonic example, these were designed to compensate for the failure of contemporary, science-oriented, society to give sufficient weight to the irrational element in human nature.[27] Limited to fifty to one hundred members, the guilds would maintain and intensify the sense of common purpose and dedication that united all "workers" within the firm, from the director and entrepreneur down, while the engineer would act as day-to-day manager and go-between to heal the "great wound"—the gap between capital and labor.[28]

If Spengler's idea of work was dominated by duty, Horneffer's focused on joy in work. This line of thinking culminated in his *The Way to Joy in Work* of 1928.[29] Here Horneffer used quotations from Luther, Goethe, Schiller, and Nietzsche to demonstrate the superiority of the German work ethic, as a preliminary to showing how its revival could solve the problem of modern work. Germany, the nation which had pioneered the welfare state, was urged to take the lead in developing a "spiritual social policy" to meet the emotional needs of modern workers, who could never be reconciled through mere improvements in their material condition. Artists, theologians, and educators could help to restore Arbeitsfreude, but it was the engineers, with their knowledge of the joy to be derived from creation and their appreciation of the beauty of technology, who could do most to enhance the German worker's innate capacity to feel "something in the presence of the

[24] Horneffer, *Ingenieur als Erzieher*, 28.
[25] Horneffer, *Ingenieur als Erzieher*, 14–15, 28–29.
[26] Horneffer, *Ingenieur als Erzieher*, 28–33.   [27] Horneffer, *Ingenieur als Erzieher*, 54–57.
[28] Horneffer, *Ingenieur als Erzieher*, 65–71.
[29] Ernst Horneffer, *Der Weg zur Arbeitsfreude* (Berlin: Hobbing, 1928).

mighty enterprise of which he forms a part" and to experience pride in mastering his work.[30]

Horneffer's devices for helping the employers win over the souls of their workers were not framed solely with the interests of industry or the economy in mind. Like Spengler he assumed that success in ending worker alienation within rationalized industry would benefit society as a whole and restore the nation to greatness. No blind supporter of the employers, Horneffer warned German businessmen that they must abandon outdated patriarchalism in favor of an improved ethic based on responsibility for the workers' welfare.[31] Nor, despite his constant references to the medieval guilds, was Horneffer simply a "reactionary." Thus, although he wanted the engineers to supplant the officer corps as educators of the nation, he insisted that the new education be built on freedom and mutual respect rather than on military discipline and obedience. Although experience in the workplace remained the best teacher of social relations, engineering schools would therefore have to place greater emphasis on personality and human values and to add courses in philosophy and the social sciences to the curriculum.[32] Only engineers educated in both science and philosophy would be able to bridge the two cultures, and reconcile Germans with their work in a technologically advanced society by helping them to develop an inner understanding of it.[33]

By appealing to employer self-interest and to the engineers' desire for increased status, Horneffer managed to get a hearing in industrial circles for his utopian ideas about joy in work. By putting "art" above "science" and by giving voice to the longing of a divided nation for reconciliation and community, he strengthened the irrational forces that the Dinta sought to harness in the battle for the workers' soul. Elements of his philosophy were absorbed into Dinta rhetoric alongside ideas taken from Spengler and inspired the Dinta as it attempted to play the role the "philosophers" had assigned the nation's engineers: that of revivifying Germany's ethic of work.

Just the same, it was personal experience rather than such ideological influences that chiefly determined the ideas about work held by Arnhold, the Dinta's guiding spirit. After attending the local machine building school in his home town of Wuppertal, Karl Arnhold worked as an engineer in a local firm, then quickly became involved in indus-

[30] Horneffer, *Ingenieur als Erzieher*, 58–59.

[31] Ernst Horneffer, "Teilung der Massen," *Der Arbeitgeber* 17 (1927), 352.

[32] Horneffer, *Ingenieur als Erzieher*, 65–67.

[33] See the summary of Horneffer's address to the 1927 convention of academic Engineers, "Der Ingenieur als Kulturträger," *Technik und Kultur* 18 (1927): 213–15.

trial training. Although he was formally attached to the Wuppertal Vocational School, many of his pupils were employed by his old firm and took most of their training at their place of work, a foreshadowing of the Dinta experiment. Simultaneously, Arnhold audited courses at the Aachen TH. When the war came, he volunteered for military service. By 1917 he was in charge of patriotic training for his division and was editing the divisional newspaper.

An ardent nationalist who never accepted Germany's defeat as final, Arnhold continued to inveigh against Versailles and the reparations settlement. His equally fervent antisocialism led him to stay in the army until 1920, organizing counter-revolutionary activities. He also founded a nationalist cultural-political club in Wuppertal and was active in other associations dedicated to defending Germany against internal and external threats from the time of the Spartacus uprising in 1919 to the French occupation of the Ruhr in 1923.[34]

Although emotional nationalism and anti-Marxism remained permanent features of Arnhold's outlook, he made great efforts to obscure the "political" motives that underlay the Dinta's program. In order to gain the greatest possible support from both employers and labor, he based his pleas for consideration of the "human factor" in industry largely on "scientific" and rational considerations and stressed the economic benefits to be derived from his educational innovations.[35] Claiming to be concerned only with alleviating the shortage of skilled, responsible, and cooperative workers, he blamed the trade unions for politicizing industrial training so as to capture workers' souls and prepare them for the final assault on capitalism. At the same time, he tried to dissociate the Dinta from conservative groups like the GWS and the BNW which promoted the ideal of the works community as part of a broad program of national renewal.[36] The Dinta, he insisted, wanted to solve the problems of industry at the plant level in the interests of industry alone, without any interference from outside.[37]

On the other hand, Arnhold conceded that the Dinta's program, if

[34] Bunk, *Erziehung und Industriearbeit*, 259, n.3; *Wer ist's?* (1935), 35.

[35] See, for example, Carl Arnhold, "Industrielle Berufserziehung," *Soziale Zukunft* (1930): 35–39, and "Menschenführung im Sinne des Deutschen Instituts für Technische Arbeitsschulung," *Sozialrechtliches Jahrbuch* (1930), 118–34.

[36] To demonstrate his opposition to yellow unions, he even forced the resignation of the Berlin Dinta representative, who as business manager of Dunkmann's Institute for Applied Sociology had publicly urged the creation of national, anti-Marxist Werkvereine financed by the employers. See "Neues zur wirtschaftsfriedlichen Arbeitnehmerbewegung," *SP* 36 (1927): 264–68.

[37] Carl R. Arnhold, "Das Dinta und die Gewerkschaften," *Wirtschaftliche Nachrichten für Rhein und Ruhr*, 10 February 1927, 149–56.

successful, would influence worker behavior far beyond the factory gates and set the Dinta on a course that made confrontation with the unions unavoidable. This erupted in a battle of pamphlets between his associate Dr. Paul Osthold (1894–?),[38] and Fritz Fricke (1894–1961), speaking for the free trade unions.[39] Fricke denounced the Dinta as an agency of the capitalists out to destroy the trade union movement in order better to exploit the workers.[40] Identifying it with yellow union-ism, he charged that it had initiated the fight for the soul of the worker in order to secure the victory of the Werksgemeinschaft principle over the ideal of *Wirtschaftsdemokratie*, economic democracy, recently adopted as official policy by the SPD.[41] For his part, Osthold admitted that the Dinta was trying to reconcile the workers to the existing order and that it hoped to do so without resorting to material incentives which he claimed Germany could not afford. He also charged that whereas the Dinta desired to solve current problems in a spirit of co-operation, the Marxists were deliberately poisoning relations between capital and labor. Thus each side accused the other of initiating the conflict that both were determined to continue to the death.

The fight for the soul of the German worker was basically a struggle for power. Its main weapon was education. The Dinta's efforts to bring industrial training under employer control directly challenged the pat-tern of vocational schooling inherited from the Second Reich, which state governments in the Weimar period, with strong support from the labor movement, were seeking to improve and universalize.[42] On the other hand, the Dinta could fairly argue that it was carrying out edu-cational reforms which the socialist trade unions had themselves called

[38] Paul Osthold, *Der Kampf um die Seele unseres Arbeiters* (2d ed.; Düsseldorf: Industrie Verlag, 1928). After distinguished war service that included a period as prisoner of war and won him the Iron Cross class I and II, Osthold studied history, economics and philosophy at Münster and Königsberg, took part in the *Ruhrkampf*, and was active in patriotic and veterans organizations. He helped start the Dinta in 1925 and worked as Arnhold's assistant until 1928 when he became editor of the *Deutsche Bergwerkszeitung*. See *Wer ists?* (1935).

[39] On Fricke, see *IBD/CE*.

[40] Fritz Fricke, *Sie suchen die Seele* (2d enl. ed; Berlin: ADGB, 1927), and "Grundlagen und Methoden der neuen psychologischen Arbeitspolitik der Unternehmer," *Gewerkschafts-Zeitung*, 21 May 1927, 285–86 and 28 May 1927, 301–302.

[41] Fricke, *Sie suchen die Seele*, 49–50. Fricke conceded that the Dinta was founded before economic democracy became a declared trade union objective. However, it had already been extensively debated at both the trade union and SPD annual conventions of 1925. See Mi-chael Schneider, *Unternehmer und Demokratie* (Bonn-Bad Godesberg: Verlag Neue Gesell-schaft, 1975), 85–90.

[42] For a comparative historical treatment of British and German vocational training that puts the Dinta into a wider context, see Peter William Musgrave, *Technical Change, the La-bour Force and Education. A Study of the British and German Iron and Steel Industries, 1860–1964* (London: Pergamon, 1967), especially 108–127.

for at their 1919 congress in Nuremberg, and that it sought to inculcate attitudes to work with which the labor movement had no real quarrel. When it promoted education for work *through* work, used aptitude tests to assign students to appropriate courses of study, combined practical skills training with theoretical schooling in the sciences and economics and with physical education, or sought to turn out skilled and flexible workers imbued with an ethic of hard, disciplined work, the Dinta maintained that it was meeting the needs of modern industry in a way that Marx, himself, would have approved.[43]

Of course, the issue was less what and how German workers were to be taught, than where and by whom. The Dinta's attempt to give industry total control over the education of its recruits ran into opposition from both the free trade unions and the Christian unions. For organized labor feared precisely what the Dinta desired, namely that young workers in Dinta schools would fail to develop proletarian or occupational bonds and instead become loyal members of the employer-dominated works community. In fact, the Dinta did everything it could to ensure this outcome. Carefully selected on the basis of the latest psychotechnical tests, young men, after a three-month probationary period, were subjected to intensive training which lasted, in the case of skilled workers, for three years. Initially concentrated in separate workshops, they were only gradually introduced to the factory proper lest their natural love of work be destroyed by premature exposure to the realities of industrial labor and the negativism of the older employees. Pupils were subjected to long hours in the training workshops, which were designed to teach careful use of time and materials and expected to be self-supporting, They also had to study relevant theoretical subjects and spend at least two periods a week outside working hours on sport. Close ties were maintained with the families, particularly the fathers, and the homes were regularly inspected to ensure that conditions for learning were right. Meanwhile, their sisters were taught to keep house and budget carefully with the money given them, ideally after having worked a full five-day week on tasks deemed suited to women, such as sewing worker uniforms or fashioning cement sacks.[44]

Arnhold vigorously promoted his educational model throughout the country. Like Adolf Friedrich of the *Anstalt für Arbeitskunde*, he spoke

[43] According to Osthold, Marx had fully understood the educational potential of combining practical productive work with instruction and gymnastics: the Dinta formula. Paul Osthold, "Sie suchen die Seele," *Der Arbeitgeber* 18 (1928): 130.

[44] Karl Arnhold, "Ausbildung und Schulung von Arbeitern in Grossbetrieben," in *Die menschliche Arbeitskraft im Produktionsvorgang* (Düsseldorf: Verlag Stahleisen, 1925), 15–23; "Neuzeitliche Lehrlingsausbildung," *Das Werk* 9 (1929): 59–62.

at innumerable conferences, and many of his addresses to industry and reform groups subsequently appeared in print. In addition, he instituted a Dinta journal which was published continuously from 1929 to 1943. Entitled *Arbeitsschulung*, "education for work," this quarterly was primarily meant for Dinta supporters, but subscriptions were also available to members of the general public.[45] It carried articles by Arnhold and his close associates interspersed with items reprinted from other sources commenting on the Dinta's fight for the soul of the German worker.[46]

Originally the Dinta was meant to turn young men just out of school into highly skilled specialists capable of doing quality work—flexible enough to serve in a variety of capacities, enthusiastic about their jobs, and loyal to their employers. Later, Dinta education was extended to those without the ability to aspire to full apprenticeships, on the grounds that all could benefit from basic manual training and be rendered more valuable to their firms,[47] but the main emphasis throughout was on the skilled trades. In this domain, the Dinta was potentially in conflict not only with the vocational schools maintained by state and local authorities, but also with other industry-sponsored organizations such as the Arbeitsausschuss für Berufsausbildung (Working Committee for Vocational Training) and the Deutsche Ausschuss für Technisches Schulwesen, DATSCH (German Bureau for Technical Education). The former was established in 1925 by the RDI and the VdA, in cooperation with the artisan associations, as a first response to recently introduced draft legislation for a national Vocational Training Program.[48] Its executive director was Franz Schürholz of the DATSCH. Already well established by the 1920s as a leader in the area of industrial training, the DATSCH was founded in 1908 by the VdI and a group of machine-building concerns to determine the requirements of industry for skilled workers and to prepare detailed curricula for industrial apprenticeships. After the war, rapid expansion of its sphere of influence put it in a strong position to oppose the newly formed Dinta as an unneeded rival.[49]

---

[45] RKW, *Der Mensch und die Rationalisierung* 1, 155.

[46] E.g., Dr. R. Kaufmann, "Um die Seele des Arbeiters," *Arbeitschulung* 1 (1 October 1929): 19, reprinted from the *Vossische Zeitung* (Berlin) of 13 January 1927; and Karl Arnhold, "Arbeit als Dienst am Volk," *Arbeitsschulung* 3 (1932): 99–104. After 1941, the journal appeared as *Arbeit und Betrieb*.

[47] Arnhold, "Ausbildung und Schulung," 20.

[48] Wolfgang Muth, *Berufsausbildung in der Weimarer Republik* (Stuttgart: Franz Steiner, 1985), 375–79, 444–82; Kastl, "Die wirtschaftspolitische Voraussetzungen für Deutsche Qualitätsarbeit," RDI, *Tätigkeitsbericht*, 37 (October 1927): 35–36; Ludwig Rennschmid, *Der Lehrling in der Industrie* (Jena: Gustav Fischer, 1931), 64–67.

[49] On the origins of the DATSCH, Muth, *Berufsausbildung*, 348–52; Musgrave, *Technical*

Instead the DATSCH cooperated fully with the Dinta and even defended it against its critics.[50] It did so despite the fact that some of its leaders had serious reservations about the ideological language with which Dinta spokesmen promoted their experiment. Schürholz himself preferred a "scientific" approach to technical training and had no desire to concern himself with the worker's soul. Deploring excessive talk about the meaning of work and the need for Arbeitsfreude, he argued that work was a social task aiming at maximum production, that it must therefore be rationally organized, and that the workers could find compensation in their free time for any perceived deficiencies of their jobs.[51] Nor did Schürholz wish to chain the worker emotionally to a particular firm. Although he hoped that the spirit of works community would eventually arise spontaneously out of the modern cooperative work process, he believed that educators had an obligation to encourage labor mobility.[52]

There is no doubt that Schürholz's approach made industry-sponsored technical training palatable to many who distrusted the Dinta's ideology: employers anxious to avoid confrontation with the unions, educators in Germany's vocational and technical schools, social reformers, and organized labor. By declaring its willingness to cooperate with the Dinta, the DATSCH substantially helped the new institute to gain legitimacy in the eyes of people not otherwise inclined to welcome business initiatives in the sphere of vocational education.[53]

In its fight for the soul of the worker the Dinta did not confine itself to industrial training. Arnhold doubted that much could be done to change the attitudes of the adult worker directly, but he recognized the importance of minimizing tensions in the workplace—if only to prevent the dissipation of the community ethos Dinta apprentices brought

---

Change, 152; Theo Wolsing, *Untersuchungen zur Berufsausbildung im Dritten Reich* (Kastellaun/Düsseldorf: Aloys Henn, 1977), 75.

[50] Franz Schürholz, *Grundlagen einer Wirtschaftspädagogik* (Erfurt: Kurt Stenger, 1928), 89–93.

[51] Schürholz, *Grundlagen einer Wirtschaftspädagogik*, 82–83. In any event, he was convinced that modern youth already possessed an industrial ethos that would enable it to adapt to the requirements of modern work. Ibid., 19.

[52] Schürholz, *Grundlagen einer Wirtschaftspädagogik*, 30–31.

[53] Franz Schürholz, "Industrie und Volkserziehung," *Sozialrechtliches Jahrbuch* (1930), 91–105. Schürholz defended industry's educational role, and called for non-ideological cooperation between employers and unions in the important task of preparing young Germans for modern work. For a purportedly "objective" comparison between DATSCH and Dinta, see Rennschmid, *Lehrling in der Industrie*, 68–85. Supervised by Adolf Weber of Munich, Rennschmid had full access to Dinta sources. Although sympathetic to the latter's aims, he cautioned that industry-based vocational training would lead to genuine *Betriebsgemeinschaft* only if the trade unions and the state were involved.

with them into the factory on completion of their program. The Dinta therefore encouraged employers to adopt advanced scientific management practices, including the use of the latest psychotechnical methods to place workers, and to offer opportunities for skills development. Furthermore, Arnhold advocated a comprehensive Werkspolitik, a modern, scientific version of the patriarchal company welfare program instituted in the past by firms like Krupp and currently propagated by Winschuh and others. To give their workers a sense of belonging, companies were urged to set up suggestion boxes, involve workers in accident prevention programs, and institute works evenings where the boss could speak directly to the workers. They were also encouraged to hire social workers to free individual employees from work- or family-related stress, and so liberate their energies for joyful labor.[54] Sport and leisure activities, courses for family members, and sheltered workshops for those whom age or injury had rendered incapable of doing their old jobs were other measures suggested for maintaining morale.

Finally, Arnhold proposed to enhance the spirit of Werksgemeinschaft through works newspapers. Drawing on his journalistic experience during the war, Arnhold had already established the *Hüttenzeitung* of the Schalker Verein in 1921 to counter revolutionary unrest in the mines. Eventually, the Dinta developed a network of similar *Werkzeitungen* as part of its effort to persuade the workers in all Dinta enterprises to identify with their plant and their company, thereby restoring joy in work. Although focused on the individual factory, these papers were expected to adhere closely to a prescribed model and were centrally edited and printed at Dinta headquarters. By 1930 there were already eighty-five such Dinta publications, with a weekly circulation of 500,000 copies, while a youth supplement, *Das Jugendland* ("The Land of Youth"), achieved an average weekly circulation of 100,000.[55]

Arnhold soon discovered that a further component to the Dinta's program was required, namely the training of managers, or, as he preferred to call them, *Führer*. There was a desperate shortage of teachers with the requisite skills and attitudes to staff his new industrial training establishments, and of individuals qualified to implement Werkspolitik in a properly scientific manner. Building on his war experience of good and bad leadership, Arnhold sought to make management training a major facet of Dinta work. However, the effectiveness of the short

[54] Arnhold, "Menschenführung," 121, 128–31.

[55] Bunk, *Erziehung und Industriearbeit*, 232–38. Heinz von Gruben, *Die Werkzeitschrift als Mittel der betrieblichen Sozialpolitik* (Munich, 1957), 122–25. See also the dissertation by Adelbert Klein, *Die Werkzeitschrift als Teil der betrieblichen Sozialpolitik* (Berlin/ Charlottenburg: Rudolf Lorentz, 1939).

courses instituted for foremen and supervisory personnel was unproven, and his efforts to involve the higher ranks of management in further education met with little response.[56]

His attempt to train a corps of Dinta engineers met with greater success. Dinta engineers were taught to be both technicians and educators and were expected to develop the leadership ability that would enable them to act as intermediaries between management and workers, as well as to set a good example to those beneath them in the works hierarchy. As bearers of the community ideal, they were to serve as role models by personally demonstrating the joy to be derived from dedication to work.[57]

Although Arnhold cooperated with the technical universities which educated the bulk of graduate engineers, he was determined to make his Dinta engineers a breed apart. Producing up to one hundred engineers a year, he sought to maintain and enhance the values inculcated during the initial training period by fostering an *esprit de corps* through continuing education programs. Moreover, each graduate was expected to wear an emblem symbolizing his membership in, and allegiance to, the Dinta, which had to be returned if he failed to work in the true Dinta spirit. Once a year, in conjunction with the annual meeting of the Society of the Friends of the Dinta, all came together for a week to exchange experiences and to learn from such notables as Atzler, Dessauer, Giese, and Riedel.[58] In these, and other ways, it was made clear that they had a dual loyalty: to the firm that employed them and to the Dinta itself. For although formally dedicated to the cause of Werksgemeinschaft, the Dinta engineers, like the Dinta company papers, were expected to look beyond the bounds of their particular works community and think of themselves as agents of national renewal, along the lines sketched out by ideologues like Spengler and Horneffer.

Arnhold attempted to harness the irrational in human beings in order to restore joy in work and the spirit of community, but he insisted that the Dinta approach the problem of work in an essentially scientific and rational (*sachlich*) spirit.[59] In addition to remolding the German

[56] Bunk, *Erziehung und Industriearbeit*, 226–28.

[57] Peter C. Bäumer, *Das Deutsche Institute fur Technische Arbeitsschulung (Dinta)*. Probleme der sozialen Werkspolitik, I. ed. Goetz Briefs. Schriften des Vereins fur Sozialpolitik, vol. 181 (Munich: Duncker & Humblot, 1930), 125–27; Carl Arnhold, "Industrielle Führerschaft im Sinne des Deutschen Instituts für Technische Arbeitsschulung (Dinta)," in *Probleme der sozialen Betriebspolitik*, ed. Goetz Briefs (Berlin: Julius Springer, 1930), 11–17.

[58] This society, according to Bunk, *Erziehung und Industriearbeit*, 229–32, was established in 1928. "Gesellschaft der Freunde des Dinta," in RKW, *Der Mensch und die Rationalisierung* 1, 155, gives fall 1929 as the founding date.

[59] E.g., Arnhold, "Menschenführung," 118–20.

worker,[60] the Dinta therefore expected its engineers to accommodate the "human factor" in the production process by reforming management practices wherever this could be done at reasonable cost. Arnhold also drew a number of Germany's leading experts on the psychology and physiology of work into the Dinta's orbit. Member firms were encouraged to establish their own psychotechnical testing divisions, and the Dinta itself established a psychotechnical research laboratory.[61] In addition, a Dinta-affiliated research institute in Gelsenkirchen studied the problems of heavy labor and of personnel selection.[62] It was Arnhold's hope that further research would turn up practical and cost-effective ways to apply the science of work to all the technical and human problems associated with industrial labor.

By 1930 the Dinta had expanded from its original base in the Ruhr mining district to involve around three hundred large and small firms in a number of industries and in most regions of the country.[63] Furthermore, Arnhold was extending its influence into the agricultural sector where he believed the "human factor" to be particularly important.[64] Programs for the semi-skilled and unskilled also began to loom larger in the Dinta's overall endeavor of turning Germany's young people into highly qualified, cooperative, and diligent members of the labor force. While an extensive network of Dinta Werkzeitungen spearheaded industry's campaign to conquer the soul of the nation's adult workers, the rapidly growing corps of enthusiastic and dedicated Dinta engineers upheld the organization's ideals in a manner that appealed to a troubled nation in search of strong leadership. Although insistent that the Dinta was a patriotic organization addressing the problems of rationalized industry in a uniquely German way, Arnhold could proudly report that foreigners were starting to take the Dinta seriously and that the Russians, in particular, had begun to copy some of its innovations.[65]

---

[60] Paul Osthold, "Das Problem der technischen Arbeitsschulung," *Das Werk* 5 (1926): 489–91.

[61] "Dinta und industrielle Psychotechnik," RKW, *Der Mensch und die Rationalisierung* 1, 154.

[62] Founded in 1925 by Arnhold, Professor Wallichs of the Aachen TH and Professor Poppelreuter of the University of Bonn, this institute was administratively linked with the Dinta from 1929. See "Forschungsstelle für industrielle Schwerarbeit, Vereinigte Stahlwerke A.G., Schalker-Verein, Gelsenkirchen," in ibid., 184–85; Bäumer, *Dinta*, 73–74; Bunk, *Erziehung und Industriearbeit*, 204–210.

[63] Bunk, *Erziehung und Industriearbeit*, 239; "Verbreitung des Dinta-Gedankens in Theorie und Praxis," RKW, *Der Mensch und die Rationalisierung* 1, 155. The latter referred to Dinta activity in the coal, potash, steel, machine-building, textile, rubber, cement, and building industries, and in the following regions: Rhineland-Westphalia, central and south Germany, Silesia, German Austria. See also Arnhold, "Industrielle Führerschaft," 11.

[64] Arnhold, "Menschenführung," 120.   [65] Arnhold, "Menschenführung," 131–32.

When one seeks to account for the Dinta's rapid spread and the attention given it by contemporaries, one is struck first of all by the lack of originality of its program. Although the war and its aftermath undoubtedly made efforts along these lines more important and potentially rewarding, the idea that industry must engage in a battle for the soul of its workers had before 1914 already given rise to many of the initiatives subsequently developed by the Dinta.[66] Works-based industrial training schools already existed before the Weimar period, and many of the social welfare schemes proposed by Arnhold echoed ideas that had been implemented by progressive firms inside and outside Germany for decades. Thus, social workers had frequently been employed in U.S. factories and offices before 1914, leading Weimar bourgeois and socialist reformers alike to urge that this practice be stripped of its patriarchal characteristics and adopted in Germany as a way to humanize the workplace.[67] Similarly, company newspapers antedated the Dinta, as did the management ideology that sought to base the reconciliation between capital and labor on the works community, and the belief that the nation's engineers were best equipped to serve as agents of this rapprochement. Finally, with respect to the application of science to the problems of industrial labor, the Dinta was but a small part of a broad movement that had been well under way before the war.

What, then, set the Dinta apart from its rivals and enabled it to capture public attention to an extent not granted to them? Along with the missionary fervor and skill with which the indefatigable Arnhold promoted its objectives, I would argue that the Dinta's success, like that of the NSDAP, was due precisely to its ability to blend into a unique amalgam ideas that were already in the air. By claiming that it had found a way to reconcile ideological opposites such as Sachlichkeit and irrationalism, that it knew how to diminish conflict between management and labor, and that through proper training and example it could help people to come to terms emotionally with the sometimes harsh realities of modern life and work, the Dinta gave contemporaries the impression that it offered a total solution to the problem of work. At the same time, the very fact that the Dinta tackled the problem from several directions at once enabled it to attract support from a variety of groups and individuals who saw merit in one or another aspect

[66] See the introduction to Peter Dehen, *Die deutschen Industrie-Werkschulen in wohlfahrts-, wirtschafts- und bildungsgeschichtlicher Beleuchtung* (Munich: A. Hüber, 1928).

[67] Frieda Wunderlich, *Fabrikpflege. Ein Beitrag zur Betriebspolitik* (Berlin: Julius Springer, 1926); Ludwig Preller, "Fabrikpflege und Wohlfahrtspflege," *Arbeiterwohlfahrt* 2 (April 1927): 193–98.

of its program without necessarily condoning all its activities or sharing its pro-business outlook and totalitarian aspirations.

As far as the ideology of work is concerned, Arnhold, who prided himself on being a practical man rather than an intellectual, made no attempt to work out a genuine synthesis between the Arbeitsfreude ethic of Horneffer and Spengler's duty version. Thus, in an article on industrial training in the GSR's *Soziale Praxis*, he argued that skilled workers might be expected to develop an occupational ethic, come to understand the social value and meaning of their work, and thereby achieve a positive attitude toward their jobs, but he reserved judgment on whether this work ethic should be rationally founded in a sense of duty or emotionally based on joy in work.[68] Instead of entering into the debate about the possibility of joy in work in industrial society, he concentrated on the main point of his message, namely the importance of propagating a modern ethic of work that would turn every German into a "high quality wheel in the great machine that is the economy."[69] By skirting the issue in this fashion, Arnhold managed to get support both from Arbeitsfreude enthusiasts and from those who believed it essential to imbue the younger generation with a sense of duty in order to compensate for the loss of joy in work.[70] Similarly, by purporting to offer an objective and scientific solution to the problem of work created by the presence of the irrational in human beings, he enabled the Dinta to win adherents among both the advocates and the opponents of the Neue Sachlichkeit.

Arnhold also managed to persuade various reform groups that the Dinta's program overlapped with their own. In the key area of industrial training he won support not only from the DATSCH but from the more progressive vocational school teachers who realized that old-style handicraft methods were no longer sufficient for the needs of industry, that people were best educated for work through work, that practical experience in the factory could be an invaluable adjunct to theoretical schooling, and that systematic social and ethical education was desirable. Agreement on such points made it possible for the Dinta and the vocational schools to cooperate on a practical level, despite the potential for friction arising from the disparity of interests.[71]

[68] Karl Arnhold, "Technische Arbeitsschulung," SP 38 (1929): 488–89.

[69] Arnhold, "Technische Arbeitsschulung," 489.

[70] See e.g., Günther Krenzler, *Arbeit und Arbeitsfreude* (Freiburg i. B.: Gutenberg, 1927), 114–15, where the Dinta is firmly identified with the *Pflichtmoral der Arbeit* ("the duty ethic of work").

[71] Carl Arnhold, "Arbeitsschulung im Rahmen des Betriebs gemäss den Grundsätzen des Dinta" in Frankfurt a. M., Soziales Museum, *Industrielle Arbeitsschulung als Problem. Fünf Beiträge über ihre Aufgaben und Grenzen* (Berlin: Industrieverlag Spaeth & Linde, 1931), 42.

Dinta support for an enlightened Werkspolitik assured Arnhold a sympathetic hearing from all who were endeavoring to solve the problem of alienation by humanizing the workplace or reforming the conduct of industrial relations. Thus Briefs of the Berlin TH endorsed the Dinta as a serious attempt to cope with the conflicts that made the industrial enterprise the social storm center of the current epoch[72] and helped train Dinta engineers. Another convert, Karl Thalheim of the Commercial College in Leipzig, praised the Dinta for utilizing the latest findings of applied psychology and sociology as part of an industry-based social policy that made practical sense from the social as well as the economic point of view.[73]

The Dinta also gained friends among proponents of Werksgemeinschaft, including Dunkmann who believed that the Dinta's approach could help to minimize if not entirely remove conflicts of interest within the firm.[74] His associate Vorwerck regarded the Dinta as part of the *völkisch* movement that considered reform of industrial relations a means to the greater end of national greatness.[75] Both the GWS, with which both Vorwerck and Dunkmann were closely connected,[76] and the industry-sponsored BNW headed by Paul Bang (1879–?) of the Pan-German League had high hopes for the Dinta. Bang, a prominent antisemite and close colleague of Hugenberg, favored the idea of Werksgemeinschaft as a way of shoring up the authority of management threatened by the forces of democracy and socialism. Contributing to a pamphlet series put out by the Gesellschaft 'Deutscher Staat' (GDS), a BNW affiliate, he praised the Dinta as a major attempt to reconcile German workers with their companies and employers through occupational training.[77] Like the GWS and other anti-Marxist organizations

---

Arnhold, drawing on the experience he had gained with such an arrangement before the war, frequently instituted special classes in the local Berufsschule to supplement the instruction his Dinta pupils received in their employers' training workshops.

[72] Goetz Briefs, "Betriebssoziologie," in *Handwörterbuch der Soziologie* (1931), 47–48.

[73] Karl C. Thalheim, "Das Deutsche Institut für Technische Arbeitsschulung (DINTA) in Düsseldorf," *Minerva-Zeitschrift* 7 (1931): 19–21.

[74] Karl Dunkmann, "Werksgemeinschaft als Organisationsproblem. Eine soziologische Untersuchung," in Vorwerck and Dunkmann, *Werksgemeinschaft*, 121–23. Dunkmann's association with the Dinta dated back to 1925 when he appeared on the same platform as Arnhold and Poppelreuter at a symposium on human beings in the production process. Karl Dunkmann, "Massenpsychologie und Arbeitserfolg," in Verein deutscher Eisenhüttenleute, *Die Menschliche Arbeitskraft im Produktionsvorgang*, 3–9.

[75] Karl Vorwerck, "Die Werksgemeinschaft in historischer und wirtschaftswissenschaftlicher Beleuchtung," in Vorwerck and Dunkmann, *Werksgemeinschaft*, 25–26.

[76] Although Dunkmann denied any direct collaboration between the two organizations, the GWS reported regularly on Dinta activities in its newsletter. GWS, *Mitteilungen* 1, no. 5 (March 1927).

[77] Wilhelm Longert and Paul Bang, *Die Grundgedanken der Werksgemeinschaft* (Langen-

that took up the works community idea, the BNW evidently hoped to benefit from identifying with the much more successful Dinta and to use the Dinta for its own purposes.[78]

Perhaps more surprising is the degree of overlap between the objectives of the Dinta and those of the Werkbund. The Dinta identified itself with one of the Werkbund's primary goals when it stressed the importance of quality work as a way of both solving the nation's economic problems and restoring joy and pride in work. A second source of congruence derived from the fact that the Werkbund, in the mid-1920s, preached a functionalist aesthetic that translated into support for experimentalism in architecture and design. According to Arnhold, modern functionalism and the Dinta's approach were closely allied: just as the functionalism of engineering design produced beauty by ensuring conformity with natural law, so the Dinta, by stressing utility and economic rationality rather than arbitrary emotionalism, would foster individual and social harmony.[79] Arnhold's point was one ideally designed to appeal to progressives within the Werkbund orbit, people like Dessauer for whom both Dinta and Werkbund represented the blend of technology and art characteristic of modern culture.[80]

Although the Dinta made considerable efforts to attract support from people outside the realm of industry, extending its circle of friends in this way also created problems. Most of the outsiders who cooperated with the Dinta did so because they hoped thereby to bring its ideology and practice into accord with their particular interests. In order to pre-

---

salza: Hermann Beyer & Söhne, 1927), 21. According to Bang's foreword, the GDS had a research division that dealt with the "scientific" aspects of the works community issue. Subsequent pamphlets gave instructions on how to start a Werksgemeinschaft and reproduced letters and speeches by various individuals who had attempted to apply the concept. However, Bang noted that the Dinta offered only a partial solution because it confined its efforts to counter "Marxist spiritual contagion" to the economic realm, neglecting the broader political dimensions of organic community. Ibid., 6–8.

[78] In similar fashion, Bang tried to use the VVVD, on whose executive committee he sat from 1924, to strengthen the conservative nationalist cause. See Diehl, "Von der Vaterlands-partei," 631; Arend Moje, Die Werksgemeinschaft in Deutschland (Diss., Göttingen, 1928; Quakenbrück: Handelsdruckerei C. Trute, 1929), 83–86. Moje noted that the works community movement as such was in danger of failing and was concerned lest it drag the Dinta down with it! There is evidence that some industrialists and social reformers who supported the Dinta believed that Arnhold might be persuaded to cooperate with the trade unions. See, e.g., Dr. Ernst Kretschmer, "Sozialreformatorische Ideen und ihre Verwirklichung," Ruhr und Rhein 9 (1928) 2: 1510–13.

[79] Carl Arnhold, "Industrielle Berufserziehung," Soziale Zukunft (1930): 38.

[80] Campbell, German Werkbund, 201–202. The text of Dessauer's address on "Technik-Kultur-Kunst," to the Werkbund's 1929 convention in Breslau is reproduced in Die Form 4 (1929): 479–86. On Dessauer's connection with the Dinta, see Bunk, Erziehung und Industriearbeit, 230.

vent others from setting the Dinta's agenda, Arnhold had to spend almost as much time fending off well-meant criticism by and interference from Dinta supporters as in defending his institute against its declared enemies. Indeed, when it came to the central fight for the soul of the German worker, the Dinta at times found it hard to distinguish friend from foe.

In particular, many who shared Arnhold's anti-Marxist stance nevertheless refused to take his side against his most consistent opponents, the free trade unions. Whether this was because, like Atzler, they wished to maintain the neutrality of science,[81] or because, like Rauecker, they believed that unions were needed to prevent the worker from falling under the total domination of management,[82] the net effect was to hamper the creation of a Dinta-led crusade against the Marxist threat. At the same time, the Dinta's right-wing sympathizers accused Arnhold of failing to use all means to pursue the institute's objectives, for example by openly subscribing to the company union ideal or by joining a political anti-Marxist coalition.

Arnhold could not realistically have expected to persuade the socialist free trade unions that they had nothing to fear from the Dinta. However, he did have some grounds for hoping that the Christian trade unions might support the Dinta's efforts to engineer industrial peace. But despite the fact that the Dinta propagated an unexceptional community social ethic that paralleled what reform-minded Catholics were saying and a vocational work ethic barely distinguishable from that to which the Christian unions subscribed, the Christian unions continued to suspect that the Dinta had merely found a new way to help the industrialists weaken the labor movement. Thus Johannes Giesberts (1865–1938), a leader of the Christian miners and Centre party deputy in the Reichstag from 1905 to 1933, favored improved industrial training and recognized the need for "love, diligence, and attentiveness" in rationalized industry, but noted the role of Spengler and Horneffer in shaping the Dinta ideology, cited Dunkmann, Arnhold, and Osthold to prove that the Dinta had no intention of cooperating with the unions, and warned that Dinta management training was perpetuating reactionary attitudes.[83]

[81] Although Arnhold was greatly influenced by Atzler, and Vögler was a director of Atzler's Dortmund institute, the Dinta thought him too pro-union. See Bunk, *Erziehung und Industriearbeit*, 201, and Brady, *Rationalization*, 332 n.24.

[82] Rauecker, *Rationalisierung als Kulturfaktor*, 31–40.

[83] Johannes Giesberts, *'Dinta' und Lehrwerkstätten der Unternehmer. Die Gefährdung der Gewerkschaftsbewegung und Gewerkschaftsjugend durch Bildungseinrichtungen der Unternehmer* (Essen: Verlag des Gewerkvereins Christlicher Bergarbeiter Deutschlands, 1927); and Carl Sonnenschein, *Der sittliche Wert der gewerkschaftlichen Arbeit* (3d ed.; Duisburg: Verlag Christ-

Apart from the threat it posed to organized labor, there were other grounds on which good Christians might object to the Dinta. For one thing, the industrial work schools sought to absorb virtually all the free time of their pupils. Realizing that this could be interpreted as a threat to the family, Arnhold went to considerable pains to involve the parents of his young recruits in their schooling. But given the Dinta's quest for total control over the hearts and minds of the young, it was impossible to allay fears among the religiously minded that the Dinta might severely circumscribe the church's own opportunities to inculcate Christian values and to mold the coming generation for a life of service to the larger community.

There was also concern about the Dinta's efforts to inculcate loyalty to the company as a supreme virtue. Although both Protestants and Catholics were searching anxiously for ways to restore a sense of community, not everyone shared the Dinta's belief that the factory or enterprise constituted the natural base of a hierarchy of communities that culminated in the Volksgemeinschaft. Thus, although Dunkmann, Longert, Osthold and others spoke up in defense of the works community idea at the ESK congress of 1927 devoted to Werksgemeinschaft, the concept was sharply attacked by the two main speakers and the majority of discussants. Ludwig Heyde, editor of Soziale Praxis, took this occasion not only to deny that Werksgemeinschaft and Volksgemeinschaft constituted parts of a single continuum, but also to insist that industry was incapable of producing true community and that adoption of the Werksgemeinschaft principle would undermine any chance for recreating the much more desirable postwar Arbeitsgemeinschaft based on free cooperation between employer and worker organizations. As for Volksgemeinschaft, this rested on an inborn ethical sense that could not be forced, but only liberated.[84] For his part, Menn, a socially involved minister from Düsseldorf, maintained that the modern human being was unwilling to give up freedom of movement and contract as demanded by the Werksgemeinschaft movement. Efforts to tie a portion of the workforce to the firm were more likely to divide than to unite; community, in the first instance, required a community of the "workers" in the narrower sense, that is, trade union solidarity. For Menn as for many within the organized labor movement the only rational basis for a democratic and modern work ethic leading to genuine

---

licher Metallarbeiter-Verband, n.d.), 11–13. According to Sonnenschein (1876–1929), the unions encouraged joyful collaboration in a spirit of Christian patriotism, but believed that the qualities best suited to buttress the latter were freedom and independence.

[84] Ludwig Heyde, "Werksgemeinschaft, Arbeitsgemeinschaft, Volksgemeinschaft," ESK, Verhandlungen (1927), 95–106.

community was not the Werk or Betrieb, both temporary by nature, but the Beruf or trade.[85]

The anticapitalist and anti-technological attitudes prevalent among active Christians also worked against the Dinta, for a successful fight by industry for the soul of its workers seemed ominously to presage a victory of material over spiritual values. Thoughts of this kind seem to have influenced the Christian unions in their opposition to the Dinta.[86] They also contributed to the preference of Dunkmann and his friends in the GWS for Adolf Friedrich's more metaphysical and spiritual approach to industrial management reform and training. Friedrich based his efforts to restore an ethic of work and community on religious principles, tried to help individuals recover Arbeitsfreude by removing the inner inhibitions that prevented them from giving their all to their work; he was prepared to work with the unions rather than to strive for total control over the workers' lives and loyalties. As a result, his AfA was deemed to offer a "Christian" answer to the problem of labor alienation that avoided the narrowly psychotechnical and unnecessarily confrontational features of the Dinta's program.[87]

If the Christian unions and many bourgeois social reformers had grave reservations about the Dinta's motives and the long term implications of its program, the most consistent opposition to it came from the socialist-affiliated free trade unions. Nothing that Arnhold could say or do to dissociate himself from the more extreme advocates of Werksgemeinschaft or to demonstrate his disdain for the old-style patriarchal model of industrial management succeeded in moderating the antagonism of the workers' leaders who interpreted his fight for the soul of the German worker as a direct attack on themselves. Should the Dinta emerge victorious, they were convinced that the workers would find themselves defenseless in the face of their class enemies, who

[85] Menn, in ESK, Verhandlungen, 106–119. Representatives of the local white and blue collar (pages 124–26 and 141–143, respectively) unions backed up Menn's position in the ensuing discussion.

[86] Rauecker, Rationalisierung als Kulturfaktor, 33–34. Making an economic unit the focus of loyalties also tended to distract people from their obligations to family, local community, fatherland, and occupation. Cf. "Der Kampf um das Deutsche Institut für Technische Arbeitsschulung ('Dinta') in Düsseldorf," SP 36 (1927): 1133–34, reprinting an attack on Werksgemeinschaft from the Christian trade union press.

[87] See especially "Werksgemeinschaft-Tatgemeinschaft," in GWS, Mitteilungen (1929, no. 1): 8–9. Also attracted by the AfA's anti-materialism and insistence on the individual's joy in work was Guido Fischer, an industrial relations specialist and lecturer at the University of Munich, who began the last of ten popular lectures in 1928/29 with a quotation from Friedrich to the effect that human work must be rooted in other-worldly values. Guido Fischer, "Die Ethik der neuen Menschenarbeit," in Mensch und Arbeit. Ihre Bedeutung im modernen Betrieb (Zurich: Verlag Organisator, 1929), 95.

would exploit their labor through uncontrolled rationalization, deprive them of its just rewards, and infringe on their newly won rights as free citizens of a democracy. The more doctrinaire among them were also concerned lest Dinta-type efforts render the workers content within the "system" and thus diminish their support for parties dedicated to its destruction.

In the public confrontation between the Dinta and the unions neither side was able to deal the other a fatal blow.[88] Apart from partisan supporters who cheered on their respective spokesmen, those who witnessed the battle of words tended to get increasingly impatient with both parties, and not a few tried to effect a reconciliation by stressing common interests and appealing to the patriotic good sense of those involved. This was the approach taken by Schürholz of the DATSCH, and by Professor Max Muss (1885–?), an economist at the Darmstadt TH. Muss, who had studied with Bücher at Leipzig, insisted that no one could hope to "win" the accelerating struggle for the soul of the worker in which the parties, unions, industry, churches, and public vocational and adult education establishments were all engaged. It was his hope that in the long run individualism and its ally rationalism would produce a common Weltanschauung based on the recognition that it was reasonable and necessary to accommodate the irrational "human" factor in industry. Meanwhile, he called for continued experiments designed to diminish destructive conflicts in the workplace.[89]

Another argument was used by the economist Emil Wehrle (1891–?), on the occasion of his promotion to the rectorship of the Nuremberg Commercial College in 1926. According to Wehrle, both management and labor stood to benefit from improvements in industrial relations, but nothing was to be gained by resorting to ideological manoeuvres. Instead of seeking to win over workers' souls, Wehrle urged business to recognize that enterprises were subject to economic laws and that strictly economic criteria should therefore be applied when considering reforms. In particular he opposed the Werksgemeinschaft: as the modern industrial concern was unable to guarantee security of employment, the workers were justified in holding onto the unions, which had been created to protect their legitimate interests.[90]

[88] The acrimonious debate lasted into the postwar period! See Fritz Fricke, *Dintageist-Wirtschaftsbürger. Eine Streitschrift* (Cologne: Bund-Verlag, 1950).

[89] Max Muss, "Arbeiterseele und Wirtschaftsgesetzlichkeit. Betrachtungen zur industriellen Arbeiterkrisis," in a special issue, *Festausgabe für Karl Bücher*, of the *Zeitschrift für die gesamte Staatswissenschaft* 82 (1927): 335–36.

[90] Emil Wehrle, *Betriebsreform, ein Weg zur Reform des Arbeitsverhältnisses?* (Nuremberg: Krische, 1927), 23–38.

A number of businessmen also opposed the idea of trying to break the unions by conquering the minds of the young. All found the notion of a community of work attractive, but some also believed that trade unionism was compatible with their interests. Thus Edmund Klein-schmidt, drawing on American experience, wrote an essay for a leading Hamburg business publication in which he argued that large firms needed the unions to help sort out conflicts between supervisors and middle managers on the one hand and workers on the other, and that industry-wide wages rates determined on the basis of collective bargaining were useful in countering charges of exploitation and preventing unfair competition.[91]

Trade-union and socialist polemics directed against the Dinta undoubtedly helped organized labor to maintain its hold on the faithful and to mobilize moderates in the university and business communities. Nevertheless, some labor leaders regarded the threat posed by the Dinta and the Werksgemeinschaft movement generally as sufficiently great to justify more concrete countermeasures. The result was a two-pronged campaign to strengthen the position of organized labor. This involved, on the one hand, propagation of Wirtschaftsdemokratie, economic democracy, as an alternative to Werksgemeinschaft, and, on the other, the inauguration of a comprehensive educational and organizational effort to "immunize" the workers against the Dinta, with special emphasis on the nation's youth.

Although the two are often confused, "economic democracy" must be distinguished from "industrial democracy," towards which the works council movement of the early postwar years had taken a significant step. The works councils were meant to encourage worker participation at the level of the shop or firm; enthusiasm for this concept began to wane, however, when it became evident that the works councils were incapable of serving as effective agents of co-management and could be

---

[91] Edmund Kleinschmidt, "Der Geist der amerikanischen Gewerkschaftsbewegung. Sind die Werksgemeinschaften der neuen Welt ein Vorbild für Deutschland?" in *Der Kaufmann in Wirtschaft und Recht* 6 (1927): 8–15. The idea that chaos would result if each Werk set its own wage scale was also part of Ludwig Heyde's case against Werksgemeinschaft. See his "Werksgemeinschaft, Arbeitsgemeinschaft, Volksgemeinschaft," 103–104. Similar arguments were advanced in the ESK debate of 1927 by Hans Menck, an Altona factory owner and head of the local chamber of commerce. Just back from a visit to the Ford plants in the United States, Menck maintained that Werksgemeinschaft could only be expected to flourish in smaller firms and in a static economy, and that it was irrational to expect the mass of workers to develop occupational pride, much less a permanent attachment to their factory sufficient to weaken their loyalty to the labor movement, in a time of rapid technological change and unemployment. For his part, Menck declared himself happy to work with the trade unions and the works councils as presently constituted. ESK, *Verhandlungen* (1927): 120–21.

used by employers to manipulate "their" workers in such a way as to weaken the central unions. Soon the unions ceased to emphasize organizational efforts at the shop level and treated such works councils as managed to maintain themselves as trade union outposts, useful for transmitting directives from union headquarters, rather than as independent agents of worker power.[92]

By the mid-1920s, what remained of the idea of worker participation or co-determination had attached itself to the concept of economic democracy, which can therefore be viewed as the beneficiary of the council movement's eclipse. As developed formally by Fritz Naphtali in 1928, economic democracy effectively confined the works councils to the "social" sphere, while reserving the economic realm for the centrally organized trade unions.[93] The idea was to revive the postwar ZAG between organized business and labor as the chief means of resolving conflict, with the state acting as arbitrator where necessary. In addition, it was hoped to expand the powers of the RWR and use it as an instrument of central economic planning. At the very time when economic liberals, Werksgemeinschaft ideologists, and advocates of industry-based social policy were attempting to decentralize and at least ostensibly to depoliticize industrial relations, the trade unions proposed to use their organizational strength at the national level and their links with the SPD and Centre parties to compensate for weaknesses at the periphery.[94]

Wirtschaftsdemokratie promised to increase the ability of organized labor to set industry-wide wage schedules and to press for legislative reforms in the interests of the working class, including the enhancement of state social welfare. It thus seemed well-designed to meet the needs of the working masses in a democratic republic. Yet it never won the unreserved support of organized labor or of the parties which claimed to represent the working class. This was partly because of the

[92] Hans Mommsen, *Klassenkampf oder Mitbestimmung. Problem der kontrolle wirtschaftlicher Macht in der Weimarer Republik* (Cologne: Eurpäische Verlagsanstalt, 1978), 24; Michael Pool, *Workers' Participation in Industry* (rev. ed.; London: Routledge & Kegan Paul, 1978), 136–41.

[93] See Fritz Naphtali, *Wirtschaftsdemokratie, ihr Wesen, Weg und Ziel* (Frankfurt: Europäische Verlagsanstalt, 1966; reprint of 1928 original commissioned by the ADGB).

[94] For a brief account of the situation in the Ruhr at the time of the major industrial conflict of 1928, see Larry Peterson, "Labor and the End of Weimar: the Case of the KPD in the November 1928 Lockout in the Rhenisch-Westphalian Iron and Steel Industry," *Central European History* 15 (March 1982): 62–63. Peterson documents the weakness of the trade unions at the local level for this important region. It is no coincidence that Wirtschaftsdemokratie became official SPD policy after the 1928 elections which brought socialists into the cabinet for the first time in years. Advances at the polls, coinciding with a renewal of industrial strife, raised hopes that the state might be used to shift the balance of power between capital and labor in the latter's favor.

fear that the new policy, by encouraging the unions further to neglect their role as defenders of the workers at plant level, would accelerate the erosion of their membership base.[95] In addition, some suspected that the framers of the new program were less interested in improving conditions for the workers than they were in using "economic democracy" as a step on the road to a new socialist order.[96] No wonder, then, that even those employers willing to deal with the unions condemned Wirtschaftsdemokratie as a propagandistic device to further the socialist cause rather than as a genuine attempt solve the problems of modern industry.[97] In any event, economic democracy failed to become an effective weapon with which to combat the Dinta.

Although at first sight more promising, the attempt by the socialists and trade unions to fight the Dinta on its own ground by expanding their educational programs also proved disappointing. For one thing, the impressive hierarchy of educational institutions that culminated in the Frankfurt Academy of Labor served an elite composed of men and women already committed to the labor movement; it could hope to influence only that portion of the working class destined for leadership roles. With respect to mass education, spokesmen for labor failed to achieve a consensus about either means or ends. Most agreed that at the primary level it was necessary to encourage the creation of comprehensive schools that would provide a common education to members of all classes. In the sphere of adult education, however, some actively supported the Volkshochschulen and similar bourgeois initiatives designed to educate the workers for citizenship and cultural participation, while others advocated a strictly "socialist" education to prepare them for a future post-capitalist society.

It was in the arena of vocational training that the main battle against

[95] Hans Mars, "Neue Gewerkschaftliche Aufgaben," *Die Arbeit* 7 (1930): 393–96, and "Von der negativen zur positiven Einstellung der freien Gewerkschaften gegenüber der sozialen Betriebspolitik," in Briefs, *Probleme der sozialen Betriebspolitik*, 90–132; Otto Suhr, "Betrieb und Unternehmen," *Gewerkschafts-Archiv* 2 (1925): 370–75. Suhr did not share Mars's hopes for the reawakening of Arbeitsfreude through humanization of the workplace, but he did regard Betriebsgemeinschaft as a reasonable objective, arguing that labor had an interest in raising the productivity of the Betrieb, though not in increasing the profits of the *Unternehmen*. He therefore advocated continuing efforts to achieve union co-determination at the works level.

[96] Naphtali himself acknowledged, under pressure from the left, that complete Wirtschaftsdemokratie was not possible under capitalism. Schneider, *Unternehmer und Demokratie*, 88; Mommsen, *Klassenkampf oder Mitbestimmung*, 24.

[97] This view prevailed when "economic democracy" was extensively debated at a meeting of the RDI at Düsseldorf in 1929. Discussants included industrialists, social policy experts, churchmen, and academics; the Dinta perspective was represented by Horneffer's talk on "Individualism or Collectivism as Weltanschauung" and Osthold's on "Socialism and Democracy." See *Das Problem der Wirtschaftsdemokratie* (Düsseldorf: Industrie-Verlag, 1929).

CHAPTER XI

the Dinta had to be fought; here, too, however, there were important differences of opinion. Supporters of the Arbeitsschule or Produktionsschule found it difficult to resist the appeal of the well-equipped industrial works schools which, unlike the majority of public vocational schools, offered training for actual jobs, on the latest machines, by instructors with experience in modern production. Only the claim of the industry-based training programs (particularly of those organized by the Dinta), to control the total life of their pupils in order to mold them into passive tools of capitalism made them objectionable. As a result, much of the left's campaign against the Dinta was devoted to alerting socialist, as well as non-socialist, educators to the evil political, economic, and human implications of the Dinta program.[98] Labor leaders, maintaining that the Dinta was, itself, a reaction to union advances on the educational front, including the labor movement's considerable leisure programs, urged the unions to redouble their efforts to reach the nation's youth in order to meet the Dinta challenge.[99]

Ideally, the labor movement would have preferred to organize its own industrial training programs. Thus Gertrud Hermes, arguing that "self help is the only answer for the working class," called for the establishment of special factories owned by public authorities or worker organizations, in which young people would benefit from production training without being subjected to capitalist contamination, and where they would develop a sense of socialist solidarity.[100] In practice, however, the shortage of independent financial and human resources forced those determined to provide an alternative to industry-based workshop training to operate within the framework of the public vocational schools.

Here the chief obstacle to successful reform—apart from a chronic shortage of funds—was the inertia of a system largely staffed by people whose political outlook reflected values derived from the Second Reich and whose occupational ethic had been shaped by the rapidly vanishing world of Handwerk. One such person was Kurt Kesseler, a non-socialist pedagogue deeply imbued with the Protestant vocational ethic who advocated a religiously based education for national unity, work, and culture. According to Kesseler, the specific task of the Arbeitsschule was

[98] E.g., Eduard Weitsch, "Das Dinta also gemeinsames Problem der Gewerkschaften und der freien Volksbildung," *Die Arbeit* 4 (1927): 685–89.

[99] Karl Zwing, "Um die Seele des Arbeiters," *Gewerkschafts-Archiv* 3 (1926/2): 295–302.

[100] Gertrud Hermes, "Eine Schule der Arbeit," *Gewerkschafts-Zeitung* 35 (1925): 512. Best known for her book on the mentality of the Marxist worker, *Die Gestalt des marxistischen Arbeiters* (Tübingen: J.C.B. Mohr, 1926), Hermes, like other confirmed Marxists, opposed the works community idea and denied the possibility of humanizing work, much less that of achieving the end of alienation, under capitalism.

to produce independent characters trained to do their work with care, diligence, and precision (*Sorgfalt, Fleiss, und Genauigkeit*), and to appreciate the true value of manual labor (*Handarbeit*).[101] Because many of the unions were still based on the crafts principle, they tended to share Kesseler's attitudes toward work, and this made cooperation between them and the vocational schools relatively unproblematic. However, rapid changes in the composition of the industrial labor force during the 1920s and the associated advance of industrial unionism led an ever greater number of educators to realize that something had to be done to provide a different kind of schooling for those destined to become ordinary semi-skilled or unskilled workers.[102]

One result was a debate about whether one could realistically expect the latter to acquire a sense of vocation and to experience joy in work. Could there be such a thing as a generalized "worker vocation" (*Arbeitsberuf*), with its attendant ethos? Professor von der Aa of Leipzig was one of those who maintained that even the unskilled could benefit from a schooling that improved their attitudes to work, taught them to make the fullest possible use of their abilities whatever the limitations of their jobs, and went beyond vocational training to general, cultural, and political education.[103] Similarly, Johannes Welzel of Berlin maintained that even the unskilled could be taught to understand that their jobs were important in the larger economic context and that they could be a source of joy, because every honest occupation constituted a potential means to ethical self-development.[104] On the other side of the debate were people like the senior inspector of schools in Hamburg, who doubted whether unskilled work could be seen as a vocation and who denied that the majority of young people could develop a profes-

[101] Kurt Kesseler, "Das Problem der Arbeitsdurchseelung und die Schule," *Pädagogisches Zentralblatt* 6 (1926): 83–92. On the conservatism of the Weimar vocational schools, see the introduction by Klaus Kümmel to *Quellen und Dokumente zur schulischen Berufsbildung 1918–1945* (Cologne: Böhlau, 1980), 16–18.

[102] See *Beschulung der Ungelernten* (Wittenberg/Halle: Zentralverlag für Berufs- und Fachschulen, 1928); Muth, *Berufsausbildung*, 576–80.

[103] Karl von der Aa, "Sinn und Gegenwartsaufgaben der beruflichen Schulen," *Beruf und Schule* 12 (1932): 133–37, the text of a lecture given to the Society of Vocational School Teachers in Leipzig, February 1932. Cf. Behler, "Die Ergänzung der Berufsschulerziehung an der Arbeitsstätte und durch freie Einrichtungen für die Jugend," *Die Deutsche Berufsschule* 38 (1929), 502–514. However Behler, addressing the eighteenth "Deutsche Berufsschultag" ("Vocational Schools Conference") in Halle, also stressed the continued importance of education for skilled work.

[104] Johannes Welzel, "Zum Problem der Arbeiterschule," *Die Deutsche Berufsschule* 36 (1927/28): 335–42. Unlike Werksgemeinschaft advocates, Welzel thought that workers had every right to look around for better jobs if they were dissatisfied with their current employers; he also emphasized the importance of teaching the unskilled the correct use of leisure, on the grounds that they were particularly liable to suffer periods of unemployment.

sional consciousness, no matter what efforts were made by the schools to cultivate a work ethic based on spiritual values.[105]

Socialists were less inclined than their bourgeois counterparts to believe that the unskilled could experience Arbeitsfreude and tended to insist that efforts to inculcate a traditional Berufsethos would do more harm than good.[106] One of the main differences between the free and the Christian trade unions was that the latter sought to preserve a professional consciousness among industrial workers which the former regarded as irrelevant to present-day issues.[107] On the other hand, even within the ADGB there were those who insisted that tending machines demanded skill and a lively mind as well as manual aptitude and so could produce a sense of pride, self-worth, and responsibility, and even a feeling of joy. If this was so, it made sense for educators to encourage their students to develop positive attitudes to the kinds of jobs they were likely to find, rather than fostering romantic nostalgia for an unrecoverable handicraft past.[108]

Whether they believed in the possibility of Arbeitsfreude or not, socialists were faced with a dilemma: how could one prepare young workers to earn their living under modern conditions, which meant turning them into cooperative, skillful, and adaptable cogs in the capitalist machine, while at the same time teaching them to fight for the rights of their class and participate in the organized struggle for socialism? To reconcile these essentially unreconcilable aims, they frequently called for better-trained vocational school teachers, improved classrooms, and a reformed curriculum that would allow more time for instruction in citizenship, trade-union history and organization, economics, and

[105] J. Schult, "Das Problem der Berufsschule für die männliche 'ungelernte' Jugend," *Die Deutsche Berufsschule* 36 (1927/28): 530–36.

[106] See, e.g., Lothar Erdmann, "Zum Problem der Arbeitsgemeinschaft," *Die Arbeit* 3 (1927): 315–20, 379–90, 641–52; and Direktor Alex Menne, Frankfurt, "Der ungelernte Jugendliche in Wirtschaft und Recht," *Beschulung der Ungelernten*: 42–54.

[107] Dr. Annemarie Hermberg, "Die Ideologie der christlichen Gewerkschaftsbewegung," *Gewerkschafts-Archiv* 1 (1924): 11. According to Hermberg, the Christian unions, when they referred to the *industrielle Beruf* of the worker, thought they were saving an idea, but actually were preserving only a word.

[108] Otto Hessler, *Gewerkschaften und Berufsschule. Material für die Jugendleiter der Gewerkschaften* (Berlin: ADGB, 1930), 17; Emil Dittmer, *Gewerkschaften, Industriemenschheit und Produktionsschule* (Berlin: Verband der Gemeinde- und Staatsarbeiter, 1925), 34–39; Stadtschulrat Winkel, "Die geistige und seelische Lage des ungelernten Jugendlichen," in *Beschulung der Ungelernten*, 59–73. Winkel, the non-socialist municipal inspector of schools in Gelsenkirchen, blamed bourgeois intellectuals and doctrinaire socialists alike for perpetuating an unjustified and outdated pessimism regarding the spiritual content of modern work, and noted with satisfaction that some socialists, having abandoned this position, were prepared to teach the worker a positive attitude to his machine.

labor law.[109] In other words, the public vocational schools were to be reshaped into institutions providing up-to-date skills training comparable to that offered in the best industrial works schools, while preparing their pupils for citizenship in the democratic society of today and the socialist society of the future.[110]

Only the last part of this program led to serious differences with the non-socialist majority of vocational school teachers. Distrust of Marxism frequently encouraged many vocational instructors to embark on a battle for the souls of their pupils that paralleled the efforts of the industrial work schools in both method and intent. Thus M. Krausse of Chemnitz, while agreeing that the unions were right to fight exploitation by pressing for better wages and hours and for stronger labor legislation, insisted as well on the importance of promoting joy in work. Echoing de Man, he argued that it was incumbent on the vocational schools to free the young from the feelings of inferiority that rendered them liable to proletarian mass psychosis. He also cited Nietzsche and Heinrich Kautz (who, it should be recalled, actively collaborated with the Dinta) to support his view that vocational teachers had a responsibility to inculcate "high German work ideals," including the desire to excel. The former objective was to be achieved by adopting psychoanalytic techniques, the latter by teaching the life stories of successful entrepreneurs.[111] Given attitudes such as these, one can understand why socialist educators were sometimes impatient with their bourgeois colleagues—and why many employers were happy to draw on the vo-

[109] Otto Hessler, "Konferenz zur Besprechung gewerkschaftlicher Jugendfragen: Bericht, Beobachtetes und Kritisches," *Gewerkschafts-Archiv* 2 (1925) 2: 130–37. See Hildegard Reisig, *Die Lehren vom politischen Sinn der Arbeiterbildung* (Langensalza: H. Beyer, 1933), for a critique of Social Democratic educational theory and practice emphasizing its inherent contradictions.

[110] Hilde Rosenberg, *Die Berufsvorbereitung des Industriearbeiters* (Cologne: M. DuMont-Schauberg, 1930), 57–70. Prepared under the direction of Heimann (University of Hamburg) and published by the Municipal Vocational Training Institute of Cologne, Rosenberg's study summarized trade union attitudes to the Dinta and to vocational training generally from the socialist perspective and noted that the free trade unions dominated the trade union committee (Gewerkschaftsausschuss für Berufsausbildung) set up in October 1926 to influence the draft vocational training legislation.

[111] M. Krausse, "Was kann die Berufsschule zur Hebung der Arbeitsfreude tun?" *Beruf und Schule* (Leipzig) 10 (1930): 126–28. See also Ludwig Schwenk, *Schaffensfreude und Lebenskunst* (2d rev. ed.; Stuttgart: Holland & Josenhaus, 1925). Recommended to schools as a prize book by the *Reichsarbeitsblatt* 7 (1927): 232, this manual for young men about to begin their vocational careers held up as examples to youth outstanding industrialists like Siemens and Krupp, cultural heroes like Hans Sachs, Goethe, and Kant, and political giants like Frederick the Great, Bismarck, and Hindenburg. Schwenk was the author of several successful textbooks used in the Württemberg trade schools.

cational schools for their manpower rather than embarking on possibly costly attempts to set up their own training establishments.

Whether the attitudes of German workers were actually altered by the Dinta-led campaign for the soul of the worker remains in doubt. The superior training available in Dinta schools and the relative job security offered to those who successfully completed Dinta courses clearly proved attractive to many young people: there was never any shortage of applicants for places in its programs.[112] In addition, the relative failure of the socialist movement to capture the imagination of the nation's youth left a void which the Dinta, with its demand for total commitment and promise of joyful work and fulfillment through membership in the works community, could hope to fill.[113] Many contemporary observers declared themselves impressed by the apparent enthusiasm of Dinta trainees, their uniform and neat appearance, and their joyful bearing.[114] In addition, the Dinta's emphasis on sport and the provision of special outings and vacation trips, some in the Dinta's own holiday ship, the *Glückauf*,[115] were so appealing that they produced demands for similar labor movement programs, and sometimes even calls for education for joy in work along Dinta lines.[116] By 1930, some socialist and trade union educators were sufficiently impressed by the Dinta to seek to collaborate with it.[117]

On the other hand, there is considerable doubt that Dinta schools actually produced workers who were more productive and more biddable than those trained elsewhere. Once they became part of the general

[112] According to Bäumer, *Dinta*, 146, oversubscription was the rule in the Ruhr, where workers, despite trade union opposition, took full advantage of all the Dinta had to offer.

[113] See Johannes Voigtländer, "Vom Sinn der Arbeit," *Betriebsräte Zeitschrift für die Funktionäre der Metallindustrie* 9 (1928): 776–79. Voigtländer warned that people like Horneffer who talked about Arbeitsfreude did so to exploit labor, but agreed with the latter that the workers could only benefit from understanding their jobs and appreciating their significance for the wellbeing of the works and the economy. Nor did he object to worker participation in Horneffer's works festivals, so long as the people took part with open eyes: "Warum sollen wir nicht auch einmal auf einem solchen Werksfest tanzen? Lasst doch die Trompeten ausspielen zum Tanz! Aber lasst sie blasen: Habt Acht!" ("Why shouldn't we dance for once at such a works festival? Let the trumpets accompany the dance; but let them sound: Take care!")

[114] E.g., David Gathen, "Das Dinta," *Westdeutsche Arbeiterzeitung*, 15 January 1927, 1–2; Helmuth Speyerer, "Deutsches Institut für Arbeitsschulung in Düsseldorf," *Technik und Kultur* 18 (1927): 77–78.

[115] Pictured in Arnhold, "Neuzeitliche Lehrlingsausbildung," 62.

[116] Walter Eschbach, "Jugendbewegung und Werksjugendpflege," *Jugend-Führer* 1 (1927) no. 9: 68–69; no. 10: 77–78; Günther Meier, *Berufsschulung und Berufserziehung der Jugendlichen durch die Arbeitergewerkschaften* (Rostock: Carl Hinstorff, 1930), 107–138.

[117] Meier, *Berufsschulung*, and Otto Neuloh, *Arbeiterbildung im neuen Deutschland. Arbeit und Sozialpolitik* (Leipzig: Quelle & Meyer, 1930), 76–78.

labor force, Dinta apprentices were just as prone as their fellow workers to join a union or vote SPD or Centre. Moreover, some of them went on strike in 1931,[118] leading to the conclusion that it was easier to teach German workers skills than to capture their souls. Unfortunately, the follow-up studies of Dinta trainees necessary to answer this question have simply not been done.[119]

In any event, the Dinta was still at the experimental stage when the depression hit Germany. The crisis of 1930–33, far from ending the fight for the soul of the German worker, led to its intensification, but changes in the economic and political environment forced the Dinta, like other participants in this struggle, to modify its approach to the problem of modern work.

[118] Bunk, *Erziehung und Industriearbeit*, 255.

[119] Eva Schöck, *Arbeitslosigkeit und Rationalisierung. Die Lage der Arbeiter und die kommunistische Gewerkschaftspolitik 1920–1928* (Frankfurt: Campus, 1977), 109–110.

XII

THE PROBLEM OF WORK IN THE
CRISIS OF CAPITALISM

THE DEPRESSION of the early 1930s, with its profound impact on all aspects of German life, led many to question the assumptions on which the short-lived prosperity of the 1920s had rested. The economic crisis reinforced doubts about the future of capitalism, undermined faith in the capacity of the parliamentary system to produce the leadership needed to head off catastrophe, and gave a great impetus to extreme nationalism. Along with capitalism, democracy, and internationalism, "modernity" itself fell into increasing disrepute. Because science and reason had clearly failed to bring about a better world, it was tempting to repudiate Neue Sachlichkeit and succumb to the appeal of a new irrationalism that valued the heart rather the mind and promoted an activist blend of sentiment and will. Overall, opinion became politicized, radicalized, and polarized, with rival groups finding new scapegoats to account for what no one could understand and proposing ever more extreme remedies for a situation perceived as out of control. In the end, the Weimar Republic, already on the defensive against a multitude of foes on right and left, was delivered into the hands of Adolf Hitler who posed as the nation's savior, the agent of a national revolution that would restore German unity, prosperity, and might.

It was only to be expected that these developments would change the way people perceived and sought to deal with the problem of work. Yet because neither the novelty of the situation nor the dimensions of the crisis were immediately apparent, ideas, attitudes, and policy prescriptions spawned by the preceding years of relative prosperity proved remarkably persistent. It was tempting to believe that things would shortly right themselves of their own accord, as they had after previous troughs in the business cycle.[1] Consequently, many saw no reason to

[1] Harold James, *The German Slump* (Oxford: Clarendon Press, 1986), 343. James demon-

276

reconsider their position with regard either to ends or means, much less to jettison projects in which they were currently engaged. On the other hand, those who had all along argued that rationalization and mechanization ruled out any reconciliation between human beings and their work in the modern world felt confirmed in their gloomy views as things went from bad to worse, while doctrinaire anti-capitalists did not need the depression crisis to convince them that the problem of work could never be solved within the existing social and political order.[2]

German businessmen, too, were reluctant to change course. Continuing to rationalize their enterprises, they strove to improve productivity and increase output despite shortages of capital and shrinking markets. They also proceeded with compensatory efforts to promote Arbeitsfreude and tried to win the allegiance of the German worker through education and improved labor-management relations. Indeed, their eagerness to minimize "outside" interference, whether from the unions or the state, led many actually to expand company social policy and give greater support to the works community movement during these years. In this, they were encouraged by advocates of Werkspolitik and Werksgemeinschaft whose efforts peaked during the depression.[3]

The tendency to persist in views developed during the preceding years of stability is well illustrated by Ernst Michel (1889–1964), a lecturer in industrial sociology and social policy at the University of Frankfurt and the director of the Frankfurt Academy of Labor. In a text on industrial organization published in 1932, one which expounded a version of Betriebsgemeinschaft that was strongly influenced by Catholic social doctrine, Michel insisted that modern work could still spiritually enrich individuals provided they were successfully integrated into a functioning productive unit. The depression did lead him to assert that companies which could not promise job security in hard times had no right to demand the workers' complete loyalty as the Werksgemein-

---

strates that the German economy was in trouble throughout the Weimar period, suffering from "a high degree of instability and low growth rates," and that the German slump was abnormal "in relation both to pre-war history and to the experience of other states." Ibid., 10–11.

[2] E.g., Günther Reimann, Das deutsche 'Wirtschaftswunder' (Berlin: Vereinigung Internationaler Verlagsanstalten, 1927), a Communist attack on Taylor and Ford in which the author predicted that German rationalization would culminate in economic disaster. For a recent discussion of the link between industrial rationalization and unemployment, which after 1927/28 never dipped below one million, see Uta Stolle, Arbeiterpolitik im Betrieb (Frankfurt: Campus, 1980), 247–61.

[3] E.g., Josef Junges, "Der Wirkungsgrad Arbeit," Neue Wirtschaft (1931): 10–12. Junges maintained that greater economic efficiency was more necessary than ever, and that the answer to industry's problems was to foster a greater spirit of enterprise and innovation coupled with improvements in industrial relations along Werksgemeinschaft lines.

schaft ideology proposed. He also insisted that firms had a responsibility to tackle the problem of unemployment through such devices as job-sharing and urged firms to develop programs that would teach people to make productive use of their increased leisure. But despite these concessions to the contemporary crisis, he continued to emphasize the primary responsibility of employers to humanize work by improving human relations in the workplace.[4] Similarly, Briefs's Institute continued actively to promote the cause of company social policy after 1930, although industrial enterprises could hardly be expected to take the lead in solving the problem of work at a time when their economic viability was threatened and the scope for independent action on the part of individual companies or plants was more restricted than ever before.

One would also have expected people to spend less time during the depression worrying about joy in work and instead to focus their efforts on job creation and the provision of meaningful leisure. It did occur to some that it was perhaps inappropriate to give top priority to restoring Arbeitsfreude in a period of mass unemployment. The socialist Fritz Fricke went so far as to maintain that the lack of joy in work complained of by employers was due precisely to the workers' fear of unemployment rather than to the nature of modern production methods or Marxist poisoning of the workers.[5] Yet the realization that job security was the workers' chief concern did not prevent most reformers from concentrating, as before, on humanizing work and restoring the sense of vocation, rather than on lessening labor alienation by enabling workers to make good use of their increased free time.[6] If anything, the depression increased their determination to promote joy in work. That the unemployed suffered not only economically but also psychologically from the loss of their jobs was taken as evidence that ordinary

[4] Ernst Michel, *Industrielle Arbeitsordnung* (Jena: Eugen Diederichs, 1932), 61–72.

[5] Fritz Fricke, "Aufgaben und Grenzen technischer Arbeitsschulung," in Frankfurt, Soziales Museum, *Industrielle Arbeitsschulung als Problem*, 98–99. See also Johannes Kunz, "Der wirtschaftliche Rationalismus (Intellektualisierung und Technisierung der Wirtschaftsprozesse) in seinen Auswirkungen auf den in der Wirtschaft tätigen Menschen und seine Erziehung," *Beruf und Schule* 11 (1931): 831–36. Kunz, a vocational-school teacher, observed that the workers opposed rationalization not because it entailed soulless work but because they identified it with unemployment.

[6] German reluctance to explore the leisure option is demonstrated by Hans Eyermann, "Das Problem der Arbeitsfreude," *Christentum und Wirklichkeit*. Evangelisches Monatsheft für Gegenwartsfragen, Verlag des Vereins für innere Mission Nürnberg (1931): 85–90, 105–110; Delius, Berlin, "Die Arbeitsfreude in der modernen Wirtschaft," *Ethik* (Halle) 7 (1931): 253–54; Georg Hirsch, *Die Faulheit. Charakterologische Studien* (Halle: Carl Marhold, 1931), especially 146–48; Friedrich Markus Huebner, *Schaffen und Ruhen. Adel der Arbeit, Sinn der Erholung* (Darmstadt: Gotthard Peschko, [1933]).

people felt the need for meaningful activity and therefore could be treated as potentially joyful workers.

Germans were slow to engage in any systematic exploration of the implications of the economic crisis and the attendant mass unemployment for the nature and future of modern work.[7] But despite this tendency towards inertia, as the seriousness of the economic crisis became apparent, most reformers accepted the practical necessity of reorienting existing programs and improvising new ones. Thus the Dinta increasingly shifted the emphasis of its educational programs from the skilled to the unskilled and addressed the problem of unemployment by urging the establishment of industry-based courses to provide general preparation for work for unemployed school-leavers unable to find regular apprenticeships.[8] It also became a forceful advocate of compulsory labor service.[9]

The mass unemployment of the early 1930s played into the hands of all who wished to institute Arbeitsdienstpflicht—labor service on a comprehensive and compulsory basis—because it seemed a way of alleviating the economic misery caused by jobless youth. But the primary reason that the Dinta favored the idea was because it appeared ideally suited to inculcate the work habits and the patriotic service ethic formerly supplied by military service in those not privileged to participate in its own industrial training programs. Common currency among nationalist groups and veterans organizations, Arbeitsdienstpflicht had also been propagated since the war as a practical way of dealing with the problem of work. Thus the engineering journal *Technik und Kultur* promoted compulsory labor service as a fair and economical way to promote the physical development of the young and teach them discipline, while creating things of permanent value and taking the pressure off the welfare budget.[10] However, those within the business community who regarded industry-based worker education and Werkspolitik as preferred alternatives to state social policy tended to be distrustful of Arbeitsdienstpflicht. Many entrepreneurs feared they would lose finan-

[7] See Fritz Karl Mann, "Zur Soziologie des Berufs," *JNS* 138 (1933): 481–500. Professor of economics and sociology at the University of Cologne, Mann himself, by 1933, was prepared to contemplate radical political solutions for the problem of work.

[8] Otto Hessler, "Dinta-Vorlehre oder weiteres freiwilliges Schuljahr?," *Gewerkschafts-Zeitung* (1932): 424–25.

[9] Carl Arnhold, "Jugendnot-Volksnot," *Das Werk* 12 (1932): 345–48; Wolfgang Schlicker, "Arbeitsdienstbestrebungen des deutschen Monopolkapitals in der Weimarer Republik unter besonderer Berücksichtigung des Deutschen Instituts für Technische Arbeitschulung," *Jahrbuch für Wirtschaftsgeschichte* 1971/73: 95–122.

[10] Nicolai, "Industriearbeiter und Wirtschaft (Das Werksgemeinschaftproblem)," *Technik und Kultur* 17 (1926): 70.

cially if the state expanded its economic role and resented paying higher taxes for what they saw as simply another step on the way to state socialism.[11]

The voluntary labor service (FAD) that was instituted on a limited scale in 1931 went only part of the way towards satisfying the supporters of Arbeitsdienstpflicht. It was favored by many who opposed the bureaucratic, militaristic, and authoritarian tendencies associated with the Dinta, and who cherished very different ideas about work. Thus the free trade unions approved of labor service as a temporary makework scheme, so long as it was voluntary and did not compete with paid labor,[12] while the Christian trade unions actively welcomed the FAD as a way of nurturing the work potential and capacity for Arbeitsfreude of the unemployed, particularly of those young people who had never held jobs and so had missed out on the education for work that only work itself could supply. They also hoped that the FAD would counteract the growing radicalism of the jobless by developing in them an ethic of service to the community, and they were pleased by its emphasis on agricultural work which, while ridding the cities of a mass of unemployed, promised to provide a useful supplement to current settlement and internal colonization schemes designed to recover German land in the East and promote the unity, culture, and strength of the German people.[13]

Meanwhile, the FAD also found favor with Protestants like Dr. Herbert Jagow of the KSB who argued that labor service constituted an excellent way of combating both Marxism and Mammonism so long as it was truly voluntary and free of undue militarist coloration, and who particularly welcomed the fact that volunteers were paid very little because this would compel them to think about the deeper meaning and purpose of all work, namely service to the whole.[14] Similarly, an article in the first issue of *Jugend im Dienst* ("Youth in Service"), a periodical designed to inspire the nation's youth to participate in the FAD, argued that the FAD would make it possible to revive the Protestant-Lutheran

[11] Schlicker, "Arbeitsdienstbestrebungen," 117–18; Friedrich Syrup, "Wesen, Zweck und Erfolge des Freiwilligen Arbeitsdienstes," *Deutsche Wirtschafts-Zeitung* (Berlin), n.d., clipping in Kiel, Wirtschafts-Archiv 0013 AL 1/ A 29 1932, 0645–0646.

[12] Wolfgang Benz, "Vom freiwilligen Arbeitsdienst zur Arbeitsdienstpflicht," *VfZ* 16 (1968): 326–27.

[13] "Der freiwillige Arbeitsdienst," ZCGD 32 (1932): 162–63, and Albert Voss, "Arbeitsdienst," ibid., 222–24.

[14] Herbert Jagow, "Der arbeitsethische Sinn des freiwilligen Arbeitsdienstes," *Kirchlich-Soziale Blätter* 34 (1931): 142–46. Jagow also believed that the FAD furthered morality by encouraging sexual repression!

service ethos, thereby renewing the ethic of work and reintegrating the working class into the body of the nation.[15]

In addition to reflecting traditional values common to Catholics and Protestants, the FAD derived much of its ethos from the work camps (*Arbeitslager*) that had grown up in a number of localities since the first world war. Some of these had been sponsored by nationalist and *völkisch* groups such as the Artamanen Bund, closely linked with the paramilitary *Freicorps*, who subscribed to a "blood and soil" philosophy. However, the main impetus in the 1920s came from the youth movement.[16] For men like Rosenstock and Klatt, the work camps were not a substitute for military service, but an opportunity to teach idealism, self-discipline, and community spirit through cooperation between students and workers. Welcoming the FAD as an extended educational experiment on a nation-wide basis, they worried that state support might lead to excessive centralization and produce not free citizens but uniform and obedient soldiers of work.[17] They hoped that the FAD would compensate individuals for the loss of Beruf by providing them with a meaningful work experience while strengthening the spirit of the Volk community.[18]

Fear of the anti-individualist, militarist potential of national labor service tended to keep socialist youth aloof from the FAD despite official SPD support. The socialist youth organizations only declared in favor of the FAD in 1932 under the influence of the growing employment crisis, and in an attempt to counter the active participation of anti-republican forces that effectively exploited the rhetoric of work to attract the young.[19] Their concerns, and those of the bourgeois youth groups eager to uphold the principle of self-administration, proved well-founded. By September 1932, centralized guidelines for the education of camp leaders had been promulgated.[20] What is more, FAD

[15] Herbert Franze, "Arbeit und Nation," *Jugend im Dienst.* Führerblätter zur Gestaltung des deutschen Arbeitsdienstes (Dresden) 1/3 (November 1932): 73–76. BA/NSD 49/1.

[16] Benz, "Vom freiwilligen Arbeitsdienst," 321.

[17] Eugen Rosenstock, "Arbeitslager und Arbeitsdienst," in Eugen Rosenstock and Carl Dietrich von Trotha, *Das Arbeitslager* (Jena: Eugen Diederichs, [1931]), 146–56. Schlicker, "Arbeitsdienstbestrebungen," 102 n.28, unfairly accuses Rosenstock of serving the interests of German monopoly capital by bringing a conservative corporatist ideology into the labor camp movement.

[18] Helmuth Croon, "Jugendbewegung und Arbeitsdienst," *Jahrbuch des Archivs der deutschen Jugendbewegung* 5 (1973): 70–72. See also *Jugend im Dienst* which printed a number of essays by people associated with the earlier *Arbeitslager* movement, including Fritz Klatt.

[19] Wolfgang Uellenberg, *Die Auseinandersetzungen sozialdemokratischer Jugendorganisationen mit dem Nationalsozialismus* (Bonn: Archiv der Arbeiterjugendbewegung, 1981), 180.

[20] Friedrich Feld, "Anteil der Studentenschaft an der Entwicklung des Arbeitsdienstes," in *Hochschule und Arbeitsdienst* (Langensalza: J. Beltz, 1935), 9.

instructors tended to be not idealistic educators from the Arbeitslager movement, but people selected by the conservative veterans association—the Stahlhelm—and trained for their leadership role by the Dinta.[21] Massively infiltrated by anti-democratic elements which valued it merely as the forerunner of a comprehensive labor service, the FAD turned away from the utopian ideal of voluntary association and adopted an authoritarian-military model. Simultaneously, its ideological emphasis shifted from individual self-fulfillment through meaningful work to sacrificial service in the interests of the national community.

Originally created to alleviate youth unemployment, which was perhaps the most distressing by-product of the economic crisis,[22] the FAD never afforded more than temporary relief to a limited number of young people. At its peak in November 1932, FAD camps accommodated an impressive 280,000 men, but this must be set against the over one million youths under twenty-five who were unable to find regular work of any kind.[23] Nor did the FAD meet the expectations of those who had hoped that labor service would fulfill important educational objectives. For one thing, the FAD primarily attracted young men from the crafts and skilled trades, rather than the radicalized unskilled who were in greatest need of education for work.[24] More fundamentally, while some participants entered into the spirit of the movement and enjoyed the opportunity for group living and constructive work offered by the FAD, the majority of "volunteers" were involved only because there was nothing better available on the job market.[25] Finally, even enthusiastic FAD supporters had to acknowledge persistent problems of motivation and discipline in its camps, accompanied by resentment of the camp authorities by individuals who objected to infringements on their right to privacy.[26] All in all, it is extremely unlikely that many FAD participants either acquired superior work habits that carried over into their post-camp lives or developed a lasting capacity for joyful labor based on a new ethic of service.

Because they realized that the FAD could at best play a limited role in shaping attitudes, Germans concerned with the effect of unemploy-

[21] Schlicker, "Arbeitsdienstbestrebungen," 109.

[22] On the youth unemployment crisis, Detlev Peukert, "Die Erwerbslosigkeit junger Arbeiter in der Weltwirtschaftskrise in Deutschland 1929–1933," *Vierteljahrsschrift für Sozial- und Wirtschaftsgeschichte* 72 (1985): 305–28.

[23] Syrup, "Wesen, Zweck und Erfolge des Freiwilligen Arbeitsdienstes," 0645.

[24] "Der freiwillige Arbeitsdienst," ZCGD 32 (1932): 162.

[25] Peukert, "Erwerbslosigkeit," 323–24.

[26] See Hans Heinrich Hasse, "Zur Psychologie des Arbeitslagers," *Jugend im Dienst* 1/3 (November 1932): 82–86.

ment on the nation's capacity for work continued to seek other ways to salvage the situation. One approach was to raise the school-leaving age. The idea of extending school by one year appealed strongly to socialists and trade unionists.[27] It could count on support from those educators who believed that young people should be kept in school through the period of puberty, lest they be adversely affected by bad work conditions or inadequate supervision on entry into the workforce during this critical stage of their lives.[28] But it ran into opposition not only from people who believed that the sooner young persons faced the realities of practical work, the better,[29] but also from those who were convinced that the country simply could not afford to spend more on its schools in a time of financial stringency. In the end, cutbacks in funds available for education ruled out the implementation of this scheme.

Another suggestion for reducing the number of those seeking to join the workforce was to restrict women's work. The exclusion of women from paid employment, long supported on ideological grounds by nationalists and traditional conservatives, had already been advocated as an economic expedient during the post-1918 crisis, and the two kinds of argument were frequently used to buttress one another.[30] But despite considerable efforts to exclude women from jobs in favor of men, females soon made up about one-third of the Weimar workforce, not only because industry found female labor relatively cheap, but also because women were deemed particularly suited to tasks requiring speed and dexterity rather than physical strength or extensive training, that is, to precisely the kind of joyless labor associated with mass production and the assembly line.[31]

Pressure to reverse this trend mounted during the depression, and culminated in systematic discrimination against women workers in two-income families (Doppelverdiener). Women were encouraged to withdraw voluntarily by reminders that their true vocation lay not in paid employment but in their role as wives and mothers; many women

---

[27] Hessler, "Dinta-Vorlehre?" 424–25.

[28] Dieck, "Beiträge zum Verständnis der Industriejugend," 348–49; Otto Conrad, "Zur Berufsethik der werktätigen Jugend," Jugend und Beruf 3 (1928): 249–51.

[29] E.g., Herbert Studders, "Erziehungswerte der Berufsarbeit," SP 40 (1931): 1253–58.

[30] E.g., by Gustav Winter, an ardent nationalist and enthusiast for Taylorism who was also a virulent anti-feminist. Winter's simple solution to postwar unemployment and to any overproduction that might result from the immense rise in productive efficiency promised by scientific management was for the state to pay women to stay at home, using the surplus created by the application of Taylorism to industry. Winter, Der Taylorismus, 234–35.

[31] Gabrielle Wellner, "Industriearbeiterinnen in der Weimarer Republik," Geschichte und Gesellschaft 7 (1981): 534–54; Stollberg, Rationalisierungsdebatte, 57–62.

in good jobs, for example those in senior civil service positions, were forced to resign. But the effect on the mass of working women doing unskilled or semi-skilled work in German offices and factories was minimal.[32] Generally speaking, these women were no more prone to experience unemployment during the depression than were their male coworkers.

If schemes to limit the labor force by raising the school-leaving age and ending women's work met with failure, so did educational reforms designed to reduce the menace of unemployment by offering further training to school-leavers destined for unskilled or semi-skilled jobs. Throughout the 1920s there had been critics who warned that it made little sense to increase the number of people aspiring to skilled work at a time when rationalization and the introduction of mass production were rapidly diminishing the demand for highly-trained workers. On the whole, however, the vocational schools continued to concentrate on preparation for the crafts and skilled trades. This was not unreasonable as long as times were good; although rationalization undoubtedly increased the need for an ever larger number of "hands" to do the repetitive and limited jobs characteristic of the Ford-style assembly line and thus forced a significant restructuring of the working class, it was hard to prove that the overall effect was one of "de-skilling."[33]

Only with the coming of the depression did the picture change: people with thorough vocational training continued to be at an advantage when competing for available jobs, but many failed to find work commensurate with their expectations. Even those fortunate enough to get jobs at the end of their apprenticeship frequently were forced to take positions that underutilized their skills. At the same time, the number of workshops and industrial firms able to take on apprentices declined. In these circumstances, it was logical to expand the role of the vocational schools to include the unskilled, offering them a general work education that would prepare them for an uncertain future.

Problems arose when it came to defining an appropriate curriculum. For boys, manual training in wood and metal workshops, sometimes supplemented by gardening, was considered most suitable. The objective was to enable pupils to make simple objects of use and carry out repairs. Learning to do this kind of work was deemed psychologically beneficial because it gave individuals a way of compensating for the limited and deadening jobs they were destined to occupy. It was also

[32] Tim Mason, "Women in Germany, 1925–1940," *History Workshop* 1 (1976): 92–93.

[33] Schöck, 169–70. It is striking that the trade unions were less concerned about the problem of "de-skilling" than many bourgeois social critics who regularly listed it as one of the chief drawbacks of rationalization. See Stollberg, *Rationalizierungsdebatte*, 91–93.

thought to have ethical value because it promoted positive attitudes to work.[34] Yet it was hard to see how such training could be expected to produce people able to maintain their love of work when confronted with the realities of unskilled industrial labor, much less help them withstand the impact of prolonged unemployment. As far as girls were concerned, the problem was simpler: most agreed that it was sufficient to teach basic homemaking skills, thereby keeping female pupils out of the job market while preparing them for their "natural" vocation.[35]

Because the reform proposals discussed so far would have entailed enlarging the role of governments, they were opposed as a matter of principle both by doctrinaire liberals and by anti-republicans eager to limit the power of the Weimar state. Thus draft legislation to restructure the vocational schools, an essential preliminary to inclusion of courses for the unskilled, was already in trouble before the depression. Actively discussed since the mid-1920s, such legislation was buried in committee by 1929 due to unbridgeable conflicts of interest among employers, craftsmen, and labor, and probably would not have been passed even if the economic crisis had not aggravated these differences while making governments eager to reduce expenditure on educational programs.[36]

Those who believed that the social question could best be solved by private enterprise, and the problem of work by changing worker attitudes, were delighted by such forced retrenchment. Ernst Horneffer continued to maintain that social insurance programs undertaken to appease the workers merely served to spread the socialist gospel while providing organized labor with a valuable power base, and that legislation limiting hours of work was a betrayal of the German identity traditionally based on diligence, and would eventually lead to the police state. Rather than interfering with business in the interests of labor, Horneffer maintained that the state should compel workers do their duty and encourage them to save, both as insurance against bad times and as a source of the capital that would enable them to become independent producers in a private enterprise economy.[37] As late as 1932, Osthold similarly blamed SPD-backed social programs for extortionate

[34] Muth, Berufsausbildung, 576–78.

[35] Paul Ziertmann, "Beruf und Bildung," SP 41 (1932): 97–104; Muth, Berufsausbildung, 578–80.

[36] Muth, Berufsausbildung, 444–82.

[37] Ernst Horneffer, Frevel am Volk. Gedanken zur deutschen Sozialpolitik (4th ed.; Leipzig: R. Voigtländer, 1930). First published in 1929, 25,000 copies of this title had been printed by 1930. Also Ernst Horneffer, Der Sozialismus und der Todeskampf der deutschen Wirtschaft (2d ed.; Leipzig: R. Voigtländer, 1931), an even more hysterical attack on socialism and economic democracy.

taxes and the rising national debt and held the workers responsible for the high level of unemployment: they had pressed for wage increases that outstripped gains in productivity, and so had forced industry to replace people with machines.[38]

However, as the depression intensified, many Germans who heretofore had regarded themselves as liberal opponents of state socialism began to entertain the idea that a strong, authoritarian, national government capable of decisive action might be needed to salvage the situation. Some even became convinced that a complete transformation of the political and social order was needed in order to bring about a permanent end to class conflict, restore the spirit of community, and put Germany back on the road to prosperity and national greatness. This led, among other things, to a nation-wide debate about the possibility of reorganizing both state and economy along corporatist lines.

The corporatist debate, which had significant implications for German ideas about the meaning and future of work, drew heavily on the work of Othmar Spann (1878–?), a Viennese professor of economics and sociology whose theory of "universalism" was designed to overcome the social alienation characteristic of individualistic democracy while maintaining capitalist industrialism intact.[39] Greatly influenced by neighboring fascist Italy as it experimented with corporatist ideas, Spann owed even more to the Catholic social reform tradition with its emphasis on occupational bonds and Christian community. As a result, Spann's works were cited not only by German fascists but also by people like the Catholic labor spokesman Theodor Brauer (1880–1942), who embraced corporatism as an alternative both to the status quo and to fascism. Propounding a "democratic" version of corporatism, Brauer called for the creation of a community of work in which the individual would be considered first and foremost as part of an occupational or functional grouping.[40] At the height of the depression crisis Brauer, to meet the demands of the day, urged the Christian trade unions to defend the Weimar system.[41] But in the long run he hoped that a new society based on Beruf rather than Besitz ("property") would evolve as people learned to reject class war ideas and to develop a strong vocational ethic that respected achievement, reflected a sense of solidarity,

[38] Paul Osthold, *Die Schuld der Sozialdemokratie. Die Zerstörung von Staat und Wirtschaft durch den Marxismus* (Berlin: Verlag für Zeitkritik, 1932), especially Chapters 4 and 8.

[39] On Spann, see Lebovics, *Social Conservatism*, 109–38.

[40] Theodor Brauer, *Sozialpolitik und Sozialreform* (Jena: Gustav Fischer, 1931); "Die berufständische Idee in Sozialpolitik und Sozialreform," ZCGD 30 (1930): 359–61; and "Der Kampf um die Sozialpolitik," *Verhandlungen des 13. Kongress der christlichen Gewerkschaften Deutschlands, Düsseldorf 1932*, 368–93 (BA Z Sg. 1—63/4).

[41] Brauer, "Kampf um die Sozialpolitik," 392.

and took into account the realities of economic, political, and social life.[42]

A corporatism closer to the fascist model was advocated by another prominent Catholic, Gerhard Albrecht, long an energetic proponent of *Werksgemeinschaft* and industry-based social policy. The depression led Albrecht to advocate the creation in Germany of an anti-democratic, anti-individualist corporate state based on the works community ideal and the vocational ethic. Nevertheless, Albrecht as well remained within the tradition of Catholic social thought. For while insisting on the importance of private enterprise, he contended that the new social order must give the workers both a fair share of material goods and a sense of dignity and belonging.[43]

This element was lacking in the anti-statist "liberal" corporatism of Dr. Walter Kupsch. A Werksgemeinschaft enthusiast, Kupsch had long advocated the replacement of patriarchal private enterprise both with a modern corporate state based on the individual company (*Betrieb*) and with an alliance between industry and workers that would combine the most positive features of Bolshevism and Italian fascism.[44] Although Kupsch placed himself in a tradition that stretched from Ehrenberg to Mussolini, during the depression he continued to minimize the role of government in engineering change. The corporate transformation he wanted would come from below, through the agency of the anti-Marxist labor movement and the nationalist veterans organizations. It would produce a society in which workers would know their rights and duties, accept private enterprise, and support an ethical management model based on respect for authority and for work. In return, they would be paid on the performance principle (*Leistungs-Gedanke*) and would be encouraged to save, both in order to accumulate capital and as insurance for times of emergency.[45]

In contrast, Hans Reupke (1892–?), a lawyer and foreign trade expert employed by the RDI, developed a corporatism that was more akin to national socialism than to traditional capitalism. Reupke tried to

[42] Brauer, "Kampf um die Sozialpolitik," 381–85.

[43] Gerhard Albrecht, *Vom Klassenkampf zum sozialen Frieden* (Jena: Gustav Fischer, 1932).

[44] Walter Kupsch, *Gegenwartsfragen und Werksgemeinschaftsidee* (Berlin: Verlag des Bundes der Grossdeutschen, 1926). This pamphlet appeared as No. 6 in a series edited for the Bund by Dr. Eduard Stadtler (1886–1945), head of the reactionary Anti-Bolshevik League, who also advocated Werksgemeinschaft and the corporate reorganization of economy, society, and state. See Stadtler's *Werksgemeinschaft als soziologisches Problem* (1926), No. 7 in the same series.

[45] Dr. Walter Kupsch-Cottbus, "Die deutsche Werksgemeinschaftsbewegung: ein Rückblick und eine Vorschau," *Neue Wirtschaft* (1931), 3:3–5; and "Der Kampf um den deutschen Arbeiter," in *Nene Wirtschaft* (1931) 7:8–10.

persuade German industrialists that Italian fascism not only showed the way out of the current crisis, but offered the best hope of solving the problem of work and preserving industrial peace in the long term. In his view, Mussolini had found a way to move forward to a post-capitalist order that would safeguard private enterprise and protect the individual entrepreneur, while stripping capitalism of its damaging characteristics. It would thus vanquish the materialistic spirit that currently poisoned the relationship between employers and employees.[46] In addition to creating a totally mobilized, productive economy providing work for everyone, fascism would destroy the proletarian ethos and integrate the workers into the nation. The result would be a unified German occupational ethic conducive to industrial peace, and a new management ideology (*Führerideologie*) that would permit the employers to maintain control through application of the natural aristocratic principle while preserving workers' rights.[47] Evidently impressed by the growing strength of the NSDAP,[48] Reupke argued that changing attitudes among the nation's youth was moving Germany in this direction. At once anticapitalist and anti-Marxist, young Germans, swept up into a religious-ethical movement that had room both for the energetic entrepreneur and the honest worker, looked forward to a new fascist society in which everyone could experience the joy of creation (*Freude des Schaffens*), while sharing the inescapable burden of labor and of daily existence.[49]

Elements of Kupsch's and Reupke's thinking were combined in the corporatism of August Heinrichsbauer, publisher of a weekly newsletter subsidized by Ruhr industry. In the wake of Germany's defeat, Heinrichsbauer, while calling for the creation of a conflict-free Volksgemeinschaft to replace the democratic republic, had urged businessmen to become actively involved in politics to ensure that governments, in pursuit of "social" objectives, did not contravene the interests of the nation's producers or otherwise infringe unduly on the autonomy of the economic sphere.[50] Critical of socialist schemes for economic democracy and nationalization of key industries, he proposed a capitalist counter-ideology involving ideas of joyful work and organic commu-

[46] Dr. Hans Reupke, *Unternehmer und Arbeiter in der Faschistischen Wirtschaftsidee. Ein neues Dogma der industriellen Zusammenarbeit und des sozialen Kampfes* (Berlin: R. Hobbing, 1931), 57.

[47] Reupke, *Unternehmer und Arbeiter*, 54–57.

[48] He had secretly joined the National Socialist party in 1930. Turner, *German Big Business*, 136–37.

[49] Turner, *German Big Business*, 57–60.

[50] August Heinrichsbauer, "Sorgen des Unternehmertums," *Deutsche Bergwerks-Zeitung* 73, 26 March 1924.

nity, along the lines set out in the writings of Othmar Spann and others.[51] Unlike Kupsch and Reupke, however, Heinrichsbauer was relatively uninterested in corporatist experiments. More important was to find and further the emergence of leadership personalities, men of the caliber of Bismarck who would be capable of dealing with the urgent problems facing the nation.[52]

If Heinrichsbauer's stress on the need for strong political leadership differentiated him somewhat from the majority of corporatists, it brought him close to Paul Bang (1879–?), Hugenberg's associate in the DNVP. In the 1920s Bang had promoted a variant of organicism incorporating the works community ideal, but even then he pointedly rejected the Catholic vocational principle and the universalism of Spann.[53] While restructuring the economy along corporatist lines might be a worthy idea, Bang saw no merit in the idea of the corporate "state" on the Italian fascist model. Rather, he advocated an economy that would allow the greatest possible scope to the principle of self-government side by side with a strong state incorporating the authoritarian Prussian-German tradition associated with Treitschke and von Stein.[54]

Although the depression did not create the turn to corporatism, it undoubtedly influenced the outlook of corporatists within the orbit of big business. Some who had formerly been content to rely on a new spirit of community to deal with the problem of work now called for institutional as well as attitudinal change. Those determined to attack the trade unions before 1930 because they were strong, thereafter pursued this course with even greater vigor because they believed them to be vulnerable. Above all, the economic crisis stimulated a more intensive search for political solutions. People like Heinrichsbauer and Bang, in arguing that an authoritarian state would be in better accord than the democratic republic with the essentially elitist ideals of management (not to mention the interests of business), could count on a

[51] Schneider, *Unternehmer und Demokratie*, 173–75.

[52] August Heinrichsbauer, "Zur Kritik der 'Wirtschaftsdemokratie," *Der Arbeitgeber* 20 (1930): 397–401. By January 1933 both Reupke and Heinrichsbauer believed that Gregor Strasser, recently ousted from his high position in the Nazi party, was better suited than Hitler to lead both National Socialism and Germany into a brighter future. Turner, *German Big Business*, 321. Heinrichsbauer for some time had used his business contacts to transmit information about, and solicit funds for, the National Socialists. Ibid., 140–41, 146, 149–50.

[53] On differences within the Werksgemeinschaft movement in the pre-depression period, see Gerhard Albrecht, "Arbeitsgemeinschaft, Betriebsgemeinschaft, Werksgemeinschaft," *JNS* 128 (1928): 530–62.

[54] Paul Bang, *Werksgemeinschaft, Berufsstand und Ständestaat: Eine notwendige Auseinandersetzung* (Berlin, n.d.[1931?]), 17–18 and passim.

more sympathetic hearing. Yet no consensus emerged in these circles on precisely what needed to be done. Nor did the business corporatists manage to reconcile the idea of a community of work based on respect for all "workers" from employer to common laborer with the concept of a work hierarchy headed by the creative entrepreneur who could achieve true Arbeitsfreude in a way denied to the laboring masses destined to execute their plans.

A more consistent concept of work, one that led to a somewhat more coherent corporatism, was developed by representatives of the *Mittelstand*, that complex and ill-defined amalgam of small shopkeepers and businessmen, artisans, farmers, white-collar workers, and salaried professionals who felt themselves threatened by the big corporations on the one hand and the organized working class on the other.[55] Despite the great disparities between the groups covered by this label, all believed that the Mittelstand, as the microcosm of the nation, had a mission to speak for the whole Volk and shared a distinctive occupational ethic compatible with corporatist ideals.[56]

Interesting variants of this ideology were proclaimed during the depression crisis by the crafts organizations or Handwerk, representing the largest component of the "old" Mittelstand, and by the "new" Mittelstand of white collar employees. One of the chief ideologues of the former was the artisan leader Hans Meusch, a spokesman in the 1920s for the progressive wing of the crafts movement.[57] Although Meusch condemned both liberalism and socialism as forms of individualism based on alien economic ideas imported by the Marxists, he rejected the romantic medievalism popular among the more reactionary elements of the Mittelstand. Instead he promoted an indigenous organic universalism derived from Othmar Spann that defined individual freedom in terms of service to the Volk community.[58] Meusch claimed that Handwerk, alone, had always recognized that the social question was essentially an ethical rather than an economic problem and during the depression had assigned it the role of intermediary between big business and labor. Its mission was to lead the way to the *Ständestaat* in which

[55] For a brief introduction to the Mittelstand and its problems during the Weimar period, see Lebovics, *Social Conservatism*, 1–48.

[56] Heinrich A. Winkler, *Mittelstand, Demokratie und Nationalsozialismus. Die politische Entwicklung von Handwerk und Kleinhandel in der Weimarer Republik* (Cologne: Kiepenheuer & Witsch, 1972), 117–18.

[57] Campbell, *German Werkbund*, 198.

[58] Hans Meusch, *Berufsgedanke und Berufsstandspolitik des Handwerks* (Hannover: Vorstand des Deutschen Handwerks- und Gewerbekammertages, 1931), 94–97, 102–103. Similar views, but with fewer antisemitic and anti-intellectual overtones, had been expressed by Meusch in September 1923. Winkler, *Mittelstand*, 112, 119.

society would be based on functional estates rather than classes, each sector of the economy would have its rightful place, and all would co-operate instead of fighting one another.[59]

Meusch also claimed that Handwerk stood for a work ethic based on self-respect, pride in skill, independence, and self-reliance: both employers and employees were said to possess these qualities to a greater extent than the current system, based on the mass, allowed them to reveal. Convinced that craftsmen, with their high ethos of work, suffered more keenly from unemployment than did the common laborer,[60] he noted with satisfaction that the apparent collapse of liberal capitalism had not resulted in increased strength for the SPD. Rather, the nation's youth had remained unmoved by the ideal of economic democracy, Marxist influence was waning, and the corporatist ideal was gaining ground within the SPD's right wing as represented by the *Sozialistische Monatshefte*. In addition, Brauer, on behalf of the Christian trade union movement, was proclaiming an occupational ethic comparable to that of Handwerk.[61] Politicized by the current crisis, Meusch insisted that reform, to be successful, had to be imposed from above.[62] Yet a survey of the existing political parties convinced him that the defense of Handwerk interests could not safely be left to any of them. His "solution" was to assert that the problem of work was essentially an ethical matter that had nothing to do with party politics.

Similarly unsatisfactory was the response to the depression of the German National Union of Commercial Employees (DHV), the most right-wing and ideologically oriented of the white-collar unions then competing for the allegiance of the new Mittelstand of salaried employees. The DHV sought to further its members' economic interests while maintaining their superior status vis-à-vis the working class.[63] Forced

---

[59] Meusch, *Berufsgedanke und Berufsstandspolitik*, 62–64; Frank Domurad, "The Politics of Corporatism: Hamburg Handicraft in the late Weimar Republic, 1927–1933," in Richard Bessel and E. J. Feuchtwanger, eds., *Social Change and Political Development in Weimar Germany* (London: Croom Helm, 1981), 174–206. In the corporatist future, individuals would be rooted within the autonomous, self-regulating organic community of their corporation or Stand. But while the latter would mediate between the individual and the state, Meusch, like Bang, maintained that the Stände must, in turn, be subordinated to a strong political authority, for it was the task of the economy to serve, and of the state to rule. Meusch, *Berufsgedanke und Berufsstandspolitik*, 111–14.

[60] Meusch, *Berufsgedanke und Berufsstandspolitik*, 108.

[61] Meusch, *Berufsgedanke und Berufsstandspolitik*, 153–60.

[62] Meusch, *Berufsgedanke und Berufsstandspolitik*, 107.

[63] See Michael Prinz, "Das Ende der Standespolitik," in Jürgen Kocka, ed., *Angestellte im europäischen Vergleich* (Göttingen: Vandenhoeck & Ruprecht, 1981), 331–53. The central role of the DHV in propagating the Mittelstand occupational ethic was stressed by Hans Speier, *Die Angestellten vor dem Nationalsozialismus. Ein Beitrag zum Verständnis der deutschen*

to resort to traditional trade union methods in order to carry out the first part of its mandate, it became increasingly strident in pursuit of the second. To differentiate its constituents from the mass of ordinary laborers at a time when rationalization and the deterioration of their economic position were eroding the distinction between blue- and white-collar workers, the DHV combined an ever more radical anticapitalism with a determined defense of idealism, anti-socialism, and nationalism. Convinced that if the trend to proletarianization was to be stemmed the new Mittelstand must assume the educational mission of the old, the DHV encouraged its members to improve their vocational qualifications and to develop their intellectual and cultural interests. It also sought to imbue them with an idealistic Mittelstand ideology centered on the notion of work as selfless service to the community.[64]

Although the DHV leadership was convinced by the 1930s that political action was essential to defend white-collar interests, like organized Handwerk it had difficulty in finding a political home. Hugenberg's DNVP, firmly committed to the employers' cause and determined to dismantle the social insurance system, was deemed too reactionary, as was Hitler's NSDAP after it decided to make common cause with the DNVP in the National Front. Consequently, the DHV executive chose to support the authoritarian Brüning government and cooperated with the Christian unions in an attempt to preserve essential social welfare programs. However, many of its members succumbed to the appeal of National Socialism. The NSDAP seemed particularly attractive to the young, many of whom approved the Nazis' antisemitism and believed the party's promise to institute a new organic order based on the ideal values they had been taught to uphold, thereby ending conflict between worker and bourgeois and effecting a coalition between workers of the hand and the brain.[65]

Disgust with the DHV's political stance led a number of individuals to withdraw from it entirely. Notable among these was Gustav Hartz

---

Sozialstruktur 1918–1933 (Göttingen: Vandenhoeck & Ruprecht, 1977). A lecturer at the Deutsche Hochschule für Politik, Speier wrote this study in 1932–33 but could not publish it then because of the advent of National Socialism.

[64] Prinz, in Kocka, Angestellte im europäischen Vergleich, 341–42; Speier, Angestellten vor dem Nationalsozialismus, 83, 102–109. In pursuit of these ideals, it mounted a massive publishing and book-distribution program designed to put inexpensive editions of suitable literature into the homes not only of its own members but of the whole lower middle class. On the DHV and the Hanseatic Publishing Institute which became the chief instrument of these propaganda efforts, see Stark, Entrepreneurs of Ideology, 22–32.

[65] Prinz, "Ende der Standespolitik," in Kocka, Angestellte, 350–53; William S. Allen, ed., The Infancy of Nazism: The Memoirs of Ex-Gauleiter Albert Krebs 1923–1933 (New York: New Viewpoints, Franklin Watts, 1976), 76.

who backed Hugenberg's successful efforts to win the leadership of the DNVP in 1928.[66] In that year Hartz published a virulent attack on Weimar social policy in which he proclaimed the need for a "conservative revolution," developed a variant of corporatism that reflected the organicist ideas of both Spann and Bang, and called for a radical break with the Republic. His fury was directed primarily against the Catholic Centre party, which he held largely responsible for framing Weimar social policy; his hopes for a corporate new order rested on an alliance between Hugenberg and Hitler—the coalition, inaugurated to combat the Young Plan, which eventually brought the National Socialists to power in January 1933.[67]

By 1932 Hartz was a confirmed National Socialist who believed that a better future rested not on statistics and scientific calculations but on "emotional concepts contained in the blood."[68] Revising his views on who was responsible for the crisis of the Mittelstand and the problem of work, he now blamed the alliance of Marxists and stock-exchange Jews, rather than the Catholics, for the proletarianization of the German "workers." However, he still inveighed against the incipient welfare state and the eight-hour day, that "misbegotten offspring of its mother, Liberalism, and its father, Marxism,"[69] and called for a new relationship between employers and employees that would tie the latter both materially and spiritually to their places of work.[70]

Hartz's program for dealing with the problem of labor alienation, like that of Heinrichsbauer and other defenders of capitalist industrialism, was based on stimulating the entrepreneurial spirit in all sectors of so-

[66] Prinz, "Ende der Standespolitik," 346 n.33.

[67] Gustav Hartz, *Irrwege der deutschen Sozialpolitik und Wege zur sozialen Freiheit* (Berlin: August Scherl, 1928), 7, 25–26, enthusiastically reviewed by the engineer K. F. Steinmetz in *Technik und Kultur* 20 (1929): 9.

[68] Gustav Hartz, *Die National-Soziale Revolution. Die Lösung der Arbeiterfrage* (Munich: J. F. Lehmann, 1932), 7. This was one of three books published "for the Nazi movement" by Lehmann in 1931–32. See Stark, *Entrepreneurs of Ideology*, 223.

[69] Stark, *Entrepreneurs of Ideology*, 101–102.

[70] See Hartz's article on the crisis and reform of German social insurance in the inaugural issue of *Werk und Beruf* (October 1929), a monthly edited by Vorwerck that sought to link the Werksgemeinschaft movement with corporatism. From October 1932 to September 1933 he pursued his goals as co-publisher—with Paul Bang and Dr. Erwin Liek—of *Soziale Erneuerung* (Stuttgart, 1–3, 1932–34), a purportedly "independent" periodical that stood for an "organic" economy and a social policy founded on private enterprise. Typically, an article of January 1933 transformed the Nazi slogan "Gemeinnutz geht vor Eigennutz" ("general welfare takes precedence over self-interest") into "Eigennutz schafft Gemeinnutz" ("self-interest serves the general welfare")! *Soziale Erneuerung* (January 1933): 112–14. Liek, a Danzig surgeon, attacked socialized insurance medicine for turning the physician into a "medical technician," thereby degrading his "art" into a mere means of earning a living. See Michael H. Kater, "Hitler's Early Doctors," *JMH* 59 (1987): 47–49.

ciety. But as a former DHV official and spokesman for the new Mittelstand, he also insisted that in order to change the rootless proletarian once again into a genuine German worker, a social revolution was needed that would replace exploitative finance capitalism with a regulated economy, put people at the center of the productive process, and value service to the community above private profit.[71] Meanwhile, he joined the NSDAP's call for a state-financed compulsory labor service to tackle unemployment and deal with the problem of work.[72]

The Mittelstand's claim that it stood for the true national ideology of work had considerable merit. Like many spokesmen of big business, Mittelstand ideologues defended private property and individual enterprise while expressing a longing for a conflict-free organic society in which all productive workers would be accorded equal respect. At the same time, a work ethic comparable to that proclaimed by the Mittelstand found acceptance at the other end of the social spectrum, among both Catholic and Protestant members of the German working class. Indeed, it can be argued that there were no more ardent supporters of the Mittelstand's occupational ethic than the skilled workers, many of whom came from crafts backgrounds and carried their work ethos with them when they joined the trade union movement. Often such workers demonstrated an attachment to a particular occupation equalling that of the artisans and stronger than that of the commercial or technical employees for whom the opportunities for identification with a specific calling could hardly be said to exist.[73]

Moreover, nationalism and idealism, although promoted with particular skill and vigor by the DHV, appealed as well to workers, many of whom aspired to bourgeois status, rejected Marxist materialism, and longed for full integration into the Volk community. While quantitative information about the relative importance of these "Tory" workers is hard to find[74] and their mentality and political behavior remain the

[71] Hartz, National-Soziale Revolution, especially 44–45, 80–93, 101–104. To make his quasi-socialist ideas—which ironically bore a strong resemblance to the social Catholicism he despised (see, e.g., Paul Jostock, "Entproletarisierung," in Die Soziale Frage und der Katholizismus [Paderborn: Ferdinand Schöningh, 1931], 388–400)—more palatable to big business, Hartz stressed that the limited welfare programs that survived after the dismantling of social insurance and labor regulation would feature self-management and individual responsibility.

[72] Hartz, National-Soziale Revolution, 177–78.

[73] Speier, Angestellten vor dem Nationalsozialismus, 83. The occupational ethic and cultural aspirations of one group of German skilled workers, the typographers, is well-described in Udo Steinmetz, "Berufsverständnis und Kulturbegriff. Zu ihrem Zusammenhang im Bildungsverband der Deutschen Buchdrucker und in der Büchergilde Gutenberg (1924–1933)," a Bremen thesis of 1977 supervised by Profs. Boehnke and Emmerich.

[74] Richard F. Hamilton, Who Voted for Hitler? (Princeton: Princeton University Press, 1982), 387–89.

subject of speculation, there are indications that those who chose to support the NSDAP were motivated by ideological as well as economic concerns.

This can be illustrated by examining the ideas about work of two "renegades" from Social Democracy whose support for the idea of a German corporatism or "socialism" during the early 1930s brought them into the National Socialist orbit. Emil Unger-Winkelried (1879–?) as a young man actually preferred detail work in a large factory to a skilled occupation because he feared that the latter would diminish his ability to pursue his avocation as a worker-journalist.[75] Having joined his union and the SPD, Unger soon became a reporter for that party's chief organ, the *Vorwärts*; but disillusionment set in when he realized the prominent role played in the labor movement by Jewish intellectuals.[76] Highly idealistic, he deplored the fact that most educated Social Democrats equated socialism simply with higher wages and shorter hours.[77]

As might have been expected of such an upwardly mobile individual, Unger was eager to improve his knowledge. For a time he attended a worker-education school dominated by the anthroposophist Rudolf Steiner who, although no Social Democrat, had demonstrated a high degree of social concern and sympathetic understanding. As a result Unger became convinced that the split between worker and bourgeois would never have happened had a greater number of patriotic German academics and bourgeois intellectuals reached out in this way to the laboring masses.[78] Instead, "old Germany" had virtually driven the workers into the arms of the Jewish-dominated SPD.

The war and its aftermath completed Unger's alienation from the socialist labor movement. Upset by the SPD's contribution to wartime fragmentation, the postwar turn towards radical Marxism and internationalism, and the all-pervasive corruption by which he felt himself surrounded, Unger left the party in 1920 and helped to found an anti-Marxist "Reformsozialistische Partei" made up of other former SPD notables who felt that the party of Bebel had been taken over by Jews and other undesirables.[79] When this failed, Unger worked for the *Bremer Zeitung*, editing its weekly supplement for workers, entitled *Der*

---

[75] Emil Unger-Winkelried, *Vom Bebel zu Hitler. Vom Zukunftsstaat zum Dritten Reich. Aus dem Leben eines sozialdemokratischen Arbeiters* (Berlin: Verlag Deutsche Kulturwacht, 1934), 38, 46. Apart from this autobiographical work, little is known about Unger. See Emmerich, *Proletarische Lebensläufe* 1, 392. The personnel file in the BDC only adds his date of birth and the fact that Unger had already joined the NSDAP formally on 1.12.1931, with the membership number 738848, rather than in 1933 as indicated by Emmerich.

[76] Unger, *Vom Bebel zu Hitler*, 64.   [77] Unger, *Vom Bebel zu Hitler*, 39.

[78] Unger, *Vom Bebel zu Hitler*, 46–47.   [79] Unger, *Vom Bebel zu Hitler*, 99–100.

Deutsche Arbeiter.[80] In 1923, when his paper set up a Berlin office, he returned to the capital and sought to replicate his successful workers' weekly on a national basis. Published in the name of the Association of Nationalist Labor Leaders from 1924, *Der Deutsche Vorwärts* drew exclusively on former SPD members as contributors,[81] and addressed itself to what Unger termed the most "radical" elements of the working class.[82] By 1929 it had attained a circulation of approximately 30,000.[83] Meanwhile, the Association, whose annual conventions were attended by between three and four thousand people,[84] had become closely linked with the NSDAP, with Frick and other future leaders of the Third Reich speaking regularly at its meetings.

Both paper and association became superfluous in 1931, when Unger openly joined the NSDAP which had supported him in secret for some years. Thereafter he used his undoubted journalistic talents to aid the Nazis in their efforts to take control of the factories. All in all, there is no reason to question Unger's claim that he and the former SDP activists linked with him contributed substantially to the success of the National Socialist revolution.[85]

One who had supported Unger's fight for Germany's liberation in the 1920s was his better-known contemporary, August Winnig (1878–1956). Winnig started out as a skilled mason but quickly demonstrated superior gifts as a writer and trade union organizer. At twenty-six he was already the editor of a trade paper, and he soon joined the executive of the German Building Workers Union, one of the SPD-affiliated free trade unions. Like Unger, Winnig was disturbed by conditions within the SPD, decried the influence of Jewish intellectuals on what had started as a German workers' party, and was transformed by the war into a fervent nationalist. Again like Unger, he broke with the SPD in 1920, after a disastrous interlude as governor of East Prussia, during which he toyed with the idea of supporting the Kapp Putsch against the Republic that had appointed him, rather than springing to the Republic's defense.[86]

Thereafter Winnig earned a comfortable living as a writer and journalist specializing in labor problems. Like Unger, he continued to think of himself as a servant of the workers' cause, but increasingly it was

[80] Unger, *Vom Bebel zu Hitler*, 106.   [81] Unger, *Vom Bebel zu Hitler*, 106–110.
[82] Unger, before the war, had been encouraged in his ambitions by Clara Zetkin who belonged to the SPD left and helped to found the German communist party. See Unger, *Vom Bebel zu Hitler*, 60.
[83] *Sperlings Zeitschriften und Zeitungs Adressbuch* 55 (1929), Section 11, 446.
[84] Unger, *Vom Bebel zu Hitler*, 115.   [85] Unger, *Vom Bebel zu Hitler*, 118–19.
[86] *Wer ist's?* 9 (1928): 1705–1706; James H. McRandle, "Warrior and Worker," in *The Track of the Wolf* (Evanston, Ill.: Northwestern University Press, 1965), 95–96.

nationalism to which he dedicated his pen. Addressing audiences of both employers and workers, he became involved with a series of political groupings that shared his desire for a conservative revolution to replace the despicable Weimar democracy with a corporatist new order in which the workers' estate would play a leading role.[87] In contrast to Friedrich Naumann's bourgeois liberal followers who sought to solve the problem of work by integrating the working class into capitalist society, Winnig insisted on the need for a total reorganization of society so as to bring it into accord with the spirit of the worker.[88]

The essentials of his program were outlined in an essay of December 1924 in the *Süddeutsche Monatshefte*, republished in somewhat expanded form in 1926 as *The Belief in the Proletariat*.[89] Adopting a biological blood-and-soil approach to the problem of the work, Winnig focused on the notion of Arbeitsfreude, to which he believed everyone had a right. Unfortunately, joy in work could only be experienced by a minority under present circumstances. Even worse, the workers were not fully aware how much they suffered from the degradation of work, while the large employers, who did recognize the problem, were incapable of solving it. Werksgemeinschaft, Winnig asserted, was a slogan without content rather than an effective remedy for the ills of a soulless, superficial civilization motivated by money and characterized by decadence and inner decay.[90] On the other hand, Winnig could not share the socialists' belief that the abolition of private property would spell the end of alienation. What was required was a non-economic revolution of attitudes led by former Marxists prepared to go "beyond Marx" in their fight for the soul of the "new man" and the rejuvenation of the Volk.[91]

[87] In addition to working with Unger, Winnig for a time belonged to the circle around the "national bolshevist" Ernst Niekisch (1889–1967). In 1927 he joined the Old Socialist party of which Niekisch had been a leading member, and established a branch in Berlin. See Niekisch, *Erinnerungen eines Deutschen Revolutionärs*, 125–26. Niekisch was himself of working class origin and erstwhile communist. He rejoined the SPD in 1922 after completing a two-year prison term for his part in the Bavarian revolution of 1918–1919 only to leave it in 1926 out of disgust with Stresemann's insufficiently nationalistic foreign policy. Lebovics, *Social Conservatism*, 139–56; Uwe Sauermann, *Ernst Niekisch. Zwischen allen Fronten* (Munich: Herbig, 1980).

[88] Hannah Vogt, *Der Arbeiter. Wesen und Probleme bei Friedrich Naumann, August Winnig, Ernst Jünger* (2d ed.; Grone-Göttingen: August Schönhütte & Söhne, 1945), 52. This was the published version of Vogt's dissertation for the Göttingen Faculty of Law and Political Science.

[89] August Winnig, *Der Glaube an das Proletariat* (rev. ed.; Munich: Milavida-Verlag, 1926). This book was first published in Berlin by Ernst Niekisch's Widerstandsverlag. References are to the Munich edition.

[90] Winnig, *Glaube an das Proletariat*, 25–27.

[91] Winnig, *Glaube an das Proletariat*, 38–39.

In face of the imminent death of decadent bourgeois civilization, Winnig's only hope was that the "new man" was potentially present in the form of the as yet "healthy" worker. The model worker was neither an individual as the liberals would have it, nor a mere proletarian as the Marxists maintained. Sprung from the body of the Volk, the model worker was the product of biology and history, the carrier of "a still fresh blood, a still unbroken will, a still unexploited creative power," with a new sense of form and a totally new outlook on life.[92] Driven by the tension between the will to live and the knowledge of mortality, all people sought to create works of lasting value that would survive their demise. But unlike many of his fellow conservatives Winnig insisted that this will to work[93] was not confined to the aristocrat or the peasant, the medieval craftsman or the bourgeois, but was also fully alive in the *Arbeitertum*.[94] Indeed, he was convinced that the process of inner renewal which would enable Europe to throw off its subservience to America could only come from this source, and would do so once the workers had freed themselves from both Marxist and bourgeois hegemony.

The ends which Winnig sought to further were entirely consistent with those of the Mittelstand, and it is no coincidence that his most influential book, *Vom Proletariat zum Arbeitertum* ("from Proletariat to Workerhood"), was published by a DHV-affiliated press.[95] Nevertheless, Winnig vehemently rejected the notion that because Mittelstand values pointed the way to the future, the Mittelstand should dominate the new order. Instead of aspiring to bourgeois status, Winnig's model workers were to assume the mission of creating the new society in their own image, for it was they who possessed the most intense ethical and social idealism, as well as a superior ability, as demonstrated in the trade union movement, to subordinate individual interests to the common cause.[96]

Shaped by the experience of war and revolution, Winnig's outlook was scarcely affected by economic fluctuations or changes in the world

---

[92] Winnig, *Glaube an das Proletariat*, 28–29.

[93] Winnig throughout avoids the use of the word *Arbeit* and instead speaks of *Wirken, Werk, Werkwille*. On this linguistic pattern, see Trommler, "Nationalisierung der Arbeit," in *Arbeit als Thema in der deutschen Literatur vom Mittelalter bis zur Gegenwart*, ed. Reinhold Grimm and Jost Hermand (Königstein: Athenäum, 1979), 114–15.

[94] Although Winnig laid claim to the term, e.g., in his autobiographical *Aus Zwanzig Jahren 1925–1945* (Hamburg: Friedrich Wittig, 1951), 50–51, the use of *Arbeitertum* as a substitute for *Proletariat* goes back to the late nineteenth century when Eugen Dühring used it in his book of 1881 on the Jewish Question. See Cornelia Berning, *Vom 'Abstammungsnachweis' zum 'Zuchtwart.' Vokabular des Nationalsozialismus* (Berlin: De Gruter, [1964]), 16.

[95] August Winnig, *Vom Proletariat zum Arbeitertum* (Hamburg: Hanseatische Verlagsanstalt, 1930).

[96] Winnig, *Glaube an das Proletariat*, 36–39.

of work. However, the depression may have influenced his publication in 1930 of an even more extreme attack on modern industrial society. *Vom Proletariat zum Arbeitertum* condemned the metropolis as an asphalt jungle which had destroyed humanity's contact with nature and its sense of community, denounced the factory in both its rationalized and unrationalized form as unnatural because it destroyed joy in work,[97] and depicted his time in apocalyptic fashion as "an age without God and honor which had debased work into a thing, linked only with other things, such as utility, food and drink, housing and clothing."[98] Winnig now also gave free rein to his antisemitism. Tracing the conflict between the true German worker and the alien intellectual back to the nineteenth century confrontation between Wilhelm Weitling and the Jew Karl Marx,[99] he deplored the fact that both youth movement and trade unions, having demonstrated a praiseworthy national enthusiasm at the outbreak of war in 1914, had since fallen under Jewish-Marxist influence.[100]

Winnig produced a poetic picture of the new world that would spell the end of alienation, but he, too, was at a loss to come up with practical suggestions for how to realize his vision. While the economic crisis strengthened his conviction that capitalism was doomed, he was not at all sure how the problem of work and thus of society was to be solved. As interim measures he advocated state protection for industry, decreased dependence on foreign loans, production for the home market, and support for the agricultural sector.[101] In 1930 he evidently also still hoped to win the Christian-National unions over to his cause by persuading them to adopt a "German" position and rid themselves of Marxist influence. But as a means to reach utopia, he could only recommend a revolution of attitudes based on self-help and trust in God.[102]

For reasons which remain unclear, Winnig failed to adopt what in many ways was the logical course, namely to become a member of the National Socialist party as Unger and so many others with similar views were doing. Despite the fact that repeated efforts were made to win him over, he never actually joined the NSDAP.[103] But if Winnig refrained

[97] Winnig, *Vom Proletariat zum Arbeitertum*, 215.
[98] Winnig, *Vom Proletariat zum Arbeitertum*, 60.
[99] Winnig, *Vom Proletariat zum Arbeitertum*, 64–96.
[100] Winnig also cited the cooperation of socialist-Jewish intellectuals with capitalism, exemplified by the liberal Ullstein publishing house, as a danger to state and nation. Winnig, *Vom Proletariat zum Arbeitertum*, 148, 183–92.
[101] Winnig, *Vom Proletariat zum Arbeitertum*, 198–200.
[102] Winnig, *Vom Proletariat zum Arbeitertum*, 217.
[103] Winnig, *Aus Zwanzig Jahren*, 56–64, indicates that he had been greatly tempted by

from committing himself to Hitler, from 1931 he served the Nazi cause as a "fellow traveler"—for example, by supporting the recently reorganized National Socialist Factory Cell Organization (NSBO).[104]

Meanwhile, the National Socialists praised his *Vom Proletariat zum Arbeitertum* in highest terms as the "anthem of the German Worker" and encouraged its wide distribution as an effective polemic against Jewish Marxism and materialism.[105] What is more, the organ of the NSBO, published between 1931 and 1934, called itself *Arbeitertum* in apparent reference to this book and excerpted passages on Jews in the labor movement from *Vom Proletariat zum Arbeitertum* in its inaugural issue.[106]

Winnig's racist, anti-technological, and anti-urban ethos conflicted with his belief that the future rested with the soundly nationalist and miraculously de-proletarianized industrial worker. Moreover, he knew full well that Germany, to be strong, required large-scale industry and also, therefore, a modern working class. Torn like so many of his contemporaries between a longing for the good old days of joyful craftsmanship and an appreciation of current realities, he found it impossible to develop a cohesive ideology that would reconcile the feelings of his heart with the knowledge of his head. Nor can one claim that Winnig's ideas were original. Borrowing his style from Lassalle and his ideas from Nietzsche, Riehl, Paul de Lagarde, Spengler, Moeller van den Bruck, Martin Spahn, and the Young Conservatives, he combined all this with "demented visions of totalitarian, caesarist regimentation."[107] It was not so much what Winnig had to say that impressed his contemporaries as the fact that he spoke as a worker about workers,[108] and it was this that rendered his writings useful to National Socialist propagandists in their fight for the soul of the German worker.

---

offers from Strasser and Hitler. Winnig claims that it was his wife who persuaded him to say "no."

[104] On the origins and evolution of the NSBO to 1933, see Max H. Kele, *Nazis and Workers. National Socialist Appeals to German Labor, 1919–1933* (Chapel Hill, N.C.: University of North Carolina Press, 1972), 149–55, 169–75, 195–201. Winnig gave a week of lectures to Nazi labor organizers paid for by big business with money channeled through Heinrichsbauer to Gregor Strasser. Turner, *German Big Business*, 157. See also Wilhelm Ribhegge, *August Winnig* (Bonn: Neue Gesellschaft, 1973), 266–75. Ribhegge claims that Winnig, by the fall of 1932, was in a panic lest the Nazis fail to come to power, yet an article by Winnig in the Nazi *Völkischer Beobachter* (September 25/26, 1932) indicates that he thought the NSDAP was becoming too radical and "Marxist." Kele, *Nazis and Workers*, 203.

[105] Walther G. Oschilewski, "Zwischen Revolution und Gegenrevolution. Über August Winnig zum 100. Geburtstag," *Die Neue Gesellschaft* 25 (1978): 221.

[106] *Arbeitertum* 1 (1931): 8–10.

[107] Oschilewski, "Zwischen Revolution und Gegenrevolution," 221.

[108] McRandle, *Track of the Wolf*, 101.

The National Socialists also knew how to profit from the writings of middle-class conservative revolutionaries, among them Spengler, Ernst Jünger, and Hans Freyer, whose radical ideas about work and society found a wide audience in the early 1930s. Spengler's fundamental pessimism was definitely reinforced by the deteriorating economic situation. His *Man and Technics*, published in 1931, combined despairing prophesies about an impending collapse of the West due to Nordic man's losing battle with the machine with appeals for a renewal of the entrepreneurial and technological spirit.[109] Tracing the evolution of human technology through the ages, he insisted that machine culture was in its death throes. Whereas hundreds of thousands of strong, innovative talents were needed even to maintain the present technical level, western societies demonstrated an alarming loss of creative impetus:

> Faustian thought begins to be sick of machines. A weariness is spreading, a sort of pacifism of the battle with Nature. . . . And it is precisely the strong and creative talents that are turning away from practical problems and sciences and towards pure speculation.[110]

Meanwhile, sabotage by way of strikes and suicide symbolized the mutiny of the "hands" against their destiny, leading to the disintegration from below of the "organization of work . . . based on the idea of 'collective doing' and the consequent division of labor between leaders and led, heads and hands."[111]

Spengler attributed the collapse of the world banking system to sinister financial interests, which had managed to gain control over all aspects of the economy and public life as the spirit of entrepreneurial capitalism declined.[112] As for the current high levels of unemployment in the industrialized countries, these were due to the shift in the center of gravity of production away from the West to inferior peoples on the periphery who lacked the inner relationship to technology characteristic of the Nordic race.[113] At best, the emergence of a new technical elite might suffice to stave off the inevitable day when the non-white peoples, using western technology, would succeed in undermining Faustian civilization.[114]

If the ideas about work in *Man and Technics* were not particularly

[109] Oswald Spengler, *Der Mensch und die Technik. Beitrag zu einer Philosophie des Lebens* (Munich: C. H. Beck, 1931; translated as *Man and Technics. A Contribution to a Philosophy of Life* (New York: Alfred A. Knopf, 1932). References are to the English version.

[110] Spengler, *Man and Technics*, 97.   [111] Spengler, *Man and Technics*, 99.

[112] Lebovics, *Social Conservatism*, 165–66.   [113] Spengler, *Man and Technics*, 102–3.

[114] Spengler, *Man and Technics*, Chapter 5: "The Last Act: Rise and End of the Machine Culture."

new, they were well-suited to the mood of Germany in the early 1930s. Spengler's insistence on the superior value of the "work" of entrepreneurs and engineers buttressed the self-esteem of people whom many blamed for having precipitated the current crisis through errors of omission or commission. At the same time, his anti-Marxist "German" or "Prussian" socialism, based on the notion of an indigenous and unique valuation of work, corresponded perfectly to the nationalist and anti-capitalist mood now ascendant among the educated. Finally, by equating technology with creative activity and struggle, and by covering what was ostensibly a defense of technical rationality based on historical "evidence" with an overlay of cultural pessimism and emotive racialism, Spengler's *Man and Technics* successfully pandered to the irrationalist strand in contemporary discourse.[115] All this was put to good use by National Socialist propagandists eager to stress the affinity between Hitler and Spengler in order to win elite support.[116]

An irrationalist technological modernism similar to that espoused by Spengler also informed Ernst Jünger's *Der Arbeiter*, surely the most original work of German literature to deal explicitly with our topic during the depression.[117] When *Der Arbeiter* first appeared in 1932, Jünger (1895–?) was already well-known as the author of *Storm of Steel*, a semi-autobiographical glorification of modern mechanical warfare that idealized those hardened by it as "princes of the trenches" and praised the spirit of community allegedly generated among them.[118] After an unhappy stint in the peace-time army, Jünger had devoted himself to literature and contributed extensively to right-wing journals.[119] It was only with *Der Arbeiter*, however, that he once more reached a wider public. In it, Jünger delineated an "ideal type" of modern worker modelled on the warrior portrayed in *Storm of Steel*, a "new man" at one with the machine, who would use technology to create a totally mobilized industrial society that would supersede degenerate bourgeois civilization.

[115] For an analysis of Spengler's "idealist" interpretation of technology, see Herf, *Reactionary Modernism*, 64–69.

[116] E.g., Paul Krumm, *Der Deutsche Sozialismus nach Adolf Hitler. Oswald Spengler und der Aufstieg des Nationalsozialismus* (Leipzig: Verlag 'Das neue Deutschland,' 1932). *Das Neue Deutschland* was a "monthly for the German freedom movement and national socialist Weltanschauung."

[117] Ernst Jünger, *Der Arbeiter. Herrschaft und Gestalt* (2d ed.; Hamburg: Hanseatische Verlagsanstalt, 1932). A fourth edition appeared in 1941.

[118] Ernst Jünger, *In Stahlgewittern. Ein Kriegstagebuch* (1st ed.; Leipzig: R. Meier, 1920; 3d and subsequent editions, Berlin: E. S. Mittler, 1922–). By 1942, over 200,000 copies had been sold. See Robert Wohl, *The Generation of 1914* (Cambridge: Harvard University Press, 1979), 57, 253–54.

[119] Herf, *Reactionary Modernism*, 92–100.

Imbued with a spirit of heroic realism diametrically opposed to the materialist and individualist bourgeois ethos, Jünger's worker would subscribe to an ethic of duty far removed from traditional morality. Thus the dignity of the individual, Arbeitsfreude, the humanization of work, and similar concerns of Weimar reformers had no place in Jünger's utopian scheme.[120] Projecting into the future tendencies that he claimed to discern in contemporary society and culture, Jünger predicted the coming of a worker-state inhabited by depersonalized, robot-like worker-soldiers, uniform in their machine-like demeanor, replaceable cogs in the productive process content to do their duty in the knowledge that those in command set goals for which it would be happiness to sacrifice and die.[121]

Jünger's vision, with its unambiguous embrace of the technological future, must have seemed more a nightmare than an ideal to most of his contemporaries. Yet *Der Arbeiter* presented in extreme and powerfully poetic form a number of ideas about work and society long current in right-wing circles. The worker-warrior analogy, like Spengler's notion of a Prussian socialism, dated back to Arthur Moeller van den Brucks's *Der preussische Stil* of 1916, which had stressed how the German work ethic, characterized by soberness and devotion to duty, was indebted to the Prussian military tradition.[122] Also common currency throughout the Weimar years were Jünger's global definition of work and the worker that transcended all boundaries of occupation and class, his vehement rejection of materialism, and his emphasis on identity of purpose between leaders and led. However, *Der Arbeiter* undoubtedly benefited from the tendency, increasing under the impact of the depression, for people to believe that bourgeois capitalism and parliamentary democracy were doomed. The very radicalism of its critique of the status quo ensured it a hearing among intellectuals during these years of crisis.

At the same time, those actually involved in the productive process did not know what to make of his book, for Jünger's "worker" bore no resemblance to anything to be found in the real world. Whereas Spengler could be put to use to buttress entrepreneurial ideology, Jünger's attacks on the bourgeoisie rendered him suspect in business circles. The business journal *Der Arbeitgeber*, in a critical review, acknowledged *Der*

---

[120] For Jünger's views on Arbeitsfreude, see Vogt, *Der Arbeiter*, 52–71. Citing passages from *Der Arbeiter* dealing with the man-machine relationship, Vogt shows that Jünger was aware of the problem of joy in work, but argues that he failed to recognize its full significance.

[121] Vogt, 52–91; Herf, *Reactionary Modernism*, 100–104; McRandle, *Track of the Wolf*, 101–104.

[122] McRandle, *Track of the Wolf*, 88.

Arbeiter's utility as an attack on historical materialism, but noted its lack of realism, the contradictions in Jünger's presentation, and the "Marxism" of some of his conclusions, including the rejection of nationalism as a bourgeois concept. Although the reviewer welcomed Jünger's attempt to integrate the workers into the nation, he accused him of failing to acknowledge that industrialism and its associated work ethic were a product of the bourgeoisie. To the extent that the *Bürger* was the real bearer and leader of the world of work, he could identify with Jünger's *Arbeiter*, but he would be reluctant to accept the culture-less, de-Christianized future of which Jünger was the prophet.[123]

Having decided to reject both nationalism and socialism as anachronistic holdovers from the bourgeois nineteenth century,[124] Jünger deliberately distanced himself from the NSDAP. Moreover, like many other conservative revolutionaries, he despised the Hitlerites as social and intellectual inferiors. Nevertheless, he spoke their language when he glorified the worker as warrior, stressed the revolutionary nature of the front experience, and elaborated the vision of a self-imposed dictatorship based on total dedication to labor and dominated in all its aspects by the Worker. Whatever his intent, his expressed desire to see the middle-class republic replaced by a workers' state organized as a "democratic dictatorship"[125] played into the hands of the National Socialists.

Unlike Spengler and Jünger, Freyer (1887–1969) was a successful academic.[126] This lent weight to his pronouncements on work and society, although the relatively inaccessible language he employed to present his conservative revolutionary views limited their popular appeal. The influence on his thinking of both the prewar youth movement and contemporary Marxism was reflected in his *Habilitationsschrift* on economic thought in nineteenth-century philosophy, published in 1921. Here Marx appeared together with Hegel as a legitimate heir to the German idealist tradition with its emphasis on freedom and progress.[127] Moreover, although he felt the attraction of the work ethic pro-

[123] Hans F. Menck, "Zu Ernst Jüngers 'Der Arbeiter,' " *Der Arbeitgeber* 22 (1932): 534–36.
[124] *Der Arbeitgeber* 22 (1932): 235–38.   [125] Jünger, *Der Arbeiter*, 254–56.
[126] From 1925 he was professor of sociology at Leipzig. On Freyer, see, most recently, Jerry Z. Muller, *The Other God that Failed. Hans Freyer and the Deradicalization of German Conservatism* (Princeton: Princeton University Press, 1988).
[127] Hans Freyer, *Die Bewertung der Wirtschaft im philosophischen Denken des 19. Jahrhunderts* (Leipzig: Forschungsinstitut für Psychologie, 1921; reprint Hildesheim: Georg Olms Verlagsbuchhandlung, 1966), 97. References are to the 1966 edition. See the appreciative analysis of this book in an otherwise hostile essay by Irving Fetscher, "Hans Freyer: Von der Soziologie als Kulturwissenschaft zum Angebot an den Faschismus," in Karl Corino, ed., *Intellektuelle im Bann des Nationalsozialismus* (Hamburg: Hoffmann und Campe, 1980), 181–85.

pounded by such romantics as Carlyle and Ruskin, also products of German idealism, Freyer recognized that theirs was a purely "metaphysical" solution that lacked the practical force needed to breathe spirit into modern industry and thus overcome capitalism from within.[128]

Convinced that neither left-wing utopianism nor right-reactionary romanticism were appropriate to solve the problem of work, Freyer called for a dynamic, holistic approach that would provide a scientific, empirical basis for an understanding of work, vocation, civilization, and culture. With references to Wundt as a noble forerunner, he welcomed the efforts of Moede and other Germans to transform narrowly practical American industrial psychotechnics into a serious experimental economic psychology that gave a proper place to both "the spirit in the economy" and "the complete dependence of economic performance on the mental and spiritual structure of the individual worker."[129] The next step was to create a "genetic social psychology" rooted in the Volk that reflected what the German historical school had already discovered in the nineteenth century, namely that "the economy is not nature, but spirit, not the domain of causal laws, but the object of historical, psychological, and philosophical-ethical understanding."[130] Such a discipline would stimulate systematic social-psychological investigations directed toward solving the key problem raised but not adequately resolved by nineteenth-century evolutionary thinkers from Saint Simon to Spencer: how to achieve a synthesis between the values of technology and those of the spirit and thus create a culture that would equal or surpass capitalism with respect to technical-productive achievements while reflecting a superior, non-materialist, morality.[131]

Although opportunism may have played a part in his espousal of National Socialism,[132] it was above all Freyer's longing for an ethically transformed economic order that led him to "fascism." In 1931, he announced that the "Revolution from the Left," based on the bourgeoisie and proletariat, had exhausted its forces, and that the "dialectic" of history guaranteed that the future would belong to the "Revolution from the Right."[133] Rejecting corporatism and other schemes that re-

[128] Freyer, *Bewertung der Wirtschaft*, 154–59.   [129] Freyer, *Bewertung der Wirtschaft*, 127.
[130] Freyer, *Bewertung der Wirtschaft*, 128–29.
[131] Freyer, *Bewertung der Wirtschaft*, 146–48.
[132] The charge of opportunism was one of many brought against Freyer in 1935 by a National Socialist critic. See IfZ, National Archives MA -141/4 T81 Roll 194, Bl.0345315-333, June 6, 1935 (name of author illegible). For a brief discussion of Freyer's relationship with Nazism, see Jerry Z. Muller, "Enttäuschung und Zweideutigkeit. Zur Geschichte rechter Sozialwissenschaftler im 'Dritten Reich'," *Geschichte und Gesellschaft* 12 (1986): 300–316.
[133] Hans Freyer, *Revolution von Rechts* (Jena: Eugen Diederichs, 1931). A single edition of

lied on changes in economic organization to overcome the class conflict characteristic of industrial society, Freyer instead called for a radical break with the past, a demonstration of force to emancipate the state from society and free individuals by making them part of the historical Volk community.[134] Only a political movement resting on the power of the Volk would be able to destroy the "industrial society" produced by nineteenth-century revolutions and replace it with a genuine socialism that would at last enable both modern technology and the social principle to come into their own. This position was reinforced in Freyer's 1933 essay on the philosophy of work which once more repudiated existing society based on interests and the pluralistic party state in favor of a new fascist political order dedicated to the Volk "as it might be." Only thus would it be possible once more to transform Arbeit into Beruf and to restore the harmonious social order on which the idea of calling depended.[135]

The high level of abstraction on which Freyer chose to operate and his lack of regard for current realities limited his impact on contemporaries. Like the writings of other radical conservatives, his pronouncements both reflected and heightened the fevered atmosphere of the times, but his elitist ideas were ill-suited to serve as the focus of a mass movement such as that represented by the NSDAP. For this reason, it is not fair to hold Freyer and his right-wing fellows responsible for either the collapse of the Republic or the victory of National Socialism.

The inability of these intellectuals to have any direct influence on events during the economic crisis was matched by that of their democratic counterparts, the "ethical socialists." Instead of advocating authoritarian solutions to the problems of contemporary society, the latter believed that the Weimar Republic represented a stage on the way to a post-capitalist society in which the benefits of modern production would be combined with the restoration of the dignity of labor and individual freedom. While dreaming of a brighter future, they therefore fought a rearguard action in defense of the Republic.

Closest to turning ethical socialism into a practical political program was Heimann,[136] who during the 1920s had done his best to persuade German Social Democracy to develop a program of reform that would combine pressure for a massive extension of state social programs with measures calculated specifically to address the problem of work, rather

---

three thousand copies was printed. See also Struve, *Elites Against Democracy*, 373, and Fetscher, "Freyer," 185–90.

[134] Freyer, *Revolution von Rechts*, 52–53, 59–71.

[135] Hans Freyer, "Zur Ethik des Berufes," *Ethik des Berufes*, 10–21.

[136] See Chapter 10, above.

than leaving such matters to well-meaning bourgeois reformers or to agents of industry like the Dinta who fostered cooperation between management and labor purely in order to further the interests of their employers. Heimann had also warned the Social Democrats not to underestimate the popular appeal of the notion of national community, however fraudulent. Convinced that Marxism itself had originated as a natural reaction to the workers' exclusion from the community, and that "community represents the great longing of restless people in this unquiet age," he had stressed the need for active struggle against the Volksgemeinschaft ideology propagated by the capitalists.[137]

The depression crisis, while it reinforced Heimann's determination to press forward towards an ethically-based socialism on a democratic basis, rendered him more doubtful about the prospects for reform under capitalism and less confident that rationalization could serve the interests of the workers. For the first time he conceded that it might be necessary to restrain technical progress in order to humanize work and prevent technological unemployment.[138] However, the aspect of the current crisis that most affected Heimann's thinking was not mass unemployment, but rather the astonishing increase of political support for National Socialism. Determined to stall the Nazi bandwagon, he tried to persuade himself and others that the devastating effects of the depression on the economic and social status of the Mittelstand had created the conditions for an alliance between it and the working class that could be harnessed to the cause of ethical socialism. Instead of allowing the National Socialists to exploit the situation for their own aggrandizement, Heimann urged Social Democracy to extend its appeal beyond the working class and to demonstrate that it had something to offer the nation as a whole. By binding the Mittelstand to the socialist cause, the SPD could prevent it from turning to labor's enemies for a solution to its problems.[139]

Heimann believed that the SPD could engineer its breakthrough to the Mittelstand by emphasizing that only socialism could both overcome the loss of meaning in work and combat the insecurity currently experienced by workers and middle classes alike. Admittedly, the problem of work differed somewhat between peasants, factory workers, white-collar employees, and other strata of the population, but all

---

[137] Eduard Heimann, *Die sittliche Idee des Klassenkampfes und die Entartung des Kapitalismus* (Berlin: J.M.W. Dietz, 1926), 40, 90. In the conclusion, Heimann acknowledges his debt to Marx, Hegel, Tönnies, Rathenau, Wilbrandt, de Man, and the dialectic theology of Karl Barth.

[138] Heimann, *Sozialistische Wirtschafts- und Arbeitsordnung*, 51–59.

[139] Eduard Heimann, *Sozialismus und Mittelstand* (Potsdam: A. Protte, 1932).

longed for freedom and rootedness in work. By stressing the human bond between work and "property," he hoped to persuade both the Mittelstand and the working class that their goals could only be attained within the context of a productive industrial economy inspired by the principle of collectivism.[140]

In his attempt to win Mittelstand support for ethical socialism, Heimann deliberately used terminology similar to that employed so effectively by National Socialist propagandists. Thus, he asserted that physically and spiritually "rooted" work was the prerequisite for true citizenship, and that people, when they strove for "a new form in which their working life would develop a new content," would also be fighting to turn the German Volk into a genuine nation.[141] But he failed to persuade the SPD to do likewise, nor is it likely that the socialists could ever have overcome Mittelstand distrust by adopting this tactic. Instead, it was the Nazis who—for the first time in German history—managed to create a political movement that bridged the gulf between the Mittelstand and significant portions of the working class. If anything, Heimann's use of "Nazi" words and phrases, by obscuring the fundamental difference between the ethical socialist position and that of the NSDAP, actually made it easier for Hitler to destroy the Republic.

To conclude this chapter, let us look at someone who, unlike the intellectuals discussed above, allied himself with Hitler and thus succeeded in turning his corporatist, Mittelstand, and conservative revolutionary beliefs into effective political action. Walther Darré (1895–1953), an agronomist and farmers' advocate, had for years espoused a racist "blood-and-soil" ideology that assigned to the German peasantry a central role in solving the problems of work and society. By the early 1930s he was a committed National Socialist and had contributed significantly to the NSDAP's electoral success by helping to formulate its agricultural program. He also played an important role in the first years of the Third Reich.[142]

Even before the onset of the depression, German agriculture had been in a state of crisis. The farmers' perception that industry and finance were gaining at their expense had produced a siege mentality that expressed itself politically in anti-government rural protest movements. By the late 1920s, these were providing fertile ground for Na-

---

[140] Heimann, *Sozialismus und Mittelstand*, 11–14.

[141] Heimann, *Sozialismus und Mittelstand*, 16.

[142] See Anna Bramwell, *Walther Darré and Hitler's Green Party* (Abbotsbrook, England: Kensal House, 1985).

tional Socialist agitation.[143] Darré, who was put in charge of the NSDAP's agrarian campaign after he joined the party sometime in 1930,[144] not only gave voice to the fears of the nation's farmers and promised practical remedies, but also provided them with a counter-ideology designed to defend agrarian interests against the modernizing forces that had steadily undermined the position of agriculture within the national economy since the last decades of the nineteenth century.

Darré's ideological position, whose essential features were fully developed before he became a National Socialist, is of considerable interest in the context of the German debate about work. Directing attention away from the urban working class, which had generally been seen as the chief locus of disaffection, to the nation's independent farmers, Darré represented the peasantry as the source of all that was good in the German work ethic and assigned this sector of the Mittelstand a key role in building the new Germany. Independent and self-reliant, German peasants were deemed to be masters of their craft, diligent workers proud of their occupation, dedicated to the success of their "enterprise," the farm, with a "feeling for the organic interplay of forces in the work as a whole," and a devotion to duty that curtailed egotism and accepted service as "the most noble deed of the free man."[145] In other words, Darré claimed for the *Bauerntum*, the independent peasantry, what Meusch attributed to the craftsmen and Winnig to the *Arbeitertum*.

Darré justified his emphasis on what was after all a rapidly diminishing element in German society by positing an intimate relationship between race, culture, and agricultural labor. Attributing all positive aspects of the German past to the "Nordic" peasantry, he designated the admixture of impure blood that had increasingly polluted the Germanic Volk since the advent of Christianity as the source of all evil. If the healthy peasant tradition was once more to permeate the whole of German culture and restore the nation to greatness, what was needed, in Darré's view, was a legally enforced program of deliberate human breeding. Only those of sound Germanic peasant stock should be al-

---

[143] On the Mittelstand protest movements in relation to National Socialism see Hans-Gerd Jaschke, *Soziale Basis und soziale Funktion des Nationalsozialismus. Studien zur Bonapartismus-theorie* (Opladen: Westdeutscher Verlag, 1982), 169–79. Although agriculture would have constituted a separate estate in any corporate reorganization of society, the German farmers considered themselves part of the Mittelstand.

[144] The exact date of Darré's joining the party is in dispute. See Barbara Miller Lane and Leila Rupp, eds., *Nazi Ideology before 1933* (Austin, Tex.: University of Texas Press, 1978), xx–xxi, and Bramwell, *Darré*, 78–79.

[145] R. W. Darré, *Das Bauerntum als Lebensquell der Nordischen Rasse* (Munich: Lehmann, 1929), excerpted in Lane and Rupp, *Nazi Ideology before 1933*, 103–106.

lowed to procreate, and encouraged to do so.[146] Specifically linking race and labor, he called on the nation to return to the "old German marriage law": "fused with the goals of breeding and with the prerogatives of rank," this "law" had served "as a filter which permitted complete procreation only to that blood which had been tested in constructive work."[147]

Darré sought to give his notions a scientific aura by drawing on what he knew of plant and animal breeding, and also employed historical and cultural arguments of the kind popularized by Spengler. Throughout Darré's discourse, references to modern genetics occur side by side with allusions to German tradition and law, and to the Germanic Weltanschauung which these, in turn, were thought to reflect. Convinced that the superiority of particular races could be demonstrated by their greater ability to create a high culture, he acknowledged that the historian and the ethnographer, as well as the geneticist, were needed to help determine what races and individuals should be allowed to perpetuate themselves.

The depression, along with the more intimate knowledge of the immediate problems facing German agriculture that derived from his work as head of the Nazi's farm propaganda division,[148] led Darré to modify his program somewhat. After 1930 he no longer presented systematic breeding as the sole means for effecting the desired national revolution. Instead, Darré now stressed the importance of establishing an autarchic economy totally self-sufficient with respect to foodstuffs,[149] and, abandoning specific references to the Bauerntum, called for the creation of an organic national state that would enable *all* working Germans to "feel at home."[150] He also drew far enough away from biological-historical determinism to assign education an important role in restoring the nation's strength: farmers would have to be taught "to regard *labor on the soil not only from the point of view of profit* but also as an *honorable service* to the German people."[151]

What Darré espoused in the early 1930s was a radical, scientistic, version of traditional *völkisch* nationalism. Dating back to the nine-

[146] R. W. Darré, Neuadel aus Blut und Boden (Munich: Lehmann, 1930), excerpted in Lane and Rupp, Nazi Ideology before 1933, 111–17.

[147] Lane and Rupp, Nazi Ideology before 1933, 114.

[148] See Lane and Rupp, Nazi Ideology before 1933, 130–31. Commenting on Darré's "Landstand und Staat," published in the Völkische Beobachter, April 19 and 21, 1931, Lane attributes changes in Darré's message in part to the influence of the NSDAP, of which he had recently become a full-fledged member.

[149] Lane and Rupp, Nazi Ideology before 1933, 130.

[150] Lane and Rupp, Nazi Ideology before 1933, 134.

[151] Lane and Rupp, Nazi Ideology before 1933, 132; author's emphasis.

teenth century, this nationalism had been intensified by the experience of war and defeat and by the treatment accorded to Germany as a result of Versailles and the reparations settlement; it reached new heights, however, in the depression years, when Germany, like the other industrialized countries, sought to resolve what was essentially a crisis of international finance and trade by resorting to nationalist expedients. Given the circumstances, it is no wonder that *Deutsche Arbeit*, present as a subtheme in German discourse about work since the days of Riehl, returned to a position of prominence that it had not enjoyed since the immediate postwar period. Among the major effects of the depression on German thinking about work, one must include the fact that people were now more ready to believe that Germany was different from, and better than, other nations and that German interests would be best served by rejecting all foreign ideas and institutions.

Nevertheless, even now there was no agreement among nationalists on just what was "German." Within the anti-democratic camp, modernists and anti-modernists continued the battle for supremacy, with each claiming that what they favored was German and what they hated either American or Jewish or Bolshevik or all these rolled into one. Darré was one of that new breed determined to devise a revolutionary nationalism blending traditional with modern elements. Like Riehl, on whose descriptions of the virtuous peasant he drew, he wanted the best of traditional values to carry over into the modern world. But unlike Riehl, Darré insisted that a solution for the nation's ills could be found only if Germans were prepared to shed traditional inhibitions that hampered the adoption of modern eugenics and prevented them from contemplating revolution. It was the crisis atmosphere of the depression years that enabled the radical variant of nationalism espoused by people like Darré to flourish. Adopted by the National Socialists, it smoothed their way to power and eventually put them in a position to determine not only *what* but also *who* was "German."

XIII

NATIONAL SOCIALISM AND THE
PROBLEM OF WORK

BEFORE 1933 the National Socialists laid great stress on their capacity to solve the problem of work. Not only did the NSDAP claim that it alone had the will and ability to restore full employment; its leaders also promised to address the deeper problem of alienation. Catering to the prevailing anticapitalist mood, they espoused a "German socialism" designed to restore joy in work and to reintegrate the workers into the body of the nation. A class-free Volksgemeinschaft was to be created, one based on an altruistic work ethic. Trumpeting the slogan "*Gemeinnutz geht vor Eigennutz*" (common good takes precedence over self-interest), already embedded in the original 25-point program of the NSDAP of 1920,[1] the National Socialists painted an inspiring picture of a third and greater Reich in which all would use their talents and abilities to strengthen Germany. In return, workers, whether of the brain or the hand (*Stirn oder Faust*) would be honored for their contributions (*Ehre der Arbeit*) and achieve status commensurate with their performance (*Leistung*).

While the National Socialist ideology of work can be broadly summarized in this way, on closer inspection it becomes clear that it represented an amalgam of several fundamentally incompatible strands. As a result, it was hard for both party members and outsiders to determine what the Nazis actually stood for. But the lack of a consistent set of principles and objectives, far from being an obstacle to success, helped the NSDAP in its quest for electoral support and provided it with a useful degree of political flexibility when it first came to power.[2]

---

[1] Reproduced in Lane and Rupp, *Nazi Ideology before 1933*, 40–43, and briefly analyzed in Eberhard Jäckel, *Hitler's Weltanschauung* (Middletown, Conn.: Wesleyan University Press, 1972), 68–74.

[2] This was also true of other facets of Nazi ideology. See, e.g., Woodruff D. Smith, *The Ideological Origins of Nazi Imperialism* (Oxford University Press, 1986), who analyzes the com-

It only created serious problems once the National Socialists were firmly in the saddle and had to decide which of their promises to implement. When it became necessary to determine the implications for policy of the ideals so confidently blazoned forth before 1933, the Nazi ideology of work revealed its internal contradictions and its potential for divisiveness.

Despite the questionable intellectual merits of Nazi ideology and the fact that a diverse set of economic, social, political, and personal factors helped determine the course of events that brought Hitler to power, no explanation of this momentous development is complete that fails to include the appeal of National Socialist ideals to the minds and hearts of Germans. This chapter will analyze the role played by ideas about work in early Nazi doctrine, examine how the NSDAP used them to gain support from various sectors of German society before 1933, and explore responses to the establishment of the Third Reich by Germans actively concerned with the problem of work during the Weimar years.

From the time of its birth, National Socialism claimed to embody the best spirit of "German" work. Anton Drexler, founder in 1919 of the German Workers' Party out of which Hitler's NSDAP was to grow, proudly identified himself as a worker and a socialist and presented his party as uniquely qualified to champion the true interests of the nation's workers. He set forth his views on work in an autobiographical essay of that year as part of an elaborate, ultra-nationalist conspiracy theory of the war, defeat, and revolution that laid the blame for Germany's misfortunes on the Free Masons and, above all, on the Jews.[3] Drexler identified the latter with western capitalism out to exploit defeated Germany, insisted that the SPD and the trade unions were manipulated by Jews serving the interests of foreign capital, and accused Jewish leftists like Kurt Eisner, the Bavarian social democrat who had started the revolution in Munich in the name of the working masses, of being the workers' enemies. How else could one explain the workers' failure to carry the November revolution through to its logical conclusion?

According to Drexler, it was the Jews' inadequacy as workers that drove them to use such means to secure dominion over working humanity. Warning the "creative workers" and "working *Führer*" of the

---

posite nature of Nazi imperialist ideology and the multiple functions it served, and Herbert Mehrtens's discussion of Nazi ideas about the natural sciences in *Naturwissenschaft, Technik und NS-Ideologie*, ed. Herbert Mehrtens and Steffen Richter (Frankfurt: Suhrkamp, 1980), 15–87.

[3] Anton Drexler, *Mein politisches Erwachen. Aus dem Tagebuch eines deutschen sozialistischen Arbeiters* (Munich: Deutscher Volks-Verlag, 1919), 40–41.

nation that Jewish capitalists were even trying to take over leadership of the antisemitic movement in order to render it harmless, he urged them to join forces against Jewish finance and the West.[4] Germany's salvation could only be assured if productive citizens of all classes rejected the Marxist ideology of class conflict and worked together to create a truly German—as distinct from Jewish-Marxist—socialism. By characterizing the Jews as parasites battening on the industrious German people, and by redefining "the worker" to include everyone engaged in productive activity, Drexler effectively linked antisemitism with both anticapitalism and anti-Marxism, thereby injecting into Nazi ideology the notion, long a staple in the European tradition,[5] that work and race are inextricably linked.

Hitler, who joined Drexler's party in its first year and quickly achieved prominence within it by dint of his extraordinary oratorical ability, not only found Drexler's ideas about work personally congenial, but recognized their political potential.[6] Proceeding to carve out a niche for the National Socialists in the anti-Republican front, he elaborated on the work-race theme in a remarkable speech of 1920.[7] An enthusiastic audience of over two thousand people at the Hofbräuhaus in Munich heard him define the German or "Aryan" work ethic as one based on duty. Forced to contend with a harsh climate under cold northern skies, the Aryan forefather had learned to work not for himself, out of egoism, but in order to preserve the tribe as a whole. The Aryan tradition also emphasized physical and mental health and devotion to a deep, spiritual, inner life. For these reasons, Germans could not regard work in Biblical terms as a curse and a punishment from God. Indeed, if a paradise of leisure existed, the Germans, addicted to strenuous activity, would be unhappy in it.[8] By contrast, Jews were born parasites and exploiters of the labor of others; lacking an ethic of work, they were incapable of creating a culture or of building a state.[9] As Hitler put it,

---

[4] Drexler, *Mein politisches Erwachen*, 34–35.

[5] Examples from the nineteenth century are Vacher de Lapouge who contrasted the Aryan's capacity for honest work with the Jew's love of speculation, and Francis Galton who listed intellect, zeal, and devotion to work among inherited abilities. See George L. Mosse, *Toward the Final Solution. A History of European Racism* (New York: Howard Fertig, 1978), 59–62 and 74.

[6] Robert G. L. Waite, *The Psychopathic God. Adolf Hitler* (New York: Basic Books, 1977), 114–16.

[7] Text and commentary in Reginald Phelps, "Hitlers Grundlegende 'Rede über den Antisemitismus,' " *VfZ* 16 (1968), 390–440.

[8] Phelps, "Hitlers Grundlegende Rede," 401–4.

[9] Phelps, "Hitlers Grundlegende Rede," 405.

Aryanism signifies an ethical conception of work leading to . . . socialism, community consciousness, "Gemeinnutz vor Eigennutz"—Judaism
means an egotistical conception of work and thus Mammonism and materialism, the absolute contrary of socialism.[10]

Subscribing to a labor theory of value as extreme as that of Marx,
Hitler defined "capital" (workshops, factories, and machines) as embodied labor and maintained that its value derived solely from its capacity to serve as means of production. Nevertheless, he warned, it was
both senseless and futile to seek to end alienation by combating industrial capitalism in Marxist fashion. Instead, like Drexler, he insisted
that the real enemy responsible for the corruption and degradation of
honorable toil was "unproductive" loan and stock exchange capitalism,
that is, "Jewish" finance capital.[11] What was needed to solve the problem of work and achieve a "German" socialism was to combine nationalism with antisemitism. Salvation lay in battling the Jewish idea of
Volk and work, and in expelling the Jews.[12]

While racist antisemitism remained an essential feature of his ideology, during the depression Hitler tended to allude less directly to the
Jewish menace. Confident that Germany's antisemites had already
been won over, and could in any case read between the lines, he found
it expedient to moderate his tone so as not to alienate those sectors of
the population (including the business community) who were disdainful of vulgar racism, while continuing to woo Germany's laboring
masses with promises of "a Reich of honor and freedom—work and
bread."[13] Moreover, because he was primarily interested in attaining
power in order to pursue his foreign policy objectives, Hitler gave relatively little attention to the problem of alienation in his speeches before 1933. Convinced that Germany's failure to achieve victory in the
World War had been due in large part to the inability of the imperial
regime to maintain national unity, Hitler offered himself to the elec-
torate as a strong leader capable of creating a truly united Volksgemeinschaft that would succeed where the Kaiser had failed. All talk of a
moral and social revolution centered on a new yet quintessentially German work ethic was but a means to this end.[14]

[10] Phelps, "Hitlers Grundlegende Rede," 406.
[11] Phelps, "Hitlers Grundlegende Rede," 409–11.
[12] Phelps, "Hitlers Grundlegende Rede," 417.
[13] Election speech of July 15, 1932, cited in Max Domarus, Hitler. Reden und Proklama-
tionen 1932–45, kommentiert von einem deutschen Zeitgenossen (Neustadt a. d. Aisch, 1962),
1:117.
[14] Interesting on Hitler as a social revolutionary is Rainer Zitelmann, Hitler. Selbstverständ-
nis eines Revolutionärs (Hamburg: Berg, 1987). Zitelmann correctly emphasizes this aspect of

The NSDAP's chief ideologist, Alfred Rosenberg (1893–1946), like Hitler, tended to emphasize the "national" rather than the "socialist" element in National Socialism. By doing so, he believed that the NSDAP could wean patriotic German workers away from the Jewish-controlled SPD. Accusing the latter of corruption and of having failed to represent the true interests of the German worker, he asserted that the Nazi swastika stood for an alliance between the hammer, the head, and the sword, rather than between the hammer and the purse.[15]

Yet Rosenberg took pains to explain that what he had in mind was not simply a Marxism minus the Jew, but rather the creation of an organic racial community based on cooperation between intellectuals and manual workers and on the exclusion of the un-German enemy.[16] Insisting that economics was secondary to politics, he maintained that socialism was essentially a means to defend the cultural values of the Volk and strengthen the state to ensure its freedom in the struggle for survival between races and peoples. For him as for other contemporary advocates of a German socialism, "socialism" did not involve national-izing production or redistributing the nation's wealth in accordance with principles of social justice, but rather represented the restoration of honor to German work, the treatment of all Germans as workers, and the replacement of a society based on class conflict with a *völkisch* community of work.[17]

As editor of the National Socialists' *Völkischer Beobachter* and orga-nizer of the *Kampfbund für Deutsche Kultur* ("Fighting League for German Culture"), Rosenberg undoubtedly contributed to Nazi victory. But his ponderous disquisition in *The Myth of the Twentieth Century* of 1930 on race, "race soul," and culture was ill-suited to attract a mass following to the NSDAP. It was left to others within the party to turn the notion of a national "socialism" based on a new ethic of work into a potent instrument of electoral politics.

We have already seen how Darré used ideas about work similar to those of Hitler and Rosenberg to win rural support for the NSDAP. In urban areas, concern with the problem of work was exploited most en-

---

Hitler's outlook, but fails to link it sufficiently with the racial and foreign political elements central to his Weltanschauung.

[15] Alfred Rosenberg, "Der Verrat am deutschen Arbeitertum" (1926) in Alfred Rosenberg, *Reden und Aufsätze von 1918–1933*, vol. 1 of *Blut und Ehre*, ed. Thilo von Trotha (Munich: Eher, 1934), 34; see also the extended version in *Kampf um die Macht. Aufsätze von 1921–1922*, ed. Thilo von Trotha (Munich: Eher, 1937), 484–503.

[16] Alfred Rosenberg, "Deutscher Student und deutscher Arbeiter" (1922), *Kampf um die Macht*, 161–64.

[17] Alfred Rosenberg, "Nationaler Sozialismus oder Nationalsozialismus" (1923), in *Kampf um die Macht*, 252–54, and "Soldat und Arbeiter" (1925), *Blut und Ehre* 1, 122–23.

ergetically by the men around Otto and Gregor Strasser. Often designated the Nazi "left," the Strassers together with Joseph Goebbels managed to establish the NSDAP in the industrialized west and north in the late 1920s. Gregor Strasser (1892–1934), who had participated in the unsuccessful Hitler Putsch of 1923, achieved prominence within the party soon after Hitler's release from prison and was promoted to chief party organizer in 1932. Because he fell out of favor in December of that year and was murdered during the party purge of July 1934, his ideas played no role in the Third Reich. During the *Kampfzeit*, however, the time of struggle before Hitler's accession to the chancellorship in January 1933, anyone who wished to know what the party stood for would have had to take Strasser's statements into account.

Strasser's version of "German socialism" included such "radical" economic measures as profit-sharing. It was buttressed by high-sounding statements about the need to replace the spirit of materialism—said to characterize both capitalism and Marxism—with an ethos stemming from "organic life itself" that would put work above property and prize achievement more than dividends. While conceding that differences among individuals would persist under National Socialism, Strasser insisted that distinctions of status and reward would in future rest not on wealth and ownership, as under capitalism, but on degrees of achievement and responsibility.[18] Rejecting Marxist egalitarianism, he stressed the idea of achievement or *Leistung* as a way of reassuring middle-class audiences that his socialist rhetoric need not be taken too seriously. Translated into the economic realm, the idea that the individuals, races, and nations that had proved their superiority in the competitive struggle for survival had a right to rule enabled Strasser to preserve, within his "German socialism," the essentials of capitalism: wages related to productivity, promotion on the basis of merit, free competition, and the right of those who rose to the top to control the means of production. Combined with a community of work, the achievement principle could also be expected to evoke a positive response among advocates of Werksgemeinschaft. The fact that a number of individuals within the business community proved ready to explore with Strasser the possibility of cooperation with the NSDAP demonstrates the effectiveness of these tactics.

Strasser also appealed to conservative nationalists. Stressing soldierly virtues, he espoused the cause of compulsory labor service as a replacement for military conscription and as the best way to foster the spirit of

---

[18] Gregor Strasser, "Gedanken über Aufgaben der Zukunft," *NS-Briefe* (15 June 1926), excerpted in Lane and Rupp, *Nazi Ideology before 1933*, 88–89.

honor and duty required to build the Third Reich. His original scheme of 1925 for *Arbeitsdienstpflicht* envisioned a compulsory one-year labor service during which all German males would be required to learn a trade. As an alternative, young men would be allowed to opt for a voluntary two-year stint in the army as preparation for leadership. Dubious about the feasibility and efficacy of blood tests, Nordicization, and similar measures of selection advocated by the racist wing of the party, Strasser thought this "Prussian" method would bring forward the biological elite best fitted to rule and most worthy of honor.[19] During the depression, when public opinion had in any case begun to favor an ethic of work based on duty rather than joy, Strasser proclaimed compulsory labor service as a central feature of the NSDAP's full employment program: necessary to restore Germany's economic health, it also constituted a valuable educational device with which to combat the Bolshevik spirit and to inculcate a German "idea of state."[20]

Flanked by such patriotic and conservative statements, Strasser's radical economic proposals lost some of their terror. But his ability to establish a reputation for himself as a Nazi "moderate"[21] also owed something to the fact that Goebbels (1897–1945) and his followers were espousing an even more extreme form of "socialism." A relative latecomer, having joined the NSDAP only in 1925, Goebbels quickly proved his worth as a party propagandist and organizer, first in the Rhineland and then in Berlin. Despite his own middle-class background, he insisted that only the proletariat would be able to liberate Germany from the "fetters of capitalism" and made it his objective to wean German workers away from Marxism and transform them into bearers of a successful National Socialist revolution. Where Hitler proposed to solve the problem of work and save Germany by eliminating Jewry, and where Rosenberg pinned his hopes for a victory of the German race soul on the creation of the Volk community, Goebbels thought it necessary for National Socialism to distance itself from and go beyond "bourgeois" antisemitism to espouse a policy combining radical socialism with aggressive nationalism.[22]

In his propaganda, Goebbels blamed capitalism for alienating and dehumanizing workers, so that the worker ceased to be "a lively human being . . . a shaper of things" and became merely "a gear in a factory

[19] Strasser, "Gedanken über Aufgaben der Zukunft," 90–94.

[20] Gregor Strasser, "Arbeit und Brot," from *Kampf um Deutschland* (Munich: Eher, 1932), excerpted in Lane and Rupp, *Nazi Ideology before 1933*, 140.

[21] Turner, *German Big Business*, 311–12.

[22] Joseph Goebbels, "Die Radikalisierung des Sozialismus," *NS-Briefe* (15 October 1925), excerpted in Lane and Rupp, *Nazi Ideology before 1933*, 80.

devoid of understanding or comprehension."[23] He also expressed his views on work and his determination to identify National Socialism with the cause of the laboring masses in a novel. *Michael*, published in 1929, tells of a middle-class veteran who abandons his studies and his girl to seek fulfillment as a miner. It glorifies work as a source of self-esteem and personal identity, as well as a means by which the individual can establish links with the soil and his fellow men.[24]

Forced by the depression crisis to compete more energetically than ever for the soul of the German worker, Goebbels changed his line somewhat. In an important speech given on October 1, 1931, at the Berlin Sportpalast and subsequently published as a pamphlet,[25] Goebbels accused not capitalism but Marxism of degrading the worker into a proletarian and depriving work of its moral worth. Whereas the Marxists lacked the creative force to give work a new meaning, the Nazis would teach workers to take pride in their achievements and to view themselves as valued members of the national community. Goebbels thus presented the NSDAP as the only party capable of revitalizing the German work ethic. He also maintained that the National Socialist state, run on the principle of discipline and authority that had so successfully built up the party, alone had the capacity to bring the workers' struggle for social justice to a victorious conclusion. He insisted, however, that the final objective of the NSDAP was not social justice but national grandeur: the mission of the workers was to "conquer Germany" for socialism so that Germany might go on to conquer the world.[26]

If the more conservative elements in German society found Goebbels's anti-capitalist propaganda alarming, they were even more upset by the NSDAP's attempts to conquer the streets and to extend the political struggle directly into the workplace. While the party's storm-troopers (SA, *Sturmabteilung*) marched and fought on their party's behalf, the NSBO under the leadership of Johannes Engel and Reinhold Muchow began to organize workers into Nazi cells within enterprises in different parts of the country. Four years after its formation in 1928 the NSBO with its 300,000 members had secured the election of rep-

[23] Joseph Goebbels, "Warum Arbeiterpartei?" *Der Angriff* (23 July 1928), as quoted in Turner, *German Big Business*, 65.

[24] James D. Wilkinson, *The Intellectual Resistance in Europe* (Cambridge: Harvard University Press, 1981), 12–13.; Klaus Theweleit, "Ich-Zerfall und Arbeit," in *Männerkörper: Zur Psychoanalyse des weissen Terrors*, vol. 2 of *Männerphantasien* (Frankfurt: Roter Stern, 1978), 270–74.

[25] Joseph Goebbels, *Vom Proletariat zum Volk* (Munich: Franz Eher, 1932), especially 18–24.

[26] Goebbels, *Vom Proletariat zum Volk*, 24.

resentatives to the works councils in competition with the traditional parties of the working class and had demonstrated the NSDAP's devotion to the cause of labor by occasionally supporting strikes.[27] Whatever doubts the party leadership might have had about the wisdom of this course, Muchow was determined to present the NSBO cells as agents of a revolution that would free German workers from the clutches of their betrayers, as a symbol of the "Arbeitertum of the future" and as an augury of an imminent "transformation of political and social relations."[28]

Judging by the NSBO's bi-monthly *Arbeitertum* and its monthly newsletter, *Der Deutsche Arbeiter*, little except the rejection of internationalism distinguished the program of the NSBO from that of the Communists. With its call for "Freedom and Bread," and promises of radical social change, the NSBO could hope to win over to the NSDAP not only unaffiliated workers and members of the yellow unions (with which the NSBO was often, mistakenly, identified), but also a number of radicalized trade unionists disillusioned with the established left-wing parties.[29]

Our brief survey of statements by leading Nazis about the problem of alienation demonstrates that by the early 1930s the National Socialists were expressing views that fitted in well with those canvassed by groups and individuals representing most sectors of society. Popular perceptions of Nazi intentions with respect to this issue, as well as Hitler's promises to put the country back to work and create a new society that would bridge class divisions, undoubtedly contributed substantially to the movement's ability to transform itself during the depression from a fringe phenomenon into the nation's largest party. In turn, the ability of National Socialism to attract support from all social classes and occupational groups, including large numbers of ordinary "workers," undoubtedly made its claim to be the agent of a new Volksgemeinschaft more plausible.

What is more, the National Socialists managed to appropriate and redefine for their own use the closely related notion of "German work," *Deutsche Arbeit*. Exploiting their compatriots' heightened sense of nationalism and the widespread longing for national renewal, they argued

[27] Kele, *Nazis and Workers*, 149–55, 169–72.

[28] Reinhold Muchow, "Die erste Durchbruchsschlacht der N.S.B.O.," in Roland Böttcher, *Erfolge Nationalsozialistischer Betriebszellen. Arbeitertum*, special issue (Spring 1931), 1–2.

[29] For an excellent summary of the controversy about relations among the NSDAP, the KPD, and the German "working class," see Conan Fischer, "Class Enemies or Class Brothers? Communist-Nazi Relations in Germany 1929–33," *European History Quarterly* 15 (1985): 259–79, and the subsequent discussion, 454–71.

that Germans were bound together not only by blood, but also by a shared ethic of work and capacity for work. By so doing, they were able to win over many sincere idealists and social reformers who would not have been attracted to a program of racial discrimination or imperialist expansionism, along with members of the Mittelstand who were most prone to regard their own approach to work as a defining national characteristic. But at the height of the depression, nationalism was not confined to the middle classes. When radicalized workers were faced with the choice between the KPD, with its rhetoric of class conflict and proletarian internationalism, and the patriotic NSDAP, Hitler's talk of Germany as a land of work and of all true Germans as workers in a common cause undoubtedly helped to ensure that it was the Nazis rather than the communists who became heirs to the Weimar Republic—which both parties were doing their best to subvert.

When first appointed German Chancellor in January 1933, Hitler had to share authority with Hugenberg's German Nationalists. It took him about two years to dismantle what remained of the Weimar constitution, impose his will on government and party, and gain the legitimacy needed to set the nation on a new, National Socialist, course. During this initial phase of the Third Reich, his task was made significantly easier by the fact that influential members of the German elite convinced themselves that the Nazis sincerely desired to tackle the problem of work. Not particularly unhappy about the Republic's demise, these people, like the majority of middle-class German professionals and academics, very much wanted to believe that the new government would bring in the reforms they had long advocated.[30]

For a time it did look as if the Nazis were serious about overcoming the barriers of class and status that heretofore had hampered efforts to solve the problem of modern work. Many reformers consequently hurried to put forward their own ideas for resolving the national crisis. The resulting plethora of projects quickly revealed a major conflict between those who hoped to establish a corporate state more or less like that with which Italian Fascism was experimenting and the advocates of a second revolution leading to a genuinely socialist new order. In addition, anti-modernists confronted enthusiasts for "progress" determined to shape the Third Reich in accordance with their technocratic vision, and conservatives who believed in the need to restore traditional Christian values clashed with racist radicals seeking a "biological" cure for the nation's ills. Often confusingly enmeshed with one another, these

[30] See Konrad H. Jarausch, "The Crisis of German Professions 1918–33," *JCH* 20 (1985): 379–98

various schemes became part of a debate about work in many respects similar to that which had been set off by the revolutionary crisis of 1918/19.

However, by the mid-1930s, the new regime had made certain choices that set limits to the debate in this, as in other, areas of national life. It had also become evident that Germany's new rulers, although happy enough to capitalize on the initial willingness of many prominent individuals to give them the benefit of the doubt, were not inclined to listen to people of independent mind. Disdainful of intellectuals as a class and applying their own criteria, the National Socialists cast aside many who would have continued to serve them loyally had they been permitted to do so.

Among those destined to be discarded early on was Bang of the DNVP, who had been briefly raised to a position of influence by his close association with Hugenberg. Convinced that his ideas about Werksgemeinschaft were about to be realized, Bang welcomed the destruction of the trade unions in early May of 1933 and did his best to demonstrate that he, too, stood for a German socialism. In an essay of June 1933, he used National Socialist terminology to define socialism as "the taming of the principle of self interest through the ideal of the common welfare," proposed that the idea of class and class war be replaced with the corporatist principle of occupational groupings, and argued that industrial relations should henceforth be founded on a new leader-follower ethos. Warning against excessive reliance on structural as against attitudinal changes, as well as against the identification of the idea of "calling" with the interests of a particular group or job category, he redefined Beruf in terms of obligation to the common task and to the Werk, both to be embedded in an authoritarian political and economic community dominated by the nation.[31]

Despite this public restatement of his ideas in National Socialist garb, Bang failed to gain a foothold in the Third Reich. Instead, he disappeared from the scene after Hugenberg's resignation on June 26 and the dissolution of the DNVP the next day. However, others continued to propagate similar views, for example Professor Weddigen (1895–?) of the University of Jena.[32] Weddigen placed himself in the tradition of Riehl, Bismarck, Abbe, Zwiedineck-Südenhorst, Spann, and Albrecht, and claimed that this tradition culminated in the corporatist National Socialism embodied in the Law for the Organization

[31] Paul Bang, "Zum berufständischen Aufbau," Soziale Erneuerung (1933), 9:265–75.

[32] Walter Weddigen, ed., Deutsche Sozialpolitik (Berlin: Junker und Dünnhaupt, 1935). See also Enno Heine, Arbeit und Kapital im Ständestaat im Gegensatz zum Staate der Vergangenheit (2d ed.; Berlin: Carl Heymanns, 1934).

of National Work of January 1934. This law established the framework for an occupational reorganization of the economy and, along with other government measures like the destruction of independent trade unions, seemed to lead straight towards a German corporatism of the kind favored by Bang and other conservative nationalists.

Both reflecting and giving substance to this illusion was the creation in May 1933 of the National-Sozialistisches Institut für Ständewesen (National Socialist Institute for Corporatism) in Düsseldorf. Financed by the steel magnate Fritz Thyssen and Dr. Klein of IG Farben, the Institute offered courses on business and economics that stressed the principle of cooperation between business and labor along Werksgemeinschaft lines. It also sought to practice what it preached by involving workers alongside representatives of management in its activities.[33] Among the Institute's instructors was Walter Heinrich of the University of Vienna who maintained that corporatism was fully compatible with National Socialism because the latter regarded both employers and employees as "soldiers in the ranks of the economic army of the nation." Insisting that corporatism was neither Marxist-utopian nor capitalist-reactionary, Heinrich urged that everything possible be done once again to root the individual worker in an economic community, so as to restore joy in work and bridge the destructive gap between work and life that prevented the emergence of true Volksgemeinschaft.[34]

Another indication that the National Socialists were sympathetic to corporatism as a solution to the problem of work was the creation of an Amt für ständischen Aufbau ("Bureau for Corporatist Reconstruction") within the NSDAP's head office. However, the strongly anticapitalist and interventionist "corporatism" espoused by these Nazis bore little resemblance to the conservative version favored by big business. Whereas people like Bang and Heinrich regarded corporatism as a device for securing economic self-regulation for private enterprise within a national framework, in the hands of the Nazis it became a weapon for subordinating capitalist interests to the National Socialist state.

In this guise it proved particularly attractive to professional engi-

[33] On the founding of the Institut für Ständewesen, see Schneider, *Unternehmer und Demokratie*, 181. Further details can be found in its own publications including the *Programmatische Richtlinien* of 1933, and in the course calendars for 1933, 1934, and 1935. The Institute published a weekly, originally entitled *Braune Wirtschafts-Post* and renamed in 1934 *Der Nationalsozialistische Wirtschaftsdienst des Westens*.

[34] Walter Heinrich, *Die Soziale Frage. Ihre Entstehung in der individualistischen und ihre Lösung in der ständischen Ordnung* (Jena: Gustav Fischer, 1934), 161–63, 195. Heinrich's book was based in part on lectures given at the Institute, but the course calendars indicate that he was only briefly associated with it.

neers. The pattern linking the engineers with corporatism had already been established in the NSDAP's early days by Gottfried Feder, an engineer himself, who served as the party's foremost economics expert during the *Kampfzeit*.[35] One of its active promoters in the early years of the Third Reich was an engineering professor, Willy Müller, who had been greatly influenced by a trip to Fascist Italy in 1927. In the first issue of the NSDAP's social policy journal, Müller assigned the state a major role in transforming industrial relations, and called for the creation of a Reichsamt für Arbeitskultur ("Federal Department for Work Culture") whose job it would be to cultivate "a higher ethical conception of work" based on "honor, justice and decency in the work relationship" as the foundation for the corporatist new order.[36]

Similarly inclined to support a National Socialist corporatism that promised to check the power of big business were certain Christian trade unionists, like Brauer, and leaders of the organized Mittelstand who saw corporatism as the modern expression of the occupational principle exemplified by the medieval guild system. However, corporatism during this period remained primarily a device promoted by big business to defend its economic interests against both its small competitors and the state. As such, German corporatism was bound to fall foul of the Nazis, dedicated as they were to the primacy of politics over economics. In November 1937 its fate was sealed with the dismissal of Hjalmar Schacht, Reich Minister of Finance since 1934 and creator of the Reich Economic Chamber that had seemed set to become the apex of a corporatist "Organization of Industry."[37] The extent of its defeat was symbolized by the rejection of Othmar Spann's application for party membership after the *Anschluss* with Austria in 1938 and the emigration in 1939 of Fritz Thyssen, an early supporter of Hitler, and chair since 1935 of the board of the Institut für Ständewesen.[38]

As far as Germany's engineers were concerned, the main attraction of National Socialism was not so much corporatism as the belief that

[35] See Lane and Rupp, *Nazi Ideology before 1933*, 32–40.
[36] Willy Müller, "Arbeitskultur," *N.S. Sozialpolitik* 1 (1933): 80–84. Müller wanted his new department to have both policing and educative functions. In cooperation with the NSBO and the German Labor Front (DAF), it would be able to compel managers as well as wage earners to conform to the new ethic of work, if necessary by excluding the ineducable among them from leadership roles in the economy.
[37] Tim Mason, "The Primacy of Politics," in S. J. Woolf, ed., *The Nature of Fascism* (London: Weidenfeld & Nicolson, 1968), 177.
[38] Avraham Barkai, *Das Wirtschaftssystem des Nationalsozialismus. Der historische und ideologische Hintergrund, 1933–1936* (Cologne: Berend von Nottbeck, 1977), 94–96; David Schoenbaum, *Hitler's Social Revolution* (1st ed. 1966; reprint New York: Norton, 1980), 121–24. References are to the 1980 edition.

the Nazis intended to put the technical expert in command and would use their power to realize the ideal of production for use instead of for profit. This had been the message of a popular pamphlet of 1932 by a Nazi engineer, Peter Schwerber. Writing for a series sponsored by Feder, Schwerber argued that engineers should be given a major role not only in industry but also in political affairs, on the grounds that they were the best spokesmen for the new, post-capitalist age that would emerge after the destruction of Jewish finance.[39] Soon after the inauguration of the Third Reich, this was followed up by Rudolf Heiss who edited a book of essays entitled *The Mission of the Engineer in the New State.* Heiss, who had joined the NSDAP in March 1933,[40] welcomed the Third Reich on the grounds that it would honor all the creative elements in the nation and fuse them with Technology.[41]

Engineers did in fact make a remarkably successful adjustment to the new regime, generally managed to advance their careers, and in many instances were rewarded with leadership positions in line with their aspirations.[42] One of the most successful was the Dinta's Arnhold, who organized the DAF's vocational training branch to spread the model of the Dinta engineer along with Dinta-style skills and management training to all parts of the country. Other technologically trained individuals also did well in the Third Reich. Robert Ley, who became head of the DAF, was an industrial chemist formerly employed by IG Farben. Even greater power was attained by Fritz Todt, builder of the autobahnen, and by Albert Speer, the National Socialist architect who headed the DAF's Beauty of Labor (Schönheit der Arbeit, SdA) program from its creation in January 1934: during the war, Todt and Speer, in turn, served as Minister of Armaments and Munitions.

Much less successful in keeping on good terms with the National Socialists were a number of reform-minded academics who in 1933 had hoped that Hitler shared or could be converted to their views. For ex-

---

[39] Peter Schwerber, *Nationalsozialismus und Technik* (2d ed.; Munich: Eher, 1932).

[40] Information from the party membership card in the BDC, which shows that Heiss was associated with the Karlsruhe TH's Institute for Refrigeration Technology.

[41] Rudolf Heiss, ed., *Die Sendung des Ingenieurs im neuen Staat* (Berlin: VdI-Verlag, 1934), 26–27. In the same volume, Heinrich Hardensett, author of an earlier work that had favorably contrasted the technician with the capitalist, claimed that only the engineer, inspired by the desire to create rather than to exploit, was capable of realizing genuine community, and restoring joy in work. For this reason, leadership in industry was to be reassigned to technical people, selected on the basis of objective criteria that took both idealism and knowledge into account. Heinrich Hardensett, "Vom technisch-schöpferischen Menschen," in *Sendung des Ingenieurs,* 12–17; Herf, *Reactionary Modernism,* 181–88.

[42] See Gert Hortleder, *Das Gesellschaftsbild des Ingenieurs* (Frankfurt: Suhrkamp, 1970), 124–29, and Karl-Heinz Ludwig, *Technik und Ingenieure im Dritten Reich* (Düsseldorf: Droste, 1974).

ample, the industrial sociologist Briefs, in a management text of 1934, argued at some length that the Nazi victory had laid the foundation for the reforms of management practices, worker attitudes, and state social policy needed to overcome alienation at its source in the workplace.[43] Convinced that Nazism spelled the end of the Marxist devaluation of work, Briefs welcomed the destruction of the trade unions as a demonstrative act proving that the Nazis had no intention of overturning the capitalist status quo. He also welcomed the new labor laws for their stress on the importance of the enterprise as the basic unit of the Volksgemeinschaft. Finally, he maintained that recent legislation upholding the honor of labor could serve as a model for other nations and had good words for the SA, which he claimed had raised the workers' social status, and for the SdA division of the DAF which had started to sponsor practical reforms of the work environment at the plant level.

Despite his enthusiasm for what he deemed to be the Nazi ideology of work, Briefs, a devout Catholic and supporter of the Republic, refused to join the NSDAP and soon came under intense pressure from his National Socialist students. These not only questioned the continued relevance of his work, but showed themselves unconvinced by his apparent conversion to Nazism. Forced to curtail his lectures as early as the summer of 1934, Briefs was unable to prevent the purge of Jews from the Berlin Institute's staff or to obtain the funding needed to secure its continued existence. Fearing for his personal safety, he accepted a visiting professorship in the United States in 1934 and two years later decided to relinquish his academic tenure and emigrate on a permanent basis.[44]

Somewhat more tenacious was Brauer of the University of Cologne. Editor since 1917 of the Catholic monthly *Deutsche Arbeit*, Brauer had always stressed the "Germanness" of his corporatist ideas as well as their roots in the Christian social tradition: as ideologist of the Christian Trade Unions he had promoted the creation of a community of performance (*Leistungsgemeinschaft*) on the basis of "Germanic character."[45]

[43] Goetz Briefs, *Betriebsführung und Betriebsleben in der Industrie* (Stuttgart: Ferdinand Enke, 1934), 131–42.

[44] Wilke, "Briefs," 347. See also Thomas Hahn, "Industriesoziologie als Wirklichkeitswissenschaft? Zwischen Empirie und Kult," in Urs Jaeggi et al., eds., *Geist und Katastrophe. Studien zur Soziologie im Nationalsozialismus* (Berlin: Wissenschaftlicher Autoren-Verlag, 1983), 191–206. Wilke leaves open the question whether Brief's public statements of 1934 represented his convictions or were merely expedients to secure the publication of his text and/or ensure his personal safety; Hahn, who emphasizes the concordance between Brief's previously expressed views and Nazi policies, concludes that he was sincere in his pro-Nazi stance.

[45] Brauer, *Sozialpolitik und Sozialreform*, 74, and "Die berufsständische Idee in Sozialpolitik und Sozialreform," 383–84.

After 1933 Brauer not only supported the incorporation of the Christian unions into the DAF, but also declared himself in favor of Nazi racist doctrine. A member of the "Kreuz und Adler" ("Cross and Eagle") society founded by vice-chancellor von Papen to reconcile Catholics and Nazis, he published a book on the Catholic in the Third Reich, and contributed to the periodical *Zeit und Volk* ("Time and People") that represented German Catholics as the most genuine defenders of the Reich idea.[46] Yet, like Briefs, Brauer failed to persuade the Nazis of his loyalty and was eventually forced into exile.[47]

Just how powerful the temptation was for Catholic social reformers to come to terms with National Socialism is illustrated by the case of Ernst Michel. Despite the fact that the regime, by March 1933, had already closed the Frankfurt Academy of Labor, of which he was the director,[48] Michel continued to promulgate his reform ideas and in the process did his best to find things about National Socialism that deserved praise. As late as 1937 he not only gave the Nazis credit for developing a unique organization of labor, for stressing "national work" as a fundamental ethical principle in propaganda and law, and for giving due weight to the social honor and dignity of the worker, but also asserted that in order to solve the problem of alienation, it was necessary to develop the social possibilities of the modern factory as a "racially appropriate ordering of available labor power."[49] Only in the following year did he finally abandon his attempts at accommodation and opt for "inner emigration."[50]

A kind of inner emigration was also the eventual response to Nazism of the philosopher Martin Heidegger (1889–1976), probably the most

[46] See Guenther Lewy, *The Catholic Church and Nazi Germany* (New York: McGraw-Hill, 1964), 46, 108, 365; Klaus Breuning, *Die Vision des Reiches. Deutscher Katholizismus zwischen Demokratie und Diktatur* (Munich: Max Hueber, 1969), 183–85; Michael Schneider, *Die christlichen Gewerkschaften 1894–1933* (Bonn: Neue Gesellschaft, 1982), 714–19, 762. Bernard Zimmermann-Buhr, *Die katholische Kirche und der Nationalsozialismus in den Jahren 1930–1933* (Frankfurt: Campus, 1982), analyzes the grounds on which Catholic theologians and intellectuals justified ideological support for National Socialism, despite reservations about the racist element in Nazi doctrine and opposition to the ruthlessness of National Socialist methods. See especially 72–93 and 108–11.

[47] Brauer, honorary professor at Cologne since 1928, tried unsuccessfully to get a regular university post as late as Spring 1935. He emigrated to the U.S. in 1937, but only relinquished his honorary professorship in 1940. See Ludwig Geck and Bernhard Ridder, *Theodor Brauer. Ein sozialer Kämpfer* (Cologne: Kolping-Verlag, 1952).

[48] Otto Antrick, *Die Akademie der Arbeit in der Universität Frankfurt a. M. Idee, Werden, Gestalt* (Darmstadt: Eduard Roether, 1966), 45.

[49] Ernst Michel, *Sozialgeschichte der industriellen Arbeitswelt* (Limburg: Gebr. Steffen, 1937), 99–100, 121.

[50] After retraining as a psychotherapist, Michel went into private practice in Frankfurt. *Internationales Soziologenlexikon* (1980), s.v. Michel, Ernst.

prestigious German academic to lend his name to the National Socialist cause during the regime's first years. Appointed Rector of the University of Freiburg in 1933, Heidegger became an enthusiastic party
member in May of that year, used his position publicly to praise the
new regime, and actively supported student participation in the labor
service on the grounds that it constituted a prime educational device
to imbue the new academic generation with a proper attitude to work
and community, while creating a much-needed bond between workers
of the brain and the fist.[51]

Possessed of a romantic reverence for the peasantry whose rootedness
(Bodenständigkeit) he valued greatly,[52] Heidegger believed at first that
the Nazis shared his ideals. However, by 1935 he became convinced
that Nazism had been perverted by technology and was deviating from
the path of true German being.[53] Having already resigned from the rectorship in February 1934 when it had become apparent that he could
exercise no real control over developments in the university,[54] he soon
withdrew entirely from the public sphere, but not before the damage
had been done. By supporting the Hitler movement at the start, when
it was weakest, by vigorously promoting a "German" work ethic indis-
tinguishable from that to be found in Mein Kampf or the propaganda of
the Labor Service,[55] and by failing at any point explicitly to repudiate
National Socialism, Heidegger helped to give ideological legitimacy to
a regime many of whose actions he undoubtedly deplored.[56]

The above examples should suffice to illustrate the difficulty that educated Germans with established reputations faced when trying to determine how they should react to National Socialism. In part, their
troubles stemmed from the erroneous assumption, based on an overes-
timation of their own importance, that the nation's new rulers would
be happy to listen to their advice on how best to resolve the problem
of work and would welcome their cooperation in resolving the national
crisis. But the difficulty of charting a tenable course was compounded

[51] Heidegger's views on work are documented in Guido Schneeberger, Nachlese zu Heidegger (Bern: Buchdruckerei Suhr, 1962), and analyzed in relation to National Socialism by
Georges-Arthur Goldschmidt, "Travail et National-socialisme," L'Allemagne d'Aujourd'hui
(1973): 11–22.

[52] Goldschmidt, "Travail et National-socialisme," 18, and Schneeberger, Nachlese zu Heidegger, Doc. 185.

[53] Herf, Reactionary Modernism, 114–15

[54] Wistrich, Who's Who in Nazi Germany, 126–28.

[55] Goldschmidt, "Travail et National-socialisme," 14–17.

[56] For a balanced discussion of Heidegger and National Socialism, touching on the relationship between his pro-Nazi views and his philosophical position, see George Steiner, Heidegger (Hassocks, Sussex: Harvester Press, 1978), 111–21.

by the fact that the National Socialists, after they came to power, continued to disagree among themselves. Quite apart from the growing
discrepancy between ideal and reality, this meant that it was genuinely
hard to judge exactly what constituted official policy.

With respect to the ideology of work, differences among party
spokesmen were due in part to the existence of separate and rival authorities within the movement. The "Nazi" work ethic was actively
propagated, among others, by the National Labor Service (RAD), the
Hitler Youth (HJ), and the DAF, each of which directed its message to
the general public as well as to its designated clientele. Making the
situation even more bewildering was the range of positions on key
points of ideology taken up by individuals within each of these organizations.

For example, several versions of the work ideal coexisted within the
RAD. As a professional soldier its chief, Konstantin Hierl (1875–
1955), wanted RAD camps to teach the military virtues of obedience
and subordination. Apparently assuming that people only worked
when forced to do so, Hierl relied on strict discipline to inculcate an
ethic of duty instead of attempting to foster free conformity with communal goals in the spirit of the pre-Nazi FAD.[57] Hierl also thought that
the RAD had a mission to renew the tie between blood and soil through
labor on the land.[58] By contrast, some members of the younger generation within the RAD sought to carry over the ideals of the Weimar
FAD into the extended, compulsory Nazi scheme. Thus the engineer
Helmut Stellrecht (1898–?), who had come up through the youth
movement, served at the Front, and fought with a *Freicorps* after the
war, warned against excessive over-organization of the RAD and called
for a new style of leadership that would combine the values of the FAD
with military virtues. Whereas Hierl and his like were prone to pit
Pflicht against *Freude*, Stellrecht, citing Winnig, argued that the two
were compatible and, indeed, that the "Germanic idea of work" entailed viewing work as a blessing and as freely chosen service to community.[59] The RAD should therefore produce people who would serve
the community through their labors not just out of a sense of duty but
also with inner joy.[60]

[57] Benz, "Vom freiwilligen Arbeitsdienst," 346–47.

[58] Konstantin Hierl, "Arbeitsdienst," in *Deutsche Sozialisten am Werk*, ed. F. C. Prinz von
Schaumburg-Lippe (Berlin: Deutscher Verlag für Politik und Wirtschaft, 1936), 113–16.

[59] Helmut Stellrecht, *Der Deutsche Arbeitsdienst. Aufgaben, Organisation, Aufbau* (Berlin:
E. S. Mittler, 1933), especially 1–12, 18–23; Benz, "Vom Freiwilligen Arbeitsdienst," 339–
44; Karl Christoph Lingelbach, *Erziehung und Erziehungstheorien im nationalsozialistischen
Deutschland* (Weinheim: Julius Beltz, 1970), 130–46.

[60] See also Fritz Mang, *Der Deutsche Arbeiter im Dritten Reich*, vol. 2 of *Sozialismus im Dritten*

Although the militarist ethos eventually dominated the RAD, the youth movement influence carried over long enough to make the Labor Service and through it National Socialism attractive also to many older conservatives, people who would have found a labor service organized along exclusively military lines incompatible with their attitudes to work. Heidegger certainly fell in this category, as did the popular *völkisch* author Walter Beumelburg (1899–?), who not only welcomed the Nazi RAD as a legitimate successor to similar movements going back to Napoleonic times, but proceeded to extol it as a step to utopia based on a new ethos that would enable Germans to view work once more as an end rather than a means to obtain consumer goods, and to prize it as the best weapon against inner distraction (*Zerreissung*).[61]

Similar internal ambivalence was present in the Hitler Youth (HJ). Despite a tendency towards regimentation and a growing emphasis on para-military training, there were genuine efforts to carry on the youth movement tradition of relying on persuasion rather than compulsion in instilling positive attitudes towards work. Even more than the RAD, the HJ seems to have attracted leaders who believed that duty need not be onerous and that work could be a source of joy. On the other hand, the HJ's capacity to further joy in work on a significant scale was limited by its initial reliance on voluntary participation and, even more, by its function as an organizer of after-school activities.[62]

Of all the National Socialist organizations to address the problem of work, the "German Labor Front" (*Deutsche Arbeitsfront*, DAF) was most consistently dedicated to the promotion of Arbeitsfreude. Already in 1925 Robert Ley, who was to become the DAF's head after the Nazis came to power, had emphasized the connection between creativity and personal fulfillment, and had insisted that it was essential to make work once more the individual's highest good. At that time, he believed the way to do this was to bring wages into accord with the creative capacities of every worker and improve the link between human being and

---

Reich (Berlin: Paul Hochmuth, 1937), 7. As late as 1937, Fritz Mang (1904–?), an Austrian-born DAF activist, argued that as organized by the National Socialists, the RAD represented an important weapon in the fight to realize "German socialism." Stripping manual laborers of their inferiority complex and intellectuals of their pretensions to higher status, it would restore joy in work and complete the integration of the workers into the Volksgemeinschaft.

[61] Walter Beumelburg, *Arbeit ist Zukunft. Ziele des deutschen Arbeitsdienstes* (Oldenburg: Gerhard Stalling, 1933). See also Liselotte Klose-Stiller, *Arbeitsdienst für die weibliche Jugend in Schlesien 1930–1945. Versuch einer Würdigung der Arbeit weiblicher Jugendlicher im Einsatz für die Allgemeinheit* (Garmisch-Partenkirchen, 1978), especially 40–42. Klose-Stiller claims that Hierl shared this ideal of work and regarded the RAD as a continuator of the FAD tradition.

[62] On the educational role of the HJ, see Peter D. Stachura, "Das Dritte Reich und Jugenderziehung: Die Rolle der Hitlerjugend 1933–1939," in Manfred Heinemann, ed., *Erziehung und Schulung im Dritten Reich* (Stuttgart: Klett-Cotta, 1980), 1:90–112.

work through better vocational training, job placement, and workplace design.[63] Later in the decade, while working for IG Farben, Ley became a supporter of the Dinta, which expressed notions about humanizing industrial work through skills training and reformed management practices that paralleled his own.[64]

Formed in 1933 on the ruins of the German trade union movement and reorganized in 1934, the DAF seemed destined to dominate Germany's domestic affairs. By appointing Ley to lead it, Hitler put him in a position to reform labor relations and reshape German attitudes to work. Ley, convinced that one of National Socialism's primary objectives was to make work once more a blessing rather than a curse, began at once to tackle the problem of work on all fronts. While the SdA under Albert Speer was created to improve workplace design and produce a clean, bright, and attractive work environment, Arnhold's vocational training branch was assigned the task of raising the general level of skills and inculcating good work attitudes. The DAF also promoted the spirit of works community through organized activities involving all "workers" from the boss on down: works festivals initiated by company-based youth troops, the *Werkscharen*, and leisure programs sponsored by its "Strength through Joy" (*Kraft durch Freude*, KdF) division. Finally, to reach a wider public, it sponsored a major exhibition devoted to German work in conjunction with the second Nazi May Day celebrations of 1934 and organized an architectural competition in the same year for a "House of Labor" (*Haus der Arbeit*). The latter, meant to demonstrate the principle of *Volksgemeinschaft*, attracted over six hundred entrants, among them such avant-garde architects as Walter Gropius and Mies van der Rohe.[65]

By such means the DAF sought to prove that it took seriously the challenge of restoring joy in work. Whether Ley and his associates acted out of concern for the individual worker or whether they were motivated solely by the desire to ensure domestic tranquility and in-

[63] See the documents in Wolfgang Jünemann, ed., *Werksgemeinschaft* (Frankfurt: Moritz Diesterweg, 1938), 52–54.

[64] John Gillingham, "The 'Deproletarianization' of German Society. Vocational Training in the Third Reich," *Journal of Social History* 19 (1986): 425. Gillingham implies that Ley got many of his ideas from Arnhold who "devised a good portion of what passed for Nazi labor ideology as well as many of the peculiar institutions set up to promote it"; but it is just as likely that the two had independently adopted notions about the humanization of work, then very much in vogue.

[65] See Winfried Nerdinger, "Versuchung und Dilemma der Avantgarden im Spiegel der Architekturwettbewerbe 1933–1935," in *Faschistische Architekturen*, ed. Hartmut Frank (Hamburg: Hans Christians, 1985), 75–81. The project was scrapped after Hitler decided none of the plans submitted were good enough.

crease the productivity of German industry at minimum cost while preparing the nation for war, was and remains subject to debate. Although the latter most likely is a fair description of Hitler's stance,[66] Ley was probably sincere in his desire to solve the problem of alienation and to make the German worker happy both as producer and consumer. But whatever Ley's motives, the fact remains that he secured the active participation in DAF projects of thousands of individuals from all walks of life, many of them volunteers, and there can be no doubt that a good proportion of these people cooperated with the DAF because they genuinely believed that it intended to carry on and extend German efforts to humanize the world of work and nurture Arbeitsfreude. In turn, DAF propagandists intensively exploited evidence of popular involvement to create a picture of a nation united as never before, and on its way to a happier, more prosperous, and peaceful future.[67]

DAF spokesmen were still calling for workplace reforms on the eve of war. In 1939 Hermann Textor, formerly of the NSBO,[68] cited de Man to the effect that Germans were congenitally unsuited to monotonous work and longed for personal, creative labor. To make the best possible use of the nation's talents and restore joy in work it was therefore necessary to give priority to the reform of work and of the economy as a whole.[69] Similarly, a practical handbook published jointly by the health divisions of the NSDAP and the DAF used the demand for Arbeitsfreude to justify extensive reforms in the working conditions of both men and women.[70]

Other DAF spokesmen adopted the belief widely held by Weimar experts that the problem of work could be solved simply by changing attitudes. This view was eloquently expressed in 1933 by Willi Börger, recently appointed as lecturer on "German socialism" by the faculty of

[66] See Hans-Gerd Schumann, *Nationalsozialismus und Gewerkschaftsbewegung. Die Vernichtung der deutschen Gewerkschaften und der Aufbau der 'Deutschen Arbeitsfront'* (Hannover: Norddeutsche Verlagsanstalt O. Goedel, 1958), 145.

[67] Cf. "Arbeitsstolz und Arbeitsfreude—Bausteine nationalsozialistisher Sozialpolitik," *NS.-Sozialpolitik* 4 (1937): 194–97 which, having identified the Nazis as proponents of Arbeitsfreude, claimed they had "made it possible for the worker to express his personality on the job and to sustain his joy in work and his social capacities in the workplace." See also Anton Riedler, *Politische Arbeitslehre. Einführung in die weltanschauliche Begründung des Arbeitsrechtes* (Berlin: Wirtschaftsverlag A. Sudau, 1937), 90–93, who argued that only the Nazis, with their emphasis on Life, could bring about the needed reforms of work and the workplace.

[68] Information from personnel card, BDC. Born 1913, Textor was listed as a Catholic living in Munich.

[69] Hermann Textor, *Völkische Arbeitseignung* (Frankfurt: Forschungsinstitut für Arbeitsgestaltung, 1939).

[70] Hermann Hebestreit, *et al.*, *Schutz und Erhaltung der Arbeitskraft* (Berlin: Otto Elsner, 1939).

Cologne University. An NSBO activist, National Socialist member of the Reichstag, and one of the first labor trustees (*Treuhänder der Arbeit*) to be appointed under the new labor law, Börger flatly maintained that, where the right spirit prevails, "work gives joy and people take pleasure in their tasks, even when these are hard."[71] It was in this spirit that the DAF devised ever new methods to instill the correct Nazi work ethic. For instance, a KdF pamphlet of 1935 gave detailed instructions for creating a spirit of community in the workplace through the organization of works festivals and printed several spoken choruses (*Sprechchöre*) glorifying work, for use on such occasions.[72]

The National Socialists not only tried to persuade Germans that the Third Reich intended to promote Arbeitsfreude, it also sought to project this image of the Hitler regime to the world at large. The chief vehicle for this was the International Central Office "Freude und Arbeit" (FuA), established in 1936 with headquarters in Berlin. The FuA's first project, the 1936 "World Congress for Leisure and Recreation," met in Hamburg under the honorary chairmanship of Hitler's deputy, Rudolf Hess, and was presided over by Ley. With sixty-one countries represented, it focused on the problem of leisure rather than of work, but the German participants made a point of stressing the intimate connection between the two. Holding up the KdF with its Beauty of Labor division as a model to the world, they insisted that industrialized nations needed to deal with the whole human being, from morning to evening, with emphasis on the workplace, for the mutual benefit of employers and workers. In Ley's own words, "We must remove from labor the connotation of burden, disgrace, inferiority and oppression, and once more make work a joy for mankind."[73]

[71] Willi Börger in the DAF's *Arbeitertum* (15 September 1933) quoted in *Ruhr und Rhein*, 19 September 1933.

[72] Otto Schmidt, ed., *Arbeit, Ehre, Freiheit. Ein Handbuch Nationalsozialistischer Gemeinschaftsfeier*, commissioned by the NSG. 'Kraft durch Freude,' Gau Württemberg-Hohenzollern (Stuttgart: NS.-Presse Württemberg, 1935). Similar handbooks for use by the Nazi Werkscharen included Fritz Irwahn's *Feste der Arbeit* and *Betriebsappelle und Kameradschaftsabende*, published in repeated editions between 1934 and 1944 by the Hanseatische Verlagsanstalt in Hamburg. Although the DAF rejected the parallel [see Alwin Rüssser, *Die Werkfeier. Auftrag und Erfüllung* (Frankfurt: Moritz Diesterweg, 1940), 21] the DAF, by these and other means, promoted a National Socialist cult of work similar to that which Ernst Horneffer had advocated in the 1920s. Despite an early declaration of faith in the *Führer* [see his *Oswald Spengler* (Stuttgart: Fr. Frommanns, 1934)], Horneffer failed to gain acceptance from the Nazis who held his Masonic past against him, as well as his former affiliation with the DDP and his alleged philosemitism. Information from Horneffer file, BDC, and IfZ MA-141/6 0347259-68 (National Archives T81 R196). On the Nazi cult of work, Hans-Jochen Gamm, *Der braune Kult. Das Dritte Reich und seine Ersatzreligion* (Hamburg: Rütten und Loening, 1962), Chapter 6.

[73] Robert Ley, address to the first committee of the World Congress, reproduced in *Welt-*

By giving work a central place in their approach to the newly perceived problem of leisure, the National Socialists showed themselves to be heirs to a distinctively German tradition. Rather than being modelled on the Italian Dopolavoro,[74] the KdF probably derived its recreational programs on similar activities sponsored in the Weimar period by the white-collar unions.[75] It should also be recalled that the Weimar Dinta had encouraged employers to organize leisure programs in order to secure the joyful allegiance of their workers.

While maintaining that recreation must be subordinated to work, DAF spokesmen nevertheless refused to espouse the rather dour "duty" version of the work ethic propounded by many conservatives. Repeatedly attacking the churches for emphasizing sin, humility, and penance in their exhortations, Ley explicitly rejected puritanism and insisted on the right of people to enjoy the whole of life.[76] Considered to be intimately connected, both Arbeitsfreude and Lebensfreude were part of the National Socialist message as projected by the DAF. In the words of Heinrich Härtle (1909–?), a party member and SS activist since 1927, "We do not only work in order to live, we also live in order to work. And after doing our duty at work, we should experience a noble joy in life."[77]

---

kongress für Freizeit und Erholung (Hamburg: Hanseatische Verlagsanstalt, 1937), 202–204. Addressing the plenary session on July 24, 1936, the Strength-through-Joy official Horst Dressler-Andress likewise maintained that it was wrong to draw a firm line between work and leisure, ibid., 69–73. See also "Schönheit der Arbeit" by the engineer Karl Kretschmer, ibid., 310–16, and "Joy in work through the beautiful and enthralling [fesselnde] work place" by an engineer-cum-company manager, Werner Stöhr, ibid., 347–51. The latter stressed that beautification projects must be regarded not as a palliative for poor wages but as a supplement to reasonable ones.

[74] For a recent account contrasting the KdF and the Italian Dopolavoro, on which the former was often thought to be modelled, see Victoria de Grazia, The Culture of Consent. Mass Organization of Leisure in Fascist Italy (Cambridge: Cambridge University Press, 1981), 72–74. The difference between the German and Italian organizations was commented on at the time, in a study of the work ethic published by Siemens. See Werner Fritsche, Das Arbeitsethos. Der Mensch und seine Arbeit (Bad Homburg: Siemens Studien-Gesellschaft für Praktische Psychologie, 1936), 89–93.

[75] See Allen, Infancy, 178–79.

[76] See, e.g., Robert Ley, Ein Volk erobert die Freude (Berlin: Verlag der DAF, 1937), 3–4; and Unserer Sozialismus. Der Hass der Welt (Berlin, Verlag der DAF, n.d.), a 24-page pamphlet of which 500,000 copies were distributed, apparently in early 1940, before the attack on France.

[77] Heinrich Härtle, Die Nationalsozialistichen Grundlagen der Arbeitspolitik (n.p., n.d.), 21. Produced jointly by the Hauptamt NSBO and the Schulungsamt of the DAF, which Härtle had joined in 1936, this 23-page pamphlet, meant for internal use only, developed the thesis of Germanic affirmation of life, spoke of Nazism as a new religion, and equated service to the Volk with worship. From 1940, Härtle headed the academic division of the Amt Rosenberg; later, after a period of service at the front, he became an inspector of SA leadership-training

But just as in the past, so during the Third Reich opinion remained divided on whether or not it was possible to recreate joy in work in modern industry. Proponents of both positions could cite prominent Nazis in support of their views on the future of work. Thus, while Hess shared Ley's insistence on the importance of counteracting the monotony associated with modern production methods by promoting Arbeitsfreude in the workplace,[78] Goebbels accepted the loss of joy in work and sought to compensate for it through leisure and recreation. Exposed to incessant Nazi propaganda, it was all too easy for Germans to hear what they wished to hear and to ignore the rest, rather than to attempt the difficult task of assessing the essential character of the regime.

Undoubtedly many Germans in these early years were genuinely impressed by the regime's prompt action in dealing with the unemployment crisis and applauded the vigor with which the basis for "German socialism" had been laid. By 1935, the creation of the DAF, elaboration of a new system of labor law, and the introduction of a variety of social policy and educational reforms designed to bring forth a "new man" all made plausible the Nazis' claim that they were well on the way to transforming the German masses into happy and productive workers capable of finding personal fulfillment in service to the Volk community, full citizens in a prosperous and powerful nation living at peace with its neighbors.

However, things soon began to change. Once they had destroyed or subverted all organizations capable of challenging their rule, the National Socialists felt ready to embark on their mission of purifying and strengthening the biological substance of the nation in preparation for the realization of Hitler's foreign policy objectives. The Nuremberg racial laws of 1935 and the reintroduction of conscription in that year were followed in 1936 by the promulgation of the first Four-Year Plan, designed to speed German rearmament and prepare the nation for war. Coupled with the achievement of full employment, these measures profoundly affected economy and society and had profound implications for National Socialist propaganda regarding work and the worker, even before the war compelled the Nazis to amend their social policies and make corresponding adjustments to their rhetoric.

---

programs. See the *Lebenslauf* in his BDC file, and Raimund Baumgärtner, *Weltanschauungskampf im Dritten Reich. Die Auseinandersetzung der Kirchen mit Alfred Rosenberg* (Mainz: Matthias Grünewald, 1977), 40–41.

[78] See Rolf Seubert, "Berufserziehung und Politik," in Ingrid Lisop et al., *Berufs- und Wirtschaftspädagogik* (Kronberg: Scriptor, 1976), 88, quoting a letter of 15 January 1934 from Hess to the Dinta.

The only thing that remained constant throughout was their determination to elaborate and enforce certain attitudes to work. In the following chapter, we shall examine how the Nazi ideology of work changed during the later phases of the Third Reich and explore how it was used to establish priorities, to justify choices to the party and the people, and to influence German thinking about work.

XIV

WORK AND THE WORKER IN THE THIRD REICH

ONCE THE National Socialists felt themselves in a position to implement their ideals, certain ideological elements and policy options proposed by the movement on its way to power were pushed aside in favor of others that had previously been submerged. As far as work was concerned, the eventual losers included not only corporatism but also "German socialism." Among the winners were the concepts of Leistung and Deutsche Arbeit. Adhered to throughout, the ideal of a national community of work or Volksgemeinschaft was itself periodically reinterpreted in accordance with the current requirements of National Socialist Germany. Far from losing their controversial character "work" and "the worker" continued to be the subjects of debate to the last days of the Third Reich.

Even after the Röhm purge of summer 1934 emasculated the SA and put an end to hopes for a "second revolution," the DAF energetically sponsored "German socialism." But as the rearmament drive intensified and the regime's demands on the economy increased, it found itself on the defensive. Implementation of Göring's Four-Year Plan of 1936 strengthened big business and industry not only in relation to other sectors of the economy, but also vis-à-vis party and state. This meant that major employers could more easily resist encroachments by DAF reformers on their internal autonomy. By 1938, a combination of the DAF's foes managed to ensure that this organization, although still ubiquitous as an instrument of party propaganda, had lost its ability to act independently and impose its will in the economic and social policy domain.[1]

Meanwhile, the need to improve efficiency and raise the productivity of labor strengthened the "modernists" within the NSDAP, people

[1] Gerhard Beier, "Gesetzentwürfe zur Ausschaltung der Deutschen Arbeitsfront im Jahre 1938," AS 17 (1977): 301.

who believed that the new Germany could only thrive by utilizing science and technology to the full. They gained at the expense of those who, fearing the potentially negative physical and psychic consequences of further rationalization, had wanted to believe that National Socialism meant to reverse the trend towards size and impersonality in industry and to halt the simultaneous shift from agricultural to urban pursuits. Gradually, such individuals either moved to the sidelines or withdrew totally from the public arena.

Those reformers who chose to cooperate with the regime after the mid-1930s were put in a difficult ideological position when it became apparent that the desire to humanize work and promote Arbeitsfreude was in conflict with the needs of economy and state. Their dilemma was clearly stated, though not resolved, by Otto Goebel, a professor at the Hannover TH. Goebel reminded his engineering students that human work is not only performed *by* people, but also *for* them, and that everything possible must be done to prevent work from being used against human beings and to render it joyful. At the same time he insisted that economic considerations must be given first place for the sake of both individual and Volk.[2] Under these circumstances, it is understandable that National Socialists found it expedient to talk less about joy in work and to expatiate, instead, on the virtue of striving to maximize individual performance or Leistung, even at the cost of personal sacrifice.

One could, of course, promote Leistung and Arbeitsfreude together, for example by asserting that the sense of mastery and achievement deriving from good work done well was in itself an important source of joy in work. This belief seems to have lain behind the DAF's emphasis on skills training and behind its support for the idea of occupational competitions, culminating in the *Reichsberufswettkampf*. But, as time went on, those for whom the primary concern remained the happiness and wellbeing of the worker could do little more than maintain, rather plaintively, that joyful work was also more productive and that workplace reforms would eventually pay off in terms of higher output and profits.

Aware that too much talk of Arbeitsfreude was bound to appear hypocritical in a period characterized by wage restraint, conscription, and direction of labor, Nazi propagandists after the mid-1930s adjusted their disquisitions on the German work ethic accordingly. In the early years of the Four-Year Plan the regime evidently still believed that it could ensure greater productive effort by drawing on the national tra-

[2] Otto Heinrich Goebel, *Das Wirtschaftsganze im Blickfeld des Ingenieurs* (Berlin: J. Springer, 1937), 75–84.

dition of personal and cultural idealism. Even the Nuremberg Party Congress of 1937, dedicated to Work, still demonstrated a certain ambivalence; although it featured a rally of massed workers marching with spades held like guns, it concluded pacifically with a performance of Wagner's *Meistersinger*, proclaimed as the "Song of Songs of the German Middle Ages," the highpoint of "German effort, creativity, strength of character, and joy in life."[3] But as time went on propagandists were increasingly prone to employ the language of combat in relation to work, referring to German workers as "soldiers of labor" engaged in the "battle" for higher production.

The transition to a more rigorous ethic of work can be traced in the writings of Karl Arnhold. As head of the DAF's bureau for vocational training and management, Arnhold, always ambivalent about joy in work, continued to give lip service to Arbeitsfreude but laid ever great stress on duty, service, and subordination of the individual to the demands of the community. Addressing the World Congress for Leisure and Recreation in 1936, he continued to maintain that industry must put the human being at the center and that every job must be designed so as to give scope to spiritual forces;[4] but by 1938 he squarely placed the onus for improved performance (Leistung) on the individual who was urged to work for the Volk within the framework of the Four-Year Plan.[5] Only when war began did Arnhold give free rein to his militarist inclinations. Insisting that Germans abandon any distinction between private and working life or between worker and warrior, he now advocated soldierly obedience to military-style leadership and adherence to a single set of values: fulfillment of duty, courage, risk, and sacrifice.[6]

The principle of Leistung, itself an ethical concept deeply rooted in the German tradition, proved particularly suited to the needs of a regime bent on preparing the nation for war. Clearly, the Third Reich stood to gain if people developed their skills and tried to get ahead. Not only would those who succeeded be more willing to accept Hitler's rule; by stimulating competition and upward mobility, the performance principle helped to create the new elite needed to direct the affairs of the Third Reich. According to Otto Dietrich (1897–1952), chief press

[3] Otto Dietrich, introduction to the commemorative volume, *Parteitag der Arbeit*.

[4] *Weltkongress*, 352–56.

[5] Karl Arnhold, *Das Ringen um die Arbeitsidee* (4th ed.; Berlin: Verlag der DAF, 1938), 155–59, and "Leistungssteigerung," *Monatshefte für NS.-Sozialpolitik* 5 (1938): 217–21. See also Artur Axmann, *Olympia der Arbeit: Arbeiterjugend im Reichsberufswettkampf* (Berlin: Junker und Dunnhaupt, 1937), 14, where the *Reichsberufswettkampf* is linked with the Four-Year Plan's efforts to raise productivity as part of the fight for freedom and independence.

[6] Karl Arnhold, *Wehrhafte Arbeit. Eine Betrachtung über den Einsatz der Soldaten der Arbeit* (Leipzig: Bibliographisches Institut, 1939).

officer of the NSDAP since 1931, Nazism was "a brilliantly conceived system of personality selection" that laid the groundwork for the solution of all the Volk's problems, including the social question.[7] Insisting that there was no contradiction between the "person" (*Persönlichkeit*) and community in Nazi ideology, Dietrich went on to maintain that Hitler had invented a "Socialism of *Leistung*" based on a new way of thinking about work and that this represented the "Archimedes point" from which to destroy the old world of individualism, liberalism, and Marxism. The performance principle would dispel Spenglerian gloom with a new optimism and serve as the bridge to a more glorious future.[8]

The *Leistungslohn* (performance wage) was designed to reconcile the interests of individual, employer, and state by rewarding superior effort. Along with accelerated vocational training, monetary incentives undoubtedly did help to overcome the deficiencies in the labor force produced by the depression, as well as the special problems created after 1936 by the shortage of skilled workers.[9] From the regime's perspective, it had the advantage of keeping the general level of wages down while giving the appearance of fairness. It also made the task of control easier by increasing wage differentials, thereby fragmenting the working class. Above all, the performance wage, by benefiting the strong at the expense of the weak, conveniently meshed with the Social Darwinist element in Nazi ideology that came to the fore in the late 1930s.[10] Even after the war had started, when the regime depended more and more on external discipline, compulsion, and terror to achieve its aims,[11] Ley continued to argue that pay should be linked to productivity, with rewards for superior performance, spoke of the right to fair wages, and claimed that National Socialism was fully compatible with a "healthy materialism."[12]

But if a work ethic based on Leistung enabled the National Socialists to justify measures to promote voluntary improvements in productivity through wage incentives, to encourage skills training, and to inculcate respect for individual achievement, they were not blind to its disturb-

[7] Otto Dietrich, *Revolution des Denkens* (Dortmund: Westfalen-Verlag, 1939), 32–33.

[8] Dietrich, *Revolution des Denkens*, 34.

[9] Rudi Schmiede and Edwin Schudlich, *Die Entwicklung der Leistungsentlohnung in Deutschland* (2d ed.; Frankfurt: Campus, 1977), 291–313.

[10] Tilla Siegel, "Lohnpolitik im nationalsozialistischen Deutschland," in Carola Sachse, ed., *Angst, Belohnung, Zucht und Ordnung* (Opladen: Westdeutscher Verlag, 1982), 124–37. A revised English version of this essay has appeared as "Wage Policy in Nazi Germany," *Politics and Society* 14 (1985): 1–52.

[11] Detlev Peukert, *Volksgenossen und Gemeinschaftsfeinde. Anpassung, Ausmerze und Aufbegehren unter dem Nationalsozialismus* (Cologne: Bund-Verlag, 1982), 214.

[12] Robert Ley, *Unserer Sozialismus* (Berlin, 1940).

ing implications. On the practical level, the performance principle, by putting a premium on individual initiative and personal advancement, raised expectations—with regard both to the potential of self-realization through work and the extent of monetary rewards—that the regime was neither willing nor able to meet. It thus reinforced the inclination of workers, in what was by then a period of full employment, to change jobs in pursuit of better conditions and higher wages, something that could not be tolerated if the regime's objectives were to be achieved. As a result, the National Socialists were compelled more and more to intervene directly in the economy, thereby limiting the rights of self-determination of both employers and workers.

The Leistungslohn also created problems from the ideological point of view, for by making concessions to the selfish and materialist element in human nature, it seemed to abandon the ideal of work as selfless sacrifice in the interests of the Volk. To resolve the fundamental tension between productive individualism and Volksgemeinschaft, some suggested that the Leistungslohn need not be based on job performance alone, but also could take into consideration service to the community and political conformity.[13] Others, while approving of freedom for individuals to pursue their personal career goals, warned that this could only be granted within the framework of the politically possible.[14] Still others used Hitler's known views on the natural selection of the elite to support their contention that community interests were best served if market forces were permitted to see to the distribution of labor.[15] But in the end it proved impossible to disguise the fact that the adoption of policies designed to encourage individuals to better themselves created ideological difficulties for a regime whose declared objective it was to further national solidarity.

By strengthening the idea of calling or vocation (Berufsgedanke), the performance principle also endangered the works community concept (Betriebsgemeinschaft) on which so much of Nazi social policy was based. The DAF itself was torn between a belief in the desirability of lifelong

[13] E.g., Heinrich Härtle, Weltanschauung und Arbeit (Berlin: Die DAF-Schulung, 1940), 5–9; DAF Zentralbüro Berufswettkampf, Richtlinien für den Berufswettkampf aller schaffenden Deutschen, 1938), 6 (IfZ Db.67.01); Theodor Hupfauer, Mensch, Betrieb, Leistung (Berlin: DAF, 1943). Hupfauer, stressing the value of competition, fair wages, and wage incentives as motivators, suggested the use of a Gemeinschaftsleistungslohn (group wage rate) to raise productivity.

[14] Hermann Textor, Deutsche Arbeitsgestaltung (Berlin: DAF Zentralbüro, Amt Soziale Selbstverantwortung, 1939), 11.

[15] Albert Lohkamp, Inhalt und Bedeutung des Rechts auf Arbeit in Vergangenheit und Gegenwart (Würzburg: Konrad Triltsch, 1939).

dedication to a particular occupation[16] and the fear that people with superior occupational qualifications would be both more individualistic and more inclined, as in the past, to develop loyalties to those in the same profession or trade rather than to their employers.[17] While the tendency to association could be held in check through legal and extra-legal controls, the regime's insatiable demand for skilled labor made it ever more difficult to persuade qualified people to put the interests of the works community above their own.[18] In this situation, the best ideological response was to remind Germans that their primary loyalty must be to the nation. Thus the DAF invoked patriotism as a sanction for cooperation between labor and management by casting the Betriebsgemeinschaft as the basic unit of the larger Volksgemeinschaft, and the Leistungsprinzip was interpreted in terms of individuals' obligation to develop their abilities to the full so as better to serve the public welfare.

In their attempt to stimulate maximum performance through appeals to patriotism, the National Socialists found the Deutsche Arbeit theme to be particularly useful. Exploiting this ideological weapon, they initially drew on the words of earlier writers to demonstrate that Deutsche Arbeit and Arbeitsfreude were inextricably linked, and that Germans were unique in their desire for and capacity to experience joy in work. Thus, the 1934 reprint of an anthology entitled *Work Brings Joy*, first published in 1927, began and ended with quotations from Carlyle, but consisted for the most part of excerpts from German authors who had emphasized work's joys, among them Schiller, Goethe, Riehl, Nietzsche, and Naumann.[19] The equation of German work and joyful work reached its pinnacle in the regime's promotion of the "international" *Freude und Arbeit* movement: in addition to hosting the international congress in Hamburg in 1936, which was timed to coincide with the Olympics, the German branch published the association's journal in four languages, helped to organize a second major conference on Joy and Work in Rome in 1938, and, in preparation for the latter,

[16] See especially DAF, Arbeitswissentschaftliches Institut, *Jahrbuch* (1937): 378.

[17] That this fear may have been justified is illustrated by the rapid professionalization of German psychology during the Third Reich. See Ulfried Geuter, *Die Professionalisierung der deutschen Psychologie im Nationalsozialismus* (Frankfurt: Suhrkamp, 1984).

[18] For examples of texts that addressed this problem by subordinating Beruf to Betrieb and Volk, see Erich Rochholz's sociological study of labor law, *Betriebsgemeinschaft und Betriebsordnung* (Würzburg: Konrad Triltsch, 1938), and Helmut Mühlberg, *Beruf und Betriebsgemeinschaft* (Frankfurt: M. Diesterweg, 1941). Mühlberg, the director of a vocational school, drew heavily on statements by Hitler and Ley to show young workers the why and wherefore of their occupations within the larger economic and national context.

[19] *Arbeit bringt Freude! Worte grosser Denker* (Leipzig: L. Wagner, 1934).

put together an extensive international bibliography on all aspects of the problem of work.[20]

By espousing internationalism, in the sense of cooperation between distinct and proudly independent peoples directed at solving common problems, the National Socialists sought to reassure the world that, all appearances to the contrary, the new Germany intended to make German work a factor for peace between nations. They were aided in this endeavor by such holdovers from the Weimar period as Rauecker who believed that Germany could best serve the international community by successfully tackling its own problem of work. Using Riehl's dictum regarding the uniqueness of each nation's approach to work, Rauecker defended Nazi social policy innovations (including withdrawal from the ILO) from an inter-nationalist perspective![21]

What is more, from the early years until the outbreak of war, the National Socialists regularly proclaimed "work" and "peace" as the twin goals of their "German revolution." The 1934 Berlin exhibition "German Volk-German Work" was dedicated to this theme,[22] as was a popular history of the movement in which the author insisted that despite Jewish propaganda to the contrary, domestic and international peace were the foundation of all Germany's work of reconstruction, and constituted its mission to Europe and the world.[23] In the same vein, Axmann maintained in 1937 that vocational competition demonstrated the younger generation's determination to devote its energies to constructive work and its longing for peace.[24] Even after the annexation of Austria in 1938, that enthusiastic exponent of German socialism Willi Börger proclaimed that National Socialism stood for freedom, the preservation of traditional values (including the German work ethic), and peace![25]

[20] *Freude und Arbeit: Bibliographische Materialien zum 3. Weltkongress 'Arbeit und Freude' in Rom, 1938* (Berlin: Zentralbüro "Freude und Arbeit," 1938).

[21] See especially Rauecker's essay on Riehl's *Deutsche Arbeit* in *N.S.-Sozialpolitik* 2 (1934/35): 42–45 (signed B.R.); his *Social Policy in the New Germany* (Leipzig: August Pries, 1937); and his "Der Weg zu neuer Arbeitsgesinnung. Die Berufserziehung im Dienst der Gemeinschaftsidee," *Berliner Tageblatt*, 25 July 1938, commenting on an international congress for vocational training recently hosted by Germany.

[22] A copy of the exhibition manifesto can be found in Museum of Modern Art, Mies van der Rohe Archive, "Deutsches Volk-Deutsche Arbeit" (n.p., n.d.). See also the review of this exhibition by the engineer K. S. von Schweigen, "Deutsches Volk-Deutsche Arbeit!" *Technik und Kultur* 35 (1934) 5:95–98.

[23] Walther Gehl, *Der Deutsche Aufbruch 1918–1936* (2d enl. ed.; Breslau: Ferdinand Hirt [1937]), 157–60.

[24] Axmann, *Olympia der Arbeit*, 14–16.

[25] Willi Börger, *Vom deutschen Wesen* (popular edition, 4th printing; Würzburg: Konrad Triltsch, 1939), 62–80, 158.

But Deutsche Arbeit also had a less benign aspect. As war loomed on the horizon, the National Socialists used the concept to demand that individuals sacrifice their happiness to the interests of the nation and employed assertions about the superiority of "German work" to persuade the nation that it had a patriotic duty to "liberate" German territory and extend the country's borders, if necessary by force of arms.

This implied the equation of Deutsche Arbeit with freedom, a notion already used during the Kampfzeit as a political tactic to woo nationalists opposed to the Versailles and reparations settlements. Incorporated in the National Socialist slogan: "Der deutschen Arbeit wollen wir den Weg zur Freiheit bahnen" ("Our aim is to pave the way to freedom for German work"), it became in the last years of Weimar a standby of NSBO spokesmen and other Nazi propagandists.[26] After 1933 the alleged necessity of liberating German work served to justify a variety of policies, including autarky (freedom from dependence on foreigners), centralized planning (freedom from domestic discord based on the pursuit of private interest), and, above all, the quest for Lebensraum (freedom to secure additional territory in which the energy and virtues associated with German labor would be able to manifest themselves). Thus, by 1942 a party tract justified Germany's wartime conquests by combining the popular theme of Germany as a "Volk ohne Raum," "a people without living space," with a plea for the liberation of German work from dependency on foreigners.[27]

It is important to remember that the "work equals freedom" idea was never a monopoly of the German right-wing. The socialist labor movement had long promoted work as a means to liberate the working class from exploitation through the victory of proletarian internationalism.[28] Admittedly, National Socialism severed the connection between the work-freedom theme and internationalism and, instead, linked it with German nationalism through the Deutsche Arbeit concept, but the Nazi's usage was sufficiently similar to that of the Left to attract additional support from that source.

What is more, the Nazis continued to exploit the idea that "every [kind of] work liberates, when the worker can feel himself its master," an idea which middle-class reformers had used in the 1920s to reconcile the German worker with the discipline and hierarchy of the modern

[26] See, e.g., the title page of Schwerber, *Nationalsozialismus und Technik* (1932). Both the NSBO and the Institut für Ständewesen used this as their motto.

[27] Hansfritz Sohns, *Um die Freiheit der Arbeit*. Nationalpolitische Aufklärungsschriften 11 (Berlin: Paul Hochmuth, 1942).

[28] See Trommler, "Nationalisierung der Arbeit," 121; Glaser, *Im Umfeld des Austromarxismus*, 153–56.

factory.[29] In the Third Reich Arnhold similarly promoted the cause of vocational training by insisting that mastery of a job enables the individual to experience a sense of freedom;[30] while in 1938 Friedrich, recently appointed head of the division for vocational training and productivity in the *Reichswirtschaftskammer*, declared that struggle is essential to freedom, and that healthy Germans are driven to strive and create because they know that only a free life is worth living.[31]

Although they referred to recognizable psychological principles and employed language made familiar by earlier socialists and social reformers, Arnhold and Friedrich clearly meant something different by "freedom" than had the friends of German labor. For them as for other National Socialists it signified not absence of restraints, but voluntary acceptance of discipline and duty. But defining "freedom" in this way was not something the Nazis invented. Indeed, the effective use to which they were able to put the equation of freedom—so defined—with the German or Prussian concept of duty derived from the fact that the former was rooted in nineteenth-century idealism, and had long been employed to strengthen the work ethic by nationalist authors. Thus in 1925 an article in the leading business journal drew on the authority of Carlyle, Schiller, Kant, and Krupp to prove that "feeling for duty, sense of responsibility, and self-discipline" were three facets of true inner freedom, best practiced and demonstrated in profession and work.[32] Two years later, a philosophy thesis submitted at the University of Halle drew on the duty-freedom ideas of Fichte and Kant to support the belief that the leisure ethic was inappropriate for "good Germans."[33]

In the Third Reich it became fashionable to link the work ethic with this "German" idea of freedom.[34] Thus Friedrich Würzbach claimed that Nietzsche had defined freedom in terms of self-directed labor, willingness to accept difficulties, and readiness to make personal sacrifices

[29] See Peter Petersen, "Sozialbiologische Probleme der Berufsschule," in Peter Petersen and W. Zimmermann, eds., *Die Aufgaben des neuen Berufsschulwesens und die Berufsschulgemeinde* (Weimar: Hermann Böhlaus, 1925), 128. Petersen was professor of pedagogy at the University of Jena.

[30] Arnhold, *Ringen um die Arbeitsidee*, 159.

[31] Adolf Friedrich, *Grundaufgaben der Menschenführung im Betrieb* (n.p., n.d.), 17. Friedrich was addressing a scientific congress of the German Steel Construction Association in Berlin. An idealistic convert to National Socialism, Friedrich replaced his Weimar motto "God-Man-Work" with "Honor-Volk-Service" in 1933, joined the SS, and taught management at the Mining Academy in Clausthal. Subsequently, he served for two years at Four-Year Plan headquarters. See Bunk, *Erziehung und Industriearbeit*, 151.

[32] G. Made, "Innerer Wert der Arbeit," *Arbeitgeber* 15 (1925): 34–35.

[33] Otto Donath, "Vom Ethos rationalisierter Arbeit" (Inaugural diss., Halle, 1927).

[34] For its political implications, see Leonard Krieger, *The German Idea of Freedom* (Boston: Beacon Press, 1957).

and demand them of others, and consequently that the Nazis were being true to Nietzsche's legacy when they talked of liberty as the freedom to struggle and strive ever upward. In Würzbach's view, National Socialism subscribed to a dynamic Nietzschean concept of freedom based on the *Führer*'s will, one that entailed self-abnegation and suffering as the price for the creation of a new community and the establishment of the thousand-year Reich.[35] Similarly, the director of the Institute for Labor Policy (*Institut für Arbeitspolitik*) in Cologne, having described the German character in terms of drives towards honor, loyalty, and freedom, defined the last as the "inner readiness" to work hard out of "a sense of responsibility and obligation vis-à-vis the community of the Volk."[36]

During the last phase of the Third Reich such arguments were the rule rather than the exception. Thus in 1944 Ley, summing up the work-freedom version of Deutsche Arbeit in an essay entitled "Our Work Liberates," explained that work and struggle are twins arising out of the everlasting laws of life: both become a burden if taken to the point where they exceed human powers, but, nonetheless, that burden is more bearable than a life without them. Writing at a time when Germany was already on the defensive, Ley argued that there is a higher freedom consisting of selection and development, one that rests on the ability of diligent individuals to make their way within an enlarged Lebensraum capable of meeting the essential needs of the race. German freedom could be enjoyed by the individual only as part of an orderly, strong, and healthy national community, to be achieved through battle and conquest by German workers, peasants, and soldiers.[37] In the same year an RAD instructor insisted that, for Germans, "Work is law, and our freedom consists in accepting that law proudly and in an upright manner, as our life-fate."[38]

At its worst, "work liberates" became the notorious "Arbeit macht frei" ("Work makes free") inscribed above the gates of the Auschwitz labor and death camp, apparently to taunt Nazism's most miserable victims. However, the man who placed this slogan there, Rudolf Höss

[35] Friedrich Würzbach, *Arbeit und Arbeiter in der neuen Gesellschaftsordnung, nach Aphorismen von Nietzsche* (Berlin: Deutsches Verlagshaus Bong & Co., 1933), 15–23. This was based on an earlier radio address.

[36] Franz Horsten, *Die nationalsozialistische Leistungsauslese. Ihre Aufgaben im Bereich der nationalen Arbeit und praktische Vorschläge für ihre Durchführung* (2d ed.; Würzburg: Konrad Triltsch, 1938), 18–19. This *Habilitationsshrift* was part of a series on German socialism edited by Börger.

[37] Robert Ley, "Unsere Arbeit macht uns frei," *Arbeit und Wirtschaft* (June 1944): 51–55.

[38] Ludwig Götting, *Die Arbeit als Erziehungsmittel im Reichsarbeitsdienst* (Berlin: Zentralverlag der NSDAP/Franz Eher, 1944), 51.

(1900–1947), seems to have been one of those Germans who genuinely believed in the bond between work and freedom. A devout National Socialist who rose through SS ranks to become the Commandant of Auschwitz, Höss had found strenuous work essential for the maintenance of his personal psychological balance and sense of identity.[39] He also claimed to have learned from his own imprisonment in the 1920s, as well as from his administrative apprenticeship at the Dachau concentration camp, that regular, disciplined labor was essential to counteract the degrading effects of prison conditions and could help to develop the qualities of character that would prepare inmates for eventual freedom.[40] When put in charge of the new concentration camp at Auschwitz, Höss did his best to remain true to the *Arbeit macht frei* principle which he brought with him from Dachau. While dutifully accomplishing the job of mass murder assigned to him, he nevertheless attempted, incredible as it may now seem, to run Auschwitz as a labor camp,[41] dedicated to production and run according to enlightened principles of scientific management. These included rational job placement and apprentice training for young prisoners to develop their aptitudes and educate them for, and through, work. Such policies showed the importance Höss attached to perpetuating proper German attitudes to work among those in his charge, even in the shadow of death.[42] For Höss, at least, *Arbeit macht frei* was more a statement of faith in a widely proclaimed national principle than an expression of cynical disdain for those held in subjection.

As the radical racism that had always been at the heart of National Socialist ideology expanded into all spheres of national life, the capacity to produce "German work" became a means of identifying true members of the Volk. Conversely, the unwillingness or inability to work as a good German should was taken to indicate racial inferiority. In conjunction with biological criteria, it eventually became a warrant for discrimination, persecution, exploitation, or even—in the case of gypsies and Jews—for genocide.[43] For by labelling certain individuals

[39] Theweleit, *Männerphantasien*, 268–70.

[40] Rudolf Höss, *Kommandant in Auschwitz. Autobiographische Aufzeichnungen* (Stuttgart: Deutsche Verlags-Anstalt, 1958), 62–64; John K. Roth, "Holocaust Business: Some Reflections on 'Arbeit macht frei,' " *Annals of the American Academy of Political and Social Science* 450 (July 1980): 76–77.

[41] On Auschwitz as a "work camp," see Robert J. Lifton, *The Nazi Doctors. Medical Killing and the Psychology of Genocide* (New York: Basic Books, 1986), 155–57.

[42] See Rudolf Höss, "Krakauer Aufzeichnungen," November 1946 (photocopy in IfZ, F 13/8, 00444–00455), six pages of jottings on the question of prison labor made while Höss was in Allied custody.

[43] Detlev Peukert, *Volksgenossen und Gemeinschaftsfremde* (Cologne: Bund-Verlag, 1982),

and groups as "alien" on the grounds that their approach to work deviated from established community standards, the National Socialists were able to render acceptable to the German public a whole range of domestic measures that might well have been rejected had they been justified in terms of biology alone. Among other things, this use of "German work" generated support for policies aimed at systematically excluding Jews from certain types of employment, subjecting unsatisfactory workers to enforced labor in so-called "Work Education Camps,"[44] or killing, through the "euthanasia" program, those inmates of mental hospitals judged to be incapable of productive labor.[45] Applied to other nations, the connection between work and race helped to legitimize the conquest of Lebensraum in the East and subjection of the indigenous population to German settlers who were deemed, on racial grounds, to have the right to monopolize all higher positions in the hierarchy of work.[46]

The Third Reich also linked work with race in other, ostensibly less punitive, ways. While the "blood-and-soil" ideology proved particularly useful to opponents of industrialization and urbanization, racial arguments were also employed by people whose chief concern was the problem of industrial work. Operating on the assumption that hereditary factors were of fundamental importance, the National Socialists sought systematically to apply "racial science" in the spheres of vocational guidance, placement, and training, as well as in the domain of management.

This was no easy or straightforward task as soon became apparent. The Munich psychologist Albert Huth, for example, in a text for practitioners (of which each chapter was headed by quotations from leading Nazis), analyzed racial characteristics as clues to psychological and mental capabilities at some length, despite the fact that his own research had shown that a definite correlation between physical build and

---

246–50; Leo Kuper, *Genocide. Its Political Use in the Twentieth Century* (New Haven: Yale University Press, 1981), 121.

[44] See Hans Buchheim, "Die Aktion 'Arbeitsscheu Reich' " (1959), in *Gutachten des Instituts für Zeitgeschichte* (Stuttgart: Deutsche Verlags-Anstalt, 1966), 2:189–95; Hans Auerbach, "Arbeitserziehungslager" (1963), in ibid., 196–201; Wolfgang Franz Werner, *'Bleib übrig.' Deutsche Arbeiter in der nationalsozialistischen Kriegswirtschaft* (Düsseldorf: Schwann, 1983), 178–92.

[45] Lifton, *Nazi Doctors*, 65–68.

[46] Ludolf Herbst, *Der Totale Krieg und die Ordnung der Wirtschaft* (Stuttgart: Deutsche Verlags-Anstalt, 1982), 154–55. See also the wartime anthology, *Arbeit und Waffe. Worte an Arbeiter und Soldaten*, ed. Herwarth von Renesse (Berlin: Nordland, 1940), especially the introduction by Ley and the Goebbels excerpts. Friedrich Griese, *Unsere Arbeit ist Glaube* (2d ed.; Berlin: Eher, 1942), 68–69, defended Nazi aggression on the grounds that Germans excel as workers.

mental-attitudinal characteristics could only be established in eleven percent of subjects.[47] Similarly, the engineer Karl Bourges, convinced that attitudes to work were inherited, that Nordics were most capable of producing high quality work, and that all Germans possessed at least some Nordic blood, insisted that racial criteria must be employed in industrial management; yet he acknowledged that the German population was racially mixed and that it was extremely difficult to measure and define the relevant variables.[48]

Not everyone was deterred by such considerations. Thus Friedrich considered National Socialist racial doctrine an invaluable adjunct to the study of the relationship between human beings and work. While he admitted that the German population was not racially homogeneous, he proclaimed his belief in the existence of the "race soul" posited by Rosenberg and asserted that inherited traits could be discovered and put to good use in job placement.[49] Maintaining that racial science was the great gift of the Nazis to the Volk, Friedrich eventually went so far as to offer his services to the SS Race and Settlement Head Office.[50]

DAF spokesmen regularly used racial arguments to back up their calls for reform. Thus Ley maintained that the German worker was innately superior, "too good to be treated as a coolie," and therefore called for the abolition of the unskilled labor force through universal vocational training.[51] During the war, he justified the use of foreigners (and women!) to do the nation's menial work on the grounds that German men were destined by their blood for higher things, including the warrior's role.[52] Similarly Hermann Textor argued that the DAF could only achieve its reform objectives with respect to management attitudes and work organization if the changes corresponded to the racial attributes of the workforce. Thus Jews worked only for money, while Russians and other people of lower race avoided taking responsibility and so had to be treated as "coolies." Only German workers were so constituted as

[47] Albert Huth, *Seelenkunde und Arbeitseinsatz* (Munich: Max Schick, 1937).

[48] Karl Bourges, *Abstammung und Beruf. Ein Beitrag zur nationalsozialistischen Menschenführung* (Düsseldorf: Verlag Stahleisen, 1938), 15–16.

[49] Adolf Friedrich, *Grundlagen der Leistungsertüchtigung* (Berlin: Otto Elsner, 1939), 1:55. See also Adolf Friedrich, "Unsere Menschenführung im Lichte des Nationalsozialismus," Vorträge über Menschenführung 31, Vereinigte Stahlwerke A.-G, Bergbaugruppe Hamborn, 19 June 1933 (DF).

[50] See BDC, letter of 11 January 1939 to the head of the *Rasse- und Siedlungshauptamt*, asking for an early appointment.

[51] *Arbeit, Volk und Staat. Auszüge aus Reden, Erklärungen und Aufsätzen Adolf Hitlers und seiner Mitarbeiter* (typescript; Berlin: Zentralarchiv der Deutschen Arbeitsfront, ca. 1935), 14–15. (LC)

[52] Similarly, Härtle, *Weltanschauung und Arbeit*, 4–5, spoke of the Nordic-Germanic capacity for war and work as affirmations of life.

to want free and responsible work and could be counted on never to abuse whatever freedom was accorded them. From this it followed that one would do best to treat them as colleagues rather than as subordinates, by providing maximum opportunities for personal involvement and Arbeitsfreude.[53]

Although opposed to racism in principle, the German labor movement had not proved immune to antisemitism in the Weimar years.[54] Thus it was not surprising that after 1933 former blue collar workers and others closely associated with organized labor should not only find Hitler's racial policies acceptable, but also consider them a reason for supporting his regime. One such was Winnig who stressed the mission of the biologically youthful Arbeitertum to rejuvenate state and society through the medium of the *Führerstaat*.[55] Another example was the sociologist Karl Valentin Müller (1896–1963), whose suggestions for solving the problem of work by limiting the reproduction of inferior peoples and individuals through mass sterilization had been published in a respected trade union publication in 1925.[56] Having welcomed the Third Reich, and having been accepted by it, Müller advocated the reform of industrial relations to incorporate a Leistungsprinzip based on hereditary selection, with environmental and educational influences demoted to a peripheral role. He also proposed a eugenics policy, because he was convinced that it was necessary not only to train and encourage quality workers, but also to breed them. Finally, Müller hoped that the reforms he outlined would enable the elite of skilled workers to compensate for the destruction of their trade unions by developing an *esprit de corps* within the framework of the Third Reich.[57]

[53] Textor, *Deutsche Arbeitsgestaltung*, and Hermann Textor, *Völkische Arbeitseignung* (Berlin: Wilhelm Limpert, 1939 for the Forschungsinstitut für Arbeitsgestaltung, Frankfurt).

[54] See Donald L. Niewyk, *Socialist, Anti-Semite, and Jew. German Democracy Confronts the Problem of Anti-Semitism 1918–1933* (Baton Rouge, La.: University of Louisiana Press, 1971).

[55] August Winnig, *Der Arbeiter im Dritten Reich* (Berlin: Buchholz und Weisswange, 1934). See also his antisemitic popular reader, *Die grosse Prüfung*, vol. 2 of *Arbeiter und Reich* (Leipzig: Teubner, 1937). Winnig initially welcomed the Nazi revolution as a great homecoming for the German workers and compared Hitler's Werk ("creation") to a many-faceted crystal giving off colors in ever new combinations and relations. As a good Christian, he eventually lost his enthusiasm for the Nazis, although perhaps not as early as 1935, as he later claimed. BA Kl.Erw.470: Nachlass August Winnig, letter of 4 July 1946 to Carl Severing, and his autobiographical *Aus Zwanzig Jahren 1925 bis 1945* (Hamburg: Friedrich Wittig, 1951), 56–64, 83–85. In any case, his antisemitism remained. See Wilhelm Ribhegge, *August Winnig* (Bonn: Neue Gesellschaft, 1973), 266–93.

[56] Karl Valentin Müller, "Gewerkschaften und Bevölkerungspolitik," *Gewerkschafts-Archiv* 2 (1925): 205–213, and "Amerikanisches: Arbeiterschaft und Rassenproblem," ibid., 249–56.

[57] Karl Valentin Müller, *Der Aufstieg des Arbeiters durch Rasse und Meisterschaft* (Munich: J. F. Lehmanns, 1935). The superior Nordic minority was to be given hereditary titles, job security, better housing, and preferential access to settlement opportunities. Müller, whose

Other working class advocates believed that National Socialism would serve labor interests by allowing the racial occupational spirit of the skilled German worker to flourish, by re-establishing the industrial worker's link with the soil, and by encouraging regional variation based on racial differences.[58] What Nazi "experts" had to say on the subject of race and work provided good grounds for thinking that the Third Reich was moving in this direction. Thus Arnhold and Giese argued that each region of Germany has its own racial character or *Gautyp*, and so urged that local differences be taken into account when formulating personnel and other management policies.[59] In other words, they adopted a "tribal" approach to the problem of work close to that favored in the nineteenth century by Riehl—a circumstance that undoubtedly contributed to the latter's popularity in the Third Reich.[60]

While regional differences with respect to attitudes to work in general and preference for certain occupations in particular do exist in Germany, Volkskunde, as practiced in the Nazi period, was unable to shed much light on them or to produce information useful to those concerned with the problem of modern industrial labor.[61] What is more, the regime from the mid-1930s on needed to stimulate labor mobility, and therefore was more interested in circumventing than accentuating those features of the workforce that might hamper this process. Finally, the Volkskunde approach, with its emphasis on diversity, ran counter to a major objective of National Socialist racial doctrine: to provide a biological basis for the Volksgemeinschaft.

There was also a fundamental, if unacknowledged, contradiction between the Nazis' emphasis on heredity and their belief in the possibility of creating the new National Socialist man through education and changes in the environment. Thus Arnhold of the DAF's vocational training branch, without subjecting his premises to philosophical ex-

---

book bore the Nazi imprimatur, subsequently lectured on population policy and social anthropology at both the University of Leipzig and the Dresden TH. From 1954–1958 he was General Secretary of the International Institute of Sociology in Rome. *Internationales Soziologenlexikon* (1980), s.v. Müller, Karl Valentin.

[58] See, e.g., Christian Rheinschmied, "Der Berufsgeist des deutschen Metallarbeiters," *Der Betriebswart* (formerly *Betriebsräte-Zeitschrift*) 14 (25 September 1933): 201–203. Rheinschmied was a spokesman for the metal workers' union.

[59] Karl Arnhold, "Ingenieuraufgaben zwischen Mensch und Maschine," *Das Werk* 16 (1936): 99–103; Fritz Giese, "Gautyp und Betriebsgeist. Arbeitswissenschaftliche Richtlinien," *Arbeitsschulung* 6 (1935): 11–18.

[60] On Riehl and National Socialism, Geramb, *Riehl*, 562–93.

[61] For a scholarly attempt to apply Volkskunde to industry in the Third Reich, see Wilhelm Brepohl, "Das Ruhrvolk und die Volkstumsforschung," *Rheinische Vierteljahrsblätter* 7 (1937): 341–72. Brepohl's work is evaluated in Johannes Weyer, "Die Forschungsstelle für das Volkstum im Ruhrgebiet (1935–1941)—Ein Beispiel für Soziologie im Faschismus," *Soziale Welt* (1984): 124–45.

amination,[62] not only assigned great importance to vocational training, but also sought to restructure the workplace in accordance with psychosocial principles and to improve the mental health of the workers, foster a spirit of community, and contribute to the drive for higher productivity through psychotherapy.[63] Furthermore, he tried to reconcile educational and racial perspectives on German work by promoting the instructional use of certain materials, notably iron: Arnhold thought that this substance corresponded most fully to the Germanic nature. But he also argued that because working with it required disciplined individual effort, it was ideally suited to reinforce the inherited traits characteristic of German manhood at its best: fighting spirit, intellect, and the capacity to cooperate with others in a big factory setting.[64]

The ingenuity displayed by Arnhold and Riedel in adapting National Socialist racism to their own area of expertise was also exhibited by people in other professions. Thus the economist Walter Thoms of the University of Heidelberg attempted to put the works community on a biological footing by defining the Betrieb as an expression of the race soul, essentially distinct from the capitalist, alias Jewish, enterprise. After outlining new accounting principles based on work effort and performance, Thoms called for the creation of a "biology of the firm" that would be racial, *völkisch*, and political in character.[65] Here, the

[62] Given the anti-intellectualism of the Third Reich, it is not surprising that the question of exactly how racial science fitted into the picture was never resolved on a theoretical level. One possible solution, the heritability of acquired characteristics, was hinted at by the philosopher Willi Zimmermann who believed that people were shaped by their occupations and that the resulting "types" could in turn be nurtured by suitable eugenics policies. In *Arbeit als Weltanschauung*. Kant-Studien Ergänzungshefte 1 (Berlin: Pan, 1937), 13–14, while seeking to convert Germans to a full-fledged gospel of work based on the Kantian imperative, he indicated that this new work ethic, too, would be genetically transmitted to future generations.

[63] Geoffrey Cocks, *Psychotherapy in the Third Reich. The Göring Institute* (New York: Oxford University Press, 1985), 196–202. According to Cocks, it was Arnhold who provided the link between the DAF and the Göring Institute of Psychotherapy. This eventually led to a formal association between the two during the war.

[64] Karl Arnhold, "Eisen Erzieht," *Arbeitertum* 3 (1 October 1933): 20–22, repeated in *Arbeitsschulung* 11 (1940): 50–51; Arnhold, *Mensch und Arbeit*. 5. Studienkonferenz der Deutschen Reichsbahn-Gesellschaft (Berlin: Verkehrswissenschaftliche Lehrmittelgesellschaft, [1934]), 24–26. Arnhold's associate Riedel, somewhat less militaristic in his outlook and more restrained in his enthusiasm for modern technology, wanted apprentices to work with wood as well as iron, because he believed wood to be especially suited to the development of creativity and individuality. Johannes Riedel, "Eisen und Holz in der Arbeitserziehung," *Arbeitsschulung* 7 (1936): 9–14.

[65] Walter Thoms, "Der Betrieb als Glied des Volkslebens," in *Gegenwartsfragen der Wirtschaftswissenschaft*, ed. Heinrich Hunke and Erwin Wiskemann (Berlin: Junker und Dünnhaupt, 1939), 160–88. This was a *Festschrift* for Gottl-Ottlilienfeld who in 1934 claimed that

idea that true community can only exist among people of like blood, a commonplace of National Socialist rhetoric,[66] was given academic respectability and linked with the view that German work was unique and therefore needed to develop its own organizational forms.

The churches, too, succumbed to this kind of thinking on occasion. Protestant nationalists had in the aftermath of the First World War already denigrated allegedly "Jewish" attitudes to work and thus contributed to the separation of Germans and Jews.[67] This kind of attack, relatively rare in the Weimar period when Jews were still able to defend themselves[68] and enjoyed the full protection of law, flourished in the Third Reich. Sanctioned by the regime, such ideas were especially prevalent among the so-called German Christians who repudiated the Old Testament and presented Jesus as an Aryan. But racist thinking about German work also infected those who stood aloof from this government-backed movement. Thus the former religious socialist Wünsch defined work quite sensibly as the essential prerequisite for human existence and explained its importance for the individual and the economy in neutral terms; he then went on, however, to insist that the individual and economic life were unable to build genuine community and must therefore at all times be subordinated to family and Volk,[69] the latter defined as a racial and spiritual community based on

his economic thinking over the preceding four decades had coincided with National Socialist doctrine in all essentials. Gottl was awarded the Goethe Medal in 1938, presumably for his support of Hitler and of National Socialist racial policies. See the introductory essay to Friedrich von Gottl-Ottlilienfeld, *Zeitfragen der Wirtschaft: Über Bolschewismus, Autarkie und Deutscher Sozialismus* (Berlin: Junker und Dünnhaupt, 1934); and *Internationales Soziologenlexikon* (1980), s.v. Gottl-Ottlilienfeld.

[66] See, e.g., A. Krüger, *Aufgabe und Sinn des Arbeitsdienstes* (Berlin: Deutscher Arbeitsdienst, 1935), 29–30, and DAF Schulung, *Der Nationalsozialismus und Du* (2d ed.; Berlin, 1941), 24.

[67] See, e.g., Walter Liek, *Der deutsche Arbeiter und das Judentum.* Deutschlands Erneuerung, Flugblatt 1 (Munich: J. F. Lehmann, 1920), 9–11; and Max Kloss, *Der sittliche Gehalt der Arbeit und die Entsittlichung der deutschen Arbeit durch Marxismus, Versailles und Dawes* (Langensalza: Hermann Beyer, 1926), an expanded version of a talk first given at a Dresden meeting of the society "Deutscher Staat," October 1925. A shorter version was published in the *völkisch Deutscher Volkswart* 8 (Neblung-November [sic!], 1925), 2:33–41. Kloss (1873–?), an engineer, contrasted the Jewish idea of work as curse with the Christian concept of work as service and went on to argue that the latter was close to the racially and climatically determined German belief that work is struggle. Campaigning against the Dawes Plan, he claimed public success for his slogan DAWES = Deutsche Arbeiter Werden Elende Sklaven! He joined the NSDAP in 1933.

[68] As an example of one such defense based on religious texts about work, see Simon Bernfeld, "Wertschätzung der Arbeit in Bibel und Talmud," *Centralverein Zeitung* (1924), Supplement 48:14–15.

[69] Georg Wünsch, *Evangelische Ethik des Politischen* (Tübingen: J.C.B. Mohr, 1936), 26, 409–418, 645–49.

353

blood, soil, heredity, and "acknowledgement of the irrational depths of all that exists."[70] This belief allowed him to defend the *Führerprinzip*, condone the regime's anti-Jewish measures, and support eugenics policies like sterilization of the "unfit,"—although he did express the hope that Christianity would be permitted to mitigate the rigors of the Führer's initiatives.

While some Protestant theologians employed racist arguments to establish that Christianity was the natural ally of National Socialism, most preferred to use biblical references for this purpose. Thus Czirják demonstrated that the new National Socialist work ethic had Christian roots and approved the enthusiasm with which the National Socialist revolution was "cleansing Germany of all alien ideas, for the sake of the Volk and of Christianity."[71] More soberly, Preisker (1888–1952), emeritus professor of Theology at Breslau, used the New Testament to explain Luther's views on work and showed that the latter were fully compatible with the "modern" German work ethic based on joyous affirmation of life.[72] Korth also used scriptural texts to prove that Christianity supported an ethic of work akin to that of National Socialism, although he distanced himself from the German Christians by drawing on both Old and New Testaments.[73]

Less inclined than Protestants to support National Socialism politically, Catholics, too, occasionally used racist language in their disquisitions on work.[74] Nevertheless, their susceptibility to the appeal of racism cannot explain why so many members of the educated middle class, both Protestant and Catholic, were willing to serve the new regime. In general, the need to work in order to survive, often coupled with personal ambition, probably played a bigger part than ideological conviction in determining their behavior. After years of joblessness or underemployment, intellectuals of all ages were delighted by the limitless opportunities for "joyful work in the national cause" that the Third

[70] Wünsch, *Evangelische Ethik*, 649. Wünsch drew on K. V. Müller to buttress his anti-egalitarian, antisemitic position on work and race. See 647, n.1.

[71] Czirják, *Sinn der Arbeit*, Foreword. See Chapter 10, above.

[72] Herbert Preisker, *Das Ethos der Arbeit im Neuen Testament*. Aufbau im 'Positiven Christentum' Nr. 19 (Gnadenfrei in Schlesien: Gustav Winter, 1936), 3.

[73] Konrad Korth, *Arbeit—ein Fluch? Das Zeugnis der Bibel und des christlichen Glaubens*. Der Heliand: Deutsch-protestantische Hefte 58 (Berlin: Verlag des Evangelischen Bundes, 1939).

[74] According to Tal, *Christians and Jews in Germany*, 94, the idea of Jews as cunning and unscrupulous nomads incapable of sharing the German's love of work was already a frequent theme in Catholic as well as Protestant writings during the Second Reich. In the 1920s the Christian unions, in their eagerness to differentiate themselves from the "atheist" socialist workers' movement, were especially prone to emphasize Catholic adherence to the dominant national ethic of work. Both Brauer and Michel, as we have seen, adopted racial terminology in their disquisitions on work after 1933.

Reich provided. Professional spirit and patriotism also help to account for the exemplary way in which even those who did not think of themselves as National Socialists continued to carry out their functions.

Yet it would be wrong to ignore the impact on these people of the Nazis' promise to effect a *rapprochement* between workers of the brain and the hand within a new Volksgemeinschaft. Although designed to appeal to all classes, this concept was particularly attractive to middle-class intellectuals, many of whom were proud to serve the new Germany as "workers of the brow," undeterred by Hitler's blatant anti-intellectualism and the regime's determination to stamp out ideological dissent. For their part, the Nazis continued to need "brain workers" inherited from earlier regimes to fill traditional positions in economic and academic life, staff the burgeoning civil service, and bolster party formations like the DAF and the SS.

Apart from the minority deemed unacceptable by the new authorities, those who had been concerned with the problem of work in the Weimar period continued to play a considerable role in the Third Reich, particularly in the areas of education and propaganda. Indeed, one can argue that their endeavors received greater support from the National Socialists than from any earlier government. The DAF's vocational training branch under Arnhold[75] and its Beauty of Labor program headed by Speer[76] were but two of the many Nazi agencies that addressed the problem of work in a substantive way while inculcating the "National Socialist" ethic of work as service to the Volk. Another was the *Arbeitswissenschaftliches Institut*, or AWI ("Science of Work Institute") of the DAF, established in 1935 by Ley to stimulate the science of work while ensuring that those contributing to it remained under party control.[77] Over the years, holdovers from Weimar took the lead in preparing AWI reports on a great variety of work-related topics, including profit-sharing, fatigue and productivity, company social policy, wage incentives, and social work training: holdovers from Weimar also staffed the AWI's active "History of Work" department which re-

[75] See, in addition to Arnhold's own writings, Rolf Seubert, *Berufserziehung und Nationalsozialismus* (Weinheim: Beltz, 1977); Georg Fischer and Harald Scholtz, "Stellung und Funktion der Erwachsenenbildung im Nationalsozialismus," in Heinemann, ed., *Erziehung und Schulung um Dritten Reich*, 2, 153–61; Gillingham, "The 'Deproletarianization' of German Society," 423–32.

[76] See especially Anson G. Rabinbach, "The Aesthetics of Production in the Third Reich," *JCH* 10 (1976) 4: 43–74; and Chub Friemert, *Produktionsästhetik im Faschismus. Das Amt 'Schönheit der Arbeit' von 1933 bis 1939* (Munich: Damnitz, 1980).

[77] Robert Ley, *Die Wissenschaft im Dienste der Sozialordnung* (typescript; Berlin: DAF, AWI, 24 August 1942), 20.

wrote the story of "German work" in accordance with National Socialist views.[78]

Although frequently subject to direction by or interference from outsiders whose authority rested solely on party loyalty, authoritative contributors to the science of work continued to publish in their areas of
expertise in Hitler Germany. The extent to which they chose to make
concessions to the Nazi ethos, however, and their motives for doing so,
varied significantly between individuals. Thus both Atzler and Moede
published in the party-sponsored monthly *N.S.-Sozialpolitik*,[79] but only
Moede, who had joined the NSDAP in 1933, adopted racist terminology and acknowledged that the totalitarian demands of the state made
it necessary to take hereditary factors into account when assessing aptitudes.[80] Moede also cited National Socialists in the introduction to
his 1935 textbook on psychotechnics, praised the regime for giving
workers their honor back while increasing productivity, and set out
guidelines for all "Schaffen des Menschen mit Stirn und mit Faust,"
Nazi rhetoric signifying mental and manual labor.[81] Yet the bulk of this
book could easily have been written five years earlier, and he never
ceased to express his indebtedness to precursors and to colleagues
abroad "who have remained true to German Wissenschaft."[82] Given
Nazi insistence that the Third Reich marked a revolutionary break with
the past, this in itself could be interpreted as a form of resistance.[83]

Because the National Socialists were particularly eager to repudiate
the Weimar heritage, they seem to have found it somewhat easier to
tolerate the work of specialists whose reputations were established in
the Wilhelminian era. One such was Richard Seyfert (1862–1940),
author of the standard text on Arbeitskunde. First published in 1909,

[78] A conference on the history of work was held in Berlin in 1937. DAF, AWI, *Protokoll der Tagung der Abteilung "Geschichte der Arbeit" am 18.10.1937*, LC, incomplete typescript, ninety-four pages, dated Berlin, November 1937. Margrit and Helmuth Schuster, "Industrie-soziologie im Nationalsozialismus," *Soziale Welt* (1984): 94–123, stress the continuity be-tween Weimar industrial sociology and that of the Third Reich, with emphasis on the role of the DAF and its AWI.

[79] Atzler's "Gestaltung der Arbeitspause" appeared in vol. 4 (1937), Moede's "Der Mensch in Betrieb und Wirtschaft" in vol. 6 (1939).

[80] Moede, "Der Mensch in Betrieb und Wirtschaft," 61.

[81] Walther Moede, *Arbeitstechnik. Die Arbeitskraft: Schutz-Erhaltung-Steigerung* (Stuttgart: Ferdinand Enke, 1935). Moede taught at the Berlin TH until 1945 and served several times as president of the Association of German Applied Psychologists. Geuter, *Professionalisierung der deutschen Psychologie*, 576.

[82] Moede, *Arbeitstechnik*, vii.

[83] For evidence that similar behavior was so interpreted on occasion, see the letter of de-nunciation dated 26.11.38, signature illegible, in Ludwig Geck's BDC file, attacking Geck for asserting, in an article in the *Internationale Rundschau der Arbeit* (1937), that the Nazis had taken all their ideas from academic and entrepreneurial pioneers of earlier days.

his *Arbeitskunde* was republished twice after 1933, despite Seyfert's insistence that the essential principles of company social policy had already been established long before by men like Abbe and Krupp.[84] But the uneasy blend of old and new in the science of work during the Third Reich is perhaps best illustrated by a National Socialist compendium on Arbeitskunde that appeared shortly after the outbreak of the war.[85] Edited by Karl Peppler (1897–?), a former administrator of the DHV and SA activist who became one of the DAF's chief social policy experts,[86] this elegantly produced book, unlike that of Seyfert, was intended for the edification of the general public. Each contributor discussed recent changes in his area of expertise in the light of the past, but only in order to establish the revolutionary character of National Socialist policies affecting work and society. As the foreword explained, the major gains attributable to the Nazi revolution, which had put the "value and evaluation of creative work" in the forefront of national life, could best be demonstrated by looking at the historical development of the various disciplines such as labor law or social insurance.

While all of Peppler's authors agreed that the regime's efforts to solve the problem of alienation and create a Volksgemeinschaft, although rooted in German tradition, represented something radically new in the nation's history, they differed markedly in their assessment of Nazism's aims and achievements. Indeed, the book as a whole can be said to sum up the National Socialist debate about work and community at a time when the Third Reich was at the peak of its power. For this reason, it is worth examining a few of these essays more closely.

The chapter on the emergence and development of the DAF was written by Gerhard Starcke (1907–?), a dedicated young DAF publicist who had joined the party in 1930.[87] Starcke maintained that the DAF had grown "organically," rather than in accordance with a preconceived plan, but that it nevertheless consistently implemented Nazi ideology. He also emphasized his respect for traditional science, for example by playing down the race issue that had been featured in his earlier book on the NSBO.[88] Now it was Volksgemeinschaft that rep-

---

[84] Admittedly, the book was updated somewhat to take Nazi innovations into account. Richard Seyfert, *Arbeitskunde als Bildungsmittel zu Arbeitsinn und Arbeitsgemeinschaft* (11th ed.; Leipzig: E. Wunderlich, 1940), especially 306–314.

[85] Karl Peppler, ed., *Die Deutsche Arbeitskunde* (Berlin: Stubenrauch, 1940, for Bibliographisches Institut A. G. Leipzig).

[86] *Deutsche Führer-Lexikon*, s.v. Peppler, Carl. Peppler was publisher of *N.S.-Sozialpolitik*.

[87] Peppler, *Deutsche Arbeitskunde*, 172–99; Starcke, *Lebenslauf*, BDC personnel file.

[88] Gerhard Starcke, *NSBO und Deutsche Arbeitsfront* (2d rev. ed.; Berlin: Rainer Hobbing, 1934), 81.

resented the key term in Nazi doctrine. According to Starcke, the birth of the Third Reich constituted the victory of reason and good sense. National Socialism had restored social harmony and made work the core of life and a source of joy. The major task ahead was to give the entire Volk access to the beauties of the world and to conquer for it a place in the sun commensurate with the magnitude of German achievement.

By contrast, Heinz Marr, although quick to welcome the advent of the Third Reich,[89] showed himself unimpressed by DAF reform efforts or the prospects for beauty and joy in work opened up by National Socialism.[90] His chapter on "Industrial Work," having traced the evolution of the modern factory system, gloomily concluded that Arbeitsfreude was impossible whatever the social system, and that the totalitarian state would therefore have to tackle the problem of work by propagating an ethic of soldierly service as the basis of Volksgemeinschaft.[91] Fortunately, in Marr's view, Germany's Protestant heritage had uniquely prepared the nation's industrial workers both to accept the separation of home and factory, play and work, and to acknowledge disciplined, heroic, and manly struggle as the order of the day—although, under the influence of the Hitler-Stalin pact of 1939, he admitted that the other totalitarian powers—Italy and European Russia—had developed similar anti-romantic attitudes towards, and ways of utilizing, industrial labor.

Rejecting the early National Socialist emphasis on agriculture and the crafts, Peppler's compendium accurately reflected current concerns by focusing on modern industry. One of the most interesting contributions in this connection was the survey of German work in song and literature by the DAF's Ernst Kunsdorff.[92] Kunsdorff (1887–?), who had joined the NSDAP in 1932,[93] duly acknowledged the achievements of non-Nazi forerunners including Riehl, but insisted that an entirely new literature was needed to mirror the joyous world created by the Na-

[89] See Heinz Marr, "Der Einbruch des Nationalsozialismus in das deutsche Parteiensystem und die Wendung zum totalen Staat," in *Die Massenwelt im Kampf um ihre Form. Zur Soziologie der deutschen Gegenwart* (Hamburg: Hanseatische Verlagsanstalt, 1934), 447–576, and his essays on industrial relations in *Deutsches Volkstum* 18 (1936): 684–92, 833–42, 923–29.

[90] Marr's loss of control over the Gesellschaft für Werkspolitik (renamed "Gesellschaft für Sozialwissenschaft" in 1937) to the DAF's Arnhold in 1938 may have spurred his dislike of the DAF. See Gesellschaft für Sozialwissenschaft, *Jahresbericht* 30 April 1938 and *Mitgliederverzeichnis* 31 December 1938 (Kiel).

[91] Heinz Marr, "Die Industriearbeit," in Peppler, *Deutsche Arbeitskunde*, 115–38.

[92] Ernst Kunsdorff, "Die Deutsche Arbeit in Lied und Literatur," Peppler, *Deutsche Arbeitskunde*, 432–56.

[93] BDC, "Parteistatistische Erhebung 1939," in Kunsdorff's personnel file.

tional Socialist revolution. Happily he hailed the emergence of a new generation of worker poets who sang of a society in which manual and intellectual work had been reconciled and labor restored to honor. Although prose writers lagged in doing justice to the realities of contemporary life, he also saw a tendency to get away from the *Blut und Boden* ("blood-and-soil") narratives written to formula in the early years of the Third Reich. At last, novels, too, were beginning to deal with the modern industrial worker, the stratum of society in which, he alleged, the National Socialist work ethos—defined as a compound of Arbeits-freude and patriotism—was most at home.

The "intellectuals" who contributed to Peppler's *Deutsche Arbeits-kunde* did not achieve consensus on major points. If the book nevertheless succeeded as a work of Nazi propaganda, this was because it demonstrated the dedication of "workers of the brow" to the new Germany. Exemplifying the spirit of Volksgemeinschaft that it wished to propagate, it represented the "high culture" end of a continuum of propaganda materials designed to persuade Germans of all classes that the Third Reich embodied the highest ideal of German work and served the common welfare. At the other extreme of this continuum lay Leopold von Schenkendorf's well-designed collector's album of cigarette cards (distributed by Salem Cigarettes of Dresden) which depicted a joyful nation at work under Nazi leadership. Published to commemorate the first anniversary of Hitler's regime, it sold for RM1.[94] In between, a plethora of propaganda publications ran the gamut from coffee-table items to cheap pamphlets intended for mass distribution. Good examples of the former are *The Honor Book of Work*, published in 1934 with an introduction by Ley,[95] *Memorials of German Work*, a lavish two-volume publication that incorporated the views on German work by leading Nazis and was heavily subsidized by industry;[96] and Arnhold's elegantly produced *The Law of Community*.[97]

Among propaganda works meant for a wider public were numerous anthologies of worker literature,[98] and a photographic celebration of

[94] Leopold von Schenkendorf, *Der Staat der Arbeit und des Friedens. Ein Jahr Regierung Adolf Hitler* (Altona-Bahrenfeld: Cigaretten-Bilderdienst, [1934]). Copy in NN. Von Schenkendorf was an SA *Sturmführer*.

[95] *Das Ehrenbuch der Arbeit*, ed. Herald Torf (Düsseldorf: Friedrich Fleeder, 1934).

[96] *Denkmal Deutscher Arbeit. Ein Werk von Deutscher Kraft und Tüchtigkeit für Jugend, Schule, Arbeitsdienst, Gewerbe, Industrie und Handel*, ed. Arthur Göpfert, Dresden, MdR (Leipzig: Alfred Hans, 1934–35).

[97] Karl Arnhold, *Vom Gesetz der Gemeinschaft* (Berlin: DAF, n.d.).

[98] See, e.g., Wolfgang Jünemann, *Werkgemeinschaft* and *Werktätiges Volk* (Frankfurt: Moritz Diesterweg, 1938); and Hans Mühle, ed., *Das Lied der Arbeit. Selbstzeugnisse der Schaffenden. Ein Querschnitt durch die Arbeitsdichtung der Gegenwart* (Gotha: Leopold Klotz, 1935).

Volksgemeinschaft entitled *Workers of Brow and Fist* that interlarded portraits of peasants, publishers, artists, professors, entrepreneurs, National Socialist leaders, and other German "workers" with uplifting quotations about work and Volk.[99] Popular pamphlets included Friedrich Griese's *Our Work Is Faith*,[100] a paean to German work addressed to members of the RAD and to Germany's front soldiers, the true bearers of German Geist, and Hans Munter's *Why Does the German Worker Back Hitler?*[101]

The production of this extensive propaganda literature was possible only because countless members of the educated classes, including scholars, journalists, artists,[102] publishers, and skilled typographers were prepared to work actively for the National Socialist cause. In turn, the elaborate propaganda apparatus of the Third Reich offered people with the requisite knowledge and skills unprecedented opportunities to serve their country and be well paid for doing so. For these individuals, as indeed for all professionals willing to conform to the requirements of the new Germany, the community of work proclaimed by National Socialism came close to realization.[103]

More problematic was the attitude of Germany's manual workers. Had these workers, too, accepted the new work ethic and come to feel at home in the National Socialist Volksgemeinschaft? Insisting that all loyal and productive Germans were "workers," the Nazis abjured the language of class when talking of the problem of work. Nevertheless, they continued to give particular attention to industrial wage-laborers, not only because of the numerical importance of this group, but also because they had reason to doubt the degree to which the "proletariat" had been integrated into the body of the nation.

For propaganda purposes, it was often thought convenient to act as if Volksgemeinschaft had been realized. Thus Goebbels, in a speech to the Hamburg *Freude und Arbeit* Congress of 1936, claimed that Na-

Mühle's anthology, which appeared with the National Socialist imprimatur, was an expanded version of a 1928 publication entitled *Das proletarische Schicksal!*

[99] Erich Matthes, ed., *Arbeiter der Stirn und Faust, ein nationales Besinnungsbuch* (Leipzig: im Matthes Verlag, 1934).

[100] Friedrich Griese, *Unsere Arbeit ist Glaube* (Berlin: F. Eher, 1940; second printing 1942). Griese was a successful novelist.

[101] Hans Munter, *Warum steht der deutsche Arbeiter zu Hitler?* (Berlin: Deutscher Verlag, 1940; 2d enl. ed., 1941). This work also appeared in English, Spanish, Portuguese, Belgian, Swedish, and Dutch.

[102] The depiction of work in National Socialist art is briefly discussed by Berthold Hinz, *Art in the Third Reich* (New York: Pantheon Books, 1979), 110–17, 148–59, and 194–95.

[103] Not all Nazi propagandists came from the middle class. See, e.g., Achim Holtz, *Nationalsozialist—warum?* (Munich: Karl Zeleny & Co., 1936), a popularization of Nazi racist and economic doctrines by a former blue-collar worker turned SS fighter.

tional Socialism had already succeeded in giving work a new ethical value and had opened the "way to the nation" for the German worker.[104] Similarly, Ley and his associates proceeded on the assumption that the DAF's social and educational initiatives had produced happy and loyal workers ready to do their all for the nation and their Führer, and that only a recalcitrant minority, congenitally incapable of German work or infected by inappropriate attitudes carried over from Marxism and Catholic trade unionism,[105] still posed a threat.

Hitler, on the other hand, frequently acknowledged that it would take fifty or even a hundred years of education to overcome the obstacles to the achievement of true community.[106] Since these obstacles were the product of centuries of hatred and discord, time was needed to root out ideas of class struggle and create a situation where all would realize that "mind and fist, brow and hand, intelligence and strength" belonged together and completed one another.[107] The Führer allowed his followers to do what they could to improve working conditions through the Beauty of Labor program and to foster harmonious industrial relations in the Betriebsgemeinschaft, but he, personally, was not particularly interested in such matters.[108] Without illusions about the speed with which his "revolution" could be accomplished, he continued to worry about the Arbeiter and was fully prepared to enforce compliance, pending the time when National Socialist racial and educational policies would have succeeded in creating the new German who would instinctively value work as service to the community and selflessly contribute to the greater Germany of the future.

Those National Socialists who nonetheless attempted to convert workers from acquiescence to enthusiastic support found a useful instrument in the works newspaper. Developed in the Weimar period by the Dinta and others engaged in the "fight for the soul of the German worker," Werkzeitungen proliferated in the Third Reich. They now had a dual purpose: to propagate the works community ideal in the

[104] Weltkongress für Freizeit und Erholung, Bericht, 72.

[105] Typical expressions of DAF anti-Catholicism were Heinrich Härtle's Berufsständische Vereine als Machtinstrumente des politischen Katholizismus. DAF-Schulung Folge C, Heft 1 (Berlin, 1937), and Vom Ständesstaat zur Priesterherrschaft. Eine Abrechnung mit Othmar Spann (Berlin: Die DAF Schulung, 1938). The DAF attacked both "internationalist" political Catholicism and the Catholic corporatist tradition based on the occupational ethic.

[106] See, e.g., his May Day speech at the Berlin Lustgarten in 1935, in Norman H. Baynes, ed., The Speeches of Adolf Hitler April 1922–August 1939 (London: Royal Institute of International Affairs, 1942), 1:987.

[107] Speech to the DAF at Nuremberg, 11 September 1937, Baynes, Speeches of Adolf Hitler, 945–46.

[108] Albert Speer, Inside the Third Reich. Memoirs (New York: Macmillan, 1970), 57.

interests of management, and to carry the political message of the
NSDAP into the workplace.[109] Indeed, once Arnhold had transferred
his attentions from private industry to the DAF, the primary objective
of these papers became a political one: namely, to convert the workers
to National Socialism.[110]

Whereas the works newspapers dated back to earlier times, the
Werkscharen were a National Socialist invention. Initially comprised of
young male converts to National Socialism who were given blue uniforms to impress onlookers and develop *esprit de corps*, these DAF-spon-
sored work troops sought to further the National Socialist version of
Betriebsgemeinschaft by organizing communal activities involving the
spoken word and song. But unlike the works newspapers, the Werkscharen could not survive into the war, at least in their original guise.
From May 1939, membership was broadened to include workers belonging to the Nazi women's organizations—the NS-Frauenschaft and
NS-Frauenwerk—as well as men enrolled in SA, SS, and DAF formations. Distinctive uniforms were no longer issued. Moreover, wartime
directives totally subordinated the Werkscharen to management and
restricted them to an educational and propagandistic role.[111]

Perhaps the most popular National Socialist initiative aimed at the
working masses, apart from the extension of paid holidays, was the
DAF's Strength through Joy (KdF) program. Although the double burden of job and home meant that women workers had no true leisure
time, and so found KdF programs irrelevant,[112] and although many
working class men could not afford to participate, the organized leisure
activities sponsored in the 1930s by the KdF undoubtedly redounded to
the credit of the regime beyond the limited circle of those who took

[109] The process of politicization can be readily traced in the *Siemens-Mitteilungen* and in
Das Werk, published since 1920, from 1926 by the United Steel Corporation. Cf. Adelbert
Klein, *Die Werkzeitschrift als Teil der betrieblichen Sozialpolitik* (Berlin/Charlottenburg: Rudolf
Lorentz, 1939), and Robert A. Brady, *The Spirit and Structure of German Fascism* (New York:
Viking, 1937), 151, both of which stress continuity with the Weimar Dinta papers.

[110] Albert Klöckner, "Die Werkzeitung als Gestaltungsmittel betrieblicher Führung," *Arbeitsschulung* 6 (1935), 1:19–20. By the time of its absorption into the DAF, the Dinta already
had over one hundred papers under its direct control. A good example of the papers that
appeared under the auspices of the Works Newspaper division of the DAF press office, was
Arbeit ist Leben. The organ of the Berlin printing and publishing house Wilhelm Limpert
which had won an award as a model enterprise in a national *Musterbetrieb* competition, *Arbeit
ist Leben* deluged Limpert workers (whom it addressed as "work comrades") with uplifting
sermons on the glory of work; during the war it attempted to keep up morale by maintaining
that Germany was engaged in a just "defensive" struggle for both freedom and Lebensraum.

[111] BA Sammlung Schumacher 287 (Werkscharen 1935–1940). Memorandum "Werk-
schar" from Obergruppenführer Jüttner of the "Oberste SA-Führung," 10 April 1940, explaining the current status of these formations in relation to other party organizations.

[112] Claudia Koonz, *Mothers in the Fatherland* (New York: St. Martin's Press, 1987), 199.

part.[113] In addition, the DAF's Beauty of Labor division demonstrated National Socialist concern for the workers by encouraging employers to do such things as improve lighting and institute attractive works canteens.

How many workers were converted by these reforms to National Socialism during the peacetime years of the Third Reich we do not know. Class conflict within the enterprise was not abolished: throughout the period of the first Four-Year Plan, however, National Socialist reforms do seem to have been effective in furthering the cause of Volksgemeinschaft. Only with the coming of war, when many popular programs had to be curtailed, did it become necessary once again to rethink the National Socialist approach to the problem of work.

In hindsight, the Second World War can be regarded as the logical outgrowth of Hitler's racist convictions and expansionist intentions. However, it is important to remind ourselves that most Germans, including many National Socialists, were dismayed at the outbreak of hostilities. Quite a number had cooperated with the Hitler regime because they believed that National Socialism, by unifying the nation and putting it back to work, would enable Germany to assume its rightful place in the community of nations *without* resort to force. Even in the first phase of the war it was still possible to hope that peace would soon be restored through a German victory. As a result, morale remained high. However, as the conflict dragged on, the fundamental lack of enthusiasm of the German public for a war of aggression compelled the regime to make ever greater efforts to manipulate opinion so as to maintain work discipline.[114]

Already before 1939 the drive for higher production had subjected German workers to increasing regulation and stress. Once Germany was at war, and especially in the later phases of the conflict when shortages multiplied and the nation's cities were subject to aerial bombardment, the pressure on civilians was hardly less than that experienced by workers inducted into the armed forces. By the 1940s the worker-warrior analogy, originally a device to reproduce the "front spirit" of community in the workplace and foster productivity in the name of patriotism, had been transformed into a frightening reality.

To counteract the adverse effects of prolonged effort on an increasingly weary population, the National Socialists relied heavily on propaganda. Particularly in the first few years, the war was presented

---

[113] Werner, 'Bleib übrig,' 31.

[114] Shifts in wartime public opinion are clearly traced in Marlis G. Steinert, *Hitler's War and the Germans*, ed. and trans. by Thomas E.J. de Witt (Athens, Ohio: Ohio University Press, 1977).

as one of defense against Jewish-dominated nations determined to destroy Germany out of jealousy of National Socialism's great achievements; workers of all classes were urged to do their duty and prove their mettle by laboring long and hard for victory. In addition to propagating an ethic of duty and service, Nazi spokesmen stressed the Social Darwinist concept of struggle, the racist version of Deutsche Arbeit, and the Leistungsprinzip. These aspects of the ideology of work were now employed not only to justify the war itself, but also to render acceptable the brutal exploitation of foreign workers and of Germans designated as enemies of the Volk.

Nevertheless, the National Socialists knew full well that propaganda alone was incapable of maintaining labor productivity. Thus in 1938 Göring declared proudly that Germany was now the "land of labor," its workers prepared to raise their productivity and work overtime because they had learned the meaning of obligation to the nation. Yet he also insisted that compulsion, incompatible with joy in work, could coexist with duty.[115] The Nazis accordingly instituted a whole range of disciplinary measures to supplement the internalized categorical imperative allegedly characteristic of the German worker. Absenteeism, slackness, or refusal to accept employment were subject to a spectrum of penalties that ranged from fines and other monetary sanctions to "reeducation" through forced labor in worker-education or concentration camps.[116]

On the other hand, in trying to attract building workers to the *Westwall*, the massive defensive bulwark constructed as part of the Four-Year Plan, the Nazis had already discovered before the war that improved working conditions, measures to preserve the health of the workforce, and non-material incentives such as organized leisure programs could do more to ensure compliance with national goals than either exhortations or penalties.[117] After 1939 it became even more essential to extract additional production from the shrinking civilian workforce without precipitating a rise in the general level of wages. Consequently the NSDAP, while talking loudly of duty and sacrifice,[118] redoubled efforts to make the necessary work less burdensome, and to demonstrate concern for workers' welfare. Moreover, as it became necessary to re-

[115] Hermann Göring, speech of 10 September 1938, excerpted in Timothy Mason, *Arbeiterklasse und Volksgemeinschaft. Dokumente und Materialen zur deutschen Arbeiterpolitik 1936–1939* (Wiesbaden: Westdeutscher Verlag, 1975), 677–80.

[116] See Werner, *'Bleib übrig,'* 27–33, 178–89; and Stephen Salter, "Structures of Consensus and Coercion. Workers' Morale and the Maintenance of Work Discipline, 1939–1945," in David Welch, ed., *Nazi Propaganda* (London: Croom Helm, 1983), 88–116.

[117] Mason, *Arbeiterklasse*, Doc. 115, 681–88. Skeptical of such efforts, Mason points out that *Westwall* volunteers were also offered high wages!

[118] See, e.g., Mason, *Arbeiterklasse*, 1192–1200, a speech by Ley of 19 November 1939, published November 20 in the *Völkischer Beobachter*.

cruit and train young people, women, and foreigners to replace the skilled male workers who joined the armed forces in increasing numbers more attention was paid to redesigning the production process and adapting the work environment to accommodate these categories of labor.

Such thinking lay behind the continued expansion of vocational training programs in wartime, despite jurisdictional conflicts between party and business organizers and between the DAF and other party organizations, and despite widespread concerns about the long-term effects of lessening the period of apprenticeship, training the unskilled, and catering to women.[119] Although the quality of these programs was less than ideal,[120] many workers undoubtedly benefitted from the opportunities created by this extension of skills training. The National Socialist vocational education policies must be classed as a popular feature of the Third Reich. How effective they were in converting labor to a National Socialist ethic of work is another question.

The trend towards mass production, which gained momentum after Speer took over as Minister of Armaments and Munitions in 1942, was not greeted with the same widespread approval. Determined to achieve maximum output with limited human resources to meet the demands of total war, Speer systematically encouraged the employment of "Taylorist" techniques by the industries within his sphere of influence; and the latter, no longer concerned about resistance from organized labor, were happy to comply. However it is worth noting that "rationalization" continued to have the most adverse impact on those near the bottom of the hierarchy of work, people whose interests had never been adequately represented by the German trade unions.

The lowest category of workers, comprising German and foreign slave laborers, was in any case regarded as expendable, and so could be worked to, and frequently beyond, the point of death. Somewhat

[119] For details, see Seubert, *Berufserziehung und Nationalsozialismus*, Fischer and Scholtz, "Stellung und Funktion der Erwachsenenbildung im Nationalsozialismus," and Gillingham, "The 'Deproletarianization' of German Society."

[120] For a critical contemporary view, see L. Hamburger, *How Nazi Germany has Mobilized and Controlled Labor* (Washington, D.C.: Brookings Institution, 1940). Hamburger, who taught at the University of Geneva, deplored the fate of the artisans under National Socialism, commented unfavorably on the system of compulsory apprenticeship and the watered-down training provided, and warned that the Third Reich was constructing a system of "industrial feudalism." Hans Kellner, "Arbeits- und Berufspädagogik," *Zentralblatt für Arbeitswissenschaft* 1 (April 1947), 1:105–109, likewise denied that any real progress was made in industrial pedagogy during the Third Reich, despite the large sums devoted to it by the Nazis; and Karl C. Lingelbach, *Erziehung und Erziehungstheorien im nationalsozialistischen Deutschland* (Weinheim: Julius Beltz, 1970), especially 123–46, argues that the efforts of National Socialists to inculcate a sense of discipline and a duty ethic tended to stifle the spontaneity and intellectual independence desirable in the modern worker.

greater care had to be taken of the next category up, German women. Because the National Socialists valued women in their biological role as mothers, they felt compelled to concern themselves with the health of these workers, at least during the child-bearing years. To protect the unborn child, the DAF encouraged modifications of the work station, transfer of pregnant women to less hazardous jobs, maternity leave, extra paid holidays, and additional rest breaks for working mothers.[121]

While much of this remained on paper, women wage-earners did receive special treatment, particularly after 1939, when their ranks were swollen by the increasing numbers of middle-class individuals assigned to industrial work. These newcomers required additional training and special indoctrination to prepare them psychologically for the monotonous tasks most were expected to perform. Determined to get the most out of their women workers, the National Socialists also paid particular attention to their health and comfort in the workplace.[122] Firms were warned to take into account the fundamentally different attitude to factory work of women due to their displacement from their natural environment, the home,—for example by allowing them to make their workplace homelike, that is clean, orderly, and attractive. In addition, female social workers (*soziale Betriebsarbeiterinnen*) were employed in increasing numbers to see to the welfare of employees and to improve their attitude to work.[123]

Reversing the position originally taken by Nazi propagandists, special efforts were made during the war to persuade women and their families to abandon the traditional view that labor for family and home was woman's true profession.[124] The right of women, even those on the assembly line, to develop an inner relationship with their work and derive satisfaction from it, was openly defended by industrial psychologists in the Third Reich as they sought to convince male managers and supervisors to improve their treatment of women workers, for the sake of the women and for the good of the country.[125]

[121] Hermann Textor, *Die Arbeitspolitik im Dritten Reich: Erhaltung und Förderung der nationalen Arbeitskraft* (Berlin: Paul Hochmuth, 1937).

[122] See, e.g., *Schutz der werktätigen Frau. Sonderveröffentlichung des Reichsarbeitsblattes* (Berlin: Verlag für Sozialpolitik, Wirtschaft und Statistik, 1941), especially 17–22 on workplace design and clothing; and Hebestreit, *Schutz und Erhaltung*, 65–69.

[123] Carola Sachse, "Hausarbeit im Betrieb. Betriebliche Sozialarbeit unter dem Nationalsozialismus," in Sachse, ed., *Angst, Belohnung*, 209–274.

[124] See, most recently, Annemarie Tröger, "The Creation of a Female Assembly-Line Proletariat," in Renate Bridenthal, ed., *When Biology Became Destiny. Women in Weimar and Nazi Germany* (New York: Monthly Review Press, 1984), 237–70.

[125] E.g., Adolf Friedrich, "Innere Arbeitsverbundenheit der Frau," *Die Deutsche Sozialpolitik* 1 (February 1945), 1:2–3, and Martha Moers, *Der Fraueneinsatz in der Industrie. Eine psychologische Untersuchung* (Berlin: Duncker & Humblot, 1943). Moers (1877–1966), who had

Women in the Third Reich also enjoyed new opportunities for relatively skilled and interesting employment outside the home. Rapid growth of the largely female social-work profession was a feature of the period.[126] So was expansion of the bureaucracy, which increased the amount of low-paid and tedious clerical work available to women, but provided many others with their first opportunity to develop skills and experience joy in work as teachers or as leaders in the National Socialist women's organizations and the women's labor service.[127] Finally, women found new scope for their abilities in the various voluntary agencies that proliferated under the aegis of the party.[128]

There was a growing tendency among National Socialists, especially during the war, to argue that German women had a duty to utilize all their abilities to serve the Volk, even if this meant allowing them to undertake a wide range of tasks originally reserved for men. Just the same, Hitler continued to insist that women belonged in the home, to oppose total mobilization of women, and to promise that they would be returned after the war to their natural domain.[129] Moreover, there is evidence that the majority of women shared his traditional views on women's role, even if most rejected the radical racism on which his attitude towards women's work was largely based.[130] Attempts to persuade those who could afford to remain at home that they had an ob-

worked with Moede in Berlin and Poppelreuter in Bonn during the 1920s, in 1940 joined the staff of the DAF's Institute for the Psychology of Work and Labor Education. See Geuter, *Professionalisierung der deutschen Psychologie,* 576.

[126] The benefits of this vocation for the individual woman were spelled out by the DAF Women's Bureau in a recruiting pamphlet: *Soziale Betriebsarbeit* (Berlin: Frauenamt der Deutschen Arbeitsfront, n.d.), 15. See also *Weltkongress für Freizeit und Erholung,* 214, where the head of a rubber goods factory explained how doing social work in industry would give women a chance to raise their sense of self while using their characteristic gifts to raise company morale.

[127] See Gertrud Scholtz-Klink, *Die Frau im Dritten Reich. Eine Dokumentation* (Tübingen: Grabert, 1978), a celebration of opportunities for working women available in the Third Reich by the unrepentant National Socialist former head of the DAF's Women's Bureau; also Klose-Stiller, *Arbeitsdienst für die weibliche Jugend.* Both these women, who clearly enjoyed their own work in the Third Reich, tried to teach others to adopt the same positive attitude to their jobs.

[128] See Hauptamt für Volkswohlfahrt, *Deine Arbeit—Dein Werk. Vom Sozialismus der Tat* (Berlin: Eher, 1942). Published on the occasion of the organization's tenth anniversary, this volume praised the work done by women volunteers, for example, as nurses, family counselors, and youth workers.

[129] Dorte Winkler, *Frauenarbeit im Dritten Reich* (Hamburg: Hoffmann und Campe, 1977), 28–33 and passim; Leila Rupp, *Mobilizing Women for War: German and American Propaganda, 1939–1945* (Princeton: Princeton University Press, 1978), 11–50.

[130] The links between Nazi racial ideology and attitudes to women's work are discussed in Gisela Bock, "Racism and Sexism in Nazi Germany: Motherhood, Compulsory Sterilization, and the State," in Bridenthal, *When Biology Became Destiny,* 271–96.

ligation to seek outside employment met with only limited success.[131] Meanwhile, women who worked out of economic necessity or because they were compelled to do so by the government, did so for the most part grudgingly.[132] Resentful of individuals who were exempt, they tended to shrug off exhortations to do their patriotic duty and instead looked for ways to lighten the double burden of work and family which a high proportion of them had to bear. Female workers in armaments firms were reported to have lower productivity and higher sickness and absenteeism rates than men; women, along with conscript labor and the young, continued to demonstrate relatively poor work-discipline throughout the war.[133]

The only manual workers who seem to have maintained a degree of joy in work throughout the war were the relatively few adult males exempted from military service because their skills were essential for war production. Members of this elite did manage to exhibit a potent ethic of work. However, it is difficult to establish how much this owed to National Socialist convictions or was correlated with approval of the regime. Some undoubtedly accepted the National Socialists' claim that their movement represented a development from rather than a repudiation of proletarian socialism—a view which the Third Reich had sought to foster by converting labor's May Day into a festival of German work.[134] A recent oral history of Krupp workers indicates that the pride in work and strong sense of self-worth demonstrated by Krupp employees, while often combined with an appreciation for the benefits offered by the Third Reich, did not reflect specifically National Socialist attitudes to work.[135] Indeed, it has been argued that their work ethic, based on the tradition of the organized working class, may have made these skilled workers relatively immune to National Socialist propaganda rather than more inclined to succumb to Nazi blandishments.

[131] Jill Stephenson, "Nationalsozialistischer Dienstgedanke, bürgerliche Frauen und Frauenorganisationen im Dritten Reich," *Geschichte und Gesellschaft* 7 (1981): 555–71.

[132] On women's reluctance to work harder, as well as their stubborn refusal to submit to factory discipline in the period of rearmament and during the war, see Winkler, *Frauenarbeit*, 62, 95, 99, 129–30, 182–91. See also Mason, *Arbeiterklasse*, Doc. 221, 1180–81, one of many reports complaining of women's resistance to full-time work and overtime.

[133] Salter, in Welch, *Nazi Propaganda*, 98–99; Mary Nolan, "Workers and National Socialism," in Charles S. Maier, ed., *The Rise of the Nazi Regime* (Boulder, Colo.: Westview, 1986), 93.

[134] See, e.g., Walther Pahl, "Der Feiertag der Arbeit und die sozialistische Arbeiterschaft," *Gewerkschafts-Zeitung*, 29 April 1933, 259–62.

[135] Ulrich Herbert, "Die guten und die schlechten Zeiten. Überlegungen zur diachronen Analyse lebensgeschichtlicher Interviews," in Lutz Niethammer, ed., *Die Jahre weiss man nicht, wo man die heute hinsetzen soll. Faschismus-Erfahrungen im Ruhr-Gebiet* (Berlin: J.H.W. Dietz, 1983), 90–91.

More pragmatically, the willingness of these men to work hard can be attributed in large part to memories of the depression and to the knowledge that military service would be demanded of those who failed to give satisfaction.[136]

A similar study of Bremen workers in the Third Reich concludes that whereas the shipyard workers tended to be anti-Nazi, their fellows in that city's modern aeronautics and automotive works were inclined to support the regime. Fascinated by technology and eager to contribute to the common effort in a spirit of Betriebsgemeinschaft, especially those employed by the Focke-Wulff Musterbetrieb exhibited a work ethic totally in accord with "Nazi" values. In addition to demonstrating pride in their personal achievements, their firm, and its product, they were grateful for the substantial economic, social, and cultural benefits bestowed upon them in return for their superior work.[137]

Apart from programs specifically designed to appease the country's manual workers, the National Socialists successfully used a general appeal to patriotism to minimize worker resistance and thus obviate the need for drastic sanctions. When called upon to serve their country in its hour of need, working-class Germans were just as prone to respond positively as members of other classes. There is also evidence that they shared National Socialist views on the superiority of German work. Thus, many German miners feared that foreign workers would hold down group productivity and thereby lower wages, disliked working with foreigners, and took it upon themselves to discipline these outsiders, "sometimes with undue force."[138] Finally, like Germans in other sectors of society, members of the working class frequently succumbed to Hitler's personal appeal. Accepting the Führer's authority as legitimate, the majority tended to support him even as they clashed with officialdom, objected to specific National Socialist policies, or criticized developments that adversely affected their particular interests.[139]

Although it is hard to generalize about worker attitudes and mo-

[136] Herbert, "Gute und schlechte Zeiten," 95 n.10.

[137] Hans-Josef Steinberg, "Die Haltung der Arbeiterschaft zum NS-Regime," in Jürgen Schmädeke and Peter Steinbach, eds., Der Widerstand gegen den Nationalsozialismus (Cologne: Piper, 1985), 867–73. Nazi labor policy also seems to have been relatively successful among the Ruhr miners, redounding to the credit of the regime despite the fact that morale-boosting improvements were generally introduced on the employers' initiative, rather than at the behest of the party's DAF, which Ruhr industry did its best to keep at arms length. See John Gillingham, Industry and Politics in the Third Reich. Ruhr Coal, Hitler, and Europe (London: Methuen, 1985), 56, 164.

[138] Gillingham, Industry and Politics, 121.

[139] On the integrative power of the Hitler myth, see Ian Kershaw, Der Hitler-Mythos. Volksmeinung und Propaganda im Dritten Reich (Stuttgart: Deutsche-Verlagsanstalt, 1980).

tives,[140] one must conclude that manual workers were not immune to National Socialism, and found numerous aspects of Nazi work propaganda congenial. Terror always remained in the background, but in the last years of the Third Reich extreme measures were seldom needed to keep Germans at work. It was foreign workers who were the chief, if not the sole, inmates of the Gestapo-run worker education camps, and the majority of these disciplinary institutions were only established in 1944.[141] On the other hand, the remarkable tendency of Germans to keep on working hard under appalling circumstances does not prove that they had all become good Nazis. What looked like high morale and loyalty to the firm can largely be accounted for by the absence of practical alternatives to staying on the job, combined with the need to cooperate with one's fellows in order to survive in the face of catastrophe.[142]

The experience of war forced enormous changes on National Socialism. As late as 1939, an idealistic young Austrian could still identify it with the cause of joy in work, peace, and the end of alienation.[143] But by 1942 the Third Reich had virtually abandoned the Arbeitsfreude ideal and had become, in the words of Albert Speer, a "slave state."[144] An armed camp surrounded by foes bent on its destruction, Nazi Germany had overburdened its agricultural sector, put its craftsmen once more on the defensive, and run its factories increasingly according to "American" methods of mass production, using foreign slave labor or women forced to neglect their families in order to replace men in essential jobs. Meanwhile business was excused for the duration from proceeding with the costly implementation of "German socialism." Of all the National Socialist ideas for solving the problem of work, the only project pursued with vigor during the last years of the war was the one proposed by Hitler in the 1920s: the elimination of the Jews.

Yet even as the military situation deteriorated, and while the "Final Solution" was in full swing, a few National Socialist ideologues continued to canvas more traditional approaches to the problem of work. Evidently eager to convince both themselves and their fellow citizens that

[140] The problem of assessing public opinion in the Third Reich is perceptively discussed in Ian Kershaw's *Popular Opinion and Political Dissent in the Third Reich. Bavaria, 1933–1945* (New York: Oxford University Press, 1983).

[141] Werner, *'Bleib übrig,'* 178.   [142] Werner, *'Bleib übrig,'* 259–63.

[143] Erich Ernst Köllinger, *Die Arbeitsfreude.* Dissertation, Innsbruck, 1939. Based entirely on National Socialist sources, this was the last extended disquisition on joy in work to be published in the Third Reich.

[144] Albert Speer, *Der Sklavenstaat. Meine Auseinandersetzungen mit der SS* (Stuttgart: Deutsche Verlagsanstalt, 1981).

the war had meaning, they insisted that the current deterioration of work was purely temporary and that the Third Reich would fulfill its promises once hostilities ceased. In the ensuing debate about the future of work in the postwar world, the DAF once more took the lead. Prevented from realizing its goals in the short run, it assured the nation that National Socialism, after the war, would finally be in a position to produce a nation without proletarians, a Germany in which all would achieve a high standard of living and work joyfully and cooperatively for the Volk community.[145]

DAF spokesmen also persisted in identifying National Socialism with modernization. Convinced that a severe shortage of labor would continue after the war, they argued for a "scientific" approach to the problem of work that would combine ideology with rationality. Only by fully utilizing Germany's human resources with the help of advanced technology and modern management techniques would it be possible to achieve the necessary level of productivity.[146] In addition, the DAF projected into the postwar period the idea of Germany as a pace-setter, with a mission to show other industrial nations how to overcome the alienation of labor.[147] Even in 1944, when the end was near, the DAF optimistically predicted that Germany would take the lead after the war in mastering the social question on a continent-wide basis.[148]

Prominent among those who speculated about the nature of German work in the postwar world was Speer, who shared the DAF's preference for modernity, but was prepared, if necessary, to make a permanent

[145] Marie-Luise Recker, *Nationalsozialistische Sozialpolitik im Zweiten Weltkrieg* (Munich: R. Oldenbourg, 1985), 82–154, 297–98.

[146] Dr. Theodor Bühler, "Wissenschaft und Sozialordnung," *Arbeit und Wirtschaft* 7 (1943): 95–99. Writing in a DAF publication designed to explain the party line to its own people, Bühler stressed the need to combine research and faith, science and Weltanschauung, and to inculcate belief in victory and a better postwar world. The DAF's AWI yearbooks for 1940/41 devoted to "Postwar Social Objectives" are analyzed in Herbst, *Totaler Krieg*, 151–53.

[147] The belief in Germany's international mission to solve the problem of work was also used in wartime to justify German domination over Europe, notably by Winschuh. This Weimar proponent of Werkspolitik welcomed the birth of a European new order under National Socialist guidance because he was convinced that only the Nazis knew how to end class conflict and restore the "Christian-Germanic" work ethic based on joy, honor and duty. See Josef Winschuh's "Der Arbeiter," section five of *Gerüstete Wirtschaft* (Berlin: Frundsberg-Verlag, 1940) and *Der Unternehmer im neuen Europa* (Berlin: Buchholz und Weisswange, 1941). Like several other books used in preparation for this study, the last bears the stamp "Ordensburg Sonthofen, Seminar 'Deutsche Arbeit.' " It would be interesting to discover more about this "Seminar." For a brief description of the *Ordensburgen*, Nazi institutions of higher learning established with the object of creating a new elite, see Schoenbaum, *Hitler's Social Revolution*, 269–71.

[148] See Theodor Bühler, "Europa ohne Proletarier," *Die Deutsche Sozialpolitik* (1944), 2:13–14.

sacrifice of Arbeitsfreude in the interests of higher output. Persuaded that the postwar demands of the domestic and export markets could only be met if Germany continued to turn out mass-produced quality goods, he was impatient with those who moaned about the damaging individual and social consequences of modern work or allowed ideological considerations to influence policy. Only a pragmatic approach, one that accepted the permanence of industrial modernization, could in his view meet Germany's needs in war and the peace to come.[149]

These attitudes put Speer into direct conflict with the SS, which had become the dominant ideological force within the Third Reich. Towards the end of the war, the result was a high-level debate between Speer and SS General Otto Ohlendorf on the future of German work. Ohlendorf (1907–1951), an economist whose influence derived from his positions in the SS security service (SD), the federal retail trade organization (Reichsgruppe Handel), and, from 1943 on, the Ministry of Economics (RWM), clung to a backward-looking Mittelstand ideology close to that propagated during the depression by Hitler and his economic adviser at that time, Otto Wagener.[150] Undeterred by the necessities of war, he wanted to keep joy in work on the national agenda. He was convinced that it was essential to combat the trend toward size and impersonality in industry lest Germany, after the war, find it impossible to provide its citizens with the kind of work that would protect and enhance its racial values. Maintaining the *völkisch* variant of National Socialism which Hitler appeared to have abandoned in favor of Speer's technological rationalism, he spoke of the ideal economy as one dominated by the small private enterprise where work retained its crafts character and where personal initiative and sense of individual responsibility could thrive. What is more, Ohlendorf insisted that the workspace (Arbeitsraum) could and should remain the main focus of a person's life: once production was redesigned to enable the individual to experience a release from strain "in work and through joy in work," there would be no need for organized mass leisure along KdF lines.[151]

Ohlendorf, himself of peasant origin, had deep reservations about modern economic developments and a decided preference for the val-

---

[149] Speer, *Sklavenstaat*, details his running battle with the SS ideologues, and his efforts during the last months of the war to prevent the destruction of Germany's industrial installations and economic infrastructure that Hitler had ordered.

[150] Speer, *Sklavenstaat*, 122. Wagener's views are summarized in Turner, *German Big Business*, 139–41. On Ohlendorf's background and career, see Wistrich, *Who's Who in Nazi Germany*, 225–27, and Herbst, *Totaler Krieg*, 182–88.

[151] June 1944 Speech by Ohlendorf to local NSDAP economic advisers, cited in Speer, *Sklavenstaat*, 123–24, 128, and Herbst, *Totaler Krieg*, 326–27.

ues associated with the peasantry and the crafts over those linked with industry; he had, however, no intention of taking Germany back to its agrarian past. What he wanted was a modern economy without the "American" production methods that Speer was encouraging, without the Leistungsprinzip that put a premium on maximum production and relied on wage incentives, and without the statist "collectivism" towards which Ley and the DAF seemed to be tending. Taking up the notion of a "third way," one already popular in the 1920s, Ohlendorf envisioned a uniquely German economic system distinct from both "Capitalism" and "Bolshevism." His ideal was a society in which industrial concentration and growth would be limited so as to retain a human scale and in which restrictions on the economic role of the State would allow individual initiative to flourish.[152]

What was characteristically "National Socialist" about Ohlendorf's position was not his desire to humanize production and preserve joy in work, but the fact that these ideas were intimately related in his Weltanschauung to a race-based nationalism that regarded honor, freedom, responsibility, honesty, and truthfulness as specifically "Germanic" values. Ohlendorf, who had joined the NSDAP in 1925 at the age of eighteen, subscribed unquestioningly to Hitler's racial views and had no qualms about the methods which Himmler's SS employed to carry out the Führer's will. The same man who opposed modern economic developments because of their damaging impact on the individual and favored extensive reforms to solve the problem of work, thought it his duty to serve as commander of an SS *Einsatzgruppe* engaged in murdering Jews, gypsies, and Communist functionaries as the German army advanced into Russia in June 1941. Like Höss and others SS "idealists," Ohlendorf was prepared to labor mightily to carry out his Führer's wishes, in the hope of asserting German supremacy and thus expanding the scope for "German work."

The debate about the problem of work continued during the war not only among National Socialists but also among their most determined foes. The resistance groups, which for years had plotted to overthrow the Third Reich and nearly managed to kill Hitler in July 1944, differed among themselves on how work should be organized and industrial relations dealt with in a post-National Socialist Germany.[153] All they could agree on was the need to take into account what had happened

---

[152] Herbst, *Totaler Krieg*, 327.

[153] Michael Schneider, "Zwischen Standesvertretung und Werksgemeinschaft. Zu den Gewerkschaftskonzeptionen der Widerstandsgruppen des 20. Juli 1944," in Schmädeke and Steinbach, *Widerstand gegen den Nationalsozialismus*, 520–31.

to work and the worker in the Third Reich, and the importance of integrating labor into the national community.

Most willing to take Nazi innovations as a point of departure was Carl Friedrich Goerdeler (1884–1945), the former Mayor of Leipzig and designated head of the prospective post-Hitler government. A conservative nationalist with traditional social views, Goerdeler had originally supported Hitler and had no fundamental objections to many of the changes initiated by the National Socialists. Thus his memoranda of 1940/41 about the aims of the resistance suggested that the DAF should be retained in modified form, with compulsory membership for all over eighteen. He also proposed that the Labor Trustees continue to arbitrate industrial conflicts and that the proscription of strikes and lockouts be upheld. Only later, under pressure from the trade unionists within the resistance, did he return to his own earlier belief that trade union participation in the administration of social programs would be a good way to integrate the working class into the nation; he then repudiated the DAF model in favor of a centralized, powerful, but autonomous national trade union.[154]

The problem of worker alienation was approached somewhat differently by the "Kreisau circle" around Helmuth James Graf von Moltke (1907–1945). Driven into opposition by religious abhorrence of National Socialism, Moltke and his associates were more radical than Goerdeler in their rejection of the Third Reich, and more determined to punish those involved in its evils. But although they would not have said so, most were no more eager than Goerdeler to undo major changes brought about by National Socialism, including the abolition of collective bargaining, the rejection of economic liberalism, and the destruction of parliamentary democracy—all of which they believed had facilitated Hitler's rise to power. In the spirit of the voluntary labor camps of the 1920s, in which many of them had participated,[155] they subscribed to the works community ideal and so tended to prefer company unions to a unified national trade union upholding the interests of labor. Politically, the Kreisau group hoped that Hitler's dictatorship would yield to an above-party Christian state headed by

[154] It was Goerdeler's hope that this new German Trade Union would form part of a self-administered corporatist structure that, ideally, would culminate politically in a constitutional monarchy. Schmädeke and Steinbach, *Widerstand gegen den Nationalsozialismus*, 523–25.

[155] See Eugen Rosenstock-Huessy's autobiographical, *I Am an Impure Thinker* (Norwich, Vt.: Argo Books, 1970), 168. Many of Rosenstock's friends became associated with the Kreisau resistance.

men of principle who would make the common welfare the measure of their actions.[156]

The few Social Democrats and trade unionists of the July resistance did not blame the rise of National Socialism on either economic or political democracy. In their case, the collapse of Weimar produced a determination to overcome the fragmentation of the labor movement along political and religious lines, a fragmentation that had prevented joint democratic action in pursuit of working-class interests and in defense of the rule of law. Formulated as early as April 1933, plans for a unified trade union or *Einheitsgewerkschaft* were quickly adopted and pushed on their bourgeois co-conspirators.[157] But if historical considerations were paramount, it is highly likely that the experience of enforced unity within the DAF and the solidarity derived from shared suffering, made it easier to contemplate postwar economic cooperation among trade unionists of all stripes. Reinforced by Nazi Volksgemeinschaft propaganda, these factors also help account for the willingness of working-class leaders to cooperate with "bourgeois" elements in efforts to replace the corrupt dictatorship with a popular government dedicated to peace, decency, and social justice and capable of dealing effectively with the problem of work.

[156] Schneider, "Zwischen Standesvertretung und Werksgemeinschaft," 525–29.
[157] Schneider, "Zwischen Standesvertretung und Werksgemeinschaft," 522–23.

XV

JOY IN WORK, GERMAN WORK?

THE COLLAPSE of the Third Reich in the spring of 1945 meant that neither the National Socialists nor their principled opponents were able to determine the future of German work. At the war's end, Germany found itself at the mercy of its conquerors, all of whom were determined to prevent its resurgence as an economic and military power, and some of whom toyed with the idea of returning it to a pre-industrial state. In the chaos of defeat, it would have been hard to predict that Germans would soon recover their will and capacity to work and that each of the three successor states to emerge from the ashes of the Third Reich—Austria, the Federal Republic of Germany (FRG) and the German Democratic Republic (GDR)—would, within less than two decades, become a modern industrial nation capable of competing successfully on the world market.

Perhaps less surprising in view of what had gone before, although still astonishing given the desperate situation in 1945, was the almost instant resumption of the debate about work. The decision for or against "socialism" was rendered urgent by pressure from the capitalist West on the one hand and the Soviet Union on the other, but attention was also given to the deeper problems of modern work that were thought to exist irrespective of the system of ownership and social distribution. By the 1950s, Germans in the FRG were once more arguing about Arbeitsfreude much as they had during the Weimar years,[1] and they did so, for the most part, without reference to National Socialism.[2]

---

[1] See, e.g., Maximilian Pietsch, *Von Wert und Würde menschlicher Arbeit* (Frankfurt: Josef Knecht, 1952); Adolf Grimme, "Vom Sinn der Arbeit," in *Selbstbesinnung. Reden und Aufsätze aus dem ersten Jahr des Wiederaufbaus* (Braunschweig: Georg Westermann, 1953), 152–68; Kurt Görsdorf, *Arbeitsfreude-Leistungsanstieg. Neue Wege erfolgreicher Arbeitspsychologie* (Munich: Verlag Moderne Industrie, 1958); Christian von Ferber, *Arbeitsfreude. Wirklichkeit und Ideologie. Ein Beitrag zur Soziologie der Arbeit in der industriellen Gesellschaft* (Stuttgart: Ferdinand Enke, 1959).

[2] For an early exception, see Fritz Fricke, *Dintageist-Wirtschaftsbürger. Eine Streitschrift* (Co-

In the 1960s and early 1970s, at the height of the student move-ment, the debate about the meaning of work altered its character and became more vigorous. Some members of the "New Left" now proposed to overcome alienation and further the cause of "human liberation" by rejecting work entirely along with the other values of bourgeois capi-talist society. To this end they initiated a variety of individual and com-munal experiments on the fringes of society. But critics of this "alter-native" vision continued to maintain the centrality of work for human existence. Frequently appealing to the authority of the early Marx, they sought new ways to humanize the workplace and improve the quality of working life.

In the mid-1970s, "humanization" enjoyed the backing not only of business and government but also of the German Trade Union Feder-ation (DGB), formed after the Nazi collapse. DGB unions placed a great deal of emphasis on workplace reform, ignoring warnings from the Marxist Left that, in the FRG, such efforts constituted capitalist or even "Fascist" manipulation of the workers rather than a genuine at-tack on the problem of alienation in the spirit of Karl Marx, the pre-conditions for which existed only in socialist states like the GDR.[3] Ten years later, the service sector of the economy had surpassed manufac-turing in importance, the computer revolution was having immense effects on the organization and nature of work, and mass technological unemployment seemed to have become a permanent feature of modern life. These and other changes brought about renewed debate on the relative value of work and leisure, their modes of interaction, and the potential for joy of modern work.[4]

Although everyone seemed to have an opinion on the subject, efforts in the 1980s to find out "scientifically" what contemporary Germans actually thought about work led to inconclusive results. As in the past, publications on the subject tell us more about the outlook of the re-searchers than about the attitudes of their subjects. A prime example is

logne: Bund-Verlag, 1950). Warning that the *Gesellschaft für Arbeitspädagogik* (GEFA) in Düsseldorf, under Karl Arnhold, was once more propagating the Dinta spirit, Fricke reminded his readers that the backers of the Weimar Dinta had helped Hitler to power, and that Arn-hold had played a prominent role in the Third Reich.

[3] For the view from the GDR, see Rudhard Stollberg, *Arbeitszufriedenheit. Theoretische und Praktische Probleme* (Berlin: Dietz, 1968), and Akademie für Gesellschaftswissenschaften beim Zentralkomitee der SED, Institut für Marxistisch-Leninistische Soziologie, *Körperliche und geistige Arbeit im Sozialismus. Eine soziologische Analyse* (Berlin-Ost: Dietz, 1980).

[4] Inaugurated in the early 1970s with the publication of Wolfgang Nahrstedt's *Die Entste-hung der Freizeit* (Göttingen: Vandenhoeck & Ruprecht, 1972), this discussion recently led to the publication of a series of television scripts and interviews on the subject of work and leisure. See Gunter Myrell *et al.*, eds., *Arbeit, Arbeit über alles. Arbeit und Freizeit im Umbruch* (Cologne: Verlagsgesellschaft Schulfernsehen/CVK, 1985).

a report of the Allensbach opinion research institute in which Elisabeth Noelle-Neumann and her co-author, Burkhard Strümpel, disagree about the importance of joy in work. Although both based their conclusions on attitude surveys which showed that Germans are less happy about, or involved with, their work than the inhabitants of other industrial nations, Noelle-Neumann upheld the traditional view that Arbeitsfreude is essential for a truly human existence and the prerequisite for fruitful leisure, while Strümpel applauded the trend away from the work-centered orientation and towards a lifestyle focused on the satisfactions to be derived from leisure and consumption.[5]

The continuing debate about German work since the demise of National Socialism clearly deserves historical treatment in its own right. It is a story that must be told in order to make a proper assessment of the place of National Socialism in German history. But the fact that Germany is now a divided nation, and that the postwar period is already longer than the Weimar and National Socialist eras combined, means that considerably more research—and another volume!—would be needed for an adequate treatment of the subject. At this point it is possible only to hazard a few tentative generalizations, confined to the FRG, bearing on the question of historical continuity.

One thing that can be said with certainty is that 1945 did not represent a major break in the German tradition with respect to work. The German work ethic survived the Hitler years and proved its worth in the chaotic postwar world; to this day, although there is widespread concern that the Arbeitsethik has finally been lost, Germans live up to their erstwhile reputation as diligent producers of quality work. To what extent other factors are responsible for the impressive work performance of Germans remains unclear. With respect to the immediate postwar period, there is considerable doubt that the willingness to work hard, along with the comparative absence of industrial strife that played such a role in speeding the process of recovery, simply represented further manifestations of traditional German attitudes. One could plausibly argue that German hard work at this time was a typically human response to national catastrophe. Alternatively, one could interpret it as a consequence of National Socialist efforts to foster Betriebsgemeinschaft and Volksgemeinschaft.[6]

---

[5] Elisabeth Noelle-Neumann and Burkhard Strümpel, *Macht Arbeit Krank? Macht Arbeit Glücklich?* (Munich: Piper, 1984).
[6] Conversely, it has been termed "an instinctive act of expiation for the evil of the war and of Nazism" and as a "frenetic attempt at forgetfulness." See the review by Peter Graves of John Ardagh's *Germany and the Germans. An Anatomy of Society Today* (London, Hamish Hamilton), in *The Times Literary Supplement* of 15 May 1987, 520.

To assess whether the latter played a role, it is necessary to ascertain whether the Third Reich actually altered how working Germans thought and felt about their work, and whether any changes that did take place were in line with National Socialist intentions. As we have shown in the preceding chapters, these intentions are themselves hard to interpret, for Nazi ideologists of work differed among themselves on key points. Whether worker attitudes changed as a result of Nazi propaganda is even more difficult to determine. Given the complexity of attitude research at the best of times and the further problems created in Hitler's Germany by the absence of independent labor organizations, opposition parties, and opportunities for the free expression of personal opinion, it seems virtually impossible to say anything useful about the extent to which German workers adopted "National Socialist" attitudes to work.

The Nazis, themselves, wondered to what extent they had been successful in imbuing the German worker with their version of the work ethic. In an attempt to keep abreast of public sentiment, they largely relied on the reports of factory inspectors and of the security police. In addition, they searched for behavioral evidence to substantiate their claims. Thus the engineer who headed the DAF's branch for productivity, vocational training, and management maintained that workers' willingness to make suggestions for improving productivity, a consequence of a campaign to extend the practice of actively soliciting worker input to all enterprises, proved that they were genuinely eager to work for Kultur and Lebensraum. [7]

Historians seeking to clarify the relationship between the National Socialists and the German working class have drawn on the same sources, but have also attempted to supplement and correct National Socialist official records and statements of intent by eliciting oral testimony and exploiting the sparse autobiographical worker literature. In addition, they have used the reports on worker opinion of the Social Democratic underground, which monitored developments between 1933 to 1940. [8] But the limitations of the evidence, combined with the tendency of historians to approach questions from the perspective of their political preferences and attitudes to work, have made it impossible to achieve consensus. All one can say at this stage is that there was a greater degree of worker support for National Socialism both before and after 1933, and more overlap between "Nazi" and working-

[7] Herbert Steinwarz, *Das betriebliche Vorschlagswesen als nationalsozialistisches Führungsinstrument* (Berlin: DAF Lehrmittel-Zentrale, 1943).

[8] *Deutschland-Berichte der Sozialdemokratischen Partei Deutschlands (Sopade) 1934–1940* (Frankfurt: Peter Nettelbeck, 1980).

class attitudes, including attitudes to work and Volk, than most friends of labor would like to think.[9] All in all, Hitler's non-working-class subjects had good grounds for believing that the Third Reich had gone a long way towards solving "the social question" and the problem of work.[10]

However, this still leaves open the question of continuity. In somewhat circular fashion, a number of postwar authors have tried to infer the extent of working-class support for Nazism, and of National Socialist influence on attitudes to work, from the behavior of German workers in the postwar period. For example, the sociologist Ludwig Geck, who himself worked for the DAF, claimed in 1953 that the exemplary cooperation between labor and management in the immediate postwar years showed that National Socialist policies designed to nurture Betriebsgemeinschaft had been effective.[11] More recently, Lothar Kettenacker has argued that the "embourgeoisement" of workers in the German Federal Republic can be taken as evidence for the success of Nazi efforts to integrate the worker into the Volksgemeinschaft.[12] Finally, Josef Mooser, while denying that the working class of the FRG has vanished into the broader mass of Arbeitnehmer ("employees") or has become bourgeois in lifestyle and outlook, acknowledges that the workers have lost their proletarian ethos in part because National Socialist efforts to integrate them on an individual basis into the Volksgemeinschaft were successful.[13]

Since the 1960s, there has been considerable argument about

[9] See Lothar Kettenacker, "Hitler's Impact on the Lower Middle Class," in Welch, Nazi Propaganda, 20–21. Kettenacker warns that it would be wrong to think the working class immune to Nazi promises of full employment and social harmony, or to underrate the impact on the workers of Hitler's speeches which stressed that what mattered was the socialization of human beings rather than of machines.

[10] See Tim Mason, introduction to Sachse, Angst, Belohnung, 18. Although still convinced that the German working class was essentially anti-Nazi, represented a genuine threat to the regime, and was kept under control primarily by compulsion and external restraints, Mason here acknowledges that bribery and pacification played a major part in securing worker compliance.

[11] Ludwig H. A. Geck, Soziale Betriebsführung (2d rev. ed.; Munich: C. H. Beck, 1953), 88–89.

[12] Lothar Kettenacker, "Sozialpsychologische Aspekte der Führer-Herrschaft," in Gerhard Hirschfeld and Lothar Kettenacker, eds., Der Führerstaat. Mythos und Realität (Stuttgart: Klett-Cotta, 1981), 116–18. Sebastian Haffner, Anmerkungen zu Hitler (Munich: Kindler, 1978), 50–53, makes a similar claim for the GDR, which he sees as the continuation of the social community successfully created by Hitler.

[13] Josef Mooser, "Abschied von der 'Proletarität'. Sozialstruktur und Lage der Arbeiterschaft in der Bundesrepublik in historischer Perspektive," in Werner Conze and M. Rainer Lepsius, eds., Sozialgeschichte der Bundesrepublik Deutschland. Beiträge zum Kontinuitätsproblem (Stuttgart: Klett-Cotta, 1983), 143–86.

whether the changes in postwar attitudes that could reasonably be as-
cribed to National Socialism were in line with Nazi intentions, or
whether they should be regarded as the unwanted product of ongoing
social processes of modernization forced on the Third Reich by the demands of modern war.[14] Even if one rejects as overly simplistic the anti-
modernist interpretation of National Socialist ideology implicit in the
latter view, it seems likely that social policy initiatives undertaken during the Third Reich played a bigger role in changing attitudes than did
Nazi attempts to create a "new man" through propaganda and indoctrination.[15] Pointing to the popularity among young workers of Nazi
offerings like payment for performance, education, and holidays, Peukert concludes that such developments furthered the emergence of a
purely instrumental relationship to work after the war.[16] Similarly,
Spode has maintained that the more generous provision of paid holidays helped to dissolve the proletarian milieu.[17] John Gillingham has
made the same claim for the extension of vocational training to wider
circles.[18] Finally, National Socialist measures to prevent arbitrary dismissal, improve sickness and pension benefits, and diminish Mittelstand privileges have been credited with lessening the division between
blue- and white-collar workers, and consequently with contributing to
the greater social homogeneity thought to characterize the Federal
Republic.[19]

On the other hand, one can argue that none of these developments
were due to "National Socialism." On the whole, it makes little sense
either to give National Socialism credit for postwar developments
thought to be positive or to blame it for things that have since gone
wrong. Our survey has shown that the Nazis had few original ideas for
solving the problem of work. The Third Reich merely offered reformers

[14] The latter argument dates back to Schoenbaum, *Hitler's Social Revolution* (1966), and
Ralf Dahrendorf, *Society and Democracy in Germany* (1st ed. 1967; reprint New York: Norton,
1980). More recently, the argument has resurfaced among historians of National Socialism
as a theoretical debate between "intentionalists" and "functionalists," starting with essays by
Tim Mason, Klaus Hildebrand, and Hans Mommsen in Hirschfeld and Kettenacker, *'Führerstaat'* (1981).

[15] Welch, *Nazi Propaganda*, 2, argues that propaganda was in any case more effective in
confirming existing trends and beliefs than in changing ideas and attitudes, while Ian Kershaw, "How effective was Nazi Propaganda?" in Welch, *Nazi Propaganda*, 180–201, maintains
that class differences, status perceptions, and religious loyalties were left fundamentally unaltered by Nazi Volksgemeinschaft propaganda.

[16] Peukert, *Volksgenossen*, 136–40.

[17] Hasso Spode, "Arbeiterurlaub im Dritten Reich," in Sachse, *Angst, Belohnung*, 275–328.

[18] Gillingham, "The 'Deproletarianization of German Society.' "

[19] Recker, *National-sozialische Sozialpolitik*, 300; Prinz, "Sozialpolitik im Wandel der
Staatspolitik," in Bruch, *Weder Kommunismus noch Kapitalismus*, 236–38.

an opportunity to implement on a national scale projects they had conceived but seldom been in a position to develop fully in the Weimar
years. What is more, after the war it turned out that those German
sociologists, social psychologists, industrial engineers, management
specialists, and educators who had fled National Socialism had ideas
about work very similar to those held by their former colleagues who
had successfully negotiated the transition from Weimar to Third Reich.
People from both groups frequently worked side by side in an attempt
to realize objectives originally developed in the 1920s, by means appropriate to the new democracy. Only the change of generations that took
place in the 1960s, when those who had played an important role in
the Weimar period faded out of the picture,[20] would seem to have significantly altered how people in the FRG think about work.

In any event, by the 1980s those who claimed that citizens of the
Federal Republic sought their primary satisfaction in leisure and consumption rather than work no longer referred to National Socialism in
their explanations for this change of attitudes. According to Noelle-
Neumann, the German media are to blame for fostering an ethos inimical to the preservation of the traditional valuation of work essential
for human happiness. Strümpel for his part considers the changed relationship between human beings and work to be a natural, even
healthy, response to the deterioration of work in advanced industrial
society.

The apparent homogenization of attitudes to work in the FRG,
whether or not it can be attributed in whole or in part to National
Socialism, raises the fundamental question of whether class has ever
been a significant determinant of such attitudes in Germany. German
"workers" seem to have adhered to an ethic of work hardly distinguishable from that of their "bourgeois" compatriots long before Hitler appeared on the scene. Indeed, one might conclude that such success as
the Nazis had in pacifying the working class stemmed in large part from
their clever use of the idea of "German work" as a unifying national
principle.

This leads us to our final question: are "Joy in Work" and "German
Work" still linked with one another today? There can be no doubt that
the problem of alienation and the related quest for Arbeitsfreude con-

[20] See, e.g., Volker R. Berghahn, *The Americanization of West German Industry, 1945–1973*
(Leamington Spa, Warwickshire: Berg, 1986), 11, who notes the disappearance at this time
of the older generation of managers "deeply moulded by the specific national characteristics
of German industry during the interwar period." Mooser, in Conze and Lepsius, *Sozialgeschichte der Bundesrepublik Deutschland*, 162, comments on a corresponding break of continuity with respect to the working class.

tinue to play a major part in discussions about work, and that German scholars have written extensively on the subject since the war. On the other hand, I would claim that there has been an important change in the connection between Joy in Work and German Work since the days of the Third Reich. Discredited by the excesses of Hitler's Reich and thwarted by the division of the country, German nationalism was forced to the fringes in the immediate postwar years and has only recently begun to regain its respectability. As a result, the problem of work has increasingly tended to be treated in an international rather than in a German national context.

Although postwar German philosophers of work are frequently referred to in the contemporary literature, along with earlier German writers on work like Marx, Nietzsche, Freud, and Max Weber, Germans can no longer claim primacy in what by now has become a truly international debate. A short list of the most influential books on the problem of modern work would still include a number of publications by Germans, but it would assuredly be incomplete without *The Anatomy of Work* by the Frenchman Georges Friedmann or *Labor and Monopoly Capital* by the American Harry Bravermann.[21] Moreover, writers on the science of work in the FRG are no longer inclined to think of themselves as contributors to a continuous and valuable German tradition. Those concerned with "humanization" are much more likely to claim the American Hawthorne experiments and the writings of Elton Mayo as precursors than to acknowledge a debt to such German innovators as Münsterberg, Hellpach, Rosenstock, or Michel. It is symptomatic that by the 1970s the American-derived term *Arbeitszufriedenheit* ("job satisfaction") had virtually displaced the German *Arbeitsfreude*.[22]

The same thing holds true at the practical level. Admittedly, postwar legislation in the FRG dealing with industrial democracy (*Mitbestimmung*) owed much to the general revulsion against the repressive features of National Socialist industrial organization and promised to implement ideas firmly rooted in the German socialist and Naumannite traditions. But although subsequent attempts to extend worker control and participation have been watched with interest by other industrial

---

[21] Georges Friedmann, *The Anatomy of Work. The Implications of Specialization*, trans., Wyatt Rowson (London: Heinemann, 1961); Harry Bravermann, *Labor and Monopoly Capital: The Degradation of Work in the Twentieth Century* (New York: Monthly Review Press, 1974).

[22] E.g., Hans-Jurgen Albers, *Zufriedenheit in Arbeit und Ausbildung. Die individuelle Stellung zum Beruf und zur Ausbildungssituation* (Trier: Spee, 1977); Emil Walter-Busch, *Arbeitszufriedenheit in der Wohlstandsgesellschaft. Beitrag zur Diagnose der Theoriesprachenvielfalt betriebspsychologischer und industriesoziologischer Forschung* (Bern: Paul Haupt, 1977).

countries,[23] few Germans now proclaim a national mission to solve the world's problems: Germans instead seem content to follow the lead of others. This has been true even in the area of social policy, where Germany had been an innovator since the days of Bismarck: the modern welfare state owes more to Sweden or Great Britain than to Germany.[24]

Germans have also contributed less than one might have expected to the international "quality of working life" movement that reached its peak in the 1970s.[25] Major innovations have tended to come not from Germany but from Scandinavia, where the Swedish Volvo automotive factories introduced group work along the lines of the Lang-Hellpach proposals of the 1920s, and from Japan whose approach to business management, reflecting an ethos akin to that characteristic of major German firms in the Weimar and Nazi periods, has become the object of nearly universal admiration and imitation. More recently, it has been suggested that a number of small firms of northern Italy, experimenting with post-Fordist systems of industrial organization designed to obviate the alienation attendant on the extreme division of labor, have succeeded in developing a "high-technology cottage industry" that restores joy in work without sacrificing the benefits of technological progress.[26]

The FRG continues to demonstrate an outstanding ability to adapt to the demands of modern work, thanks to the presence of a well-educated and highly trained workforce, a strong and reasonably cooperative labor movement, a tradition of quality and good design going back to the pre-World War One period, and a progressive corps of managers willing to incorporate ideas and practices developed elsewhere. But on the ideological plane, it seems to regard itself as just one industrial country among many. In particular, intellectuals in both Germanies have tended to repudiate the national tradition of work associated with Riehl; taking the internationalist Marx as their guide, they no longer believe their country has a special mission to overcome labor alienation and thus solve the problem of modern work.

Despite the division of their nation, there is no reason why Germans cannot make further contributions in this area, but whether there will

[23] The German contribution is placed in comparative perspective by Poole, *Workers' Participation in Industry*.

[24] Hans Günter Hockerts, "Ausblick: Bürgerliche Sozialreform nach 1945," in Bruch, *Weder Kommunismus noch Kapitalismus*, 263.

[25] See, generally, Louis E. Davis and Albert B. Cherns, *The Quality of Working Life*, 2 vols. (New York: Free Press, 1975).

[26] Charles F. Sabel, *Work and Politics: The Division of Labor in Industry* (Cambridge: Cambridge University Press, 1982). The only mention of Germany in this comparative study relates to developments of the 1920s.

ever be a revival of Deutsche Arbeit in the sense of a "German" idea of work will depend on whether the "myth" of German uniqueness is reborn. If it is, then it is highly likely, though not certain, that the notion of German work will recover its former high place in the national self-image. For the moment, it would seem that only a small minority is inclined to move in this direction.[27] The link between "Joy in Work" and "German Work" that many Germans had attempted to preserve through all vicissitudes of national life since the days of Riehl, and that the National Socialists had done their best to elaborate and cement, may well have been permanently broken.

[27] See Noelle-Neumann and Strümpel, 272–73, where Noelle-Neumann refers to her earlier "Brauchen wir mehr Nationalstolz?" published in the *Frankfurter Allgemeine Zeitung*, 6 August 1982, 10. Basing her conclusions on an international study of national pride, Noelle-Neumann maintained that, among Germans, the loss of a positive attitude to work is correlated with a lack of national self-esteem. For her, a restoration of a true spirit of nationalism would go hand in hand with a recovery of joy in work.

SELECT BIBLIOGRAPHY

PRIMARY SOURCES

To include all the primary sources cited—themselves only a fraction of those con-sulted in the course of research for this book—would overburden this bibliography. I have therefore decided to confine myself to a note on archives and special collec-tions, and a list of those newspapers and periodicals of the period examined system-atically. Other primary materials are fully documented in the notes, and can be located by looking up the relevant individual, organization, or subject in the index.

I. Archival Sources and Special Collections

The following archives and libraries were particularly valuable as sources of hard-to-find printed items and/or biographical information. Some of the most useful files are listed by name.

Bayerische Staatsbibliothek, Munich. Outstanding general collection.
Berlin Document Center. [Cited as BDC]. NSDAP personnel files on specific indi-viduals.
Bundesarchiv, Koblenz. [Cited as BA].
    1. Sammlung Schumacher, 122, 223, 237, 239, 262, 330—National Social-ist documents, DAF etc.
    2. Z Sg. 1, Sg. 2—pamphlets, series, and other published materials relating to a variety of non-governmental associations.
    3. NSD 49 (Deutscher Arbeitsdienst), 50 (DAF), 51 (NSBO).
    4. Kl. Erw. 461 (Bernhard Otte), 470 (August Winnig).
    5. R11 (Reichswirtschaftskammer).
Deutscher Gewerkschaftsbund, Archiv und Bibliothek, Düsseldorf. Useful source of la-bor periodicals.
Deutsches Zentralinstitut für Soziale Fragen, Berlin. Books, pamphlets, and periodi-cals dealing with social issues.
Diakonische Werk der Evangelischen Kirche, Central-Blbliothek der Inneren Mission, Berlin. [Cited as Ber. Ev]. The Protestant counterpart of the Volksverein collec-tion in Mönchengladbach.
Friedrich-Ebert-Stiftung, Bonn. Current books and periodicals.
Historische Kommission zu Berlin. Strong reference collection. Particularly useful on social and economic history, and social policy.
Institut für Weltwirtschaft, Kiel. The library was an excellent source for books and serials. The Institute's *Wirtschaftsarchiv* has a great deal of newspaper material conveniently available on microfilm.
Institut für Zeitgeschichte, Munich. [Cited as IfZ]. In addition to the library, the following archival files contained particularly helpful information:

1. Db 36, 61, 66, 67, 77.
2. Fa 176.
3. MA (National Archives, Records of the NSDAP, copy): 116 (Willy Hell-pach) 141 (Hans Freyer, Adolf Friedrich, Ernst Horneffer); MA 609.
4. RK 20, 21.

Library of Congress, Washington. [Cited as LC].

Nachlass Adolf Friedrich. [Cited as DF]. Published and unpublished materials, in the possession of Friedrich's daughter, Dorothée Friedrich.

New York Public Library, Arents Collection [Cited as NN].

Volksverein Bibliothek und Stadtbibliothek, Mönchengladbach [Cited as VB]. Outstanding collection of books, pamphlets, and periodicals formerly belonging to the Catholic Volksverein.

Werner-von-Siemens-Institut für Geschichte des Hauses Siemens, Munich. [Cited as Siemens]. Library contains valuable pamphlets, and works newspapers published by Siemens. I did not use the Institute's archive.

II. Newspapers and Periodicals Examined Systematically

Akademie der Arbeit in der Universität Frankfurt am Main. *Mitteilungen*. Frankfurt (1925–30).

Die Arbeit. Berlin (1924–33).

Arbeit und Beruf. Bernau and Berlin (1921–34).

Arbeit und Betrieb. See Arbeitsschulung.

Arbeit und Wirtschaft. Schulungsamt der DAF. Berlin (1941–44).

Der Arbeiterpräses. Praktisches Handbuch für die Leiter und Freunde der katholisch-sozialen Bewegung. Berlin (1919, 1923–25).

Arbeitertum. Blätter für Theorie und Praxis der nationalsozialistischen Betriebszellenorganisation. Berlin (1931–34).

Arbeiterwohl. Organ des Verbandes katholischer Industrieller und Arbeiterfreunde. Berlin (1888–1904).

Arbeiterwohlfahrt. Berlin (1926–29).

Der Arbeitgeber. Zeitschrift der Vereinigung der deutschen Arbeitgeberverbände. Berlin (1921–33).

Die Arbeitsschule. Zeitschrift für Arbeitserziehung und Werkunterricht. Leipzig (1936–42).

Arbeitsschulung. Dinta, Düsseldorf (1929–43). From 1941 on as *Arbeit und Betrieb*.

Archiv für angewandte Soziologie. See Institut für angewandte Soziologie.

Archiv für Frauenarbeit. Berlin (1913–22).

Archiv für Sozialwissenschaft und Sozialpolitik. Berlin (1912–33).

Beiträge zum deutschen Arbeits- und Sozialversicherungsrecht. Würzburg (1938–40).

Beruf und Schule. Zeitschrift des Landesvereins Sachsen der Lehrkräfte an beruflichen Schulen. Leipzig (1930–33).

Betrieb und Gewerkschaft. Zeitschrift für marxistische Strategie und Taktik. Berlin (1929–33).

Blätter für den religiosen Sozialismus. Berlin (1920–27).

Die Bücherwarte. Berlin (1926–33).

Chronik der Arbeit. Hamburg (1924–27).

Correspondenzblatt der Generalkommission der Gewerkschaften Deutschlands. See *Gewerkschaftszeitung.*

Deutsche Arbeit. Monatschrift für die Bestrebungen der christlich nationalen Arbeiterschaft. Berlin and Cologne (1916–33).

Deutsche Arbeitsfront, Arbeitswissenschaftliches Institut. *Jahrbuch.* Berlin (1936–41).

Deutsche Arbeits-Korrespondenz. Berlin (1936–37).

Die Deutsche Berufsschule. Deutscher Verein für Berufsschulwesen, Leipzig (1924–30).

Deutsche Hochschule für Politik. *Berichte.* Berlin (1923–).

Deutsche Republik. Frankfurt (1926–29).

Die Deutsche Sozialpolitik. Gemeinschaftsarbeit der Zeitschriften 'Soziale Praxis' und 'Monatsheft für NS-Sozialpolitik,' zugleich Kriegsausgabe der Zeitschrift 'Soziale Zukunft.' Berlin (1944–45).

Deutsche Werksgemeinschaft. Wochenzeitung der werksgemeinschaftlichen Arbeiterbewegung. Berlin (1924–33).

Deutschland-Berichte der Sozialdemokratischen Partei Deutschlands (SOPADE) (1934–1940; reprint Frankfurt, 1980).

Evangelisch-Sozial. Vierteljahrsschrift für die sozial-kirchliche Arbeit. Leipzig (1929–33).

Evangelisch-Sozialer Kongress. *Verhandlungen* (1925–31).

Die Frau. Monatsschrift für das gesamte Frauenleben unserer Zeit. Berlin (1923–31).

Frauenarbeit. Organ des Verbandes katholischer Vereine erwerbstätiger Frauen und Mädchen Deutschlands. Berlin (1921–31).

Freude und Arbeit. Official Organ of the International Central Bureau Joy and Work, Berlin (1936–41).

Gesellschaft für deutsche Wirtschafts- und Sozialpolitik, Berlin. *Mitteilungen* (1927–32). From 1931 on as *Neue Wirtschaft.*

Gesellschaft für Soziale Reform. *Schriften.* Jena (1901–1931).

Gewerkschafts-Archiv. Monatsschrift für Theorie und Praxis der gesamten Gewerkschaftsbewegung. Jena (1924–33).

Gewerkschafts-Zeitung. Hamburg, Berlin (1903–1933).

Glückauf. Berg- und Hüttenmännische Zeitung. Essen (1925–33).

Institut für Angewandte Soziologie. *Unterrichts-Briefe*, Series A. Berlin (1926–33). From 1929 on as *Archiv für angewandte Soziologie.*

Jahrbuch der Christlichen Gewerkschaften (1924–27).

Jahrbuch des Allgemeinen Deutschen Gewerkschaftsbundes. Berlin (1925–31).

Jahrbuch für Sozialpolitik. Leipzig (1930–31).

Jugend und Beruf. Berlin (1926–37).

Jugend-Führer. Mitteilungen für die Leiter der Jugend-Abteilungen der Gewerkschaften. Berlin (1926–29).

Jungsozialistische Blätter. Berlin (1926–28).

Kirchlich-Soziale Blätter. Kirchlich-Sozialer Bund. Berlin (1927–31).

Kölner Sozialpolitische Vierteljahresschrift. Cologne (1926–32). Title varies.

Kulturwille. Monatsblätter für Kultur der Arbeiterschaft. Leipzig (1925–31).

Materialblätter für Wirtschafts- und Sozialpolitik. Gewerkschaftsbund der Angestellten. Berlin (1926–32).

Neue Blätter für den Sozialismus. Berlin (1930–31).

Neue Wirtschaft. See Gesellschaft für deutsche Wirtschafts und Sozialpolitik.

N. S.-Sozialpolitik. Stuttgart and Berlin (1933–39).

Reichsverband der Deutschen Industrie. *Tagungsberichte*. Berlin (1924–27, 1929).

Riehlbundhefte. Schweidnitz (1924–26).

Ruhr und Rhein. Wirtschaftszeitung. Essen, Düsseldorf (1920–34).

Siemens-Mitteilungen. Siemensstadt (1923–39).

Soziale Arbeit. Berlin (1935–36).

Soziale Erneuerung. Stuttgart (1932–34).

Soziale Praxis. Berlin (1926–33).

Soziale Revue. Katholische internationale Monatsschrift. Munich (1923–33).

Sozialistische Bildung. Berlin (1929–33).

Sozialistische Monatshefte. Stuttgart (1904–32).

Ständisches Leben. Blätter für organische Gesellschafts- und Wirtschaftslehre. Berlin, Vienna (1931–35).

Technik und Kultur. Verband deutscher Diplomingenieure. Berlin (1920–33).

Technik und Wirtschaft. Monatsschrift des Vereines deutscher Ingenieure. Berlin (1921–25).

Das Werk. Monatsblätter der Montangruppe der Siemens-Rheinelbe-Schuckert-Union. Düsseldorf (1920–36). From 1926 on, Monatsschrift der vereinigten Stahlwerke A.G. Subtitle varies. Cf. *Siemens-Mitteilungen*.

Werk und Beruf. Monatsschrift für den berufsständischen Gedanken. Berlin (1929–34). Subtitle varies. Merged into *Ständisches Leben*, 1935.

Wirtschaft und Arbeit. Monatsschrift für das Deutsche Wirtschaftsleben. Berlin (1933, 1936–37).

Zentralblatt der Christlichen Gewerkschaften Deutschlands. Berlin (1925–27, 1933).

SECONDARY WORKS

The list below includes works that provided important information or ideas, whether or not they are directly cited in the text. I have omitted items dealing solely with specific individuals. Certain journal titles have been abbreviated. See the list of abbreviations.

Akademie für Gesellschaftswissenschaften beim Zentralkomitee der SED, Institut für Marxistisch-Leninistische Soziologie. *Körperliche und geistige Arbeit im Sozialismus. Eine soziologische Analyse*. Berlin: Dietz, 1980.

Albers, Hans-Jürgen. *Zufriedenheit in Arbeit und Ausbildung. Die individualle Stellung zum Beruf und zur Ausbildungssituation*. Trier: Spee, 1977.

Der alltägliche Faschismus. Frauen im Dritten Reich. Berlin: Dietz, 1981.

Anthony, P. D. *The Ideology of Work*. London: Tavistock Publications, 1977.

Antrick, Otto. *Die Akademie der Arbeit in der Universität Frankfurt a. M. Idee, Werden, Gestalt.* Darmstadt: Eduard Roether, 1966.

Arendt, Hannah. *The Human Condition. A Study of the Central Dilemmas Facing Modern Man.* Garden City, N.Y.: Doubleday Anchor Books, 1959.

Aretz, Jürgen. *Katholische Arbeiterbewegung und Nationalsozialismus.* Mainz: Matthias-Grünewald, 1978.

Argyle, Michael. *The Social Psychology of Work.* London: Allen Lane, 1972.

Ascher, Abraham, "Professors as Propagandists. The Politics of the *Kathedersozialisten.*" *Journal of Central European Affairs* 23 (1963): 282–302.

Ash, Mitchell G. "Academic Politics in the History of Science. Experimental Psychology in Germany, 1879–1941." *Central European History* 13 (September 1980): 255–86.

Auerbach, H. "Arbeitererziehungslager 1940–1944." (1963), in *Gutachten des Instituts für Zeitgeschichte* 2. Stuttgart: Deutsche Verlags-Anstalt, 1966.

Bajohr, Stefan. *Die Hälfte der Fabrik. Geschichte der Frauenarbeit in Deutschland 1914 bis 1945.* Marburg: Verlag Arbeiterbewegung und Gesellschaftswissenschaft, 1979.

———. "Weiblicher Arbeitsdienst im 'Dritten Reich'. Ein Konflikt zwischen Ideologie und Ökonomie." *VfZ* 28 (1980), 331–57.

Baritz, Loren. *The Servants of Power. A History of the Use of Social Science in American Industry.* Middletown, Conn.: Wesleyan University Press, 1960.

Barkai, Avraham. *Das Wirtschaftssystem des Nationalsozialismus. Der historische und ideologische Hintergrund, 1933–1936.* Cologne: Verlag Wissenschaft und Politik Berend von Nottbeck, 1977.

Barkin, Kenneth D., "Conflict and Concord in Wilhelmian Social Thought." *Central European History* 5 (March 1972): 55–71.

Baumgärtner, Raimund. *Weltanschauungskampf im Dritten Reich. Die Auseinandersetzung der Kirchen mit Alfred Rosenberg.* Mainz: Matthias-Grünewald, 1977.

Baumgartner, Alois. *Sehnsucht nach Gemeinschaft. Ideen und Strömungen im Sozialkatholizismus der Weimarer Republik.* Paderborn: Ferdinand Schöningh, 1977.

Baxter, Brian. *Alienation and Authenticity. Some Consequences for Organized Work.* London: Tabistock Publications, 1982.

Beier, Gerhard. *Das Lehrstück vom 1. und 2. Mai 1933.* Frankfurt: Europäische Verlagsanstalt, 1975.

———. "Dokumentation. Gesetzentwürfe zur Ausschaltung der Deutschen Arbeitsfront im Jahre 1938." *AS* 17 (1977): 297–335.

Bell, Daniel. *Work and its Discontents.* Boston: Beacon Press, 1956.

Bendele, Ulrich. *Sozialdemokratische Schulpolitik und Pädagogik im wilhelminischen Deutschland. Eine sozialhistorisch-empirische Analyse.* Frankfurt: Campus, 1979.

Bendix, Reinhard. *Work and Authority in Industry. Ideologies of Management in the Course of Industrialization.* New York: Wiley, 1956.

Benz, Wolfgang. "Vom freiwilligen Arbeitsdienst zur Arbeitsdienstpflicht." *VfZ* 16 (1968), 317–46.

Berg, Peter. *Deutschland und Amerika 1918–1929.* Lübeck: Matthiesen, 1963.

Berghahn, Volker R. *The Americanization of West German Industry, 1945–1973.* Leamington Spa: Berg, 1986.

Bergmann, Waltraut et al., *Soziologie im Faschismus 1933–1945. Darstellung und Texte.* Cologne: Pahl-Rugenstein, 1981.

Berning, Cornelia. *Vom 'Abstammungsnachweis' zum 'Zuchtwart.' Vokabular des Nationalsozialismus.* Berlin: De Gruyter, [1964].

Bernsdorf, Wilhelm, ed. *Wörterbuch der Soziologie,* 2d ed.; Stuttgart: Ferdinand Enke, 1969. S.v. "Arbeit" by D. Bell, and "Arbeitsfreude" by Chr. v. Ferber.

Bernsdorf, Wilhelm and Horst Knospe, eds. *Internationales Soziologenlexikon.* 2d ed. Stuttgart: Ferdinand Enke, 1980.

Bessel, Richard and Mathilde Jamin. "Nazis, Workers and the Uses of Quantitative Evidence." *Social History* 4 (1979), 111–16.

Bessel, Richard and E. J. Feuchtwanger, eds. *Social Change and Political Development in Weimar Germany.* London: Croom Helm, 1981.

Best, Fred, ed. *The Future of Work.* Englewood Cliffs, N.J.: Prentice-Hall, 1973.

Bibliographie der deutschen Zeitschriftenliteratur, 1896–1964.

Birnbaum, Bruno. *Organisation der Rationalisierung Amerika-Deutschland.* Berlin: R. Hobbing, 1927.

Bock, Hans Manfred. *Syndikalismus und Linkskommunismus von 1918–1923. Zur Geschichte und Soziologie der Freien Arbeiter-Union Deutschlands (Syndicalisten), der Allgemeinen Arbeiter-Union Deutschlands und der kommunistischen Arbeiter-Partei Deutschlands.* Maisenheim am Glan: Verlag Anton Hain, 1969.

Boese, Franz. *Geschichte des Vereins für Sozialpolitik 1872–1932.* Schriften des Vereins für Sozialpolitik 188. Berlin: Duncker & Humblot, 1939.

Bollenbeck, Georg. *Zur Theorie und Geschichte der frühen Arbeiterlebenserinnerungen.* Kronberg: Skriptor, 1976.

Bott, Hermann. *Die Volksfeindideologie. Zur Kritik rechtsradikaler Propaganda.* Stuttgart: Deutsche Verlagsanstalt, 1969.

Brady, Robert A. *The Rationalization Movement in German Industry.* Berkeley: University of California Press, 1933.

———. *The Spirit and Structure of German Fascism.* New York: Viking, 1937.

Bramsted, Ernest K. *Aristocracy and the Middle Classes in Germany. Social Types in German Literature 1830–1900.* Rev. ed. Chicago: Chicago University Press, 1964.

Braverman, Harry. *Labor and Monopoly Capital. The Degradation of Work in the Twentieth Century.* Foreword by Paul M. Sweezy. New York: Monthly Review Press, 1974.

Breipohl, Renate. *Religiöser Sozialismus und bürgerliches Geschichtsbewusstsein zur Zeit der Weimarer Republik.* Zürich: Theologischer Verlag, 1971.

Breuning, Klaus. *Die Vision des Reiches. Deutscher Katholizismus zwischen Demokratie und Diktatur (1929–1934).* Munich: Max Hueber, 1969.

Bridenthal, Renate, Atina Grossman, and Marian Kaplan, eds. *When Biology Became Destiny. Women in Weimar and Nazi Germany.* New York: New Feminist Library/Monthly Review Press, 1984.

SELECT BIBLIOGRAPHY

Briefs, Goetz, ed. *Das Bild des Arbeiters in der katholischen Sozialbewegung.* Festschrift für Prälat Dr. Franz Müller. Cologne: Balduin Pick, 1960.

Bruch, Rüdiger vom. "Bürgerliche Sozialreform und Gewerkschaften im späten Deutschen Kaissereich. Die Gesellschaft für Soziale Reform (GSR) 1901–1914." *IWK* 15 (1979), 581–610.

———. *Wissenschaft, Politik und öffentliche Meinung. Gelehrtenpolitik imn Wilhelminischen Deutschland (1890–1914).* Husum: Matthiesen, 1980.

———, ed. *'Weder Kommunismus noch Kapitalismus.' Bürgerliche Sozialreform in Deutschland vom Vormärz bis zur Ära Adenauer.* Munich: C. H. Beck, 1985.

Buchheim, Karl. *Deutsche Kultur zwischen 1830 und 1870.* Frankfurt a. M.: Akademische Verlagsgesellschaft Athenaion, 1966.

Buchholz, Wolfhard. "Die nationalsozialistische Gemeinschaft 'Kraft-durch-Freude.' Freizeitgestaltung und Arbeiterschaft im Dritten Reich." Munich dissertation, 1976. [Photocopy].

Büttner, Hans Wolfgang. *Das Rationalisierungs-Kuratorium der deutschen Wirtschaft.* Düsseldorf: Droste, 1973.

Bullen, Roger J., H. Pogge von Strandmann, and A. B. Polonsky, eds. *Ideas into Politics. Aspects of European History 1880–1950.* London: Croom Helm, 1984.

Bunk, Gerhard P. *Erziehung und Industriearbeit. Modelle betrieblichen Lernens und Arbeitens Erwachsener.* Weinheim and Basel: Beltz, 1972.

Burchardt, Lothar. "Technischer Fortschritt und sozialer Wandel. Das Beispiel der Taylorismus Rezeption." In *Deutsche Technikgeschichte,* ed. Wilhelm Treue, 52–98. Göttingen: Vandenhoeck & Ruprecht, 1977.

Calkins, Kenneth R. "The Uses of Utopianism. The Millenarian Dream in Central European Social Democracy before 1914." *Central European History* 15 (June 1982): 124–48.

Campbell, Joan. *The German Werkbund. The Politics of Reform in the Applied Arts.* Princeton: Princeton University Press, 1978.

———. "Social Idealism and Cultural Reform in the German Arts and Crafts, 1900–1914." *The Turn of the Century. German Literature and Art 1890–1915,* ed. Gerald Chapple and Hans J. Schulte, 311–25. Bonn: Bouvier Verlag Herbert Grundmann, 1981.

Clayre, Alasdair. *Work and Play. Ideas and Experience of Work and Leisure.* London: Weidenfeld and Nicolson, 1974.

Cocks, Geoffrey. *Psychotherapy in the Third Reich. The Göring Institute.* New York: Oxford University Press, 1985.

Conrad, Else. *Der Verein für Sozialpolitik und seine Wirksamkeit auf dem Gebiet der gewerblichen Arbeiterfrage.* Jena: G. Fischer, 1906.

Conze, Werner. "Vom 'Pöbel' zum 'Proletariat.' Sozialgeschichtliche Voraussetzungen für den Sozialismus in Deutschland." *Vierteljahrsschrift für Sozial- und Wirtschaftsgeschichte* 41 (1954): 333–64. In *Moderne Deutsche Sozialgeschichte,* ed. Hans-Ulrich Wehler, 111–36. 2d ed. Cologne: Kiepenheuer & Witsch, 1968.

———. "Arbeit" and "Beruf." In *Geschichtliche Grundbegriffe. Historisches Lexikon zur Politisch-Sozialen Sprache in Deutschland,* ed. Otto Brunner, Werner Conze and Reinhart Koselleck. Stuttgart: Klett, 1972–.

Conze, Werner and Ulrich Engelhardt, eds. *Arbeiter im Industrialisierungsprozess. Herkunft, Lage und Verhalten.* Stuttgart: Klett-Cotta, 1979.

Conze, Werner and M. Rainer Lepsius, eds. *Sozialgeschichte der Bundesrepublik Deutschland. Beiträge zum Kontinuitätsproblem.* Stuttgart: Klett-Cotta, 1983.

Croon, Helmuth. "Jugendbewegung und Arbeitsdienst." *Jahrbuch des Archivs der deutschen Jugendbewegung* 5 (1973): 66–84.

Crusius, R., G. Schiefelbein, and M. Wilke, eds. *Die Betriebsräte in der Weimarer Republik von der Selbstverwaltung zur Mitbestimmung. Dokumente und Analysen.* 2 vols. Berlin: Olle & Wolter, 1978.

Dahrendorf, Ralf. *Society and Democracy in Germany.* Garden City, N.Y.: Doubleday, 1967.

Davis, Luis E. and Albert B. Cherns. *The Quality of Working Life.* 2 vols. New York: Free Press, 1975.

Dawson, William Harbutt. *The German Workman. A Study in National Efficiency.* New York: Scribner, 1906.

De Grazia, Sebastian. *Of Time, Work, and Leisure.* Garden City, N.Y.: Doubleday, 1962; reprint Anchor Books, 1964.

De Grazia, Victoria. *The Culture of Consent. Mass Organization of Leisure in Fascist Italy.* Cambridge: Cambridge University Press, 1981.

Denk, Hans Dieter. *Die christliche Arbeiterbewegung in Bayern bis zum ersten Weltkrieg.* Mainz: Matthias-Grünewald, 1980.

Deutsche Akademie der Künste, Berlin. *Literatur im Klassenkampf. Beiträge zur sozialistischen Literatur der Weimarer Republik.* Dortmund: Weltkreis Verlag, 1973.

Diedrich, Karl-Friedrich. *Entwicklung und Stand der sozialen Betriebsgestaltung.* Munich: Wilhelm Steinebach, 1951.

Diehl, James M. "Von der 'Vaterlandspartei' zur 'Nationalen Revolution': Die 'Vereinigten Vaterländischen Verbände Deutschlands (VVVD)' 1922–1932." *VfZ* 33 (1985), 617–39.

Dorsch, Friedrich. *Geschichte und Probleme der angewandten Psychologie.* Bern and Stuttgart: H. Huber, 1963.

Dräger, Horst. *Volksbildung in Deutschland im 19. Jahrhundert.* Dokumentation zur Geschichte der Erwachsenenbildung, vol. 1. Braunschweig: Georg Westermann, 1979.

Eckhardt, Jochen. "Deutsche Arbeitsfront, Arbeiterklasse, imperialistische Sozialpolitik in Betrieben und forcierte Aufrüstung 1936–1939." *Jahrbuch für Geschichte* 27 (1983): 75–107.

Elwitt, Sanford. " 'Economie sociale' and the Discipline of Labour. Social Science and Social Engineering in France, 1860–1900." *Europa* 2, no. 2 (Spring 1979): 21–34.

Emmerich, Wolfgang. *Zur Kritik der Volkstumsideologie.* Frankfurt: Suhrkamp, 1971.

———, ed. *Proletarische Lebensläufe. Augobiographische Dokumente zur Entstehung der zweiten Kultur in Deutschland.* 2 vols. Reinbek bei Hamburg: Rowohlt, 1974.

Evans, Richard J., ed. *The German Working Class 1888–1933. The Politics of Everyday Life.* London: Croom Helm, 1982.

393

Fabian, Anne-Marie, ed. *Arbeiterbewegung, Erwachsenenbildung, Presse*. Festschrift für Walter Fabian zum 75. Geburtstag. Cologne: Europäische Verlagsanstalt, 1977.

Fähnders, Walter. *Proletarisch-revolutionäre Literatur der Weimarer Republik*. Stuttgart: J. B. Metzler, 1977.

Fähnders, Walter and Martin Rector. *Linksradikalismus und Literatur. Untersuchungen zur Geschichte der sozialistischen Literatur in der Weimarer Republik*. 2 vols. Reinbek: Rowolt, 1974.

Feldman, Gerald D. and Irmgard Steinisch. "Die Weimarer Republik zwischen Sozial- und Wirtschaftsstaat. Die Entscheidung gegen den Achtstundentag." *AS* 18 (1978): 353–439.

Ferber, Christian von. *Arbeitsfreude. Wirklichkeit und Ideologie. Ein Beitrag zur Soziologie der Arbeit in der industriellen Gesellschaft*. Stuttgart: Enke, 1959.

———. " 'Arbeitsleid' in der Wohlstandsgesellschaft." *Soziale Welt* (Dortmund) 15 (1964): 289–99.

Fink, Eugen. *Grundphänomene des menschlichen Daseins*. Freiburg: Karl Alber, 1979.

Fischer, Conan. "The SA of the NSDAP. Social Background and Ideology of the Rank and File in the Early 1930s." *JCH* 17 (1982): 651–70.

———. "Class Enemies or Class Brothers? Communist-Nazi Relations in Germany 1929–33." *European History Quarterly* 15 (1985): 259–79.

Fischer, Wolfram. *Wirtschaft und Gesellschaft im Zeitalter der Industrialisierung. Aufsätze-Studien-Vorträge*. Göttingen: Vandenhoeck & Ruprecht, 1972.

———. "Die Pioneerrolle der betrieblichen Sozialpolitik im 19. und beginnenden 20. Jahrhundert." In *Betriebliche Sozialpolitik deutscher Unternehmen seit dem 19. Jahrhundert*, ed. Wilhelm Treue and Hans Pohl, 34–51. Wiesbaden: Franz Steiner, 1978.

———. "Labor-Management and Indeustrial Relations in Germany 1870–1930." In *Labor and Management*. Proceedings of the Fourth Fuji Conference, ed. Keiichiro Nakagawa, 99–123. Tokyo: University of Tokyo Press, 1979.

Franzoi, Barbara. *At the Very Least, She Pays the Rent. Women and German Industrialization, 1871–1914*. Westport, Conn.: Greenwood Press, 1985.

Frauen und Wissenschaft, ed. Gruppe Berliner Dozentinnen. Berlin: Courage, 1977.

Fricke, Dieter. "Bürgerliche Sozialreformer und die Zersplitterung der antisozialistischen Arbeiterorganisationenen vor 1914." *Zeitschrift für Geschichtswissenschaft* (Berlin-East) 23 (1975): 1177–98.

Friedmann, Georges. *The Anatomy of Work. The Implications of Specialization*. Translated from the French by Wyatt Rowson. London: Heinemann, 1961.

Friemert, Chup. *Produktionsästhetik im Faschismus. Das Amt 'Schönheit der Arbeit' von 1933 bis 1939*. Munich: Damnitz, 1980.

———. "Faschismus und Ideologie auf betrieblicher Ebene." In *Faschismus und Ideologie*. Argument-Sonderband 62 (1980), 227–54.

Fromm, Erich. *The Sane Society*. New York: Holt, Rinehart and Winston, 1955.

———. *Arbeiter und Angestellte am Vorabend des Dritten Reiches. Eine sozialpsychologische Untersuching*. Ed. Wolfgang Bonss. Stuttgart: Deutsche Verlags-Anstalt,

1980. English translation: *The Working Class in Weimar Germany. A Psychological and Sociological Study*, by Barbara Weinberger. Cambridge: Harvard University Press, 1984.

Fürstenberg, Friedrich, ed. *Industriesoziologie, Vol. 1: Vorläufer und Frühzeit 1835–1934*. Soziologische Texte. 2d ed. Neuwied: Luchterhand, 1966.

Gamm, Hans-Jochen. *Der braune Kult. Das Dritte Reich und seine Ersatzreligion. Ein Beitrag zur politischen Bildung*. Hamburg: Rütten & Loening, 1962.

Gasman, Daniel. *The Scientific Origins of National Socialism*. London: Macdonald, 1971.

Geary, Dick. *European Labour Protest 1848–1939*. London: Croom Helm, 1981.

Gellately, Robert. *The Politics of Economic Despair. Shopkeepers and German Politics 1890–1914*. London: Sage, 1974.

Geuter, Ulfried. *Die Professionalisierung der deutschen Psychologie im Nationalsozialismus*. Frankfurt: Suhrkamp, 1984.

Giersch, Reinhard. "Von der 'Nationalsozialistischen Betriebszellenorganisation' zur 'Deutschen Arbeitsfront' 1932–1934." *Jahrbuch für Geschichte* 26 (1982): 43–73.

Gilbert, James B. *Work without Salvation. America's Intellectuals and Industrial Alienation, 1880–1910*. Baltimore: Johns Hopkins, 1977.

Gillingham, John. *Industry and Politics in the Third Reich. Ruhr Coal, Hitler, and Europe*. London: Methuen, 1985.

———. "The 'Deproletarianization' of German Society. Vocational Training in the Third Reich." *Journal of Social History* 19 (Spring 1986): 423–32.

Gladen, Albin. "Die berufliche Aus- und Weiterbildung in der deutschen Wirtschaft 1918–1945." In Wilhelm True and Hans Pol, eds., *Berufliche Aus- und Weiterbildung in der deutschen Wirtschaft seit dem 19. Jahrhundert*. Wiesbaden: Steiner, 1979, 53–73.

Glaser, Ernst. *Im Umfeld des Austromarxismus. Ein Beitrag zur Geistesgeschichte des österreichischen Sozialismus*. Vienna: Europa Verlag, 1981.

Görsdorf, Kurt. *Arbeitsfreude-Leistungsanstieg. Neue Wege erfolgreicher Arbeitspsychologie*. Munich: Verlag Moderne Industrie, 1958.

Goldschmidt, Georges-Arthur. "Travail et National-Socialisme." *Allemagne d'Aujourd'hui* (1973) 2:11–22.

Gottschalch, Holm. "Historische Stationen auf dem Leidensweg der Arbeitsfreude im Spiegel psychologischer Theorien und empirischer Erhebungen. Materialsammlung und Typologie zum Arbeiterbewusstsein." *Soziale Welt* (Göttingen) 30 (1979): 439–68.

Grebing, Helga, ed. *Geschichte der sozialen Ideen in Deutschland*. Munich: Günther Olzog, 1969.

Greifenhagen, Martin. "Demokratie und Technokratie." In Claus Koch and Dieter Senghass, eds., *Texte zur Technokratiediskussion*, 54–70. Frankfurt: Europäische Verlagsanstalt, 1970.

Grenner, Karl Heinz. *Wirtschaftsliberalismus und Katholisches Denken. Ihre Begegnung und Auseinandersetzung im Deutschland des 19. Jahrhunderts*. Cologne: J. P. Bachem, 1967.

Groh, Dieter. "Intensification of Work and Industrial Conflict in Germany, 1896–1914." *Politics and Society* 8 (1978): 349–97.

Gruben, Heinz von. *Die Werkzeitschrift als Mittel der betrieblichen Sozialpolitik.* Munich, 1957.

Guillebaud, Claude William. *The Works Council. A German Experiment in Industrial Democracy.* Cambridge: Cambridge University Press, 1928.

———. *The Social Policy of Nazi Germany.* Cambridge: Cambridge University Press, 1941.

Guitton, Paul. "Le travail attrayant. Essai historique précédé s'une analyse théorique de l'Idee de Travail." Doctoral dissertation, Rennes, Faculty of Law, 1935.

Gutman, Herbert. *Work, Culture and Society in Industrializing America. Essays in Working-Class and Social History.* New York: Knopf, 1976.

Halter, Martin. *Sklaven der Arbeit—Ritter vom Geiste. Arbeit und Arbeiter im deutschen Sozialroman zwischen 1840 und 1880.* Frankfurt: Peter Lang, 1983.

Hamann, Richard and Jost Hermand. *Stilkunst um 1900. Epochen deutscher Kultur von 1870 bis zur Gegenwart,* vol. 4. Munich: Nymphenburger Verlagshandlung, 1975.

Hamburger, L. *How Nazi Germany Has Mobilized and Controlled Labor.* The Brookings Institution Pamphlet No. 24. Washington, D.C., 1940.

Hamilton, Richard F. *Who Voted for Hitler.* Princeton: Princeton University Press, 1982.

Hanisch, Ernst. *Konservatives und Revolutionäres Denken. Deutsche Sozialkatholiken und Sozialisten im 19. Jahrhundert.* Vienna: Geyer, 1975.

Harney, Klaus. *Die preussische Fortbildungsschule. Eine Studie zum Problem der Hierarchisierung beruflicher Schultypen im 19. Jahrhundert.* Weinheim: Beltz, 1980.

Haumann, Heiko, ed. *Arbeiteralltag in Stadt und Land. Neue Wege zur Geschichtsschriebung.* Argument-Sonderband 94. Berlin: Argument Verlag, 1982.

Hausen, Karin, ed. *Frauen suchen ihre Geschichte.* Munich: C. H. Beck, 1983.

Haworth, J. T. and M. A. Smith, eds. *Work and Leisure.* Princeton: Princeton Book Co., 1976.

Hayes, Peter. *Industry and Ideology. IG Farben in the Nazi Era.* New York: Cambridge University Press, 1987.

Heinemann, Manfred, ed. *Erziehung und Schulung im Dritten Reich.* 2 vols. Stuttgart: Klett-Cotta, 1980.

Heitzer, Horstwalter. *Der Volksverein für das katholische Deutschland im Kaiserreich 1890–1918.* Mainz: Matthias-Grünewald, 1979.

Hentschel, Volks. *Geschichte der deutschen Sozialpolitik 1880–1980. Soziale Sicherung und kollektives Arbeitsrecht.* Frankfurt: Suhrkamp, 1983.

Herbert, Uli. "Erkundungen im Revier. Drei Arbeitsleben bei Krupp." *Journal für Geschichte* (1982): 16–22.

Herbst, Ludolf. "Die Krise des nationalsozialistischen Regimes am Vorabend des Zweiten Weltkrieges und die forcierte Aufrüstung." *VfZ* 26 (1978): 347–92.

———. *Der totale Krieg und die Ordnung der Wirtschaft. Die Kriegswirtschaft im Spannungsfeld von Politik, Ideologie und Propaganda 1933–1945.* Stuttgart: Deutsche Verlagsanstalt, 1982.

Herf, Jeffrey. *Reactionary Modernism. Technology, Culture and Politics in Weimar and the Third Reich.* Cambridge: Cambridge University Press, 1984.

Hermand, Jost and Frank Trommler. *Die Kultur der Weimarer Republik.* Munich: Nymphenburger Verlagshandlung, 1978.

Heron, André. "Der Taylorismus. Grundsätze, Methoden, Doktrin." *Kursbuch* (Berlin) 43 (1976): 1–13.

Herzberg, Frederick. *Work and the Nature of Man.* Cleveland: The World Publishing Company, 1966.

Hinrichs, Carl. *Preussentum und Pietismus. Der Pietismus in Brandenburg Preussen als religiös-soziale Reformbewegung.* Göttingen: Vandenhoeck & Ruprecht, 1971.

Hinrichs, Peter. *Um die Seele des Arbeiters. Arbeitspsychologie in Deutschland, 1871–1945.* Cologne: Pahl-Rugenstein, 1981.

Hinrichs, Peter and Lothar Peter. *Industrielle Friede? Arbeitswissenschaft, Rationalisierung und Arbeiterbewegung in der Weimarer Republik.* Cologne: Pahl-Rugenstein, 1976.

Hinz, Berthold. *Art in the Third Reich.* New York: Pantheon, 1979.

Hirschfeld, Gerhard and Lothar Kettenacker, eds. *Der 'Führerstaat': Mythos und Realität. Studien zur Struktur und Politik des Dritten Reiches.* Stuttgart: Klett-Cotta, 1981.

Hock, Wolfgang. *Liberales Denken im Zeitalter der Paulskirche. Droysen und die Frankfurter Mitte.* Münster: Aschendorf, 1957.

Hoff, Alois. "Gewerkschaften und Rationalisierung. Die freigewerkschaftliche Rationalisierungsdebatte 1924–29." Dissertation, Diplom-Volkswirt. Berlin, 1975.

Homburg, Heidrun. "Anfänge des Taylorsystems in Deutschland vor dem Ersten Weltkrieg. Eine Problemskizze unter besonderer Berücksichtigung der Arbeitskämpfe bei Bosch 1913." *Geschichte und Gesellschaft* 4 (1978), 170–94.

Horn, Norbert and Jürgen Kocka, eds. *Recht und Entwicklung des Grossunternehmen im 19. und frühen 20. Jahrhundert.* Göttingen: Vandenhoeck & Ruprecht, 1979.

Hortleder, Gert. *Das Gesellschaftsbild des Ingenieurs. Zum politischen Verhalten der technischen Intelligenz in Deutschland.* Frankfurt: Suhrkamp, 1970.

Hüttenberger, Peter. "Nationalsozialistische Polykratie." *Geschichte und Gesellschaft* (1976), 417–42.

International Biographical Dictionary of Central European Emigrés 1933–1945. 3 vols. Munich: K. G. Saur, 1980–1983.

Israel, Joachim. *Alienation from Marx to Modern Sociology. A Macrosociological Analysis.* Boston: Allyn & Bacon, 1971.

Jäckel, Eberhard. *Hitler's Weltanschauung. A Blueprint for Power.* Middletown, Conn.: Wesleyan University Press, 1972.

Jäckel, Ebergard and Axel Kuhn, eds. *Adolf Hitler. Sämtliche Aufzeichnungen, 1905–1924.* Stuttgart: Deutsche Verlags-Anstalt, 1980.

Jaeggi, Urs, ed. *Geist und Katastrophe. Studien zur Soziologie im Nationalsozialismus.* Berlin: Wissenschaftlicher Autoren-Verlag, 1983.

James, Harold. *The German Slump. Politics and Economics 1924–1936.* Oxford: Clarendon Press, 1986.

Jantke, Carl and Dietrich Hilger. *Die Eigentumslosen. Der deutsche Pauperismus und die Emanzipationskrise in Darstellungen und Deutungen der zeitgenössischen Literatur.* Freiburg: Karl Alber, 1965.

Jarausch, Konrad H. "The Crisis of German Professions, 1918–1933." *JCH* 20 (1985): 379–98.

———. "The Old 'New History of Education'. A German Reconsideration." *History of Education Quarterly* 26 (Summer 1986): 225–41.

Jaschke, Hans-Gerd. *Soziale Basis und soziale Funktion des Nationalsozialismus. Studien zur Bonapartismustheorie.* Opladen: Westdeutscher Verlag, 1982.

Jay, Martin. *The Dialectical Imagination. A History of the Frankfurt School and the Institute of Social Research, 1923–1950.* Boston: Little, Brown, 1973.

Joyce, Patrick. *Work, Society, and Politics. The Culture of the Factory in Later Victorian England.* New Brunswick, N.J.: Rutgers University Press, 1980.

———, ed. *The Historical Meaning of Work.* Cambridge: Cambridge University Press, 1987.

Kahn-Freund, Otto. *Labour Law and Politics in the Weimar Republic.* Edited by Roy Lewis, Jon Clark, translator. Oxford: Blackwell, 1981.

Kaiser, Rolf and Hermann Loddenkemper. *Nationalsozialismus—totale Manipulation in der beruflichen Bildung?.* Frankfurt: Peter Lang, 1980.

Kater, Michael H. "The Work Student: a Socio-Economic Phenomenon of early Weimar Germany." *JCH* 10 (1975): 71–94.

———. "Die 'Technische Nothilfe' im Spannungsfeld von Arbeitunruhen, Unternehmerinteressen und Parteipolitik." *VfZ* 27 (1979), 30–78.

———. *The Nazi Party. A Social Profile of Members and Leaders, 1919–1945.* Cambridge: Harvard University Press, 1983.

———. "Hitler's Early Doctors: Nazi Physicians in Predepression Germany." *JMH* 59 (1987): 25–72.

Kele, Max H. *Nazis and Workers. National Socialist Appeals to German Labor, 1919–1933.* Chapel Hill, N.C.: University of North Carlina Press, 1972.

Kelly, Alfred, ed. *The German Worker. Working-Class Autobiographies from the Age of Industrialization.* Berkeley, Calif.: University of California Press, 1987.

Kellner, Douglas, "On the Philosophical Foundation of the Concept of Labor." *Telos* 16 (Summer 1973): 1–8.

Kershaw, Ian. *Der Hitler-Mythos. Volksmeinung und Propaganda im Dritten Reich.* Stuttgart: Deutsche-Verlagsanstalt, 1980.

———. *Popular Opinion and Political Dissent in the Third Reich: Bavaria 1933–1945.* Oxford: Oxford University Press, 1981.

Kirkpatrick, Clifford. *Nazi Germany. Its Women and Family Life.* Indianapolis, Ind.: Bobbs-Merrill, 1938; reprint, New York: AMS Press, 1981.

Klages, Helmut. *Geschichte der Soziologie.* 2d ed. Munich: Juventa, 1972.

Klemperer, Klemens von. *Germany's New Conservatism. Its History and Dilemma in the Twentieth Century.* Princeton: Princeton University Press, 1968.

Klemperer, Victor. *LTI. Notizbuch eines Philologen.* Berlin: Aufbau Verlag, 1949.

Klose-Stiller, Liselotte. *Arbeitsdienst für die weibliche Jugend in Schlesien 1930–1945. Versuch einer Würdigung der Arbeit weiblicher Jugendlicher im Einsatz für die Allgemeinheit.* Garmich-Partenkirchen, 1978.

Klotzbach, Kurt. *Bibliographie zur Geschichte der deutschen Arbeiterbewegung 1914–1945*, 3d ed. Bonn: Volker Mewttig, 1981.

Kocka, Jürgen. "Industrielles Management. Konzeption und Modelle in Deutschland vor 1914." *Vierteljahrsschrift für Sozial und Wirtschaftsgeschichte* 56 (1969): 332–72.

———. *Die Angelstellten in der deutschen Geschichte, 1850–1980. Vom Privatbeamten zum angestellten Arbeitnehmer.* Göttingen: Vandenhoeck & Ruprecht, 1981.

———, ed. *Angestellte im europäischen Vergleich.* Göttingen: Vandenhoeck & Ruprecht, 1981.

Koonz, Claudia. *Mothers in the Fatherland.* New York: St. Martin's Press, 1987.

Korff, Gottfried. "Volkskultur und Arbeiterkultur. Überlegungen am Beispiel der sozialistischen Maifesttradition." *Geschichte und Gesellschaft* 5 (1979): 83–102.

Kouri, E. I. *Der deutsche Protestantismus und die soziale Frage, 1870–1914. Zur Sozialpolitik im Bildungsbürgertum.* New York: Walter de Gruyter, 1984.

Kretschmar, Gottfried. *Der Evangelisch-Soziale Kongress. Der deutsche Protestantismus und die soziale Frage.* Stuttgart: Evangelisches Verlagswerk, 1972.

Krieger, Leonard. *The German Idea of Freedom. History of a Political Tradition.* Boston: Beacon Press, 1957.

Kühnl, Reinhard. *Die nationalsozialistische Linke, 1925–1930.* Meisenheim: Anton Hain, 1966.

Kümmel, Laus, ed. *Quellen und Dokumente zur schulistischen Berufsbildung 1918–1945. Quellen und Dokumente zur Geschichte der Berufsbildung in deutschland, A/2.* Cologne: Böhlau, 1980.

Kuper, Leo. *Genocide. Its Political Use in the Twentieth Century.* New Haven: Yale University Press, 1981.

La Vopa, Anthony J. "Vocations, Careers, and Talent: Lutheran Pietism and Sponsored Mobility in Eighteenth Century Germany." *Comparative Studies in Society and History* 28 (April 1986): 255–86.

Lane, Barbara Miller and Leila J. Rupp, eds. *Nazi Ideology before 1933. A Documentation.* Austin: University of Texas Press, 1978.

Lebovics, Herman. *Social Conservatism and the Middle Class in Germany, 1914–1933.* Princeton: Princeton University Press, 1969.

Lees, Andrew. *Revolution and Reflection. Intellectual Change in Germany during the 1850's.* The Hague: Martinus Nijhoff, 1974.

Lethen, Helmut. *Neue Sachlichkeit, 1924–1932. Studien zur Literatur des 'Weissen Sozialismus.'* Stuttgart: J. B. Metzler, 1970.

Lidtke, Vernon. *The Alternative Culture. Socialist Labor in Imperial Germany.* New York: Oxford University Press, 1985.

Lifton, Robert J. *The Nazi Doctors. Medical Killing and the Psychology of Genocide.* New York: Basic Books, 1986.

Lindenlaub, Dieter. *Sozial- und Wirtschaftsgeschichte. Richtungskampfe im Verein für Sozialpolitik.* Wiesbaden, 1967.

———. "Firmengeschichte und Sozialpolitik zur Wissenschaftsgeschichte der Nationalökonomie in Deutschland vor dem ersten Weltkrieg." In *Wissenschaft,*

Wirtschaft und Technik, ed. Karl-Heinz Manegold, 272–85. Munich: Bruckmann, 1969.

Lingelbach, Karl Christoph. *Erziehung und Erziehungstheorien im nationalsozialischen Deutschland*. Weinheim: Julius Beltz, 1970.

Linse, Ulrich. *Anarchistische und anarchosyndikalistische Jugendbewegung 1918–1933*. Frankfurt: Dipa, 1976.

Lisop, Ingrid, Werner Markert, and Rol Seubert, eds. *Berufs- und Wirtschaftspädagogik. Eine prolemorientierte Einführung*. Kronberg: Scriptor, 1976.

Literatur der Arbeiterklasse. Aufsätze über die Herausbildung der deutschen sozialistischen Literatur, 1918–1933. Berlin: Aufbau-Verlag, 1974.

Löwith, Karl. *From Hegel to Nietzsche. The Revolution in Nineteenth-Century Thought*. Trans. David E. Green. Garden City, N.Y.: Doubleday Anchor Books, 1967.

Ludwig, Karl-Heinz. *Technik und Ingenieure im Dritten Reich*. Düsseldorf: Droste, 1974.

Ludwig, Martin H. *Arbeiterliteratur in Deutschland*. Stuttgart: J. B. Metzler, 1976.

McRandle, James H. *The Track of the Wolf. Essays on National Socialism & Its Leader, Adolf Hitler*. Evanston, Ill.: Northwestern University Press, 1965.

Maden, Paul. "Some Social Characteristics of Early Nazi Party Members, 1919–23." *Central European History* 14 (1982): 34–56.

Mai, Gunther. "Die Nationalsozialistische Betriebszellenorganisation. Zum Verhältnis von Arbeiterschaft und Nationalsozialismus." *VfZ* 31 (1983): 573–613.

Maier, Charles S. "Between Taylorism and Technology. European Ideologies and the Vision of Industrial Production in the 1920s." *JCH* 5 (1970) 2:27–61.

———. *Recasting Bourgeois Europe. Stabilization in France, Germany, and Italy in the Decade after World War I*. Princeton: Princeton University Press, 1975.

———. "The Factory as Society." In *Ideas into Politics*, ed. Roger J. Bullen, 147–63. London: Croom Helm, 1984.

———, ed. *The Rise of the Nazi Regime. Historical Reassessments*. Boulder: Westview Press, 1986.

Manuel, Frank E. and Fritzie P. Manuel. *Utopian Thought in the Western World*. Oxford: Basil Blackwell, 1979.

Marshall, Paul, ed. *Labour of Love. Essays on Work*. Toronto: Wedge Publishing Foundation on behalf of the Christian Labour Association of Canada, 1980.

Mason, T. W. "Labour in the Third Reich 1933–1939." *Past and Present* 33 (April 1966): 112–41.

———. *Arbeiterklasse und Volksgemeinschaft. Dokumente und Materialien zur deutschen Arbeiterpolitik 1936–1939*. Wiesbaden, Westdeutscher Verlag, 1975.

———. "Women in Germany, 1925–1940." *History Workshop*, 1 (Spring 1976): 74–113, and 2 (Autumn 1976): 5–32.

———. "National Socialism and the Working Class, 1925–May 1933." *New German Critique* 11 (Spring 1977): 49–93.

Mattheier, K. J. "Werkvereine und wirtschaftsfriedlich-nationale (gelbe) Arbeiterbewegung im Ruhrgebiet." In Jürgen Reulecke, ed. *Arbeiterbewegung an Rhein und Ruhr*. Wuppertal: Peter Hammer, 1974.

Mayer, Arno J. *The Persistence of the Old Regime. Europe to the Great War*. New York: Pantheon, 1981.

Meakin, David. "Decadence and the Devaluation of Work. The Revolt of Sorel, Péguy and the German Expressionists." *European Studies Review* 1 (1971): 49–60.

———. *Man and Work. Literature and Culture in Industrial Society*. London: Methuen, 1976.

Mehrtens, Herbert and Steffen Richter, eds. *Naturwissenschaft, Technik und NS-Ideologie. Beitrage zur Wissenschaftsgeschichte des Dritten Reiches*. Frankfurt: Suhrkamp, 1980.

Merkle, Judith A. *Management and Ideology. The Legacy of the International Scientific Management Movement*. Berkeley: University of California Press, 1980.

Merton, Robert K. *Social Theory and Social Structure*. New York: Free Press, 1968.

Meyer, Klaus. *Arbeiterbildung in der Volkshochschule. Die 'Leipziger Richtung.' Ein Beitrag zur deutschen Volksbildung in den Jahren 1922–1933*. Stuttgart: Ernst Klett, 1969.

Mitzman, Arthur. *Sociology and Estrangement. Three Sociologists of Imperial Germany*. New York: Alfred A. Knopf, 1973.

Mohler, Armin. *Die Konservative Revolution in Deutschland 1918–1932. Ein Handbuch*. 2d rev. ed. Darmstadt: Wissenschaftliche Buchgesellschaft, 1972.

Mommsen, Hans. *Klassenkampf oder Mitbestimmung. Problem der kontrolle wirtschaftlicher Macht in der Weimarer Republik*. Cologne: Europäische Verlagsanstalt. 1978.

Mommsen, Hans and Ulrich Borsdorf, eds. *Glück auf, Kameraden. Die Bergarbeiter und ihre Organisationen in Deutschland*. Cologne: Bund, 1979.

Mommsen, Hans, Dietmar Petzina, and Bernd Weisbrod, eds. *Industrielles System und politische Entwicklung in der Weimarer Republik*. Düsseldorf: Droste, 1974.

Mosse, George L. *The Crisis of German Ideology. Intellectual Origins of the Third Reich*. London: Weidenfelt & Nicolson, 1970.

———. *Toward the Final Solution. A History of European Racism*. New York: Howard Fertig, 1978.

———. *Masses and Man. Nationalist and Fascist Perceptions of Reality*. New York: Howard Fertig, 1980.

Mühlberger, Detlef. "The Sociology of the NSDAP. The Question of Working-Class Membership." *JCH* 15 (1980): 493–512.

Muller, Jerry Z., "Enttäuschung und Zweideutigkeit. Zur Geschichte rechter Sozialwissenschaftler im 'Dritten Reich.' " *Geschichte und Gesellschaft* 12 (1986): 289–316.

Munich, Institut für Zeitgeschichte. *Gutachten des Instituts für Zeitgeschichte* 2 (Stuttgart: Deutsche Verlags-Anstalt, 1966).

Murard, Lion and Patrick Zylberman, eds. *Le Soldat du travail. Guerre, Fascisme et Taylorisme*. Special Issue of *Recherches* (Paris), 32/33 (September 1978).

Musgrave, Peter William. *Technical Change, the Labour Force and Education. A Study of the British and German Iron and Steel Industries, 1860–1964*. London: Pergamon, 1967.

Muth, Wolfgang. *Berufsausbildung in der Weimarer Republik*. Wiesbaden: Franz Steiner, 1985.

Myrell, Gunter, ed. *Arbeit, Arbeit über alles. Arbeit und Freizeit im Umbruch*. Cologne: Verlagsgeschelschaft Schulfernsehen/CVK, 1985.

Nadworny, Milton J. *Scientific Management and the Unions 1900–1932. A Historical Analysis*. Cambridge: Harvard University Press, 1955.

Nahrstedt, Wolfgang. *Die Entstehung der Freizeit*. Göttingen: Vandenhoeck & Ruprecht, 1972.

Nelson, Daniel. *Managers and Workers. Origins of the New Factory System in the United States, 1880–1920*. Madison: University of Wisconsin Press, 1975.

Nerdinger, Winfried. "Versuchung und Dilemma der Avantgarden im Spiegel der Architekturwettbewerbe 1933–1935." In *Faschistische Architekturen. Planen und Bauen in Europa 1930 bis 1945*, ed. Hartmut Frank, 65–87. Hamburg: Hans Christians, 1985.

Neufeld, Michael J. " 'He Who Will not Work, Neither Shall He Eat': German Social Democratic Attitudes to Labor, 1890–1914." M.A. Diss., University of British Columbia, 1976.

———. "Taylorism, Trade Union Leadership and Technological Change. 'Scientific Management' and the German Free Union, 1908–1923." Unpublished seminar paper, Johns Hopkins University, Modern European Seiminar, 1979.

Nicholls, Anthony and Erich Matthias, eds. *German Democracy and the Triumph of Hitler. Essays in recent German History*. London: George Allen and Unwin Ltd, 1971.

Niethammer, Lutz, ed. *Die Jahre weiss man nicht, wo man die heute hinsetzen soll*. Berlin: J.H.W. Dietz Nachf., 1983.

Niewyk, Donald L. *Socialist, Anti-Semite and Jew. German Democracy Confronts the Problem of Anti-Semitism 1918–1933*. Baton Rouge, La.: University of Louisiana Press, 1971.

Noakes, Jeremy. *The Nazi Party in Lower Saxony 1921–1933*. London: Oxford University Press, 1971.

Noakes, Jeremy and Geoffrey Pridham, eds. *Documents on Nazism, 1919–1945*. London: Jonathan Cape, 1974.

Noelle-Neumann, Elisabeth and Burkhard Strümpel. *Macht Arbeit krank? Macht Arbeit glücklich? Eine aktuelle Kontroverse*. Munich: Piper, 1984.

Nolan, Mary. *Social Democracy and Society. Working-Class Radicalism in Düsseldorf 1890–1920*. Cambridge: Cambridge University Press, 1981.

Oberschall, Anthony. *Empirical Social Research in Germany 1848–1914*. Paris: Mouton, 1965.

Olbrich, Josef, ed. *Arbeiterbildung in der Weimarer Zeit. Konzeption und Praxis*. Braunschweig: Westermann, 1977.

Opitz, Reinhard. *Der deutsche Sozialliberalismus 1917–1933*. Cologne: Pahl-Rugenstein, 1973.

Osterroth, Franz. *Biographisches Lexicon des Sozialismus*. Hannover: S. H. Dietz, 1960.

———. "Der Hofgeismarkreis der Jungsozialisten." *AS* 4 (1964): 525–69.

Pätzold, Gunter, ed. *Die betriebliche Berufsbildung 1918–1945*. Quellen und Dokumente zur Geschichte der Berufsbildung in Deutschland, A/1. Cologne: Böhlau, 1980.

Pankoke, Eckart. *Soziale Bewegung—Soziale Frage—Soziale Politik. Grundfragen der deutschen 'Sozialwissenschaft' im 19. Jahrhundert*. Stuttgart: Ernst Klett, 1970.

Passerini, Luisa. "Work Ideology and Consensus under Italian Fascism." *History Workshop* 8 (1979): 82–108.

Patch, William L., Jr. *Christian Trade Unions in the Weimar Republic. The Failure of 'Corporate Pluralism.'* New Haven: Yale University Press, 1985.

Peabody, Dean. *National Characteristics*. Cambridge: Cambridge University Press, 1985.

Petrick, Fritz. *Zur sozialen Lage der Arbeiterjugend in Deutschland 1933 bis 1939*. Berlin (East), 1974.

Peukert, Detlev. "Ruhr Miners under Nazi Repression, 1933–1945." *International Journal of Oral History* 1 (June 1980): 111–27.

———. "Arbeiteralltag—Mode oder Methode." *Arbeiteralltag in Stadt und Land*. Argument-Sonderband 94, 8–39. Berlin, 1982.

———. *Volksgenossen und Gemeinschaftsfremde. Anpassung, Ausmerze und Aufbegehren unter dem Nationalsozialismus*. Cologne: Bund, 1982.

———. "Die Erberbslosigkeit junger Arbeiter in der Weltwirtschaftskrise in Deutschland 1929–1933." *Vierteljahrschrift für Sozial- und Wirtschaftsgeschichte* 72 (1985) 3:305–328.

Peukert, Detlev and Jürgen Reulecke, eds. *Die Reihen fast geschlossen. Beiträge zur Geschichte des Alltags unterm Nationalsozialismus*. Wuppertal: Peter Hammer, 1981.

Phelps, Reginald H. "Hitlers Grundlegende Rede über dem Antisemitismus." *Vierteljährshefte für Zeitgeschichte* 16 (October 1968): 390–440.

Pietsch, Maximilian. *Von Wert und Würde menschlicher Arbeit*. Frankfurt: Josef Knecht, 1952.

Pinson, Koppel S. *Modern Germany. Its History and Civilization*. 2d ed. New York: The Macmillan Company, 1966.

Poole, Michael. *Workers Participation in Industry*, rev. ed. London: Routledge & Kegan Paul, 1978.

Popitz, Heinrich, ed. *Technik und Industriearbeit*, 2d ed. Tübingen: J.C.B. Mohr, 1964.

Preller, Ludwig. *Sozialpolitik in der Weimarer Republik*. Stuttgart: E. Mittelbach, 1949; reprint, Düsseldorf: Droste, 1978.

Rabinbach, Anson G. "The Aesthetics of Production in the Third Reich." *JCH* 11 (1974) 4:43–74.

Recker, Marie-Luise. *National-Sozialistische Sozialpolitik im zweiten Weltkrieg*. Munich: R. Oldenbourg, 1985.

Reich, Nathan. *Labour Relations in Republican Germay. An Experiment in Industrial Democracy, 1918–1933*. New York: Oxford University Press, 1938.

Reichling, Norbert. *Akademische Arbeiterbildung in der Weimarer Republik*. Münster: LIT, 1983.

Reifner, Udo, ed. *Das Recht des Unrechtstaates. Arbeitsrecht und Staatsrechtwissenschaften im Faschismus.* Frankfurt: Campus, 1981.

Reinisch, Leonhard, ed. *Die Zeit ohne Eigenschaften. Eine Bilanz der zwanziger Jahre.* Stuttgart: W. Kohlhammer, 1961.

Die Religion in Geschichte und Gegenwart. 2d ed., 1927–1932; 3d. ed., 1957–1965.

Reulecke, Jürgen. *Sozialer Frieden durch soziale Reform. Der Centralverein für das Wohl der arbeitenden Klassen in der Frühindustrialisierung.* Wuppertal: Peter Hammer, 1983.

Reulecke, Jürgen and Wolfhard Weber, eds. *Fabrik, Familie, Feierabend. Beiträge zur Sozialgeschichte des Alltags im Industriezeitalter.* Wuppertal: Hammer, 1978.

Riesman, David. "The Themes of Work and Play in the Structure of Freud's Thought," Chapter in *Individualism Reconsidered and other Essays.* Glencoe, Ill.: Free Press, 1954.

Ringer, Fritz K. *The Decline of the German Mandarins.* Cambridge: Harvard University Press, 1969.

Ritter, Gerhard A. *Staat, Arbeiterschaft und Arbeiterbewegung in Deutschland. Vom Vormärz bis zum Ende der Weimarer Republik.* Berlin: J.H.W. Dietz, 1980.

————, ed. *Arbeiterkultur.* Königstein: Anton Hein, 1979.

Rivinius, Karl Josef. *Die soziale Bewegung in Deutschland des neunzehnten Jahrhunderts.* Munich: Heinz Moos, 1978.

Rock, Reinhard. *Hauszeitschriften deutscher Unternehmen. Genesis und Analyse eines Public Relations-Instruments.* Frankfurt: Harri Deutsch, 1972.

Roche, Georges. "Nouvelles classes moyennes et idéologie: les ingénieurs sous la République de Weimar." *Revue d'Allemagne* 10 (1978): 49–74.

Rodgers, Daniel T. *The Work Ethic in Industrial America 1850–1920.* Chicago: University of Chicago Press, 1978.

Roth, Hermann. "Die nationalsozialistische Betriebszellenorganisation (NSBO) von der Gründung bis zur Röhm-Affäre (1928–1934)." *Jahrbuch für Wirtschaftsgeschichte* 1 (1978): 49–66.

Roth, John K. "Holocaust Business: Some Reflections on 'Arbeit macht Frei!' " In *Reflections on the Holocaust*, Annals of the American Academy of Political and Social Science 450 (July 1980): 68–82.

Roth, Karl-Heinz, ed. *Die 'andere' Arbeiterbewegung und die Entwicklung der kapitalistischen Repression von 1880 bis zur Gegenwart. Ein beitrag zum Neuverständnis der Klassengeschichte in Deutschland.* Munich: Trikont, 1974.

Rülcker, Christoph. *Ideologie der Arbeiterdichtung 1914–1933. Eine Wissensoziologische Untersuchung.* Stuttgart: J. V. Metzler, 1970.

Rürup, Reinhard, ed. *Wissenschaft und Gesellschaft. Beiträge zur Geschichte der Technischen Universität Berlin 1879–1979.* Berlin: Springer, 1979.

Rupp, Leila J. "Mother of the Volk. The Image of Women in Nazi Ideology." *Sign* (Winter 1977): 362–79.

————. *Mobilizing Women for War: German and American Propaganda, 1939–1945.* Princeton: Princeton University Press, 1978.

————. "Klassenzugehörigkeit und Arbeitseinsatz der Frauen im Dritten Reich." *Soziale Welt* 31 (1980) 2:191–205.

Sabel, Charles F. *Work and Politics. The Division of Labor in Industry.* Cambridge: Cambridge University Press, 1982.

Sachse, Carola, ed. *Angst, Belohnung, Zucht und Ordnung. Herrschaftsmechanismen im Nationalsozialismus,* with an introduction by Tim Mason. Opladen: Westdeutscher Verlag, 1982.

Saldern, Adelheid von. *Mittelstand im 'Dritten Reich'. Handwerker-Einzelhändler-Bauern.* Frankfurt: Campus, 1979.

Saul, Klaus. *Staat, Industrie, Arbeiterbewegung im Kaisserreich.* Düsseldorf: Bertelsmann, 1974.

Schad, Susanne Petra. *Emprical Social Research in Weimar Germany.* Paris: Mouton, 1972.

Schäfer, Hermann P. "Die 'Gelben Gewerkschaften' am Beispiel des Unterstützungsvereins der Siemens-Werke, Berlin." *Vierteljahrschrift für Sozial- und Wirtschaftsgeschichte* 59 (1972): 41–76.

Scharfe, Martin. "Pietische Moral im Industrialisierungsprozess." In *Religion und Moral,* ed. Burkhard Gladigow, 27–47. Düsseldorf: Patmos, 1976.

Schick, Manfred. *Kulturprotestantismus und soziale Frage. Versuche zur Begründung der Sozialethik, vornehmlich in der Zeit von der Gründung des Evangelisch-sozialen Kongresses bis zum Ausbruch des ersten Weltkrieges (1890–1914).* Tübingen: J.C.B. Mohr, 1970.

Schlicker, Wolfgang. "Arbeitsdienstbestrebungen des deutschen Monopolkapitals in der Weimarer Republik unter besonderer Berücksightigung des Deutschen Instituts für technische Arbeitsschulung." *Jahrbuch für Wirtschaftsgeschichte* (1971) 3:95–122.

Schmädeke, Jürgen and Peter Steinbach, eds. *Der Widerstand gegen den Nationalsozialismus. Die deutsche Gesellschaft und der Widerstand gegen Hitler.* Munich: Piper, 1985.

Schmiede, Rudi and Edwin Schudlich. *Die Entwicklung der Leistungsentlohung in Deutschland,* 2d ed. Frankfurt: Campus, 1977.

Schmieder, Eberhard. "Arbeitsethos. Eine Einführung in seine Geschichte." *Schmollers Jahrbuch* 79 (1959): 299–337, 429–62.

Schneider, Michael. *Unternehmer und Demokratie. Die freien Gewerkschaften in der unternehmerischen Ideologie der Jahre 1918–1933.* Bonn: Neue Gesellschaft, 1975.

———. *Die christlichen Gewerkschaften 1894–1933.* Bonn: Neue Gesellschaft, 1982.

———. "Religion and Labour Organization: The Christian Trade Unions in the Wilhelmine Empire." *European Studies Review* 12 (1982): 345–69.

Schöck, Eva C. *Arbeitslosigkeit und Rationalisierung. Die Lage der Arbeiter und die kommunistische Gewerkschaftspolitik 1920–1928.* Frankfurt: Campus, 1977.

Schoenbaum, David. *Hitler's Social Revolution. Class and Status in Nazi Germany 1933–1939.* Garden City, N.Y.: Doubleday, 1966: reprint, New York: Norton, 1980.

Scholder, Klaus. *Die Kirchen und das Dritte Reich.* Frankfurt: Ullstein, 1977.

Scholtz-Klink, Gertrud. *Die Frau im Dritten Reich. Eine Dokumentation.* Tübingen: Grabert, 1978.

Scholz, Otfried. *Arbeiterselbstbild und Arbeiterfremdbild zur Zeit der industriellen Revolution. Ein Beitrag zur Sozialgeschichte des Arbeiters in der deutschen Erzähl- und Memoirenliteratur um die Mitte des 19. Jahrhunderts.* Berlin: Colloquium, 1980.

Schraepler, Ernst, ed. *Quellen zur Geschichte der sozialen Frage in Deutschland.* 2 vols. 2d rev. ed. Göttingen: Musterschmidt, 1960.

Schulz, Gerhard. *Faschismus-Nationalsozialismus. Versionen und theoretische Kontroversen 1922–1972.* Frankfurt: Ullstein, 1974.

Schumann, Hans-Gerd. *Nationalsozialismus und Gewerkschaftsbewegung. Die Vernichtung der deutschen Gewerkschaften und der Aufbau der 'Deutschen Arbeitsfront.'* Hannover: Norddeutsche Verlagsanstalt O. Goedel, 1958.

Schuster, Margrit and Helmuth Schuster. "Industriesoziologie im Nationalsozialismus." *Soziale Welt* (1984): 94–123.

Schwabe, Klaus. "Anti-Americanism within the German Right 1917–1933." *Amerikastudien* 21 (1976): 89–107.

Schweitzer, Arthur. *Die Nazifizierung des Mittelstandes.* Stuttgart: Ferdinand Enke, 1970.

Seeman, Melvin. "The Urban Alienations: Some Dubious Theses from Marx to Marcuse." *Journal of Personality and Social Psychology* 19 (1971): 135–43.

Seubert, Rolf. *Berufserziehung und Nationalsozialismus. Das berufspädagogische Erbe und seine Betreuer.* Weinheim: Beltz, 1977.

Sewell, William H. *Work and Revolution in France. The Language of Labor from the Old Regime to 1848.* New York: Cambridge University Press, 1980.

Shanahan, William O. *German Protestants Face the Social Question.* vol. 1: *The Conservative Phase 1815–1871.* Notre Dame: University of Notre Dame Press, 1954.

Shepard, Jon M. "Technology, Alienation and Job Satisfaction." *Annual Review of Sociology* 3 (1977): 1–21.

―――. "Alienation Studies." *Annual Review of Sociology* 1 (1975): 91–123.

Sherwood, John M. "Rationalization and Railway Workers in France: Raoul Dautry and Les Chemins de Fer de l'Etat, 1928–1937." *JCH* 15 (July 1980): 443–74.

Siegel, Tilla. "Wage Policy in Nazi Germany." *Politics and Society* 14 (1985): 1–52.

Simon, Yves R. *Work, Society and Culture,* ed. Vukan Kvic. New York: Fordham University Press, 1971.

Skrzypzak, Henryk. "From Carl Legien to Theodor Leipart, from Theodor Leipart to Robert Ley. Notes on some strategic and tactical problems of the German free trade union movement during the Weimar Republic." *IWK* 13 (August 1971): 26–45.

Smith, Woodruff D. *The Ideological Origins of Nazi Imperialism.* New York: Oxford University Press, 1986.

Sohn-Rethel, Alfred. *Intellectual and Manual Labour. A Critique of Epistemology.* London: Macmillan, 1978.

Sorg, Richard. *Marxismus und Protestantismus in Deutschland, 1848–1948.* Cologne: Pahl-Rugenstein, 1974.

Speier, Hans. *Die Angestellten vor dem Nationalsozialismus. Ein Beitrag zum Verständ-*

nis der deutschen Sozialstruktur 1918–1933. Göttingen: Vandenhoeck & Ruprecht, 1977.

Spencer, Elaine Glovka, "Between Capital and Labor: Supervisory Personnel in Ruhr Heavy Industry before 1914." *Journal of Social History* 9 (1975–6): 178–92.

———. "Employer Response to Unionism: Ruhr Coal Industrialists before 1914." *JMH* 48 (September 1976): 397–412.

Stachura, Peter D., ed. *The Shaping of the Nazi State*. London: Croom Helm, 1978.

Stark, Gary P. *Entrepreneurs of Ideology. Neoconservative Publishers in Germany 1890–1933*. Chapel Hill, N.C.: University of North Carolina Press, 1981.

Stearns, Peter N. "Adaptation to Industrialization: German Workers as a Test Case." *Central European History* (1970): 303–331.

———. "National Character and European Labor History." *Journal of Social History* 4 (1970): 95–124.

———. *Lives of Labour. Work in a Maturing Industrial Society*. London: Croom Helm, 1973.

———. "The Effort at Continuity in Working-Class Culture." *Journal of Modern History* 52 (December 1980): 626–55.

Steinbrinker, Heinrich. "Der Geist der Gemeinschaft. Wechselwirkungen zwischen Arbeiterjugendbewegung und 'bürgerlicher' Jugendbwegung bis 1933." *Jahrbuch des Archivs der deutschen Jugendbewegung* 10 (1978): 7–23.

Steinert, Marlis G. *Hitler's War and the Germans*, ed. and trans. by Thomas E. J. de Witt. Athens, Ohio: Ohio University Press, 1977.

Steinmetz, Udo. "Berufsverständnis und Kulturbegriff. Zu ihrem Zusammenhang im Bildungsverband der Deutschen Buchdrucker und in der Büchergilde Gutenberg (1924–1933)." Schriftliche Hausarbeit zur 1. Staatsprüfung für das Lehramt. Bremen, 1977.

Stephenson, Jill. "Nationalsozialistischer Dienstgedanke, bürgerliche Frauen und Frauenorganisationen im Dritten Reich." *Geschichte und Gesellschaft* 7 (1981): 555–71.

———. "Women's Labor Service in Nazi Germany." *Central European History* 15 (September 1982): 241–65.

Stern, Fritz. *The Politics of Cultural Despair. A Study in the Rise of the Germanic Ideology*. Berkeley: University of California Press, 1961; reprint, Garden City, N.Y.: Doubleday Anchor Book, 1965.

Stieg, Gerald and Bernd Witte. *Abriss einer Geschichte der deutschen Arbeiterliteratur*. Stuttgart: Ernst Klett, 1973.

Stollberg, Gunnar. *Die Rationalisierungsdebatte 1908–1933. Freie Gewerkschaften zwischen Mitwirkung und Gegenwehr*. Frankfurt: Campus, 1981.

Stollberg, Rudhard. *Arbeitszufriedenheit. Theoretische und praktische Probleme*. Berlin: Dietz, 1968.

———. *Arbeitssoziologie*. Berlin-Ost: Verlag Die Wirtschaft, 1978.

Stolle, Uta-Katina. *Arbeiterpolitik im Betrieb. Frauen und Männer, Reformisten und Radikale, Fach- und Massenarbeiter bei Bayer, BASF, Bosch, und in Solingen (1900–1933)*. Frankfurt: Campus, 1980.

Struve, Walter. *Elites against Democracy. Leadership Ideals in Bourgeois Political Thought, 1890–1933.* Princeton: Princeton University Press, 1973.

Stupperich, Amrei. *Volksgemeinschaft oder Arbeitersolidarität. Studien zur Arbeitnehmerpolitik in der Deutschnationalen Volkspartei, 1918–1933.* Göttingen: Musterschmidt, 1982.

Sussman, Herbert L. *Victorians and the Machine. The Literary Response to Technology.* Cambridge: Harvard University Press, 1968.

Tal, Uriel. *Christians and Jews in Germany. Religion, Politics and Ideology in the Second Reich, 1870–1914.* Trans. Noah Jonathan Jacobs. Ithaca, N.Y.: Cornell University Press, 1975.

Theweleit, Klaus. *Männerphantasien.* vol. 2, *Zur Psychoanalyse des weissen Terrors.* Frankfurt: Verlag Roter Stern, 1978.

Thomas, Keith. "Work and Leisure in Pre-Industrial Society." *Past and Present* 29 (1964): 50–66.

Tilgher, Adriano. *Work. What It Has Meant to Men through the Ages.* Translated by D. C. Fisher. New York: Harcourt, Brace [1930]; reprint, New York: Arno Press, 1977.

Trommler, Frank. *Sozialistische Literatur in Deutschland. Ein historischer Überblick.* Stuttgart: Alfred Kröner, 1976.

———. "Die Nationalisierung der Arbeit." In *Arbeit als Thema in der deutschen Literatur vom Mittelalter bis zur Gegenwart,* ed. Reinhold Grimm and Jost Hermand, 102–125. Königstein: Athenäum, 1979.

Turner, Henry Ashby. *German Big Business and the Rise of Hitler.* New York: Oxford University Press, 1985.

Uellenberg, Wolfgang. *Die Auseinandersetzungen sozialemokratischer Jugendorganisationen mit dem Nationalzialismus.* Schriftenreihe des Archivs der Arbeiterjugendbewegung 4. Bonn, 1981.

Volpert, Walter. *Die 'Humanisierung der Arbeit' und die Arbeitswissenschaft.* Cologne: Pahl-Rugenstein, 1974.

Vondung, Klaus. *Völkisch-nationale und nationalsozialistische Literaturtheorie.* Munich: List, 1973.

———, ed. *Das wilhelminische Bildungsbürgertum. Zur Sozialgeschichte seiner Ideen.* Göttingen: Vandenhoeck & Ruprecht, 1976.

Vontobel, Klara. *Das Arbeitsethos des deutschen Protestantismus, von der nachreformatorischen Zeit bis zur Aufklärung.* Bern: A Francke, 1946.

Wachtler, Günther. *Humanisierung der Arbeit und Industriesoziologie. Eine soziologische Analyse historischer Vorstellungen humaner Arbeitsgestaltung.* Stuttgart: W. Kohlmanner, 1979.

Walter-Busch, Emil. *Arbeitszufriedenheit in der Wohlstandsgesellschaft. Beitrag zur Diagnose der Theoriesprachenvielfalt betriebspsychologischer und industriesoziologischer Forschung.* Bern: Paul Haupt, 1977.

Ward, William Reginald. *Theology, Sociology and Politics. The German Social Conscience 1890–1933.* Bern: Peter Lang, 1979.

Welch, David, ed. *Nazi Propaganda. The Power and the Limitations.* London: Croom Helm, 1983.

Wellner, Gabrielle. "Industriearbeiterinnen in der Weimarer Republik." *Geschichte und Gesellschaft* 7 (1981): 534–54.

Werner, Wolfgang Franz. *'Bleib übrig.' Deutsche Arbeiter in der nationalsozialistichen Kriegswirtschaft.* Düsseldorf: Schwann, 1983.

Weyer, Johannes. "Die Forschungsstelle für das Volkstum im Ruhrgebiet (1935–1941): ein Beispiel für Soziologie im Faschismus." *Soziale Welt* (1984): 124–45.

Wiedemann, Konrad. *Arbeit und Bürgertum. Die Entwicklung des Arbeitsbegriffs in der Literatur Deutschlands an der Wende zur Neuzeit.* Heidelberg: Carl Winter, 1979.

Wiegelmann, Günther, ed. *Kultureller Wandel im 19. Jahrhundert.* Verhandlungen des 18. Deutschen Volkskunde-Kongresses in Trier, 1971. Göttingen: Vandenhoeck & Ruprecht, 1973.

Will, Wilfried van der and Rob Burns, eds. *Arbeiterkulturbewegung in der Weimarer Republik. Texte—Dokumente—Bilder.* Frankfurt: Ullstein, 1982.

Willett, John. *Art and Politics in the Weimar Period. The New Sobriety 1917–1933.* New York: Pantheon, 1978.

Winckler, Lutz. *Studie zur gesellschaftlichen Funktion faschistischer Sprache.* Frankfurt: Suhrkamp, 1970.

Winkel, Harald. *Die deutsche Nationalökonomie im 19. Jahrhundert.* Darmstadt: Wissenschaftliche Buchgesellschaft, 1977.

Winkler, Dörte. "Frauenarbeit versus Frauenideologie. Probleme der weiblichen Erwerbstätigkeit in Deutschland 1930–1945." *AS* 17 (1977): 99–126.

———. *Frauenarbeit im 'Dritten Reich.'* Hamburg: Hoffmann und Campe, 1977.

Winkler, Heinrich August. *Mittelstand, Demokratie und Nationalsozialismus. Die politische Entwicklung von Handwerk und Kleinhandel in der Weimarer Republik.* Cologne: Kiepenheuer & Witsch, 1972.

———. "Der entbehrliche Stand. Zur Rolle des gewerblichen Mittelstandes im 'Dritten Reich.' " *AS* 17 (1977): 1–40.

Wistrich, Robert S. *Who's Who in Nazi Germany.* London: Weidenfeld & Nicolson, 1982.

Wittwer, Wolfgang W. *Die Sozialdemokratische Schulpolitik in der Weimarer Republik. Ein Beitrag zur politischen Schulgeschichte im Reich und in Preussen.* Berlin: Colloquium, 1980.

Wolsing, Theo. *Untersuchungen zur Berufsausbildung im Dritten Reich.* Kastellaun/Düsseldorf: Aloys Henn, 1977.

Wright, Anthony W. "Guild Socialism Revisited." *JCH* 9 (1974) 1:165–80.

Zimmermann-Buhr, Bernhard. *Die katholische Kirche und der Nationalsozialismus in den Jahren 1930–1933.* Frankfurt: Campus, 1982.

INDEX